CONCURRENT SYSTEMS

∴

An Integrated Approach to Operating Systems, Database, and Distributed Systems

D1634474

CONCURRENT SYSTEMS

An Integrated Approach to Operating Systems, Database, and Distributed Systems

JEAN BACON

University of Cambridge

ADDISON-WESLEY
PUBLISHING
COMPANY

Wokingham, England • Reading, Massachusetts • Menlo Park, California • New York
Don Mills, Ontario • Amsterdam • Bonn • Sydney • Singapore
Tokyo • Madrid • San Juan • Milan • Paris • Mexico City • Seoul • Taipei

INTERNATIONAL COMPUTER SCIENCE SERIES

Consulting editor   **A D McGettrick**   University of Strathclyde

SELECTED TITLES IN THE SERIES

To my parents:
Samuel Goodram
and
Annie Goodram
(née Lee)

Cover designed by Chris Eley incorporating photograph © Pete Turner/The Image Bank and printed by The Riverside Printing Co. (Reading) Ltd.
Typeset by VAP Publishing Services, Kidlington, Oxfordshire.
Printed in the United States of America.

First printed 1992.

British Library Cataloguing in Publication Data
A catalogue record for this book is available from the British Library

Library of Congress Cataloging in Publication Data
Bacon, Jean, date
    Concurrent systems : an integrated approach to operating systems, database and distributed systems / Jean Bacon.
      p. cm. -- (International computer science series)
    Includes bibliographical reference and index.
    ISBN 0-201-41677-8
    1. Parallel processing (Electronic computers)   I. Title.
II. Series.
QA76.58.B33   1992
005.1'1--dc20   92-34364
                                                            CIP

Preface

The aim of this book is to equip students with an integrated view of modern software systems. Concurrency and modularity are the unifying themes. It takes a systems approach rather than a programming language approach, since concurrent programming is firmly rooted in system design. The language is an implementation tool for the system designer and programming languages are covered throughout the book from this perspective.

The formal theory of concurrency is not included. Rather, the aim is to provide a systems background to which subsequent formal study can relate. Without prior study of real systems a student can have little intuition about the basis of formal models of concurrent systems. For students about to work on the theory of concurrency the book provides a summary of essential system fundamentals.

The structure of the book is:

- **Introduction,** in which some real-world concurrent systems are described and requirements for building computerized concurrent systems established.
- **Part I,** in which the abstraction of a concurrent system as a set of concurrent processes is established and the implementation of processes in operating systems and language systems is studied.
- **Part II,** which shows how a logically single action (an operation invocation) can be guaranteed to run without interference from other concurrent actions.
- **Part III,** which shows how a number of related actions can be guaranteed to run without interference from other concurrent actions.
- **Part IV,** in which some case studies are considered from the perspective developed throughout the book.

Computer systems curriculum

I have taught operating systems, distributed systems and computer architecture for many years. Because distributed operating systems have come into widespread use comparatively recently, most curricula include them at final-year undergraduate or postgraduate level. Distributed operating systems are now commonplace and a student is more likely to be using one than a centralized time-sharing system. It is somewhat artificial to cover the functions of a shared, centralized operating system in great detail in a first course, particularly when the rate of development of technology makes it essential constantly to re-evaluate traditional approaches and algorithms.

In general, there is a tendency for closely related specialisms to diverge, even at undergraduate level. An overview of system components and their relationships is desirable from an early stage:

- Operating systems include communications handling.
- Language runtime systems work closely with (and are constrained by) operating systems.
- Real-time systems need specially tailored operating systems.
- Dedicated communications handling computers need specially tailored operating systems.
- Database management systems run on operating systems and need concurrency and file handling with special guarantees.
- Concurrent programs run on operating systems.
- Many system components employ databases.
- Distributed systems employ distributed databases.
- Distributed databases need communications.
- Distributed operating systems need transactions.

Concurrent Systems achieves this integration by setting up a common framework of modular structure (a simple object model is used throughout) and concurrent execution.

I have used this approach in the Computer Science curriculum at Cambridge since 1988, when a new three-year undergraduate degree programme started. A concurrent systems course, in the second year of a three-year degree course, is a prerequisite for further study in distributed operating systems, communications and networks, theory of concurrency, and various case studies and projects. Figure 1 suggests an order of presentation of systems material. Courses in the general area of real-time, embedded control systems would also follow naturally from this course. At Cambridge, a course which gives an overview of system software precedes 'Concurrent Systems' so the students start with some knowledge of file management and memory management. As this may not universally be the case I have included these functions in Part I of the book. I take the detailed aspects of these operating systems functions in the context of special-purpose systems' requirements after the concurrent systems material has been covered.

In the ACM Curriculum 91 for Computing (see Denning *et al.*, 1989; Tucker 1991), the general topic 'operating systems' includes distributed operating systems and communications. Curriculum 91 identifies the three major paradigms of the discipline as: **theory**, which is rooted in mathematics; **abstraction** (modelling), which is rooted in experimental scientific method; and **design**, which is

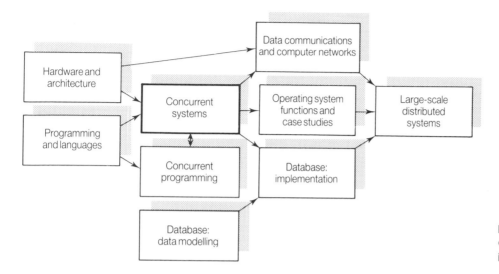

Figure 1
Concurrent systems
in the curriculum.

rooted in engineering. Theory deals with the underlying mathematics of each sub-area of computing. Abstraction allows us to model large, complex systems in order to comprehend their structure and behaviour and carry out experiments on them. Design deals with the process of implementing a system to meet a specification. The approach taken here embodies abstraction and design and establishes the basis for theory.

Audience

It is assumed that the reader will come to this material with some knowledge and experience of systems and languages. First-year undergraduate courses on programming and systems software are appropriate prerequisites.

The book is intended as a **modern replacement for a first course in operating systems** – modern in the sense that concurrency is a central focus throughout; distributed systems are treated as the norm rather than single-processor systems, and effective links are provided to other systems courses. It is also suitable as a text to be read in parallel with more traditional, specialized courses in operating systems, communications and databases. It also provides integrating and summarizing study for graduate students and practitioners in systems design including systems programming. Graduate students who are researching the theory of concurrency will find the practical basis for their subject here.

An outline of the contents

Chapter 1 describes a number of types of concurrent system and draws out requirements for supporting concurrent activities. Concurrent systems can exploit a wide range of system topologies and architectures. Although this area is not addressed in great detail their characteristics are noted for reference throughout the book.

Chapters 2 through 7 form **Part I**. System design and implementation require software to be engineered. Software engineering, which involves the specification, design, implementation, maintenance and evolution of software systems, has merited many books in its own right. This book focuses on concurrency issues, but a context of modular software structure is needed: first, to give a context for Part I, where intuition on a single logical action is needed; second, in order that the placement of concurrent processes in systems may be understood.

Modular system structure is therefore introduced in **Chapter 2** and the modular structure of operating systems is used as an extended example. The idea that a minimal kernel or 'microkernel' is an appropriate basis for high-performance specialized services is introduced here. The concepts of **process** and protocol to achieve the dynamic execution of software are also introduced.

In **Chapter 3** device handling and communications handling are covered. These topics are treated together to highlight the similarities (between communications and other devices) and differences (communications software is larger and more complex than device handling software). The communications handling subsystem of an operating system is itself a concurrent (sub)system, in that at a given time it may be handling several streams of input coming in from various sources across the network as well as requests for network communication from local clients.

Chapter 4 covers memory management. The address space of a process is an important concept, as also are mechanisms for sharing part of it. Some of the more detailed material in this chapter and the next can be omitted on a first reading or deferred in a teaching context.

Chapter 5 gives the basic concepts of filing systems. File system implementations involve data structures both in main memory and in persistent memory on disk. Both the memory management and file management subsystems of operating systems are concurrent systems in that they may have in progress both requests from clients and demands for service from the hardware.

Chapter 6 gives the detailed concrete basis for the process abstraction that is provided by operating systems. Once the process abstraction is created as one operating system function we can show how processes are used to achieve the dynamic execution of the rest of the system. Operating system processes may be used within operating system modules, while application-level processes may be located within application modules. There are several design options which are discussed throughout the book.

Chapter 7 is concerned with language systems and a particular concern is the support for concurrency. The relation between operating system and language system processes is discussed in detail. Multi-threaded processes are introduced.

Part I is mostly concerned with implementation. Knowledge of the material presented here is necessary for a thorough understanding of concurrent systems.

Care must be taken, when working at the language or theoretical modelling levels, that the assumptions made can be justified for the operating system and hardware that will be used to implement a concurrent system.

We can now work with the abstraction of a concurrent system as a set of concurrent processes. **Part II** proceeds to explain the mechanisms for ensuring that a given concurrent process can execute without interference from any other, bearing in mind that processes may be cooperating with other processes (and need to synchronize with them) or competing with other processes to acquire some resource.

Chapters 8 to 14 comprise Part II. In Part II we temporarily ignore the issues of composite operations and the need to access multiple resources to carry out some task and confine the discussion to a single operation invocation that takes place within a concurrent system.

The notion of a single abstract operation is informal and closely related to the modular structuring of systems. A process can, in general, read or write a single word of memory without fear of interference from any other process. Such a read or write is indivisible. In practice, a programming language variable or a useful data abstraction, such as an array, list or record, cannot be read or written atomically. It is the access to such shared abstractions by concurrent processes that is the concern of **Part II**. Chapters 8 to 12 are mostly concerned with 'load and go' systems that run in a single or distributed main memory. Chapters 13 and 14 start to consider the effect of failures in system components and process interactions which involve persistent memory.

Chapter 8 discusses the major division between processes which share memory, running in a common address space, and those which do not. Examples are given, showing the need for both types of arrangement.

Chapter 9 is concerned with the lowest level of support for process interactions. The architecture of the computer and the system is relevant here. It is important to know whether any kind of composite read–modify–write instruction is available and whether the system architecture contains shared memory multiprocessors or only uniprocessors.

Semaphores are introduced, with several examples of their use. Implementation issues are covered. A discussion of the difficulty of writing correct semaphore programs leads on to high-level language support for concurrency in the next chapter.

Chapter 10 looks at language primitives that have been introduced into high-level concurrent programming languages where the underlying assumption is that processes execute in a shared address space, for example, conditional critical regions and monitors.

Chapter 11 compares inter-process communication (IPC) mechanisms within systems where shared memory is available and where it is not. In both cases processes need to access common information and synchronize their activities.

Chapter 12 covers IPC for processes which inhabit separate address spaces. Pipes and message passing are discussed. The material here is relevant to distributed IPC, but the essential characteristics of distributed systems are not yet discussed.

Chapter 13 introduces the possibility that a system might crash at any time and outlines mechanisms that could be used to provide crash resilience. An initial discussion of operations which involve persistent data is also given.

Chapter 14 focuses on distributed systems. Their special characteristics are noted and the client–server and object models for distributed software are outlined. We see how an operation at one node of a distributed system can be invoked from another node using a remote procedure call protocol. Node crashes and restarts and network failures are considered. Although distributed IPC is the main emphasis of the chapter, it concludes with a general discussion of naming, location and the binding of names to locations in distributed systems.

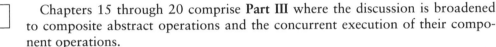

Chapters 15 through 20 comprise **Part III** where the discussion is broadened to composite abstract operations and the concurrent execution of their component operations.

Chapter 15 introduces the problems and defines the context for this study. Composite operations may span distributed systems and involve persistent memory.

Chapter 16 discusses the desirability of dynamic resource allocation and the consequent possibility of system deadlock. An introduction to resource allocation and management is given, including algorithms for deadlock detection and avoidance.

Chapter 17 discusses composite operation execution in the presence of concurrency and crashes and builds up a definition of the fundamental properties of transactions. A model based on abstract data objects is used.

Chapter 18 discusses concurrency control for transactions. Two-phase locking, time-stamp ordering and optimistic concurrency control are described and compared.

Chapter 19 is mainly concerned with crash recovery, although the ability to abort transactions for concurrency control purposes is a related problem. A specific implementation is given.

Chapter 20 extends the object model for distributed systems and reconsiders the methods of implementing concurrency control in this context. The problem of atomic commitment is discussed and a two-phase commit protocol is given as an example. A validation protocol for optimistic concurrency control is also given.

Part III has established the concept of transaction which is fundamental to all distributed systems.

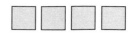

Chapters 21 through 24 comprise **Part IV,** in which a number of systems are presented as case studies. Greater depth is possible here than in the examples used earlier. An aim is to show that the approach developed throughout the book helps the reader to comprehend large and complex systems.

Chapter 21 describes the basic UNIX Edition 7 design. The design is evaluated and the process management and interprocess communication facilities, in particular, are criticized. The way these criticisms have been addressed in recent versions of UNIX (BSD 4.3 and System V.4) is then described.

Chapter 22 covers the design of microkernels. Mach and CHORUS are described in some detail because they provide binary compatibility with UNIX BSD 4.3 and UNIX System V.4 respectively. The chapter concludes with an outline of distributed systems research at Cambridge where a microkernel has been designed to support dynamic real-time systems based on ATM networks.

Chapter 23 first discusses how transaction processing monitors are implemented in terms of processes, IPC and communications. Some examples of TP systems in the area of electronic funds transfer are then given, for example, an international automatic teller machine (ATM) network.

Chapter 24 draws out the main conclusions, integrating the various parts of the book.

Although many small **examples** of hardware, systems and languages are used, two extended examples have been selected. First, the UNIX 7th Edition design illustrates so many problems of concurrent systems so well that it is frequently used as an illustrative example. The UNIX case study in Chapter 21 shows how these long-understood problems have been addressed in the current UNIX offerings. The second extended example is not such an obvious choice. I needed to show the RISC approach to computer architecture and its implications for concurrent systems. Because our local workstations are based on the MIPS R2000 I know this system well, and have used it as an example of interrupt handling, memory management, processor design and (lack of) support for concurrency.

The **appendix** presents two problems in greater depth than can be justified within a single chapter. *N*-process mutual exclusion for shared memory and distributed systems is the first. The management of a cache of disk buffers, highlighting the problems arising from concurrent access, is the second. Both are left open-ended and exercises are given.

Order of presentation

Figure 2 indicates dependencies in the material and shows how the chapters might be selected for courses emphasizing operating systems, concurrent programming or databases. It is not essential to cover everything in Chapters 4 and 5 before later chapters are taken, as discussed above. Chapter 16 can be treated

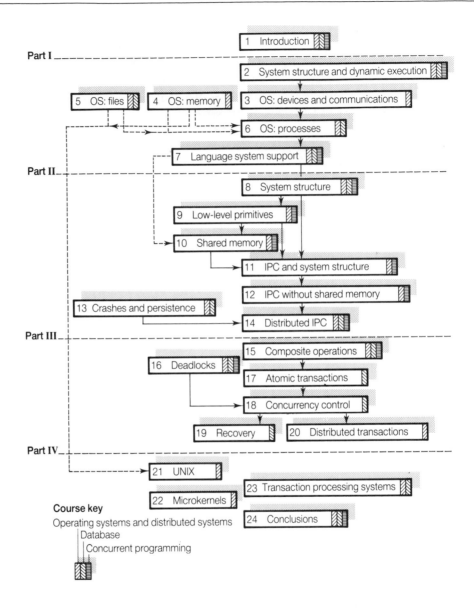

Figure 2
Presentation of the material.

similarly. Sections from these chapters are referenced when they are needed and the topics could be embedded.

The material in Part II could be taken in a different order. Although there is a flow of argument through the chapters as written, there is no inherent reason why shared-memory IPC has to come before that with no shared memory.

The book could be used for a conventional operating systems course by selecting Part I, Chapters 8 through 12 of Part II, Chapter 16 from Part III, and the UNIX case study. Distributed operating systems could be included in such a course from the start by following the whole of Parts I and II. The case studies could then include both UNIX and microkernels. Although all of Part III is not essential for such a course, Chapter 16 should be included and parts of Chapters 15 and 17 are highly desirable.

A concurrent programming course could supplement Part I (possibly excluding Chapters 4 and 5) and Part II with full details of a language to be used for project work. Chapters 15 and 16 from Part III should also be included.

A course on concurrency control in database systems would use Part III, but earlier chapters which cover operating system support for databases provide an excellent background.

Further study

The book naturally leads on to a course on large-scale distributed system design. Issues of naming, location, placement, protection, authentication and encryption are introduced but not discussed in depth. The replication of data to achieve high availability and performance is not discussed and a follow-on course would cover this aspect of large-scale system design, including protocols for keeping the data consistent. The commitment protocol of Chapter 20 is a starting point. In such a course, operating systems, databases and communications are again integrated.

Optional courses on specialized systems, such as real-time embedded control systems also follow from this material. How to achieve high performance in filing systems might be taken as another advanced topic, as might memory management, tailored for specific systems.

It is important to have a basis for correct reasoning about the precise behaviour of concurrent systems and various mathematical models are already in use (Hoare, 1985; Milner, 1989). As mentioned above, theory of concurrency might also be deemed further study.

Objective

The main emphasis of the book is system design: how to comprehend existing systems and how to design new systems. One can't write certain kinds of concurrent system in certain languages above certain operating systems. This book aims to show the reader why. Computers are marketed optimistically. Names such as 'real-time operating system' are used with little real concern for their meaning. In order to survive an encounter with a salesperson one must know exactly what one wants and must know the pitfalls to look out for in the systems one is offered. I hope the book will help concurrent systems designers to select the right hardware and software to satisfy their requirements.

Instructor's guide

An instructor's guide is available which contains the following:

- Curriculum design. An outline of parts of the ACM/IEEE-CS 'Computing Curricula 1991' is given. Uses of *Concurrent Systems* in the curriculum are discussed.
- Points to emphasize and teaching hints. For each chapter, key points, potential difficulties and suggested approaches to teaching the material are given.
- Solutions to exercises and some additional exercises. The solutions include examples of how the various designs that are discussed have been used in practice.
- A description of some environments for project work and how to get them.
- Overhead transparency masters.

Acknowledgements

I am grateful for feedback from four sets of undergraduates who have taken the course and have used the notes on which the book is based. I am also grateful to graduate students and colleagues in the systems area for their comments, based on experience. They have been tolerant of the time I have diverted from other activities in order to turn a set of lecture notes into a book. I underestimated this time, of course, and am grateful for their understanding.

Thanks are due to the often anonymous reviewers. Their comments on a first draft which was closer to lecture notes than a self-standing text motivated another year's work. I am particularly grateful to George Coulouris and Jean Dollimore for reviewing both drafts of the book and for the many suggestions they gave. Ken Moody provided substantial feedback on all aspects of the work, in particular, Part III and the appendix. Thanks also to Wu Zhixue for reading and commenting on Part III. Robert Sultana and Noha Adly Atteya undertook a great deal of reading and gave me many useful comments. Professor Chris Haynes' review provided helpful suggestions and great encouragement for the final stages of the work. I greatly appreciate the sustained encouragement of Simon Plumtree of Addison-Wesley.

Jean Bacon
Cambridge, November, 1992

Contents

9   Low-level mechanisms for process synchronization   **210**

10   Language primitives for shared memory   **249**

Introduction: Examples and requirements

CONTENTS

The aim of the book is to show what concurrent systems are, why they are important and how they may be designed and built. We shall start from an informal, intuitive definition of a concurrent system. Concurrent means 'at the same time'. The meaning of 'at the same time' is explored more deeply as we progress through the book, but initially we shall assume that the same measure of time holds throughout a system. A concurrent system must handle separate activities which are in progress at the same time. To be a little more precise, we shall consider two activities to be concurrent if, at a given time, each is at some point between its starting point and finishing point.

The broad range of types of concurrent system is introduced in this chapter and their essential characteristics are highlighted. Requirements for implementing these systems are drawn out in each case and the chapter concludes with a discussion of the requirements of concurrent systems in general. The rest of the book is concerned with meeting these requirements.

We hope to build concurrent systems which exploit new technology in emerging application areas. We need to be in a position to bring a good deal of processing power and memory to bear on a given problem and using a multicomputer system of some kind is likely to be the best way to do this. For this reason, this chapter includes a survey of the different kinds of overall system architecture on which a concurrent software system might run.

In some cases, a system is **inherently concurrent** since it is handling activities that can happen simultaneously in the world external to the computer system, such as users who want to run programs or clients who want to do bank transactions. Alternatively, it might be possible to work on parts of a problem in parallel by devising a concurrent algorithm for its solution. This is a valuable approach when an application involves a massive amount of computation and data and there is a real-time requirement for the result, such as in weather forecasting. These are **potentially concurrent applications**. At present, many problems of this type are solved, if at all, by sequential (rather than concurrent) algorithms on expensive, high-performance computers. A concurrent approach could improve matters in two ways. Either the same quality of result could be achieved at lower cost by using a number of inexpensive off-the-shelf computers, or a better model of the physical system could be built, perhaps giving rise to even more data to be processed but generating a more accurate result. Concurrent algorithms might also bring the solution of a wider range of problems within a reasonable budget.

1.1 Inherently concurrent systems

Systems which must respond to, or manage, simultaneous activities in their external environment are inherently concurrent and may broadly be classified as

- real-time systems;
- database management and transaction processing systems;
- operating systems.

In each case the implementation of the system is as likely to be **distributed** across a number of computers (**hosts**, **nodes** or **sites**) as centralized.

1.1.1 Real-time systems

The special characteristic of real-time systems is that there are timing requirements which are dictated by the environment of the computer system. It may be essential, for example, for the computer system to respond to an alarm signal in some specific time, although it may be highly unlikely that such a signal will occur and it will never be predictable. The term '**hard real-time system**' is used to indicate that the timing requirements are absolute. '**Soft real-time**' indicates that failing to meet a deadline will not lead to a catastrophe.

Another useful distinction is between **static** and **dynamic** real-time systems. In a static system an analysis of the activities that must be carried out by the system can be done when the system is designed. In a dynamic real-time system requests may occur at irregular and unpredictable times and the system must respond dynamically and with guaranteed performance. Examples are given below.

It is worth emphasizing that 'real-time' does not always imply 'very fast indeed', but rather that timing requirements are known and must be guaranteed.

Examples of real-time systems are process control systems for power stations, chemical plants etc., embedded military command and control systems, hospital patient monitoring systems, spaceflight, aeroplane and car engine controllers, air traffic control systems, robot controllers, real-time image processing and display systems, videophones and many more.

Process control

A common scenario is that data is gathered from the controlled system and analysed. This may involve simply taking a temperature or pressure reading at an appropriate time interval and checking against a safe level, or more complex data gathering across the process followed by mathematical analysis and feedback to fine-tune the system. The accuracy with which this can be done depends on the amount of data gathered by whatever measuring or sampling devices are employed and the time that can be spent on the analysis. The data gathering and analysis are predictable and periodic. The period depends on the process being controlled. The computer-controlled fuel injection system for a car engine must sample many times per second; the temperature in a furnace is sampled every few seconds; the water level in a reservoir may only need to be sampled every hour.

This periodic activity must be integrated with the ability to respond to unpredictable events. An alarm could occur, indicating that some action must be taken with high priority. Maybe the temperature of a nuclear reactor is too high and must be lowered, or perhaps gas pressure is building up in a coal mine, indicating the danger of an explosion.

Another type of non-periodic event is high-level or coarse-grained parameter tuning. This is initiated by a management system which has a high-level view of the entire system, perhaps gathered from widespread sampling. Management may also wish to make changes, such as to the relative amounts of the various materials being produced by a system. This may be less urgent than an alarm signal, but is the means by which the process is controlled as a whole.

The two types of activity may be classified as **monitoring** and **control**. Monitoring involves gathering data; control involves regular, fine-grained tuning, irregular coarse-grained tuning and response to alarms. Figure 1.1 shows these two major activities in a computer system which is part of a distributed process control system. There may be a trade-off between the accuracy of the data analysis and the system's ability to respond to events: at certain times, accuracy may be sacrificed to rapid response. But it is critical that if an alarm occurs it must get immediate attention and that certain events must have response in a specified time.

There is scope for concurrency in such systems in that many small computer systems of this kind will work together to control a large industrial or experimental process and each one may have several functions it must perform.

Not all real-time systems are distributed, multicomputer systems. A domestic appliance, a robot, a car engine, or a missile may have a single **embedded** controlling computer. The software will still have several functions to perform,

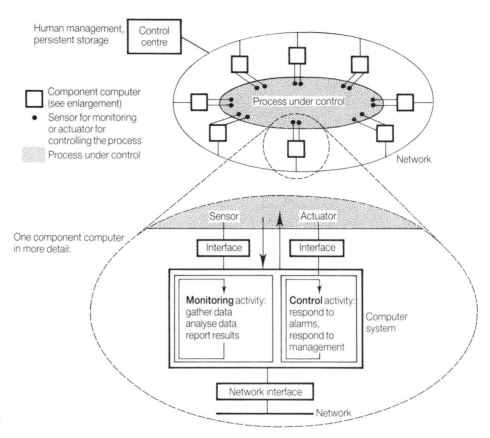

Human management, persistent storage

Control centre

☐ Component computer (see enlargement)

● Sensor for monitoring or actuator for controlling the process

▒ Process under control

Process under control

Network

One component computer in more detail:

Sensor   Actuator

Interface   Interface

Monitoring activity: gather data analyse data report results

Control activity: respond to alarms, respond to management

Computer system

Network interface

Network

Figure 1.1
Example of a distributed process control system.

associated with monitoring and control. There is, in general, a requirement for the support of separate activities.

Real-time systems of the kind described here are hard and static. Timing requirements are absolute and the system's requirements can be analysed statically at system design time. The approach is usually to design a periodic schedule for the system, allowing for the possibility of alarms in each period.

Multimedia systems

An emerging application area for high-performance networked workstations is **multimedia**: the ability to show moving pictures and hear voice in addition to the traditional display of text and graphics. Assuming the workstation has a windowing system, one or more windows could be used for video. Many applications, such as a videophone, videomail or videoconferencing, require a talking person to be displayed. In this case the video (picture) and audio (voice) must be synchronized for delivery to the workstation screen; the voice must be synchronized with lip movements.

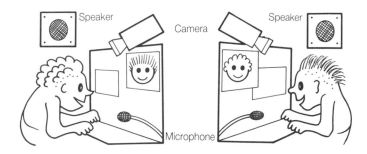

Figure 1.2
Multimedia
workstations.

Videoconferencing and videophones operate in real time. Data can be lost if the system does not keep up. Videomail requires messages which may contain text with video and voice clips to be stored and delivered to the workstation screen when the mail is read. Once the process of reading the mail starts there are real-time requirements on the system to deliver the components at an acceptable rate and in synchrony.

There are many potential applications for stored multimedia documents. For example, a database containing a museum catalogue could include a video clip of an item shown from all angles. A database on ornithology could contain text and drawings for each bird, maps of its territory, audio of the song and video of the bird in flight.

When multimedia data is stored, requests to deliver it to a workstation screen are unpredictable and the system must respond dynamically. Several requests might arrive during the same time period. To achieve acceptable performance the storage system, operating system and communications software must be able to make guarantees of a certain **quality of service**.

Video requires massive amounts of storage space and it must be transferred at a very high rate for a smooth, jitter-free picture to be seen. Taking an example from a local system, a one-minute video clip occupies over 12 megabytes of storage and the required transfer rate is 200 kilobits per second. The voice to be synchronized with the picture has lower storage and bandwidth requirements, typically 64 kbits per second. We assume that adequate amounts of storage are available for video and voice 'across a network' and that the network has enough bandwidth to deliver voice and video 'streams'. The system software design problem is to ensure that both video and voice are delivered to the workstation at a high enough rate for a good picture to be seen and synchronized voice to be heard.

The activities of delivering voice and video are separate and have different requirements for throughput, but both must get sufficient processor time to deliver the image and voice to a standard that the human observer finds acceptable. Although video requires more processing, memory and network resources, we are not too sensitive to temporary hitches in its delivery, whereas we find shortcomings in the delivery of voice infuriating (think of the inaudible announcement that comes over the loudspeaker when your train is due). There are therefore some quite complicated trade-offs to be made.

To what extent should multimedia workstations be considered real-time systems? A videophone requires video and voice to be delivered in real time; if data is corrupted it cannot be recovered except by a human user asking for a repeat. The environment dictates certain requirements for the system to be usable. It could be classified as a soft real-time system.

There is only a quantitative difference between multimedia systems and traditional timesharing systems; multimedia systems need more processing power, network bandwidth and storage capacity and software that is capable of exploiting them. There is a qualitative difference between such soft real-time systems and power station control systems, where there is an absolute requirement for response, even if some components of the system fail. This is implied by the name 'hard real-time system' for the latter.

Hard real-time applications involving real-time video might be as follows:

- An aeroplane contains a video camera. The pictures it records are compared with an internally stored map of its intended route. This is part of an automatic system for keeping the plane to its planned route and to prevent it crashing into hills or church towers.

- A factory automation system involves many mobile robots, each containing a video camera. The robots must avoid obstacles which may include other mobile robots and humans. There have been fatal accidents in systems of this kind, caused by bugs in real-time software.

- Cars of the future might contain video cameras. The car must stop if a child runs in front of it. The cars behind it must avoid crashing into it. Should the image processing software be able to distinguish between a child and a dog (or a rabbit)?

Requirements

The requirements for building a real-time system that have emerged from the above discussion may be summarized as follows:

- There is a need to support separate activities. Some may be periodic, such as gathering data (taking measurements of temperature, pressure etc.), and others unpredictable, such as responding to alarm signals.

- There is a need to meet the specific requirements of each activity, which may involve meeting time deadlines.

- There may be a need for the separate activities to work together to achieve a common goal.

1.1.2 Database management and transaction processing systems

Database applications are concerned with large amounts of persistent data, that is, data on permanent storage devices that exists independently of any running program. A typical user of a database system wants to make **queries** about the data, such as 'what is the current level of my bank account' or 'list the owners who live in Cambridge of purple Ford cars manufactured in 1990'. The owners of the database are concerned with keeping it up to date and will want to make **updates**. We assume a database management system (**DBMS**) which is responsible for interacting with users and organizing the reading and writing of the database to satisfy their requirements. The DBMS is a concurrent system since it may have to handle several clients simultaneously. The term **transaction** is used for a request from a client to a DBMS.

There are many uses for databases. Commercial systems include banking, airline and other booking systems, stock control for retailing, records of employees, and so on. Engineering systems cover such things as CAD systems, VLSI design and components databases for manufacturing. Statistical databases are held of population census data, for weather forecasting etc. Public databases are held by police, health and social service institutions. There are also library and other specialized reference systems with expert systems to assist in the formulation of queries to extract the required information from specialized databases.

In applications where it is not critical that at all times the data appears to be up to date to the current instant, updates may be batched and run when convenient, perhaps overnight. This approach simplifies the management of the database enormously and is likely to be used if at all possible. Many of the problems associated with concurrent access are avoided by this means. For example, users may accept that the value given for the balance of a bank account is not up to date; the value at the end of the previous working day may be output with a clear indication of the time at which the value was valid. There is no guarantee in such a system that there is sufficient money in an account to cover a withdrawal. The trend is towards more up-to-date and interactive use of banking databases. Stock control in a supermarket might be managed on a daily basis with consolidation of purchases and reordering of stock carried out overnight.

In some systems the activities of reading and updating data are closely related and updates cannot be deferred. It would be impossible to run an airline or theatre reservation system with an overnight batched update policy. You need to know immediately whether you have booked a seat and not tomorrow morning, and therefore each transaction needs to see the up-to-date system state. Other examples of **transaction processing systems** are the international automatic teller machine (ATM) network service, which provides cash dispensing and other banking services worldwide, and point of sale terminals. Both are discussed in Chapter 23.

There is scope for concurrency in database applications because of simultaneous requests from clients. In some kinds of database different clients are unlikely to require access to the same part of the database; it is unlikely that anyone else will be attempting to access my medical record at the same time as my doctor. Concurrent access is desirable for a fast response to queries and there are unlikely to be **conflicting** requests, that is, requests that attempt to update and read the same part of the database at the same time. Any number of

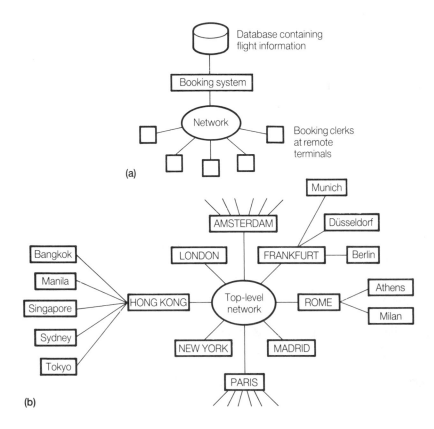

Figure 1.3
Airline booking
systems:
(a) components;
(b) part of the early
SITA private
network.

transactions which only require to read the database may be run in parallel. If it is possible to update the database as well as read it, the DBMS must ensure that transactions do not interfere with each other.

In order to respond to queries in the time-scale required, data will be copied from secondary storage (such as disk) into main memory and reads and updates will use the main memory copy. This introduces the potential problem that the copy of the data held on secondary storage becomes out of date. If the system crashes, the contents of main memory may be lost; for example, a power failure causes loss of main memory. The users of the system may have gone away in the belief that their transactions are complete and their results securely recorded. The management system must ensure that this is the case, even if writing information out to disk slows the system down. A transaction system must therefore support concurrent access and allow for system failure at any time.

Figure 1.3(a) shows the components of a transaction processing system for airline bookings. Many booking clerks can be acting simultaneously on behalf of their clients to book seats on flights recorded in a database. The administration also makes changes to the database. Figure 1.3(b) illustrates the worldwide nature of such a system. The diagram shows some of the components of the SITA (Société Internationale de Télécommunications Aéronautiques) private network as it was in the 1970s (Chou, 1977). Even then, over 200 airlines were members of this non-profit cooperative organization.

The kind of problem addressed in Part II is to book a seat on a flight correctly; it is booked but not double booked (assuming that the owners do not have an over-booking policy). The kind of problem addressed in Part III is how to implement a system which can automate the booking of an itinerary consisting of a number of connecting flights or none at all; if one connection can't be booked then none of the others are.

Requirements

The requirements for building transaction processing and database management systems that have emerged from the above discussion may be summarized as follows:

- There is a need to support separate activities.

- There is a need to ensure that the separate activities access and update common data without interference.

- There is a need to ensure that the results of transactions are recorded permanently and securely before the user is told that an operation has been done.

1.1.3   Operating systems and distributed operating systems

We shall first consider self-standing computer systems. It is useful to distinguish between single-user systems and multi-user systems; see Figure 1.4(a) and (b). Single-user systems range from small inexpensive **personal computers** to high-performance **workstations**. Multi-user systems are based on high-performance micro- or minicomputers (with a small number of users) or expensive multiprocessor mainframe or supercomputers. We consider the hardware basis for concurrent systems in more detail in Section 1.3.

In a single-user system the user's keyboard and screen are packaged with the processor(s) and memory; a single computer is perceived. The users of a multi-user system access the system via a **terminal**. Terminals are separate from the main memory, central processor(s) and shared devices such as disks and printers. A terminal might provide a graphical user interface and a windowing system and might have internal processors and memory dedicated to these functions. The old 'dumb' terminal has evolved into a special-purpose computer. A system might have large numbers of terminals, remote from the central computer, which are managed in groups by dedicated terminal concentrator computers.

A general-purpose operating system runs in the personal computer, single-user workstation or shared computer. Its purpose is to run the users' programs and to allocate the hardware resources they need such as memory, disk space, devices and processors.

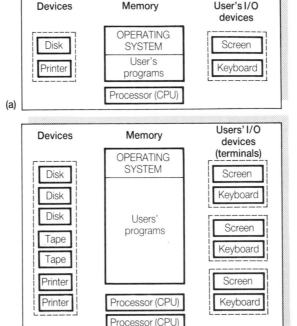

The user's keyboard and screen are likely to be packaged in a single unit together with the memory and processor(s).

The terminal devices are packaged as separate units. There may be large numbers of them, they may be remote from the computer and they may be handled by an intermediate controlling computer, a terminal concentrator.

Figure 1.4
Components of (a) single-user systems and (b) multi-user systems.

There is scope for concurrency in both single-user and multi-user systems. We shall see that devices tend to be very slow compared with processors. The operating system will attend to the devices when necessary, but run programs while the devices are busy producing the next input or performing the last output.

In a single-user system the user should be allowed to start off some lengthy computation, such as 'number crunching' or paginating a long document, and carry out other tasks, such as reading mail, in parallel. The operating system should be able to support these separate concurrent activities, running several applications and handling several devices.

There is obvious scope for concurrency in multi-user systems: running many users' programs, handling many devices simultaneously and responding to users' commands. Again, the operating system will attempt to overlap processing and device handling wherever possible. An example is a printer spooler; users' commands to print files are noted and the printing takes place in parallel with general program execution.

In comparison with the statically analysable real-time systems we considered above, the events handled by operating systems tend to be irregular and unpredictable rather than periodic. The load they must handle is dynamic. A user may start using a terminal or workstation at any time and create a heavy computational or I/O load. Although timing considerations are important they tend not to be as critical and inflexible as in real-time systems. It is desirable that a user

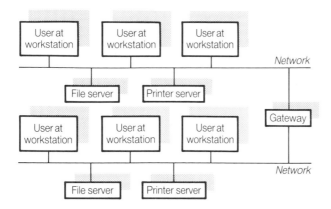

Figure 1.5
A simple distributed
operating system.

at a terminal should get a response in a short time, but the consequences of not meeting this requirement are not comparable with a nuclear power station blowing up.

A multi-user operating system must manage the **sharing** of system resources between users while ensuring that an acceptable service is given to all of them. It must respond to potentially **conflicting demands** from users for the resources it manages, such as memory, processing time and filing space. Requests will occur dynamically and some will involve a number of **related objects** which are managed by the operating system.

Consider an example involving only one user: the user gives the command to delete a file. The space the file occupies on disk will become free space and the directory entry for the file must be removed. This involves reading the directory from disk into main memory, changing it and writing it back to disk. The details of file management will be explained in Chapter 5, but it is clear that the simple operation of deleting a file involves several different operations by the operating system. The design of a file management system must allow for the fact that a crash could occur at any time, including part-way through a composite operation, and also that different users may make concurrent requests for operations such as creating and deleting files.

Distributed operating systems

Distributed systems consist of computers connected by a communications medium such as a local area network (LAN). LANs are generally owned by a single organization and span relatively small distances, typically a single building or a few adjacent buildings. A university campus network may comprise a number of interconnected LANs. A popular model of a LAN-based distributed system is that of personal workstations augmented by shared server computers available across the network, for filing, printing etc., as shown in Figure 1.5.

The workstation operating system is a single-user system with scope for concurrency as described above. The workstations may have local disks, and therefore local filing system software. However, it is likely that the local disks will be relatively small and users will run out of space. Also, users will want to share files with each other. It makes sense to store system files that everyone needs centrally rather than at every workstation. Also, users don't want the trouble of backing up their own files to guard against disk or software failures. For these reasons it is likely that file storage will be provided as a network-based service. It is also likely that a number of file servers will be needed to provide sufficient storage space and processing capacity for all but the smallest systems. These **shared servers** must respond to simultaneous requests from clients and are therefore concurrent systems. The Athena system at the Massachusetts Institute of Technology (MIT) (Treese, 1988) and the ITC system at Carnegie Mellon University (Satyanarayanan, 1985) are examples of this kind of distributed system. They provide computing services for all the students of their respective universities.

The operating systems in the computers that are part of a distributed system contain software for **communications handling**. At the lowest level, handling a network connection is similar to handling a high-speed peripheral. However, the data delivered by the network may have come from any one of the other computers in the distributed system rather than just a single device. Computers can send data at very high speed and the network is likely to deliver pieces of data from many sources in an interleaved order. The higher levels of communications software will therefore have a number of incoming communications in progress simultaneously and must deliver complete, reassembled 'messages' to the correct destinations.

The communications software must also take 'messages' from its clients and send them across the network to their intended destinations. Again, a number of requests for this service may be outstanding at a given time. A given message may contain a very large document and may be split into pieces of an acceptable size for the network hardware.

It is clear from the above discussion that a communications handling **subsystem** of an operating system is itself a concurrent system. The term 'subsystem' will be used to indicate a major functional unit within a system.

The above discussion has taken the example of a localized distributed system based on a LAN. There are many distributed systems connected by wide area networks (WANs) and communications software is in general designed to allow worldwide interaction.

Requirements of operating systems

- There is a need for the operating system to support separate activities at the application level (external to the operating system): the independent actions of its users or the multiple activities of a single user. The requirements that applications place on operating systems are dynamic and unpredictable.

- There is a need for separate activities within the operating system: it must handle simultaneous requests from a number of its clients and it must handle simultaneously active devices.

- There is a need for some of the separate activities to cooperate to achieve a common goal; an example is a printer spooler which prints files for users. It must take requests from the various users who want their files printed and liaise with whatever system components know how to control the printer and locate files on the disk.

- There is a need to manage competition for resources by separate activities.

- Separate activities must be able to read and write system data structures without interference.

- There is a need for a single task to be carried out as a whole, even when it involves a number of related subtasks. This must take into account potentially interfering concurrent activities and possible failures of the system.

The requirements on operating systems are wide-ranging. Many aspects of concurrency control have traditionally been studied in the context of operating systems, since many problems were first encountered and defined in operating system design. Chapters 3, 4 and 5 expand on operating system functions and Chapter 6 shows how they support separate activities. Part II is concerned with some of the detailed problems of cooperation and competition between related activities.

Part III explores the problems associated with composite tasks. This area has traditionally been studied in the context of database management and transaction processing systems, since these systems have stronger requirements in this area than traditional operating systems. Operating systems may tell a user that the most recent version of a file has been lost after a system crash. If a database system tells a user that a transaction is done it must guarantee that this is the case and the results of the transaction must survive any subsequent system failure. In spite of this difference in emphasis the conceptual basis both for operating systems and for database systems is the same.

1.2   Potentially concurrent applications

We now move from systems which are inherently concurrent to applications which might benefit from concurrent implementation. Parallel algorithms are not presented in detail. Rather, the aim is to show the requirements for the support of separate but related concurrent activities that will work together to achieve some result. It is also important to investigate the requirement for some degree of interaction between the parallel computations.

The general motivation for exploiting potential concurrency in an application is that some or all of the following are the case:

- there is a large amount of computing to be done;
- there is a large amount of data to be processed;
- there is a real-time requirement for the result;

● hardware is available for running the potentially concurrent components in parallel.

First, some general approaches to obtaining a concurrent solution to a problem are described.

1.2.1 Replicated code, partitioned data

Perhaps the simplest approach is to use a sequential algorithm but to **partition the data.** Figure 1.6 shows the general idea. If all the components must run to completion the overall time taken is that of the longest component (the other components have run in parallel and have finished before the longest one) plus the overhead of initiating the parallel computations and synchronizing on their completion. The speed-up achieved therefore depends on being able to divide the computation into pieces with approximately equal computation time. This is because we have assumed that the total amount of data processing to be done is the same whether it is done sequentially or in parallel. If we can divide the computation into components which require the same amount of computation time we have maximized the concurrency in the execution of the algorithm.

Examples of problems which are suited to this static partitioning of data are as follows:

● finding all the roots of a given function;

● finding the turning points of a given function;

● searching for specific values in data which has no ordering related to the values required; for example, the data may be records about people which are ordered according to their surnames. You are searching for people with a specific value in some field of their record, for example, those with an Australian grandparent.

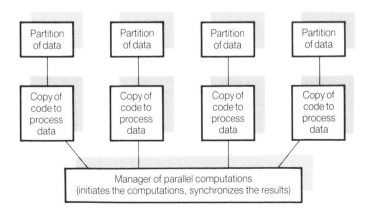

Figure 1.6
Replicated code,
partitioned data.

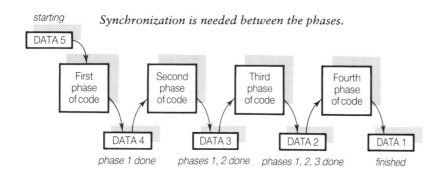

Figure 1.7
A four-stage
pipeline.

A parallel algorithm for searching might be particularly suitable for large amounts of data, some of which is in main memory and some on disk. While one parallel activity waits for more data to be brought in from disk, another can proceed with processing data in main memory.

In some applications, once a solution is found by one component all the others can cease their activity. An example is a search for a single solution to a problem or query. In this case, once the solution is found all the components which are still executing should be stopped. The system mechanisms should make it possible to do this.

1.2.2   Pipelined processing

Another simple approach is the **pipeline**. If the total function to be applied to the data can be divided into distinct processing phases, different portions of data can flow along from function to function. Figure 1.7 shows a four-stage pipeline. An example is a compiler with phases for lexical analysis, parsing, type checking, code generation and so on. As soon as the first program or module has passed the lexical analysis phase it may be passed on to the parsing phase while the lexical analyser starts on the second program or module.

The requirements here are for the separate activities executing the various phases to be able to synchronize with each other: to wait for new data to become available or to wait for the next phase to finish processing its current data.

1.2.3   Tree-structured algorithms

Many algorithms can be represented by a tree structure. For example, the evaluation of a function for given arguments may often be split into the evaluation of two (or more) subfunctions, which in turn can be split... In this case there is potential for parallel evaluation each time a branch is made as each subfunction must deliver its result to contribute to the higher-level evaluation.

Certain problems require that every branch must be evaluated in full. In other applications the tree structure is a way of dividing a search space where only one solution is required. The whole space should be traversed only if no solution exists. As soon as a solution is found the algorithm should terminate. Again, as discussed in Section 1.2.1, ongoing executions (and the process of creating new ones) should be stopped.

In other cases, such as speech recognition, the parallel branch traversals may represent alternative possibilities for a solution. Each branch has an associated probability of matching the solution and the requirement is to produce the combination of branches with the highest probability of success.

A tree structure introduces more potential parallelism than the simple, static, linear partitioning described above in Section 1.2.1. A new problem here is how to create a reasonable number of parallel computations dynamically, bearing in mind the overhead of each computation and the number of physical processors available to execute them.

1.2.4 Shared data

In Section 1.1.2 we saw that activities in a transaction processing system need to access the same shared data, such as in an airline booking system. The requirements of the application are such that the data cannot be partitioned: you have to book the seat on the flight the client wants, even if someone else is attempting to book a seat on the same flight.

The algorithms outlined above have attempted to avoid the need for concurrent activities to access shared data. We focused on parallel activities carrying out independent work. Even in these cases, their results may need to be merged into a shared data structure. Also, when one activity finishes its work it may be able to request more work from the manager or from one of the other parallel activities. In practice, interaction and cooperation between the activities are likely to be required.

Concurrent algorithms may be designed so that concurrent activities access shared, rather than strictly partitioned, data. For example, the work to be carried out is divided into units and recorded in a shared data structure. Each activity reads a work item from the shared data structure and marks it as taken. A potential problem is that the concurrent activities have to access the shared data one at a time to avoid corrupting it (we shall study this problem later). If the units of work are long relative to the time taken to get the next unit from the data structure then contention for access to the shared data is likely to be tolerable.

1.2.5 Application areas

A full treatment of the different application areas in which concurrent algorithms can be used merits a number of books, for example, Quinn (1987), Almasi and Gottlieb (1989) and Bertsekas and Tsitsiklis (1989). A brief summary is given here and detailed study is left for further reading.

In the area of numerical algorithms the modelling, or simulation, of physical systems can consume a great deal of computing power and data space. Examples are simulation of nuclear reactions and modelling the atmosphere for weather forecasting. Numerical methods based on the solution of partial differential equations, Fast Fourier and other transforms and optimization in general are candidates for parallel decomposition.

Software engineering tasks, such as the compilation of programs which comprise very large numbers of modules, are an obvious target for parallelization. A library containing the interface specifications of the modules must be available so that intermodule operation invocations can be checked.

Graphics applications, such as those involving raytracing techniques to achieve three-dimensional images, can be parallelized.

The general area of artificial intelligence has a large number of problems which require a large amount of processing power, such as voice and image recognition, natural language processing and expert systems. It is often the case that a number of solutions to a problem must be evaluated and the most likely one selected.

1.2.6   Requirements for supporting concurrent applications

Some simple approaches to designing concurrent algorithms were presented above. They illustrated the approaches of partitioning the data, statically or dynamically, and partitioning the code into a pipeline. For potentially concurrent applications we may have the option of designing an algorithm based on partitioning. For inherently concurrent applications, such as transaction processing systems, we may not have the option of partitioning the data. For some applications it may be more appropriate to use shared data. In general, in a potentially concurrent application, the separate activities are related and cooperate to achieve a common goal.

Some requirements for the support of concurrency at the application level are:

- There is a need to support separate activities.

- There is a need for these activities to be managed appropriately: to be created as required and stopped when no longer needed.

- There is a need for separate activities to synchronize with each other, and possibly to pass data when synchronized.

- there may be a need for separate activities to share the data relating to the application; alternatively, the data may be strictly partitioned.

The application will be written in a programming language and it must be possible to meet the requirements outlined here through the facilities offered by the language and the underlying operating system.

1.3   Architectures for concurrent systems

It is desirable that cheap processing power, large and fast memory and high-band-width communications media should be exploited. Conventional architectures and interconnection topologies may be used as a basis for concurrent software. Alternatively, special architectures may be appropriate for certain application areas. Some are well understood and available commercially, while some are novel and still the subject of research and evaluation. This section reviews the options available. Where appropriate, any special language system associated with the architecture is described.

A broad classification that is helpful when considering concurrent systems was given by Flynn (Bayer *et al.*, 1978). It is based on the number of independent instruction streams and data streams being processed by the system.

1.3.1   System classification

SISD: Single instruction stream, single data stream

This is the conventional uniprocessor model, with a single processor fetching and executing a sequence of instructions which operate on the data items specified within them. This is the original von Neumann model of the operation of a computer.

SIMD: Single instruction stream, multiple data stream

In this case there are many processing elements but they are designed to execute the same instruction at the same time. For this reason the processors can be simple: they do not need to fetch instructions from their private memory, but receive their instructions from a central controller. They do, however, operate on separate data items such as the elements of vectors or arrays.

Any machine that has vector or array instructions which execute in parallel can be classified as SIMD. It may be that the array processor component is a special-purpose attached processor such as in the ICL DAP (Distributed Array Processor). This component has thousands of small processors and is loaded to perform matrix calculations. A conventional SISD computer carries out this process. The very high-performance, and expensive, Cray range of computers offer vector operations of this type.

The potential increase in performance through using an SIMD processor depends on the proportion of matrix instructions in the application. It is inevitable that parts of the algorithms concerned will execute sequentially and there is overhead in loading the array processor.

This kind of concurrency is **fine-grained**, being at the level of a single instruction on a single data item, and **synchronous**, in that the operations occur together. Many application areas produce problems that require vector and matrix solutions. Some of these areas are well funded and are able to use the expensive SIMD computers, often called 'supercomputers', that have been developed specifically for this purpose. In this book we are concerned with more general-purpose concurrent systems and will not consider SIMD machines further.

MIMD: Multiple instruction stream, multiple data stream

Systems with more than one processor fetching and executing instructions are MIMD. The instructions need not be closely related and they are executed asynchronously. This is a very broad category (the classification scheme has been criticized for this reason) and includes networks of computers and multiprocessors built from separate computers.

Another broad classification that distinguishes conventional systems from experimental ones is into the categories **control-driven, data-driven** and **demand-driven**. The conventional von Neumann model of a computer is control-driven. The processor fetches and executes a sequence of instructions, the program counter acting as sequence controller. It is argued that sequencing is usually overspecified in conventional programming languages and that, very often, instructions that are written down in a sequence could be executed in parallel. The problem is how to detect automatically when instructions are independent of each other and exploit this potential concurrency.

Consider the following program fragment:

$x := a{\times}b$;
$y := c{\times}d$;
$z := x{+}y$;

In this simple example, x and y can be evaluated in parallel, but both must be evaluated before z.

An outline of the range of possible hardware on which a concurrent software system might be implemented is now given. Sections 1.3.2 to 1.3.4 consider control-driven architectures with increasing numbers of constituent computers. The data-driven and demand-driven approaches are discussed briefly in Sections 1.3.5 and 1.3.6. Finally, network-based systems are considered.

1.3.2   Conventional uniprocessors

A single uniprocessor computer may be used to implement some kinds of concurrent system. A time-sharing operating system is an example. Many users are interacting with the system simultaneously and many programs are in the process of being executed (that is, they are at some point between their start and termination) at a given time. We shall see in Chapter 6 that the fact that there is only one processor may be transparent to the programmer. At the application software level it is as though each program is executing on a dedicated processor.

An important point about uniprocessors is that the technique of forbidding interrupts may be used for controlling concurrency. Device handling, including interrupts, will be explained in Chapter 3, but the basic idea is that you can prevent the processor from doing anything other than its current activity until it reaches the end of it, when you 'enable interrupts' again. In the meantime, mayhem may have broken out and alarm signals may be pending but the processor carries on regardless. We shall expand on this technique for simplifying the design of concurrent software in Chapter 8, and Chapter 21 gives an operating system case study which uses this technique. It obviously has to be used with great care and for short periods of time. The system designer has to decide whether, and to what extent, to make use of the fact that software will run on a uniprocessor. This dependency can impose a major constraint on possible system upgrades and has often prevented the owners of commercial operating systems from improving the performance of their systems by introducing more processors. Removing such a dependency retrospectively requires a major rewrite of the heart of a system.

Starting from a uniprocessor system it is common to exploit more processing power by adding dedicated machines for specific device-handling functions. The terminal handling function might be offloaded into a separate 'front end' computer. Disk controllers have become quite complex in their functionality and contain dedicated processors. When functions have been moved to special-purpose, dedicated computers to the greatest possible extent, the next step is to move on to multiprocessors to obtain more potential concurrency.

The conventions for processor architecture evolve in response to factors such as the increase in processing power and the speed and quantity of memory. The trend for general-purpose processors is towards reduced instruction set computers (RISC) and away from complex instruction set computers (CISC). There are implications for concurrency control in RISC machines, which are discussed in Chapters 3 and 9.

There is a place for conventional uniprocessors in many large-scale concurrent systems. A process control system may consist of a number of relatively small computers placed strategically around the process being controlled. A network connects them and the system is managed automatically by software whenever possible and manually when higher-level, strategic decisions are required. A program development environment may be based on personal uniprocessor workstations and uniprocessor machines may also be used for controlling printers and file servers. This style of concurrent system was introduced above in Section 1.1.

1.3.3 Shared-memory multiprocessors

The conventional multiprocessor model is of a relatively small number of processors (ranging from 2 to about 30) executing programs from a single shared memory. Note that only one copy of the operating system and any other system software is needed. We now have the situation that software from the same memory is being executed at the same time on a number of processors. A fundamental distinction between different kinds of concurrent software is whether or not the components which run in parallel share memory.

It is more difficult to write operating systems that run on multiprocessors than on uniprocessors. Aspects of this problem are still being researched. Sometimes, to simplify the design, one dedicated processor will execute the operating system and one dedicated processor will handle all I/O. At the end of Part II the reader should understand the trade-offs involved in such decisions.

When more than some fairly small number of processors access a single shared memory, contention for memory access becomes too great. The effect can be alleviated by providing the processors with hardware-controlled caches in which recently accessed memory locations are held. If we wish to get more concurrency into a system we have to look to a different system topology.

1.3.4 Multicomputer multiprocessors

There are very many different computer system designs based on interconnected computers. Let us make the simplifying assumption that each processor accesses only its own local memory directly. The processors may be placed on a shared bus, typically up to 10–15 of them before contention becomes excessive. They communicate with each other through the control and data paths of the bus. A hierarchy of buses may be used to increase the number of processors in the system, as for example in the early Pluribus and Cm* systems (Siewiorek *et al.*, 1982).

To exploit massive concurrency we may wish to use many tens of processors. In this case their connectivity is a major design decision. It is sometimes argued that a tree structure is appropriate for a wide range of problems and that each processor should be connected to three others (its parent and two children). The Inmos transputer has four high-speed serial links for the construction of inter-connected systems. A tree-like structure could be built or indeed any topology appropriate for the application.

A crossbar switch arrangement allows any processor to communicate with any other, but only if no other processor is already doing so. It is expensive to connect everything to everything using a switching arrangement and we must not forget that a motivation for using large numbers of computers is to take advantage of inexpensive, off-the-shelf components, so the cost is important.

As network performance has increased, interconnection by this means is an alternative to multicomputer multiprocessors for some concurrent applications; the components may be loaded onto separate machines connected to a network.

A general problem with multicomputers is the complexity of the software systems required to manage them and the time to load software prior to execution. There is little advantage for general applications if loading concurrent software into a multicomputer is a lengthy and complex process, involving transfer through many computers *en route*, even if execution completes in a fraction of the sequential execution time. At present, such topologies tend to be used for software that will run indefinitely once loaded, such as in embedded control systems.

1.3.5   Dataflow (data-driven) architectures

In a conventional (imperative) programming language you have to write down a sequence of statements even when there are no dependencies between them and they could be executed in any order or concurrently. Dataflow is a response to this overspecification of sequencing.

It is also argued that conventional von Neumann computers have a fundamental design flaw in their bottleneck for memory access. Instructions are fetched in sequence and their data operands are then read or written as specified in the instruction. It is difficult to speed up program execution by fetching instructions or data in advance so you have to rely on getting them quickly when you find out where they are.

In the dataflow model, an instruction may execute as soon as its data operands are ready. Any number of instructions can execute in parallel, depending on the number of processors available. It is possible to arrange for the operations to have at most two arguments. The first argument to be ready for an operation will detect that its pair is not yet available and will wait in memory provided for the purpose. The second will detect that the first is ready, by an associative match on the memory, and they will then go off together to a processor for execution. The result of the operation will become an argument for another operation, and so on.

It is necessary to distinguish between different executions of the same operation, such as in separate calls of a given procedure and the executions of a loop in a program. To address this problem special languages have been developed for dataflow in which there can be at most one assignment to a given variable.

The concurrency made available by the dataflow approach is potentially very great and at a very fine granularity: at the machine instruction level. The challenge is to devise an architecture that can exploit the concurrency.

A problem with a data-driven approach is that unnecessary processing may be carried out for paths in a program that may never be followed; for example, in a simple if-then-else statement, both the 'then' path and the 'else' path may have been computed before the condition is evaluated. This computation may have been done in competition with other computations which were needed. To solve this problem a 'demand-driven' approach is advocated with the aim that only those values that are needed are computed. Function application has seemed attractive as a basis for this approach.

1.3.6   Architectures for functional languages

A pure functional language does not have destructive assignment statements. When a function is applied to its arguments it always produces the same result since there can be no side-effects; that is, in a functional language you can assume that $f(a) + f(a) = 2 \times f(a)$. This is not true in all imperative languages because the first call of f with argument a may have caused an assignment to some variable within the body of f (a side-effect). The second call $f(a)$ may then deliver a different result from the first.

It is argued therefore that functional languages are inherently concurrent. Any number of function applications can be carried out in parallel; as soon as the arguments are available the function can be applied. There is greater potential for controlling the concurrency than in the dataflow approach if we can defer a function application until we are sure that the result is needed: so called 'lazy evaluation'. Again, the challenge is to design a machine to exploit the idea.

Both data-driven and demand-driven architectures, and associated software systems, are still in the research domain. In the meantime, conventional von Neumann machines have exhibited a regular and dramatic increase in performance and decrease in cost with which it is very difficult to compete (Hennessy and Patterson, 1990).

1.3.7 Network-based systems

Local area networks (LANs)

A local area network (LAN) offers **full connectivity** for some number of computer systems. This contrasts with many multicomputer multiprocessor topologies as discussed above: for example, a transputer can be connected to at most four other transputers. Each transputer in a multi-transputer topology may need to handle data which comes from an external source and is destined for an external destination. In contrast, each computer on a network is only concerned with data which is sent specifically to it.

Figure 1.8 shows three basic LAN topologies, namely star, bus and ring, for the popular workstation–server model discussed in Section 1.1. In the star topology every message is first directed to a central switch which forwards it to its intended destination. The central switch is an obvious reliability hazard and should, perhaps, be a reliable multiprocessor. In a bus topology an attached computer that wants to communicate puts its 'message' addressed to its intended recipient computer on the bus. All computers monitor the bus and extract the messages addressed to them. Failure of an attached computer usually does not stop the bus from working. The problem to be solved is how to determine when the bus is free to be used. We shall see one solution in Section 3.8. In the ring topology an attached computer that wants to communicate puts its 'message' on the ring. When the message passes through the intended recipient's station it is extracted. Failure of any repeater causes the whole ring to fail and methods of duplicating the links and stations are used in applications which cannot tolerate failure.

The approach to communications handling in component computers of multi-computer multiprocessor systems and computers attached to networks is very different. This is partly because they have evolved to meet different requirements and partly because of their different emphasis on hardware and software to

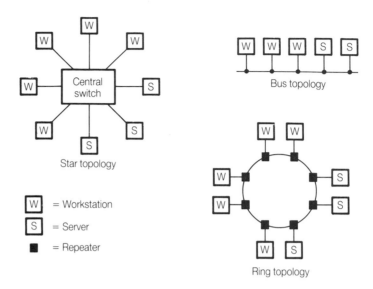

Figure 1.8
Star, bus and ring
LAN topologies.

support data transfer. The former employ **hardware protocols,** such as in a computer's internal bus, to transmit data from source to destination. The higher levels of software, which interpret the data (introduced in Section 1.1.3), tend to be much simpler than in network-based systems. The **software protocols** which the latter employ will be introduced in Section 3.9. These handle more options for sending information to different destinations, allow for loss of data due to network errors or shortage of storage space and in general are more complex.

The basic philosophy of network communications software is to regard the network as a shared resource which must be managed. For example, a user of an attached workstation may have started a background compilation, which requires several files to be read from a file server and, in parallel, may be reading mail from a mail server. Certain attached computers exist solely to support communication, for example, when two LANs are connected by a **gateway computer** or a LAN is connected to a wide area network (WAN).

A simple outline of data communication using a LAN is that a packet of information is composed by a connected computer system, addressed to some other connected computer system, and put on the LAN. The addressing information in the packet ensures that the intended destination computer will take the packet. It is a function of the software in the attached computers to compose and interpret the information.

The LAN design determines the size of the packet of information that it can accept. An Ethernet packet can contain up to 4 kbytes of data and a Cambridge Fast Ring cell contains 32 bytes, for example. This should not have to be a concern of application-level software, so communications software manages the transmission and safe reception of information between networked systems. Communications hardware and software are discussed further in Chapter 3.

LANs are widely used as a basis for program development environments. Each user has a workstation and there are shared server computers such as file servers; that is, the LAN is the interconnection medium for a distributed system, such as is described in Section 1.1.3.

The bandwidth of the LAN medium is shared by the attached computers. In certain types of LAN a proportion of the bandwidth can be guaranteed to each attached computer. This kind of guarantee can be essential for some applications. It is also important to know the overhead imposed by the communications software. The network may be able to guarantee a high, sustained throughput of data but the application software is concerned with the time taken for data to be transferred between application levels on different computers. The design of the communications software and the operating system greatly affect this, but as LAN bandwidth increases it becomes increasingly feasible for a LAN-based system to be used for many kinds of distributed application.

A single LAN, with associated communications software, can handle a certain number of attached computers. If more than this were to be attached, contention for access to the network might become too frequent, and some networks might become congested. For this reason, and also for reasons of geographic separation, a number of interconnected LANs are often used in a company or campus, sometimes called a local internet.

Wide area networks (WANs)

When computers or LANs need to be connected over long distances, wide area networks (WANs) are used, as shown in Figure 1.9. There are now many worldwide WANs which are used for applications such as electronic mail, information retrieval services, dealings on the international stock exchanges, banking, commerce and science. Figure 1.9 indicates that certain computers are dedicated to the communications handling function. A gateway computer is shown attaching each LAN and host system to the WAN and a communications subnet comprising computers called 'routers' is shown. These communications computers cooperate to route each 'message' from its source to its destination.

Like the international telephone service, basic WAN infrastructure is provided by the public telephone companies. There are also WANs with private, dedicated connections.

In general, LANs operate at 10s to 100s of megabits per second and are highly reliable. WANs comprise many different links with different characteristics; some may be slow and unreliable. A worldwide network may contain a satellite link through which a large volume of data can be transferred but with a long end-to-end delay; some computers may be attached to a WAN by telephone lines. The trend is towards the provision of high-speed connections which have the characteristics of LANs.

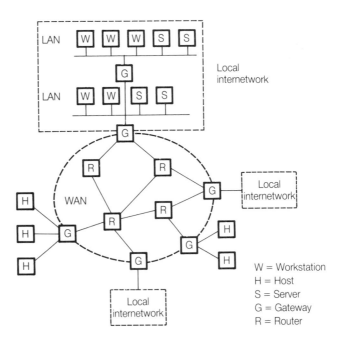

Figure 1.9
LANs connected by
WANs.

We discuss networks in more detail in Chapter 3. Chapter 22 introduces a network technology that is suitable for high-speed WAN connections and Chapter 23 includes a case study which involves the use of high-speed WANs.

1.3.8   Summary of hardware bases for concurrent systems

Figure 1.10 summarizes the topologies that might be used as the hardware basis for a concurrent system. The arrows indicate the direction of increasing concurrency achieved through different paths of development.

Architectures based on dataflow or function application are an alternative to the conventional von Neumann machine. They attempt to exploit all the potential concurrency of the application rather than that written down in a conventional programming language. Their challenge is to devise an efficient implementation, able to compete with the sophistication of current conventional processor and compiler technology. As they are still in the research domain and are often associated with specific languages they will not be considered further in this book.

The central path takes a single uniprocessor as starting point and attempts to introduce an increasing amount of processing power. Special-purpose processors can handle devices, but a major design change comes when several processors are used to execute programs residing in a single memory. Above a certain number of processors accessing a given memory, a topology comprising interconnected

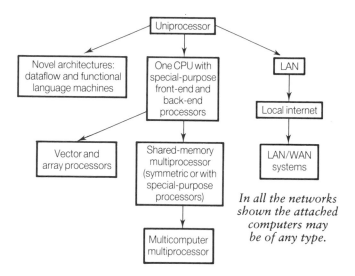

Figure 1.10
Summary of
concurrent system
topologies.

computers is necessary. There is a variety of possible interconnection structures. Vector and array processors may be seen as special-purpose multiprocessor machines.

An alternative to the complexity of the interconnection structures of multi-computer multiprocessor systems is a network. A LAN medium may be used to achieve full connectivity of a certain number of computers, but communication is achieved through software rather than hardware protocols. As LAN performance increases, networked computers can be used for distributed computations as well as the more conventional program development environments, provided that the operating system and communications software impose an acceptable and bounded overhead.

1.4   A definition of a concurrent system

The discussion so far has been based on an intuitive notion of what a concurrent system is. We have looked at a number of types of computerized system in which different activities are in the process of being executed (are at some stage between their starting point and finishing point) at the same time, that is, concurrently. Figure 1.11 shows some of the concurrent (sub)systems that have been mentioned. In each case a number of activities may be in progress simultaneously within the system, either because components of a concurrent algorithm have been started off in parallel or because a number of clients may simultaneously make demands on the system, as shown in Figure 1.12. The concurrent system may be an operating system, a subsystem within an operating system or

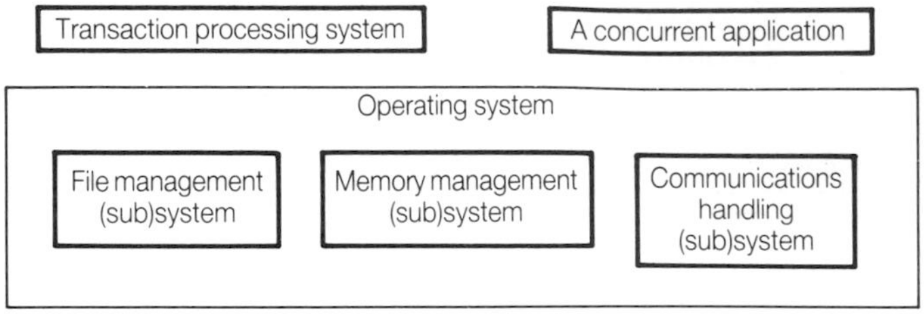

Figure 1.11
Examples of
concurrent
(sub)systems.

Figure 1.12
Concurrent activity.

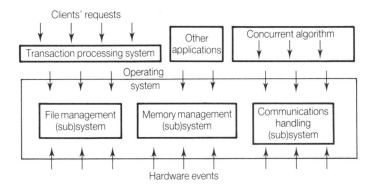

an application or service running above an operating system. In all cases, the concurrent system shown may be distributed across a number of computers rather than centralized in a single computer.

We have made an implicit assumption that it is meaningful to assert that two events happen 'at the same time'. We shall examine this assumption more deeply when we look at systems in which the time at which an event happens is defined by a clock local to the computer in which the event takes place. If many computers, each with their own clocks, are cooperating together to achieve some goal the times their local clocks indicate are not guaranteed to be the same.

We are concerned with **software systems**, implemented on a variety of hardware, in which a number of **separate activities** are in progress at the same time. The separate activities are **related** in some sense; we assume that it is possible to define the **goal** of the concurrent system. This may, however, be very general, such as 'to support the independent activities of a number of users of an operating system', or very specific, such as 'to find the most probable piece of English speech represented by some digitally encoded data'.

In some cases the separate activities may be working together closely, **cooperating**, to solve a given problem. In other cases the relation may be much looser; the concurrent activities may be independent but running above common system software and needing to share common system resources for which they must **compete**.

The activities may need to **interact with the external environment** of the computer system and may need to meet **timing requirements** when doing so.

The activities may need to use the **main memory only** of a single computer (as part of a 'load and go' program execution) or they may use main memory only, but of a number of computers in a distributed system. Finally, the activities may access or record data in persistent memory (for example, a disk-based filing system). In this case they use **both main memory and persistent memory** of a single computer or of computers in a distributed system.

1.5   Requirements for implementing concurrent systems

Some common requirements can be drawn from the discussion on concurrent systems above.

1. Support for separate activities. Examples are:
    the monitoring and control activities in a process control system;
    the running of users' programs by an operating system;
    the handling of devices by an operating system;
    the transactions of the customers of a banking system;
    the concurrent computations executing an application.

2. Support for the management of separate activities, in particular, the ability to create, run, stop and kill them, and possibly to indicate their relative priorities.

3. Support for related activities to work together. Examples are:
    parallel activities each generating part of a solution to a problem;
    device handling programs which deliver input data to, or take output data from, user programs;
    booking clerks making airline bookings on behalf of clients, when many clerks can run programs concurrently.

4. The ability to meet timing requirements. Examples are:
    that an alarm might require a response in a specified time;
    the weather forecast must be ready before the time of the forecast arrives;
    users must hear clear, smooth, recognizable speech and see non-jittering video;
    users should get response in a 'reasonable' time from systems.
    If a real-time application runs above an operating system the application must know what the operating system can guarantee and with what probability. Note that it might be necessary for the application level to indicate the priorities of its separate activities to the underlying operating system in order that timing requirements can be met. This is not possible in most current operating systems.

5. Support for composite tasks. A single task may have several components which are executed concurrently with other tasks. The system may fail after the completion of some of the subtasks but before the whole task is complete.

The rest of this book shows how these requirements are met. Part I is concerned with establishing the abstraction and implementation of **process** to meet the requirement for support of separate activities. Chapter 2 gives a high-level view of modular system structure and the dynamic execution of software by processes. Chapters 3, 4 and 5 describe operating system functions that support concurrent systems. Chapter 6 focuses on the support provided by operating systems for separate activities and the issues involved in attempting to meet timing constraints. Chapter 7 discusses the support for programming concurrent systems in high-level languages. Part II shows how related activities may work together to carry out the functions of a concurrent system. In order to keep the complexity of the presentation to a minimum, the discussion in Part II is restricted to the implementation of correct execution of a 'single operation' without interference. Part III addresses the problems of composite tasks which may involve a number of subtasks involving a single main memory, main memory and persistent memory in a single computer system, or the main memory and persistent memory of computers in a distributed system.

Exercises

1.1 (a) What is a real-time system?
 (b) Why is it useful to distinguish 'hard' from other real-time systems?
 (c) In what ways do operating systems which support real-time systems differ from those which support single-user workstations and multi-user, time-sharing systems?

1.2 Classify the following as hard real-time, real-time or non-real-time systems:
 An embedded computer system which controls the fuel mixture in a car engine
 A robot controller for a car production assembly line
 An on-line library catalogue system
 A single-user workstation which supports graphics, digitized voice and video
 A worldwide electronic mail (email) system
 A network of computers for a banking system
 A hospital patient monitoring and control system
 An on-line medical record system
 A weather forecasting system based on a model of the earth's atmosphere
 An international stock exchange computer system
 Do any of the above systems have to handle concurrent activities?

1.3 Give examples of monitoring and control activities in real-time and non-real-time systems.

1.4 (a) Define three general models for concurrent algorithms.
(b) On what kinds of hardware could you run a concurrent algorithm and expect to achieve better performance than on a uniprocessor? Are any new overheads introduced for the hardware you mention?

1.5 (a) What is a concurrent system?
(b) Can a concurrent system run on a uniprocessor computer? Give examples to justify your answer.

1.6 What is a shared-memory multiprocessor? Are any of the approaches for devising concurrent algorithms particularly suited to this kind of architecture?

1.7 What is the difference between communications handling for a multicomputer system with hardware-controlled connections between specific computers and a network-based multicomputer system?

Further reading

Further reading in the area of real-time systems may be found in Burns and Wellings (1989) and Stankovic and Ramamritham (1988). Hopper (1990) describes a multimedia workstation project.

There are many books devoted to database systems, some of which cover distributed database, for example, Bernstein *et al.* (1987), Date (1983, 1986), Korth and Silberschatz (1991), Ceri and Pellagati (1987), Stefano and Pellagati (1987), Bell and Grimson (1992).

Many books are devoted to operating systems, for example Silberschatz *et al.* (1991), Tanenbaum (1988, 1992), and Janson (1985). Distributed operating systems are the concern of Coulouris and Dollimore (1988), Sloman and Kramer (1987) and Tanenbaum and van Renesse (1985). Bayer *et al.* (1978) contains a number of classic papers which are referenced throughout this book. Communications handling is the subject matter of many books, for example, Tanenbaum (1988) and Halsall (1992).

Parallel algorithms for general or specific application areas are the concern of Quinn (1987), Manber (1989, Chapter 10) and Bertsekas and Tsitsiklis (1989). Almasi and Gottlieb (1989) include the topic as well as parallel architectures. Thakaar (1987) is a collection of papers on dataflow and functional language machines.

Siewiorek *et al.* (1981) is an excellent source of reference material on computer systems. Hennessy and Patterson (1990) motivate the design of current systems based on the characteristics of technology.

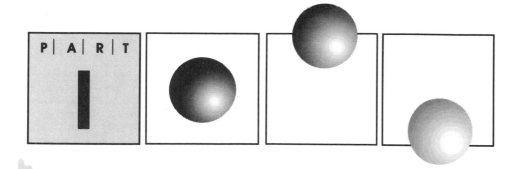

Background and fundamentals

CHAPTERS

Computer science is concerned with **exploiting technology**. A prime motivation for the study of concurrent systems is to be able to exploit current and projected processing power, memory size and speed, storage capacity and communications bandwidth. CPU performance is increasing at about 35% per annum (for microprocessors), memory size quadruples every three years, and disk performance grows relatively modestly at about 5% per annum. Local and wide area network bandwidths are increasing less uniformly but equally dramatically. The ten megabits per second local area network commonly used throughout the 1980s is being replaced by hundred megabit networks connected by gigabit backbone networks.

A major challenge for computer science is the **management of complexity,** since computerized systems which exploit the potential of technology tend to be large and complex. This is achieved by creating abstractions as a means of structuring systems, and will be a theme throughout the book. By this means a system can be comprehended as a whole at a high level of abstraction, but we can focus on any component part at any level of detail required at lower levels of abstraction. The design of software to facilitate the creation of abstractions is the first topic to be discussed in Chapter 2. The main modules within operating systems (often called subsystems) are used as examples.

We are aiming to exploit technology by bringing more processing power to bear on the solutions to problems. In order to do this we must use concurrent software systems. The introduction started from an informal, intuitive notion of what is meant by a concurrent system and proceeded to a more rigorous definition and some implementation requirements. Chapter 2 develops the abstraction of a concurrent system as a set of concurrent processes. Chapters 3, 4, 5 and 6 discuss the basic functions of operating systems with particular emphasis on the support for and use of concurrent processes. Chapter 7 considers the support for processes in programming language systems. Part I therefore establishes the process-abstraction and studies its implementation.

System structure and dynamic execution

2

CONTENTS

Computer scientists must comprehend, design and build large software systems. A high-level view of how a system is structured and how its components work together dynamically is essential for this purpose. We establish a context of **modular software structure** as a framework for looking at software systems and then progress to considering the **dynamic behaviour** of systems.

After considering modular structuring in general terms we proceed, in the next four chapters, to look at the major modules within operating systems, since these provide functions that are needed in many concurrent system.

2.1 System structure

2.1.1 Modules and interfaces

The software systems that are the concern of this book are large and complex. Such systems cannot be described and developed as one large program. The notion of a **module** is important for breaking large systems down into smaller components. Each component may then be broken down into smaller components and so on. The system can then be comprehended at any required level of detail.

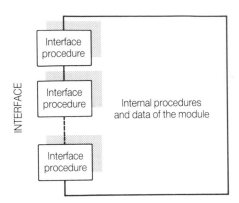

Figure 2.1
A pictorial
representation of
a module.

A module is a program unit which is used exclusively through an external **interface**. What is inside the module, its **implementation**, should be of no concern to its **clients** (see Figure 2.1). The interface is usually a set of procedures and these are specified in detail in an **interface specification** which includes the name of each procedure together with its arguments and results, each with an associated type. A programming language which supports separate compilation of modules allows compile-time type checking not only of the names of those procedures, which are called in modules external to the current module, but also of their call and return arguments.

The term **client** of a module, system or service will be used to indicate a piece of software that, when executed, invokes (makes calls to) the module. The term **user** will in general indicate a human user.

If the modules are designed carefully, they should be general enough to be used as building blocks in more than one system over reasonably long time-scales. Methods of achieving this goal conveniently and efficiently are the subject of much current work in the area of software engineering.

Because systems are large and complex it is necessary to specify each component module precisely. This acknowledges that no one can comprehend an entire system in full detail and allows small parts to be focused on at different times and by different people. Software engineering practices include **systematic procedures** for developing and documenting system components and also **formal methods** for describing system components in mathematical notation (Hayes, 1987; Somerville, 1989).

The process of modularization within systems and programming languages is often called **abstraction**; the view provided at the interface is an abstract rather than concrete view of the function provided by the module. The implementation gives the concrete realization of the abstraction. Although a syntactic specification of the interface of a module is necessary for correct use of the module it is not sufficient, in itself, to convey the meaning (or semantics) of the function provided by the module. The distinction is between **syntax** and **semantics**. For example, an interface specification of an *integer-add* operation will indicate that the operation takes two integers and delivers an integer. This does not tell us that the integer delivered must be the sum of the integers input.

2.1.2   Abstract data types

The concept of module introduced above is very general. A system designer has to decide how to decompose a system into modules. An approach to modular structuring which has gained popularity is to define a very specific form that modules can take. The idea is that each module should manage a single data abstraction and its interface should be the operations that can be carried out on data of that type. An example from operating systems is a type *file*, with operations such as *create, delete, open, close, read, write*. An example from programming is a type *stack*, with operations such as *push* and *pop*. As mentioned above, software reusability is important and a strict approach to module design makes the goal easier to achieve.

This approach is called **data encapsulation**. At the module interface there is no indication of the way the data type is **represented** internally. As discussed above, there are additional semantic requirements. The bytes we read from the file must be the same bytes that we wrote to it; the integer we pop from a stack of integers must be the integer we last pushed onto it.

Figure 2.2 illustrates this simple concept. However, the picture of a software system as a flat collection of data objects does not capture the relationships that exist between them. Figure 2.3 shows a more general case which must be handled in practice. A given abstract data type may be a composition of other types; for example a *table* may be composed of *records*, each of which contains fields such as *strings* and *integers*. Type *table* has associated operations, type *record* has associated operations, and so on.

Suppose that we want to use the type *stack* in an application but sometimes we need to use stacks of integers, sometimes stacks of reals, sometimes stacks of records and sometimes stacks of stacks. We wish the type *stack* to be **generic**,

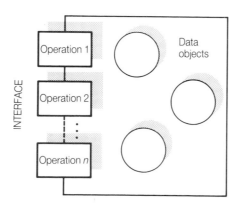

Figure 2.2
An abstract data
type.

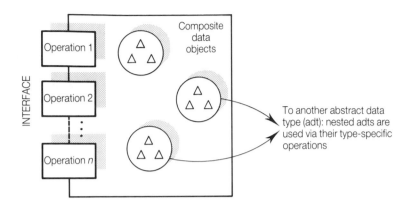

Figure 2.3
A composite
abstract data type.

illustrated in Figure 2.4. Here, a given type (such as *stack*) may be constructed from different low-level types (such as *integer, real, record*).

Figure 2.5 emphasizes a concern of this book: that data may be stored in persistent memory rather than in main memory.

2.1.3 Objects

An **object** is a generalization of an abstract data type. As with abstract data types, composite objects will have components that are also objects and each component may also have sub-objects and so on. Object-oriented systems again allow these relationships to be expressed through the type system, thus allowing data to be modelled.

In addition to providing data encapsulation, an object of some abstract type can have **more than one representation,** for example, the type *complex* can be implemented as a real part and an imaginary part or as a modulus and an argument, and the representation is not apparent at the interface. Different representations of an abstract type can coexist in a given system and the system is

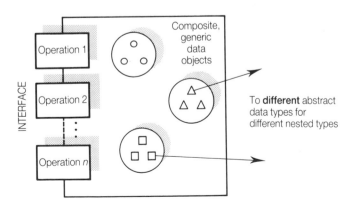

Figure 2.4
A generic abstract
data type.

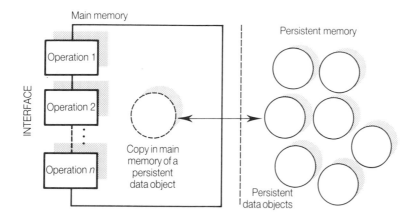

Figure 2.5
Persistent data
objects.

responsible for managing operations which involve more than one object when their representations may differ, for example, to add two complex numbers. A system which allows for different representations of objects can cope naturally with interworking between heterogeneous system components.

The ability to reuse modules was highlighted as an important motivation for using abstract data types. Object systems provide greater flexibility for creating new types from existing ones. New operations can be added, existing operations can be removed or replaced and operations may be **inherited** from other types.

Objects may be named uniquely in the entire system and, when an object is referenced by a running program, the supporting system may dynamically locate and load that object. This is the property of **dynamic binding**. Such mechanisms could be used for objects which are traditionally managed by system services (such as mail messages or icons on your screen) or the operating system (such as files) as well as for data objects defined within an application program written in an object-oriented language. Meyer (1988) provides further reading on this topic, and some object-oriented operating systems, which are being developed as research projects, will be mentioned in context in later chapters.

Current operating systems do not provide a universal object-naming scheme or a dynamic binding facility. Object-oriented software systems, such as ANSA (1989) and Comandos (Horn and Krakowiak, 1987), are being developed as **platforms** to run above standard operating systems.

2.1.4 Models applied to practical systems

The previous sections have introduced modules, abstract data types and objects. The distinctions will not be important to us until we consider distributed systems explicitly in Chapter 14. For the purposes of the earlier chapters it is usually sufficient to consider a software system as a collection of modules, each providing functions which are invoked through interface operations. We shall use the concept of an abstract interface and a concrete implementation wherever possible.

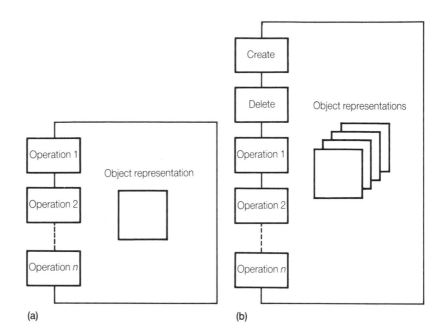

Figure 2.6
Objects and object managers: (a) an object (or instance of an abstract data type); (b) an object manager (or abstract data type).

It will sometimes be useful to distinguish between a single object of a given type and a management module that manages many or all objects of a given type. Figure 2.6(a) shows a single object with the operations appropriate to its type. Figure 2.6(b) shows a manager for objects of a given type. In this case there are operations to create a new object of the type and to delete an existing object, and operations need to indicate the particular object to be manipulated.

The notions of module and interface may be used to describe system structures at both a coarse granularity, representing an entire system or major service, and at a fine granularity, representing a single data abstraction, as we shall see throughout the book. An **operating system**, for example, may be considered as a single module, presenting a set of system calls as its external interface (see

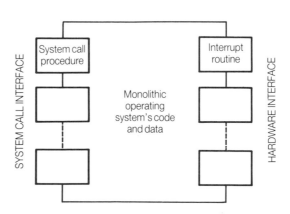

Figure 2.7
An operating system as a single module.

Figure 2.7). It can be thought of as providing an abstract machine which is easier to use than the real machine, as we shall discuss in Section 2.3. This is the model of conventional or **closed** operating systems, in which clients of the operating system are not allowed access to any internal modules except through the system calls. An operating system also has an interface to the hardware, but this is of no concern to its high-level clients. We expand on the internal modular structure of an operating system in Section 2.4.

2.2   Static structure and dynamic behaviour of a system

The type of modular specification outlined above gives a static description of the components of a system, but gives no indication of its dynamic behaviour. We know that interface procedures are called or operations are invoked on objects, but we have as yet no way of thinking about the events that may cause the invocations or the order in which invocations might take place.

As well as a data model, a **computational model** is therefore required with a notion of **active elements** or **activities** which may call interface procedures or invoke operations on objects in order to carry out a computation. Active elements have been given a variety of names in systems: activities, processes, tasks, or threads.

We shall use the term **process** for an entity which executes a program on a processor; a process is a unit of execution. The term 'process' has been used traditionally in computer science for this purpose, but over the years it has come to be used widely and often loosely outside academic computer science. For this reason, current operating systems designers have tended to avoid the term and **thread** is now more common as the unit of execution. Section 6.10 defines these terms more carefully than we are in a position to do at this stage.

A process must follow a **protocol** in order to use an object correctly, that is, a set of rules which define the order in which the object's interface operations may meaningfully be invoked. For example, a protocol for an existing file object is likely to be that the file is *opened*, a succession of *reads* and *writes* are then allowed, after which it is *closed*. If the protocol is not followed the invoker of the object may be given an error return, such as 'incorrect argument' if a file's pathname is given where an open file identifier is expected, or 'attempt to *pop* from an empty stack' if *pop* is invoked before *push*.

Again, the point should be made that the syntactic specification of the interface of a module is necessary for correct use of the module, but is not sufficient, in itself, to convey the meaning (or semantics) of the function provided by the module. In the case of the file, we require that the bytes we read from it are the same bytes that we previously wrote to it. The specification of a protocol is another means by which the intended semantics of the object is conveyed.

2.2.1   The process concept

To introduce the notion of process let us consider some analogies and see how far each can be taken.

The text of a book is comparable with the text of a computer program or the specification of a module. The activity of reading a book is comparable with the execution of a program by a process.

Two musicians sharing a score while playing a piece of music are comparable with two processes executing the same program on two processors simultaneously. Luckily, they need to turn the pages at the same time as they are playing synchronously.

I start to read a book, make a note of where I have got to and then put it down. My son picks it up, decides it looks interesting and starts to read. Over a period of time the two of us cooperate (or compete) over reading the book. This is again comparable to two processes executing a program. Since only one of us is reading at one time the analogy is with a program that for some reason may only be executed by one process at a time. In the case of the book, we can buy another copy to avoid sharing it.

I am reading a book; the phone rings; I answer the phone and go back to the book. This is comparable with a processor temporarily leaving the execution of a program to deal with an event such as a disk controller signalling that it needs attention after completing the transfer of some data.

In all cases there are the concepts of the static text and the dynamic process of reading it.

Some more formal definitions, taken from Brinch Hansen (1973a), are as follows:

data

Physical phenomena chosen by convention to represent certain aspects of our conceptual and real world. The meanings we assign to data are called information. Data is used to transmit and store information and to derive new information by manipulating the data according to formal rules.

operation

A rule for deriving a finite set of data (output) from another finite set (input). Once initiated, the operation is completed within a finite time.

computation

A finite set of operations applied to a finite set of data in an attempt to solve a problem. If it solves the problem it is called an algorithm, but a computation may be meaningless.

program

A description of a computation in a formal language.

computer

A physical system capable of carrying out computations by interpreting programs.

virtual machine

A computer simulated partly by program.

process

A computation in which the operations are carried out strictly one at a time: **concurrent processes** overlap in time. They are **disjoint** if each refers to private data only and **interacting** if they refer to common data.

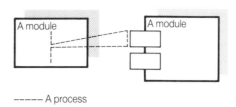

Figure 2.8
A process invoking
an operation.

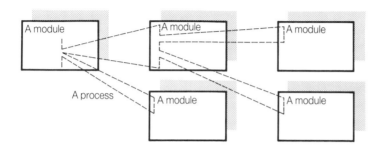

Figure 2.9
A process
executing code.

In the case of software modules, the program text specifies the modules and they are executed dynamically by processes on one or more processors. A process may move from module to module by calling interface procedures (see Figures 2.8 and 2.9).

A given module may be executed by a number of processes simultaneously. In a time-sharing system, for example, users may share a single copy of system utilities, such as editors or compilers. Each user has an associated process fetching and executing the instructions of the shared code. Figure 2.10 shows two processes executing a compiler. Here the processes are shown as cyclic, since they are likely to spend time executing a loop such as 'fetch the next statement and translate it'. There must be different input, output and data areas for the two separate compilations.

In this case the processes are disjoint rather than interacting; there is no connection between the different processes executing the compiler. Although common code is executed, there is workspace private to each process. A main concern of this book is to study the more difficult problem of interacting processes.

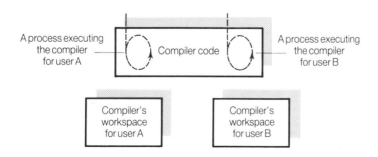

Figure 2.10
A compiler being
executed by two
processes.

2.3   Operating system functions

Our aim is to comprehend and build concurrent systems. Many of them are built to run on top of operating systems of some kind; others are subsystems which form part of operating systems (see Figure 1.12). It is therefore necessary to understand what an operating system can provide for any application which runs above it and also to understand what the operating system may be hiding or making inaccessible. A study of the concurrent subsystems within operating systems fulfils both of these purposes: it explains the services they provide for the application level and also some of the details of the lower levels which are hidden from the application. We do not wish to study operating systems for their own sakes, and the details of many of the internal algorithms used within current operating systems are left for specialized texts in that subject. The fact that operating system design is changing in response to developments in technology makes such an approach desirable.

The functions of an operating system are broadly:

- *To manage resources*
  The resources are typically processors, devices, disk space for files, memory for loaded programs and communications connections to other machines. The operating system is responsible for allocating resources, often dynamically on demand, for resolving any conflicts that might arise over access to resources and for responding to events associated with them.

- *To provide a service for its clients, which may be utilities, applications or human users*
  Hardware is difficult to program, and the system and its users must be protected from the errors that would be made if uncontrolled access to hardware was allowed. The operating system handles the raw hardware and provides a high-level interface to it. In a single-user system a high-level interface is a convenience; in a multi-user system it is essential to prevent interference between users. This may be described as creating a **virtual machine** (a number of virtual resources) that is easier to use than the real machine (the real hardware resources); see Figure 2.11.

The operating system manages resources and provides high-level interfaces for their use. An implication of this is that clients of the operating system must be prevented from accessing the resources other than through these interfaces. We shall study the **protection mechanisms** that are used to enforce this in Chapter 3. The basic idea is that the operating system is privileged to carry out certain functions (such as device handling) and its clients are prevented from carrying out these functions. The part of the operating system which is privileged is often called the kernel, although, as we shall see below, conventional 'kernels' have become larger than is implied by this definition.

If we take a time-sharing system as an example of an operating system there may be many users simultaneously sitting at terminals controlling their program executions, typing input to editors and so on. In Chapters 3 and 6 we show how

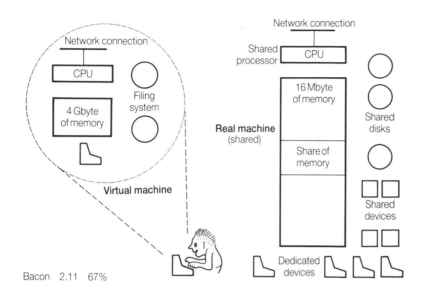

Figure 2.11
A virtual machine
and a real
machine.

it is possible for more users to run simultaneously than there are hardware processors to execute their programs or respond to their commands. In Chapter 3, **device handling** is considered in some detail, followed by an introduction to communications handling. In Chapter 6, sharing the available processors between the users is the focus; this is where we see how the processes introduced here are implemented.

The operating system is also concerned with **memory management.** It must allocate memory to running programs, both on initial loading and when data areas need to exceed their initial storage allocation. It must also interface with memory management hardware, set up the hardware and deal with any errors caused by a running program, as we shall see in Chapter 4. In a system with many users or many processes per user, the memory management subsystem is itself a concurrent system, since it may at any time be in the process of handling more than one request from its clients. Also, throughout the book we shall be concerned with whether memory can be shared between components of a concurrent system.

Most systems require storage that persists independently of the currently executing programs. The provision of such storage through **file management** functions is described in Chapter 5. Again, the file management subsystem of an operating system is itself a concurrent system and will be used as an example throughout the book. Some aspects of the internal implementation of filing systems are given in Chapter 5 and support this example.

2.4   How operating system services are invoked

There are two ways of invoking operating system services:

● a process may make system calls;

● a user may give commands to a process running a command interpreter program.

Once a process is executing a program it may request operating system services by making system calls. The set of system calls is the interface to the operating system module through which the operating system functions are invoked. Section 3.2 explains in detail how this entry into the operating system can be made.

First, a process must be created to execute the program. Some main memory must be allocated for the purpose, and the file comprising the load module of the program to be run must be loaded into that memory. Some processor time must be allocated to the process to run the program. A process executing the **command interpreter** program initiates these activities (by making system calls) in response to a command from a user. It must be part of system initialization to ensure that such a process is ready to receive commands. In a multi-user system, we can envisage a process executing the command interpreter program on behalf of every active user.

A **command interpreter** therefore causes system utilities or user programs to be loaded and run. It is concerned with initiating process creation (through system calls to the operating system) and with process management.

Current workstations and terminals typically have **graphical user interfaces**. Instead of typing out a command, users use a mouse device to move a cursor across the screen to indicate an object that they wish to use or to select an item from a system menu. Clicking the mouse, for example to open a file icon for editing, is equivalent to giving a command to a command interpreter.

2.5   Operating system structure

An operating system is a very large piece of software; for example, Sun's UNIX kernel (the basic functions described above and shown in Figure 2.12) occupies over a megabyte. Figure 2.7 gave a simple picture of an operating system as a single module with an interface comprising system calls. Figure 2.12 shows some of the internal modules in a conventional **closed** operating system, such as would be found in a personal workstation or a time-sharing system. The system calls can be partitioned into those which invoke file storage services, those which request terminal I/O, those which request network communication, and so on. The term **subsystem** is often used for the major internal modules of operating systems.

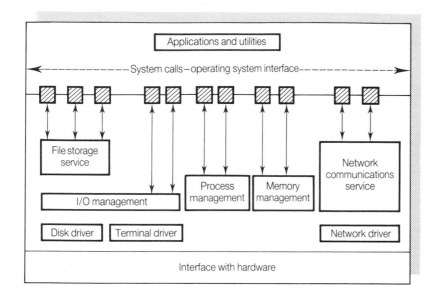

Figure 2.12
A typical closed operating system structure.

As operating systems grew in size a great deal of research effort was devoted to considering how best they should be structured. One proposal was to impose a strictly layered structure on the functions introduced above. The idea is that each layer in the hierarchy creates a single abstraction. Any layer uses the services provided by lower layers and provides a service for layers above it. An advantage is that a change at a given level does not affect lower levels. The research systems THE (Dijkstra, 1968) and Venus (Liskov, 1972) explored this design idea. In practice, systems have not been designed with their functions in a single strict hierarchy. This is because of the difficulty of choosing one specific layering of functions. In THE, for example, a memory fault could not be reported to the operator's console because the console manager was placed above memory in the hierarchical structure. We consider this example again in Chapter 9.

Certain modules fall naturally into a hierarchical relationship and this is exploited in system design. For example, a module concerned with driving a disk comes naturally 'below' a module concerned with providing a file service. A layered structure is used for communications software, as we shall see in Chapter 3.

If a concurrent system is to be built on distributed hardware many of the component computers may have very limited functionality. A component of a process control system may be dedicated to monitoring the process; a component of a distributed system may be dedicated to providing a file storage service or to function as a gateway between networks, concerned only with communications handling. Such components do not need to run a complete operating system, neither would the many programming support utilities provided for human users be needed there. Figures 2.13 and 2.14 illustrate this point.

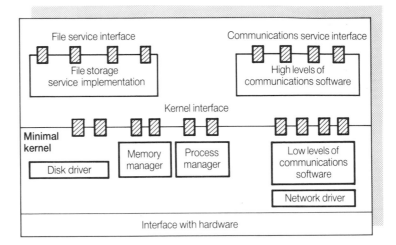

Figure 2.13
A file server.

For this reason an **open** operating system structure is advocated (Lampson and Sproull, 1979). The idea here is that those functions which are needed universally, by every component of a system, form a **minimal kernel**, sometimes called a **lightweight kernel** or **microkernel**. The phrase '**kernelization** of an operating system' is also coming into use. These names tend to be used now rather than 'open operating system', partly to avoid confusion with the term 'open system' which was also coined in the 1970s for use in communications standards. In the latter case the term means that a system is open to communication in a heterogeneous world.

To give an example, if a computer has no local disks because storage is provided across the network, then modules concerned with storage need not be present in that component of the system. Figure 2.13 shows a dedicated file server with disk handling in the kernel and the file service module running at user level. Figure 2.14 shows a dedicated gateway computer; its function is to receive data from one network and transmit it on another. In the figure, high-level communications handling is shown outside the operating system, but this might not be feasible if very high performance is required. In both cases memory management is shown but this could be very simple for dedicated servers.

A small kernel has the advantage of being easier to engineer and maintain. Also, the services that are implemented above rather than within the kernel can easily be recompiled and loaded and may therefore be changed (or omitted in certain configurations as we have seen).

We shall see in Chapter 6 that processes that are executing kernel functions run at higher priority than user-level processes. We shall see in Chapter 3 that they may be privileged to carry out certain functions that are forbidden to user-level processes.

There has been a good deal of experimental work on what should be included in a minimal kernel (see Chapter 22). Every computer has at least one processor, some memory and at least one device, for example, a terminal or network

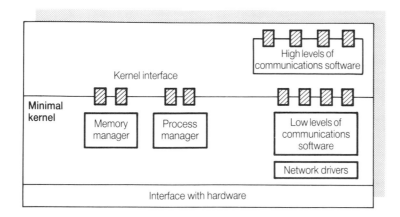

Figure 2.14
A gateway.

connection. The aim is to implement efficient mechanisms in the kernel and as much as is reasonable at user level. If you are sure that you *always* want a particular function to run as fast as possible, whatever applications the kernel is to support, you should include it in the kernel. You then give it priority over every function you might ever implement at user level. This is a difficult decision to make. There is a trade-off involved between making a service part of the kernel, and therefore fast but inflexible, and keeping the kernel as small as possible for maintainability and low overhead. Any particular function may provide a **slower service** when it is located at **user level** than when it is provided as part of the kernel.

The **kernel overhead** is the time spent in the kernel between an event occurring and the user-level process that is interested in it being scheduled. In real-time systems it is essential to be able to **bound** this time; the requirement is to be able to express the maximum possible delay rather than to obtain high speed as such. A minimal kernel makes this feasible. The requirements of the applications that run above a minimal kernel can be expressed by indicating the relative priorities of these user-level processes.

With good design, the minimal functionality of the kernel should lead to low overhead and the potential for high performance, which is essential for many network-based server computers. Any inefficiency in a kernel design affects every application, however high its priority.

To summarize, a microkernel-based system has the following potential advantages:

- The system configuration can be tailored for dedicated servers.
- A small kernel is easier to engineer and maintain.
- The services which now run above the kernel are easier to engineer, tune, update and maintain.
- The time spent executing the kernel can be bounded.
- The kernel provides efficient basic mechanisms; policies are expressed flexibly at user level. Programmers can control the relative priorities of user-level software.

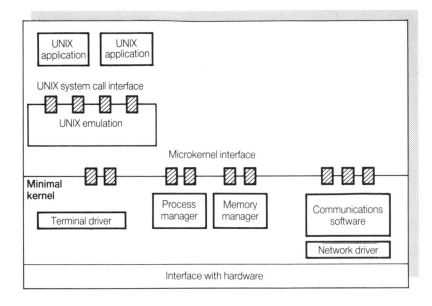

Figure 2.15
Emulation of an
existing operating
system above a
microkernel.

A potential disadvantage is that a given service will respond more slowly to its clients if it is implemented at user level instead of inside the operating system.

A microkernel should be able to form the basis for a traditional operating system which provides a programming support environment. A problem in moving to a new operating system design is that a vast amount of software has been written to run above the old operating system. Ideally, a microkernel should provide a set of abstractions from which higher-level services can be built. It should be possible to build a conventional operating system interface above a microkernel and run existing software above that. This approach has been taken by several microkernel projects, as we shall see in the case studies in Part IV. Figure 2.15 shows the basic idea. The UNIX emulation can take UNIX system calls and translate them into calls on the microkernel's services.

Finally, Figure 2.16 shows the microkernel itself split into separate modules, each with its own interface. We shall discuss alternative approaches to system structuring and alternative methods of invoking the services offered by modules through their interface operations throughout this book.

Figure 2.16
A fully
modularized
microkernel.

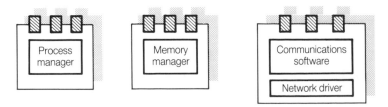

2.6 Summary

We need a way to think about complex software systems. The basic functionality of a system can be described in terms of **modular** software structure. By distinguishing between the **interface** and **implementation** of a module it is possible to create abstractions, that is, to focus on what a module does rather than how it does it. A specification of the modules of a system does not tell us how it is executed dynamically, a computational model is also needed.

The concept of **process** was introduced as the means by which dynamic execution of software is achieved. A process performs its computation by invoking the interface operations of modules. A **protocol** defines the correct orderings of operation invocations. An outline of some typical operating systems' modular structure was given and major functions, or **subsystems**, were highlighted. A conventional **closed operating system structure** was compared with an **open** structure based on a **minimal kernel** or **microkernel**. The potential advantages of a microkernel-based system were outlined and we discussed the criteria for deciding what should be included in a microkernel. Existing operating systems' interfaces can be provided above the microkernel so that existing application software can continue to be used.

In this chapter we have deliberately taken a high-level, abstract view of concurrent systems. In the rest of Part I we study the implementation of the abstractions that have been introduced here.

Exercises

2.1 What are modules, abstract data types and objects?

2.2 What is a process?

2.3 Describe how a program, comprising a number of object code files, is loaded and run by an operating system. Which operating system functions are invoked in order to create the required environment for the program to run?

2.4 (a) What are the main functions of operating systems in general?
  (b) What functions would you expect to be present in operating systems for:
   (i) A process control computer with a sensor for monitoring, an actuator for control and a network connection for reporting to and receiving commands from a control centre?
   (ii) A dedicated, network-based filing machine or 'file server'?
   (iii) A computer dedicated to controlling the communications passing between two networks, that is, a 'gateway' computer?

(iv) An autonomous personal computer?

(v) A single-user workstation with services available across a network?

(vi) A machine dedicated to managing and answering queries on a database?

2.5 (a) What is meant by a closed operating system structure?

(b) What is a microkernel?

(c) What are the advantages and disadvantages of closed operating systems and microkernel-based systems?

2.6 Relate the definitions of modules and processes to the structure of operating systems. How might modules be used? How might processes be used?

In a strict hierarchy of modules a process executing in a module at a given level may invoke only lower-level modules. Is it possible to arrange the operating system functions we have encountered so far into a strict hierarchy? What are the advantages and disadvantages of a layered structure?

Section 9.6 describes the strictly layered structure of the THE operating system and Exercise 9.5 describes the layers of the Venus operating system.

Operating systems: Device and communications management

3

CONTENTS

3.1 Overview

The kinds of hardware on which a concurrent system might be built were outlined in Chapter 1. In most application areas we do not have to program devices directly but are likely to use an operating system in each component of the system. An operating system provides a high-level interface to the hardware which abstracts away from the specific details of how each device is programmed. This makes life easier for the programmer, but as designers of concurrent systems we have to take care that nothing crucial is lost in this process: that the interface we use gives us the performance and functionality we require. For example, if a hardware event must have a response within a specified time we need to understand all that can happen in the software system that responds to the event. Some operating system designs make them unable to guarantee to meet timing requirements. For this reason, a concurrent system designer needs to know the basics of how devices are controlled.

Some devices are dedicated to a particular task, such as the terminals allocated to individual users, or sensors and actuators for monitoring or controlling industrial processes. Others, such as disks, printers and network interfaces, are shared among users. Both types are managed by the operating system. We consider the low-level interface between devices and the software which controls them. This study forms the basis on which software design decisions can be taken, in particular, the allocation of processes to modules concerned with device handling. Hardware events are one source of concurrent activity in a system; we need to study the precise mechanisms involved.

When a program is loaded and runs it may contain errors which are detected by the hardware. For example, the arithmetic logic unit (ALU) may detect a division by zero or an illegal address; the address of a data operand may be at an odd byte address when an even one is expected. Whenever such a program runs it will cause the same errors at the same point in the execution. These can be classified as **synchronous** hardware events.

In the next chapter we shall see that a program may not all be in main memory. When a 'page' that is not in memory is referenced the hardware signals a 'page fault'. Page faults are synchronous events because they are caused by running programs and must be handled before the program can continue to run.

When a program runs, events may occur in the system that are nothing to do with that program. The disk may signal that it has finished transferring some data and is ready for more work; the network may have delivered a packet of data. Such events are **asynchronous** with program execution and occur at unpredictable times.

These aspects of the interaction of a process with the hardware are considered in detail, as is the system call mechanism through which a user-level process may request use of a device.

The network connection of a computer may be considered at a low level as just another device. However, it is a shared device and computer–computer communication can generate a large volume of data associated with multiple simultaneous process interactions. The communications handling subsystem is therefore a large concurrent system. The design of communications handling software is introduced in the later sections of the chapter, although a complete study would require a book in its own right (Comer, 1991; Halsall, 1992; Tanenbaum, 1988).

3.2   Device management

In this section the basics of how devices are controlled by program are given. Figure 3.1 gives an operating system context for all the levels associated with I/O handling.

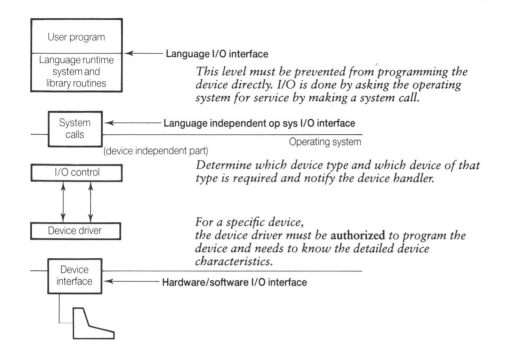

This level must be prevented from programming the device directly. I/O is done by asking the operating system for service by making a system call.

Determine which device type and which device of that type is required and notify the device handler.

For a specific device, the device driver must be **authorized** *to program the device and needs to know the detailed device characteristics.*

Figure 3.1
Device handling subsystem overview.

In Section 2.3 it was pointed out that programs running above the operating system must be prevented from programming devices directly. This section will show how this restriction can be enforced and how users may request input or output by making a system call, since they are not allowed to program it for themselves (see Section 3.4). Figure 3.1 indicates this difference in privilege between the operating system and the user level. It is clear that when a system call is made a mechanism is needed to change the privilege from user (unprivileged) to system (privileged).

Three interfaces are indicated. The lowest-level interface is with the hardware itself. Only the operating system module concerned with handling the device needs detailed information on its characteristics, for example, the amount of data that is transferred on input or output. The operating system creates a higher-level interface, creating virtual devices that are easier to use than the real hardware. This interface is language independent. Finally, the language libraries offer an I/O interface in the form of a number of procedures that are called for doing I/O. These may differ from language to language and from the operating system's interface. Each language system must invoke the operating system's system call interface on behalf of its programs.

Processes are required to execute these modules. This is discussed in detail in Chapter 6; in particular, Figure 6.1 shows processes allocated to the modules of Figure 3.1. First, the device handling function of the operating system is developed.

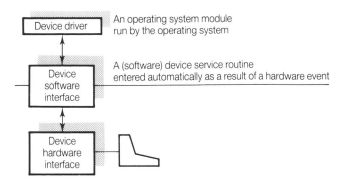

Figure 3.2
Hardware–software
interface.

In Figure 3.1 an interface between the device hardware and the operating system software is shown. Figure 3.2 focuses on this interface and shows a hardware component and a software component. Section 3.2.2 describes one form of hardware interface to a device and Sections 3.2.3–5 introduce the lowest level of software interface and the mechanism by which it is invoked by hardware.

3.2.1   Processor and device speeds

It is important to realize that devices are, in general, very slow compared with processors. This was always the case, and the gap has widened, since processor speeds have increased faster than device speeds and are likely to continue to do so. Consider a user typing ten characters a second to an editor and suppose the processor executing the editor executes an instruction in a microsecond. The disparity in these speeds becomes more obvious if we scale them up. If we scale one microsecond up to one second then on this scale the user types a character once a day while the processor executes an instruction every second. Current processors would be more likely to be executing more than ten instructions per second on this scale whereas users keep on typing at the same speed. An alternative way of expressing this relative speed is that in 1980 the processor could execute about 40 000 instructions while you typed a character; in 1990 it could execute about 1 250 000 instructions.

Current workstations and terminals typically have graphical user interfaces which have been made possible by these increases in processor speeds and memory sizes. As you type to an editor which is displaying a page of your text in a window, your screen changes significantly as you type. There is a good deal of processing to be done as a result of the input of a character.

In many concurrent systems disk storage is needed. Although disk density has doubled every three years, disk access time is limited by the electromechanical nature of the device and has only increased by a third between 1980 and 1990. An example illustrates the increase in capacity and performance and decrease in cost:

In 1963 an 80 megabyte storage system on 32 cartridges cost £100,000. The data rate was 50–100 kilobits per second and it took 50–200 milliseconds to position the heads.

In 1986 a 765 megabyte storage system on 8 cartridges cost £1000. The data rate was 2 megabits per second and it took 2–35 milliseconds to position the heads.

In 1992, the HP C3010 has a formatted capacity of 2000 megabytes on 19 surfaces, an average seek time of 11.5 milliseconds, a transfer rate of 10 megabits per second from the disk buffer to a SCSI-2 bus. The cost is US$3.75 per megabyte.

Section 3.2.6 shows how disks are programmed.

Many computer systems are network-based. Current networks in widespread use, such as Ethernet, typically operate at 10 megabits per second, but 100 megabit through to gigabit networks are becoming available. We shall consider communications handling later in this chapter, but it is clear that an operating system has less time to handle communications devices than peripherals.

For a comprehensive coverage of the characteristics and performance of processors, memory and I/O see Hennessy and Patterson (1990).

3.2.2   A simple device interface

Figure 3.3 shows a simple device interface which has space to buffer a single character both on input and on output. An interface of this kind would be used for a user's terminal, for some kinds of network connections and for process control systems. In the case of a user terminal, when the user types, the character is transferred into the input buffer and a bit is set in the status register to tell the processor that a character is ready in the buffer for input. On output, the processor needs to know that the output buffer is free to receive a character and another status bit is used for this purpose. The processor can test these status bits and, by this means, output data at a speed the device can cope with and input data when it becomes available.

3.2.3   Polling and interrupts

Device programming can be done by testing status bits in the interface (Section 3.2.2), in which case the interface sits passively, with the bits indicating the device's status, and the processor must test these bits to determine when to transfer data to the interface on output or from it on input. This is called **polling** the device. The device management subsystem could test each device in turn or perhaps test some devices more frequently than others. This is a very simple and reliable method and could be the best way to handle devices in small systems; an outline of a program of this kind is used as an example in Section 7.3. Polling is a bad method for time-critical systems because an event could occur immediately after its device had been tested and would not be seen until that device was

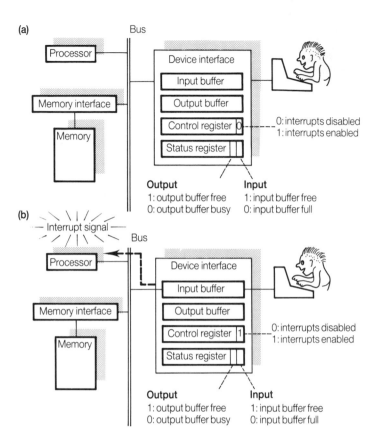

Figure 3.3
A simple device
interface with (a)
interrupts disabled
and (b) interrupts
enabled.

tested again. Also, it is not a good use of processor time to cycle round all the devices, periodically testing which ones are ready for attention.

An alternative is to use **interrupts** if the mechanism is available in the hardware. Figure 3.3(b) shows interrupts enabled in the control register in the device interface. If this is done, the interface will actively signal the processor as soon as data is in the input buffer on input and as soon as the output buffer becomes free for the next item of data on output (Figure 3.3(b)). This permits the fastest possible response to devices but is more complex to program than polling. We assume that the interface, when sending an interrupt signal to the processor, can identify itself and indicate the priority level that has been assigned to it (see Section 3.2.4).

Now suppose that the processor is fetching and executing instructions from an arbitrary program when it receives an **interrupt signal** from a device. Assuming that handling the device is more important than continuing to execute the program, an **interrupt** should occur from the program to an **interrupt service routine** (see Figure 3.4). It must be possible to resume the interrupted program, and this implies that the program counter (at least) must be saved before it is set

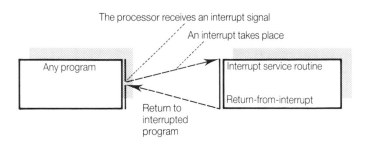

Figure 3.4
An interrupt.

up for the interrupt routine. Also, the contents of any processor registers that are used by the interrupt routine must be saved before they are used and subsequently restored. In general, we say that the **processor state** of the interrupted program is saved on the interrupt so that the processor can be used by the interrupt routine. The saved state must be restored by the time the program is resumed.

All computers have **hardware** to effect this transfer, and a typical mechanism is described in the following sections and illustrated in Figure 3.5. The program counter (PC) and processor status register (PSR) are saved by hardware. At the end of the routine, assuming we are to return immediately to the interrupted program, a special return instruction will restore both the PC and the PSR. Any

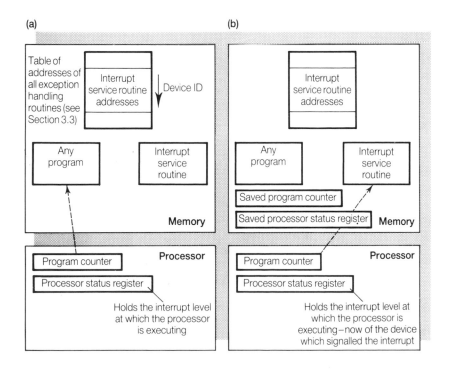

Figure 3.5
The interrupt
mechanism:
(a) before the
interrupt is taken;
(b) after the
interrupt is taken.

other registers that are used by the interrupt service routine are saved at the start of the routine and restored at the end of the routine by software. Note that the hardware mechanism may cause writes to memory in order to store the PC and the PSR.

3.2.4 Interrupt handling: priorities

Computer systems typically have a large range of device types. Some must be handled with great urgency, for example, a sensor reading from a nuclear reactor which signals a danger level. Others should be handled promptly to keep the system running smoothly, for example, file transfer from disk. We have seen in Section 3.2.1 that a system has no difficulty in keeping up with a human typing characters on a keyboard.

Each source of interrupt signal is therefore assigned a priority. Not only can a normal program be interrupted by the arrival of an interrupt signal, but execution of a service routine for a low-priority interrupt may be interrupted by the arrival of a higher-priority interrupt signal. The processor status register indicates the priority level at which the processor is executing. An interrupt signal with a higher priority causes an interrupt; an interrupt signal with a lower priority is held **pending** until the higher-priority interrupt service routine has finished, that is, until exit from its service routine. Nested interrupts are handled by using a stack structure; the PC and PSR are stored on a stack each time an interrupt occurs and restored from the stack when a return from interrupt instruction is executed.

3.2.5 Interrupt vectors

Each device has an associated interrupt service routine. When an interrupt is to take place (on a priority basis) the address of the correct interrupt routine must be set up by hardware in the program counter. A dedicated area of main memory is used to hold these addresses. The device interface identifies itself when sending an interrupt signal to the processor, and this allows the correct service routine address to be selected from the table. This table is shown in outline in Figure 3.5 and Figure 3.6 gives more details.

As well as the addresses of device interrupt service routines the addresses of all exception handling routines are held there (see Section 3.3). Notice that, although the transfer of control from the interrupted program to the interrupt service routine is carried out by the hardware interrupt handling mechanism, this table access is another reference to main memory and adds to the expense of the mechanism.

3.2.6 Direct memory access (DMA) devices

A simple interface has been used as an example in the above sections. An interrupt is associated with the transfer of every character. Some device interfaces

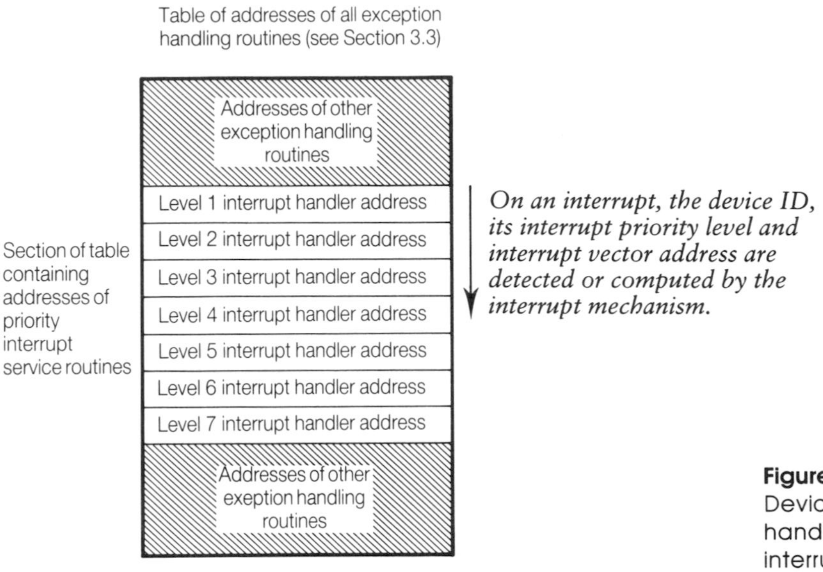

Table of addresses of all exception
handling routines (see Section 3.3)

Section of table
containing
addresses of
priority
interrupt
service routines

| Addresses of other exception handling routines |
| Level 1 interrupt handler address |
| Level 2 interrupt handler address |
| Level 3 interrupt handler address |
| Level 4 interrupt handler address |
| Level 5 interrupt handler address |
| Level 6 interrupt handler address |
| Level 7 interrupt handler address |
| Addresses of other exeption handling routines |

*On an interrupt, the device ID,
its interrupt priority level and
interrupt vector address are
detected or computed by the
interrupt mechanism.*

Figure 3.6
Device interrupt
handling and
interrupt vectors.

will transfer a block of data into or out of memory and will interrupt the
processor only after the whole transfer is complete. This requires a more complex interface and a simple processor is dedicated to the task of controlling the
data transfer. Devices of this kind are called direct memory access (**DMA**)
devices. This kind of interface is often used in communications; a whole packet
of data coming in from the network is placed in memory. Another example is a
disk controller.

A disk controller is a simple processor with registers for holding the disk
address, memory address, and amount of data to be transferred. After this information has been passed to it by a central processor, together with the instruction to proceed with the disk read or write, the disk controller transfers the
whole block between disk and main memory without any intervention from the
central processor (see Figure 3.7). When the block transfer is complete, the disk
controller signals an interrupt. The processor can execute some other program
in parallel with the transfer.

During the transfer the disk controller is transferring data to or from memory
at the same time as the processor is fetching instructions from memory and
reading and writing data operands in memory. The memory controller ensures
that only one of them at once is making a memory access. The disk controller
may access memory between an instruction fetch and a data access which is part
of the instruction execution; this is called **cycle stealing**. DMA slows down the
rate at which the processor executes instructions.

A hardware-controlled cache for holding recently used instructions and data
(or a separate cache for each) will help to reduce this contention. Instructions and
data can be accessed in the cache at the same time as the disk controller accesses

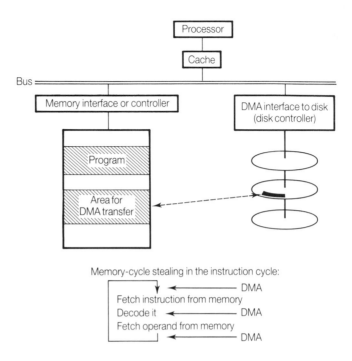

Figure 3.7
Direct memory
access.

main memory. In Chapter 4 we take a closer look at the memory hierarchy in a computer system, including hardware-controlled caches.

Modern disk interfaces have become more sophisticated than that described above. A technique called **scatter-gather** allows the programmer to specify a number of blocks of data to be written to one place on the disk by a single command (gather), or a single area of disk to be read into a number of memory locations (scatter). This is particularly useful when a logically contiguous area is dispersed in the physical memory when paged memory management is used (see Chapter 4). A similar technique is described for a network interface in Section 3.8.

3.2.7 Memory-mapped I/O

In the above sections we have assumed that we can transfer data to a device. There are two approaches to achieving this: by a special set of I/O instructions or by memory-mapped I/O. The latter approach is used in modern machines. The idea is that physical memory addresses are allocated to device interfaces, and input, output, status checking and control are achieved by reading and writing these memory locations. No extra instructions are needed for these purposes. The simple interface described in Section 3.2.2 would have memory addresses assigned for the single-byte input, output, status and control registers.

3.2.8 Timers

Timers are handled among the devices of a computer system. They are available as programmable chips and are almost always used with interrupts enabled, although some programmable timers allow a polling mode of use. Other devices signal an interrupt to indicate that data is ready on input or more data can be output. Timers are used just to generate timing information, usually in the form of interrupts.

A timer interface may be programmed to generate an interrupt after some specified period of time, then do nothing until further instructed. Alternatively, it may be set up to generate interrupts periodically. We can count them and use them, like clock ticks, as a basis for all timing in a system. The rate at which interrupts are generated is programmable and some of the uses that are made of timers require a fine time grain. The range of rates at which timing interrupts can be arranged to occur depends on the specific device and is typically from 1 microsecond to 65 milliseconds.

Examples of the use of timers in a system are as follows:

- *Time of day*. Systems which perform functions for human users, such as printing and filing, are expected to maintain the correct date and time. This can be based on the clock ticks described above. Typically, the system maintains a count which is decremented on a timer interrupt. The size of the count is such that it decrements to zero after a second's worth of clock ticks. A time of day counter which is maintained to a one-second granularity from some base value can then be incremented. A 32-bit counter at one-second granularity would overflow after 136 years.

  An alternative way of maintaining the time of day is to arrange to receive a signal from an external radio station or satellite. Transmission is typically once a second at an accuracy of the order of a millisecond. This is likely to improve, and processors are likely to have the capacity to receive a more frequent signal in the future (see Chapter 14).

- *Managing the time for which processes run on processors*. A timer interrupt is a mechanism for stopping a running process.

- *Accounting for CPU usage*. Clients may be charged for their use of a processor.

- *Providing an alarm clock service for processes* so they can delay for a specific length of time or until some time of day arrives.

- *For monitoring the system and its clients*. For example, a profile of the amount of time being spent on various tasks can be built up by noting the value of the PC at regular intervals.

3.3 Exceptions

The above section has introduced device programming and has placed this function within the operating system. The interrupt mechanism is used to transfer control from any running program (inside or outside the operating system) to an interrupt service routine which is part of the operating system. The processor state is set to 'privileged' by the interrupt mechanism and the minimum necessary processor state (the PC and processor status register) is saved so that the interrupted program can be resumed later.

The operating system is entered by this means when a device signals that it needs attention. The mechanism can be generalized to be the standard means by which the operating system is entered.

Note that the interrupt signal from the device has, in general, nothing to do with the program that is running when it occurs. Such interrupts occur asynchronously at unpredictable times.

3.3.1 Exceptions caused by a running program

When a program runs it may cause a number of error conditions to be generated in the hardware. All of these conditions may be signalled as interrupts, as described above for devices, and handled by interrupt service routines. The more general terms **exception** and **exception handling routine** tend to be used to include device and other types of interrupt. Examples are:

- The ALU may detect a division by zero, or two's complement overflow on addition or subtraction.
- The addressing hardware may be given an odd byte address for an instruction fetch when instructions must be aligned on even byte boundaries.
- An illegal bit pattern may be found for an operation code by the instruction decode logic.
- Memory outside the range of the available physical memory may be addressed.

All of these are caused by the program that is running. If the program was restarted, they would occur again at the same point; unlike device interrupts they are predictable. In almost all cases the program cannot continue after the error condition has occurred. The error handling is **synchronous** with the program execution. Device interrupts are **asynchronous** and might or might not be handled immediately they occur, depending on the relative priorities of the running program and the interrupting device.

In the next chapter we shall see that a program may not all be in main memory. When part of a program (a 'page') is to be accessed for a data operand or an instruction the addressing hardware signals that it is not present in memory (a 'page fault' interrupt). This kind of hardware event is caused by the running program, but will not necessarily occur at the same point of every program execution. When the program is run on another occasion, the operating system may have space for more of its pages, or different pages, to be in memory, so the same page faults may not occur. That is, the points at which page faults can occur are predictable to the operating system, but whether they occur or not on a given run depends on which pages are in main memory.

When a page fault does occur it must be handled before the program can continue; that is, the page that is being referenced must be transferred into memory by the operating system. The program execution can then continue from the instruction which caused the page fault. The page fault handling is synchronous with the running program.

Another source of exception associated with a given program is an attention interrupt or break. The user has decided to abort the program run and has pressed the attention key. In this case, the program execution could continue for some time before being aborted. The event is asynchronous.

3.3.2   System (privileged) mode and user (unprivileged) mode

Suppose a call for an operating system service (a system call) is implemented as a simple procedure call. A user process would simply enter the operating system and start to execute system code. The system code might well go on to program devices or change the contents of hardware registers. Assuming the system code is correct there is no problem. Notice, however, that privileged actions are being carried out by a user process. Now suppose that a user process executes similar privileged actions when executing an application program at user level. How can we allow the former but not the latter? That is, how can we prevent a process from executing privileged actions when it is executing an application but allow it to execute privileged actions when executing the operating system?

For this reason, processors are designed to run in at least **two modes** or **states**. In **user mode** certain privileged instructions, such as enabling and disabling interrupts, are forbidden. If code executing with the processor in user mode attempts to execute a privileged operation the processor generates an exception. A privilege violation of this kind is synchronous with program execution. The associated exception handling routine handles this error. If the processor is executing in **privileged** or **system mode** the execution of the same instruction proceeds without interruption. It is therefore necessary to arrange for operating system code to be executed in the privileged state. We have seen how this is achieved for exception handling routines: the exception mechanism sets the state to privileged.

It could be argued that in a single-user system there is no need to protect the operating system or hardware from corruption. The user suffers but the program can be debugged and run on a rebooted system. (One hopes that the program errors have not corrupted the filing system!) A similar argument can be applied to dedicated server computers or embedded systems, that is, any system that runs a single application. In these cases the same software runs indefinitely and it may be argued that once this has been developed and tested then the overhead of protection checks is unnecessary. However, large software systems will have residual bugs and protection checks can help to locate and confine them. Most non-trivial systems benefit from protection from error and malice.

3.3.3   The system call mechanism

When a user requests a service which requires privileged actions to be carried out it is necessary to switch the processor state from user mode to privileged mode. The exception mechanism is usually employed for this purpose; we force a system call to generate an exception. Instructions called **software interrupts** or **traps** are designed specifically for this purpose. The fact that such instructions cause an exception has the side-effect that the processor state is changed to privileged as part of transferring control to the interrupt service routine. The interrupt service routine can then pass control to the required system call procedure.

The mechanism just described is usually the standard method for entering the operating system on a machine where privileged state is used. In this case, a system call is like a procedure call with a change of state; in an unprotected system, a system call is just a procedure call. In general, if the processor has only two states, the system designer must choose which modules should run under privileged state and which need not.

3.3.4   Summary of the use of the exception mechanism

Figure 3.8 shows the table of addresses of exception handling routines for the Motorola MC68000 processor. This example brings together the various types of exception we have discussed.

Figure 3.9 shows a sequence of events which illustrate nested interrupt handling and trap handling. A user program is running when an interrupt from a device at priority level 3 occurs (1). The service routine for that device is entered (2). As part of the transfer mechanism the processor status register and PC of the user program are saved and then set up for the interrupt service routine; the PC is loaded from the table of addresses of interrupt service routines; the status register is set to level 3 and privileged state. Part-way through execution of this interrupt service routine a higher-priority device interrupts (3). Its service routine is executed (4). This completes and the interrupted PC and processor status are restored to return to the interrupted level 3 routine (5). This completes and we return to the interrupted user program (6). The user program makes a system call and a trap instruction is executed by a library routine (7). The trap service routine is executed. The priority level in the processor status register is not changed but the state is set to privileged. The routine completes and control is returned to the interrupted user program (8).

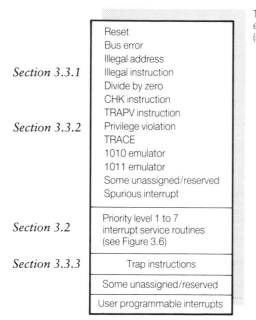

Table of addresses for 256
exception handling routines
(see Section 3.3)

Figure 3.8
Example of
exceptions from the
Motorola MC68000.

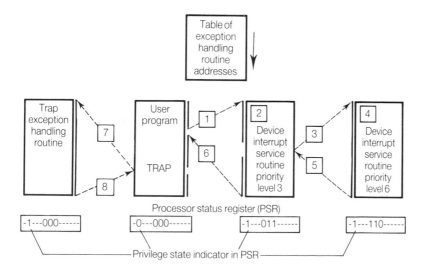

Figure 3.9
An example
showing nested
interrupts.

3.3.5   User-level exception handling

In the above discussion we have seen the low-level mechanism for detecting certain errors and the first stage of dealing with the errors in an exception handling routine. In many cases the error will be fatal and the process will be aborted, but before this happens an error message should be given to an on-line user or written to a log file. This is not a high-priority activity and should not be done by the operating system (and certainly not by an interrupt routine!). Error handling should be done in the context of the user process that caused the error. Error handling routines are typically provided as part of a programming language library and their addresses are made available to the operating system so that control can be transferred to the correct place when an error occurs. When a process is created and initialized the address of its normal start and the address of an initial error handling routine are recorded (see Section 6.3.1 and Figure 6.4).

UNIX signals are an example of a mechanism for signalling exceptional conditions, see Section 21.10. A signal is a flag which is set in the kernel and detected on return to the application. Also, some programming languages have an exception facility to allow users to name certain error conditions and to supply procedures for handling them. The language library can then pass control to the user's routine when appropriate.

3.4   Multiprocessors

The discussion so far has considered only a single processor. We should consider how exceptions and interrupts are managed on multiprocessors.

When a program runs on a processor, any exceptions it causes are signalled to that processor. These include errors, system calls and page faults, all of which are synchronous.

The handling of asynchronous exceptions, such as those caused by interrupts from a peripheral device, will depend on the details of the multiprocessor configuration. An installation may include dedicated devices, such as user terminals, shared devices such as disks, and possibly system management devices, such as an operator console. One option is that each hardware device is allocated to a single processor, which issues all instructions to control that device. Interrupts generated by the device are always signalled to that same processor. A lot of multiprocessor systems are based on this model for I/O.

In a shared-memory multiprocessor the action of a DMA device is essentially independent of the processor that initiates a particular transfer. Provided that each processor has a private stack for saving the processor state, an interrupt signalling the end of a DMA transfer may be handled on any processor. A system configured so that shared devices may be controlled by any processor is more flexible than one in which a process requiring access to a given peripheral device must be run on a particular processor.

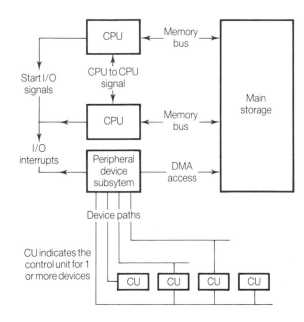

Figure 3.10
IBM's System/370
XA configuration.

The IBM System/370 mainframe architecture provides for multiprocessor configurations that share main memory. Each processor has a dedicated page of memory which is used for such purposes as saving the processor state on interrupt, and interrupts may therefore be handled without interference between processors. In the first version of the System/370 architecture introduced in 1970 each peripheral device was allocated to a single processor. As technology advanced the original design was found inadequate in various ways, and in 1982 the System/370 Extended Architecture (XA) became available. There are two major changes for XA, both recognizing that processors at the top end of the range had become limited by the architecture. First, there is a 31 bit addressing mode in addition to the previous standard of 24 bit addresses (see Chapter 4). Secondly, the configuration for peripheral devices was modified so that any processor may control any device (see Figure 3.10). I/O devices are usually configured so that there is more than one path to a shared peripheral, such as a disk drive.

There are other considerations to be taken into account in a multiprocessor system. If a user aborts a program by depressing the attention key, the processor that takes the interrupt must be able to interrupt the processor on which the program is running; there is a requirement for inter-processor interrupts.

We saw in Section 3.2.8 that a timer is a particular kind of device that can be set to generate interrupts. Two types of timing service are needed, one based on the time in the world outside the computer ('real time'), the other measuring the computation time of a given process. The real-time clock in any processor should tick provided the processor is alive, regardless of whether it is performing any computation. The **timer resolution** (the length of a tick) will depend on the processor design. Either the operating system or an application program may require action to be taken at a particular time; it is important that the act of informing the program of the time carries a low overhead. In a uniprocessor system the timer will interrupt the processor on which the program runs. In a multiprocessor system a given processor may take timer interrupts, update various counts in the operating system's data structures and detect whether any time limits have expired. In this case, the processor running a program which needs to take action must be interrupted; an inter-processor interrupt mechanism is again required. Alternatively, each processor may have its own timer, and the interrupt will occur on the processor on which the program runs. In the latter case it will be necessary to synchronize the timers on the various processors, and there should be system support to achieve this.

Timing individual processes in execution is essential in many applications, and it can also be useful when debugging. Most processors have an interval timer which can be read from within an executing process, usually by entering a trap routine. It is also possible to interrupt a process after a specified computation time has elapsed. This interval timing service may or may not be provided by the same clock that maintains the real time.

3.5 CISC and RISC computers

Throughout the 1980s there was a move towards simpler processors. If the instruction set is simple and instructions are of equal length, techniques such as instruction pipelining can more easily be used to achieve high performance. If the processor is simple, the chip fabrication time and therefore time to the marketplace is faster. There may also be space on the chip for cache memory or address translation (see Chapter 4).

When real programs were measured it was found that the complex instructions and addressing modes, designed to support specific data structures, are rarely used by compiler writers. Their complexity implies inflexibility and they are never quite right for the job in hand. The virtual disappearance of assembly language programming means that the machine instruction set need not be high level and attempt to 'bridge the semantic gap' between the programmer and the machine. Compact code is no longer an aim, since current machines have large address spaces, typically 32 bits for a 4 gigabyte address space, and physical memory is cheap.

These arguments have led computer design from **Complex Instruction Set Computers (CISC)**, which were in the mainstream of architectural development until the early 1980s, to the current generation of **Reduced Instruction Set Computers (RISC)**, mentioned in Section 1.3.2. An excellent treatment is given in Hennessy and Patterson (1990). Some aspects of RISC designs are similar in their simplicity to the minicomputers of the 1970s and the early generations of microprocessors. Other aspects, such as the address range, have outstripped early mainframes.

3.5.1 The RISC approach to interrupt handling

The exception handling mechanism described in Section 3.3 aims to support the requirements of operating systems. A good deal of mechanism is provided and has to be used whenever an exception occurs. A large table in main memory is indexed on every exception to extract the appropriate exception handling routine address; the program counter and processor status register are saved on a stack in main memory. The approach described is based on that used in the Motorola 68000 series, the DEC VAX series and other CISC machines.

In the area of exception handling a fresh look at the real requirements of the operating system is in order. It is argued that a fast, simple mechanism may be more appropriate than a very general one, and that complex cases can be handled by software. One obvious way of achieving speed-up is to avoid saving the state in main memory and instead to use processor registers. Another is to avoid accessing main memory to find the address of the exception handling routine.

Avoiding the saving of state in memory

It is very often the case that the interrupted program is not resumed after the exception is serviced; a fatal error might have been signalled by the exception in which case control passes to a user-level library routine to give an error message and abort the program; or an interrupt may have made a high-priority process runnable and the interrupted process is temporarily suspended. If the state of the interrupted process has been put on a stack in memory it will have to be copied elsewhere in memory (see Chapter 6) rather than set up again in the hardware. It would surely be better for a small amount of state to be saved in registers and copied from there by the exception handling routine when necessary. Special registers could be provided to hold a small amount of state, such as the interrupted program counter and the previous processor status register.

Avoiding table lookup of an interrupt routine address

Table lookup can be avoided by having a 'first-level interrupt handler': a single exception handling routine that is executed in response to every exception. Such a routine can determine the cause of the exception by testing values in processor registers etc. Interrupt decoding is therefore carried out by software instead of by hardware. This first-level interrupt handler may handle a simple exception and return control to the interrupted process with minimum overhead. Alternatively, it may be necessary to pass control to another routine. In this case it might be necessary to enable interrupts selectively; that is, the routine may be executed at some appropriate priority interrupt level.

The address of the first-level interrupt handler can be set up in the PC as part of the hardware interrupt mechanism, thus avoiding a table lookup in memory. Also, interrupts will be disabled as part of the hardware interrupt mechanism. If the handling of the exception requires another routine to be called (see above), or processor registers to be used, then state can be saved as necessary. This can be done safely because interrupts are disabled.

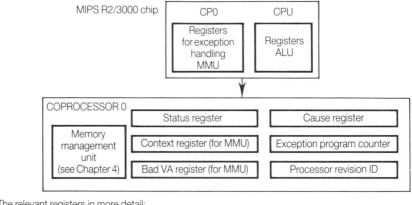

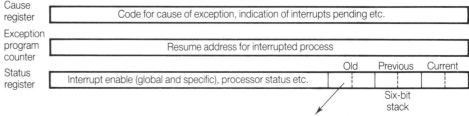

Figure 3.11
Exception
handling in the
MIPS R2000/3000
coprocessor 0.

Figure 3.11 shows the support for exception handling in the on-chip system control coprocessor of the MIPS R2000/3000. The cause, status and exception program counter (EPC) registers are relevant to this discussion and are shown in more detail in the figure. The status register contains a three-level (six-bit) stack; each level has a processor status bit (privileged, unprivileged) and a global interrupt enable/disable bit.

On an exception, the exception handling mechanism:

● puts the resume address for the interrupted process in the exception program counter (EPC) register;

● pushes a new two-bit entry onto the six-bit stack. This sets the processor status to privileged and disables interrupts globally;

● sets up the PC to the address of one of three exception handling routines. Except on reset and certain memory management exceptions this is the address of a general routine. These addresses can be known to the hardware.

The return from exception (RFE) instruction pops the status stack by two bits. This can follow, and be executed indivisibly with, a transfer of control to the required address: the normal arrangement for pipelined branch instructions.

This discussion has highlighted those aspects associated with making the interrupt mechanism as fast as possible. A complete description of the registers and the handling of specific exceptions for the MIPS processor is given by Kane (1989).

3.6   User-level input and output

Low-level mechanisms for performing input and output have been described in some detail. Application programs are, in general, not allowed to program at this level, and must ask the operating system to do I/O on their behalf. We now consider this top-down application-driven view of I/O programming, shown in Figure 3.12.

A general point is that I/O statements should be made as general as possible. Ideally, a given program should be written with I/O statements that can be bound to different devices for a given execution. The language-level I/O is in terms of logical devices which can take or deliver arbitrary amounts of data. A **stream** facility is often provided by languages as well as single character and string I/O. An application can set up a number of named input and output streams and send or deliver arbitrary numbers of bytes to or from them.

The operating system interface is used by the language libraries. This is likely to support the input or output of a single character or a string of characters. A detailed example for a specific operating system is given in Chapter 21.

3.6.1   Buffers and synchronization

The application level can request input or output of an arbitrary amount of data; the device concerned can transfer a fixed amount. Data buffers are needed between the I/O modules which are invoked by the application (top-down) and those which are executed in response to device events (bottom-up). Figure 3.13 shows the general idea. The top-down software can place the data to be output in one or more buffers. We then need a mechanism for telling the lower levels that there is work to do. Similarly, when a device delivers data it is placed in one or more buffers by the low levels and the high levels must be told there is work to do. We are seeing a requirement for processes to **synchronize** with each other.

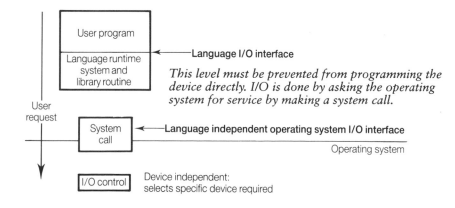

Figure 3.12
Top-down
invocation of I/O.

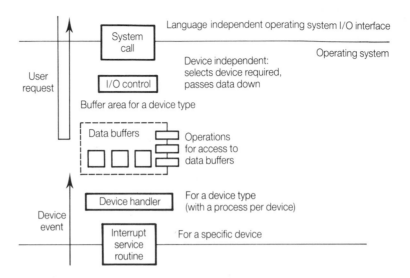

Figure 3.13
I/O buffers.

There is likely to be a buffer area for user terminals, one for disk blocks, one for network communications, and so on. Figure 3.13 shows the data buffers as abstract data types or objects. We assume interface operations such as *acquire-buffer, release-buffer, write bytes into buffer* and *read bytes from buffer*. We are not concerned here with the details of buffer space allocation, but rather to draw out the requirement for synchronization between processes.

A general point is that the device handler should be able to start work as soon as possible on a large amount of output, before the top level has put it all into a number of buffers. Similarly, on input the high level may be able to start taking data from a buffer as soon as one is full. Care must then be taken that the processes synchronize their accesses to the buffers. Chapters 9 and 10 discuss this problem in general and solutions are given there.

In the case of characters input from terminals, the device handler must look at each character before deciding whether to put it into a buffer. The character might indicate that the program should be aborted or that output to the screen should be halted until further notice.

This chapter emphasizes the general structure of an I/O handling subsystem in terms of modules and processes. Chapter 21 gives an example of how terminal handling and disk handling are done in one particular operating system.

3.6.2   Synchronous and asynchronous input and output

When a user-level process makes a request for input or output, the following may be the case:

- The request can be satisfied by a transfer of data from or to a buffer in memory. For example, a previous DMA transfer may have delivered a block of data and the user may request a few bytes at a time. In this case there is no need for the process to be delayed. Control can be returned to it with the data on input, or with the transfer to the device scheduled to take place on output.

- The request cannot be satisfied immediately. For example, the required data may not already be in a buffer in memory and it may be necessary to perform physical device input. On output, the system's policy may be such that a limited amount of buffer space can be allocated to a single process and physical output must be performed before the whole output request can be satisfied.

System designs differ in the options available to the user-level process when a delay is necessary. A **synchronous** I/O policy indicates that the user-level process is blocked when a delay is necessary until the request can be satisfied. An **asynchronous** option means that, if a delay is necessary, control can be returned to the user-level process, which can proceed with its work and pick up the requested input or acknowledgement of output in due course. In some systems, user-level processes can specify whether they require synchronous or asynchronous I/O when they make a request.

The UNIX system offers only synchronous I/O, often referred to as 'blocking system calls'. The IBM System/370 allows the user-level process to select synchronous or asynchronous I/O as required.

3.7   Communications management

Distributed systems running on computer networks were introduced in Section 1.1.3 and local area network (LAN) topologies and wide area networks (WANs) were introduced in Section 1.3.8. An operating system for a computer with a network connection must have a communications handling function. The network connection of a computer may be considered at a low level as just another device. It has an interface and is handled by device-driving software. The characteristics of the network interface will depend on the network concerned. Each network is designed to deliver **packets** of data to its attached computers via their network interfaces. Sometimes the packets are of variable size, up to some maximum size, while sometimes the data arrives in fixed size cells. Section 3.8 gives examples of packet sizes and interfaces.

Communications handling differs from the device handling function we considered above because the network connection is shared and networks are often faster than devices. We considered terminal handling where one user process has one device and there is a duplex connection between them. We considered disk DMA interfaces. In this case many processes share the use of a filing system on a number of disks and there can be several outstanding data transfers in progress, initiated on behalf of different processes. In Section 3.2.1 we saw an example of a disk with a data transfer rate of rate of 2 Mbits per second. It is commonplace for networks to operate at 10 Mbits per second and rates of 100s to 1000s

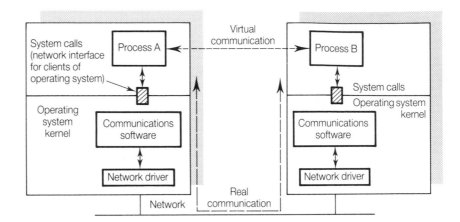

Figure 3.14
Communication
between processes
on different
machines.

Mbits per second are coming into use. Disk speeds are unable to increase dramatically because of the electromechanical nature of the device.

In the case of communications handling, the network connection is shared. Several local processes can request to communicate with external processes and their requests may be in progress simultaneously. Also, external processes may autonomously request to communicate with local processes. Computer–computer communication can generate a large volume of data associated with these multiple simultaneous process interactions. The communications handling subsystem is therefore a large concurrent system. It must handle simultaneous inputs and outputs for very large volumes of data. The subjects of data communications, networks and protocols merit complete books, but we need an overview of this function if we are to understand how processes on different computers can cooperate to achieve the goals of a concurrent system. Also, specialized texts on communications do not cover how these systems may be implemented in terms of processes.

In some distributed systems a network connection may be the only peripheral a computer has. In others, a workstation may have a local keyboard and screen, but may use the network for file access. Yet another arrangement is for a workstation to have a local disk and filing system augmented by a network file service. Also, applications may be implemented as concurrent processes spread across a number of computers.

Processes on different machines may need to communicate with each other. A client process may invoke a server function or peer processes may need to exchange information. Figure 3.14 shows the basic requirement, with process A on one machine and process B on another. The *virtual communication,* shown as direct between process A and process B, may in practice be achieved by a system call to the operating system which organizes data transfers across the network: the *real communication* shown in the figure.

We now look at the low-level aspects of communications networks, those concerned with network interfaces and drivers. We then proceed to the higher levels of communications software in Section 3.9.

3.8   Communications networks, interfaces and drivers

A given computer might be connected to a local area network (LAN) or a wide area network (WAN). Perhaps the most common (and most general) topology is that of interconnected LANs connected by WANs to form an internetwork. Figure 1.9 shows local networks of workstations and servers with WAN connections. For generality, it also shows some host computers directly attached to the WAN. Some concurrent systems span large-scale or even global networks, for example, electronic mail systems, information retrieval services and the private networks of companies with widely dispersed branches.

A computer's network connection is handled by the operating system in much the same way as a device. The network has an interface and the operating system contains a driver for the interface. Aspects of relevance to the network connection are the method that is used to access the network medium and the interface between the network hardware and the attached computer (see Figure 3.15). For example, some networks require active connections which participate in the transmission of packets from one network link to the next, whereas in others the network connection is just a passive tap. These issues are not relevant to the concurrent software structures we are considering here. We discuss interfaces briefly in Section 3.8.3.

Above the driver are higher levels of software implementing communications services and protocols (see below). There are system calls to give the operating system's clients an interface to the communications service. The basic structure is similar to that of the I/O subsystem, with communications initiated both top-down and bottom-up and with the requirement for data to be buffered.

Some examples of LAN characteristics are given in Table 3.1. These examples illustrate two major approaches to LAN design, the bus and ring topology. Their access methods and some interfaces for them are described briefly below. A complete description can be found in Hopper *et al.* (1986) and Halsall (1992).

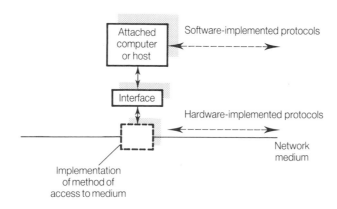

Figure 3.15
Medium, access method and interface.

Table 3.1   Characteristics of LANs

Ethernet	10 Mbit s^{-1}	variable size packets with up to 4Kbytes of data
IEEE 802.4 token bus	10 Mbit s^{-1}	variable size packets, 96 to 8 kbytes
FDDI token ring	100 Mbit s^{-1}	variable size packets, typically 96 bytes
Cambridge Ring (CR)	10 Mbit s^{-1}	fixed cell size with 2 bytes of data
Cambridge Fast Ring (CFR)	100 Mbit s^{-1}	fixed cell size with 32 bytes of data
Cambridge Backbone Ring (CBR)	1 Gbit s^{-1}	fixed cell size with 32 bytes of data

Some network interfaces use DMA; they deposit an assembled block of data into main memory then signal an interrupt. Others interrupt the processor every time a packet arrives at the network interface.

We shall not discuss the packet structure in detail. In all cases we assume that the packets that are transmitted onto the network have control information as well as data so that the source and destination of the transmission can be determined by the network hardware and errors can be detected and recovery procedures invoked. Our main concern is the software systems in the attached computers. As network users we need to be aware of the data transmission rates they can sustain and with what guarantees.

3.8.1   Ethernet

Ethernet is a LAN designed at Xerox Palo Alto Research Center (PARC) (Metcalfe and Boggs, 1976) and a prototype was operational there in 1976. It is a broadcast bus type of network whose medium is a coaxial cable named the 'ether'. The access method (for an attached computer) is **carrier sense multiple access with collision detection** (CSMA/CD). In this scheme a potential transmitter listens to the communications medium to determine whether there is already a transmission in progress on the network. If the ether is quiet the transmission goes ahead. Since it is possible that another station initiates a transmission at the same time, a packet collision can occur. In order to detect this, each station listens to the transmission of its packet and if corruption is detected the transmission is aborted. To avoid transmissions which have collided being retried in phase, a random back-off period is used before retransmission takes place. This period increases exponentially on repeated collisions.

Ethernets were originally intended for 'office' applications, but have come to be used widely during the 1980s. In practice they work well at light loads, typically 10% of capacity. As processors continue to increase in performance and multiprocessors become more widely used Ethernets will become more heavily loaded. As load increases, so does the chance of contention and the possibility of delay. The network is monopolized while a transfer takes place, which, together with the probabilistic nature of the access mechanism, means that timing guarantees cannot be made for applications that need them.

3.8.2   Ring-based LANs

Several ring-based networks have been developed over the years. One method of controlling access to the ring is to employ a unique circulating **token**. When a computer receives the token from the ring it may delay transmitting it until it has placed its own packet onto the ring. Only one computer may be transmitting at one time. IBM Zurich have developed a token ring (Bux *et al.*, 1982); another is FDDI (fiber distributed data interface) (Burr, 1986; Ross, 1986).

The Cambridge Ring networks are based on the **slotted ring** principle (Hopper and Needham, 1988). The first was operational in 1976 at the University of Cambridge Computer Laboratory. A ring of given length can carry a fixed number of cells, constantly circulating. Each carries a leading bit indicating full or empty. A station assembles a cell it wishes to transmit and inserts it into the first available empty packet. A packet makes a complete circuit of the ring and the destination station copies the cell and marks it as received. Other responses may also be indicated. When the cell returns to its sender, the response is noted and the packet is marked empty and passed on. Notice that the sender may not reuse this packet. This is called an 'anti-hogging' mechanism and ensures that all stations have an equal chance of using the medium. This allows timing guarantees to be made.

If a small fixed packet size is used, a given piece of data to be transferred is split for transmission and reassembled after reception. Software immediately above the interface must handle this; that is, higher-level protocols implemented in software manage the transmission of larger packets (see below). If a larger, variable packet size is used, as in Ethernet, some communications can be achieved by the transfer of a single packet. It will still be necessary to split some 'messages' into packet-sized portions and reassemble them at the destination. This is called 'segmentation and reassembly'.

3.8.3   Examples of network interfaces

Because of the commercial success of Ethernet in a wide variety of applications, a great deal of effort has been expended on producing high-performance interfaces for it. Examples are the DEQNA (DEC, 1986) and LANCE (AMD, 1985) interfaces. Both employ a ring of transmit descriptors and a ring of receive descriptors in main memory. The transmit descriptors indicate buffers containing data to transmit as packets and the receive descriptors indicate buffer space to use for incoming packets. Transmission and reception is done by DMA from and to these buffers defined by the descriptors in the rings. An interrupt may be generated on the emptying or filling of a buffer by the interface. Concurrent access by the interface and the host computer to the descriptor rings could cause errors, and a protocol is employed to ensure correct access. By using large packets and a suitable memory system a host can, in theory, achieve close to 100% utilization of an Ethernet with one of these interfaces.

The Cambridge Fast Ring and Cambridge Backbone Ring are used primarily in a research environment. No interface supporting DMA access has yet been built for the CFR so all data must be moved between the host memory and the interface using processor cycles. The CFR can buffer only one 'cell' of 32 bytes. So far, only a single type of interface (for the VME bus) has been built for the CBR (Greaves *et al.* 1990). It contains four transmit FIFO buffers and one receive FIFO buffer. Each buffer has a capacity of 256 cells of 32 bytes per cell. It can be programmed to interrupt on every cell received or only when a cell containing an end of frame bit is detected. A version offering DMA has been designed.

3.9   Communications software

A communications **protocol** is a set of rules for controlling communication. It may define a particular, ordered sequence of messages to be used in a communication. The order is agreed by convention between the communicating entities to satisfy their requirements. A simple example, taken from a different context, is:

message: ' Hi beta, this is alpha, are you receiving me? OVER'
reply: 'Yes alpha, this is beta, I'm receiving you. OVER'

The above two messages implement a **connection establishment** protocol.

An example of an **application protocol** (see Figure 3.16) is a client's interaction with a file server, for example:

file-id =   **open** (*filename, write-mode*)
data-bytes = **read** (*file-id, byte-range*)
               close (*file-id*)

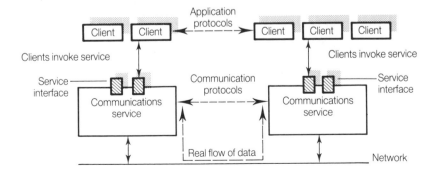

Figure 3.16
Service interface
and protocol.

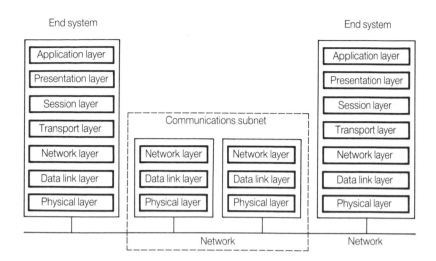

Figure 3.17
The ISO reference model for OSI.

The client must obey certain rules for interacting with the file server. The operations must be invoked in the right order and the correct arguments must be passed. In this example the client must **open** a file before reading it. The server replies with a *file-id* for subsequent use by the client. The client passes the *file-id* when it wants to read data from the file.

Communications software implements services and protocols to allow information to be transmitted between computers. A service interface to the communications software is specified so that its clients may indicate which services and protocols they require. Figure 3.16 shows this scheme.

This simple picture does not express the many functions of communications software. The communications service shown in Figure 3.16 must have a great deal of internal structure and is always described in terms of layers with functions associated with each layer. The lowest layer is concerned with the physical network and the highest with applications concerns. The next section gives a standard definition of the various layers of communications functions.

3.9.1 The ISO reference model for Open Systems Interconnection

The International Standards Organization's (ISO) reference model for Open Systems Interconnection (OSI) (see Figure 3.17) provides a framework for discussion and comparison of communications software. Standard protocols and service interfaces have been specified for some of the levels. The reference model is itself a standard: ISO-7498 (see ISO, 1981 and Zimmerman, 1980).

The network architecture shown in Figure 3.17 is deliberately all-embracing and most networks map onto a subset of it. It may represent a network comprising any number of connected LANs and WANs. The two **end systems** indicate a

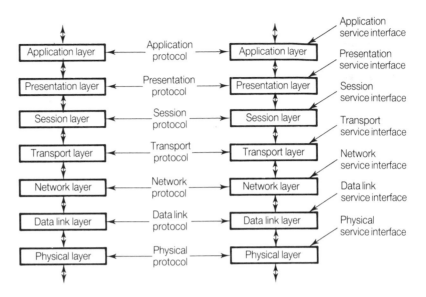

Figure 3.18
Protocols and
service interfaces.

source and sink of communication and the **communications subnet** may comprise any number of intermediate (gateway) computers which cooperate to transfer information between the end systems.

The reference model provides a framework for modular, layered software. Each layer provides a service interface to the layer above and protocols for communicating with the corresponding layer in other systems. Figure 3.18 gives the general idea. Figure 3.19 shows how data to be transmitted is passed down the layers. At each level a header, and possibly a trailer, is added as defined for the particular layer protocol to be used. At the receiving end system each layer strips off its header and trailer and passes the data up to the layer above. The highest level interprets the data according to an application protocol. Figure 3.20 shows a simple example of a small amount of data to be transmitted between two application processes. By the time it has reached the lowest level and is ready for

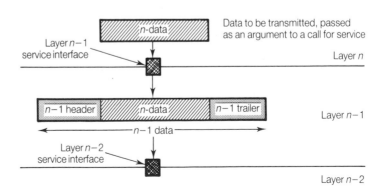

Figure 3.19
Data packaged for
transmission by a
protocol.

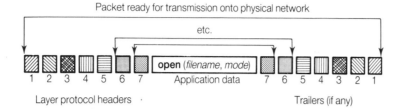

Figure 3.20
Example of data
packaged for
transmission.

transmission to the network it has accumulated a protocol header from each
layer (and possible also a trailer). The figure assumes a network which allows
this data to be transmitted as a single packet.

Figure 3.18 shows the protocols between the seven reference model layers and
the service interface for each layer. The layers were chosen to give useful
abstractions; a brief definition of the function of each layer is given below.

The **physical layer** is concerned with transmitting uninterpreted bits across a
communication channel from one computer to another and with managing the
connection.

The **data link layer** is mainly concerned with taking a raw transmission facility and turning it into a link that appears to be free from errors.

The **network layer** is concerned with transmitting data from a source to a destination across (possibly a number of heterogeneous) networks. It must determine a route for the data packets and must attempt to avoid congestion in the
network by controlling the number of packets transmitted.

The **transport layer** is concerned with transmission from end system to end
system. It provides hosts with a standard service. A number of different qualities
of service are appropriate to this level. One major distinction is between a
connection-oriented service and a **connectionless service**. The transport layer is
usually the highest level of communication service in the operating system and
the session layer provides an interface to the operating system's communication
service (see Figure 3.21).

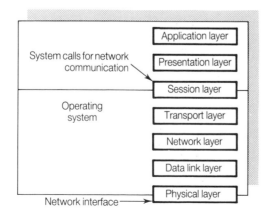

Figure 3.21
ISO reference
model layers in a
typical operating
system.

The **session layer** allows clients of an operating system on one machine to establish and use sessions with clients of an operating system on another machine.

The **presentation layer** is concerned with the representation of data. In the extreme case, the communicating end systems may run on different hardware, with different operating systems and with different implementations of language systems. Even in this case, a standard data representation allows arguments such as strings, integers etc. to pass from a client to a service. Some more homogeneous examples are considered in Chapter 14.

The **application layer** contains a number of standard protocols that are of general use. The remote procedure call (RPC) protocol discussed in Chapter 14 is an example. We shall study an RPC package that contains application, presentation and session layers. Other examples are file transfer protocols, electronic mail, remote login remote job entry, virtual terminals and many others. Any service program may define an application protocol that its clients must use when invoking it.

3.9.2   Connection-oriented and connectionless communication

There are two fundamentally different kinds of service that a layer can offer to the layer above it: **connection-oriented** and **connectionless**. In a connectionless service a data item being transmitted by a protocol is sent as a separate unit, unrelated to any previous communication at that level. The data is sent as a so-called **datagram** which contains full addressing information.

A connection-oriented service requires that a connection or **virtual circuit** is set up between the communicating entities. In this case data items are sent along the connection, and are identified only by the virtual circuit concerned and not by full addressing information.

There are variations of both styles of service. In outline, the trade-offs are as follows:

● It takes longer to decode a datagram to determine which process it should be delivered to.

● It takes time to set up and tear down a connection. If a communication consists, for example, of a single request followed by a single reply the overhead of a connection is unnecessary.

● Use of a virtual circuit implies that the computers implementing communications must retain state about the connections that have been set up. Several computers might be involved if communication is taking place across interconnected LANs or WANs. A problem is that if any computer fails, the connections that are routed through it will have to be re-established.

For some applications, such as client–server interactions, connections seem to be unnecessary. We shall see a request–response protocol implemented above a datagram service in Chapter 14. For other applications, such as the transfer of a voice or video stream from a server to a workstation, a connection seems to be essential. The time for each packet to be decoded afresh is likely to be prohibitive.

In the past, connection-oriented services, X.25 for example, were notorious for being heavyweight and therefore inappropriate for a large number of distributed applications. New protocols are now in use which implement lightweight virtual circuits (McAuley, 1989). Techniques that achieve efficiency are:

- The circuit is not set up by a separate connection establishment protocol, including an end-to-end acknowledge before data can be sent along it. As soon as the first hop is ready the data can go.

- A circuit can easily be broken and re-established.

- There is no multiplexing above the datalink level; each application-level process-to-process connection has a separate virtual circuit.

Applications which use this style of protocol are described in Section 22.4.

3.10   Communications handling within an operating system

Figure 3.21 gives an example of how the ISO layers might be provided in a typical operating system.

There are a large number of different protocol hierarchies. Taking a local example, the UNIX systems at the University of Cambridge Computer Laboratory are configured with over 20. It is therefore important for operating systems to allow their clients to select the protocol hierarchy they require. Figure 3.22 shows a commonly used protocol hierarchy in relation to the ISO layers in an Ethernet-based UNIX system. Section 21.16 shows how network communications are set up and used in this system.

We have seen the need for synchronization between user-level processes requesting to send or receive data and the hardware carrying out physical I/O. We also discussed the use of I/O buffers on input and output (see Figure 3.13). Similar synchronization and buffering arrangements are needed for network I/O. Chapter 6 discusses how software, including I/O and networking software, may be executed by processes.

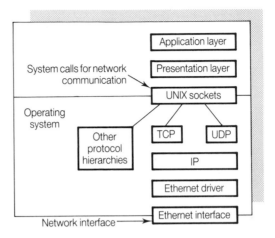

Figure 3.22
The ARPA protocols
in an Ethernet-
based UNIX system.

TCP = Transmission Control Protocol (a connection-oriented transport service)
UDP = User Datagram Protocol (a connectionless transport service)
IP = Internet Protocol (network level)

3.11 Summary

The hardware is one source of events, and therefore of concurrent activity, in a concurrent system. We have seen how the hardware may signal an event, such as the arrival of a unit of data, and how events are handled by software. Hardware events may be classified as those which are caused by (and must be handled synchronously with) a running program and those which are external and may be handled asynchronously.

Some concurrent systems may need to meet timing requirements. For such systems it is necessary to understand how events arrive and the mechanism for handling them. It is also important to realize that, although the hardware may be fast enough to meet timing requirements, software policies could make it impossible to guarantee them. We shall see more of this in Chapter 6. So far, we have seen that an operating system provides a convenient, high-level interface for device handling, and therefore hides the details.

In a concurrent system processes may need to interact with devices and communicate with other processes which may be across a network. The communications subsystem must handle simultaneous requests from local users and interleaved communications data arriving across the network. Other computers are likely to generate more data than local peripherals. Because of this potential volume and complexity, careful modular structuring is required. The most general case is when unlike systems need to communicate, and the ISO OSI standards are designed to address this. The ISO reference model is used to describe and compare all communications software.

The next chapters cover memory management and file management functions. If the reader has some knowledge of these topics already these chapters may be omitted. The main thrust of the argument continues in Chapter 6. There, we see how the processes we introduced as an abstraction in Chapter 2 are implemented by the operating system. We can then study how processes may be used to handle devices and run users' programs.

Exercises

3.1   By looking in Hennessy and Patterson (1990), for example, find out the following:
(a) The execution times of typical instructions of CISC computers such as the VAX series, the IBM System 370, the Motorola 68000 series, the Intel 8086 and 80x86 series.
(b) The execution times of typical instructions of RISC computers such as the Motorola 88000, the SPARC, the MIPS R23000 and the Intel 860.
In both cases note the instruction lengths and their functionality.

       Now find out the rate at which networks and peripherals, such as terminals, printers, disks and RAM used as disks, can accept or deliver data and also the unit of data that is accepted or delivered.

3.2   What are the advantages and disadvantages of handling devices by a polling scheme compared with an interrupt-driven approach? In what kinds of system does the application dictate which approach must be taken?

3.3   How many memory accesses are made during the hardware exception handling mechanisms described in Sections 3.2 and 3.5? Estimate the total time to achieve the transfer of control from the interrupted program to the exception handling routine in both cases.

3.4   You have hardware support for seven priority interrupt levels. On what basis would you assign these priorities?

3.5   What is direct memory access (DMA)? How can (a) a single block and (b) several blocks of data be transferred between main memory and a disk or network?

3.6   Processors are usually designed to execute in one of two (or more) privilege states, for example, user and supervisor mode.
(a) When and how is the state change from user to supervisor mode made?

(b) When and how is the state change from supervisor to user mode made?

(c) Which instructions would you expect to be privileged (executable only in supervisor mode)? What is the mechanism for preventing them from being executed in user mode?

3.7 An application should be able to send an arbitrary amount of data to be output to a device. Devices transfer a fixed amount. How is this achieved?

3.8 Error conditions are often detected at a low level in a system, such as in an exception handling routine. Why should they not be dealt with immediately? Devise a method to allow error handling at user level within the context of the application that caused the error.

3.9 How are exceptions handled in a shared-memory multiprocessor?

3.10 Compare and contrast peripheral I/O and network I/O.

3.11 Define wide area networks and local area networks (see also Section 1.3.8).

3.12 Compare and contrast the Ethernet with a ring-based LAN. Which design type will guarantee bandwidth between connected systems? What kind of applications need such guarantees? Are the guarantees usually made to the application level?

3.13 What is meant by connectionless and connection-oriented communication?

3.14 Which of the ISO layers would you expect to be implemented inside an operating system?

3.15 How do you think the ISO layers might be implemented in terms of the modules and processes introduced in Chapter 2? Try this question again after reading Chapter 6.

Operating systems: Memory management

4

CONTENTS

4.1 Memory management

An operating system function is to allocate memory to processes. As explained in Section 2.4, a command interpreter will take a command to run a program, request memory from the operating system, load files into the memory and cause a process to be created to execute the program. When a process runs, its data structures may need to grow beyond the initial memory allocation and it must be possible for more memory to be requested from the operating system. The operating system must keep track of free physical memory and must record the allocations it has made to each process.

We shall first take an architectural view of main memory in the context of the storage hierarchy of a computer, and then go on to study issues such as protection and sharing which are relevant to concurrent systems design.

4.2 The memory hierarchy

Figure 4.1 shows a typical computer system's memory hierarchy. There is a trade-off involved in using storage devices which involves size, speed and cost. The CPU registers are the fastest but smallest store. A large proportion of the machine's instructions will access data from CPU registers and compiler writers must organize their use to optimize program execution time. The design of the processor and the hardware-controlled cache are not our concern here but as system designers we need a broad view of current and projected sizes and speeds. An excellent summary is given in Hennessy and Patterson (1990).

The **cache** is small and fast compared with main memory and acts as a buffer between the CPU and the memory. It contains a copy of the most recently used memory locations: address and contents are recorded there. Every address reference goes first to the cache. If the desired address is not present we have a **cache miss**. The contents are fetched from main memory into the CPU register indicated in the instruction being executed and a copy is retained in the cache. It is likely that the same location will be used again soon, and, if so, the address will be found in the cache, in which case we have a **cache hit**. If a write occurs, the hardware not only writes to the cache but also generates a **write-through** to main memory.

In a uniprocessor operating system the cache can be considered as transparent. The designer of an operating system for a shared-memory multiprocessor needs to know how the processors' caches operate. It might be that more than one processor has the same writeable data value cached, for example. These issues are not relevant to memory management.

The concern of this chapter is main memory. Instructions must be in main memory in order to be fetched and executed by a processor. Any data operand referenced by an instruction must be in main memory for the instructions to execute successfully. Our expectations of what 'a reasonable amount of main memory' is have changed over the years and will continue to do so, roughly: 1970, 64 kbytes; 1980, 1 Mbyte; 1990, 16 Mbytes; 2000, a gigabyte? There are

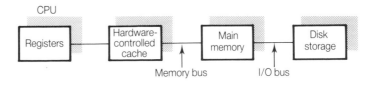

Figure 4.1
The memory
hierarchy.

already 200 Mbyte WSI (wafer scale integration) main memory devices available and many different options for disk storage.

From a system designer's point of view an important property of main memory is that it is in general volatile; that is, if there is a power failure the information stored there is lost. This is a daunting prospect if one has 200 Mbytes of it! Non-volatile memory is available, but is more expensive than conventional volatile memory. Disk storage, on the other hand, is non-volatile and much system design effort is concerned with writing information safely out to disk to guard against loss of main memory on a crash. We shall return to this topic in Chapter 13, and throughout Part III.

4.3 The address space of a process

We shall make use of the concept of the address space of a process (the range of addresses available to it) throughout the book. The concept is important for naming (addressing), protection and system structure and we need to examine it in some detail.

Some machine language instructions contain addresses, for example:

LOAD a specified processor register with the contents of an address;

STORE the contents of a processor register in an address;

CALL a procedure at some address;

JUMP or BRANCH to an address.

The instructions have an address field which contains a representation of a memory address. The number of bits allocated to an address is an architectural decision. Many early computers' instruction sets had only 16 bit address fields, which allowed only 64 kbytes of memory to be addressed directly. A typical figure is now 32 bits which allows 4 gigabytes (Gbytes) to be addressed. We say that such an architecture gives a **virtual address space** of 4 Gbytes. The amount of physical memory configured into a given computer system is likely to be much smaller than this.

The important concept is the virtual address space of a process. An address can be anywhere within the virtual address space, but must be **bound** to a physical memory address before the instruction execution can be carried out.

Object code addresses are produced by system software: a compiler and/or an assembler. Any realistic program should be developed as separate modules which are then linked and loaded into memory. When the compiler or assembler is translating a single module, it does not know (except in very simple systems) where the module will be loaded in the physical memory of the computer. Translators must therefore adopt a convention about the addresses to use in the code they output. Let us assume that translators output code for each module as though it would start from address zero in memory. A linker can take a sequence of such modules and create a single load module by adjusting the (relative) addresses in all but the first module. The addresses in this composite load module are still relative to its start. The basic principle is illustrated well by this simple example, using address zero as the start of a single program module. However, a compiler has the whole virtual address space at its disposal and modern compilers have more elaborate conventions for use of the virtual address space.

We now consider what happens when such a module comes to be loaded into physical main memory. The operating system is responsible for managing memory and we assume that it will give the loader a base address from which to load the module. The important question is whether the loader should adjust all the relative addresses in the module, converting them to absolute physical addresses, before loading it. This is called **static relocation** or **static binding**. If this was done, then once a program was loaded into memory the addresses in it would be fixed and the code or data at these addresses could not be moved in memory. The only flexibility available to an operating system would be to move the program out to backing store and then later move it back into main memory into exactly the same place. It would be possible to move a module to a different place in main memory only if the relocation information (the location of relative addresses within the module) was retained with the module and the translation from relative to absolute addresses was carried out by software every time the module was moved.

In a system which is dedicated to a single task, such as monitoring an industrial process or providing a service, it might be the case that once a program is loaded in memory it runs there indefinitely. In this case the static binding of addresses (at load time) just described might be appropriate. All the processes executing in such a system would share the same **physical address space**. They are all using the absolute machine addresses of the available physical memory. They would not be protected from each other, should addressing errors occur, nor would any operating system code be protected from application-level processes, unless some additional hardware was provided (see Section 4.5).

We now consider the possibility of keeping the loaded addresses relative to the start of a program. The advantages of doing this are:

- a given program can run anywhere in physical memory and can be moved around by the operating system;
- it might be possible to protect processes from each other and the operating system from application processes by whatever mechanism we employ for isolating the addresses seen by processes.

To realize these advantages we must have a mechanism to bind the virtual addresses within the loaded instructions to physical addresses when the instructions are executed. Much of this chapter is concerned with how to do this.

Figure 4.2 illustrates the concept we have just introduced, that of the virtual address space of a process. The process sees a virtual machine in which it has access to a virtual address space starting from address zero. The real machine is shared by a number of processes, and we see the virtual memory of the process occupying a portion of real physical memory. Since this address translation is

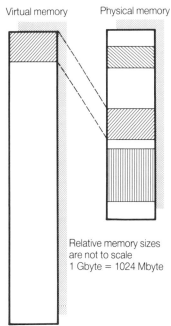

The size of virtual
memory is defined
by the number of
bits in an address,
e.g. a 32 bit address
gives a 4 Gbyte
virtual memory.
The user's program
is shown here
starting from
address zero.

Virtual memory   Physical memory

The size of physical
memory is likely to be
much smaller than
virtual memory,
typically a few
megabytes.

The user's program
is shown here
starting at some
arbitrary address
and sharing the
memory with other
programs.

Relative memory sizes
are not to scale
1 Gbyte = 1024 Mbyte

Figure 4.2
Virtual memory and
real memory.

part of every instruction fetch or data fetch from memory it has to be integrated
closely with the hardware instruction cycle. We now consider various forms of
hardware mechanism which support and extend the basic idea introduced here.

4.4   Dynamic relocation hardware

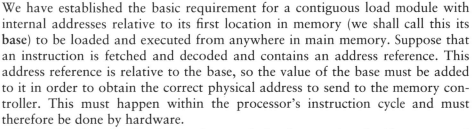

We have established the basic requirement for a contiguous load module with
internal addresses relative to its first location in memory (we shall call this its
base) to be loaded and executed from anywhere in main memory. Suppose that
an instruction is fetched and decoded and contains an address reference. This
address reference is relative to the base, so the value of the base must be added
to it in order to obtain the correct physical address to send to the memory controller. This must happen within the processor's instruction cycle and must
therefore be done by hardware.

Dynamic relocation hardware, for translating from a virtual address to a real
address at runtime, was first used in the early 1960s. It is now commonplace for
computers to have memory management units (MMUs) and these may take a
variety of forms. A simple development of memory management hardware and
its use by operating systems is given below. A summary of MMUs is given in the
appropriate sections and a detailed example is described in Sections 4.11
and 4.12.

4.5   Protection hardware

Simply adding a base address to each address reference made by a program does not help to confine those address references to the memory allocated to the program; that is, relocation hardware does not provide a protection function. Before relocation hardware came into use protection registers had already been provided for many computers. Again, various forms were available, but the basic idea was usually to check each address reference against values set up in hardware registers. For example, when a process was selected to run, the operating system would load its upper and lower bounds into two registers for this purpose. It was natural to combine the relocation and protection function in a single set of registers.

4.6   Relocation and protection of a single contiguous segment

The simplest form of dynamic relocation hardware is a single **base register**. The operating system must load this as part of setting up the state of a process before passing control to it. This register can also function as a lower bound protection register and a second register (we shall call it the **limit register**) can be used to delimit the upper bound of the program. Figure 4.3 shows a typical instruction execution cycle augmented with protection checks and address relocation.

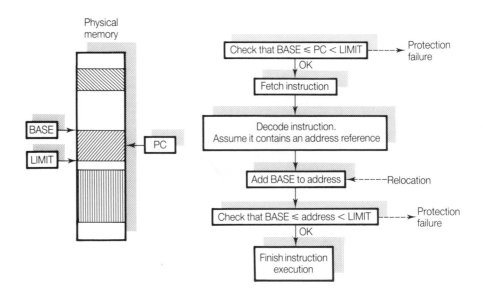

Figure 4.3
Instruction execution with protection checks and relocation.

4.7   Several segments per process

In practice it is not very useful for a program to have to occupy a single contiguous range of physical addresses. With such a scheme it would not be possible for two processes to share the code of a compiler (the example used in Figure 2.10). The difficulty is in arranging for the two executions of the compiler to access different data areas. This can be achieved, transparently to the program, if the system has two base registers and two limit registers, thus allowing two separate segments per process. Figure 4.4 shows two processes sharing a compiler and Figure 4.5 shows relocation (and protection) hardware to realize this scheme. The most significant bit of an address is taken as a segment identifier: 0 indicates the data segment (segment 0) and 1 indicates the code segment (segment 1). If this bit is 0 then base register 0 is used for relocation. If it is 1 then base register 1 is used.

With two separate segments it is easy to implement a more sophisticated protection scheme than access/no-access to physical memory. We can implement different modes of access to the segments and set these up for each individual process when it comes to run. The system might support separate *read, write* and *execute* rights, for example. Any process sharing a code segment could be set up to have only *execute* rights to it. A process would have *read* and *write* rights for its own data segment. Instruction execution would then include a check of the type of access required.

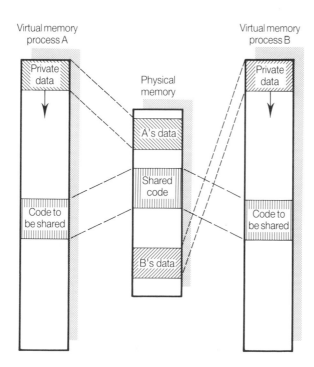

Figure 4.4
Two processes share a code segment but have private data segments.

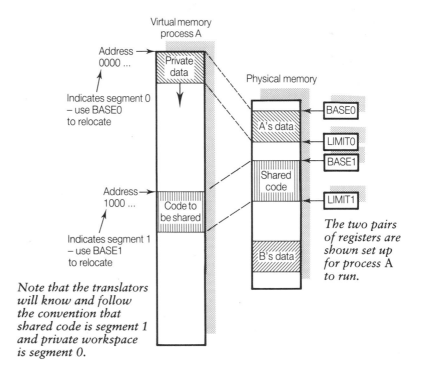

Virtual memory process A

Address 0000 ...

Indicates segment 0 – use BASE0 to relocate

Address 1000 ...

Indicates segment 1 – use BASE1 to relocate

Private data

Code to be shared

Physical memory

A's data

Shared code

B's data

BASE0

LIMIT0

BASE1

LIMIT1

The two pairs of registers are shown set up for process A *to run.*

Note that the translators will know and follow the convention that shared code is segment 1 and private workspace is segment 0.

Figure 4.5
Relocation and protection hardware for two segments.

Within a single program it is usual to have separate areas for code and data areas, for example, code, stack and heap. Language systems have conventions on how the virtual address space is arranged and a common scheme is shown in Figure 4.6. Here, we see a code segment, which will not grow in size, followed by a data area which may well grow. At the top of the virtual address space we see the stack growing downwards in memory.

To realize an arrangement of this kind with one segment only, the stack would have to be very much closer to the heap than indicated here or we should not have enough physical memory to load the segment, even though most of it is the empty gap between the heap and the stack. There would be no possibility of sharing the code (or any of the data) and no possibility of different kinds of access checks on the separate parts. As the two data areas grow they might well collide and this would require software to create more space by moving the data. If we had only two segments we would probably use one for the code and heap (and be unable to protect them differently) and the second for the stack. This would at least allow the two data areas to grow without colliding. Three segments would be preferable.

It is easy to generate examples where it would be nice to have four or more segments per process. The segment is the unit of protection and sharing, and the more we have, the more flexible we can be. In the evolution of mainframe computers the provision of large numbers of segments per process was an early aim; Multics is an early example (see Bensoussan *et al.*, 1972; Saltzer, 1974).

Figure 4.7 shows how a virtual address may be split into segment number and byte offset within segment. The hardware support for dynamic address

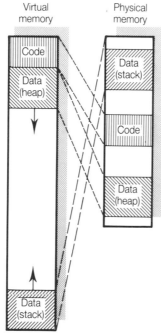

The user's program is shown here starting from address zero. After the code comes a growing data area (the heap). The stack is in a separate data area and grows towards the heap.

The code area and two data areas are shown separately relocated. This would require three segments per process and corresponding relocation and protection hardware.

Figure 4.6
A common convention for using virtual memory.

translation must be extended to support many segments. The operating system must keep a segment table for each process in which the location of each segment is recorded. These tables need to be in fast memory, perhaps pointed to by a processor register.

If a process can have many segments, only those currently being used for instruction fetch and operand access need be in main memory. Other segments could be held on backing store until they are needed. It might be that some segments need never come into main memory on a given program run, for example, those containing error handling routines might not be needed.

To achieve this we must decide how a segment is brought into main memory when it is needed. For example, what should happen when a transfer of control is about to be made to a segment that is not in main memory? It is not desirable for the compiler to attempt to foresee the need for such transitions. Only the operating system, at runtime, knows how much main memory is available and where it has chosen to place the segments of the currently active process.

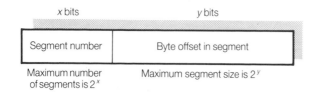

Virtual address: address field of an instruction.

Figure 4.7
A virtual address for a segmented system.

The mechanism that is used is that the address translation hardware allows a segment to be addressed that is not present in main memory. An addressing exception is generated when this happens and is handled by the operating system, possibly with hardware assistance. The general concept here is called **virtual memory**. A program's segments are located throughout the memory hierarchy and the operating system, in response to addressing hardware exceptions, effects the necessary segment transfers. We shall explore this concept again in the next section in the context of paging.

Topics that are left for further study are:

- the detailed design of the tables the operating system must keep for the segments of each process, the type of access the process has to each and where each segment is currently located in main memory and/or on disk;

- how the main memory and backing store is allocated to the segments of processes;

- how the operating system and memory management hardware interact in specific systems.

Details of memory management hardware that supports segmentation are not given here, but examples are the Burroughs B5000 (Siewiorek *et al.*, 1981), the PDP-11 series and, more recently, the Intel 80286 (Ciminiera and Valenzano, 1987; Hennessy and Patterson 1990, pp. 445–9).

In summary, the advantages of segmented virtual memory are:

- The virtual address space of a process is divided into logically distinct units.

- Segments are the natural units of access control, that is, the process may have different access rights for different segments.

- Segments are the natural units for sharing code and data objects with other processes.

The disadvantage is that it is inconvenient for the operating system to manage storage allocation for variable-sized segments. After the system has been running for a while the free memory available can become fragmented. Although the total free memory might be far greater than the size of some segment that must be loaded, it might be that there is no contiguous area large enough to hold it. This problem can be solved by moving segments that are not needed out to disk and moving them back if they come into use again. The segments of processes that are not running, perhaps because they are blocked, waiting for lengthy I/O, are obvious candidates for rejection to backing store. This is called **swapping**.

4.8 Paging

In the preceding sections we have developed a requirement for a process to have several segments which can be of arbitrary size. The kind of hardware that would support segmentation has been introduced.

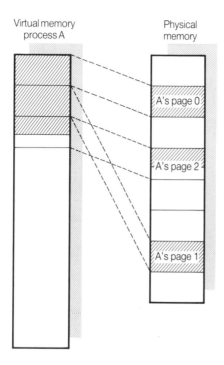

Virtual memory
process A

Physical
memory

A's page 0

A's page 2

A's page 1

Figure 4.8
Paging.

A memory management scheme that solves the physical storage allocation problem associated with segmentation is called **paging**. Blocks of a fixed size are used for memory allocation so that if there is any free store it is of the right size. Memory is divided into **page frames** and the user's program is divided into pages of the same size. This is transparent to the programmer, unlike segmentation. Figure 4.8 illustrates paging for a process with a single segment. All the pages in this example are shown in main memory.

In systems where program sizes are unpredictable and programs are loaded dynamically, the limited size of physical memory can cause problems. As outlined above for segmented systems, a portion of the disk storage (or a separate, dedicated, high-speed device) can be used as an extension to main memory and the pages of a process may be in main memory and/or in this backing store. The operating system must manage the two levels of storage and the transfer of pages between them. It must keep a page table for each process to record this and other information. Note that a main memory page base address is sufficient to locate a page; pages are of fixed size, so there is no need to record an upper bound.

Dynamic relocation hardware (paging hardware) is needed to translate from a virtual address to a physical address at instruction execution time. Figure 4.9 shows the general idea of virtual to physical address translation by a memory management unit (MMU). Before a page can be addressed it must have an entry set up by the operating system in the table shown. This table is looked up associatively as part of every address reference.

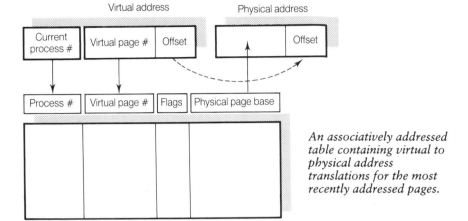

Figure 4.9
Outline of the
paging hardware
function.

An associatively addressed table containing virtual to physical address translations for the most recently addressed pages.

The virtual page number is extracted from the virtual address, the process's identifier is appended and an associative lookup with the (process #, virtual page #) fields is initiated. If a match is found an access check is made, based on the information recorded in the flags, for example, is a write being attempted to a page where the access is read only? If all is well, the physical page base, taken from the matched table entry, is appended to the offset from the virtual address to form the complete physical address. The 'flags' field will indicate the access rights allowed and other information; see Section 4.11 for an example.

If an address reference is made to a page which is present in main memory but which does not have an entry in the table, the address translation fails. A table entry must be made for that page. Memory management hardware differs in the assistance it provides to the operating system to achieve this.

If an address reference is made to a page which is not present in main memory the address translation will fail. No match will be found in the table, and the addressing hardware will raise an exception, called a '**page fault**'. The operating system will handle the exception.

A detailed example of paging hardware is given below in Section 4.11 and the hardware–operating system interaction in Section 4.12. Paging hardware was first used in the UK Atlas computer in 1960 (Kilburn, 1962).

Notice that **virtual memory** is created by this scheme. There is no need for an entire program to be loaded in main memory; indeed, a program can be larger than physical memory. When a new page is addressed, to fetch an instruction or access a data operand, it is brought into main memory on demand. This is called **demand paging**. An alternative approach is to attempt to predict which pages will be needed by a process (its current **working set**) and to load them in advance.

Topics which are left for further study are:

● The detailed design of the tables the operating system must keep for the pages of each process, the type of access the process has to each and where each is currently located in main memory and/or on disk. Section 4.8.1 is relevant to the management of large, paged virtual address spaces.

- How the main memory and backing store is allocated to the pages of processes.

- The algorithms that are used to determine which pages of a process should be in main memory, for example, those which compute the current **working set** of pages of a process. An algorithm is also needed to decide which page should be rejected from main memory to make space for a new page which is to be brought in as a result of a page fault, and so on.

As main memory becomes larger, the criteria for algorithms of this kind will change. Many paging algorithms date from the mid 1970s when physical main memory was a scarce resource. A current trend is to integrate file I/O and memory management by allowing a file to be mapped into the virtual address space of a process. It is then demand-paged into memory rather than read through I/O buffers. This approach is motivated and described in Section 5.7 and examples of its use are given in Chapter 22. Its use would affect the choice of paging algorithms for a system and the methods available for their selection (Mapp, 1991).

4.8.1 Inverted page tables

The assumption has been made above that the operating system will hold a page table for each process. If the virtual address space is large, the page tables are potentially large (for example, 4096 entries for a 1 kbyte page size and a 4 Gbyte virtual address space) and a process's page table must be in main memory when a process is running. We shall see in Section 4.9.1 that it is likely that pages will be allocated sparsely in clusters, within the virtual address space rather than in a single contiguous region.

A single main memory page table (sometimes called an inverted page table) might be used by the operating system. Physical main memory is likely to be relatively small, and a single page table could be used to record which page of which process occupies each page frame of physical memory. Compared with holding a page table per process this is potentially economical in both space and searching time.

In the above sections on segmentation and paging we have left the detailed design of the process segment and page tables for further study. In all schemes it is necessary to be able to record the fact that a given page may be both in main memory and on backing store. For example, when a page is brought into main memory, the copy on backing store still exists. The inverted page table approach provides a convenient way of storing this information.

A page table per process can be managed by the operating system, in addition to the single main memory page table, to indicate the backing store location of the process's pages. The main memory page table can record whether a writeable page has in fact been written to. The operating system can use this information to decide whether a page needs to be copied to backing store before it is overwritten in main memory. In outline:

1. A process makes an address reference to a new page which does not have an entry in the associative address translation table (see Figure 4.9).

2. The operating system (or hardware) searches the main memory page table for that page of that process.

3. If the page is in main memory it will have an entry in the main memory page table and is given an entry in the associative address translation table. The instruction execution is restarted and, this time, the address translation completes.

4. If the page is not in main memory it will not be found in the main memory page table. The operating system can consult the processes page table to locate that page on backing store and can initiate its transfer into main memory. An entry in the associative address translation table must be made for the page as described above.

A scheme of this kind was used effectively at a time when main memory was small (see Morris and Ibett, 1979), and is currently used in Hewlett-Packard's Precision Architecture.

4.9   Paged segments

The arguments for having several segments per process (for protection and sharing) still hold in a system which uses paging for physical storage management. The two concepts can be combined so that each segment of a process is divided into pages. Figure 4.10 illustrates the idea for the simple case of two segments per process and Figure 4.11 shows how a virtual address may be interpreted when both segmentation and paging hardware are used. An example of an MMU which supports both segmentation and paging is that used in the Motorola 68020, the MC68851 device (Milenkovic, 1990).

An alternative scheme is for the operating system to manage segments without hardware assistance and for paging hardware only to be used, as described in the next section.

4.9.1   Software-supported segments, hardware-supported pages

Note that the hardware in a paged segmented system need only know about pages. The page is the unit of physical storage allocation and the hardware must perform virtual to physical address translation and signal a page fault if the translation cannot be done. Segmentation need only be supported by software, and the positioning in the virtual address space and maximum size of a segment

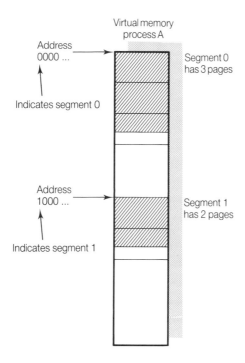

Figure 4.10
Paged segments illustrated for two segments per process.

are then no longer dictated by the requirement for the hardware to extract a fixed portion of the virtual address as segment number. The memory management unit used as an example in Section 4.11 is of this kind. A 32 bit address is interpreted as a 20 bit virtual page number with a 12 bit offset. The operating system manages a number of segments in each process's virtual address space in an implementation of UNIX on this machine.

The compilers in a system and the operating system share conventions on how the virtual address space is used: the virtual addresses at which the user code and the data areas start, for example. A single page table for the whole address space would be too large and most pages would be unused. The operating system can keep a page table for each segment and can note the access allowed to each page of that segment.

Note that this scheme allows a large **sparse virtual address space** to be managed. The pages are allocated in clusters (within segments, sometimes called

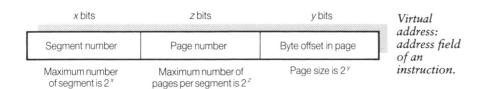

Virtual address: address field of an instruction.

Figure 4.11
A virtual address for a paged segment.

regions when used in this way) which are widely dispersed in the virtual address space according to software conventions. Access control can be as fine-grained as desired since it is specified for each segment. An extension of this idea is that a separate page table can be used for each 'object' in a virtual address space (see Section 5.8).

4.9.2 Copy-on-write paging hardware

We have seen that segmentation allows processes to share a portion of their address space. In this case the sharing processes see a single copy of the segment and any change made by any process is seen by all.

It is often the case that a copy of a writeable data area of one process is required by another. We shall see examples in Part II, when we consider how information is transferred between cooperating concurrent processes, and in the case studies in Part IV. Suppose a data area is to be copied from one process's address space into another's and that both processes are allowed write access to their private copies of the data. The data will be copied into new physical pages of memory and new page table entries will be set up for these pages for the process with the new copy. The two processes now have separate physical copies of the pages and separate page table entries for them.

Suppose that in practice it is unlikely that either process will write to the data area, or perhaps each will write to a very small portion of a large data area. An example is that when a new process is created in the UNIX operating system, a replica of the address space of the creating process is made for the created process. The first thing the created process does is usually to discard most of its inherited address space and run a completely new program, making the copying a waste of time.

Some paging hardware offers a 'copy-on-write' option. The idea is that the process which is to receive the copy of the data is given new page table entries which point to the original physical pages. Only if either process writes to a page of the data area is a new copy made of that page. To support this the hardware must have a 'copy-on-write' flag which is set for each page of the copied data for both processes. When the 'copy' is made, both processes are given copy-on-write access to all the pages of the segment. When a write access is made, an access protection exception is raised and a physical copy of the page is made and entered in the page table of the writing process. The access rights of both processes can now be set to write access and the copy-on-write flags unset.

4.10 Address translation in the storage hierarchy

Figure 4.1 shows the storage hierarchy of a computer system. Figure 4.12 extends the picture to include address translation. The PC will contain a virtual address which must be translated to a real address before an instruction is

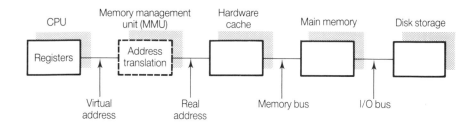

Figure 4.12
Address translation
in a memory
hierarchy.

fetched. When the processor decodes an instruction, extracts an address field
and computes the address of an operand, this is a virtual address. It must be
translated to a real address, dynamically, by hardware at runtime, before it can
be used to read or write memory. The above sections outlined the kind of
address translation that might be done.

4.11   An example of a memory management unit (MMU): MIPS R2000/3000

Figure 4.13 shows the basic design of the MIPS R2000 (also R3000) chip. As
well as a RISC processor there is also a system control coprocessor on the chip.
This includes a memory management unit which is shown in more detail in the
figure. The MMU contains a table with space for 64 entries. This is called a
translation lookaside buffer (TLB). Each non-empty entry in the TLB indicates a

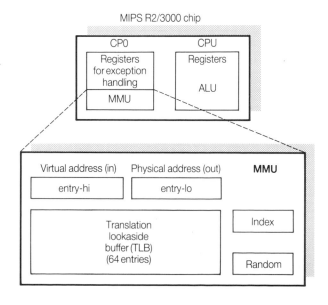

Figure 4.13
An example of an
MMU: the MIPS
R2000/3000 .

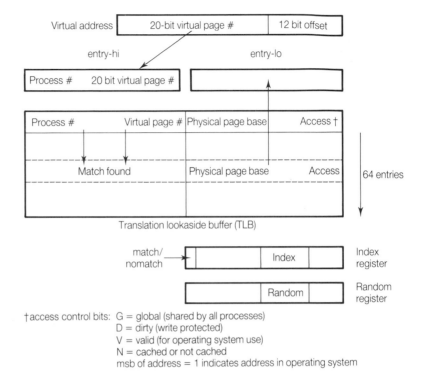

Figure 4.14
MIPS R2000/3000
address translation.

page in the virtual memory of a process and its corresponding location in physical memory (see Figure 4.14). The TLB is managed by the operating system; before a page can be addressed it must be in main memory and have an entry in the TLB. The MMU contains four registers: entry-hi, entry-lo, index and random. The operating system uses them to insert or replace entries in the TLB; the addressing hardware uses them to perform address translation. We are concerned here with the address translation function; the next section covers the interface with the operating system.

The virtual memory system supports pages of 4 kbytes, so a 32 bit address is divided into a 20 bit page number and a 12 bit offset. Every time a virtual address is to be translated (to fetch an instruction or read or write a data operand), the process number and virtual page number are entered in the entry-hi register. They are compared associatively with all the corresponding virtual addresses stored in the table (a 'TLB probe') and if a match is found the index register indicates this and the position of the matched entry in the TLB. The matched TLB entry is then read and the physical address of the base of that page is then available in entry-lo. The 12 bit offset can then be appended to the page base to give the physical address required.

In addition to the basic address translation function described above, there is some support for access control policies to be enforced.

- There is basic protection of the operating system from user processes. If the processor is executing in user state and an address reference is made to the operating system's area (the most significant bit of the address is 1; see Figure 4.15) then an exception is raised.

- It is possible for a page to be made shareable by all processes, indicated in a global (G) access control bit. In this case all process IDs will be deemed to match.

- A further bit D (dirty) is for controlling write access. An exception is raised if a write access is attempted to a page which is write-protected in this way.

- The valid (V) bit is provided for use by the operating system. If everything matches but V indicates invalid then an exception is raised. A page may be referenced by another process while being paged in, for example.

- The N bit is for mapped access to pages which are not cached: it indicates whether the cache or main memory should be accessed for this physical address.

Only 64 pages are mapped at any time; the 64 pages accessed most recently by all the processes which have run on this processor. In fact, many pages need not be mapped. For example, much of the operating system kernel needs to be resident permanently in main memory. Such kernel pages must not be 'paged

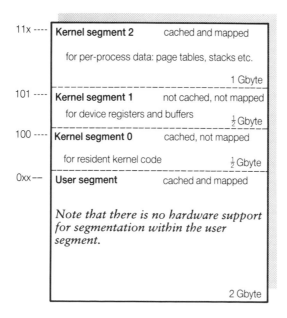

Figure 4.15
MIPS R2000/3000
virtual address
space.

out' and can be mapped directly onto some specified area of main memory, bypassing the address translation hardware. Figure 4.15 shows the arrangement of the virtual address space supported by the MIPS R2/3000. The operating system occupies half of every process address space. Operating system code is in a kernel segment which is cached but not mapped; device registers and buffers are in a kernel segment which is neither cached nor mapped. Operating system data, such as process page tables and data areas, is both cached and mapped, as is the user segment.

The hardware therefore supports a user segment and three operating system segments. When an operating system is implemented on this architecture it is likely to support more user-level segments within the one known to the hardware. UNIX supports three user-level segments, for example, a code segment and two data segments.

4.12   An example of operating system page fault handling: MIPS R2000/3000

If a process accesses a new page the virtual address will be passed to the MMU as described above but no match will be found. The address translation hardware signals an exception and the exception handling routine passes control to the memory management module within the operating system. If the page is already in main memory all that needs to be done is to make a TLB entry. This is done by putting process number and virtual page number in entry-hi and the physical page base and the required values of the access control bits in entry-lo.

The operating system can specify which TLB entry should be loaded with the contents of entry-hi and entry-lo by setting a value in the index register and executing 'write to TLB'. Alternatively, a random entry can be chosen by using the index value in the random register by executing 'write random to TLB'. The former is chosen if a TLB entry is known to be free or if the operating system is running an algorithm to compute which page entry to replace, based on usage information.

If the page is on backing store the operating system must consult its memory management tables to find out where it is located. It must find, or make, a free page in main memory and must start the transfer into memory of the required page. While this (DMA) transfer is in progress, some other process may be scheduled to run on this processor. When the transfer completes, indicated by a disk interrupt, the operating system can enter this page in the TLB. When the process which caused the page fault is next scheduled, it must be restarted at the instruction which caused the fault, and this time the address will be translated successfully.

4.13   Memory management hardware in system design

Is memory management hardware always needed in a computer system? If the system is very small and simple and needs to be very cheap, such as a low-end PC, a memory management unit may not be justifiable.

In some systems, once software is loaded it remains resident and runs indefinitely. The software may have to be resident in main memory to guarantee real-time response. The system may be dedicated to a specific function and have nothing equivalent to error-prone or malicious user programs. It could be argued that memory management hardware is unnecessary in such cases; there is certainly no need for virtual memory. The protection afforded by memory management hardware is useful, however. The memory management access controls can be set up so that an instruction which causes an illegal attempt to write or transfer control outside the module in which it occurs can be trapped. As software grows in size, this support for debugging will become increasingly important.

In systems where program sizes are unpredictable, programs are loaded dynamically and the system is shared by several users the limited size of physical memory can cause problems. In this case virtual memory is essential. It is also desirable that the various independent programs should be protected from each other and the operating system should be protected against them.

Memory mapping can be used to avoid the inefficiency of copying data. Examples are: the transfer of data between a network or I/O buffer and the address space of a process; the transfer of data between processes; and the copying of an address space on process creation. In some cases (when source and destination both need access to the data after the transfer) the copy-on-write facility will be useful (see Section 4.9.2); in others a simple transfer of data by remapping is all that is needed.

Single-user networked workstations are now more common than multi-user systems. Workstation operating systems typically have to deal with only a small number of processes at any time. Memory technology is such that 4 Mbyte units will soon be available at reasonable cost and a 64–128 Mbyte memory will soon become feasible. It might be argued that all software will be able to fit in a main memory of this size and virtual memory techniques will become redundant. Application program sizes have continued to grow, however, and system software such as graphical user interfaces has become very large. It is likely that virtual memory techniques will continue to be needed, but the assumptions on which they are based have changed dramatically.

Although disk density has doubled every three years for the past twenty years, disk access time has lagged behind and has only increased by a third in the past ten years. As processor speeds continue to increase, disk access will increasingly be a bottleneck. New technology such as non-volatile RAM or power-backed RAM disks is likely to be used for virtual memory swap space. Perhaps a 'memory server' across a high-speed network will support virtual memory better than a local disk can.

In the next chapter we consider massive, persistent disk-based storage systems (filing systems) as opposed to the use of disks as an extension to main memory as described above. After that, we consider how file I/O and memory management might be integrated.

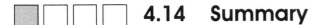 ## 4.14   Summary

Memory management of some kind is necessary in every component computer of a concurrent system. In some cases it can be very simple, when resident software runs indefinitely. In other cases demands on memory are dynamic. Even in the case of permanently resident software it is likely that unpredictable demands will be made on data space, for example, for buffer space for packets coming in from a network.

Segmentation was considered as a means of structuring a process's address space and of sharing some parts with other processes while keeping other parts private. Hardware support was outlined but details were left for further study. Paging mechanisms were also discussed. These are transparent to the programmer.

Memory management is relevant to the concurrent system designer because it is through memory management that processes may share memory. Also, the memory management subsystem is itself a concurrent system. It is invoked on initial program loading to arrange physical storage allocation; it has an interface for client programs which need to expand their data areas during a program run; and it is entered as a result of hardware events such as page faults.

Exercises

4.1 Outline the basic memory management functions of an operating system.

4.2 Describe how copies of instructions and data are held in the various levels of a memory hierarchy: permanent disk storage, backing store for main memory on disk, main memory, cache memory and processor registers. When are transfers of data made between the various levels? In each case, indicate whether the transfer involved is controlled by hardware or the operating system and explain the interface between the hardware and the operating system.

4.3 What is the virtual address space of a process? How large is the virtual address space for address lengths of 16, 24 and 32 bits? How does a separate address space per process protect processes from each other and the operating system from processes?

4.4 Give examples of why processes might wish to share parts of their address spaces. What kind of memory management hardware would support this sharing? How can memory protection be enforced when sharing is allowed?

4.5 What are the advantages and disadvantages of running the operating system in the address space of every process? What are the advantages and disadvantages of running the operating system as a separate process with its own address space? (Bear this question in mind while reading the rest of the book.)

4.6 Why do systems which use segmented memory management have to solve the problem of fragmentation of main memory? Why do segmentation and swapping go together?

4.7 Is segmentation transparent to the application programmer and/or the language implementer? Is paging transparent? What service is segmentation hardware designed to provide? What problem is paging hardware designed to solve?

4.8 (a) How can a large data structure which is in the address space of one process be made shareable by some other process so that they both see the same copy of the data?
(b) How can a large data structure be transferred from the address space of one process to that of another without copying the data?
(c) How can a copy of a large data structure which is in the address space of one process be given to another process? If it is unlikely that both processes will write to the same part of the data structure, how could the system avoid giving them a copy each?

4.9 (a) How many entries would there be in a process page table in a system with 32 bit addresses and a 1 kbyte page size?
(b) How might the processes page tables be organized to avoid a large number of page table entries for a sparsely populated virtual address space?
(c) It has been suggested that a main store page table (sometimes called an inverted page table) might be used, instead of a page table per process for pages in main store. What are the advantages and disadvantages of this approach?

5

Operating systems: File management

CONTENTS

5.1 File management

Chapter 2 introduced the major subsystems within operating systems. Every component computer in a system has some main memory and at least one device, even if this is only a network connection, so some form of memory management and device management is always needed. Not every system needs file management; a dedicated network gateway or a node of a process control system are examples of those that do not. Even a workstation might not have a local disk. In this case the user needs assistance in retrieving files from remote file servers across a network.

The relative and projected performance of processors and disks, described in Section 3.2.1, should be borne in mind throughout this section. I/O will become a bottleneck in future systems and very large main memories will be used to compensate for relatively poor I/O performance; that is, a great deal of information will be cached in main memory, some of which may be non-volatile.

We shall first discuss file management functions in general terms and then consider them in the context of a distributed system. Finally, some current trends towards increasing performance and integrating memory management and file management will be described.

5.2   An overview of filing system functions

Filing systems provide:

- **a storage service:** clients do not need to know about the physical characteristics of disks, or where files have been stored on them. The filing system should take steps not to lose a file that has been entrusted to it, even if there are hardware faults or software crashes.

- **a directory service:** clients can give convenient text names to files and, by grouping them in directories, show the relationships between them. Clients should also be able to control the sharing of their files with others by specifying who can access a given file and in what way.

Figure 5.1 illustrates a typical interaction between a file service and a client. We shall see later that filing system designs differ, particularly when they are serving a distributed system. Interactions between the component modules of the file service are not shown.

We assume that a file is created with some text name such as *exercise1.c* or *chapter5*. The client quotes this name in order to use the file again. In (1) the client calls an operation such as *open-file* with the text name as an argument. Another argument will specify whether the client wants to read only or read and write the file. The directory service will carry out an **access check** to ensure that

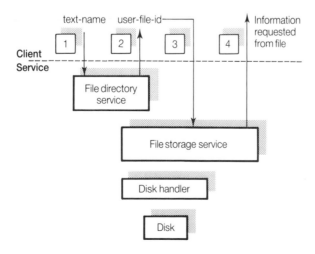

Figure 5.1
A client interaction with a file service.

this client is **authorized** to access this file in the way specified. The directory service is responsible for translating the text name into a form which enables the file storage service to locate the file on disk; we call this **name resolution**. In order to do this it may need to call on the storage service and the storage service may need to call the disk handler to read the disk.

A filing system stores very large numbers of files, only a few of which are in use at any time. At (2) the filing system is ready for the client to use this file. It will have set up information about the file in its tables in main memory. It returns a **user-file-identifier** (user-file-id, or UFID) for the client to use in subsequent requests to read or write the file, shown at (3). At (4) the storage service returns the portion of the file that was requested at (3).

Notice that the initial request must give a filename that allows the file to be identified uniquely in the filing system. The user-file-id may be a temporary name for use by the process and might be something like 'my open file number 7'.

A potential problem that arises because files can be shared is concurrent requests for access to the same file. Another function of filing systems is therefore **concurrency control**. A crude approach is based on the argument that many clients can safely read a file at the same time but only one should be allowed to have write access. A filing system could enforce such a policy by noting whether a file has been opened for reading, and if so by how many clients, or for writing, in which case any subsequent requests to read or write would be refused. This is called **mandatory concurrency control**. A file is said to be **locked** for reading or writing.

Current thinking is that this approach is too inflexible. Many applications, such as distributed database management systems, may wish to have write access to different parts of the same file, and it is tedious if the underlying mechanisms enforced by the operating system prevent it. Indeed, the multiple writers are usually multiple instances of the same program in a distributed system and are designed to work together. For this reason, operating systems may now allow simultaneous write access to files. They may, as an optional extra, provide a **locking service** to help the clients cooperate with each other. A client may be able to request a shared lock or an exclusive lock on a file and be told whether locks have already been taken out and, if so, by whom. Clients may also be given an advisory warning on a request to open a file if the file is already open for a potentially conflicting access mode. Filing systems differ in the concurrency control services they offer. We shall return in Section 5.6 to other ways in which a filing system design may differ from that implied by the above interaction.

A filing system is a concurrent system since it may have to handle simultaneous requests from clients. Consider a computer dedicated to providing a file service for clients at workstations on a network and assume that a number of clients' requests are outstanding. The server takes a request and starts to work on it. The disk must be read, so, rather than wait for the (electromechanical) disk to deliver the required data, the server starts to work on another request. We shall now consider some of the internal algorithms and data structures so that we can take filing systems as an example throughout the book.

5.3   File and directory structure

As far as the file storage service is concerned, the objects it stores (files) are unstructured sequences of bytes. The filing system must be able to identify each file uniquely in the filing system and, to achieve this, will associate an identifier with a given file (we shall call this the system-file-identifier, SFID).

A **directory** is a structured object and comprises a list of entries, each of which associates a text name with information on the named object, including its SFID. The directory service will use the storage service to store directories. A directory is therefore given a SFID by the filing system. This is discussed further in Section 5.4, and Figure 5.4 gives an example of a directory object with associated operations.

A very simple filing system could hold the names of all files in a single directory. This was done in some early systems and in some small personal computer systems, but has the following disadvantages:

- The directory would be very large and held on disk. Looking up a given filename in it would take the directory service a long time.

- Different users might use the same text names for their files. Unique text names could be achieved by appending the owner's name to each filename. Grouping each user's files into a separate directory is an obvious rationalization. This would give a two-level hierarchy. This was provided in some early systems such as TOPS10 for the DecSystem 10.

- Users typically store a great deal of information in a filing system and some support for **organizing this information** is desirable. Convenient grouping within a user's files should be supported for easy location and access control; for example, users should be able to keep files of different types in different directories and group files that they are likely to use together in the same directory.

Therefore, although a directory hierarchy is not essential in theory, it is now provided in practice by most filing systems. Directories are created and named by clients of the filing system through requests to the directory service which in turn invokes the storage service. The filing system keeps a top-level or **root directory**. Figure 5.2 shows a simple example.

5.3.1   Pathnames and working directories

In a hierarchical filing system, files and directories are named relative to the top level root directory, that is, the full name of each file and directory is a **pathname** starting from the root. The examples below use / as a separator between components of a pathname and a pathname starting with / is assumed to start from the root.

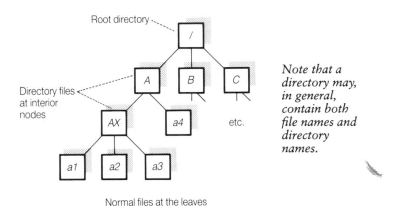

Figure 5.2
A filing system.

/A/AX	is the full pathname of the directory *AX* of Figure 5.2. Directory *AX* is recorded in directory *A* which is recorded in the root directory.
/A/AX/a2	file *a2* of Figure 5.2 is recorded in directory *AX* which is recorded in directory *A* which is recorded in the root directory.

A pathname can be long and tedious to use. Most systems have the concept of a **current working directory** and names can then be relative to this as well as full pathnames. For example the name *a1* can be used for the file */A/AX/a1* if the current working directory of the user has been set to *AX*. When a user logs in there is usually a procedure for establishing an initial working directory.

5.3.2   File sharing: access rights and links

A major advantage of a generally accessible filing system is that stored objects (files and directories) can be shared. One means of supporting and controlling this sharing is to allow the owner of each object to indicate who may use it and in what way. When a user who is not the owner attempts to access the object, the access rights are checked and access is granted or denied accordingly.

An alternative way to support sharing is to allow new directory entries to be set up to point to existing objects. Such entries are called **links**. The idea is that an authorized sharer can give a new name to the object instead of remembering the owner's pathname. A given object is no longer defined to have a unique pathname and the naming tree becomes a general directed graph (see Figure 5.3(a)). Systems may restrict the use of links so that a link can be set up to a file but not to a directory (Figure 5.3(b)). Figures 5.9 and 5.10 show how links are implemented.

5.3.3 Existence control

When links are allowed the system must have a policy about what it means to delete a file or directory. If the owner wishes to delete an object but there are links to it from other users' directories, then should the object be deleted or not,

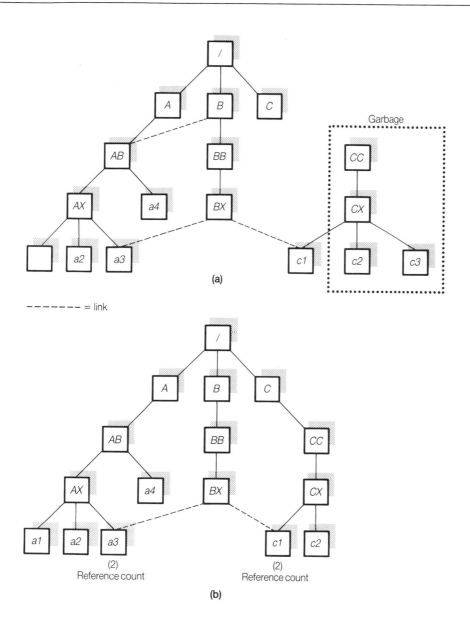

Figure 5.3
Graph structured
filing systems:
(a) general naming
graph; (b) links to
files but not
directories.

and if not, who should pay for its storage? The consensus on existence is that *an object should be kept in existence while there is a valid pathname for it.*

A request to delete an object therefore results in the requester's directory entry for that object being removed, but it does not necessarily result in the stored object being removed. A valid pathname might still exist to it because of a link that has been set up. On the other hand, if the last directory entry has been removed, the file (or directory and subtree below it) are inaccessible and have become garbage (Figure 5.3(b)).

This general area is called **existence control** and is another filing system function. One mechanism for achieving existence control is called **garbage collection**. All the objects that can be accessed from the root of the filing system are marked during garbage collection and unmarked objects can be deleted. Another mechanism is called **ageing**. When an object is touched in any way it is allocated a count which is decremented periodically. If the count decrements to zero before the object is touched again, it may be deleted by the filing system (or archived to tape, because in this case it may still be accessible from the root). It is the responsibility of the clients of the filing system to touch their objects more frequently than the timeout period.

If links may only be set up to files and not to directories, existence control is greatly simplified. It is then possible to keep a reference count for each file and detect when the last reference to it has been removed by a delete. UNIX takes this approach for hard links (see Section 21.6). If this restriction is not made, existence control is a more complex task involving higher overhead; for example, the filing system could carry out garbage collection.

5.4   The filing system interface

The filing system interface will contain operations such as those listed below. Filing systems differ, however, so this set of operations should not be considered definitive. The operations are given in general terms because filing system interfaces may differ in syntax.

UFID is used as an abbreviation for the user-file-identifier introduced in Section 5.2 above and illustrated in Figure 5.1. This may or may not be the same as the system-file-identifier, SFID, introduced in Section 5.3. The filing system may return a given user UFIDs 0,1,2,3 etc. for the files currently in use, whereas the SFID is unique within the filing system. We assume that the SFID is for internal use and is a reference to information on the file or directory, including its location in the storage system, see Figure 5.5.

Note that when a file or directory is created its name is recorded in a directory: the pathname argument is intended to indicate both the name of the newly created object and the superior directory in which this name is to be recorded.

Error returns are not given.

- **Directory service**

  Operations available to clients of the filing system

Operation	Arguments	Returns
create directory	pathname of directory	done
delete directory	pathname of directory	done
list directory contents	pathname of directory	list of directory contents

set access rights to file or directory	pathname of file or directory, users/rights specification	done
link	pathname of directory, pathname of file or directory	done
create file	pathname of file	done
delete file	pathname of file	done
open file	pathname of file, read/write	UFID

● **File storage service**
Operations available to clients of the filing system

Operation	Arguments	Returns
read file	UFID, byte-range, where to put bytes in memory	bytes requested
write file	UFID, byte-range to write, where to find bytes in memory	done
close file	UFID	donc
position pointer	UFID, position for pointer in bytes	done

5.4.1   The directory service as type manager

Note that a directory cannot be read and written arbitrarily by clients of the filing system, but can be accessed only through the interface operations on directory objects such as *list directory contents* and *create directory*. A directory can therefore be regarded as an example of an **abstract data type** with associated operations (see below). We can think of the directory service as the owner or **type manager** of directories which it stores as files on the lower-level storage service. Figure 5.4 gives an example of a directory with associated interface operations. Creating a file or directory includes making an entry for it in a superior directory as well as allocating storage for it. Deleting a file or directory includes

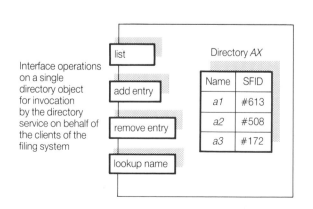

Interface operations on a single directory object for invocation by the directory service on behalf of the clients of the filing system

One possible implementation of a directory is illustrated here.

Figure 5.4
A directory object.

removing a directory entry. The operations on directory objects shown in Figure 5.4 are as follows:

Operation	Arguments	Returns
lookup name in directory (for pathname resolution and access checking, see below and Section 5.5)	name, pathname of directory	SFID
add entry to directory (to implement creation of a file or directory)	name, pathname of directory	done
remove entry from directory (to implement deletion of a file or directory)	name, pathname of directory	done

5.4.2   Notes on the directory service interface to filing system clients

The directory service is concerned with pathname resolution and access checking. Suppose a file is to be opened. To resolve the pathname of the file the directory service must read each component directory in the path in turn in order to locate and read the next component. Section 5.5 gives more information on how this is implemented. The file's entry is looked up in the final directory component and an identifier for the file (UFID) is returned to the client.

The directory service will check whether the user is authorized to carry out the specified operation on a file or directory. The access allowed is set by the owner. The link operation requests a new directory entry to be made for an existing file or directory as discussed above in Section 5.3.2. Implementation details and examples are given in Section 5.5.1 below.

5.4.3   Notes on the file service interface to filing system clients

These operations assume that a file has been opened successfully and the user has been given an identifier (UFID) for use in subsequent requests. The arguments for **read and write** operations must include the position in the file (byte-range) of the bytes that are to be read and the main memory location for the bytes to be read to or written from. The byte-range in the file is likely to be specified not as start-byte, finish-byte but as start-byte and count. The start position can then be taken as an implicit pointer held by the system which is positioned at the start of the file initially. For sequential file access the user need never worry about positioning the pointer but can just request to read the next n bytes. The operation **position pointer** has been included for use by applications which need random access. This style of operation is convenient in a centralized system but can be a problem in distributed systems. A request might be repeated because of network congestion or server failure and restart. We shall discuss this in Chapters 13 and 14.

The **close** operation tells the system the file is no longer needed, so any data structures it is holding in main memory on the file can be removed after the file and its metadata (information on the file or 'data on the data') are safely recorded on disk.

5.5   The filing system implementation

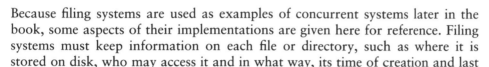

Because filing systems are used as examples of concurrent systems later in the book, some aspects of their implementations are given here for reference. Filing systems must keep information on each file or directory, such as where it is stored on disk, who may access it and in what way, its time of creation and last access, etc. A typical information block is shown in Figure 5.5.

Different filing systems may store this information in different ways. An important point is that several links (directory entries) may exist for a given file or directory. The method of storing information on the file should ensure that there is only one copy of it. If the information was kept with the directory entry, for example, not only would this make directories large but it would also cause the information to be replicated when links were set up. The information is needed to locate the file or directory on disk, so that part certainly cannot be stored with the file. A common approach is to use a table where each entry is a block of information on a file or directory. We shall call this a **metadata table** because it holds data about the data stored in files and directories. Figure 5.5 shows such a table and Figure 5.6 makes it clear that the files, directories and metadata table recording information on them are all stored permanently on disk.

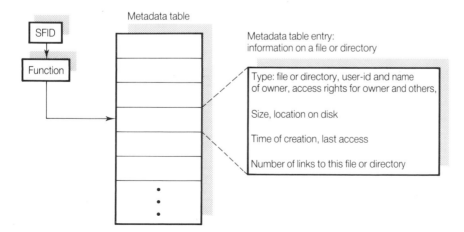

Figure 5.5
A metadata table
for a filing system.

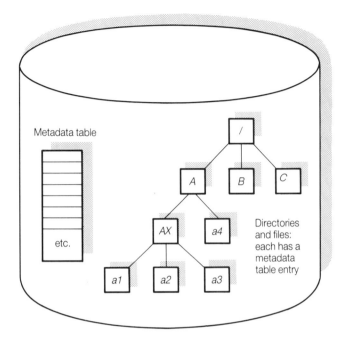

Figure 5.6
A filing system on
disk.

It is important that the entry on a given file or directory should be located quickly. A good algorithm is needed to convert a SFID into the correct entry in the table. The method used in the UNIX system, which is a simple index into the table, is described in Section 21.6. An alternative is a hashing function.

Figure 5.7 outlines data structures, typical of those used within filing systems, that are held in main memory when a file is in use. The case where two users have opened the same file is illustrated. User A has UFID 3 allocated for the file and user B has UFID 5. The file has a single SFID and a single metadata table entry.

Two main memory filing system data structures are shown. The system open file table has an entry for each sharer of the file. This allows for concurrent sharers of a file to have their own position pointer into it for reading and writing. The active file information table contains entries with information similar to that held in the metadata table. Figure 5.8 expands on this. Additional information that is likely to be held is the SFID and concurrency control information, that is, whether the file is open for reading or writing and by how many readers and/or writers.

Figure 5.7 also shows a buffer area for disk blocks. Recall Figure 3.10 and Section 3.6.1 where I/O buffering was introduced. It is likely that this buffer area is also used as a cache. Disk access is slow and the system will aim to satisfy as many read requests as possible from the cache.

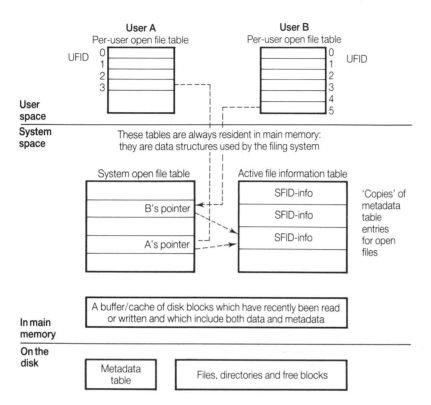

Figure 5.7
Data structures used by a filing system.

File systems differ in the semantics of their **write** operations. A successful write might indicate that the data has been written to disk or might mean only that the data has reached the buffers in (volatile) memory. In this case it would be lost on a power failure. File system policies differ over whether they attempt

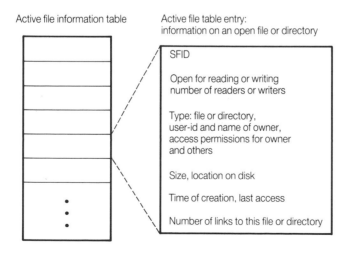

Figure 5.8
An active file table in main memory.

to write out the write buffers to disk as soon as possible or whether they attempt to avoid physical disk writes by keeping data in memory as long as possible. The advantage of the latter approach is that the data in a disk-block-sized buffer may be changed several times in quick succession by user-level writes of arbitrary byte sequences. Data written out may also be re-read from the cache.

Keeping the data in memory allows a fast response to a write request at the risk of data loss and file system inconsistency on a power failure. Another reason to delay a given write is that the disk handler may be able to achieve higher performance if it reorders the writes to allow the arms to sweep across the surface of the disk and back instead of moving back and forth in response to requests in the order that they arrive.

There is scope for using non-volatile memory as a write cache both to achieve secure, asynchronous writes and to improve disk-head scheduling performance.

5.5.1 Hard links and symbolic links

The link operation requests a new directory entry to be made for an existing file or directory, as discussed above in Section 5.3.2. If the access is allowed the new name is added with the SFID of the existing file. This is called a **hard link**. Figure 5.9 gives an example.

Note that the SFID has been defined as a unique file identifier within a single filing system. The hard link mechanism as described above can therefore only be used within a single filing system.

We can create a unique, system-wide identifier for a file as:

> filing system identifier, file-identifier within system,

that is, filing system identifier, SFID (filing-system-file-identifier).

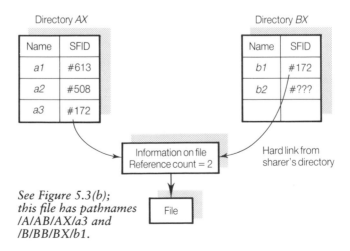

Figure 5.9
Example of a hard link.

See Figure 5.3(b); this file has pathnames /A/AB/AX/a3 and /B/BB/BX/b1.

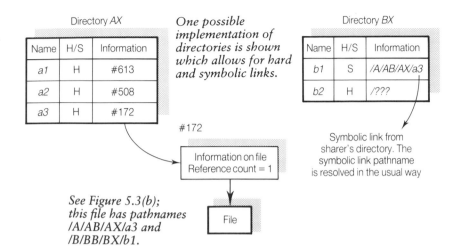

Figure 5.10
Example of a
symbolic link.

An alternative form of link, called a **soft link** or **symbolic link**, involves entering the new name with a pathname for the existing object, instead of its SFID. Figure 5.10 gives an example of a symbolic link within a single filing system. A possible implementation of directories is shown there which allows an entry to contain either an SFID (or hard link) or a symbolic link. Exercise 5.10 suggests an alternative.

In practice, symbolic links are most useful for allowing accesses between different filing systems, in particular to allow access to remote filing systems.

5.6   Network-based file servers

The previous sections have presented general principles that are relevant to filing systems in general: for single-user workstations, centralized time-sharing systems or distributed systems. We now focus on the special properties of network-based filing systems for distributed systems.

We are not concerned here with how network communication is invoked between the client of the file service and the service. We shall discuss this later in Chapter 14. Neither are we concerned with how a number of file server machines work together to provide a service. That is the concern of a more advanced course on distributed operating systems such as Coulouris and Dollimore (1988) or Mullender (1989). Even less are we concerned at this stage with the problem of how to manage more than one copy of a file.

A question we should address is where the functions we have discussed above are provided:

- naming and pathname resolution
- access control
- existence control
- concurrency control.

5.6.1   Open and closed storage architectures

Figure 5.11 shows two ways in which a network file service can be provided. In the first case, a single file service comprising a directory service and storage service is provided. The only way to use the storage service is through the directory service; we have a closed storage service architecture. This enforces a single naming convention and access control policy on all clients.

Note that, although the architecture is closed, the service components might be distributed; for example, the storage service component might be provided remotely and the directory service in a client workstation, perhaps as a component of a closed operating system. In this case, the user invokes the local directory service which invokes the remote storage service. The user does not interact directly with the storage service.

In the second case we see the service interface at the level of the file storage service; recall the file service interface operations given in Section 5.4. The names used at the interface are SFIDs and not pathnames. This allows a network-based file storage service to support different client operating systems, each with its own directory service. It also allows direct use of the file storage service by clients, such as a mail service. A mail service does not need to use pathnames for messages and, since the mail service is the owner of all messages while they are in transit, it has no need for fine-grained access control. Messages may be taken from and delivered to filing systems by the clients of the mail service. Again, as discussed in Section 2.4, we see an **open architecture** providing a more general and flexible service than a closed one.

Figure 5.11
Storage service architectures: (a) closed; (b) open.

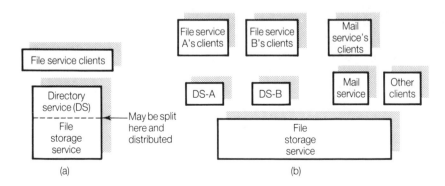

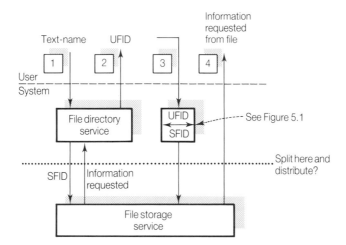

Figure 5.12
Client interaction
with a closed file
service.

5.6.2   The storage service interface

We have argued that the **interface** of a network-based file service should be at
the file storage service level and should be **open** for general use. Figure 5.12
extends the simple picture of a closed architecture presented in Figure 5.1 in the
light of the implementation details we have seen in Section 5.5 and so that we
can see the implications of separating the directory service from the storage service and of making the storage service interface open. Roughly, we see the directory service dealing with pathnames and the storage service dealing with SFIDs.

Figure 5.13 shows a possible interface for a network storage service. Let us
assume that the interface that was previously invoked from within a closed file
service is now both remote and open to invocation across a network by any
client.

5.6.3   Location of function

We should consider the location of filing system functions with this proposed
division of functionality.

Naming and **name resolution** is the responsibility of the clients of a storage
service defined at this level. As we have discussed above, an open interface
allows a number of different naming schemes and access control policies to be
supported. Note that a given directory service will store its directories on the
storage service. The directory service is the owner of its directories. To resolve a
pathname the directory service will need to fetch each component of the pathname in turn from the storage service in order to look up the SFID of the next
component in a directory.

The **existence control** function is closely associated with the naming graph.
(Recall that an object should be kept in existence if it is accessible from the root
of the naming graph.) The storage service level sees only a flat SFID-to-file

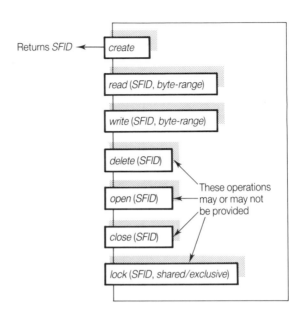

Returns *SFID*

create

read (*SFID, byte-range*)

write (*SFID, byte-range*)

delete (*SFID*)

open (*SFID*)

These operations may or may not be provided

close (*SFID*)

lock (*SFID, shared/exclusive*)

Figure 5.13
The storage service interface.

mapping and has no knowledge of the internal structure of the files (including directories) it stores. This appears to place the existence control function at the directory service level; that is, in an open environment each client of the storage service would have to carry out its own existence control.

This model of the world is not fully general. It does not allow for the possibility that stored objects might be shared by different kinds of client; for example, a file might represent a video clip and be embedded in a mail message. The owner of the file wishes to delete it. Is its SFID still in an active mail message? The Cambridge File Server (Birrell and Needham, 1980) provided both an open interface at the storage service level and support for existence control. This was achieved by maintaining a skeletal naming graph within the storage service. The CFS interface contained no delete operation and asynchronous garbage collection was carried out periodically.

Figure 5.13 shows a delete operation in the storage service interface. Who should be able to invoke this operation? Recall that to delete a file means that a directory entry is to be removed. This interaction is between the directory service and its clients and the directory service decides whether the material may also be removed. If there is no sharing between different types of client of the storage service each can detect and delete garbage.

An alternative approach is that the storage service ages its objects and can delete (or archive) an object when its time expires. The clients of the service should keep their objects alive by touching them within the defined time period. A *touch* operation could be provided for this purpose. A directory service, or any service which uses the storage service, can perform this service on behalf of its clients.

Current filing systems tend to make restrictions which simplify these issues. If only files and not directories can be shared, a reference count can be kept with each file. Also, current systems tend not to support the open interface and full generality of sharing we have set up here. Users often work within a closed but distributed environment. Future filing systems will need to support a variety of types of objects, such as voice, video, database, mail etc., and more general solutions than those currently in use will be needed.

The **concurrency control** function cannot easily be placed at the client level since, even within a single client type, there may be many instances of the client, such as a directory service, and any one might have opened a file. It would be necessary for all the clients which could access a file to communicate to achieve concurrency control. We assume that there is one copy of a given file and a natural place to implement concurrency control is where the file is stored. The storage service might provide shared and exclusive locks on files, as discussed in Section 5.2. An alternative is to provide a separate lock service which clients are trusted to use. If the storage service is stateless it cannot provide this service (see Section 5.6.4).

The storage service does not know about the internal structure of files and is likely to provide concurrency control at the granularity of whole files. If a client of the storage service, such as a database management system, requires arbitrarily fine-grained concurrency control (that is, locking of components of structured objects), this must be provided above the storage service level, within the client application or in some new service.

In a centralized system **access control** is carried out during pathname resolution, when a file is opened (for reading or writing) or a directory operation is invoked. In a distributed system these access checks must still be carried out during pathname resolution.

In a closed, but distributed, system the clients of the storage service are all instances of the client operating system's directory service; they may be authenticated as such by the system mechanisms. The storage service is said to have a **protected interface**. In an open system the storage service interface can be used directly by a number of different clients. Access control is therefore needed at the storage service level so that the files stored there cannot be read or written by unauthorized clients. We discuss this further in Section 5.6.5.

5.6.4 Stateless servers

A widely used network file service is Sun's NFS (see Coulouris and Dollimore, 1988). Although in practice NFS is associated with UNIX systems, its design is sufficiently general to support other clients. The storage service interface of NFS is at the file service level and not the directory service level.

In the above sections we have made an implicit assumption that a file is opened before it is read and/or written, then closed after use. We assumed that the filing system would keep information on all the files that are open. If this is done in a network filing system we have the situation where a file service computer could fail but its clients could continue running. Any state held by the server is lost on a crash, which gives us a problem on restarting the server.

In order to avoid this problem the designers of NFS chose to implement a stateless server. Stateless servers do not hold information on behalf of particular clients. They will probably optimize the service they give by remembering which files have been used recently and by having their data and metadata ready in a cache. A service that is specified as stateless cannot provide a concurrency control function.

5.6.5 File identifiers and protection at the storage service level

The network storage service must guarantee to protect the information that is entrusted to it from unauthorized access. We assume that the underlying system provides an **authentication service** so that the storage service has secure knowledge of who is invoking it. There are two basic approaches to access control.

1. *Access control lists*

   The storage service keeps access control information on each file it stores as described in Section 5.3.2. The owner specifies who may access the file and in what way. Each time a read or write request is made, the storage service checks that the initiator of the request has the access rights required, then uses the SFID to locate the file internally.

   Note that the directory service represents directories as files stored on the storage service. (Recall Figure 5.4 and the notion of the directory abstraction and the directory implementation). Only the directory services may read and write their directories arbitrarily; users of the directory service access directories through their type operations via the directory service. As far as the storage service is concerned, a directory service is the owner of its directories. The directory service needs to implement a higher-level access control policy for its clients.

   A general comment on the access list approach is that we may wish to be able to express fine discriminations on who or what may access each file. For example, we may wish to give various groups of people subtly different rights and we may wish to exclude certain individuals who belong to those groups from having the group's privilege. Also, a name on an ACL may itself represent a list. If this is so, the mechanism does not scale well, and access list checking could become too great an overhead, particularly if it is carried out every time a file is accessed and not just once for all when a file is opened.

2. *Capabilities*

   In this case, the storage service does not record who may access a file and in what way. Instead, possession of an identifier, of a carefully designed form, is taken as proof of the right to access the file. An identifier that is used in this way is called a file **capability**. Figure 5.14 shows a typical format for a capability.

| Access rights | Unique identifier within filing system | Check digits |

Figure 5.14
A typical format for
a capability.

A capability must not be forgeable; that is, it must not be possible to invent a number and use it to access some arbitrary file. For this reason, capabilities contain sparse random numbers so that if you invent a number of the right length you are very unlikely to hit on one that maps onto a file.

It is possible to encode access rights within capabilities so that the storage service can discriminate read and write access rights, for example. It must be impossible for the user of the capability to change the access rights encoded in it. If you change a capability in any way it must be rejected by the storage service. Section 14.9 discusses capabilities in a more general context and explains how they may be constructed and checked.

We assume that the underlying system is such that it is not possible to eavesdrop on network communication and pick up and use capabilities that are being transmitted.

We have outlined how the functions of a storage service can be provided in a distributed environment. Further study should be carried out in the context of a discussion of distributed systems architecture.

5.7 Integrating virtual memory and storage

We have seen files used for persistent storage, and main memory for the storage of running programs and data. The most common programming language abstraction for stored data is the file; files are named and used explicitly in programs.

We have seen in Section 5.5 that the filing system maintains a cache of buffers in main memory and that users' requests are satisfied from those buffers. This means that on a read, data is first written into the system buffers and then copied to the application. On a write, data is copied into system buffers, then written to disk. The efficiency of file input and output could be improved if this copying was avoided.

The integration of virtual memory and file I/O is an attractive idea. Memory management is concerned with the organization of disk backing store for running programs and with the transfer of pages between main memory and disk. File management is concerned with the organization of the file store and with the transfer of blocks of files between main memory and the disk to satisfy I/O requests. A file comprises a number of disk blocks or disk 'pages'; a segment comprises a number of memory pages. There is obvious scope for the integration of file management and memory management. As well as rationalizing the system design, performance gains should result, since a page is transferred directly into the memory area of a process and not via a system buffer.

Several operating system designs have used this idea (Bensoussan, 1972; Lampson and Sproull, 1979; Wilkes and Needham, 1979). The Multics design unified the concepts of file and segment; when a file was opened it was mapped as a segment into the address space of a process. Others have provided an option to map files in virtual memory as well as access them conventionally; for example, UNIX BSD 4.3 specified but did not implement this option, while Sun OS extended and implemented this specification.

A file-mapping facility is used as follows:

● Instead of opening a file a process makes a system call to map the file, or part of the file, into its address space. As virtual address spaces are now typically of the order of gigabytes, this is feasible. The process may specify the virtual address where the file should be mapped or the operating system may decide and return the address. The operating system creates appropriate page table entries, marking the pages as not present in memory initially.

● As the file is addressed in memory it is moved in by the memory management mechanisms of the system, such as demand paging. The page table entries are filled in with the physical page base addresses in the usual way.

● The process may specify whether the file is to be mapped private or shared and will indicate the mode of access allowed, such as read, write, execute.

Note that the file store on disk and the backing store for memory management, often an area of the same disk, have been unified. Once the mapping is noted by the operating system, pages may be read directly from the file. Updated pages may be written back to the file. An insertion or deletion in the middle of a file must be handled in both styles of system. The usual approach is to create a new file (see your local editor).

Although several past systems have employed this technique it has not become popular with programmers, who appear to prefer the familiar file abstraction. However, large virtual address spaces and relatively slow disks combine with programming language developments to make this approach increasingly attractive. IBM's OS/2 (Cook and Rawson, 1988; Kogan and Rawson, 1990), Mach and Chorus (see Chapter 21) provide memory-mapped files. Also, persistent programming languages have been designed and object-oriented interfaces have been provided as extensions to operating systems. This approach will provide a higher-level, and therefore more attractive, interface for programmers.

5.8   Mapping objects in virtual memory

In the previous section we saw that a file could be mapped into the virtual address space of a process. An extension to this idea is often used in **object-oriented systems**. Modules, abstract data types and objects were introduced in Chapter 2. Recall that a data object can only be accessed through the operations associated with its type; see Figure 5.15 (and recall Figure 5.4).

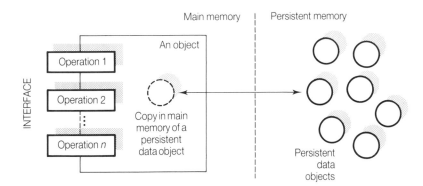

Figure 5.15
Persistent data
objects.

The following assumptions form the basis of this object-oriented approach to system design:

- Typed objects are defined and used in programming languages.
- An object may be made **persistent** and stored in persistent storage. It then exists independently of the running program that created it and may be used later by any program that knows its name.
- Each persistent object is identified uniquely in a system.
- Given an object's identifier it can be located in the persistent storage of the system.
- For simplicity, we assume that there is a single copy of a persistent object.

In a system of this kind, programmers may work with a higher-level abstraction for persistent storage than unstructured files, that of typed objects. We shall not study such systems in great detail, but it is interesting to note here that the object abstraction may fit very well with the desire to integrate virtual memory and persistent storage. When a persistent object is to be used by a process it may be mapped into the address space of the process and demand-paged between persistent store and main memory as described above for files.

5.9　Summary

Filing systems may be thought of as a service offered above an operating system kernel rather than a mandatory part of every kernel. Network-based filing systems are common and users' workstations may or may not have local filing systems. Traditional centralized operating systems, however, offer filing system services as part of a resident kernel and some system designs reflect an evolution from centralized to distributed systems.

We have studied filing systems because they are an example of a concurrent system. Many clients may simultaneously have requests outstanding. We shall consider how a filing system may have several client requests in progress simultaneously.

The data structures that a filing system is likely to use have also been discussed in some detail. This is so that the problems of interference between processes doing work on behalf of different clients simultaneously can be studied. We have also considered the data structures held permanently on disk and the data structures held in main memory on currently active files. We shall be concerned with the problems of updates to data structures in main memory being safely written out to disk. We shall also be concerned with the consistency of the data structures held on disk in the presence of concurrency and crashes.

We have studied the basic functions provided by a filing system as part of a storage architecture and have gone on to consider how best these functions might be distributed. An open architecture allows many different types of client to be supported. We outlined how we might build such an open architecture by distributing the functions of a filing system.

The role of disk-based filing systems is likely to change dramatically as processor performance continues to increase relative to disk speed and increasingly large amounts of main memory are used. In the meantime, techniques for improving the efficiency of filing systems will be used.

File input and output is inefficient because data is copied into system buffers and again into user space. We discussed the integration of virtual memory and storage through mapped files. Several operating system designs have used this idea and, in general, programmers have found the storage model presented by this approach rather low-level and complex. A current trend is to provide programmers with a model of persistent objects. Objects, rather than files, could then be mapped into the address spaces of processes.

Exercises

5.1   Which component computers of what types of system would you expect to have local disks with associated disk management software and filing system software?

5.2   What are the advantages and disadvantages of providing filing system software inside and outside the operating system?

5.3   Explain how a directory may be considered as an abstract data type or object.

5.4   How might the modules and processes introduced in Chapter 2 be used to implement a filing system? (Chapters 6, 7 and 8 will give a full explanation, although enough ideas have been presented in this chapter for a first attempt to be made.)

5.5   Is a multi-level filing system such as a tree structure essential or just convenient in a multi-user system? How might a two-level system be used?

5.6   How can file sharing be supported in a filing system? What additional problems over normal file sharing are introduced if directory sharing is also allowed?

5.7   In what ways might a filing system provide concurrency control, that is, control of the simultaneous use of a shared file or directory? What are the advantages and disadvantages of the methods you suggest?

5.8   What are the functions of the directory service level and the file storage service level of a filing system?

5.9   File protection is achieved by a combination of authentication and access control (authorization). Describe different kinds of access control policies that you might wish to implement. Discuss how these policies could be implemented.

5.10   Contrast the access control list approach to file protection with the capability approach. Could both methods be combined in a filing system?

5.11   Sketch an implementation of symbolic links held as separate (small) files. Outline the corresponding directory implementation.

5.12   In some systems a file must be opened before it is used, and the filing system maintains a context for open files; other filing systems are 'stateless'. What are the advantages and disadvantages of these approaches?

5.13   It has been proposed that an immutable filing system should be used. Once a file is named by the filing system it may not be changed. A new filename must be generated if a change must be made to a file. Directories are still to be mutable. What are the advantages and disadvantages of this approach?

5.14   Filing systems often attempt to hold as much current data and metadata as possible in main memory. The advantage is to be able to satisfy clients' read and write requests faster than if a disk had to be read or written. What are the possible dangers of this approach? Which application areas could not tolerate it?

5.15   Take the file service operations given in Section 5.4 and work out a modular design with file service interface operations and nested modules for directory object management and file object management.

6 Operating systems: Process management

CONTENTS

In the previous chapters we have considered a static description of a software system as a number of modules and the functions of some of the major operating system modules. The concept of 'process' as an active element which causes the modules to be executed dynamically was introduced briefly. We now return to and develop this concept in order to satisfy the requirement, established in Chapter 1, that separate activities should be supported in concurrent systems. This support, as provided by operating systems, is now examined in detail. We show that one function of an operating system is to create the abstraction of a set of concurrent processes. Having created this abstraction, processes may be used to execute both operating system and application modules.

6.1   Use of processes in systems

The designers of early operating systems solved the problems of concurrency and synchronization in an *ad hoc* way. It was always necessary to support synchronization between programs doing input or output and the corresponding devices, to take account of the great disparity in processor and device speeds. During the 1960s the concept of process came to be used explicitly in operating systems design, for example in Multics (Corbato and Vyssotsky, 1965), THE (Dijkstra, 1968) and RC4000 (Brinch Hansen, 1970).

One aspect of designing a concurrent system is to decide where processes should be used. A natural assignment is to allocate a process wherever there is a source of asynchronous events. In an operating system, for example, a process could be allocated to look after (synchronize with) each hardware device. If a user switches on a terminal and presses the attention key, an operating system process is waiting to respond. In an industrial control system a process could be allocated to each monitoring sensor and controlling actuator.

Another natural allocation of processes is to assign at least one process to each independent unit of work comprising a loaded program, data and library. Such a process will make system calls on the operating system to request service, for example, to request input, output, use of a file etc.

Figure 6.1 shows two active processes assigned to execute the static modules of Figures 3.9 and 3.10. One executes the user program and makes library and system calls to do I/O; the other programs the device, taking requests from user programs and transferring data to or from the device. We have made an assumption in the figure: that a user process enters the operating system (with a change of privilege as discussed in Section 3.3.2) and executes the top level of the operating system. This is only one way in which the operating system might be designed (see Section 6.10).

We have assumed that processes exist in a system and have outlined how they might be used. We now focus on how they are supported and managed by the operating system. We assume that there is a process management module within the operating system which 'knows about' a number of processes, such as those handling devices and those executing users' programs.

6.2   Processes and processors

There are often far fewer processors than the processes we should like to use in a system. If this was not the case we could dedicate a processor permanently to each process. When the process has something to do, it executes on its processor: when it has nothing to do its processor idles. In practice, the operating system must perform the function of sharing the real processors among the processes. We shall see that this function can be regarded as creating **virtual**

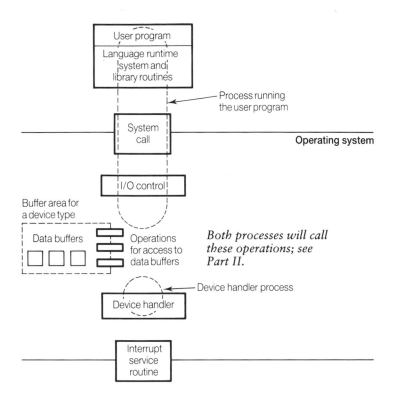

Figure 6.1
Part of a device
handling subsystem
showing processes.

processors, one for each process; that is, the operating system is simulating one processor per process.

In Section 2.5 we saw that interrupts from devices may be given a priority ordering and that the handling of a low-priority interrupt is temporarily abandoned if a high-priority interrupt arrives, and is resumed after the high-priority interrupt has been handled.

This idea can be applied to processes as well as to the interrupt routines which are entered by a hardware mechanism. A user process may be busily inverting a large matrix when an interrupt arrives (and its service routine is executed) to say that a block of data that was requested from the disk is now in memory and the disk is free to accept further commands. The disk handling process should run as soon as possible (to keep a heavily used resource busy), and then maybe the matrix program should resume or maybe the data from disk was awaited by some more important user process which should run in preference to the matrix program. We assume that the operating system process management function will implement a policy such as that outlined here.

Consider two processes in detail: Figure 6.2 is a time graph and shows two device handler processes (such as the one shown in Figure 6.1) sharing a single processor. It also shows when their respective devices are active and when the associated interrupt service routines (ISRs) run on the processor. We assume

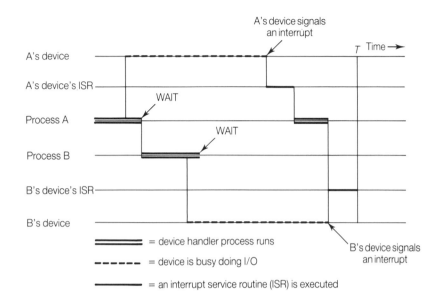

Figure 6.2
Time graph of two
device handler
processes.

that an ISR does not run as part of any process. An example of an alternative
approach is given in Chapter 21.

Initially, process A runs, starts its device then gets to a point where it can do
no more until the device completes its activity. It must be possible for the
process to indicate this fact to the process management function, shown here as
WAIT. When a process executes WAIT it changes its state from **running** to
blocked. Process B is then run on the processor, starts its device then WAITs. If
only A and B are available for running then the system becomes idle. In practice,
there may be some other process that can be run. The next event shown in the
graph is that A's device signals an interrupt which is taken by the processor and
A's interrupt service routine is entered. This makes process A able to run again
– its state changes from **blocked** to **runnable** and then to running when it is
selected to run on the processor. While process A is running, B's device signals
an interrupt which is taken by the processor, interrupting process A. B's interrupt service routine is executed and finishes at time T, shown in the graph.

A policy decision must be made over what should happen at time T. In some
operating systems, the policy is that process A must resume whatever the relative priorities of A and B. The justification is that A has not voluntarily executed
a WAIT and should be allowed to continue until it does so. This is called **non-
preemptive scheduling**. The UNIX operating system schedules kernel processes
(those executing the operating system) in this way. The advantage is simplicity –
a process can be assumed to have tidied up its data structures, and not be hog-
ging some valuable resource if it is allowed to finish its current task. The disadvantage is slow response to hardware events. Non-preemptive scheduling is
useless if fast response to unpredictable events is required; for example, alarm
signals or other events in hard real-time systems.

6.3   Process state

The discussion of Section 6.2 highlights that a process may be in a number of distinct states, illustrated in Figure 6.3:

- running on a processor: RUNNING state;
- able to run on a processor: RUNNABLE state;
- unable to run on a processor because it is awaiting some event and cannot proceed until that event arrives: BLOCKED state.

The transition from running to runnable occurs when the process does not voluntarily give up its processor (by asking to be blocked while waiting for an event to occur) but is forcibly preempted from its processor either because it has used up its allotted time and must make way for another process or because some higher-priority process has become runnable as a result of an interrupt.

6.3.1   Saving process state

If a process can be preempted from its processor at any instant, it is the responsibility of the operating system to make sure that it can be resumed in exactly the same state. The contents of the memory allocated to the process will be unchanged but the contents of any processor registers must be saved, since they will be used by the processes which run subsequently.

The operating system keeps a data block, often called a **process descriptor**, for each process that it supports. When a process is preempted or blocks voluntarily, the processor state, which includes the program counter and contents of registers, is saved in the process descriptor. Other information is also held here, such as the process's state (blocked or runnable) and its start address (see Figure 6.4). Information on the memory allocated to the process may be held here in a simple system or elsewhere if large page tables are involved (see Chapter 4). Other information such as that associated with open files and other resources

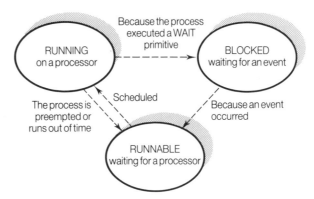

Figure 6.3
States and state transitions of a process.

Process ID
Priority (see Section 6.6)
Process state
Reason for waiting
Record of events (see Section 6.4)
Area for saving registers,
    including PC, stack pointer, general-purpose registers
Start address
Exception address (see Section 3.3.5)
Time slice (see Section 6.6.2)
Time left this run
Links for data structures

Figure 6.4
A process
decriptor.

allocated to the process may be kept here or in a second process environment data structure at user level. This kind of information is only needed when the process is running and is quite large and variable in length. Information that must be in the process descriptor is that which is needed when the process is not in main memory (for example a record of event(s) the process is awaiting). We are now seeing the detailed implementation of the process abstraction.

6.3.2 Context switching

The process of saving the state of a process and setting up the state of another is called **context switching**. The instructions that are executed in performing these operations and the frequency at which context switching happens are an overhead at the lowest level of a system. When we consider alternative ways of supporting communication between processes in Part II we shall consider the context switches that are necessary to implement the various methods. Context switching overhead is relevant to many aspects of system structuring.

6.4   Synchronizing with the hardware – events and the WAIT operation

We have seen above that the operating system's support for processes must include the provision of a WAIT operation to allow processes to synchronize with the hardware. The term **event** will be used to include the arrival of an interrupt signal from a device.

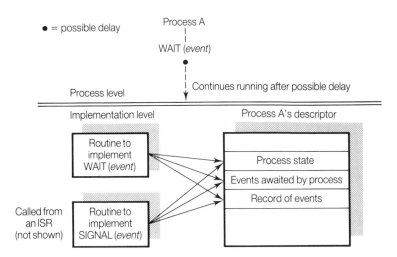

Figure 6.5
Process
synchronization
with events.

This operation might be provided as a WAIT for one specific event, for any one event or for one of a selected set of events. Possible hardware events are relatively small in number and are known at system design time. This set of possible events can easily be encoded in data structures. As shown in Figure 6.4, the process descriptor could encode the reason the process is blocked and the events of interest to this process that have occurred, see below. Figure 6.5 shows one way of implementing process–event synchronization. The assumption here is that it is well known which processes will wait on which events. An example is a dedicated device handler that synchronizes with a single device.

Figure 6.5 shows the process level and the implementation level for a WAIT for a specific event. When the process executes WAIT, control is transferred to the routine which implements WAIT. Assuming that the event of interest has not already occurred, the process state is set to *blocked* and the event it is waiting for is recorded in the 'events awaited by process' slot. Some other process is then run. When the event occurs, we assume that a routine SIGNAL(*event*) is executed which causes the process state to be set to *runnable* and the reason for waiting to be removed. The process will be selected to run again in due course. This assumes that the system design is such that a dedicated process waits for each event so SIGNAL(*event*) operates on the appropriate process descriptor. Section 6.4.2 takes a more general approach.

An event might arrive while the process that would be interested in it is still busy on some previous task, and hasn't yet got around to waiting for it. Another possibility is that the process set a device in motion, but was preempted from its processor before it could execute WAIT for event in order to synchronize with the device. It is essential that the operating system should not unset the interrupt and ignore the event if no process is waiting for it. This was a 'feature' of some early operating system designs. In Figure 6.5 the operating system notes that the event has occurred in the 'record of events' slot. This is sometimes called a **'wake-up waiting'**. When the process requests to wait for the event it can continue running and need never enter the blocked state.

6.4.1   Race conditions

Consider the following sequence of events:

A process executes WAIT(*event*).
The WAIT routine checks that the event is not already recorded.
  The hardware signals an interrupt to indicate the event has occurred.
  The interrupt handler invokes the SIGNAL(*event*) routine.
    The SIGNAL routine checks that the process is not waiting for the event.
    The SIGNAL routine records that the event has occurred ('wake-up waiting').
  Interrupt processing terminates and the WAIT routine resumes execution.
The WAIT routine sets the state of the process to BLOCKED ('wait-on-event').

The sequence of actions recorded here is often called a 'race condition'. Following it:

● the process is BLOCKED, waiting for the event to be SIGNALLED;

● the event has been SIGNALLED, and is available marked 'wake-up waiting'.

The process will wait indefinitely for the event if this is allowed to happen. For this reason the WAIT and SIGNAL routines must be implemented as indivisible, **atomic**, or **primitive** operations by some means. We shall discuss how this might be done in Part II.

6.4.2   Event and process objects

The design described in Section 6.4 has encoded hardware event information in the process descriptors, assuming that specific processes are dedicated to handling the various events. A more general approach is to separate the event data structure from the process data structure.

Recall that in Section 2.1 abstract data types and objects were introduced. We can implement events and processes in this way. An event object comprises an internal data structure representing an event plus interface operations SIGNAL(*event*) and WAIT(*event*), as shown in Figure 6.6. The figure also shows process objects with operations to BLOCK and UNBLOCK a process. We discuss this further in Section 6.9.

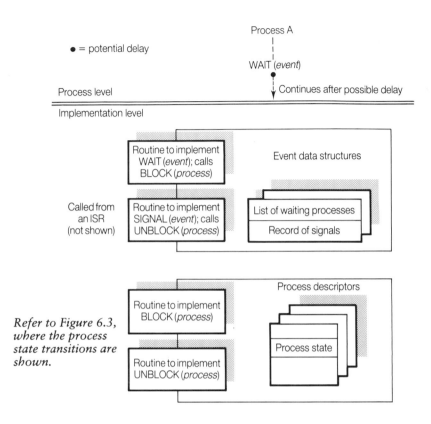

Figure 6.6
Event and process
objects.

When a process executes WAIT(*event*), the process identifier is recorded in the event data structure and the BLOCK(*process*) routine is called, causing the representation of the process state to be changed from blocked to runnable. A SCHEDULE routine (not shown) could then be called to decide which process to run next. Process scheduling is discussed in the next section.

When an event occurs, the SIGNAL(*event*) routine is invoked. If one or more processes are recorded as waiting for the event, one of them (or perhaps all of them, depending on the system policy) can be made runnable by invoking UNBLOCK(*process*). Again, scheduling is invoked after this. If no process is awaiting the event its occurrence is recorded as a wake-up waiting in the event data structure.

6.5   The process data structure

The operating system must handle many processes and will maintain a data structure holding their descriptors. This could be set up in a number of ways. The aim is that the operating system should be able to choose and run the highest-priority process as quickly as possible. Selecting a process to run on a processor is called process **scheduling.** The selection policy determines which process will be selected and is effected by the **scheduling algorithm**. Setting up a process state in the processor's registers is called **dispatching**. Figure 6.7 shows one possible data structure, an array or table of process descriptors; many alternatives are possible.

6.6   Process scheduling – general approaches

When a free processor is available the operating system must select a runnable process (if one exists) to run on it. The **scheduling policy** of the system determines which process is selected.

The mechanisms to effect this policy must be as efficient as possible since they are an overhead on every process, however urgent. The design of the data structures representing processes and the algorithms for inserting and removing processes into and out of them is therefore important. In this section, scheduling policies appropriate for meeting the requirements of systems of different types are discussed.

6.6.1   Unary, binary and general scheduling

In certain cases the selection of the next process to run can be simplified.

Unary scheduling: in the case where the system is idle (all processes are blocked, waiting for events) and an event occurs which makes some process runnable then that process is clearly the one that should run. No others need be considered and scheduling can be bypassed.

Binary scheduling: when a process is running it is by definition the most important, highest-priority process. If that process does something to make another process runnable then the choice of which one to run is between the two processes concerned. No others need be considered. Similarly, if an event occurs while a process is running which makes another process runnable, the choice is, again, between the two processes.

General scheduling: when the process that is running terminates or blocks, waiting for some event, a general schedule must be carried out.

6.6.2   Process behaviour and priority

Operating system processes have known function and duration, and in many systems are put into a permanent, **static fixed-priority** ordering. Figure 6.7 gives an example of how the information on processes might be held in a process management module and shows system processes handled separately in this

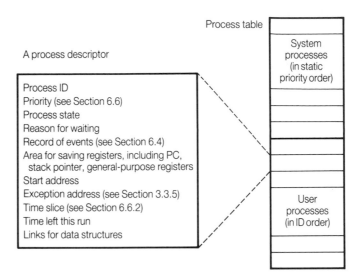

Figure 6.7
A possible process
structure.

way. They are in fixed-priority order and the operating system's scheduler will first search from the top of the table for a runnable system process.

In some application areas, such as process control, the function and duration of all processes may be known at system design time and it may be appropriate to assign them a static fixed-priority ordering. It may be possible to analyse the timing requirements of all processes and pre-specify a schedule which meets them. This kind of system is discussed further in Section 6.8.

In a multi-user system, the nature of application processes is unknown to the operating system and their behaviour will change during a typical program run, for example, from a data input phase to a processing phase to an output phase. In interactive systems, one user cannot be kept waiting while another indulges in a long bout of number crunching, so a **time slice** is allocated to a process when it begins to run. The process descriptor may indicate the length of the time slice to be allocated to this process and will have a record of the time left to this process on this run. This time must be decremented every time the clock interrupts and when it reaches zero the process is out of time. There may also be some indication of process priority.

Figure 6.7 shows one way of recording all the processes in a system. One or more queues of runnable processes may be chained through the user processes in this table, using the link fields in the process descriptors, as indicated in Figure 6.8. When a process becomes runnable it is added to the end of the appropriate queue.

Processes doing input or output usually become blocked very soon and do not get to the end of their time slices. They may also be using shared system resources, such as the filing system's disks, which should be kept running to the greatest extent possible. Figure 6.9 gives an alternative view of a high-priority

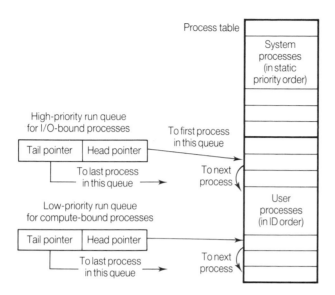

Figure 6.8
Run queues
through the
process structure.

and a low-priority run queue. When a process becomes runnable after being blocked it is allocated to the high-priority run queue. If it continues to block before using up its time slice it will always be scheduled from the high-priority queue. If a process runs to the end of its time slice it is moved to the end of the low-priority queue. Only if a high-priority queue is empty is a low-priority queue examined. In practice, processes may stay blocked for long periods (see Section 3.2.1) and the high-priority queue is often empty.

In summary, system processes have highest priority and are scheduled according to a static fixed-priority scheme. User processes which have blocked and

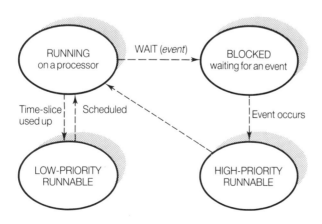

Figure 6.9
Run queues with
priority based on
recent activity.

have become runnable again are next highest and user processes which run to the end of their time slices are lowest.

Figure 6.10 shows a refinement of this general idea.

- As before, system processes are of highest priority and are handled in static, fixed-priority order. They are not shown in the figure.

- There is a high-priority queue for user processes that blocked, waiting for certain events such as a page fault, and are now runnable.

- There is a medium-priority queue for user processes that were blocked, waiting for resources which are less critical for system performance (for example, devices such as dedicated terminals or tape drives), and are now runnable.

- The low- and lowest-priority queues are for processes that use up their time slice. Two queues allow for an allocation of two priority levels for processes when they are not doing I/O. More queues could be used if required by the applications supported by the system. Alternatively, a single queue, ordered according to process priority (instead of first come first served) could be constructed. Process priority may be assigned statically (in response to application requirements) or computed dynamically, depending on recent CPU usage.

The idea of multiple queues can be extended as required in a system.

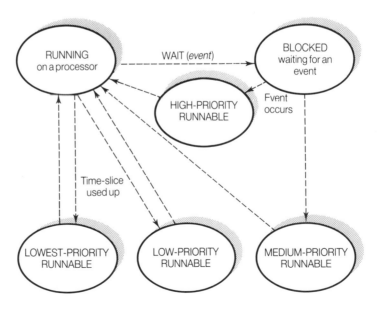

Figure 6.10
More run queues with priority based on recent activity.

6.7 Scheduling for shared-memory multiprocessors

Section 1.3.3 introduced shared-memory multiprocessors and Chapter 3 discussed the allocation of devices to processors and interrupt handling. Chapter 4 described the memory hierarchy in a computer system, including a hardware-controlled cache and an address translation unit. In a shared-memory multiprocessor each processor has a separate cache and address translation unit.

A given processor may have a local run queue for the device handlers of any dedicated devices it might have. There are also likely to be one or more global run queues. A possible approach is that a processor, on becoming free, should execute code such that it first examines its local run queue and, if that contains no runnable process, should take a process from the global run queue(s). Note that the global run queues are writeable data structures and adding or removing a process will involve more than one read or write of memory. It must be ensured that these data structures remain correct in the presence of simultaneous attempts to update them. This is important in all systems, but requires particular attention in a multiprocessor. Mechanisms to ensure this are the subject matter of Part II.

In the introductory chapter we saw that an application might best be programmed as a number of concurrent processes. In Chapter 7 we consider how the component processes of a concurrent program might be specified and supported by the language run-time system and the operating system. A general point is that an application should be able to indicate to the operating system that it has a number of processes and to give their relative priorities for scheduling purposes. It is then possible to run them simultaneously on the processors of a multiprocessor. Section 6.11 considers this requirement and gives an introduction to **multi-threaded processes**.

Scheduling algorithms for multiprocessors form an active research area. One approach to process scheduling for shared-memory multiprocessors is to allocate the process at the top of the run queue to the first processor that becomes free. This policy ignores the fact that a process may have run very recently on a particular processor and may have built up a useful state in both the cache and the address translation unit. It might have blocked for a high-priority event and be runnable again in a very short time. If a process has been blocked for some time then its state is likely to have been superseded by that of more recent processes. In the case of a page fault, for example, the process should clearly continue to run on the same processor.

It might be appropriate to allow a process to 'busy wait' on a page fault. This will be described in more detail in Chapter 9, but the idea is to keep the process scheduled and running instead of blocking it and doing a context switch to another process. The waiting process might execute in a tight loop until it is interrupted by the arrival of the required page.

Another factor to take into account is the relationships between groups of processes. If certain processes are designed to work closely together then the ideal arrangement may be for them to be scheduled simultaneously on the multiple processors of the multiprocessor. Bad performance could result from ignoring this kind of relationship; for example, a process runs, then tries to communicate with a partner. The partner is runnable but not scheduled. The first process is blocked and the partner is scheduled on the same processor. It picks up the pertinent information from the first process, acts on it then tries to send back an answer. Its partner is not scheduled, and so on.

The counter-argument is that if the processes are sharing data it is better for them to run on the same processor so that the same cache is used. If they run on separate processors and are sharing writeable data the overhead of keeping the caches coherent will be introduced.

6.8   Process scheduling to meet real-time requirements

Although preemptive scheduling with carefully chosen process priorities may ensure optimum use of resources it may not be sufficient to ensure that a number of processes meet their timing requirements in a real-time system.

Real-time systems were introduced in Section 1.1. There we defined two kinds of real-time process: those which are periodic and carry out some cyclic activity like data sampling and analysis, and those which must respond to unpredictable events in a specified time. A real-time scheduler must ensure that all processes satisfy their timing constraints.

Another example was introduced in the discussion on multimedia workstations in Section 1.1.1. A video and voice stream must be delivered to a workstation so that the voice is synchronized with the moving lips of the person in the picture. Although video generates far more data than voice, and is therefore likely to be managed at higher priority, the voice stream must be allowed a small proportion of time periodically. Conventional scheduling might well allow the voice to fall behind.

It is relatively easy to schedule a number of periodic processes. The processor time can be divided up in a suitable way and allocated to them in the same way as the time slices described above. A static analysis is usually carried out and a schedule determined. It is more difficult to incorporate response to unpredictable events. Should the system designer allow for the worst possible case of all events arriving at the same time (or very close together) or take some probabilistic model of when they might arrive and live with a low probability of bursty behaviour?

A model of an aperiodic process is that it becomes ready to run when a particular event occurs, it must then compute for a known length of time and, in competition with other processes, it must complete in some specified time. We assume that the system has process preemption.

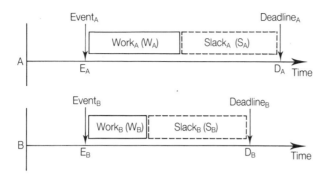

Figure 6.11
Processes in a real-time system.

Figure 6.11 shows two processes A and B each with a known computation time (work$_A$ and work$_B$) and a known length of time in which the work must be completed. The graph shows this as a **deadline (D), work time (W)** and **slack time (S)** for each process. The first graph in Figure 6.12 shows one possible sequence of events for the two processes. First process A's event occurs and process A is scheduled. Before process A's work is complete, process B's event occurs. The scheduler now has to decide whether to schedule A or B. The scheduler has the information to compute the deadlines of A and B and the remaining slack time of A and B.

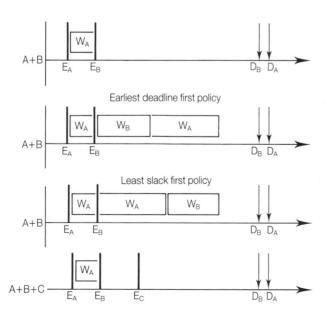

Figure 6.12
Real-time scheduling.

An **earliest deadline first** policy would cause process B to be selected. B then completes before its deadline by the value of its slack time. If a third process then comes along the option of using up some of B's slack time (by delaying B) has been lost.

An alternative strategy is to schedule first the process with least remaining slack time, provided that they can both meet their deadlines. The third graph of Figure 6.12 shows this **least slack first** policy for A and B. The fourth graph shows the event for a third process C occurring. It is left as an exercise for the reader to compare the two policies with respect to work done and slack time left for A and B at time E_c.

This discussion does not take into account that the processes might be delayed, waiting for resources, thus unavoidably using up slack time. Scheduling decisions would then have to be reconsidered. The periodic processes mentioned above would also have to be scheduled. The aim here is to introduce, through very simple examples, the issues that are involved in scheduling for real-time systems so that the reader has a basis for evaluating any operating system that is claimed to be 'real-time'. It also emphasizes that there is further study to be done in this area (Burns and Wellings, 1989).

6.8.1   System structure and response to events

The ability to meet the requirement for a process to be scheduled in some bounded time after an event occurs is affected by the overall operating system design as well as the specific scheduling algorithm it employs. Some operating systems are executed 'procedurally'; that is, operating system code is executed 'in-process'. When a user process makes a system call it becomes a system process and enters the operating system. Such systems tend to have very few dedicated system processes and much of the work that is done by one process may be on behalf of others.

An example is that in UNIX an interrupt is serviced in the context of whatever process is running when it occurs. Another example from UNIX is when a process waits in the kernel for an event, the event occurs and the process is about to return to user mode to respond to the event. Before returning to user mode the process executes system code to determine whether any process is due to be woken up after asking to be delayed for a certain length of time. A high-priority process could therefore be required to act as an alarm clock for any number of low-priority processes between receiving the event for which it was waiting and responding to it.

This style of system design makes it difficult to compute how quickly a process can be guaranteed to run after an event occurs. There is an indeterminate amount of system code that may be executed as part of any process. The alternative design approach is to have the operating system executed by dedicated processes and to request service from them. System structure is discussed further in Section 6.10 and in Part II.

6.9 Process abstraction and implementation

The above sections have shown the details of how processes may be implemented. Figure 6.13 shows two layers: the high-level process abstraction and the layer supporting the abstraction. The function of the support layer is to provide an environment in which concurrent processes may exist. The support layer can be thought of as being at a low level within an operating system, so that processes may be used to execute operating system functions, such as device handlers and the memory management subsystem. Figure 6.14 gives an alternative view of Figure 6.13, showing the process management module as an abstract data type, located within an operating system. The representation of processes (the various process data structures) is hidden and the interface contains operations on processes.

Figure 6.15 highlights the general idea that a single operation at the process level may be implemented by a routine at the level below. The invocation mechanism might be a simple procedure call from within the operating system to the process management module or a system call from an application process running above the operating system. At the process level, the operation appears to be a single indivisible instruction. An operation of this kind is sometimes called a 'primitive': for example, WAIT(*event*) could be referred to as a synchronizing primitive. The implication for the implementation of the operation is that it is atomic, to avoid the race conditions discussed in Section 6.4.1. If the operation invocation blocks the process there will be a delay before the process continues.

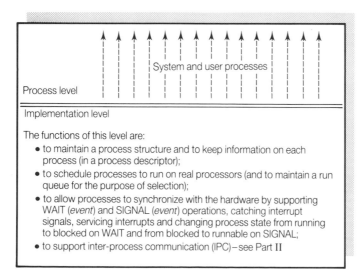

Figure 6.13
Supporting concurrent processes.

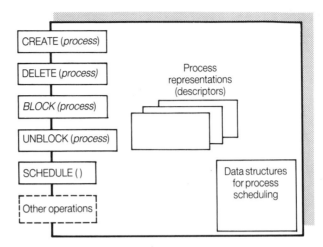

Figure 6.14
Process
management
module, alternative
view.

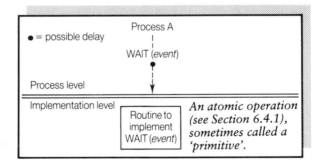

Figure 6.15
Implementation of
operations.

There has been no indication in the above discussion that the processes supported are other than completely independent of each other. In Chapter 8 the need for processes to communicate will be motivated and mechanisms for achieving interprocess communication (IPC) will be described throughout Part II.

6.10 Operating system structure and placement of processes

As a result of the material studied in Chapters 3, 4 and 5 we can now put together the notions of static modules of code and their dynamic execution. We shall use an operating system as an example. We have seen how one operating system function is to support processes. We now consider how processes might

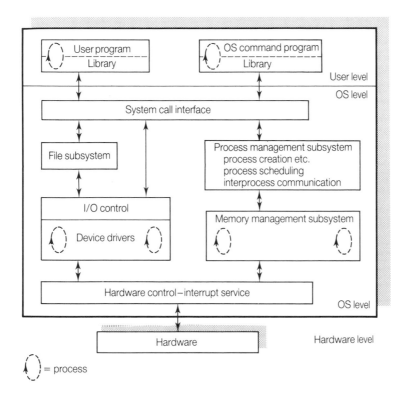

Figure 6.16
Outline of OS
modules with
processes.

be used in the implementation of an operating system. Figure 6.16 shows the major components of a traditional, closed operating system and gives a possible placement of processes to achieve dynamic execution of the system. Processes are allocated as follows:

- A single process is allocated to each user-level activity: a user program execution or a command execution. This assumes that each of these activities is a single sequential process. We shall consider concurrent programs in the next chapter.

- A process is allocated to handle each device instance. Such a process will wait for and respond to device interrupts and be given work to do by the high level of I/O management (see Sections 3.6 and 6.1). Data will be passed between the high and low levels via buffers (see Section 3.6).

- Some memory management processes are indicated to respond to address translation faults, to allocate main memory to processes, and to move processes into and out of main memory as necessary (see Section 4.12). A process which is concerned with swapping other processes between main memory and backing store must be guaranteed to be resident in main memory itself.

- Certain modules are shown with no permanent allocation of processes. It is assumed here that the code is executed in the context of the user process as a result of a system call. In this case, a state change from user state (unprivileged) to system state (privileged) is necessary as discussed in Section 3.3.2.

  Section 8.1 discusses different ways of using processes within a module such as a filing subsystem. An alternative that could have been shown here is a number of permanently allocated processes. Exercise 6.11 expands on one implication of these two alternative models of execution of an operating system.

- The process management module cannot itself be implemented as processes (see Section 6.9).

In Chapter 21 a different approach is shown in a case study on the UNIX operating system. UNIX takes an extreme position and minimizes the number of processes which are bound to modules. There are no device handler processes and virtually the whole kernel is executed 'in-process'. Interrupt handling is executed in the context of whatever process happens to be running when the interrupt occurs. Exercise 6.10 discusses one aspect of this further.

6.11　Introduction to multi-threaded processes

In the discussion in Section 6.10 we saw that a number of processes might execute in a single module of the operating system. In Chapter 7 we shall see a number of processes executing a concurrent program. A common requirement is for a number of processes to share an address space and all the resource allocations that are associated with the address space. We have two separate concepts here:

- the unit of execution (the unit of scheduling by the operating system);
- the memory and other resources with which the unit of execution is associated.

In this chapter we have shown how processes, the units of execution, can share a processor. The process descriptor contains the processor state, including the program counter. Section 6.5 indicated that the memory allocated to the process might be recorded in the process descriptor or elsewhere, for example, as a page table associated with the process. In some operating systems it is possible for a number of processes to share the same memory management information and other resources, such as open files. Such processes are often called **lightweight processes** or **threads**, and the system is said to support **multi-threaded processes**. The term 'lightweight' is used to indicate that the context switching overhead is low. There is no need to change the memory management or other resource information on a context switch. In other operating systems

Table 6.1   Microkernel terminology.

Microkernel	Unit of execution	Unit of resource allocation
Mach	thread	task
Chorus	thread	actor
Mayflower	lightweight process	domain
Wanda	thread	process or address space
V	thread	team
Amoeba	thread	cluster

this is impossible: each process is defined to have a separate address space. Such systems are said to have a **heavyweight process** model because the overhead on a context switch is high.

If an operating system is to run on a shared-memory multiprocessor it is important that multi-threaded processes are supported. The separate threads of a process can then be scheduled to run simultaneously if processors are free.

Most of the 'microkernels' which have been developed recently run on multi-processors and support this facility; most traditional, closed operating systems do not. There is a great disparity in the terminology used for these concepts; see Table 6.1.

The process supported by traditional operating systems is equivalent, in this terminology, to an address space with one thread, a task with one thread, a process with one thread etc. We shall return to this general area in Chapter 7 and in Part II.

6.12   Summary

We have seen how the abstraction of a concurrent system as a set of concurrent processes is implemented as one of the functions of an operating system: **process management**. We have also seen that processes may be used within the operating system itself, for example as device handlers. Operating system designs vary in the way in which processes are used. A brief introduction to the requirement for processes to share an address space and other resources was given. We distinguished between the unit of execution and the unit of resource allocation.

When a concurrent system is to be designed and implemented above an operating system it is important that the requirements on the operating system are understood. We have seen that **preemptive process scheduling** is necessary for a system to have any hope of supporting real-time response to events and that, in addition, specially tuned real-time process scheduling algorithms may be required for certain application areas.

In practice, a concurrent system will be written in a high-level language and the next chapter considers how the potential concurrency provided by the operating system may be carried through to an application written in a concurrent programming language.

Exercises

6.1   Discuss how you would wish to allocate processes in the systems that were described in the introduction, for example:
(a) an industrial process control system
(b) a multiaccess (time-sharing) computer
(c) a powerful personal workstation
(d) a transaction processing system
(e) a parallel searching algorithm to run on a shared-memory multiprocessor
(f) a multiphase compiler to run on a shared-memory multiprocessor.

6.2   How would you simulate one processor per process in a uniprocessor and a shared-memory multiprocessor?

6.3   List everything that might be considered part of the state of a process. Which of these items must always be in main memory and which could be swapped out to backing store when the process was not running?

6.4   (a) Design a method of implementing synchronization between a peripheral and a single process which is dedicated to managing it.
(b) Design a method of implementing synchronization between a peripheral and a process which is currently waiting for it to deliver data but is not dedicated to this task.
(c) Design a method of implementing synchronization between any hardware device and one or more processes.

6.5   Design a data structure which implements the representation of the processes known to an operating system. You should consider whether your system has a significant number of dedicated system processes and, if so, whether they will be held separately from user processes. What operations would you expect to provide at the interface of a process management module?

6.6   (a) When does a general schedule need to be carried out in a multi-access system?

(b) How can a process in a multi-access system be scheduled differently when it is in a compute-bound phase from when it is doing input or output?

(c) How many processes would you expect to be active in a single-user workstation, a dedicated gateway computer and a dedicated file server?

(d) How would you expect processes to be scheduled in a multimedia workstation (see Section 1.1)?

6.7 How does scheduling for real-time systems differ from scheduling for multi-access systems?

6.8 What approaches can be taken to scheduling for shared-memory multi-processor systems?

6.9 Recall the layered communications software described in Chapter 3. Consider the situation when several user processes have made requests for network input or output.

(a) How might the layers be executed by processes?

(b) How might synchronization between user-level processes and the arrival or transmission of data at the network be arranged?

(c) Where might network buffers be located with respect to the ISO layers?

(d) Why would it be a bad idea to have a process execute each of the ISO layers?

6.10 For a given modular operating system structure, what is the minimum set of dedicated, resident system processes that can be used? How does the rest of the operating system get executed in this case?

How would you design to maximize the number of dedicated system processes?

For both of the approaches indicated above, discuss where a separate address space could be used for protection purposes. Assume that the system provides a mechanism for a process to make requests of the operating system. We have studied one such mechanism in Section 3.3.2. We shall expand on this in Part II.

6.11 In what circumstances might it be advantageous to use several threads of control within a single process?

6.12 Section 6.9 introduced a process management module and pointed out that, as this module implements the process abstraction, it cannot itself be implemented in terms of processes.

Within an operating system, the interface operations of the process management module may be called as simple procedures. In Section 6.4, for example, we saw the WAIT(*event*) operation invoking the BLOCK(*process*) operation.

In Section 6.10 it was mentioned that an operating system might be executed by a set of system processes taking users' requests or might instead be executed 'in-process'. For both of these models of execution, discuss how the invocation of process management can be incorporated into the model. (The problem to address is, if you are executing the operating system yourself, what happens when you block yourself?).

Language system support for concurrency

7

CONTENTS

Concurrent systems are almost invariably programmed in a high-level language. We now consider how concurrency can be supported at the language level. First, we review relevant language-level aspects of the execution of a program by a sequential process. Then we consider how concurrency might be supported within a language.

7.1 Process state in language systems and operating systems

Chapter 6 defined the state of a process as far as the operating system is concerned, that is, the information stored on a process by the process management module of the operating system. It includes the value of the program counter and the contents of other hardware registers; information about any ongoing interaction of the process with the hardware, such as events the process is waiting for and events of interest to the process that have already occurred; the files a process has opened; and the memory that has been allocated to the process.

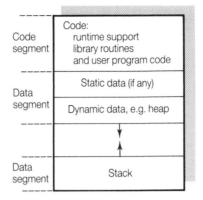

The user-level of the virtual address space of a process.
  The operating system may support three segments, which are used as shown (refer to Chapter 4).

Figure 7.1
A common storage arrangement for a single process.

A process which is executing a program, originally written in a high-level language, also has a language-level state comprising the values of variables which are accessible to the process at a given time. These are stored in data areas in the memory allocated to the process. Chapter 4 described some memory management schemes based on segmentation. One simple arrangement (Figure 7.1) is that a process has a code segment, which includes the runtime support and library code as well as the user-level code, and two data segments, one for the static data and the **heap** and one for the **runtime stack**. The use of these data areas is discussed in more detail below.

This level of the process state is of no concern to the operating system, as it is stored safely in the memory allocated to the process and, unlike processor registers, is not used by any other process. Rather, it is the concern of the **runtime system** which is responsible for managing the dynamic execution of a program by a process. Figure 7.2 gives an overview. Here we have moved from the literal

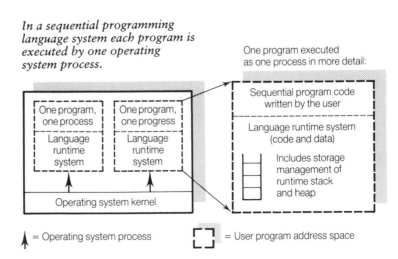

Figure 7.2
One program, one process: runtime system support of user-level program.

view of the arrangement of the virtual address space of the process in the seg-ments allocated by the operating system. We show that the user-level code runs within a framework provided by the runtime system. The runtime system code manages the storage needed by the user program when it is executed. Note that there is a **single thread of control** within which the runtime system and the user level code is executed. For example, when the program is loaded and the operat-ing system passes control to the process, this is likely to be to the runtime system code in the first instance. When the runtime system has initialized its data struc-tures etc. it will pass control to the user code. When the user code runs, it makes procedure calls into the runtime system for service.

We now examine the language-level process state in some detail. It is assumed that the reader is familiar with a high-level sequential language such as Pascal or Modula-2 or 3 and has already encountered the basic ideas of language imple-mentation, such as the allocation of storage for variables on a runtime stack. This section revises these ideas and highlights the essentials of the state associated with a process in a language system.

7.1.1   Procedures and activation records

The programs or modules introduced in Section 2.1 have a finer-grained struc-ture which may be defined in terms of procedures. When a procedure is called at runtime it must be allocated storage space for local variables etc. One function of the language runtime system is to acquire storage space from the operating system (if a data segment needs to grow in size) and to allocate this space as required by the running program.

Programming languages vary over where variable declarations can be made and the degree of nesting of declarations that is allowed. We shall assume for simplicity that storage space is associated with modules and procedures and that procedure declarations are not nested. Chapter 7 of Aho *et al.* (1986) gives a comprehensive treatment of this topic.

At compile time the variables declared in each module or procedure are noted and an **activation record** is created for each procedure which defines the data space that will be needed when the procedure is called. When the module is entered, by procedure call at runtime, a stack frame containing control informa-tion and storage space for the variables is set up from the associated activation record. For any procedure activation, storage must be available as follows: for the call parameters before the call; for the return address at call time; and, dur-ing the procedure execution, for local variables, any further procedure call para-meters and the return parameters for this activation.

At runtime, some specific sequence of module entries and procedure calls is followed and the stack structure reflects this dynamic sequence, as shown in Figure 7.3. The variables become accessible (addressable) by the process when the stack frame containing them is set up.

When the process exits from the procedure by executing a *return* instruction the stack frame associated with that procedure is removed from the stack. The

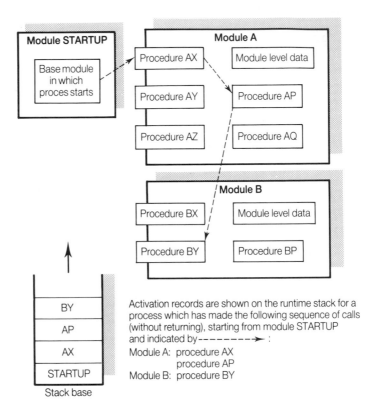

Figure 7.3
Modules,
procedures and
the runtime stack.

Activation records are shown on the runtime stack for a
process which has made the following sequence of calls
(without returning), starting from module STARTUP
and indicated by- - - - - - - - -▶ :
Module A: procedure AX
                   procedure AP
Module B: procedure BY

frame pointer is reset to the stack frame of the calling procedure. The calling
procedure may pick up return parameters from the stack. Note that all the state
associated with the procedure activation is lost on exit from it; indeed, the space
on the stack will be reused if the process calls another procedure from its
current context.

7.1.2   The heap and garbage collection

The abstract data types described in Section 2.1 maintain the state of their data
objects independently of any of the operations being called. A stack structure is
therefore not appropriate for the storage of such objects, since stack storage dis-
appears on procedure exit. A data structure called a **heap** is used for the storage
of such long-lived objects. A client may create a new object of the type and will
receive a reference to the object for use as a parameter for subsequent calls.
Object references may be placed on the stack as input and output parameters in
the usual way.

It may also be convenient to use a heap for the storage of large objects or
where it is impossible to determine the size of an object at compile time; that is,
if the language allows data structures to be created dynamically and their size

may depend on some runtime calculation or input data. In these cases a reference to an object may be put on the stack in place of the object itself. The language CLU takes this approach to an extreme in that all data is stored in the heap and the stack contains only references; the language is said to have pointer semantics.

Whenever storage space is allocated from the heap there is a problem over reclaiming it when it has fallen out of use. In some languages it is the responsibility of the programmer to deallocate unwanted storage. The problem here is that programmers make errors and may forget to deallocate storage. Storage allocation and deallocation is one of the most common sources of programming errors. Continuously running programs (that is, systems of some sort) are particularly susceptible to this form of error, which is called a **storage leak** and is a common cause of system crashes.

Another example is that storage may be deallocated when there are still references to it. Any use of such a reference is an error.

The alternative policy is that the language system automatically reclaims storage space by detecting when variables can no longer be reached. This is called **garbage collection**. It may be carried out synchronously, in which case execution halts until garbage collection completes, or asynchronously (also called **on-the-fly**) in parallel with program execution. There are heated debates in the systems area about whether it is worth putting up with your program going away to (synchronous) garbage-collect from time to time to avoid the possibility of a crash due to a storage leak. This is a choice that has to be made when a system implementation language is chosen. The ideal of efficient, transparent, asynchronous garbage collection is difficult to achieve.

7.2   Concurrent systems built from sequential programs with system calls

Chapter 6 showed how a single process, supported by the operating system, is used to execute a single user-level application. This model is assumed in the discussion on language systems presented in Section 7.1. Each user-level process is typically independent of all others and need only interact with the operating system (by means of system calls). Section 6.4 showed how the operating system allows a process to synchronize with the hardware by means of a WAIT primitive and event signalling. This interaction with the hardware is typically done by an operating system process (that is, a process executing operating system code) acting in response to a request by a user process. In a concurrent system it may also be necessary for user-level processes to synchronize and share information with each other.

In Chapter 1 a range of concurrent systems was described, and an aim of the book is to show how to write software to implement them. For some applications it may be appropriate to use a sequential programming language. Each unit of the concurrent system may be a single sequential process and the operating system may provide **system calls to allow interaction with other processes** in addition to the system calls for requesting operating system service. Many concurrent systems are written in sequential programming languages, for example, in C or C++ above UNIX.

The characteristics of the systems for which this approach is appropriate are that the units to be run concurrently are relatively large; the concurrency is **coarse-grained** rather than **fine-grained**. Also, interactions are likely to be relatively infrequent: perhaps an occasional synchronization rather than frequent cooperation involving extensive use of common information. That is, the processes are likely to be **loosely coupled** rather than **tightly coupled**.

A major problem with the approach is portability of the concurrent system. The processes have made use of an operating system interface (a number of system calls) that has been provided to allow interactions between processes. If the system is to be able to run on any other operating system it is necessary for the same interface to be present. Syntactic differences can be allowed for when the code is ported, but semantic differences between operating systems are likely to occur in this area.

7.2.1   Shared data

The above discussion has made the implicit assumption that the processes that execute the separate programs share no data. In Chapter 4 we saw that segmentation hardware allows processes to share part of their address spaces. The operating system may impose restrictions on fully general sharing. For example, the original UNIX design supported three user-level segments, one code segment and two data segments; the code segment could be shared but not the data segments. Many current UNIX systems are still like this.

If it is possible for processes to share data segments then the extended system call interface discussed above would have to support a more closely coupled interaction between the processes than we have assumed so far. The portability problem could be increased by this requirement.

For this reason, standard interfaces, such as the POSIX interface for C programs running on UNIX systems (IEEE, 1988), have been developed. Such an interface runs as a standard set of library routines and allows a concurrent system to be developed in a sequential programming language augmented by library calls. A similar package, the 'C threads package', is provided for the Mach operating system. We shall not be in a position to discuss the features of such packages until the end of Part II.

Part II makes a major distinction between processes which can share data objects (access them directly) and processes which share no data. In this chapter we are concerned with language-level support for concurrency and will return to architectural issues in Chapter 8. In the initial discussion here we make the simplifying assumption that if a concurrent program comprises several processes, they all share a single address space and are managed by a single runtime system.

7.3   Evolution of concurrency in programming languages

We now explore the support for concurrency that might be provided by a **concurrent programming language**. We take the extreme position that an entire concurrent system is to be written as a single concurrent program. For generality, we take the model that the concurrent system to be programmed is to run above a minimal operating system and explore the resulting requirements on the language system and the operating system for different types of application. In practice, some of the examples below are likely to be implemented as special-purpose systems with integrated operating system functions.

A number of concurrent programming languages (that is, languages with syntax for expressing concurrency) have been developed. Examples of the different approaches taken in different concurrent programming languages are given throughout Part II. In this chapter we explore how more than a single **thread of control** might be supported in a concurrent program. That is, we return to the requirement, established in Chapter 1, that separate activities should be supported in a concurrent system and examine how separate activities might be represented in a single program.

7.3.1   Examples

We consider some examples (A–D below) of concurrent systems and attempt to see how they could be programmed as a single concurrent program running above a minimal operating system.

Our first attempt in each case is to use a sequential programming language to program the separate activities involved. We then explore the use of coroutines and language-level processes. An important conclusion that will be drawn is that it is not sufficient to write a concurrent system in a concurrent programming language without knowing how the operating system on which the program is to run supports concurrency.

A A file server is to run on a dedicated uniprocessor machine available to its clients across a network. It takes requests from clients and can be working on a number of requests at the same time. For example, it may need to wait for the disk to be read on behalf of one client, so starts work on behalf of another. Figure 7.4 shows the static modular structure. Refer to Figure 2.13, Chapter 5 and Section 8.1 for background and related information.

B A simple operating system must control a number of devices and a device handling subsystem (Figure 7.5) is to be written in some appropriate programming language. A device handler may finish its immediate task and may need to wait for more data to be input or output. It must not lose track of what it was doing, however. If it was filling a buffer with characters coming

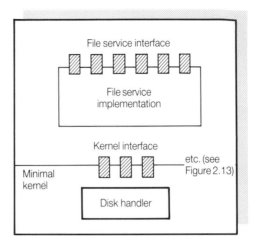

Figure 7.4
A: a dedicated file server.

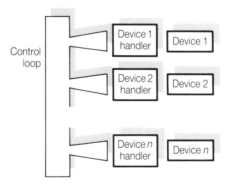

Figure 7.5
B: a device handling subsystem.

in from the network, the buffer and associated counts and pointers should still be there when that device is serviced again.

C Figure 7.6 shows a computerized control system for a chemical plant which carries out periodic data gathering, analysis and feedback, as described in Section 1.1.1. The computer system should also respond to alarm signals which are infrequent and unpredictable, but of very high priority.

D A shared-memory multiprocessor is available and a parallel algorithm is proposed to search for a particular value in a large amount of stored data. Parallel activities should execute code to search a partition of the data, see Section 1.2.1. A management activity is needed to start off the correct number of parallel searches, allocate partitions of the data to them and be ready to receive the result and stop the searches when the result is found.

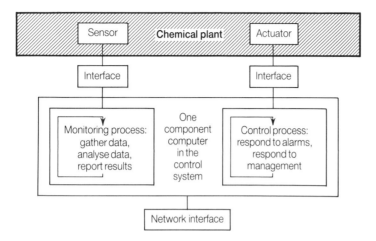

Figure 7.6
C: chemical plant
controller.

7.3.2 Programming a concurrent system in a sequential programming language

Although many procedures may be active at any time, because of nested or recursive calls, there is only one thread of control, one stack and one heap when a program that was written in a sequential programming language is executed (Figure 7.7).

It is therefore difficult, and unnatural, to write independent subsystems (collections of related procedures or modules) within a single program or to manage simultaneous activation of such code on behalf of a number of clients. There is no assistance for implementing a subsystem which may get to a point where it must wait for an event, remember where it got to and resume later (as discussed in Section 6.4). In particular, it is not possible to freeze the runtime stack at some point and go back to it later. There is a single runtime stack which is used on behalf of whatever computation runs when the waiting computation can no longer run.

It would be extremely tedious to attempt to program A, B or C as a single sequential program and D would revert to a sequential algorithm running on a single processor. At any point where a wait was required, state would have to be saved by the programmer and resumed correctly at the appropriate time. There would be no chance of achieving a fast response to events (which C must have) as there is a single thread of control and the operating system sees only one process. If an interrupt occurs, the state of the process is saved, a wake-up waiting is recorded and the process is resumed (Chapter 6). Whatever the desired effect of the interrupt might be within the concurrent program, there is no immediate transfer of control. The program could be written to test from time to time to see which events had happened using a polling system with interrupts disabled or a WAIT(*set of events*) primitive and to transfer control accordingly.

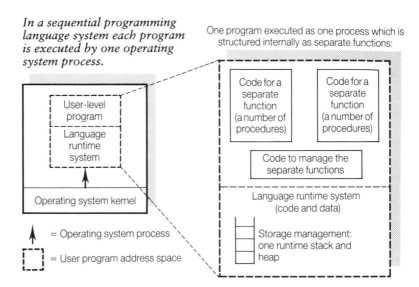

In a sequential programming language system each program is executed by one operating system process.

One program executed as one process which is structured internally as separate functions:

Figure 7.7
Sequential language, separate activities in user-level code.

It would therefore be out of the question to use such a scheme for C (because timing requirements could not be guaranteed to be met) and highly undesirable for A and B, even if they are to run on a uniprocessor.

It would be impossible to exploit a multiprocessor with such a computational model. Since any internal structuring is transparent outside the program and there is only one thread of control it is only suitable for execution as one process on one processor.

In summary, if separate activities are implemented within a single program written in a sequential programming language:

● There is no assistance from the runtime system or the operating system for managing them as separate activities.

● If one activity must be suspended (because it cannot proceed until some event occurs) and another resumed, the user-level code must manage state saving and (later) restoring.

● There is no possibility of making an immediate response to an event by a transfer of control within the user-level code. After an interrupt, control returns to exactly where it was within the process.

7.3.3   Coroutines

Some programming languages, for example Modula-2 and BCPL, provide **coroutines** for expressing independent subprograms within a single program. The motivation for having a single program with internal coroutines is that data can be shared where appropriate but private data is also supported; each coroutine has its own stack. The language provides instructions to create and delete a

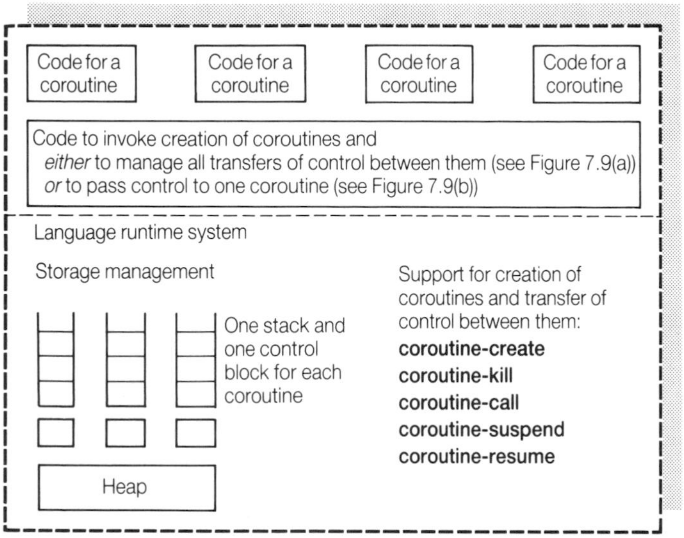

Figure 7.8
Language support
for coroutines.

coroutine and to allow a coroutine to suspend its execution temporarily but retain its state. Control may be passed explicitly from the suspending coroutine to another. Alternatively, control may be returned to the caller of a coroutine when it suspends. Figure 7.8 gives an overview of how coroutines are supported.

When a coroutine activation is created, the name of the associated code module, the start address and the space required for the stack are specified.

co-id := **coroutine-create**(*name, start address, stack size*);

A stack is initialized and a control block is set up for the coroutine activation which holds the stack pointer and the start address. At this stage, the coroutine is in the suspended state at the main procedure entry point. Later, when the coroutine is suspended, the control block will hold the address at which execution will resume. An identifier *co-id* is returned for use in subsequent references to this coroutine activation.

kill(*co-id*)

frees the space occupied by the activation. The coroutine scheme must specify who can execute **kill**. It is likely that suicide is illegal and that one cannot kill a dynamic ancestor. We assume that an **active list** is maintained by the coroutine management system of the dynamic call sequence of coroutines, see below.

At any time at most one of the coroutine activations can be running. Two types of control flow can be used:

call(*co-id*)   % pass control to the activation *co-id* at the address specified in its control block. *co-id* is deemed to be a child of the caller and is added to the active list.

> **suspend**   % pass control back to the parent of this child on the active
> list. Remove the executor of **suspend** from the active list.
>
> **resume** (*co-id*) % remove the executer of **resume** from the active list, pass
> control to the activation *co-id* and add it to the active list.

Figure 7.9 shows these alternatives. Note that to use **call** (*co-id*) repeatedly would cause the active list to grow indefinitely. We assume that **suspend** or **resume** is executed when a coroutine cannot proceed until some condition becomes true. Note that this supension is voluntary; that is, the coroutine executes until **suspend, resume** or another **call**.

We can program example A by creating a coroutine activation for each client of the file server. The same code may be executed for each client and they may share system data but each will have a separate stack for private data. The arrangement of a main loop which decides which coroutine to call, followed by **suspend** in the coroutine (Figure 7.9(a)), is appropriate for this application.

Example B could be programmed using a coroutine scheme. However, there is only one thread of control through the program and the sequence of control is

Figure 7.9
Alternatives for management of transfer of control in a coroutine system.
(a) A parent **calls** coroutines in turn, which pass control back to it by **suspend.**
(b) A parent **calls** a coroutine. This resumes a coroutine at the same level which **replaces** it on the active list.

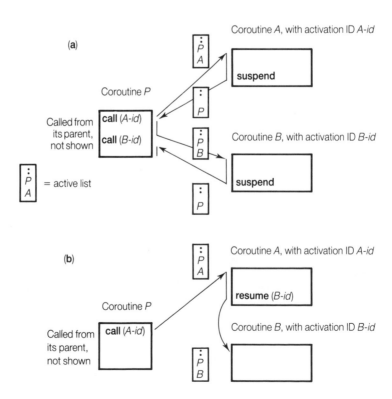

programmed explicitly; that is, the device handlers are called in an order that does not depend on whether they have work they can do. It would therefore be tricky to make sure that a high-priority device was polled from its coroutine often enough relative to a low-priority device, and impossible to respond instantly to any particular device.

An interrupt service routine would be entered automatically (see Section 3.2), but after that we would return to our predefined sequence of control, no matter how high the priority of the interrupt, since the operating system is aware only of one process and not of its internal coroutine structure.

It would therefore be impossible to program the monitoring and control activities of example C using coroutines. The chemical plant might blow up before we tested to see whether an alarm signal came in. The only way to take effective action on an alarm would be for the interrupt service routine to do all the work. This might be appropriate in a crisis situation, but is unsuitable as a general approach for achieving timely response.

A multiprocessor cannot be exploited using coroutines since there is only a single thread of control. D cannot be programmed as a concurrent algorithm to exploit a multiprocessor.

In summary, if separate activities are implemented as coroutines within a single program:

- The runtime system supports creation of coroutine activations, shared and private data and transfer of control between activations.

- The scheduling of the coroutine activations must be implemented in the user-level code. Explicit transfer of control takes place at user level.

- There is a single thread of control. Scheduling of coroutines and execution of coroutines takes place within this single thread.

- There is no possibility of making an immediate response to an event by a transfer of control within the user level code. After an interrupt, control returns to exactly where it was within the process.

- Suspension is voluntary; control stays with a coroutine (except for interrupt and return) until it executes **suspend** or **resume**. It may therefore be assumed that any shared data structure that is accessed by a coroutine is left in a consistent state by it; it cannot be preempted part-way through updating a data structure.

- Transfer of control between coroutine activations involves very little overhead, typically of the order of ten machine instructions. The address for resumption is stored in the control block and the activation list is managed. There is no need to save data.

The Tripos operating system (Richards *et al.*, 1979) was written in BCPL and has a coroutine structure. A filing system (example A) and device handling (example B) were included. Tripos was designed as a single-user system and a single shared address space is used for the operating system and applications.

7.3.4   Processes

Some programming languages, such as Mesa, Concurrent Pascal, Pascal Plus and occam, support processes within a program. Again, as described above for coroutines, a program may be written to contain independent subprograms. Each subprogram is now executed by a separate process as defined by the language system. Like coroutines, each process has its own stack, but unlike coroutines, control is managed by an 'outside agency' and is not programmed explicitly within the subprograms. The outside agency is a process management module within the language runtime system (Figure 7.10).

A process may need to wait for a shared, language-level resource or for another process to complete a related activity. A wait operation is provided and will be implemented as a procedure call to the language runtime system. Another process will then be selected to run.

A major question in system design is the relationship between the language-level processes and the processes known to the operating system. It might be that the operating system can only support one process for one program. In this case the 'process' defined in the concurrent programming language is not a fully fledged operating system process. The (sub)processes within the program are managed internally by the language system which effectively re-implements a process scheduler. The language system is multiplexing one operating system process among subprocesses known only to itself.

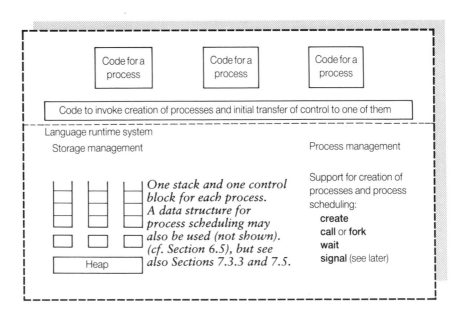

Figure 7.10
Language-level support for processes.

The scheme is similar to a coroutine scheme, but the application programmer does not have to program the transfer of control between the language level processes. Process scheduling is provided by the runtime system.

A problem with this scheme is that if any one of the language-level sub-processes makes a system call to the operating system to do I/O and becomes blocked then no other subprocess in the program can run. Recall that an operating system might only provide system calls for I/O which are synchronous (Section 3.6.2). This is operating system dependent; for example, UNIX system calls are synchronous, IBM MVS calls may be synchronous (in QSAM) or asynchronous (in BSAM). Even if the subprocess were to use the language-level process management module as an intermediary for the purpose of making a system call, a blocking system call made by the manager will still block the whole process. This is a fundamental problem if the operating system sees only one process.

If the subprocesses defined in a program may be made known by the language system to the operating system they become operating system processes (or they may be called **threads** as defined in Section 6.11). They are then scheduled by the operating system to run on processors and may run concurrently on the separate processors of a multiprocessor. Each may make an operating system call and block without affecting any of the others.

The operating system may note the groupings of such language-level processes, that is, their association with an address space. Various terms have been used for these concepts. The terms **lightweight process** and **thread** may be used for what we have above called a language-level subprocess, known to the operating system. The term **process** or **address space** or **domain** may be used to indicate the unit of resource allocation for a related set of threads. An operating system is said to support **multi-threaded processes** if it provides facilities for a process to make its internal threads known. We shall revisit these system issues in Section 7.5 and Chapter 8.

7.3.5 Comparison of concurrency tools for examples A, B, C and D

The issues that have been highlighted in the above discussions are:

1. *Blocking, synchronous calls to the operating system*
   If an operating system provides only synchronous system calls and a concurrent program runs as a single operating system process, then no component of the program can run while the operating system regards the process as blocked.

2. *Response to events*
   An application which does not need rapid response to events may choose to run with interrupts disabled and use a polling system rather than one which is event-driven.

Suppose we are running with interrupts enabled. If a process (which is known to the operating system) is running and an event of interest to it occurs, a record of the event is made (in the process descriptor or an event data structure) and the process is resumed. A response to the event can only be made when a WAIT(*event*) call is made to the operating system.

Suppose a process (known to the operating system) makes a WAIT(*event*) call to the operating system and is blocked, waiting for the event to occur. When the event occurs, rapid response to it can only be achieved if the process is scheduled immediately by the operating system, preempting whatever process was running when the event occurred.

3. *Voluntary suspension and integrity of shared data structures*
   If a coroutine or process can run until until it suspends voluntarily (apart from interrupt and return) then it can be arranged that the shared data structures that it accesses are left in a consistent state before it suspends. A simple way of ensuring data integrity is therefore achieved at the expense of prompt response to events.

A **coroutine** scheme can be used for examples A and B, provided that immediate response to events is not required and that the operating system offers asynchronous (non-blocking) system calls. It would be inadequate for example C, where instant response to an alarm is essential, and for D, which must exploit a multiprocessor by having multiple threads of control that are known to the operating system to achieve speed-up from a concurrent algorithm.

Figure 7.11 shows a coroutine associated with each device and a polling loop in which the coroutines associated with the devices are called in turn and the devices are polled from within the coroutines. Such a scheme could be used with device interrupts disabled. In this case, data could be lost if a device was not polled often enough and a second data item arrived before the first had been detected and transferred from the interface. It can be arranged that the devices with the shortest critical times or the highest throughput are polled more frequently than other devices.

If interrupts are enabled, the interrupt service routine for a device could transfer a small amount of data onto the stack associated with the corresponding coroutine or could set a flag to indicate that a block of data had arrived in memory. A ring of buffers can be exploited by some interfaces (see Section 3.8.3). After execution of the interrupt service routine control returns to the interrupted instruction.

In considering the use of processes, let us first assume that the concurrent program runs as a **single operating system process**. We shall call the language-level processes subprocesses for clarity. For A each client's request is handled by a subprocess which executes the file service code. In B each device handler is a subprocess as shown in Figure 7.12. The way in which the subprocesses might be used is as discussed above for coroutines.

The scheme is inadequate for example C, where instant response to an alarm is essential, and for D which requires the subprocesses to be scheduled to run on

Assuming that a coroutine activation has been created for each device,
a polling loop could be implemented as follows:

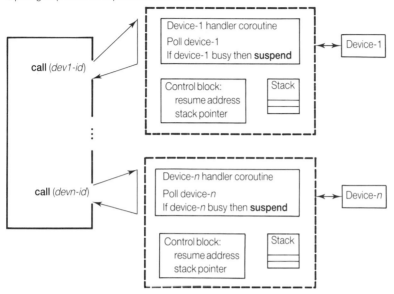

Figure 7.11
Coroutines for a
device handling
subsystem.

Assuming that a process activation has been
created to handle each device, we have:

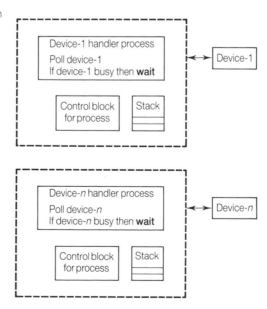

Note that
wait
*passes control
to this module
and is not a
system call to
the operating
system.*

Figure 7.12
Language-level
processes for a
device handling
subsystem.

separate processors of a multiprocessor. The only difference between coroutines and language-level subprocesses is that subprocess scheduling is provided by the language runtime system, whereas coroutine scheduling must be written by the application programmer.

Now let us suppose that the operating system sees each language-level process as a separate process or thread and consider whether C and D can now be programmed. The parallel search activities of D can be programmed as processes which may run on separate processors. For C we have further requirements on the operating system. Suppose the data gathering process is running. An interrupt arrives to indicate that an alarm condition has developed; the interrupt service routine passes control to the process manager to change the state of the control process from waiting to runnable. It is a high-priority process and therefore should run immediately, preempting the data gathering and analysis. The operating system must support this.

The process scheduling policy of the operating system is therefore crucial. If the scheduling algorithm is **non-preemptive** a process may continue to run until it blocks. Even if an interrupt occurs and the corresponding interrupt service routine is executed, control passes back to the interrupted process. The process scheduling algorithm is only invoked when the current process blocks, in spite of the fact that a high-priority process may have been made runnable. It might be the case that the requirements of A and B could be met with non-preemptive scheduling, but it is essential to have **preemptive process scheduling** for C, as described in Section 6.6. Even this may not be sufficient for implementing real-time systems in general. Approaches to scheduling for real-time systems were introduced in Section 6.7.

Two further points should be made concerning the use of an operating system process (or thread) for each language system (sub)process:

- There is more overhead on a switch, even between threads of the same process, if the operating system is involved. We saw that a switch between coroutines or between language-level processes involves very little overhead. A switch between processes known to the operating system involves an entry into the operating system, and the saving of state such as the contents of processor registers (see Section 6.3.1).

- We can no longer make the assumption that data structures are in a consistent state on a process switch. The concurrent program might run on a multiprocessor, in which case separate processes might access shared data structures at the same time. If the concurrent program runs on a uniprocessor the same problem arises if we have preemptive scheduling.

We have deliberately considered examples of concurrent systems which have a wide range of requirements. We have taken a general model that an application written in a concurrent programming language might be expected to run on some minimal operating system and have seen the requirements on the operating system.

7.4 Implementation of processes in language systems

7.4.1 Specification, creation and suicide of processes

In some languages a special kind of procedure call indicates that a new process should be created to execute the call and should run in parallel with the caller, sharing the address space of the caller. The modular software specification does not indicate which modules will be executed in parallel. Processes are created dynamically to execute the modules of the system. Mesa, Modula-3 and CCLU (see Chapter 14) follow this style.

Figure 7.13 shows an example of syntax that may be used to create a process to perform a specific function, after which it is deleted: FORK, for procedure call with process creation, and JOIN, for child process deletion and return. Note that the parent and child will need to synchronize at JOIN; that is, one will get there first and must be able to wait for the other. In some cases the child process will need to pass the results of its work to its parent and the parent may need to interact with the child. How this is done is the subject matter of Chapters 9 and 10. This use of FORK should not be confused with the UNIX **fork** system call which causes a new process, with its own separate address space, to be created by the operating system.

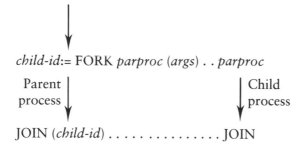

$child\text{-}id$:= FORK $parproc$ $(args)$ . . $parproc$

Parent process
Child process

JOIN ($child\text{-}id$) . . . . JOIN

Figure 7.13
Process creation and termination using FORK and JOIN.

An alternative approach to achieve process creation is to allow a new kind of module to be declared as a process; that is, a process is defined as a syntactic unit in a program. For example, a device driver for devices of a particular type might be programmed in general and specific device drivers for specific devices created as process activations.

process *iodriver (dev:device, buffer-size:integer)*
% a routine to transfer characters to the device from a buffer on output
% a routine to transfer characters from the device to a buffer on input
. . .
end *iodriver* % this specifies a general device driver

We now need to set up a separate process for each device. We assume in this example that this is done at system initialization, that the processes will run indefinitely and are not managed by their creator; a *process-id* is not returned. Process creation is achieved here by what looks like a normal procedure call to the process module. For example:

iodriver (*dev1*, 1000)   % this creates a device handler process for *dev1*
iodriver (*dev2*, 50)   % this creates a device handler process for *dev2*

We now have two device driver processes, each with its own stack and input parameters specifying the name of the device to be handled and a buffer count for data input or output. The processes are created and are candidates for scheduling. When control is passed to such a process it runs from its start address.

A more general scheme, allowing for process management through use of the process identifier, might be as follows:

p1-id := **process-create** (*iodriver, dev1*, 1000)   % to create a device handler
                                 process for *dev1*

p2-id := **process-create** (*iodriver, dev2*, 50)   % to create a device handler
                                 process for *dev2*

Subsequent calls may make use of the returned process id. For example:

kill (*p1-id*)
signal (*p2-id*)

Languages may allow **dynamic process creation** at runtime as in the examples above. The first approach allowed dynamic creation and removal of processes; the second showed specification of a process in a program with dynamic instantiations of it at runtime.

A language system may insist on knowing the number of processes that will run in a given program and may create them statically. occam is an example (Inmos, 1984).

A general classification of styles of concurrent program is that modules may be passive and processes may call procedures to execute the module code, as in the first example above, or modules may be active and have permanent, internally bound processes, as in the second example above. We shall explore these alternative structures throughout Part II.

7.4.2 Parental control of processes

A design issue is the degree of control or influence a creator (parent) process should have over a process it creates (child). Once a process is created it is likely to be independent of its parent for scheduling purposes and may be able to outlive its parent. If a *child-process-id* is returned when a process activation is created, this can be used to control the process.

If the system has the notion of process **priority** then it is necessary to indicate the priority of a process when it is created. Obviously, safeguards are needed if this is in the hands of normal users and the priority specified is likely to be relative to that of the creator and its other children. The implementor of a concurrent system will have a view of the relative priorities of its component processes.

We have seen in Section 7.4.1 that it might be appropriate for a process to **commit suicide** on completion of its work and for its parent to receive the results of the work. It might also be necessary or desirable in certain circumstances to **kill** a running process. A debugging process may detect that the system being debugged is acting erroneously and its execution should be terminated. A command interpreter process which has loaded a program and has created a process to execute it may detect, or be told by the operating system, that an error state has arisen in its child; or the human user that started a program execution may abort it. In example D above, a number of processes are searching for a single solution to a problem. As soon as one of them finds the solution all the others should be terminated. There is therefore a general need for external control of running processes, and a mechanism to achieve this should be provided.

Processes known to the operating system can be controlled. The interrupt mechanism starts the removal of control from a running process. For example, a break character typed by the user may be interpreted as a command to abort the current user program execution. The act of typing the character forces an interrupt service and the break character indicates that the process associated with that user should not be restarted from where it was interrupted but should be aborted. In the case of example D an inter-processor interrupt (see Section 3.4) is needed to achieve immediate termination of the searching processes once the result is found.

For language-level processes which are not known to the operating system, external control of running processes is more difficult. Each process may need to be programmed to 'check in' with a manager periodically so that it can be stopped.

A universal requirement is the ability to **synchronize** with a created process. The process was created to do work in parallel with the creator. Mechanisms for finding out that the work has been done and for acquiring the results of it are needed. It is often necessary to combine the partial solutions to a problem that have been obtained by parallel processes, for example. This is part of a more general requirement discussed throughout Part II.

7.4.3   Exception handling in programming languages

User-level exception handling was introduced in Section 3.3.5. The idea was that error handling routines which output error messages to the user or write them to a log should run in the context of the program causing the error rather than as part of the operating system. We saw that a compiler could pass not only the start address of a program to the operating system but also the address of an exception handling routine. In Section 6.3.1 we saw that the process descriptor could contain such an address.

As well as error routines, typically provided as part of a library, the application may name exceptions and provide handlers for them. This is another means by which transfer of control from one part of a program to another can be achieved as a result of the occurrence of some event or condition. Some programming languages offer an extensive exception handling facility. Examples are CLU (Liskov *et al.*, 1981) and Modula-3.

7.4.4   Storage allocation for language-level processes

Section 7.3.4 discussed language-level processes and Figure 7.10 gave a simple representation of a process management module within the language system and a stack associated with every process. We assume that the concurrent program runs in a single address space and that instead of a single 'run-time stack' we now have a number of stacks.

In a system with a storage allocation model, such as that shown in Figure 7.1, it is likely that the process stacks will be allocated in the stack segment and that all processes will share the heap segment. The convenience of an easily extensible single stack growing towards a heap, as used for a sequential program implementation, has been lost with this arrangement. An alternative is to use the heap for the process stacks. In every case a maximum stack size will need to be specified explicitly (or implicitly as a default value) on process creation. If this size is exceeded because of a greater depth of procedure call nesting than foreseen, the multiple stack data structure will have to be adjusted or a new, larger stack allocated for that process in the heap.

Language-level storage allocation schemes will not be studied in depth in this book and for more information the reader should consult, for example, Aho *et al.*, (1986).

7.5   Operating system and language system processes: summary

Section 7.1 outlined the state associated with a process in a language system environment. When a sequential programming language is used, one language system process is managed as one operating system process (Figure 7.14(a)). When a concurrent programming language is used the programmer, explicitly or implicitly, may set up a number of concurrent processes (Figure 7.14(b), (c)). If these may be made known to the operating system, through a system call, we have the situation shown in Figure 7.14(c). We saw in Section 6.11 that modern operating systems are likely to support threads as well as processes, that is, **multi-threaded processes**. Processes are then the unit of resource allocation and threads the unit of scheduling.

In summary, the programs indicated in Figure 7.14(a), (b) and (c) will run as operating system processes, each in a separate address space. We then have two separate concepts: language-level subprocesses that are not known to the operating system, and language-level subprocesses that are also known to the operating system.

Unfortunately, a standard terminology does not exist which distinguishes between them. The same terms 'thread' and 'lightweight process' are used for both concepts. We shall attempt always to be specific about whether the language-level subprocesses are or are not known to the operating system.

Each language-level process must have a separate stack; in some implementations they may share the heap storage area and may share some data structures in the heap. The stacks and heap are concerns only of the language system.

If the language-level subprocesses are known to the operating system, they are scheduled independently and can WAIT for synchronous I/O separately. While one blocks, waiting for I/O, another thread of the same process can run. This is essential if the concurrent program is to run on a multiprocessor.

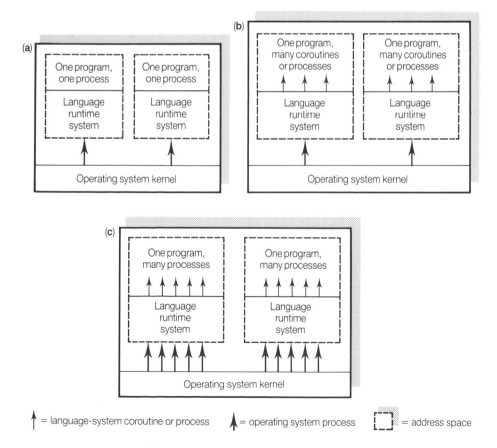

Figure 7.14
Implementation of concurrent processes.
(a) Sequential programming language.
(b) Concurrent programming language without operating system support.
(c) Concurrent programming languages with operating system support for internal processes.

For a real-time system to be able to make timing guarantees it is certainly necessary for threads to be scheduled preemptively and it may, in addition, be necessary for special priority-based or deadline-based scheduling to be used (see Section 6.8).

When implementing a concurrent system in a concurrent programming language it is necessary to know about the operating system and hardware on which the system will run. Specific points are summarized below.

 ## 7.6 Summary of Part I

In Chapter 1 we established the requirements for implementing concurrent systems:

1. support for separate activities;
2. support for the management of separate activities;
3. support for related activities to work together;
4. the ability to meet timing requirements;
5. support for composite tasks.

At this stage the reader should understand:

- the concept of process;
- how the process abstraction is supported by language systems and operating systems;
- the relationship between these process implementations and the implications of this relationship.

The requirement to support separate activities (1) has therefore been explored in detail. The reader should now be able to think of a software implementation of a concurrent system as a set of concurrent processes.

The requirement for the management of separate activities (2) has been discussed. We have seen how a process activation may be created from a process specification. We have discussed the need for process termination through suicide or murder.

The support for the related activities to work together in a concurrent system (3) has been motivated, but has yet to be addressed systematically. We have seen that a coroutine, or language-level process, scheme may allow simplifying assumptions to be made about the consistency of shared data structures on a coroutine or process switch. This also holds for processes managed by the operating system when they are scheduled non-preemptively, but only if the system runs on a uniprocessor. We discuss the problem in general in Part II.

The ability of a concurrent system to meet timing requirements (4) must obviously depend on hardware characteristics. It has been shown that this ability also depends on the support for concurrency provided by the operating system. If this basic level of support is not given, a real-time system cannot be programmed in a language system. It is therefore necessary to know whether the operating system schedules its processes preemptively. If not, critical timing requirements cannot be guaranteed to be met. Preemptive scheduling is a necessary condition for timing guarantees to be met, but is by no means sufficient. Scheduling algorithms were discussed in Chapter 6, both for general-purpose and for real-time systems.

We have explored the options for implementing concurrent systems. Either components are written in sequential programming languages and system calls are provided to support their interaction or a concurrent programming language is used.

In the former case there is a potential portability problem. Concurrent systems developed in this way can only run on operating systems which have compatible system calls for this purpose. Standard library packages have been developed to provide a convenient interface for some programming languages on some operating systems.

In the latter case we have examined the possible relationship between the processes (or coroutines) specified in a concurrent programming language and the processes supported by the operating system. This was shown to be operating system dependent.

The overhead involved in switching between the separate activities of a concurrent system should be taken into account. This is lowest for coroutines and language-level processes, highest for operating system (heavyweight) processes (each of which has a separate address space), and intermediate for switching between threads (known to the operating system) of the same process.

An important issue emerges from the discussion in this chapter. Even if a concurrent system is to be written in a high-level language it is necessary to have knowledge of:

- the relationship between the language system and the operating system;

- details of the operating system support for processes;

- some aspects of the hardware on which the system will run; for example, is it a uniprocessor or a multiprocessor?

Exercises

7.1 What aspects of the state of a process are of concern to an operating system and a language system?

7.2 Discuss how a sequential programming language can be used to implement a concurrent system. What assistance would you expect from a library package and operating system? What are the advantages and disadvantages of using a concurrent programming language?

7.3 What is the essential difference between coroutines and processes? If a concurrent program is to run on a uniprocessor machine, what advantages are there in using a language which supports processes? When might coroutines offer an advantage?

7.4 What are the potential problems of using a language-level 'threads package' when the operating system sees only one process? Why might such a scheme be inappropriate for a shared-memory multiprocessor?

7.5 What are essential requirements for real-time response to be achieved?

7.6 (a) What is meant by a static specification of processes in a programming language?
(b) How would you expect a static approach to be reflected in the syntax of a language?
(c) How can dynamic process creation and deletion be supported in a concurrent programming language?
(d) How might a parent process determine properties of a child process it creates, such as its name or identifier?
(e) How might a parent process be given control over a child process once it has been created?

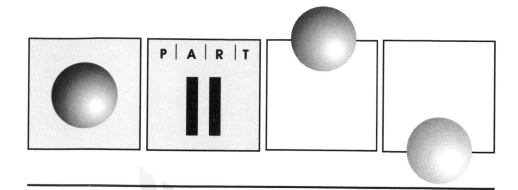

Single concurrent actions

CHAPTERS

In Chapter 1 requirements for implementing concurrent systems were established, among which were:

1. Support for distinct activities
2. Support for management of these activities
3. Support for correct interaction between these activities

We have already seen how the first requirement above can be met. Chapter 6 showed how independent activities are supported as operating system processes. If only coarse-grained concurrency is required it might be sufficient for the operating system to support synchronization and sharing of information between processes; a sequential language might be augmented by a number of system calls for this purpose. The problem is that the same system calls might not be available on another operating system. Chapter 7 showed how separate activities might be programmed and supported in a high-level language system. If concurrent processes in a language system are to be more than just a structuring convenience it is necessary for the operating system to support multi-threaded processes (see Section 7.5).

As discussed in Section 2.3, a software system may be described in terms of its functional modules and their interfaces. When we wish to understand its dynamic behaviour we need a model for how the operations of the modules are executed by processes. The set of concurrent processes which comprise a concurrent system cannot be assumed to exist in steady state. We have to consider where they should be placed, how they come into being, how their execution is started and stopped and how and when they are deleted; this is requirement 2 above. In Chapter 7 we saw alternative mechanisms that might be provided in concurrent programming languages to achieve process creation and deletion. We now go on to explore how these mechanisms can be used.

A concurrent system may be considered as a set of concurrent processes. If the processes are unrelated and never need to interact in any way our problems are over. More typically, the processes need to work together to achieve the goal of the concurrent system: partial solutions to a problem, generated by distinct processes, may need to be combined or a user process may need to request service from a system process. Support for interaction between processes is invariably required. Part II addresses this requirement in detail.

It is helpful to define a framework for considering the problems that can occur when processes execute concurrently. This allows the subject to be presented as simply as possible and in a coherent order. We first study how a 'single action', carried out by a process, can complete correctly without interference from the activities of any other concurrent process.

The notion of a single operation is informal and may be related to the modular structure of systems. A process can read or write a single word of memory without fear of interference from any other process since such a read or write is made indivisible by the hardware. In practice, a programming language variable or a useful data abstraction, such as an array, list or record, cannot be read or written in a single hardware operation. It is the access to such shared abstractions by concurrent processes that is the main concern of Part II; the discussion focuses on the execution of a single operation on a single data abstraction.

First, Chapter 8 establishes a context for this detailed study by taking a high-level view of the software structure of systems. A broad classification can be based on whether processes execute in memory which they share with other processes: in particular, whether shared data objects can be invoked. Alternatively, each process may execute in a separate address space, disjoint from that of all other processes or perhaps sharing only immutable code. In this case, processes must cooperate without the benefit of directly addressable shared data objects. The need for both styles of system is justified by a number of examples.

The model of computation underlying Chapters 9 through 12 is that a concurrent program is loaded, proceeds to execute, and builds up state in main memory. The concurrent operations we consider are on data objects in main memory and we do not, at this stage, focus on persistent data that is independent of any running program. At the end of Part II we extend the discussion to consider concurrent invocations of a single operation on persistent data. In this case it is necessary to consider system crashes in which main memory is lost: the concern of Chapter 13.

In Chapter 14 the issues which are peculiar to distributed systems are introduced: parts of a distributed computation may fail independently and there is no global, system wide, common value for time. We again restrict the discussion to the invocation of a single operation on one computer from another.

System structure

8

CONTENTS

In Chapter 4 the concept of the virtual address space of a process was introduced and we saw how virtual addresses are mapped onto physical addresses. We also saw that the virtual address space of a process may be divided into segments and that it may be possible for a given segment to be shared by many processes. It is straightforward for the code of a compiler, for example, to be shared by any number of processes while each sharer has a private data segment. We are concerned here with **shared data**.

An important distinction to be made in Part II is whether the processes being considered in a given interaction can access shared data objects directly. They may share an entire address space, and can therefore make use of shared data, as we saw in Chapter 7. They may execute in separate but segmented address spaces in which segments may be shared. If data segments can be shared by processes, again we need to consider how processes should access shared data objects.

If the processes' address spaces are completely disjoint, for example on separate machines, or are such that they cannot share data segments, we must consider how processes can share information without having access to shared data objects. Examples are now given to illustrate that both arrangements have their place in system design.

The concurrent system designer has to decide how to use processes, how many to use and where to place them. Some alternative design possibilities are examined. After this system context is established we go on to explore the support required for process interactions.

8.1   Processes sharing an address space

A file management system might be provided as a subsystem within an operating system for a centralized time-sharing system or a personal workstation. Alternatively, it might run in a dedicated file server machine across a network from its clients. Details of file service functions were given in Chapter 5, and Chapter 7 considered this example in the context of a concurrent programming language.

Examples of possible clients of a file service are: an application process requiring to read or write a data file; a command interpreter, acting in response to a user's command to run a program, initiating its loading into memory from the file store; or a compiler creating an object code file.

We assume that the module which is to implement the service has an interface which offers operations such as **open** a file for reading or writing or **read** or **write** part of an open file, etc.

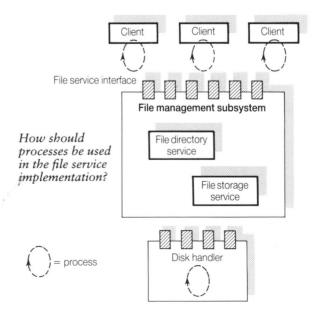

How should processes be used in the file service implementation?

Figure 8.1
A subsystem showing modular structure.

We can envisage a structure as shown in Figure 8.1 with the following components:

- clients of the service;
- a module concerned with looking up the names of files and checking whether the client making the request is in fact authorized to use the file in the way requested – the **file directory service**;
- a module concerned with locating the required piece of the file on disk, or perhaps in a buffer in main memory if there have already been some operations to read data from the file – the **file storage service**;
- a module concerned with handling the disk and with synchronizing with disk interrupts.

Recall that there is a great deal of system data recording the location of files and free storage on disk and the transactions in progress in main memory (the filing system's metadata). We assume that system data in main memory is available as shared data structures to any process which executes the file system code.

8.1.1   Placement of processes within the subsystem

As discussed in Chapter 6 it is natural to place a dedicated process in the disk-handling module. It is natural to place a process (at least one) with each client. The question of interest here is how processes should be located in the intermediate module offering the directory and file storage service. There are a number of options.

1. Use no processes at all. Allow the client processes to enter the service module by calling procedures. Note that if more than one client at once enters the module, problems could occur when they read and write shared system data (see Section 8.7.1). This is the essence of the problem to be solved in Chapters 9 and 10.

2. Use a single file manager process which takes one request for service at a time from a queue of messages. Suppose this process starts to work on behalf of one client. All other clients' requests have to wait until the file manager gets around to them. This is a wholly inappropriate arrangement for a multiprocessor. Even on a uniprocessor the file manager might find that serving one client involved a delay while waiting for data to be retrieved from disk. It would not be a good idea to keep all the other clients waiting while the (electromechanical) disk rotated. It would be better to start work in parallel on behalf of another client. To do this within a single process it would be necessary to keep track of where it had got to with client 1 while beginning to service client 2. This would effectively re-implement process management and create a multi-threaded server process.

3. Associate a set of dedicated processes with the module. The number could be chosen to reflect the number of processors available or some arbitrary, soft

limit. A sensible arrangement would be to have an interface, or listener, process and a set of worker processes to carry out requests. The job of the interface process is to take new requests, one at a time, from a queue of messages requesting service, and to assign a worker process for each. This should be done as quickly as possible so as to free the interface process for handling the next request. The set of worker processes need to share an address space in order to share file system data. This may lead to problems as mentioned in (1) above.

4. Initially, a single process is associated with the module and listens for a request. When one arrives it creates a new process to listen in its place, carries out the request and then commits suicide. It might be necessary to limit the number of processes that are created and delay some incoming requests. Again, the processes need to share an address space.

We have argued the need for simultaneous execution of the file service code by many processes. Such processes need to access common data structures associated with the file service as well as private data of relevance only to one specific client. The most suitable arrangement is that the processes share an address space. Whether processes enter the (passive) service module by calling the interface procedures or whether there are internally bound processes is a question of system design style. The trade-offs are discussed later.

8.2 Processes in separate address spaces or with shared code segments

In many systems there is a requirement for memory protection. In a multi-user system one user must not be allowed to write to or read from another user's memory indiscriminately. Also, in a multi-user system any corruption of the system software affects all users and not just the culprit and there is therefore a stronger protection requirement than in a single-user system. To satisfy this protection requirement it must be possible to control the access a process has to memory, in particular, to be able to prevent write access.

Let us first consider a process running in an address space that is disjoint from that of any other process; that is, it shares no code or data with any other process. Such a process can only fetch and execute an instruction or read or write a data operand from its own address space. This is the case if processes run on separate machines in a distributed system. It may also be arranged in a shared system, if memory protection hardware is available.

Let us now suppose that memory protection hardware supports a segmented address space and that certain code segments (such as compilers or editors, as shown in Section 2.2.1) can have 'execute only' access enforced; that is, any attempt to read or write an address in the segment would cause a protection error. The segment is protected from corruption and it can therefore be shared by many processes. To achieve this sharing the segment must be in each sharer's virtual address space and be mapped onto the same pages of physical memory for each of them. The mechanism is a system convenience to avoid wasting memory on multiple copies of identical, immutable code and is irrelevant to any consideration of a process at an abstract level. We shall consider processes which share user-level code in this way as effectively running in separate address spaces. The issue is whether it is possible for processes to share writeable data segments.

It could be argued that only system code will run in a dedicated server machine, such as a file server, and there is therefore no strong requirement for protection. However, any software may have bugs and memory protection may be useful for containing their effects. The idea is to confine an erroneous process to its own address space by using memory relocation and protection hardware. An error in the communications system should not be able to corrupt the file system, for example. There is no need for communications processes and file server processes to have access to each others' data structures and enforcing this separation by hardware can trap an error before its effects spread around the whole system. We have to pay for protection of this kind by not being able to share memory when it would be convenient, for example, when data read from a file has to be transferred across the network. We shall see how this problem is solved in Chapter 12 and in the case studies in Part IV.

As mentioned above, an example of processes occupying separate address spaces is when they run on different machines. In this case any communication between them takes place across the network via network hardware interfaces. We assume that a network (device) handler process will be allocated to synchronize with data arriving via the network interface. The network handler will alert a higher-level process that data has been transmitted. As discussed in Chapter 3, we have synchronization between the low-level and high-level communications software and exchange of data by means of a shared buffer.

When a request to synchronize with some local process arrives from a process across the network, a system process implementing a communications protocol will decode the request and decide which local process to signal. We have therefore reduced synchronization between processes on separate machines to synchronization between local processes.

8.3   Shared data segments

Memory segmentation schemes often allow only code segments to be shared at user level, as discussed above. We now consider briefly both shared data segments at user level and arrangements for sharing the entire operating system kernel.

The most general segmentation scheme allows many segments per process with arbitrary sharing. With such a scheme it would be possible for some data areas to be shared (for example, shared system tables and communication areas), but others to be private (for example, work space for a single client). This generality of sharing was a design aim of some early systems such as Multics (Saltzer, 1974), but recent systems have tended to be more restricted.

In Part II we are concerned with the problems that can arise when data is shared directly in memory by concurrent processes and with the arrangements that must be made for sharing information when there is no shared memory.

8.3.1   Sharing the operating system

In order that a process can easily make system calls to request system services, it is often arranged that the operating system code and data occupy the same part of every process's address space, typically one half of it. UNIX is structured in this way, as shown in Figure 8.2. When a process is executing in user mode it may be separate from all other processes (as in UNIX). When it requests system service by calling a system call procedure it enters a region which is shared with all other processes. Operating system code accesses shared operating system data. When concurrent processes access shared data the problems of interference mentioned in Section 8.1.1 can arise.

8.3.2   An example of support for sharing the operating system: MIPS R2000/3000

Figure 8.3 shows the arrangement of the virtual address space of the MIPS R2000/3000. Half the virtual address space is for user code and data, half for the operating system. Much of the operating system must be resident in memory, that is, it must not be swapped out to backing store and need never be moved around in memory once loaded. It is possible to make these parts of the operating system directly mapped onto physical memory, thus avoiding the need for address translation for references to them. The address translation table is a scarce resource since it has room for only 64 entries (see Section 4.11), and this is a good way of conserving it. There is also provision for some parts of the operating system not to be cached. This is for memory-mapped I/O and data areas used by DMA devices (see Section 3.2).

As discussed in Chapter 4 and above in Section 8.2, if a system supports segmentation it is possible to arrange for arbitrary segments of user-level code or data to be shared. It is common for code to be shared, for example, editors, compilers and libraries. It is less common for a system design to allow data segments to be shared, even if the hardware makes it possible. Figure 8.2 shows the

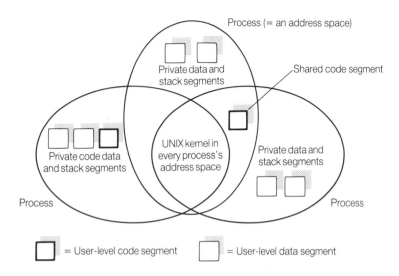

Figure 8.2
UNIX structure.

original UNIX design with three segments at user level, one for code (the text segment) and two for data. Although the text segment could be shared, it was not possible to share any data areas. Some recent versions of UNIX support shared data (see Chapter 21).

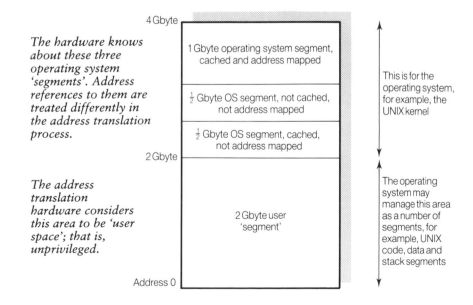

The hardware knows about these three operating system 'segments'. Address references to them are treated differently in the address translation process.

The address translation hardware considers this area to be 'user space'; that is, unprivileged.

Figure 8.3
MIPS R2000/3000 virtual address space.

8.4 Summary of process placement in the two models

The above sections have discussed the placement of processes in relation to system structure. Figure 8.4 (a), (b) and (c) illustrates these cases.

Some fundamental points are:

- Processes (often called threads in this context) may share the same address space, as described in Section 8.1 above and illustrated in Figure 8.4(a). Here we have a multi-threaded process (recall Section 6.11). The process is the unit of resource allocation and threads are the unit of execution and scheduling and the active entities which need to communicate.

- Processes may run in separate address spaces on the same machine: see Section 8.2 and Figure 8.4(b). Here we have a heavyweight process model where the process is both the unit of resource allocation and the unit of scheduling and execution.

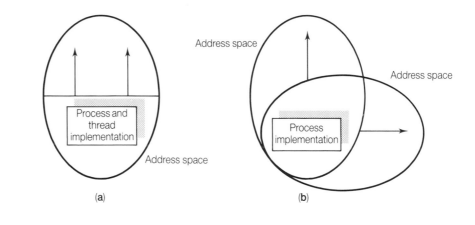

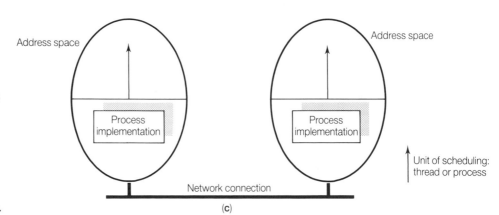

Figure 8.4
Process placement within systems.
(a) Many processes (threads) per address space.
(b) One process per address space, same machine.
(c) One process per address space, separate machines.

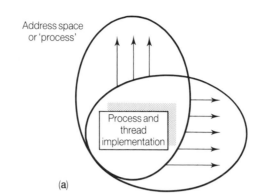

↑ Unit of scheduling:
  thread or 'lightweight'
  process

*Here we see processes
sharing a single address space.
Recall from Section 6.11 that
alternative terminology is
'multi-threaded process' or
'multi-threaded tasks'
if these processes are known
to the operating system.*

(a)

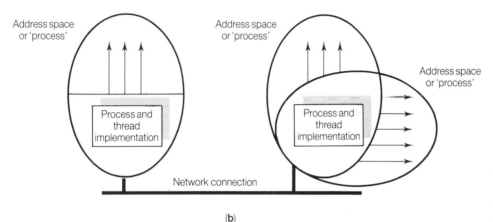

(b)

Figure 8.5
Multi-threaded
processes within
systems.

• User processes may run in separate address spaces on the same machine. System processes on this machine may share an address space. It might be that user processes become system processes when they make system calls and enter the operating system: see Section 8.3 and Figure 8.4(b).

• Processes may run in separate address spaces on different machines; see Section 8.2 and Figure 8.4(c).

To complete the picture, it should be pointed out that a thread of one multi-threaded processes may need to be aware of and interact with a thread of another multi-threaded process, as shown in Figure 8.5.

To avoid confusion in terminology we shall continue to discuss **inter-process communication (IPC)** throughout Part II. In systems where threads are the active entities, scheduled by the operating system, it would be more correct to use the term **inter-thread communication**.

8.5 Requirements for process interaction

Bearing these structural points on process placement in mind we now look in more detail at why processes might need to interact and how their interactions might be supported in a system.

1. *Processes may need to **cooperate** to carry out some task*

   Specifically, one process may need to **make a request** for service of some other process and eventually may **wait** for the service to be done. An example from Section 8.1 is a request from a process in the file management module to a disk-handler process to read the disk and to wait for the required data to be available in memory before proceeding.

   We have already seen in Section 3.2 that the disk handler process synchronizes with the disk in a similar way. It issues the commands which cause the required section of the disk to be read into memory, then waits for the DMA transfer to finish. The hardware signals an interrupt when this has happened and the process control module changes the state of the disk handler from blocked to runnable as a result. We have studied synchronization between a process and the hardware; we now have a requirement for synchronization between processes.

   It may also arise that one process reaches a point where it must ensure that some other process has carried out a certain task before continuing, for example, that one process has written some data to a file before another process can process it. An example occurs in a pipeline of processes, such as the pipelined compiler shown in Section 1.2. Each processing phase must wait for the previous phase to complete. Another example is that the process requesting I/O must synchronize with and share buffer space with a process handling device I/O, as shown in Section 3.6.

   We are seeing a general requirement for **synchronization**. A process may need to **WAIT** in order to synchronize with some other process, just as a process may need to **WAIT** to synchronize with the hardware.

   There is also the associated requirement for **sending a request** or **signalling** that some task has been carried out. When one process **WAITs**, something should, in due course, cause it to proceed again.

   In summary, cooperating processes need to synchronize with each other and to do this need to be able to WAIT for each other and SIGNAL to each other.

   This basic requirement is independent of whether they share the same address space.

2. *Processes may **compete** for exclusive use of services or resources*

   Many clients may make simultaneous requests for some service; several processes may attempt to use a resource at the same time. The system implementation must manage this competition; order must be imposed, making the processes take turns, waiting where necessary, and a choice must be made

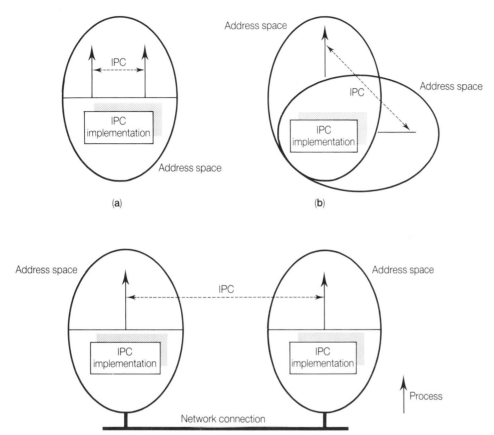

Figure 8.6
Inter-process
communication
(IPC) and its
implementation.

between processes making simultaneous demands for resources which must
be used serially.

*Competing processes need to WAIT to acquire a shared resource and need
to be able to SIGNAL to indicate that they have finished with the resource.*

Support for process interaction

Figure 8.6 shows interacting processes, and the implementation of support for
the interactions, in some of the process placement diagrams. The term inter-
process communication (IPC) is used in the figure to include the types of interaction discussed above. We now consider process interactions in more detail.

8.6   Types of process interaction

We have seen how to implement a concurrent system as a set of concurrent processes and have seen a system context for the placement of processes. We have established a requirement for processes to interact in order to cooperate together or compete for resources in order to meet the design goals of the concurrent system.

We now focus on what is interacting with what. There was an implicit assumption that two processes were involved in the interactions described in Section 8.5. If we examine the interactions more closely, we see that in some cases, specific processes are involved in an interaction. An example is a pipeline of processes (see Section 1.2) in which a given process will always need to synchronize with the same processes, those preceding and succeeding it in the pipeline. It may know their **names** in advance and happily WAIT for or SIGNAL to the appropriate process. In other cases a process may have no idea in advance which processes will require to interact with it and therefore cannot synchronize with specific, named processes.

A general classification of process interaction is described below.

One to one

The type of system in which this arrangement is appropriate is one which has a **static configuration** of interactions between individual processes. A process control system where a process reads a sensor or controls an actuator associated with the physical environment is likely to fit this model. These processes send their data to or receive commands from other known management processes. A pipeline structure is another example. The interactions which will take place are known in advance; in particular, the **names** of the processes involved are known.

Any to one

The most common example of this type of interaction is multiple clients of a single server. In this case a server process offering the service will accept a request from any potential client process. In a given interaction one client invokes one (possibly well-known) server. The server cannot know which potential client will next invoke it and needs to be able to WAIT for 'anyone' to make a request.

The ability for a system to support this style of interaction in general requires a naming problem to be solved. This is relatively easy for well-known system services; the server process name can be made known in advance to all clients. We shall see how the general problem might be solved in Chapter 14.

One to many

This style of communication may be used to notify a set of interested parties that an event has occurred. The term **broadcast** is used if a communication is sent out to 'everyone' and there is usually no record of who has and who has not received it.

A **multicast** implies that a communication is sent to a specific set of recipients. There may (in a reliable multicast) or may not (in an unreliable multicast) be an indication as to whether each individual has received it. In this case the interaction is genuinely 'one to many'.

It might be that the system does not support multicast directly and forces the one to many interaction to be implemented as a series of one to one interactions. This could be very slow if a response from a recipient had to be received before the next one to one communication could be made. Protocols have been developed to avoid this cost.

Again, naming is relevant to a discussion of multicast. At the level at which processes are interacting, a group name might be supported to indicate a list of individuals. An example of a slow version of this style of interaction is sending an electronic mail message to a distribution list. In this case the system guarantees to buffer the message until it can be delivered to its recipients.

One to many communication may also be used in fault-tolerant systems where a given task must be carried out by more than one process; for example, three processes might compute a result and vote on its value. If one process fails, the other two can still agree on the result.

Any to (one of) many

A given service might be provided by a number of anonymous processes. A client needs to request service from any free service process rather than one particular named process. The servers may execute shared service code and data concurrently, as in some of the schemes described in Section 8.1.1, or may run on separate computers in a computer network.

This communication pattern is included for completeness, but it may in practice be reduced to the cases already discussed. The problem may be solved as a naming problem; the required server may be selected by a name lookup (see Chapter 14). Alternatively, a multicast protocol may be used first to request the service. One responding server is selected and we then have one to one communication.

Many to many via shared data

Finally, as we have seen in Section 8.1, processes may be able to share writeable data. Any number of processes can communicate through a shared data structure.

We shall bear these broad categories in mind in subsequent chapters, although many refinements and alternative methods of implementation exist for each type of interaction.

8.7 A process interaction

We now consider the interactions between processes in more detail, bearing in mind the broad categories of cooperation and competition and the architectural distinction of shared data and no shared data.

8.7.1 Problems when processes share data in memory

If processes share an address space, the system designer may make use of shared data objects to effect cooperation or manage competition for resources. If shared data objects can be written as well as read by concurrent processes, problems can arise.

Consider an airline booking system, for example. The database of flight bookings will be held on disk, but read into main memory for reading and update. Let us consider the data in main memory. Suppose that the seats of a particular flight are marked as free or booked and that each process, acting on behalf of a client, has to find a free seat and book it. If the concurrent processes run on a multiprocessor, or if preemptive scheduling is used, two processes could find the same seat free at the same time and both could proceed to mark it as booked. The problem arises from uncontrolled concurrent access to shared data. (We assume that, even if the airline has an overbooking policy, booking should be implemented in a controlled way and that booking errors should not occur by accident.)

More realistically, booking might proceed on the basis of a count of the number of seats which remain unbooked on a given flight, rather than causing specific seats to be reserved. A booking process might call a procedure to book a seat on a given flight and execute code which includes a statement such as:

if *unbooked-seats* >0
   then *unbooked-seats* := *unbooked-seats* −1;

If several processes execute this code simultaneously, overbooking can still occur. First, the value of *unbooked-seats* is read into a processor register (several processes could read the same value), then the value in the register is tested, then (if the value is greater than zero) the decremented value is written to memory.

Figure 8.7(a) shows two processes executing on two processors of a multiprocessor. Both read the value of *unbooked-seats* into a register (either from their caches or from main memory) and find the value is 1. There is one seat left! They each proceed to book it.

Figure 8.7(b) shows two processes running on a uniprocessor with preemptive scheduling. Process A reads the value of *unbooked-seats* into a register and is then preempted in favour of Process B. The saved state of process A includes the values stored in the processor registers. Process B reads the value of *unbooked-seats* into a register, finds there is one seat left and books it. When Process A

(a)

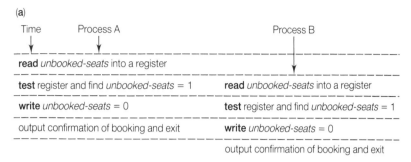

(b)

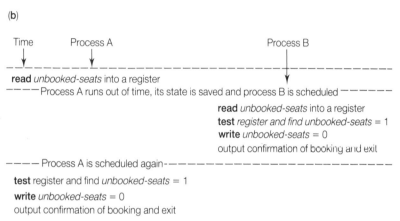

Figure 8.7
Interference
between processes
which share data.
(a) Two processes
running on two
processors of a
multiprocessor.
(b) Two processes
running on a
uniprocessor with
preemptive
scheduling.

runs again its saved state is set up in the processor registers; it finds there is one seat left and proceeds to book it.

The problem arises from uncontrolled access to shared data, but, more specifically, because the implementation of the high-level language statement given above requires several machine language instructions. This is discussed in more detail in Chapter 9.

There are many examples of concurrent systems based on a shared memory model and problems which might arise from shared data. For instance:

● In a process control environment, a count of the amount of material produced might be incremented by many processes which monitor production and decremented by processes which organize the loading and transportation of the material.

● In an operating system, a data structure might be set up to hold requests for service by some system process. In order to make a request, a process must write an entry into the data structure, managing the associated pointers and counts. In order to service a request, the system process must read an entry and manage the associated pointers and counts.

We have focused here on the problem that a single logical operation may not be implemented as a single machine-level operation. In Chapter 13 we return to the example discussed above, of booking a seat, with a different focus. Figure 8.7 showed the statement 'output confirmation of booking to client'. In practice, this must not be done before the fact that the seat is booked has been safely recorded in persistent memory. If a crash occurs, and main memory is lost, a record of the booking must persist.

8.7.2 Problems when processes do not share data in memory

Here, the problem is how to support the sharing of information, which is necessary if processes are to work together to achieve some goal. A concurrent system in which processes do not share memory requires information to be passed between processes as well as the WAIT–SIGNAL synchronization requirement established in Section 8.5 above. It is possible to support the transfer of data around the system from process to process.

The problems associated with this are:

- **Naming**: the processes involved must know each others' names in order to communicate.

    In a single centralized system we can assume that the operating system will extend the name spaces of the processes it supports so that they can communicate. We return to the need for a system-wide naming scheme in Chapters 11 and 14 when we look in more detail at interprocess communication in distributed systems.

- The time to copy data between address spaces or to move it across a network.

    Chapter 12 and the case studies in Part IV show how this time can be minimized by using memory management hardware.

- The time to context-switch between processes running in separate address spaces and the number of context switches involved (see Section 6.3.2).

At first sight it appears that no problem of concurrent access to shared data can arise if processes share no memory. However, it might be that a process is managing some data that is of interest to other processes and will carry out operations on it for them on request; the process is encapsulating a data structure. For all the reasons discussed in Section 8.1.1, the process may work on more than one such request simultaneously. We have rediscovered the need for a multi-threaded server process.

8.7.3 Granularity of concurrency

The size of a process, that is, the number of operations it comprises, is system- or application-dependent. For example, it might be appropriate to use a separate process to carry out operations on each element of a vector or array. This is **fine-grained concurrency** and would typically be used to achieve a highly parallel solution on a special-purpose architecture such as a vector or array processor. An example of **coarse-grained concurrency** is the use of one process for each user job in a time-sharing system.

The concurrent systems addressed by this book tend to require processes that fall between these two extremes.

For some concurrent systems, shared memory is highly desirable, so that data structures can be shared, and processes (threads) do not each bear the overhead of separate memory management. In this case it is relatively easy to create new processes dynamically to achieve parallel computation. A new address space, with associated memory management tables, is not needed on process creation and switching between processes does not require a switch between memory management tables.

There is often a limit to the number of processes and threads that an operating system, running on a given hardware configuration, can support. This typically depends on the **space** allocated for process management data structures, memory management tables etc., and the **time** taken to execute the algorithms which access these data structures.

As we have seen in Chapter 7, many lightweight processes known only to the language system may be multiplexed into a single heavyweight process known to the operating system. Switching between these language-level processes involves less overhead than switching between threads that are known to the operating system.

For some applications, a separate address space per process is mandatory or desirable. Many systems include subsystems of both types.

The concurrent system designer must analyse the application to determine the best decomposition in terms of:

- the number of separate activities;
- the frequency of interaction between them;
- the extent to which they need to access shared information and the granularity of access;
- the need for protection between them;
- the extent to which they need to make potentially blocking system calls.

It is important, for performance and other reasons, to decide where processes known to the operating system must be used, where threads known to the operating system are appropriate and where processes known only to the language system are sufficient. As we established in Chapter 7, it is necessary to know (or choose) the properties of the hardware and the operating system on which the system will run.

8.8 Definition of single concurrent actions

We now attempt to define a 'single' action that might be carried out by a process in a concurrent system. As stated in the introduction to Part II, such a definition must be somewhat arbitrary and is made in order to divide the material to be presented so that we can focus on it in a coherent order. We could define a single action to be a single read of main memory or a single write to main memory. There is no problem arising from such operations being carried out by concurrent processes, since each operation is guaranteed by the hardware to be indivisible or **atomic**. This definition of a single operation would not help us to focus on the problems associated with concurrent systems.

Rather, we are concerned with a higher-level or logical operation which involves more than one read or write of memory. The examples in Section 8.7 are relevant here. To book a seat is a single logical operation and involves a read, test and write of a count. A request to an operating system process to carry out some service may require a record to be written into a data structure and a pointer to be updated. In these cases we need to execute more than one machine instruction on data in main memory and to exclude other processes from that specific data abstraction until the abstract operation is complete.

The motivation given above is driven by requirement; a top-down view is taken. Andrews (1991) uses the following definition, which focuses on implementation; a bottom-up view is taken to arrive at the same intuition:

> An **atomic action** is a sequence of one or more statements that appears to be indivisible; i.e. no other process can see an intermediate state. A **fine-grained** atomic action is one that can be implemented directly by an indivisible machine instruction. A **coarse-grained** atomic action is a sequence of fine-grained actions that appear to be indivisible.

It is helpful to relate the notion of a single logical operation, or Andrews' coarse-grained atomic action, to the modular structure of systems, and in particular to the abstract data types introduced in Section 2.1.2. A single operation on a data abstraction is the intuition required throughout Part II.

This simple model of a single, logical operation carried out on a data structure in the main memory of a single computer is sufficient for most of Part II. In Chapter 13 system crashes are considered; computer systems crash and main memory can be lost. If you tell a client that a seat is booked then you must have noted the booking in persistent memory or a crash could erase the record that the booking took place. We must therefore consider operations which involve data objects stored in persistent memory.

We extend the definition of an atomic operation to include the property that any permanent effects of a completed atomic operation should survive a crash and that either the entire operation is done or none of it is. If there is a crash part-way through an atomic operation, no intermediate state created by it may persist. We dicuss how this can be achieved in Chapter 13.

In Chapter 14 an operation invocation across a distributed system is discussed. Here again the effects of an operation are visible beyond the main memory of a single system and we have to consider the possibility of crashes in the systems involved and the network connecting them.

Part III considers how several Part II-style operations may be combined into a higher-level operation. An area of concern is multiple related operations within main memory, but the main emphasis in Part III is the problem of multiple related operations on data held in persistent memory (for example in a database or file store on disk).

Exercises

8.1 (a) Why is a single process inadequate to implement a dedicated service such as a file server?

(b) Why are multiple processes each in a separate address space inconvenient for such an implementation?

(c) For what kinds of concurrent system would you expect to use a separate address space for each process?

(d) To what extent can the memory management techniques studied in Chapter 4 be used to achieve the kind of data sharing that is needed in the implementation of a service?

8.2 Consider the file service implementation given in Chapter 5. Which data structures must be accessed on behalf of every client of the service? Which data is private to an individual client? Could the memory management techniques studied in Chapter 4 be used to achieve shared service code, some shared data and some private data? (Consider the programming language storage allocation scheme outlined in Chapter 7. Assume that each process has a separate stack and that they share a heap.)

8.3 Give examples of interactions between processes that require one to one, many to one, one to many and many to many interactions.

For each example other than one to one, consider whether you could use a sequence of separate one to one interactions or whether you genuinely need an interaction involving many processes simultaneously.

8.4 Give examples of problems that can arise from uncontrolled access by concurrent processes to shared writeable data.

9 Low-level mechanisms for process synchronization

CONTENTS

Concurrent processes need to work together in order to achieve the goals of the concurrent system they comprise. They may need to synchronize and to access common information. We now look at how this requirement for interaction is met. As specified in Section 8.3:

> Cooperating processes need to synchronize with each other and to do this need to be able to WAIT for each other and SIGNAL to each other.

> Competing processes need to WAIT to acquire a shared resource and need to be able to SIGNAL the fact that they have finished with a shared resource.

The implementation of processes developed in Chapter 6 (by operating systems) and Chapter 7 (in language systems) is now extended with an inter-process communication (IPC) facility.

The operations WAIT and SIGNAL which are described in this chapter can be used for synchronization between processes executing in a shared address space or in separate address spaces. Processes in separate address spaces will be known to the operating system. They may be executing code that was originally written in a sequential programming language, in which case WAIT and SIGNAL are likely to be provided as system calls, see Section 7.2.

Processes sharing an address space are likely to be part of a single concurrent program and may or may not be known to the operating system, see Section 7.5. If they are not known to the operating system, WAIT and SIGNAL will be provided by the language runtime system only. If they are known to the operating system (as threads of a multi-threaded process), WAIT and SIGNAL may still be provided by the language runtime system in the first instance, as discussed in Section 9.5.3.

When processes share memory they are able to access common data structures, and are able to cooperate by this means, as discussed in Section 8.7. In this chapter we show how the basic WAIT and SIGNAL mechanism may be built on in quite complex ways by processes in order to synchronize their access to shared data structures. Chapter 10 shows high-level language constructs that achieve similar effects but are easier for programmers to use. Chapters 11 and 12 focus on synchronization and exchange of information between processes in separate address spaces.

9.1   Process synchronization compared with event signal and wait

Section 6.4 introduced an implementation mechanism which allows a process which is known to the operating system to synchronize with a hardware event, typically the arrival of an interrupt signal. In Section 8.5 a requirement was established that a process should be able to synchronize with another process as well as with the hardware. We shall first consider whether the familiar WAIT(*event*), SIGNAL(*event*) mechanism is suitable for process synchronization. Possible implementations of the mechanism are shown in outline in Figures 9.1 and 9.2, following Section 6.4. Figure 9.1 can be used if a dedicated process is associated with each hardware event. A process can await several events, but an event is associated with only one process. Figure 9.2 is more general and allows any number of processes to await a given event.

Some characteristics of an event synchronization mechanism are:

- In the case of hardware events, a complete list of events of interest may be specified at system design time.

  We are now moving on to consider general inter-process synchronization 'events'. A system might have a small, static number of processes, but in general we should consider a large number of processes with dynamic process creation.

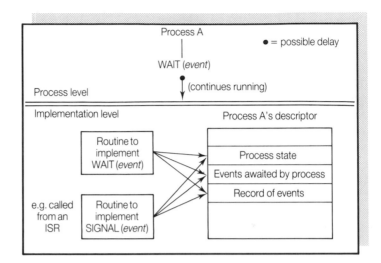

Figure 9.1
Dedicated process
synchronization
with hardware
events.

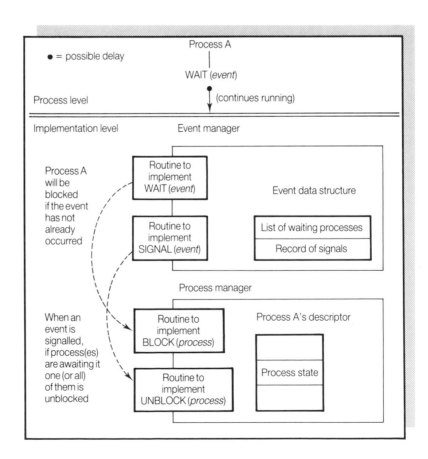

Figure 9.2
General process
synchronization with
hardware events.

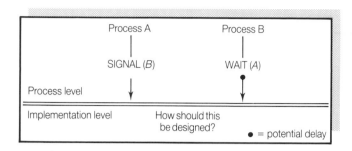

Figure 9.3
Inter-process
synchronization.

- When one process synchronizes with one hardware device, simplifying assumptions can be made. It is not necessary to allow for simultaneous execution of WAITs by processes or SIGNALs by the device. The possibility of simultaneous WAIT and SIGNAL should be allowed for, but many (uniprocessor) operating systems avoid the possibility at race conditions by forbidding interrupts for a short time while a process executes WAIT.

These two points, the naming of the processes involved in a communication and the possibility of concurrent use of the mechanism by processes, must be considered when a general inter-process synchronization mechanism is to be designed. If the communicating processes are known only to the language system and not to the operating system then only the naming problem need be considered, since in this case there can be no real concurrency at the language level. We shall in general be concerned with the case of processes known to the operating system.

Figure 9.3 shows a process-level view of an inter-process synchronization mechanism. The following points are relevant to an implementation of such a mechanism:

- A process may SIGNAL another named process. A process may WAIT for another named process.

- Must a process WAIT for a SIGNAL from one other named process only or may it specify 'any process' as the source?

- Must a process SIGNAL to only one named process or may it SIGNAL an event on which several processes may be waiting (see Figure 9.2)?

- If a SIGNAL happens before the corresponding WAIT it should be recorded in some way.

- The implementation must provide a means of recording the required source of a SIGNAL.

- If the mechanism were to be strictly one to one, an entry in the process descriptor could be used to record the required source of the SIGNAL or the actual source of the SIGNAL, depending on whether WAIT or SIGNAL happens first.

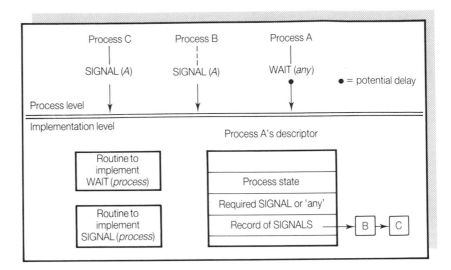

Figure 9.4
Inter-process
synchronization.

- What happens if a process expects to receive a number of signals from other processes and these arrive in advance of the associated WAITs? Will all but one be lost or can the mechanism be extended to list all signallers? This is applicable to many to one (clients to server) communication.

- If the system has a fixed small number of processes, a new entry in the process descriptor could be used to encode which of them are currently signalling a given process. In general, we assume this is not appropriate.

- If there is a large number of processes, or processes are created dynamically, an entry in the process descriptor could point to a data structure containing the list of processes currently signalling this one (see Figure 9.4).

In Section 8.6 we discussed the types of process interactions that a system might be required to support. The event mechanism of Chapter 6 could be used as a starting point for designing support for inter-process interactions. Some of the message passing mechanisms which are covered in Chapter 12 follow Figures 9.1 and 9.4; see Sections 12.6 and 12.7.

There is usually a requirement for interactions which are more general than one-to-one specifically named processes. One process should be able to WAIT for a SIGNAL from any other process. Also, a number of processes may need to synchronize their accesses to a shared data structure. A given process must WAIT for the data structure to be free if it is in use. Suppose a process has finished its access to the shared data. How should it indicate this to any processes that might be waiting to use it? Again the requirement is for one process to SIGNAL several others which are not known to it. We shall consider this problem as an alternative starting point for devising a general inter-process synchronization mechanism. The solution will resemble Figure 9.2.

9.2   Synchronization to achieve exclusive access to shared data

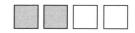

In a concurrent system many processors are simultaneously fetching and executing instructions of stored programs. The following facts relating to the conventional machine level of a computer can be asserted:

- reading a memory location is indivisible or atomic (see Section 8.8);
- writing a memory location is atomic.

There can be arbitrary interleaving of machine instruction execution from concurrent computations and therefore arbitrary interleavings of memory accesses. The possibility should be considered that between any two instructions of one computation, any number of machine instructions of any other concurrent computation could be executed. It should also be noted that a high-level language statement, even one as simple as $x := x + 1$, may be compiled into a number of machine instructions.

Now consider two processes sharing a data structure. We assume that within each process there is at least one sequence of instructions which accesses the data structure. We also assume that at least one of the processes will write to the data structure and that more than one memory location is written. An example is chaining a new record into a queue; several pointers must be written before the data structure reaches a consistent state. Figure 9.5 shows two processes, each with a **critical region** of code for the same data structure. Figure 9.6 gives a more realistic, modular representation of the way operations on shared data would be programmed in practice. Processes A and B call procedures to operate on the shared data and within these procedures are critical regions where the data must be accessed exclusively.

The problem to be solved is how a process can be given exclusive access to a data structure for an arbitrary number of reads and writes. A first attempt at a solution might be to associate a boolean variable with the data structure to indicate whether it is *free* or *busy*. The two processes agree, by convention, that they will test the variable before entering their critical regions associated with the

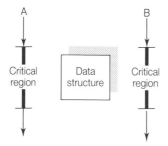

Figure 9.5
Two processes with critical regions for the same data structure.

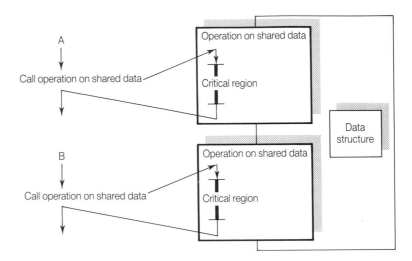

Figure 9.6
Modular
representation
of Figure 9.5.

data structure and will only enter if the region is free. Figure 9.7 shows this scheme informally, Figure 9.8(a) shows the scheme in operation for two processes running on a multiprocessor, and Figure 9.8(b) shows two processes preemptively scheduled on a uniprocessor.

The problem here is that there are several instructions involved in entering the region safely (and several memory accesses) and only a single memory access is atomic. Process A could read the boolean, find the region free, set the boolean to busy using a write instruction and proceed into its critical region. Process B could read the boolean between Process A's read and write, apparently find the data structure free and also proceed to set it to busy and enter its critical region. We are no nearer a solution.

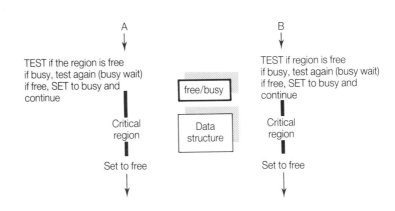

Figure 9.7
Two processes with
critical regions for
the same data
structure – first
attempt at control
by a boolean.

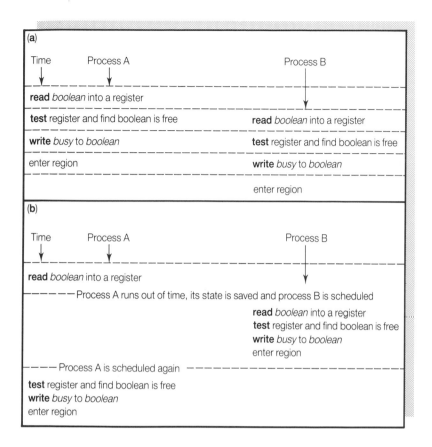

Figure 9.8
Failure to protect a critical region with a boolean. (a) Two processes running on two processors of a multiprocessor. (b) Two processes running on a uniprocessor with preemptive scheduling.

9.2.1 Hardware test-and-set or equivalent

Many computers have instructions which perform *read*, *conditional modify* and *write* of a memory location within a single bus cycle; that is, they provide an atomic, conditional update of a memory location. With such an instruction we can implement mutual exclusion on a multiprocessor. One example is a test-and-set instruction which is typically of the form:

TAS BOOLEAN;   **if** the boolean indicates that the region is free
     then set it to indicate busy and skip the next instruction
     else execute the next instruction

If the boolean was free it is now set to busy and the process enters its critical region. If the boolean was busy, the next instruction in sequence is executed (see Figures 9.9 and 9.10). This can simply jump back to try the test and set again, called a **busy wait** or **spin lock,** or can jump to some other place where a WAIT which blocks the process is implemented. This is discussed in detail in Section 9.3. Other instructions of this kind include 'increment (or decrement) memory

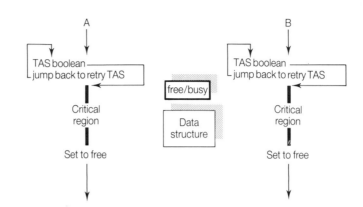

Figure 9.9
Two processes with critical regions for the same data structure – control by indivisible test-and-set of a boolean.

and set condition code' and 'compare and swap'. An example of the use of the latter is given in Section 9.10.4.

A boolean and a TAS instruction may also be used to implement synchronization, as shown in Figure 9.11, but only between two processes. A boolean, to be used as a synchronization flag, is initialized to busy. Process A executes TAS

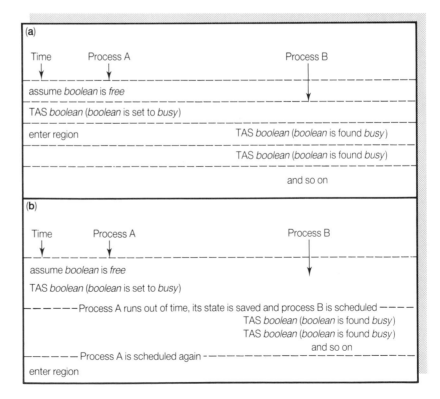

Figure 9.10
Protecting a critical region with an atomic test-and-set instruction. (a) Two processes running on two processors of a multiprocessor. (b) Two processes running on a uniprocessor with preemptive scheduling.

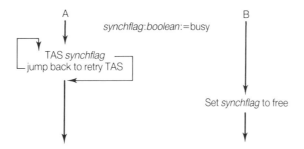

Figure 9.11
Two-process
synchronization
using TAS.

when it needs to synchronize with process B. Process B sets the flag to free. There must only be one possible signaller to set the flag to free since only one signal is recorded.

In uniprocessor systems the technique of forbidding interrupts while small sections of critical code are being executed to completion is often used within the operating system. With interrupts disabled, a process will continue to run indefinitely on the single processor. No other process can do anything. This is because the interrupt mechanism is the basis of timing and preemption as well as external device handling. The technique will not work for multiprocessors, since processes are running simultaneously and ensuring that one process continues to run on its processor without interruption does not stop another process from accessing the same memory locations while running on its processor.

Multiprocessors

If a composite instruction is used in a multiprocessor it is preferable, for performance reasons, that the instruction is such that processes read in the period when they are waiting to enter a critical region and write only once on entry. This is the case in a TAS instruction which reads, tests then writes only if the test is successful, for example, if the critical region is free. This is because each processor is likely to have a hardware-controlled cache (see Section 4.1); a read can take place from the cache alone whereas any value written to data in the cache must be written through to main memory so that all processors can see the up-to-date value. There would be severe performance penalties if several processes were busy waiting on a flag and the busy waiting involved a write to memory. Some composite instructions are defined in the exercises at the end of this chapter.

When a number of processes are busy waiting on the same flag and are scheduled on different processors, each processor's cache will contain a copy of the flag. A test-and-set on a boolean in a cache alone would not, of course, achieve concurrency control. The hardware cache control mechanisms must prevent the use of out-of-date values.

A standard mechanism is that when a memory location is written, all cached entries of that location are invalidated and the new value must be fetched from memory by the next read instruction. A more lightweight mechanism is the 'snoopy cache' designed for the DEC Firefly multiprocessor (Thacker *et al.*, 1987) which is based on the VAX CISC architecture. In this case each cache controller is designed to monitor the memory bus for addresses that it has cached in order to detect whether another processor has written a new value to any of its cached data and, if so, to pick up the updated value.

Section 9.3 describes a general mechanism, based on the semaphore data type and associated operations, which can be used to support both **synchronization** and **mutual exclusion** and which incorporates the blocking of waiting processes. Although not satisfying all the higher-level requirements established in Section 8.4, it forms the basis of many current implementations and has historic significance. In considering the implementation of semaphores we shall bring together the ideas of Sections 9.1 and 9.2.

First, we consider whether it is likely that future architectures will provide an indivisible test-and-set or equivalent instruction. The implications of not having such an instruction are outlined.

9.2.2   Trends in computer architecture and multicomputer system architecture

As hardware became more sophisticated during the 1970s, instruction sets could be relied on to provide a test-and-set, or equivalent, instruction. It is a natural extension of the instruction set of a register–memory or memory–memory architecture. In these cases instructions are typically of variable length and there are instructions which modify memory. Also CISC designs (see Section 3.5) were aiming to meet the requirements of the programmer – to bridge the semantic gap between the programmer and the hardware. Systems programmers need test-and-set instructions.

With the RISC (reduced instruction set computer) approach of the 1980s simplicity and high performance became the predominant design motivations. Fixed-length instructions are the best basis for building instruction pipelines to achieve high performance. Caches are invariably used for instructions and data to minimize the number of slow accesses to main memory. Memory access instructions are simple 'load register from (cache) memory' and 'store from register to (cache) memory' instructions and all ALU instructions operate on registers only. This style of architecture is called a **load–store architecture** and has come to predominate.

The design style was also justified by analysing the assembly code produced for many application programs by a number of compilers (see Hennessy and Patterson, 1990). It was found that the complex instructions of the CISC architecture are rarely used. Although the assembly code programs produced for RISC machines are longer than those for CISC they run significantly faster. The programs measured were sequential rather than concurrent.

Manufacturer-independent operating systems such as UNIX have become widely used and have the status of *de facto* standards. The UNIX kernel design assumes that it will execute on a uniprocessor; it raises the interrupt priority of critical code and is based on non-preemptively scheduled processes. With such a design real-time requirements cannot be met and only a limited range of concurrent systems can be supported. The difficult problems are avoided; this may be the best approach if a correct and stable operating system is required for application areas which are not time-critical. As we shall see in Chapters 21 and 22, the UNIX interface is now supported by new versions of the kernel which can run on multiprocessors and meet timing requirements.

It might be that future multicomputer architectures will be networked uniprocessors, rather than shared-memory multiprocessors. In this case, future operating systems might continue to make use of the interrupt mechanism in order to provide concurrency control, forbidding interrupts for a very short time while a flag is tested and set. As instruction times decrease and because real-time requirements remain constant as the technology progresses, this might be acceptable. In fact, the dramatic reduction in execution time has been achieved by excluding from the instruction set those composite instructions which perform ALU operations on memory. It can be argued that the time for which interrupts are forbidden on a RISC machine in order to achieve exclusive update is less than the execution time of a single complex instruction on a CISC machine.

We should therefore distinguish between the effects of forbidding interrupts for a very short time and scheduling processes non-preemptively. Preemptively scheduled processes must be a feature of any system that needs to make timing guarantees. It remains to be seen whether the trend in instruction set design will be away from support for concurrency control suitable for multiprocessors. The MIPS R2/3000 processor (Kane, 1989) has no support, for example, whereas the HP PA-RISC provides a 'read and clear memory' instruction.

DEC's *Alpha* Architecture (DEC, 1992) takes a novel approach to providing concurrency contol for multiprocessors. In addition to the normal read and write instructions there is a special read instruction (Load Memory Data into Integer Register Locked) which causes the processor to record the location read in a per-processor register and to set a per-processor locked flag. The memory controller will indicate if this location is written by another processor by unsetting the locked flag. There is also a special conditional write instruction (Store Integer Register into Memory Conditional). If the memory location has not been written since this processor read the location (with lock) then the write goes ahead, otherwise the write fails. The value of the lock flag is returned to the processor as an indication of success or failure. The process of read with lock followed by conditional write can be repeated as an entry protocol for a critical region, for example.

9.2.3   Concurrency control without hardware support

We have studied how to implement critical regions. Within a given process we can specify the phases of execution relating to a critical region as follows:

> execute non-critical code
>> execute an **entry protocol** for the critical region
>>> execute the critical region
>> execute an **exit protocol** for the critical region
> execute non-critical code

So far, we have assumed hardware support for the entry protocol and the exit protocol, through special instructions or forbidding interrupts, but it is possible to devise protocols that do not depend on such support. The appendix presents two *n*-process mutual exclusion alogrithms in detail.

Early computers had no indivisible test-and-set instructions and work was done at that time on concurrent algorithms to ensure safe test and set of a flag without hardware assistance (Dijkstra, 1965).

If shared-memory multiprocessors are to be built from RISC computers without support for concurrency control such algorithms will be needed. Lamport (1974, 1987) and others have contributed an extensive body of work in this area. A general point is that it is difficult to be sure that one has reasoned correctly about algorithms of this kind, and they are notoriously susceptible to bugs. It is important that formal techniques are developed to establish proof of the correctness of algorithms that are at the heart of all process interactions. The recent book by Andrews (1991) establishes a formal basis and gives a summary of these protocols.

The entry protocols discussed in this section have assumed that processes will 'busy wait' or 'spin lock' while they are waiting to enter their critical regions. This may be appropriate in a multiprocessor system if the wait is likely to be for a short time and a context switch to another process might waste more processor cycles than the busy waiting. We should keep the spin lock technique as an option to be used in appropriate circumstances, but we should also have the option of suspending a process to avoid busy waiting. This is covered in the next section.

9.3 Semaphores

In 1968 Edsger Dijkstra published a paper on the design of a small but carefully structured operating system called THE, which is described in Section 9.4. The design was based on a small, static number of concurrent processes which synchronized with each other and with the hardware by means of a mechanism called a semaphore.

A semaphore is a **type** of variable with operations SIGNAL and WAIT. The representation of a semaphore variable is typically an integer and a queue (Figure 9.12). The definitions of the semaphore operations are as follows:

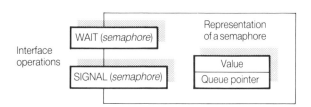

Figure 9.12
A semaphore
abstract data type.

WAIT (*semaphore*)   if the value of the semaphore is greater than zero then decrement it and allow the process to continue, else suspend the process (noting that it is blocked on this semaphore).

SIGNAL (*semaphore*) if there are no processes waiting on the semaphore then increment it; else free one process, which continues at the instruction after its WAIT instruction.

We can envisage a semaphore management module as an abstract data type manager which may be located in the operating system (for semaphores of concern to the operating system) and also in the language runtime system (for semaphores which are not of concern to the operating system); see Section 9.5.2.

If semaphores are made available in a programming language, a typical usage is as follows:

to declare a semaphore called *lock* and initialize it to 1:

    var *lock*:*semaphore* := 1;   % assuming compile time initialization

an example of use of a semaphore:

    procedure *semaphore-user*
        begin
            WAIT(*lock*);
            access data
            SIGNAL(*lock*)
        end;

We shall now cover some examples of the ways in which semaphores may be used and then look in more detail at systems implications of their implementation.

9.4   Use of semaphores

9.4.1   Mutual exclusion

A semaphore initialized to 1 may be used to provide exclusive access to a shared resource such as a data structure.

```
var data-structure : some-type,    % a shared data structure
    lock:semaphore := 1;           % a semaphore associated with the shared
                                     data
```

To use a semaphore:

```
procedure access-shared-data
    begin
        non-critical instructions
        WAIT(lock);                % start of critical region
            access shared-data-structure
        SIGNAL(lock);              % end of critical region
        non-critical instructions
    end;
```

Figure 9.13 shows one possible time sequence for three processes, A, B and C, which access a shared resource. The resource is protected by a semaphore called *lock* and is initialized to 1. Process A first executes WAIT(*lock*) and enters its critical code which accesses the shared resource. While A is in its critical region first B then C attempt to enter their critical regions for the same resource by

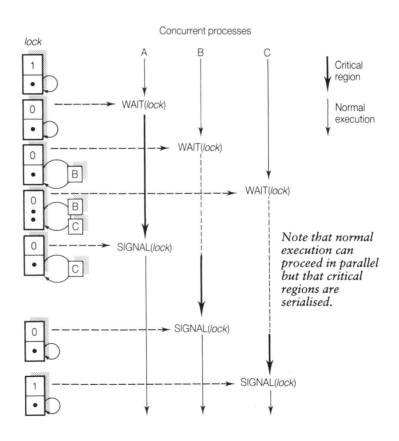

Figure 9.13
Processes
accessing shared
data protected by
a semaphore.

executing WAIT(*lock*). Figure 9.13 shows the states of the semaphore as these events occur. A then leaves its critical region by executing SIGNAL(*lock*). B can then proceed into its critical code and leave it by SIGNAL(*lock*), allowing C to execute its critical code.

In general, A, B and C can execute concurrently. Their critical regions with respect to the resource they share have been **serialized** so that only one process accesses the resource at once.

Note that an assumption has been made about the scheduling of processes waiting on the same semaphore, namely that the first process to be queued on WAIT will be the first to be freed on SIGNAL. This is an implementation decision. An alternative implementation is to free all waiting processes and make them execute WAIT again when next they are scheduled to run. In this case the scheduling algorithm of the operating system is used to select which process should proceed. Yet another alternative is to implement a scheduling policy for the semaphore queue based on some notion of process priority made available to the semaphore implementation. This is discussed further in Section 9.5.

9.4.2 Synchronization of cooperating processes

We started the chapter with the requirement that two processes should be able to synchronize their activities. A semaphore can be used for this purpose. Consider two cooperating processes. When A reaches a certain point it cannot proceed until B has performed some task. This can be achieved by using a semaphore initialized to zero on which A should WAIT at the synchronization point and which B should SIGNAL. Figures 9.14 and 9.15 show how WAIT before SIGNAL and vice versa are managed. Section 9.5.1 discusses how an attempt to execute WAIT and SIGNAL simultaneously is handled in the implementation. This use of semaphores can be generalized to many signallers of process A's semaphore. Semaphores used in this way have been called private semaphores: only one process may WAIT on the semaphore, while any number may SIGNAL.

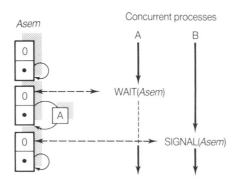

Figure 9.14
Two-process synchronization: WAIT before SIGNAL.

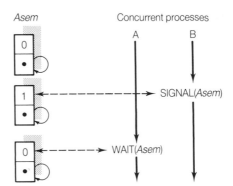

Figure 9.15
Two-process
synchronization:
SIGNAL before
WAIT.

9.4.3 Multiple instances of a resource

Allocation on demand of multiple instances of a resource can be managed by a semaphore initialized to the number of instances available. A process requests a resource instance by executing WAIT on the associated semaphore. When all the instances have been allocated, any further requesting processes will be blocked when they execute WAIT. When a process has finished using the resource instance allocated to it, it executes SIGNAL on the associated semaphore. This method could be used for dynamic allocation of devices to processes, for slots in a shared data structure etc.

Figure 9.16 shows a number of semaphores in use in the ways described in this section. The figure shows a semaphore type manager with operations to create and initialize a semaphore as well as the WAIT and SIGNAL operations that we defined above as synchronizing primitives.

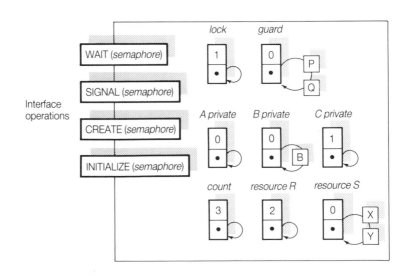

Figure 9.16
A semaphore
data type
manager in use.

9.5 Implementation of semaphore operations

Section 9.4 gave an overview of the different ways in which semaphores can be used and showed their representation as data structures. We now focus on how the operations on semaphores are implemented.

The possibility of concurrent invocation of semaphore operations by processes must be considered. This will certainly happen on a multiprocessor and will happen on a uniprocessor unless restrictions are imposed to avoid the possibility.

Approaches to scheduling the queue of processes waiting on a given semaphore are then considered.

There are system design issues concerning where the semaphore type manager should be located and how it interacts with process management. We first assume that IPC is incorporated together with process management in the operating system and examine the problem of concurrency.

9.5.1 Concurrency in the semaphore implementation

In Section 9.2 the use of an atomic test-and-set instruction on a boolean variable was shown to be sufficient to implement mutual exclusion; that is, to implement a lock on a shared resource. By this means, a data structure can be locked and a number of operations carried out on it without interference from any other process. If the boolean indicates that the shared resource is busy then the process must busy wait until the resource becomes free. Busy waiting may be acceptable on a multiprocessor for short periods of time.

The definition of semaphore operations in Section 9.3 assumes that a process's state can be changed from running to blocked by the operating system if the resource is busy when it executes WAIT(*lock*). Also, the state of some process may be changed from blocked to runnable when the semaphore is signalled. In the former case it is added to the semaphore queue; in the latter it is removed.

The implementation of the operations WAIT and SIGNAL on semaphores therefore may involve both changing the value of the semaphore and changing the semaphore queue and process state. These changes must be made within an atomic (indivisible) operation to avoid inconsistency in the system state; all must be carried out or none should be.

In any multiprocessor implementation and any unrestricted uniprocessor implementation, arbitrary numbers of WAITs and SIGNALs on the same semaphore could occur at the same time.

The requirement for mutually exclusive access to shared data therefore applies to the semaphore implementation. The operations WAIT and

SIGNAL contain critical regions with respect to the data structure representing the semaphore. But semaphores were introduced to SOLVE the mutual exclusion and synchronization problems!

It appears that we could be in danger of creating an infinite regression of WAITs: the WAIT routine which may eventually block the process contains a critical region and a process may therefore have to wait before executing it. How should this latter wait be implemented? Again, the options are:

● Forbid interrupts on a uniprocessor over the WAIT or SIGNAL operations.

● Use a test-and-set or equivalent instruction on a uniprocessor or multiprocessor.

● Associate a boolean with each semaphore (Figure 9.17). Processes may busy wait on the boolean if another process is executing WAIT or SIGNAL on the same semaphore.

● Execute an algorithm which implements a protocol to ensure exclusive access to a given semaphore while the WAIT and SIGNAL operations are executed.

Having arranged that the WAIT and SIGNAL operations are atomic it must be ensured that they will complete once they start, and hopefully without undue delay. Testing and changing the value of a semaphore will not cause delay. Changing the state of the process involves access to the process descriptor, possibly through a call to a separate module to BLOCK or UNBLOCK the process. It might be that the process descriptor is being accessed on behalf of another process, for example, to record the occurrence of a hardware event signal. If we can assume that BLOCK and UNBLOCK are guaranteed to complete in a bounded time then WAIT and SIGNAL can be given similar guarantees.

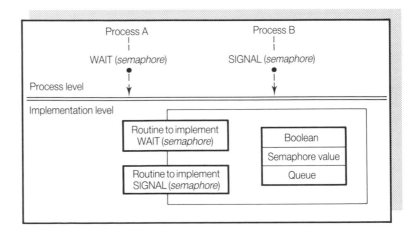

Figure 9.17
Process and implementation level of semaphores.

This is a difficult and crucial area of system design. When we have built atomic and correct WAIT and SIGNAL operations which are guaranteed to terminate we can build the rest of the concurrent system above them.

9.5.2 Scheduling the WAIT queue, priority inversion and inheritance

Section 9.4.1 indicated that processes waiting on a given semaphore might be scheduled first come first served (FCFS). Two problems can occur:

1. A low-priority process which has acquired a semaphore holds up all processes waiting on it, however high their priorities, until it signals the semaphore. It is scheduled at low priority and may be preempted while holding the semaphore, thus increasing the delay experienced by the waiting processes. This is called **priority inversion**.

2. Low-priority processes may be ahead of high-priority processes in the semaphore's queue.

A simple scheme which solves the second problem for uniprocessors is to free all waiting processes on SIGNAL. It must be arranged that each will execute WAIT again. This can be achieved by storing the appropriate value of the program counter in the process descriptor when the process is blocked. The highest-priority process is then the first to be scheduled and the first to acquire the semaphore. The disadvantage is the system overhead in repeatedly blocking and unblocking processes; a given process may have to WAIT several times before acquiring the semaphore.

This approach does not solve the problem for multiprocessors. In this case a number of the freed processes may be scheduled to run on separate processors and it cannot be guaranteed that the highest-priority process will be the first to execute WAIT and acquire the semaphore.

FCFS scheduling might be appropriate for certain types of system:

- if real-time response is not required;
- if the processes that wait on a given semaphore typically execute at the same priority;
- if semaphore queues are expected to be very short.

A system in which real-time response is required typically allows application processes to be allocated a priority. Process priority could be used to order the semaphore queue and this would solve the second problem. It would be necessary, of course, for the process priority to be made known to the WAIT (*semaphore*) routine.

The first problem can be solved by allowing a temporary increase in priority to a process while it is holding a semaphore. Its priority should become that of the highest-priority waiting process; it can be said that it runs at the priority of the 'head waiter'. This is called **priority inheritance**. A process runs at an **effective priority** which is the greater of its assigned priority and its inherited priority.

Process (or thread) scheduling for real-time systems and for multiprocessors is an active area of research. In a real-time system the time taken to respond to an event must be bounded. A process may be delayed while waiting for a resource which is protected by a semaphore. It is important to be able to bound this delay.

Some real-time systems may be analysed statically when the system is designed (see Section 1.1.1). In this case it is known which processes use which resources. For a given semaphore it is therefore known which processes may acquire it and, in particular, the highest-priority process that may ever acquire it. This is called the **priority ceiling** of the semaphore. The **priority ceiling protocol** (Goodenough and Sha, 1988) may be used to bound the delay of a process in such a system. The protocol limits the delay which results from waiting for lower-priority processes to a maximum of one critical section of one lower-priority process. The basic idea is that, even if a semaphore is free, it may only be acquired by a process if all the other semaphores that are currently held by processes have lower-priority ceilings than the priority of this process. A summary of this area may be found in Davari and Sha (1992).

9.5.3   Location of IPC implementation

Effecting process state changes, through BLOCK and UNBLOCK operations, is a function of the process management module within the operating system. If processes share memory (with write access) the implementation of semaphores can be located in the language runtime system, as shown in Figure 9.18, rather than in the operating system. The processes can invoke the operations on the shared semaphore data. Note that we are assuming that the language-level processes (or threads) are known to the operating system since the operating system is aware of their state and is being called to BLOCK and UNBLOCK processes. If the processes were not known to the operating system the semaphore type manager would reside entirely in the language's runtime system and (language-level) process management would also be implemented there.

A process which requires to access a shared, language-level resource, or needs to synchronize with another language-level process, can call the SIGNAL and WAIT operations in the semaphore type manager in the runtime system. If the semaphore value indicates that the shared, language-level resource is free the process executing WAIT can continue; there is no entry into the operating system. If the resource is busy then a call is made to the operating system's process management module to BLOCK the process. Similarly, on SIGNAL, if there is no waiting process there is no entry into the operating system. If processes are waiting, one is selected and a call is made to UNBLOCK it. This style of implementation is attractive because of its efficiency, avoiding operating system entry if no process state change is necessary; that is, avoiding a change of execution

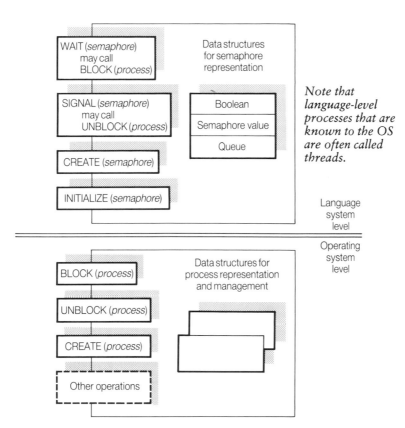

Figure 9.18
Semaphores at the language system level.

mode, saving of process state etc. The operating system data structures are assumed to be protected against concurrent access, as described in Section 9.5.1.

The above discussion has assumed that one language system process is equivalent to one operating system process (see Section 7.5). In certain implementations many language system processes are multiplexed onto a single operating system process and in this case a BLOCK request is not made to the operating system each time a multiplexed process must WAIT for a language-level resource. This style of implementation of (coroutine-like) processes is reasonable for uniprocessor systems (without real concurrency) and for operating systems such as basic UNIX which has a heavyweight process model with one process per address space. The disadvantage is that because only one process is known to the operating system, if a blocking system call is made, none of the threads may run while the blocked thread waits.

9.6 An example of semaphores in system design: the THE system

In the THE system, Dijkstra *et al.* designed a hierarchy of virtual resources managed by a strictly layered system of processes. A brief outline of its structure is as follows; see also Figures 9.19 and 9.20. The lowest level, level 0, creates virtual processors. Above this, processes exist and may communicate using a semaphore mechanism. The rest of the system may be written using these concurrency tools. All interrupts enter at this level, and all but the clock interrupt are handled at higher levels. At level 1, one process provides a one-level virtual store. It synchronizes with drum interrupts and with requests for store from higher-level processes. At level 2, one process provides virtual consoles for higher-level processes and synchronizes with their requests. It also synchronizes with console interrupts and the memory manager process. At level 3, a separate process manages each physical device. Each process synchronizes with its device's interrupts, with the memory and console manager processes, and with higher-level processes over I/O requests. At level 4, the highest, reside five user processes. In all cases where data is passed, producer–consumer style message buffering must be used, controlled by semaphores as described in Section 9.7.

In Chapter 2, modular system structure was introduced. A strictly layered system structure is a particular form of modularization. Each layer provides an abstract interface for processes at higher levels to invoke. The system can be proved correct from the 'bottom up' because processes at a given level cannot invoke operations at higher levels, so there is no problem of circular dependencies between modules.

Level 4 (user processes)	Five user processes
Level 3 (one process for each physical device)	Creates virtual devices Synchronizes with device interrupts Synchronizes with the memory manager and console process Synchronizes with requests from higher levels
Level 2 (one process)	Creates virtual devices Synchronizes with device interrupts Synchronizes with the memory manager and console process Synchronizes with requests from higher levels
Level 1 (one process)	Creates virtual memory Synchronizes with drum interrupts Synchronizes with requests from higher levels
Level 0	Creates virtual processors Provides semaphores for IPC Handles clock interrupt Acknowledges other interrupts which are serviced at higher levels

Figure 9.19
Structure of THE.

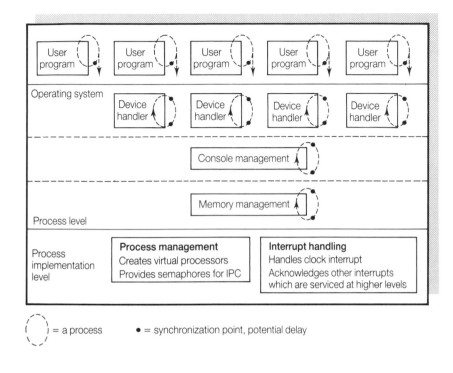

Figure 9.20
Structure of THE, showing process placement.

The problems introduced by a strictly layered design are due to the sacrifice of flexibility to achieve layering. In the THE design, for example, the console manager can invoke memory management but not vice versa. The memory manager is not able to output a message to the operator's console. If memory had been placed above the console in the design this would have been possible, but in this case the console process would not have been able to request memory for I/O buffers (Dijkstra, 1968).

The Venus operating system (Liskov, 1972) was another strictly layered design which used semaphores as the basic synchronization mechanism (see Exercise 9.5). Although strict layering makes it easier to reason about the behaviour of a system it is difficult in practice to choose the ordering of the layers, and most systems do not follow this model.

9.7 The producer–consumer, bounded buffer problem

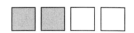

9.7.1 Use of buffers

In Section 3.6 we saw the need for **synchronization** and **data exchange** between user-level processes requesting I/O and device handlers taking output or delivering input. A user-level process should be able to make a request for an arbitrary amount of data to be output or input. The device takes or delivers a fixed amount. A data buffer allows these device-dependent characteristics to be hidden from the user level. It also allows irregular bursts of user-level processing or device activity to be smoothed out. A process engaging in a burst of activity can continue until the buffer is full.

The synchronization conditions on accesses to the buffer are as follows. If a user-level process requests input and the buffer is empty it must block until input arrives. If a device handler process finds there is no more data in the buffer for output it must block until more data arrives. If a fixed amount of space is allocated for the buffer, the user-level process must be blocked when it has filled the buffer on output until the handler has freed some space. Similarly, the device must be stopped on input until the user-level process has freed some buffer space by reading from the buffer. Access to the buffer data structure to read or write will require more than a single memory access, so atomic read and write operations must be implemented (as critical regions for example).

Terminology: There is ambiguity in the way the term buffer is used in the literature and in system design. In the main example in this section we shall discuss a single 'buffer' with a number of fixed size 'slots'. An alternative use of the term buffer is to indicate a single block of data in a 'pool of buffers'. This latter usage is often found in I/O, communication and file buffer management schemes.

There are many uses for buffers between processes. A possible use of the cyclic buffer structure we shall discuss in this section is to hold requests for filenames to be spooled to a printer. A server process takes requests from the buffer and organizes the printing of the files. Any process which invokes this service (by a system call) causes a request to be entered into the buffer. We are implementing a queue of requests in a table of fixed size.

In general, buffers may be used between user-level processes according to the needs of the application: between system-level processes or between user-level and system-level processes.

Buffers might be implemented in a number of different ways. In this section we study a **cyclic** or **bounded buffer** implementation (a classic problem in the literature on concurrency). Exercise 9.5 and the second case study in the appendix outline a method of buffer management based on a pool of buffers. In this latter case there is no specified order in which the buffers are used. It is assumed that the buffer manager will keep a data structure such as a chain of free buffers.

9.7.2   Definition of a cyclic or bounded buffer

We now study the management of a cyclic buffer and, in particular, the concurrency control that is necessary for its correct use. The buffer has a fixed number of fixed-sized slots. If the buffer is full a process which attempts to put an item into it must be blocked. If the buffer is empty a process which attempts to take something out of it is blocked. Let us label the slots $1, 2, \ldots N$. After slot N has

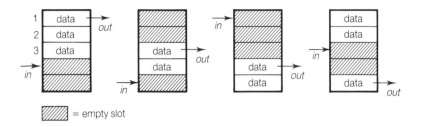

Figure 9.21
A cyclic (or bounded) five-slot buffer in use.

been filled (or emptied) the next slot to be filled (or emptied) is slot 1 again. Figure 9.21 shows a five-slot buffer in various stages of use.

The algorithms given below focus on the problems associated with access to such a buffer by concurrent processes. Details such as pointer management are not included. We consider two general problems:

1. A single producer process sends information, in blocks of a specified fixed size, to a single consumer process.
2. A single circular buffer is used between a number of producer processes and a number of consumer processes.

9.7.3   Algorithm for a single producer and a single consumer

Figure 9.22 gives a high-level view of a solution to the single producer, single consumer problem. The problem would be programmed in practice in a modular style with the buffer as an abstract data type. This general scheme is shown in Figure 9.23. The processes must synchronize over the state of the buffer. The producer must delay if the buffer is full and the consumer must delay if the buffer is empty. Figure 9.24 gives a solution using two semaphores, *items* and *spaces*; *items* is initialized to 0 indicating there are no items in the buffer initially, *spaces* is initialized to N, the number of slots in the buffer. Each time the producer inserts an item it executes SIGNAL(*items*), thus incrementing the item resource count managed by the *items* semaphore. Each time the consumer

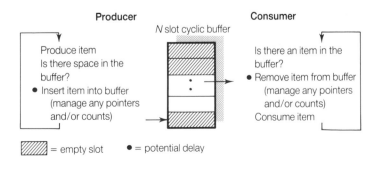

Figure 9.22
Producer – consumer outline.

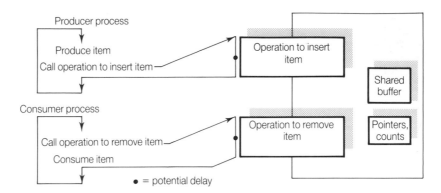

Figure 9.23
Modular representation of the producer – consumer problem.

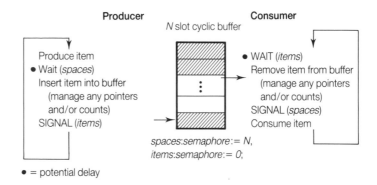

Figure 9.24
Single producer, single consumer

removes an item it executes SIGNAL(*spaces*), incrementing the space resource count managed by the *spaces* semaphore. When the buffer is empty, *items* has value zero and the consumer will block on WAIT(*items*). When the buffer is full, *spaces* has value zero and the producer will block on WAIT(*spaces*). Note that for a single producer and single consumer the buffer is not accessed under mutual exclusion since they are accessing different parts of the buffer (using different pointers). The synchronization of the processes ensures that they block before attempting to access the same slot in the buffer.

9.7.4 Algorithm for more than one producer or consumer

Figure 9.25 gives the solution for many producers and a single consumer. The many producers must access the buffer under mutual exclusion as they are using the same pointer to insert items. For many producers and many consumers, the consumer code must be similarly extended to enforce exclusive access to the buffer between consumers. One producer and one consumer could access the buffer concurrently, provided producers and consumers use different guard semaphores, such as *pguard* and *cguard*.

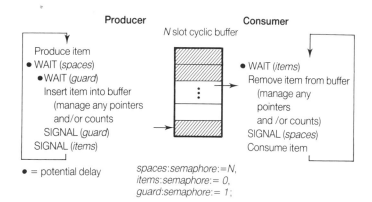

Figure 9.25
Multiple producers,
single consumer.

9.8   The multiple readers, single writer problem

A style of competition between processes which is more complex than simple mutual exclusion arises when many processes may be allowed to read a resource simultaneously (that is, they make no change to it) but writers must have exclusive access. Any solution to this problem must make an assumption about relative priorities. Here we shall assume that as soon as a writer wishes to write, all current readers are allowed to finish reading but any subsequent request to read is held up. This priority scheme is appropriate when it is important that readers read information which is as up to date as possible.

Semaphores are used to manage the situation where processes need to block.

R : *semaphore* :=0	is used to count outstanding requests to read when a writer is writing and readers are blocked on R.
W : *semaphore* :=0	is used to count outstanding requests to write when readers are reading and writers are blocked on W.
WGUARD:semaphore :=1	is used to enforce exclusive access by writers
CGUARD:semaphore :=1	is used to enforce exclusive access to the various counts which keep track of how many readers and writers are active:

    ar   is the count of active readers

    rr   is the count of active readers which are also reading

    aw is the count of active writers

    ww is the count of active writers who have proceeded to the writing phase, which they must do one at a time.

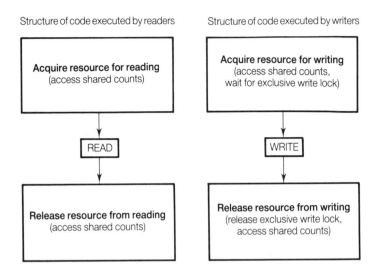

Figure 9.26
Structure of code
executed by
readers and writers.

Figures 9.26 and 9.27 show the basic structure of the code which must be executed by reader processes and writer processes. To acquire or release the resource, shared counts must be accessed under mutual exclusion. The fact that writers must write under mutual exclusion is indicated. Figure 9.29 shows this code structured in a more realistic modular fashion.

Figure 9.28 gives the algorithm in detail. Priority is given to waiting writers over waiting readers, since active readers only go on to become running readers if there are no active writers. The various counts are accessed under mutual exclusion, protected by the semaphore *CGUARD*. Processes wait to read or write on semaphores R or W respectively. The complexity of the code derives

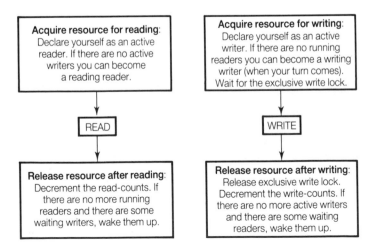

Figure 9.27
Code executed by
readers and writers
in more detail.

Code executed by readers

Code executed by writers

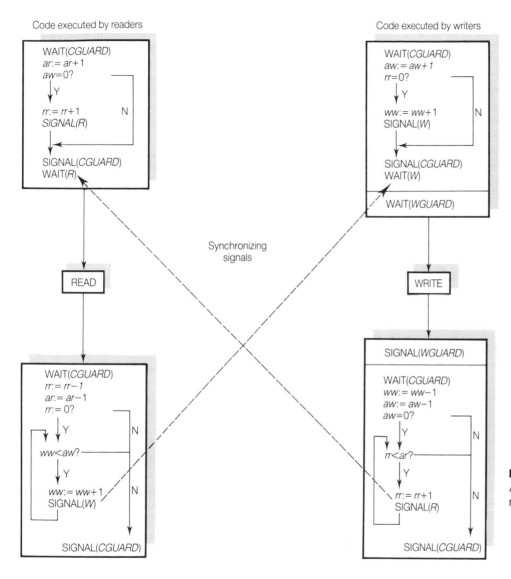

Figure 9.28
Algorithm for
readers and writers.

from the management of these two semaphores. *R* and *W* are given 'wake-up-waiting' signals in the acquire procedures if there are no active writers (for *R*) or no running readers (for *W*). Releasing the resource may involve sending synchronizing signals to waiting readers and writers (the writers proceed to write one at a time); the last running reader wakes up any waiting writers, the last active writer wakes up waiting readers.

Figure 9.29 shows a modular structure for the solution. The resource is managed within a module with interface procedures to acquire and release it for reading and writing. All delay involved in waiting on semaphores is hidden within this module.

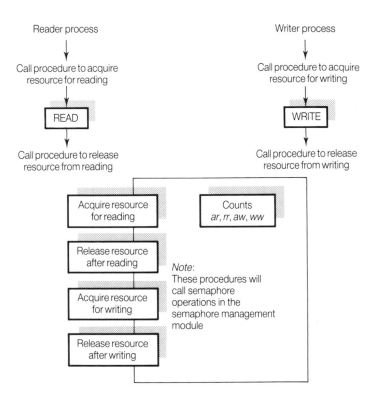

Figure 9.29
Modular structure
for readers and
writers.

9.9   Limitations of semaphores

In Section 9.1 we started by considering a synchronization facility such as
WAIT(*process-id*) and SIGNAL(*process-id*). We have now seen that semaphores
provide more generality and flexibility than a one-to-one (named-process to
named-process) scheme. WAIT (*semaphore*) can be used by many processes to
wait for one or more signalling process. SIGNAL(*semaphore*) can be used by
many processes to signal one waiting process. We have shown examples of how
semaphores can be used to solve a range of realistic problems of concurrent systems.

Suppose the semaphore type was available in a language as the only basis for
IPC. We should consider some of the concepts which are lacking in semaphore
operations that might be important, at least for some types of concurrent system. Typical problems with the use of semaphores are:

● Their use is not enforced, but is by convention only. It is easy to make mistakes in semaphore programming. It is not easy to remember which

semaphore is associated with which data structure, process or resource. It is easy to forget to use WAIT and accidentally access unprotected shared data, or to forget to use SIGNAL and leave a data structure locked indefinitely.

- The operations do not allow a test for busy without a commitment to blocking. An alternative to waiting on the semaphore might be preferable. We shall see that creating a new process so that one process may continue processing while the other waits is a standard solution which avoids this restriction.

- It is not possible to specify a set of semaphores as an argument list to a WAIT operation. If this was possible, alternative orderings of actions could be programmed according to the current state of arrival of signals. Such a facility would be difficult to implement and would introduce overhead. Again, process creation might solve the problem.

- The time for which a process is blocked on a semaphore is not limited, in the definition we have used here. A process blocks indefinitely until released by a signal.

- There is no means by which one process can control another using semaphores without the cooperation of the controlled process.

- If semaphores are the only IPC mechanism available and it is necessary to pass information between processes, in addition to simple synchronization processes must share (part of) their address space in order to access shared writeable data directly. A scheme such as producer–consumer buffering is required. The semaphore value could be used to convey minimal information but is not available to processes.

In general, if concurrency is to be made available to applications programmers, it is desirable to enforce modularity and correct use of concurrency tools wherever possible. This is the subject of the next chapter.

9.10 Eventcounts and sequencers

The data types **eventcount** and **sequencer** have been proposed (Reed and Kanodia, 1979) as an alternative to semaphores. The operations on them are designed for any combination of concurrent execution. The notion of counts of event occurrences, increasing indefinitely from the time the system is started, is used. The fact that the 32nd and 33rd occurrences of a given event are distinguished feels better, intuitively, for a multiprocessor implementation than, for example, semaphore values 1 (event 32 occurs), 0 (handled), 1 (event 33 occurs), 0 (handled), or 1 (event 32 occurs), 2 (event 33 occurs), 1 (event 32 handled), 0 (event 33 handled). Also, the values of these counts are made available to processes through the operations defined on them, and these values can be used by processes, for example, to order their actions.

Eventcounts can be represented by positive integers, initialized to zero, and have the following operations defined on them:

ADVANCE(*E*):   increment *E* (*E*:=*E*+1) and return the new value of *E*
READ(*E*):   return the current value of *E*
AWAIT(*E*, *value*):   delay the executing process until *E* is greater than or equal to *value*

In using the values returned by ADVANCE and READ, processes must take into account concurrent use by other processes.

Sequencers are used for ordering the actions of concurrent processes. Sequencers may be represented by positive integers, initialized to zero. There is a single operation available on them:

TICKET (*S*):   return the current value of *S* and increment *S* (*S*:=*S*+1)

Examples are now given to show the distinct uses of eventcounts and sequencers.

9.10.1   Use of eventcounts for synchronization

A process specifies which occurrence of an event it is waiting for, rather than just the next event of that type. We therefore introduce a local count *i* within the process for this purpose (Figure 9.30).

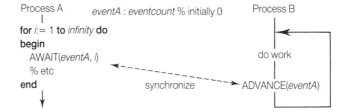

Figure 9.30
Synchronization using an eventcount.

9.10.2   Use of a sequencer to enforce mutual exclusion

Figure 9.31 shows a process competing with others to use a resource protected by the eventcount *GUARD*. The approach is analogous with taking a ticket when you enter a bakery or shoe shop. Customers are served in the order of the number on their ticket. The process first acquires a ticket, which in this example is stored in its local variable *myturn*. It then attempts to enter its critical region by executing AWAIT(*GUARD*, *myturn*). The critical region of this process is executed after those of processes with lower values returned by TICKET(*S*), that is, the order of execution of critical regions is determined by the values returned by TICKET(*S*).

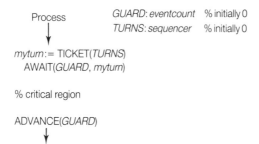

Figure 9.31
Mutual exclusion using a sequencer and an eventcount.

9.10.3   Producer–consumer, bounded buffer with eventcounts and sequencers

For a single producer and a single consumer all that is needed is synchronization. The producer must delay when the buffer is full; the consumer must delay when it is empty. They may access the buffer at the same time since the solution to the synchronization problem ensures that the consumer does not read the ith item until the producer has written it and the producer does not write into the ith slot until the consumer has read the i–Nth item from it.

Figure 9.32 outlines the solution. The eventcounts IN and OUT count the items put in by the producer and taken out by the consumer.

When there are multiple producers and consumers, a sequencer TP must be used to order the accesses to the buffer of producers and one TC for that of consumers. Figure 9.33 outlines the solution.

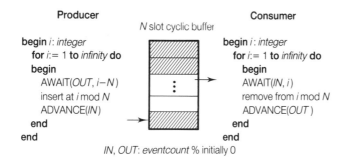

Figure 9.32
Single producer, single consumer with eventcounts.

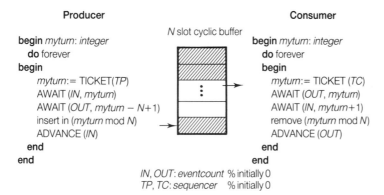

Figure 9.33
Multiple producers and consumers with eventcounts and sequencers.

9.10.4 Implementation of eventcounts and sequencers

The ADVANCE and TICKET operations must be implemented to allow any number of concurrent executions. The simple way to do this is to use a suitable instruction along the lines of a 'test-and-set' (TAS) described in Section 9.2, that is, one which offers a read–modify–write bus cycle. An example is a compare and swap (CAS) instruction. For example:

CAS *Register1, Register2, Memory*

If the contents of *Register1* and *Memory* are the same then *Memory* is overwritten by the contents of *Register2*. If they are not the same then *Register1* is overwritten by *Memory*. A condition code is set to indicate which of these took place.

This is used to implement a secure increment, assuming *Memory* contains the value to be incremented, as follows:

1. read *Memory* into *Register1*
2. write *Register1*+1 into *Register2*
3. execute CAS

If no other processes have written to *Memory* it will be as it was when it was read into *Register1* and will have been incremented by the CAS.

If *Memory* has been written since it was read into *Register1* the swap will not take place and the new value of *Memory* will be in *Register1*, ready for a retry.

9.10.5 Discussion of eventcounts and sequencers

Eventcounts and sequencers were designed with multiprocessor implementations in mind. Reed and Kanodia (1979) give further examples and alternative implementations. The fact that the operations can be executed concurrently is an important property. The fact that the values are strictly increasing helps both in implementing and using them correctly. Another advantage of the operations is that a process could be given the right to read an eventcount but not to write it.

However, a process must be trusted to provide the correct value as the second argument for the AWAIT operation. It is in the interest of cooperating processes to do so, but competing processes might attempt to jump the queue by using a lower value than that returned by a TICKET operation or an error could result in a wrong value being passed. Another problem is the potential delay or deadlock if a process acquires a ticket and then delays or dies before executing the associated AWAIT.

Eventcounts and sequencers are, like semaphores, low-level concurrency control operations and are subject to similar difficulties to those listed for semaphores in Section 9.9. There is a great deal of experience in the use of semaphores in systems but, as yet, little experience with eventcounts and sequencers.

9.11   Summary

We started with the requirement for synchronization between processes. Chapter 6 has shown how a process can synchronize with hardware events and we took this as a starting point. Operations such as WAIT(*process*) and SIGNAL(*process*) were considered and were shown to be inadequate as the basis for a general IPC scheme. WAIT and SIGNAL operations can be used for synchronization both when processes share and do not share data.

We studied how to enforce exclusive access to shared data, that is, how to make the operations on the shared data atomic. We defined critical regions within processes and specified that a process must obey an entry protocol before executing critical code and an exit protocol on leaving. We considered hardware-supported implementations of these protocols. A composite instruction can be used both on a uniprocessor and a multiprocessor; forbidding interrupts for a short time while a flag is tested and set can only be used on a uniprocessor.

The trend in general-purpose computer architecture is towards RISC computers, which are less likely to provide composite instructions than CISC computers. The techniques that are giving us very short instruction execution times are the ones that are excluding the possibility of (slow) complex instructions with ALU operations on memory. We saw that some RISC architectures are providing support for concurrency control and others are not.

System architectures based on uniprocessors connected by very high-speed networks will continue in widespread use and, for such systems, forbidding interrupts while a pair of instructions is executed is likely to be acceptable within the operating system kernel.

Software implementation of the entry and exit protocols for critical regions may be used for shared-memory multiprocessors. It is crucial that such protocols can be proved correct and it is necessary to establish a formal basis for their study. This is an important area in which a theoretical approach should be taken.

We defined semaphores and found that WAIT(*semaphore*) and SIGNAL (*semaphore*) could be used with greater flexibility and generality than WAIT(*process*) and SIGNAL(*process*). We saw semaphores used not only for synchronization between two processes but also for synchronization between a single waiting process and many signalling processes, to guard shared data and to manage resources. In these latter two cases many processes can WAIT on a semaphore. The semaphore acts as an indirect name between processes and allows more general patterns of synchronization than one to one (named process to named process).

Examples of semaphore programs were then developed, showing how processes which share an address space (writeable data space) can synchronize their access to shared information in order to work together to achieve the goals of the concurrent system. A shared cyclic buffer was implemented for one to one cooperation between processes and was generalized for many to one and many to many interactions. Resource management, allowing multiple simultaneous readers but only one writer at once, was also programmed. The solutions presented were quite complex and typically needed several semaphores.

The main disadvantages of semaphores are that programmers can easily make mistakes when using them. There is no automated enforcement of their correct use. The next chapter develops the idea that a compiler could be told which data is shared and could enforce its protection through a pair of semaphore operations.

Eventcounts and sequencers were introduced as an alternative to semaphores. The examples were reprogrammed using these datatypes.

The next chapter continues to discuss the development of support for interprocess communication for processes operating in a shared address space.

Exercises

9.1 Support for synchronization between processes and the hardware was described in Section 6.4. Concurrent processes also need to synchronize with each other. Discuss the approach of extending the methods described for process–hardware synchronization to encompass process–process synchronization. What kinds of interaction could, and could not, be supported by the designs you devise?

9.2 Examine the processor handbooks of your local machines. Explore any composite instruction definitions with a view to using them to implement semaphore operations, in particular, WAIT(*semaphore*).

You may find composite instructions in the instruction sets, such as:

TAS   (test-and-set a variable)

INC   (increment a value and set a condition code register)

CAS   *Register1, Register2, Memory* (compare and swap: if the contents of *Register1* and *Memory* are the same then *Memory* is overwritten by the contents of *Register2*. If they are not the same then *Register1* is overwritten by *Memory*. A condition code is set to indicate which of these took place.)

(a) Write the entry and exit protocols for a critical region using each of the above instructions.

(b) Show how the instructions may be used to achieve condition synchronization so that a process may delay until a condition becomes true.

You may assume that processes cooperate; that some other process which exits from the critical region or makes the desired condition true will take action to inform the delayed process.

9.3 The SIGNAL and WAIT operations, provided as primitives by a kernel, are defined to be atomic. Discuss how this atomicity can be implemented. Consider the following cases:
- hardware which provides a test and set or other composite instruction;
- a uniprocessor, both when a composite instruction is available and when none is available;
- a multiprocessor with no composite instruction.

9.4 What are the problems of designing a system with a strict hierarchical structure? What are the advantages?

The Venus operating system (Liskov, 1972) had the following levels (bottom-up): 0: hardware, 1: instruction interpreter, 2: CPU scheduling, 3: I/O channels, 4: virtual memory, 5: device drivers and schedulers, 6: user processes. Does this choice of layers solve the problems discussed for THE in Section 9.3?

9.5 A buffer object manager is to be implemented. Buffers are to be managed as a pool of fixed-sized objects. A producer process first acquires an empty buffer, then performs a number of write operations into it until it is full. A consumer process first acquires a full buffer then performs a number of reads from it until it is empty.

Each object has a header part, for holding information on the use of the buffer (such as a count and a pointer), for links so that the buffers can be chained etc., and a body part for holding data. A chain of empty buffer objects and a chain of full buffer objects are to be maintained. The object manager detects when a buffer becomes full.

Interface operations are proposed as follows:

buff-id :=	*acquire-empty-buffer ()*	% executed by producers
buff-id :=	*acquire-full-buffer ()*	% executed by consumers
return-code :=	*write-buffer (buff-id, bytes)*	% executed by producers
bytes :=	*read-buffer (buff-id, byte-count)*	% executed by consumers
	free-buffer (buff-id)	% executed by consumers

Discuss the following:
(a) use of the proposed interface operations and possible modifications;
(b) the information that might usefully be kept in each buffer header;
(c) how a full buffer, on writing, and an empty buffer, on reading, should be detected and indicated to the invoker;
(d) how exclusive access to a buffer object might be ensured;

(e) how the various chains might be updated correctly, secure from concurrent access;

(f) how the scheme compares with a cyclic buffer (see Section 9.7) for concurrent accesses by producers and consumers.

9.6 The classic **sleeping barber** problem is given as Exercise 9 of Chapter 10. Solve this problem using semaphores.

Language primitives for shared memory

10

CONTENTS

Throughout this chapter processes are assumed to be executing in a shared address space and therefore are able to share data.

The low-level primitive operations described in Chapter 9 may be made available to programmers in a high-level language. As discussed in Section 9.9 no assistance can be given to ensure they are used correctly. Some assistance could be given if the programmer could tell the compiler:

- which data is shared by processes in the program;
- which semaphore (for example) is associated with which shared data;
- where the critical regions for accessing the shared data are located in the program.

The compiler could then check and enforce that:

- shared data is only accessed from within a critical region;
- critical regions are entered and left correctly by processes.

10.1 Critical regions at the language level

To meet the above requirements, syntax such as the following is needed:

- *shared* as an attribute of any data type,

● a **region** declaration such as:

   region *<shared data>* **begin** ... **end**

The compiler could create a semaphore for each shared data declaration and could insert a WAIT(*semaphore*) operation at the start of the critical region and a SIGNAL(*semaphore*) operation at the end.

> *some-data: shared some-type*   % create a semaphore, for example, *CRsem,*
> initialize it to 1 and note that it is associ-
> ated with *some-data*
>
> .
> .
> .
>
> **region** *some-data* **do**
> **begin**   % insert WAIT(*CRsem*)
>   .
>   .
> **end**   % insert SIGNAL(*CRsem*)

Guarding access to shared data is one requirement of the tools provided for programming a concurrent system. This is an example of arbitration between processes competing for a resource. Assistance is also needed for cooperation between processes. An example is synchronizing over the state of a shared resource. A producer process cannot put data into a shared buffer if it is full and needs a mechanism to allow it to WAIT until there is space in the buffer and to allow consumer processes access to the buffer, in order to make space there, while it is waiting.

During the evolution of concurrent programming languages (see Brinch Hansen, 1973b), a proposal for this kind of synchronizing primitive, in addition to the critical region constructs described above, was for **conditional critical regions** with an associated AWAIT(*condition*) primitive. In the form proposed this was difficult to implement since *condition* could be any conditional expression, for example, AWAIT(*count*>0). It is difficult to establish whether the many conditions involving programming language variables awaited by processes have become true.

Figure 10.1 shows a solution for the readers and writers problem using conditional critical regions. Notice that the solution is much simpler (for the programmer) than the semaphore solution given in Figure 9.28. The programmer has only to be concerned with when to AWAIT. When to unblock (wake up) a process is the problem of the implementation.

An implementation of such a primitive would have the overhead of re-evaluation of the conditions on which processes were waiting each time any process left a critical region in which the shared data might have been changed. This is an unacceptable overhead, in general, in a part of the system which should be efficient. An alternative synchronizing primitive was provided in the context of monitors, as shown in the next section, but this brought back the requirement on the programmer to manage explicit signalling.

v is declared as a shared record with two integer fields
aw (active writers) and *rr* (running readers) both initially 0
writelock is declared as a shared boolean

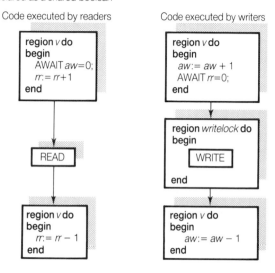

Code executed by readers

```
region v do
begin
    AWAIT aw=0;
    rr:= rr+1
end
```

```
READ
```

```
region v do
begin
    rr:= rr − 1
end
```

Code executed by writers

```
region v do
begin
    aw:= aw + 1
    AWAIT rr=0;
end
```

```
region writelock do
begin
    WRITE
end
```

```
region v do
begin
    aw:= aw − 1
end
```

Figure 10.1
Algorithm for
readers and writers
using conditional
critical regions. (The
problem is
described in
Section 9.8.)

10.2   Monitors

The critical region construct, in itself, has no way of enforcing modularity and a program might be structured as shown in Figure 10.2. In practice, as with semaphores, elaborate conventions and working practices would be used in addition to the language constructs.

A monitor has the structure of an abstract data object. In a monitor the encapsulated data is shared and each operation is executed under mutual exclusion. This is illustrated in Figure 10.3. Compared with Figure 10.2, the critical region within each process has been replaced by a call to a monitor procedure.

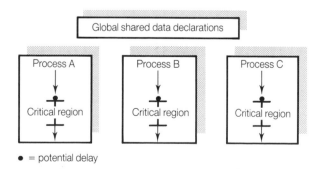

Global shared data declarations

Process A — Critical region

Process B — Critical region

Process C — Critical region

● = potential delay

Figure 10.2
Possible program
structure with
conditional critical
regions.

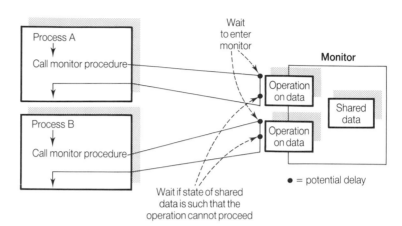

Figure 10.3
Enforced program
structure with
monitors.

The monitor implementation must ensure that only one process is active in the monitor at any time. As Figure 10.3 shows, there is therefore a potential delay and a commitment to WAIT, if necessary, on calling a monitor procedure. To implement this mutual exclusion the compiler could associate a semaphore with each monitor. Any call to a monitor procedure would involve a WAIT on the associated semaphore and return (exit the procedure) would include a SIGNAL on that semaphore.

Mutual exclusion is not sufficient for programming concurrent systems. In most of the problems solved in Chapter 9, for example, condition synchronization is also needed (the resource may be busy when you want to acquire it; the buffer may be full when you want to put something into it). This is provided in most monitor-based systems by a new type of variable called a **condition variable**. The programmer declares the condition variables that are needed by the application and the monitor implementation manages them as synchronization queues (see below). The operations on condition variables are WAIT and SIGNAL. A process may delay itself by executing WAIT(*condition-variable-name*). It is freed subsequently by some other process executing SIGNAL(*condition-variable-name*). Figure 10.4 shows a typical structure of a simple monitor procedure. On entry, the process tests whether it can proceed to operate on the shared data or whether it must wait for some condition on the data to be satisfied (for example, for the buffer to have a space for inserting an item).

The definition of condition variables used in this chapter follows those given in the original monitor proposals (Hoare, 1974; Brinch Hansen, 1973a,b). Whereas a semaphore is implemented as an integer and a queue, a condition variable is implemented only as a queue. There is therefore no notion of a wake-up waiting as discussed in Section 6.4, and the WAIT operation always queues the executing process. The definition of SIGNAL is that if there are any waiting processes then one of them is freed. If there are no waiting processes there is no effect.

Monitor procedure

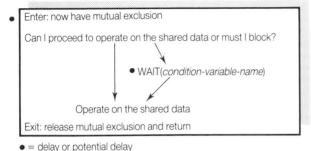

Enter: now have mutual exclusion

Can I proceed to operate on the shared data or must I block?

● WAIT(*condition-variable-name*)

Operate on the shared data

Exit: release mutual exclusion and return

● = delay or potential delay

Note that WAIT *releases the exclusion on the monitor.*

Figure 10.4
Condition synchronization under exclusion in a monitor procedure.

It is possible to use this simple definition because the SIGNAL and WAIT operations on condition variables take place within monitors under mutual exclusion. It is therefore possible for a process, under the protection of guaranteed exclusive access, to test the value of some variable, such as a count of items in a buffer, and to decide to block itself on the basis of the value of the variable, as shown in Figure 10.4. No other process can be accessing the variable at the same time nor signalling the condition variable between the test and the WAIT. That is, the fact that only one process is active in a monitor at any time makes it possible to avoid race conditions.

A process must not be allowed to block while holding a monitor lock. If a process must wait for condition synchronization the implementation must free the monitor for use by other processes and queue the process on the condition variable, as shown in Figure 10.5. If, as suggested above, a compiler associates a semaphore with a monitor to enforce exclusion, then that semaphore must be signalled when a process is blocked on a condition variable queue.

It is essential that a process should leave the monitor data in a consistent state before executing WAIT(*condition*). It might be desirable to enforce that a

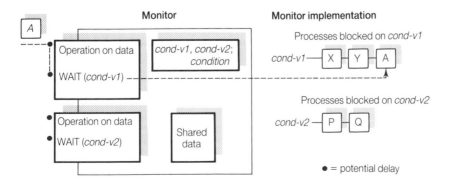

Figure 10.5
Condition variable queues.

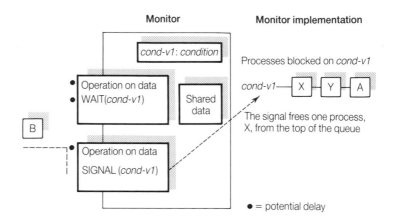

Figure 10.6
Signalling a
condition variable.

process can only read (and not write) the monitor data before executing WAIT. Alternatively, software support might be possible to ensure that the data is in a consistent state by allowing an invariant to be associated with the shared data and for assertions that the invariant is satisfied to be checked at every monitor exit point. This opens up the field of how to prove programs correct, which is outside the scope of this book.

The implementation of SIGNAL has a potential problem, as shown in Figure 10.6. The signalling process, process *B* in the figure, is active inside the monitor and a process freed from a condition queue, process *X* in the figure, is potentially active inside the monitor. By definition, only one process can be active inside a monitor at any time. One solution is to enforce that a SIGNAL is immediately followed by (or combined with) exit from the procedure (and monitor); that is, the signalling process is forced to leave the monitor. A compiler could check for and implement this. If this method is not used, one of the processes must be delayed temporarily and resume execution in the monitor later.

Let us suppose that the signaller, *B*, is allowed to continue and the signalled process, *X*, must wait. One way of achieving this without a separate mechanism is to transfer the signalled process from the condition variable queue on which it is waiting to the head of the queue of processes waiting to enter the monitor. The saved process state would ensure that the process would continue execution from the correct point when next scheduled. We are assuming that the queue to enter the monitor is scheduled first come first served, so that no other process can overtake this one, enter the monitor and possibly invalidate the condition. This may not always be the case, for example, if priority inheritance is in use (see Sections 9.5.2 and 10.2.4). The monitor operations must be such that the signaller exits without making the condition that it previously signalled false.

If instead the signalled process *X* runs, the signalling process *B* may be put at the head of the monitor wait queue. In this case there is no problem about the condition signalled remaining true but the monitor data must be in a consistent state before a SIGNAL is executed. The WAITing process has already had this constraint imposed upon it before WAITing.

The above discussion indicates that the monitor mechanisms must be implemented with great care; also, that the programmer of the monitor procedures must be aware of the constraints imposed by the mechanism.

The syntactic structure of a monitor is typically as follows:

> *monitorname* : **monitor**
>   entry-procedures <list of procedure names which are visible externally>
>   variable declarations and initialization of values
>   external procedure declarations and bodies
>   internal procedure declarations and bodies
> **end** *monitorname*;

The syntax for calling monitor procedures requires both the monitor name and the required procedure name and arguments to be specified.

10.2.1   Single resource allocator

In Chapter 9 a single semaphore, initialized to 1, was used to allocate a single resource. Processes execute WAIT on that semaphore to reserve the resource and SIGNAL on that semaphore to release it. If monitors are the only concurrency tool available, a single resource allocator would be built as a monitor with operations to reserve and release the resource. The shared data encapsulated by the monitor is in this case a boolean *busy,* initialized to false, representing the state of the resource: free or allocated. A condition variable *free* is declared and is used to allow processes to WAIT if the resource is already assigned to some other process. On releasing the resource, a process must both set *busy* to false and SIGNAL(*free*). Figure 10.7 outlines the monitor and shows a process making use of it.

In a little more detail, the syntax of the data declaration would typically be:

> **var**: *busy* : *boolean* := *false*;
>   *free* : *condition*;

and the procedures *reserve* and *release* would be coded as:

> **procedure** *reserve*()
>   **if** *busy* **then** WAIT(*free*);
>   *busy* := *true*
>   **end**;
>
> **procedure** *release* ()
>   *busy* := *false*;
>   SIGNAL(free)
>   **end**;

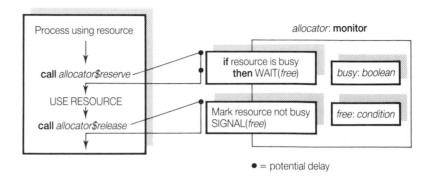

Figure 10.7
Monitor to
allocate a
single resource.

10.2.2 Bounded buffer manager

The semaphore solution to the producer–consumer, bounded buffer management problem is given in Section 9.7. The shared buffer together with associated counts and pointers may be encapsulated in a monitor. Notice that exclusive access to the buffer is always enforced by the monitor, even if there is only one producer process and one consumer process.

Synchronization over the state of the buffer is needed. A producer process needs to WAIT if the buffer is full and a consumer process needs to WAIT if the buffer is empty. Two condition variables, *notfull* and *notempty*, are therefore used. Figure 10.8 outlines the monitor structure and call sequences.

The procedures *insert* and *remove,* shown in Figure 10.8, would be coded along the following lines:

procedure *insert* (< *item*>)
    if < buffer is full> **then** WAIT(*notfull*);
    < put item in buffer>;
    SIGNAL(*notempty*)
    end;
procedure *remove*() **returns** <*item*>
    if < buffer is empty> **then** WAIT(*notempty*);
    < take item from buffer>;
    SIGNAL(*notfull*)
    end;

10.2.3 Multiple readers, single writer

The readers and writers problem is described in Section 9.8 and a semaphore solution is given there. Figure 10.9 gives an outline of the procedures required in a monitor solution. In this case the resource to be read or written is not part of the monitor data since the monitor would enforce exclusive access, preventing multiple simultaneous reads. The use made of the monitor is similar to that

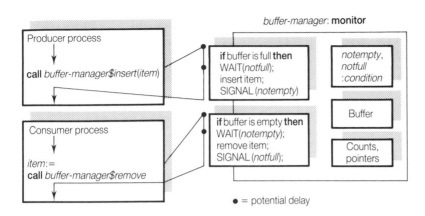

Figure 10.8
Monitor to manage
a bounded buffer.

given in Figure 10.7 for the single resource allocator. Reader processes call *startread* (which may involve delay getting into the monitor and delay getting the resource). They then read the resource, together with any other readers. After they have finished reading they call *endread* (which may involve delay getting into the monitor). Writer processes call *startwrite* (which may involve delay getting into the monitor and delay getting the resource). They then write the resource (one at a time is enforced by the monitor) and call *endwrite* (which may involve delay getting into the monitor).

The readers and writers problem has variants which require different priority schemes. If writing is relatively infrequent or it is very important that the information read is up-to-date then priority should be given to a new writer which

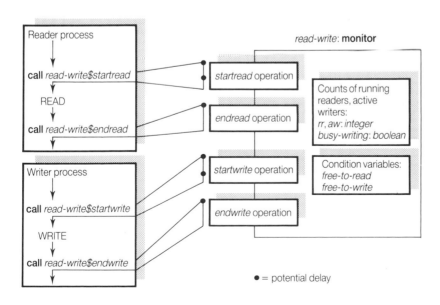

Figure 10.9
Monitor outline for
multiple readers,
single writer.

should write as soon as all current readers have finished reading. This is implemented in the solution given below. If writing is frequent and old data is better than no data for readers then a scheme which allows waiting readers in after one writer finishes may be preferable. The choice depends on the application requirements.

In the solution below, when a writer finishes writing, and if there are no other writers waiting to write, it wakes up one waiting reader by SIGNAL(*free-to-read*). Readers may all read together, however, so that a reader wakes up another reader before leaving the *startread* procedure. Each reader wakes up one more reader until no more are waiting.

An invariant on the monitor is

if *busy-writing* then *rr* = 0.

Expanding on the solution outlined in Figure 10.9 :

```
read-write: monitor
    entry-procedures startread, endread, startwrite, endwrite
    var rr, aw : integer
        busy-writing : boolean
        free-to-read, free-to-write : condition

    procedure startread ()
        if aw>0 then WAIT(free-to-read);
        rr := rr+1;
        SIGNAL(free-to-read)      % If one reader can read, all can read. Each reader
        end;                       % wakes up another, while any remain waiting.

    procedure endread ()
        rr := rr–1;
        if rr = 0 then SIGNAL(free-to-write);
        end;

    procedure startwrite ()
        aw := aw+1;
        if busy-writing or rr > 0 then WAIT(free-to-write);
        busy-writing := true
        end;

    procedure endwrite ()
        busy-writing := false; aw := aw–1;
        if aw>0 then SIGNAL(free-to-write)
                else  SIGNAL(free-to-read)
        end;
    end read-write;
```

10.2.4 Discussion of monitors

Exclusion: monitors are a crude concurrency mechanism, enforcing a restriction that whole operations on shared data are executed under exclusion. As we have seen in the examples above, we can arrange that the shared data is the condition data only, rather than the condition data plus the shared resource, if we wish to allow controlled simultaneous access to a resource (for example, multiple readers, single writer). In the language Mesa the exclusion requirement is alleviated to some extent by only enforcing exclusive execution on those procedures explicitly declared as *mutex*. This allows operations such as 'read the size of the buffer' to be invoked concurrently with monitor operations. If monitors are the only available concurrency tool it can happen that programmers define shared data abstractions unnaturally in order to make the exclusive operations as small as possible.

Synchronization over the state of the resource occurs within a mutually exclusive operation, in contrast with the flexibility available in semaphore programs. This allows simplifying assumptions to be made by the implementation. There is no need to allow for wake-up waiting signals and a process is always blocked when it executes WAIT on a condition.

The language CCLU was developed at the University of Cambridge Computer Laboratory, UK (Bacon and Hamilton, 1987) from CLU (Liskov *et al.,* 1981) and originally provided monitors. CCLU was intended for use as a systems programming language and, for this purpose, monitors were found to decrease performance unacceptably in some circumstances. The language now retains its modular structure based on abstract data types but uses critical regions within the operations when exclusive access to data objects is needed. Other properties of CCLU are motivated in the next section.

As with semaphores, a process calling a monitor procedure is committed to wait if the monitor is in use and then wait if the resource managed by the monitor is not available. If the language provides dynamic process creation, for example by means of a FORK primitive which creates a child process to run in parallel with the parent process, a child can be created to call the monitor operation and the parent can proceed in parallel. This is discussed further in the next chapter and illustrated in Figure 11.10.

Section 9.5.2 discussed how processes waiting on a semaphore might be scheduled. The same arguments apply to processes waiting to enter a monitor. Priority inversion might happen if a low-priority process is executing in a monitor and higher-priority processes are waiting. Priority inheritance could be used to solve this problem; that is, the monitor code could be executed at the priority of the highest-priority waiter.

10.3   Per-object exclusion

In the above section it has been assumed that there is a single shared data structure to be encapsulated in each monitor. This is often the case, and some examples were given. It is also a frequent occurrence that there are many objects of a given type of shared data; indeed, this is the more general case.

If we consider a module for managing files, for example, the operations *open, close, read, write* may be associated with the type file and are therefore common to all files. Each file might be subject to multiple readers, single writer exclusion. If a monitor, as described in Section 10.2, were used to implement a file management module for all files we would have an unacceptable restriction on concurrency. Only one process at a time could be executing monitor code. What is required is that, instead of a single lock protecting entry to the monitor, a lock should be associated with each data object as shown in Figure 10.10. The language CCLU offers this facility.

Each call to a manager of shared objects must include an *object-ID* as an argument. The representation of each object includes a lock. A lock can be implemented as a semaphore (for each object) and the semaphore operations can be used to achieve exclusive access to an object. This might be transparent to the programmer and each procedure then starts with a WAIT operation on the object's semaphore. This arrangement would enforce exclusive access to the object. Alternatively, locks can be made visible to the programmer, in which case a critical region can be specified anywhere within an operation. CCLU supports this latter approach and also allows the user to supply the lock operation implementations so that different kinds of access control policy can be enforced.

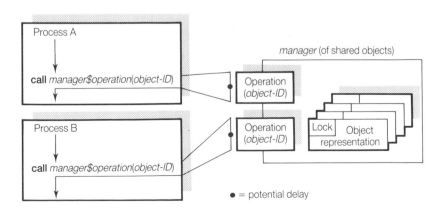

Figure 10.10
A lock per object.

10.4 Synchronization at the granularity of operations

In Chapter 9 we programmed a cyclic buffer between many producers and many consumers. In the solution, producers first checked whether a slot was free, and consumers whether an item was available; then exclusive access to the buffer was ensured among producers or among consumers. One producer and one consumer could access different parts of the buffer at the same time.

The development from critical regions to conditional critical regions and then to monitors combined concurrency control and structuring. In order to carry out an operation on a shared object a process first calls a monitor procedure, which may involve a delay, waiting to enter the monitor. Once inside the monitor the process may again be delayed if the state of the shared data is such that it cannot proceed. The operations on the condition variables used for this purpose are low-level primitives, equivalent to event or semaphore operations, and just as difficult to program correctly. Also, by putting synchronization over the state of the shared data inside the monitor procedure the need for a convention has been re-introduced. The convention of ensuring that the data is in a consistent state before a WAIT on a condition variable is executed must be observed. There might also be a convention that SIGNAL must immediately precede exit from the monitor, as discussed in Section 10.2.

An attractive idea is to allow an operation on an object to go ahead only if the object is in a state such that the operation can complete. For example, a call to put an item in a buffer should only start if there is an empty slot. Thus, a delay before starting to execute the operation would replace both a delay to enter a monitor and a synchronization delay within it.

10.4.1 Path expressions

It is possible to specify the order in which operations may be invoked on an object in the form of a **path expression** (Campbell and Haberman, 1974). The language Path Pascal (Campbell and Kolstad, 1980) uses this approach. A path expression involves only the names of the operations. The default is that they are not executed under mutual exclusion, so the path expression must express this requirement. The code of the operations no longer has to express synchronization constraints.

> **path** *name1, name2, name3* **end**   % the separator is a ,

indicates that *name1, name2* and *name3* may be executed in any order and any number of instances of each may be executed together.

> **path** *first; second; third* **end**   % the separator is a ;

indicates than one execution of *first* must complete before each execution of a *second* can start, and similarly for *second* and *third*. Concurrent executions of *first, second* and *third* are allowed provided that this restriction is followed.

path 2:(*device-type-handler*) **end**

restricts the number of concurrent executions to 2.

path 1:(*op1, op2, op3)* **end**

means that only one of the three operations can be active at any time. They are critical regions for the same single resource (managed by a monitor-like structure).

path 1:(*op1*), 1:(*op2*) **end**

indicates that a maximum of one *op1* and one *op2* can execute concurrently.

path setup; [*spooler*] **end**

[ ] are used to indicate that when one instance of spooler has started, any number of other instances can start.

path 6:(5:(*op1*), 4:(*op2*)) **end**

indicates that as many as five invocations of *op1* can proceed together and as many of four of *op2*, provided that the limit of six invocations is not exceeded.

For an N slot buffer we can write:

path N:(1:(*insert*); 1:(*remove*)) **end**

which indicates that *insert*s are mutually exclusive, *remove*s are mutually exclusive, each *remove* must be preceded by an *insert* and the number of completed *insert*s is never more than N times the number of completed *remove*s.

Because the code of the operations no longer expresses synchronization constraints we cannot express synchronization that depends on input parameters or the state of a monitor. For example, we may wish an input parameter to indicate the priority of the caller and use this value to order processes waiting to invoke a certain operation. Path expressions are therefore less flexible than conventional monitors for many problems.

As monitors are passive structures the code associated with a path expression must be executed by the caller. Only one process at once may execute this code. More concurrency could be achieved if, instead, an active process managing a monitor-like structure could decide which operations could go ahead.

10.4.2   Active objects

Because monitors are passive structures any code associated with them must be executed by the active processes using the monitor. If a process was bound to a monitor structure it could execute code that is independent of any caller. Such an active object manager can determine the state of the shared object it manages and can decide which operations on it can complete. The potential users of the object make procedure calls as though to monitor procedures.

The advantages of this scheme are that synchronization at the granularity of operations on objects has been achieved and that the operations exported to the caller can be minimal; that is, they delay the caller for the shortest possible time. Any background housekeeping can be executed by the object manager process after an operation completes.

When the manager is ready to accept an external call it must decide which set of operations it is prepared to accept a call to perform. If any such requests are outstanding, one is selected non-deterministically. This style of concurrency control is based on Dijkstra's guarded commands (1975). A scheme of this kind was proposed by Brinch Hansen (1978) for a language called Distributed Processes and is used in the Ada language (see Welsh and Lister, 1981).

The following example shows a skeleton Ada program for a bounded-buffer manager in order to highlight the relevant features of Ada tasking. It should be compared with the monitor for the same purpose shown in Section 10.2.2.

The variable *count* is assumed to hold the number of items in the buffer and is initialized to zero.

```
task-body buffer-manager is
.
.
.
begin
loop
   SELECT
      when count < buffer-size
         ACCEPT insert (parameter) do
            [code to put item into buffer]
         end;
      increment count;
      [manage pointer to next slot for insertion]
   or
      when count>0
         ACCEPT remove (parameter) do
            [code to take item out of buffer]
         end;
      decrement count;
      [manage pointer to next slot for removal]
   end SELECT
end loop
end buffer-manager;
```

Points to note are:

- ACCEPT statements are executed by, or on behalf of, external callers. It is not defined which task actually executes the instructions of the ACCEPT statement.

- Each ACCEPT statement is guarded by a condition and a call is only accepted if the associated condition is true.
- The SELECT statement allows a number of ACCEPT statements (those whose conditions evaluate to true) to be made available to external callers.
- Only the minimum necessary code need be executed in an ACCEPT statement. The count and pointers are managed by the buffer manager task.

As in a monitor implementation of a bounded buffer, the external caller calls a procedure to insert an item or remove an item. In Ada the buffer manager is an active task which will only accept for execution those calls that are able to complete. A RENDEZVOUS is said to be made between the buffer manager task and a selected client.

Exercise 10.9 gives another example, the classic 'sleeping barber' problem.

10.5 Summary

We aim to make system issues clear and then discuss how they may be programmed. We have established the areas of systems where the model of processes sharing memory is appropriate: at the application level, where lightweight processes share an address space, and at the implementation level for any type of system. Chapters 9 and 10 followed the development of concurrency tools in high-level languages for shared-memory based systems.

It is now widely accepted that programming languages should have modularization facilities with type checking across module interfaces. How best to support concurrency in high-level languages is still an open question.

We have seen that combining mutual exclusion with modularization in a monitor structure may restrict concurrency unduly. This is important if such a language is to be used for programming those parts of systems which must be efficient. Systems programmers exercise ingenuity when presented with such problems and tend to devise monitors with artificially small operations. This defeats the philosophy of natural, readable abstractions as a basis for software design. For this reason, CCLU provides modules (clusters) for data abstraction, but critical regions and semaphores for mutual exclusion and synchronization.

A monitor protects a single shared data object. We argued the need for what is effectively an object type manager with concurrency control on object instances. A monitor-like structure can be used for this purpose provided that, instead of a single monitor lock, there is a lock associated with every object.

We considered synchronization at the granularity of whole operations. The motivation is to avoid a wait for exclusive access to shared data followed by another wait if the shared data is in a state such that the desired operation cannot proceed (the buffer is full). Path expressions have been suggested to achieve this for passive structures such as monitors. Active objects can achieve the effect by executing some form of guarded command. Active objects were also shown to allow more concurrency than monitors because only those statements that need to be executed under exclusion need be exported to callers. Ada tasks with SELECT and ACCEPT statements were taken as an example.

We now return to system architecture and trace the development of support for concurrency when processes do not share memory.

Exercises

10.1 How would a compiler use semaphores to implement critical regions in a concurrent programming language?

10.2 Why is it inefficient to implement condition synchronization within a critical region using an expression involving programming language variables?

10.3 In Hoare (1974) it was proposed that the scheduling of processes waiting on a condition variable in a monitor could be priority based rather than just first come first served – a 'scheduled wait'. Syntax such as WAIT(*condition-name, priority*) could be used to indicate the ordering of waiting processes on a condition queue.

Using this construct, write an *alarmclock* monitor with procedures *wakeme(n:integer)* and *tick*. The *tick* procedure is invoked on a timer interrupt at regular intervals to maintain a value of system time. The *wakeme* procedure is to allow a process to request that it should be blocked for a number of units of time and then woken up again. The process 'priority' is to be used to order the time at which the process is awakened.

10.4 The process priority described above for Exercise 3 can also be used to wake up processes in a suitable order for writing to the cylinders of a disk. Assume that a sweep or 'elevator' algorithm is to be used to control the disk heads: that is, the heads are to move across the surface to the outermost required cylinder in one direction then are to move back in the opposite direction. The heads sweep smoothly across the surfaces and back, stopping at cylinders *en route* for processes to make data transfers.

Write a monitor with a procedure to request that the heads be moved to a given cylinder and to block the invoking process until its required cylinder is reached, and a procedure that is called by a process after it has finished making a data transfer to a given cylinder.

10.5 Rewrite the 'readers and writers' monitor operations to give priority to waiting readers over waiting writers. The application is such that it is better to read stale data quickly than to wait for up-to-date data.

10.6 Why is a monitor inadequate for managing many shared objects of the same type? How could mutually exclusive access by processes to the same data object be provided?

10.7 Why is 'synchronization at the level of operations' desirable? How might this approach be supported in a concurrent programming language? Consider the cases of both passive modules (or objects) and active modules (or objects).

10.8 Discuss how dynamic process creation can be used to avoid unnecessary delay in a monitor based system.

10.9 The **sleeping barber** problem. (We assume that the barber and his customers are male.)

A barber provides a hair-cutting service. He has a shop with two doors, an entrance and an exit. He spends his time serving customers one at a time. When none are in the shop, the barber sleeps in the barber's chair.

When a customer arrives and finds the barber sleeping, the customer awakens the barber and sits in the barber's chair to receive his haircut. After the cut is done, the barber sees the customer out through the exit door.

If the barber is busy when a customer arrives, the customer waits in one of the chairs provided for the purpose. If all the chairs are full he goes away.

After serving a customer the barber looks to see if any are waiting and if so proceeds to serve one of them. Otherwise, he sleeps again in his chair.

Write a solution to the problem for the barber process and the customer processes.

Notice that the problem is set up with a single (active) server process and many client processes. The clients rendezvous with the barber who cuts their hair while they sit. The barber can sweep up after each customer has left.

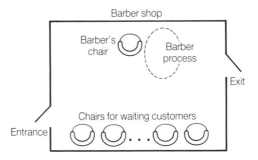

Figure 10.11
The sleeping barber problem.

We could envisage a do-it-yourself barbershop with a single pair of scissors and book of instructions. The clients would take it in turns to use these shared resources then sweep up before leaving. This would model a monitor-like approach to having a service done.

We could also envisage a number of equivalent barbers offering the service in the shop, each with a barber's chair but with a single queue of waiting customers. If the solution is to be written in a language which provides active objects, such as the Ada tasks described briefly in Section 10.4.2, the problem is trivial. The barber provides a single operation *cut-hair* which customers call. No SELECT statement is needed (because there is only one operation) and the ACCEPT statement takes a waiting customer, if any, for service. The language implementation does all the work.

If we are to solve the problem, as set, in a language which provides only monitors, or semaphores, we have to program the client and server process's rendezvous using only these tools. A solution might start from the following:

a monitor *barber-shop*

exported procedures *get-haircut* which clients call and *get-next-customer* which the barber calls.

various condition variables such as *barber-available*.

The problem as formulated above is not matched exactly by a solution along these lines. It would be necessary to specify that the barber entered the shop to see if there were waiting customers and, if not, left the shop and slept in a back room until signalled (by a bell ringing perhaps). Andrews (1991) gives several alternative solutions.

11 IPC and system structure

CONTENTS

11.1 Evolution of inter-process communication

The general theme of Part II is inter-process communication (IPC). In Chapter 8, Part II was introduced by considering system structure and the placement of processes within systems. We saw that it is often desirable for processes to share memory. For example, a server of many clients is implemented most conveniently as multiple server processes (or threads) sharing an address space.

Chapters 9 and 10 developed the inter-process communication primitives that such processes might use when programmed in a high-level language. The underlying system primitives may be based on semaphores, event queues or eventcounts and sequencers, but the high-level language programmer need not be aware of them. The compiler can create and initialize any required semaphores,

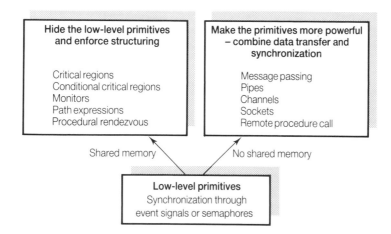

Figure 11.1
Evolution of IPC primitives.

for example, and can replace modular constructs such as critical regions by appropriate semaphore operations. This development is outlined in Figure 11.1.

Processes which comprise a concurrent system yet which run in separate address spaces, sharing no data, still need access to common information in order to work together or compete for resources; that is, IPC is also required for systems of processes with no shared memory. Two approaches to sharing information are as follows:

- Data is passed from process to process; an example of this style of process cooperation is a pipeline of processes (see Section 1.2.2).

- The common information is managed by a process. In this case the managing process will carry out operations on the data it encapsulates on request from other processes. This is called the client–server model.

    This approach can be used to support both cooperation between processes and competition. In the latter case, the server may be managing a shared resource and allocating it to processes on demand.

In both cases the IPC mechanism must support the transfer of data between processes. In the first case, data is passed around. In the second case a request must be passed which contains information on which operation is to be invoked on which shared data item. We discuss these approaches throughout the chapter.

The evolution of IPC primitives when there is no shared memory is also outlined in Figure 11.1. Both shared-memory and no-shared-memory primitives require synchronization which is provided by the low-level primitives taken as the starting point in Figure 11.1. In shared-memory systems, processes can synchronize their access to shared data by using low-level primitives. In no-shared-memory systems the IPC mechanism must support data transfer. The general approach is to combine synchronization and the transfer of data in the lowest-level IPC primitives.

One form of this is a synchronized **byte stream**; one process can send bytes in an unstructured stream, another can read bytes from the stream. If an attempt is made to read more bytes than have been written to the stream, the reading process is blocked until more bytes are available. Note that this method conveys no information about the structure of the byte stream nor of the data types that are being transmitted between the processes. The method is similar to performing file or device I/O through a library stream package. The applications which use the mechanism can, of course, interpret the byte stream as structured, typed data (for example, a stream of records, each with typed fields). The point is that the system mechanism provides no support for this.

Another form is more akin to transferring information in the form of typed arguments on a procedure call. A **message** is constructed with a header indicating the destination of the information and a body containing the arguments. There may or may not be assistance in type-checking the arguments, as we shall see in Chapter 12.

An issue to consider, as with shared memory primitives, is the assistance that can be provided to the programmer within a high-level language, and this will be covered in Chapters 12 and 14. The rest of this chapter is concerned with the system structures and system design issues associated with the two styles (shared memory and no shared memory) of IPC.

11.2 Procedural system structure

A typical design approach for a system of concurrent processes which share memory is shown in Figure 11.2. A process is associated with each source of asynchronous events, in this example an application and a device. It is assumed

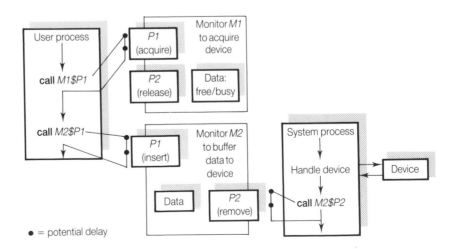

Figure 11.2
Procedural system structure (with shared memory).

that before using the device the application process must first reserve it, which it does by calling a monitor procedure. It then outputs data to the device by means of a buffer manager. A dedicated system process handles the device. It calls a monitor procedure to acquire a unit of data of the correct size, transfers it to the device and waits for the device interrupt.

The details of the example are not important. The important design points are how to use processes and how they communicate. The monitors are passive structures and the active processes thread their way through them, by calling procedures, to get those things done which involve cooperation or competition with other processes. The monitors are set up to organize queues for resources over which processes compete and to manage buffers between producer processes and consumer processes.

11.3   System structure and IPC based on no shared memory

In this model of system structure each process runs in a separate address space. There is no shared data and we cannot therefore build passive structures independent of processes to encapsulate shared data. The system must provide a mechanism for a process to send some data to another process and for the intended recipient to synchronize with its arrival. We may want to build a number of processes in a pipeline or a server which takes requests from many clients.

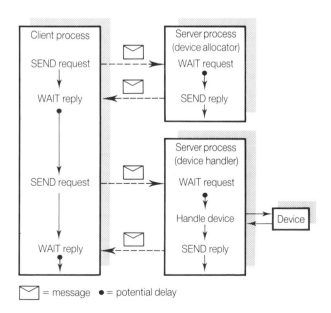

Figure 11.3
System structure with no shared memory.

In the latter case, a client process will send a request for an operation to be done on its behalf by a server process and will wait for the result, or an acknowledgement that the request has been carried out, to come back.

Figure 11.3 shows the example used above in Section 11.2 for a system with no shared memory. We now have a process responsible for allocating the device and a process which handles it. The client process first asks for permission to use the device and then sends data to the device handler process, which has subsumed the buffering function of the monitor shown in Figure 11.2.

11.4 Processes in UNIX

The UNIX process structure was described briefly in Section 8.3. Each process runs in a separate address space, but the UNIX kernel occupies part of every process's address space. When a process makes a system call and enters the kernel its status changes from user mode to system mode and it begins to execute kernel code, as shown in Figure 11.4. A process is quite likely to wait for an event while in the kernel or to access some system data structure. At any time a number of (system mode) processes may have entered the kernel. The shared memory methods of IPC discussed in Chapters 9 and 10 are relevant here; that is, UNIX processes cannot share data when they are in user mode but they can share data when they are in system mode.

System processes are scheduled non-preemptively in UNIX. If an interrupt occurs when a process is executing in the kernel the interrupt service routine is executed in the context of that process and control is always returned to the interrupted process. It can continue to run until it voluntarily chooses to WAIT for an event. It may also forbid interrupts for a short time if it is about to access a data structure that could also be accessed by an interrupt service routine. Thus many of the problems discussed in Chapters 9 and 10 are avoided and the

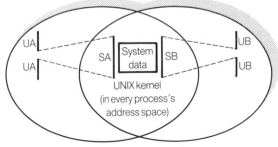

Process A (in a separate address space)   Process B (in a separate address space)

Figure 11.4
Processes in UNIX,
system-mode
communication.

UA = process A in user mode
SA = process A in system mode

Pipe for IPC between user processes in separate address spaces

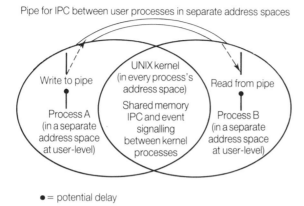

● = potential delay

Figure 11.5
Processes in UNIX,
user-mode
communication.

kernel design is kept simple. The price to be paid for this simplicity is that UNIX cannot guarantee real-time response to events and is unsuitable for running on a multiprocessor.

Processes executing in user mode in UNIX may need to cooperate over some task. Figure 11.5 illustrates the IPC facility provided for these processes which share no memory. Two processes may arrange to have a 'pipe' set up between them. A pipe is a synchronized byte stream; one process writes bytes into the pipe and the other takes them out. If the pipe is empty, the reader is delayed. If the pipe has become too 'full' for the system to hold it conveniently in main memory, the writer is delayed. There is no support for separating the byte stream into separate, structured communication. The facility is described in more detail in Section 12.3 and 21.9.

Finally, the writer of an application which is to run under UNIX may wish to use concurrent processes but may wish them to share data structures; the typical requirement for implementing a server process with many clients. In this case a coroutine or process package may be used as described in Section 7.3 and illustrated in Figure 11.6. The language system level supports many lightweight

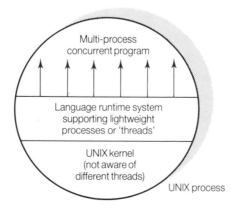

Figure 11.6
Multi-threading
over UNIX.

processes or 'threads', whereas the underlying operating system sees only one process for scheduling, blocking, waking up etc. A disadvantage of this arrangement is that if a blocking system call is made, no thread may run in the application; as far as the operating system is concerned, the process is blocked. Again, a multiprocessor could not be exploited.

11.5 Systems where shared-memory communication is appropriate

When a programmer writes a concurrent program in a language which provides shared memory IPC, the underlying system may be as follows:

- An unprotected system such as those implemented for PCs. All processes and the operating system run in a single shared address space or may use the real, unmapped addresses of the machine.
- The language runtime system may function as a simple operating system. This is the case in many real-time process control and embedded control systems.
- The program may run in a separate address space above an operating system where multi-threading is provided by the language system only or where multi-threaded processes are known to the operating system.

The program may run on a uniprocessor or a shared-memory multiprocessor and a given program may exhibit very different behaviour and performance in these different environments. The programmer should be aware of this.

11.6 Systems where shared-memory communication is not appropriate

Some areas where the programmer may find shared memory undesirable or impossible to use are as follows:

- In protected systems, such as multi-user systems, where processes run in separate address spaces.
- Between processes on different computers, such as within certain process control systems or general-purpose network-based systems.
- In systems where it is desirable to retain flexibility over where processes are loaded.

  Here, it is assumed that we want to defer the decision of which processes to load into which computers until system configuration time. Processes which use shared-memory IPC are constrained to be loaded into the same computer. IPC which does not rely on shared memory can be used between processes on the same machine or on different machines.

- In systems which have a process migration facility to achieve load balancing.
  Here, we are keeping open the option of moving a process from one machine to another when the system is running. Shared-memory IPC would prevent this.

11.7   Overview of inter-process communication

Shared-memory mechanisms for IPC were the concern of Chapter 10. IPC for systems with no shared memory has been introduced here and is discussed in more detail in Chapter 12. Figure 11.7 gives a high-level view of both styles of

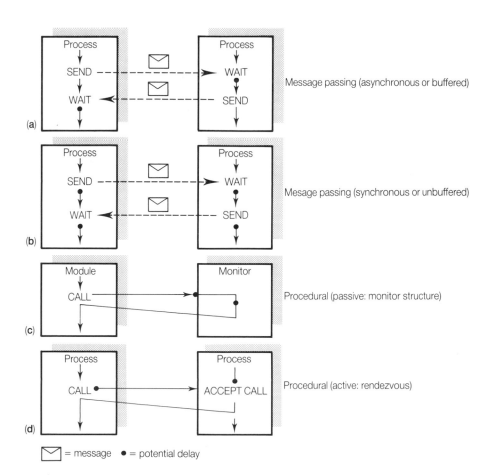

Figure 11.7
Summary of high-level IPC mechanisms.

mechanism; (a) and (b) show two approaches to **message passing** for systems with no shared memory. The IPC implementation must support the transfer of information and the synchronization of the processes involved in the transfer. In (a) a sending process is not delayed and the system must buffer information in transit if the receiver is not ready for it. In (b) the communicating processes must synchronize in order for the information to be passed directly from sender to receiver. (c) and (d) show two approaches to shared memory IPC. In both cases the initiating process makes a procedure call. In c) this is to a passive module, a monitor (Section 10.2); in (d) it is to an active module where the internally bound process chooses to accept the calls (Section 10.4.2). Method (d) is potentially suitable for processes which do not share memory, although its best known implementation is in the Ada language for processes which share memory. We shall explore this further as a 'remote procedure call' in Chapter 14.

A question which comes to mind is whether the functionality provided by the two basic approaches differs fundamentally. Are there some things you can do in one type of system but not in the other?

11.8   Duality of system structures

Lauer and Needham (1978) claim that the two basic system structures are duals: that any problem that can be solved in one of the system types has a dual solution in the other. Certain primitives for process management and IPC must be available for the argument to hold.

The functions that can be made available at the interface of a monitor, such as buffer management functions, might equally be provided by a process and invoked by a form of message passing. Figures 11.8 and 11.9 illustrate one way of achieving this dual functionality. Chapter 12 covers alternative implementations. A message can be sent to request invocation of a particular function on the data. The potential delay on entering the monitor is mirrored by the potential delay if the receiving process is not ready to receive the request. The potential delay inside the monitor procedure is mirrored by the managing process finding that it cannot proceed further with a particular request and starting work on another one; the condition queues of the monitor are mirrored by this multi-threading in the process.

A difference apparent from the figures is that the calling process in the procedural system is committed to wait in the monitor, if necessary, and does not have the option of carrying out processing in parallel. This option can be made available to the process through a FORK primitive (see Sections 7.4 and 10.4 and Figure 11.10). The parent process forks a child process to make the call to the monitor procedure. The child may be delayed in the monitor but the parent can get on with other work in parallel. The parent can synchronize with the child to obtain the result of the monitor call by executing a JOIN primitive. Assuming that the sole purpose of the child was to make the monitor call it can

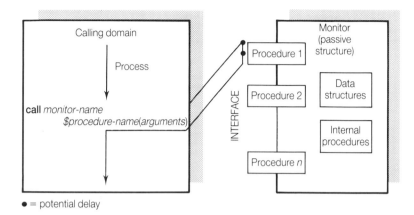

Figure 11.8
Procedural sytem
structure.

now commit suicide by executing EXIT. This scheme is feasible because
processes are 'lightweight'. They share the address space of the parent and
require only a small descriptor and a stack.

The point to emphasize is that there is no intrinsic reason for preferring
shared-memory or no-shared-memory based systems. The same functions can be
provided in each in equivalent structures and the same degree of concurrency can
be achieved. There may be implementation-dependent factors to consider which
affect performance, such as: to what extent the operating system is invoked to
get some operation done or how many context switches are involved.

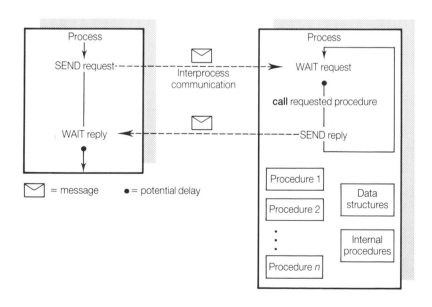

Figure 11.9
Dual functionality
without shared
memory.

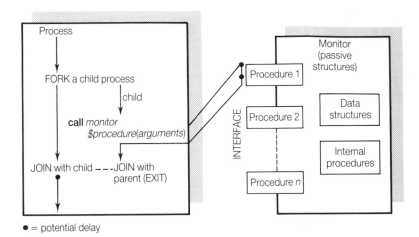

Figure 11.10
Forking a child
to make a call.

The style of working may be constrained by the hardware that has been purchased for a system or the software that must be used. If the primitives described above are available there is functional equivalence between the two styles.

11.9 Naming

Within a single concurrent program running in a shared address space we can assume that the processes know the names of the procedures to call in order to access shared data and the semaphores or condition variables to use for synchronization. We can also assume that how to invoke operating system service is well known, for example, through the specification of a system call interface.

For IPC between processes in separate address spaces to take place, a process initiating communication must know the name of the destination of the communication. Let us first assume that the processes are running in separate address spaces on the same machine. The machine has a single operating system which has full knowledge of all the processes it supports and their attributes. We can assume that system services, such as mail, which run above the operating system, also have well-known names. The operating system is able to map the name to the appropriate object to be used for IPC.

If a concurrent application is to run as a number of separate processes on the same machine it is necessary for each process to know the name of the others. When a process is created, by requesting that a named file should be loaded and a process created to execute the loaded program, the process's name (identifier) is returned by the operating system to the creator. The creator of the processes of the concurrent application may make the names available to all components. An example of a mechanism of this kind is given in Section 21.8.

Within a single machine, we can assume that the operating system will manage any name spaces that are relevant to more than a single address space. The operating system can be seen to be extending the address space of a single process by making names available to it to be used for communication.

We defer considering the problem of naming for cross-machine IPC until Section 14.9.

11.10   Summary

In Chapter 8 we considered system structures based on shared memory and no shared memory and established where each type of structure might occur in a concurrent system. We considered how processes should be placed and used in both kinds of system. In this chapter we have taken the same theme and have extended the discussion to inter-process communication.

We have seen that any task that can be accomplished using the IPC facilities of one style of system can also be accomplished with the IPC facilities of the other style of system. This has been called the **duality** property of the two styles of system structure when a mapping between specific primitives is applied.

We have already studied how concurrent processes can use shared data to achieve their goals. In Chapters 9 and 10 a number of different concurrency facilities that have been used in programming languages and operating systems were studied. In this chapter an outline of IPC without shared memory was given. In the next chapter we study this topic in detail.

We considered briefly the issue of naming in a concurrent system. Within a single computer the operating system was seen to extend the name space of the processes it supports to allow them to communicate. Naming in distributed systems is considered in Chapter 14.

Exercises

11.1 To what extent can processes which run in separate address spaces make use of kernel-provided semaphores to support their cooperation? To what extent can processes which share an address space or part of an address space make use of this facility?

11.2 How would you expect a user-level process to request a service from an operating system in a procedural system and in a non-procedural system?

How might the hardware constrain or support the choice of system structure? When do context switches take place in both cases?

11.3 (a) What is meant by the assertion that procedural and non-procedural systems may be viewed as duals of each other?

(b) Give the duality mapping of: monitor, monitor procedure, condition synchronization on a condition variable in a monitor, process, monitor procedure call, dynamic process creation.

(c) Outline how the monitors given as examples in Chapter 10, including the exercises, may be rewritten as processes. (Details of how to do this are given in the next chapter.)

IPC without shared memory

12

CONTENTS

12.1 Introduction

It is often necessary for processes to access common information in order to achieve the goals of the concurrent system they comprise. If processes do not share any part of their address spaces, in particular writeable data space, some other approach must be taken.

A first attempt at a solution might be to put the common data in a file and allow access to the file by a number of processes. This approach has been used successfully in many applications, but is shown in Section 12.2 to be inadequate as the only system mechanism for concurrent processes to share information.

The UNIX operating system supports pipes between processes, as outlined in Section 11.4. The mechanism is designed to support the pipeline model of computing; a pipe is an unstructured, synchronized byte stream between two processes. It is not able to support many to one, client–server interactions, which are often required. Details are given below in Section 12.3.

Message passing is the main topic of this chapter. Message passing may be asynchronous (messages are buffered by the message passing mechanism) or synchronous. In practice, buffering is likely to be implemented at the application level if a synchronous system is provided.

Support for process interactions which are more general than one to one may be provided by message passing systems. Alternative approaches are presented and evaluated in Section 12.5. Group naming schemes and indirection through named channels or mailboxes are included.

The implementation of asynchronous message passing within a single computer is covered. A potential efficiency problem is the need to copy data between address spaces. Methods of avoiding this are discussed. In practice, message passing is likely to be used in distributed systems and the mechanism will then be integrated with communications services. This aspect of an implementation is deferred until Chapter 14.

Synchronization with the hardware by event signalling was covered in Section 6.4. If a system is to be based on message passing then event signalling can be unified with message passing, as shown in Section 12.7.

Integration of message passing into a programming language may be achieved by providing primitives to send and receive a message. Instead, a higher level of abstraction might be created. The novel approach, used in the occam programming language, of making message passing look like an assignment which is distributed between two processes is described in Section 12.9.1. Although occam programs might reside on a single transputer, they are also intended to be written for systems comprising many transputers. The Linda high-level abstraction of a shared-memory-like tuple space is also described. Here, we apparently have content-addressable messages.

The premise of this chapter is that processes do not share writeable data. We shall assume, in the first instance, that processes are single-threaded rather than multi-threaded. Multi-threaded processes are considered in Section 12.10.

12.2   Use of files for common data

Processes do not need to share memory in order to be able to access shared files. File access is slow, however, compared with accessing data in main memory. This method of sharing information is therefore only appropriate where high-speed inter-process interaction is not required. A pipelined compiler is likely to use this method of sharing information. In this case the concurrency is coarse-grained; a great deal of work is done in each phase and the output is naturally placed in a temporary file. All that is required as an IPC mechanism is a means by which the phases can synchronize.

Some operating systems only provide for a file to be open for exclusive writing or shared reading. Again, this is appropriate for coarse-grained interactions. For example, a process opens a file for writing, writes data to it then closes the file. Other processes may read it concurrently with each other. We have seen how an operating system could implement such a 'multiple readers, single writer interlock' by a semaphore program in Section 9.8 and by a monitor in Section 10.2.3. This method of sharing information could involve long delays, but this might not be important if the waiting process had nothing else to do, such as in a pipeline of processes. In other applications simultaneous write sharing might be a natural way for the application to operate.

Other operating systems provide advisory locking of files and issue a warning if a lock is requested which conflicts with an existing lock. Applications are allowed to ignore such warnings.

It might be that a large amount of data is located in a file and that a number of processes are to cooperate over processing it. In this case, the application could require that all the cooperating processes should have the file open for writing simultaneously. The application ensures that they will each process a different part of the data in the file and therefore will not interfere with each other. For this reason, operating systems designers now tend to provide **shared locks** and **exclusive locks** rather than **read locks** and **write locks** (see also Chapter 5). It is usually left to the application software to organize correct use of the files although system storage services could support fine-grained concurrency control (Bacon *et al.*, 1991).

An alternative scheme to allow concurrent write sharing is for a data management subsystem to be implemented above the operating system. This client of the operating system would itself have many higher-level clients. It would manage files on their behalf and would cause data to be moved between disk and main memory in response to their requests. The function of such a subsystem is to manage requests for data from application processes and to ensure that reads and writes to the data do not interfere. It might also provide a higher-level view of the data, superimposing type information on the data, which the operating system stores and interprets only as a sequence of bytes.

Persistent programming languages and database management systems provide this kind of service. Here, the clients may be humans waiting for information, in which case there is all the time in the world (at the level of machine instruction execution time) to satisfy the request. The database management system does, however, have to handle concurrent requests from clients and ensure the correctness both of the stored data (the database) and the information output to clients. This topic is covered in Part III.

Part II is concerned with high-speed, relatively fine-grained inter-process interactions that cannot be achieved through file I/O. A mechanism for moving information between running processes is required.

12.3 UNIX pipes

We have seen that access to normal files is too slow for them to be used as a general mechanism for inter-process communication. The pipe in UNIX is designed to be used like a file but implemented to allow more efficient transfer of information between two processes. When a file is opened by a process a small integer file identifier is returned by the system for subsequent use when reading or writing the file. For example:

file-id   := **open** (*filename, access required*)
[*bytes*] := **read** (*file-id, byte-range-within-file*)
              write (*file-id, number and location in memory of bytes to write*
              to file, where to write bytes in file)

A pipe is created by a special system call, but a normal file identifier is returned to the creating process. This identifier may be made available to another process as described below and the pipe is subsequently read or written, in the same way as shown for files, by means of this ID. The processes must be programmed so that one writes to the pipe and the other reads from it.

              write ((*pipe*)*file-id, number and location in memory of bytes to*
              be written to pipe)
[*bytes*] := **read** ((*pipe*)*file-id, number of bytes to be read*)

The implementation ensures that a pipe stays in main memory rather than being written out to disk. For this reason there is a notional, system-dependent, maximum size for a pipe. When the pipe contains this number of unread bytes the writing process is blocked on any further attempt to write until the reading process removes some bytes. The reading process is blocked if it attempts to read from an empty file. A pipe may therefore be seen as a **synchronized byte stream** between two processes.

An obvious difference between a pipe and a file is that there is no notion of selecting where to read from or write to in a pipe. One reads the next bytes that arrive, or writes some more bytes to the pipe. The pipe is therefore a stream of bytes flowing from one process to another, whereas a file is a sequence of bytes. There is no operating system support for any structuring of the information represented by the bytes of the file or the bytes passed in the pipe.

A process is created in UNIX by means of a fork system call which causes a new address space to be created. The address space of the parent is replicated for the child. Any files the parent has opened or pipes the parent has created become available to its children. The children can be programmed to communicate via the pipes they inherit. The processes which may use a pipe are therefore the children, grandchildren or descendants in general, of the process that created the pipe.

The pipe mechanism described above has been criticized as too restrictive in that processes must have a common ancestor in order to use a pipe for communication. For this reason, some later versions of UNIX have introduced named pipes. In this case a text name with the same structure as a normal filename is associated with a pipe. Such a pipe has a permanent existence in the UNIX name space and can be opened and used by processes under the same access control policies that exist for files. There is no longer the requirement for a family relationship between the processes.

12.3.1   Use of pipes by UNIX: command composition

As indicated by the name 'pipe', the model of concurrent programming that the UNIX designers had in mind was the pipeline of processes. Applications programs may create and use pipes as described above. The system programs which implement UNIX commands are written so that the output from any command may be piped as input to another. Commands may be composed into sophisticated programs.

For example, a text file could be piped to a program which removes punctuation and creates a list of words as output. This could be piped to a program which sorts the words into alphabetical order. This could be piped to a program to remove adjacent identical words. This could be piped to a program to compare the words with those in a dictionary file and to remove words that match the dictionary. The remaining words could be output to the user's terminal: we have a spelling checker. Chapter 21 presents pipes in the context of a UNIX case study.

12.3.2   Evaluation of the pipe mechanism

There is no system support for structuring the byte stream into separate packets of information. Processes using a pipe may, of course, implement application-level protocols, above the pipe mechanism, to control their interaction. It would be possible in theory for many descendants of a common ancestor to use the same pipe, for example if they agreed to use fixed length messages, but it would be difficult to program in practice.

A pipe tends to be used as a one-way, one-to-one IPC mechanism, to support pipelines of processes. Two pipes are needed to support two-way communication between two processes. Although a process can set up a number of pipes it is impossible to test whether one pipe is empty and, if so, to read from another. One is committed to block if one reads from an empty pipe.

Section 8.6 discussed the types of process interactions that are required in systems. Pipes do not support the (one of) many to one interaction needed to implement a server with many potential clients. Nor do they support one to many or many to many interactions.

We now proceed to study a more general and flexible IPC mechanism.

12.4   Asynchronous message passing

Message passing as an IPC mechanism has been in use since the late 1960s, at the same time that Dijkstra used the semaphore mechanism in the THE operating system. Examples of the use of this mechanism are the MU5 design at

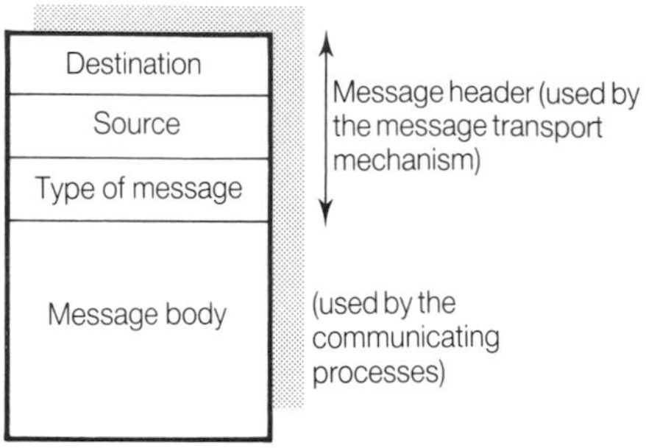

The message body comprises fields that contain typed data such as is passed as arguments on procedure call.

Destination	Message header (used by the message transport mechanism)
Source	
Type of message	
Message body	(used by the communicating processes)

Figure 12.1
A typical message.

Manchester University (Morris and Detlefsen, 1969; Morris and Ibett, 1979) and the operating system for the RC4000 (Brinch Hansen, 1970).

Message passing primitives support both synchronization and data transfer. It is argued that, even in a system structure based on shared memory, processes synchronize in order to exchange information and that supporting both in the low-level system primitives allows complex buffer management at the process level to be avoided. The counter-argument is that complex buffer management must then be done in the implementation, which is an overhead on all processes. If processes cannot access shared data structures, a system mechanism must be provided to pass data between them.

A typical message is shown in Figure 12.1. The system makes use of the message header in order to deliver the message to the correct destination. The contents of the message, the message body, are of no concern to the message transport system. The contents must be agreed between sender(s) and receiver(s). Application protocols associated with specific process interactions determine how messages should be structured by a sender in order to be interpreted correctly by the receiver.

The source of the message is likely to be inserted, or at least checked, by the system. This prevents one process masquerading as another as the source of a message; you can be sure that the message was sent by the specified process. Figure 12.1 shows a field in the message header for 'type of message'. This might be used to indicate whether the message is an initial request for some service or a reply to some previous request; it might be used to indicate the priority of the message or it might be a sub-address within the destination process indicating a particular service required. The header may contain additional fields to those shown, particularly if a message must be transported across a network (see Chapter 14). There has been an implicit assumption here that the source and destination fields of the message will each indicate a single process. This might be the case, but a more general and flexible scheme is often desirable as discussed below.

Figure 12.2 gives an outline of a message passing mechanism. Process A wishes to send a message to process B. We assume that each knows an appropriate name for the other. Process A builds up the message then executes the SEND

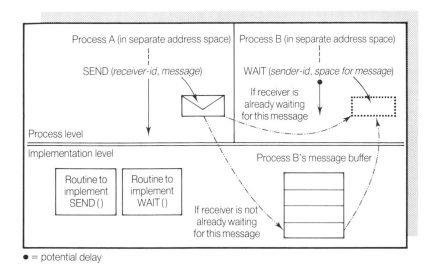

Figure 12.2
A message passing system.

primitive with parameters indicating to whom the message should be delivered and where it is (in a data structure in process A's address space). Process B reaches the point in its code where it needs to synchronize with and receive data from process A and executes WAIT (or perhaps RECEIVE) with parameters indicating from whom the message is expected and where it should be put. This assumes that:

- each knows the identity of the other;
- it is appropriate for the sender to specify a single recipient;
- it is appropriate for the receiver to specify a single sender;
- there is an agreement between them on the size of the message and its contents (an *application protocol*). We shall see that language-level type checking could be helpful here.

We also assume that (in asynchronous message passing) the sending process is not delayed on SEND; that is, there is no reason why its state should be changed from runnable to blocked. This implies that the message passing implementation must buffer messages, as shown in Figure 12.2, in the case when the destination process has not yet executed a WAIT for that message. The message acts as a wake-up waiting signal as well as passing data. A process which executes WAIT will have its state changed to blocked if there is no appropriate message waiting for it in its message buffer. When a message arrives subsequently it is delivered to the process, assuming that it satisfies the conditions specified in the WAIT primitive, and the process becomes runnable again.

Section 12.6 discusses the implementation of asynchronous message passing. The above discussion implies that the message is copied from the sender's address space into the receiver's address space, if necessary via a buffer maintained by the message passing service. Section 12.8 discusses synchronous message passing.

12.5 Variations on basic message passing

A message passing service may be provided with variations on the scheme described above, in order to satisfy the requirements of the systems which will use it. The reasons for these variations include the following:

- The communicating parties may not know, or need to know, each others' names (Sections 12.5.1, 12.5.4, 12.5.5).
- A process may need to be able to send a message to more than one process (Section 12.5.6).
- Support for discriminating between different messages that arrive for a process is desirable (Sections 12.5.2, 12.5.3).
- Processes may not want to commit to an indefinite WAIT for a single, specific message (Sections 12.5.2, 12.5.3, 12.5.8).
- Messages may become out of date in certain environments (Section 12.5.9).
- It may be appropriate for a reply to a message to be sent to some process other than the sender (Section 12.5.7).

12.5.1 Receiving from 'anyone'

In the message passing scheme outlined above we assumed that communication was one to one. It is often reasonable to assume that the sender knows the identity of the receiver (the receiver may be a well-known system service), but in many applications a process may wish to receive messages 'from anybody' in order to participate in many-to-one communication (see Section 8.6). The implementation should provide a means for a potential receiver process to specify 'from anybody', either as a default if no sender is specified or as a distinguished identifier. An alternative is to use indirection so that messages are sent and received via what have variously been called channels, ports or mailboxes (see later subsections).

12.5.2 Request and reply primitives

The message system may distinguish between requests and replies and this could be reflected in the message passing primitives. For example:

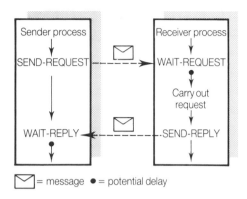

Figure 12.3
Message-based
client–server
interaction.

SEND-REQUEST   (*receiver-id, message*)

WAIT-REQUEST   (*sender-id, space for message*)   *WAITS for a request, when one comes sender-id & message will be set*

SEND-REPLY   (*original-sender-id, reply-message*)

WAIT-REPLY   (*original-receiver-id, space for reply-message*). *WAITS for original receiver to pick*

A typical interaction is illustrated in Figure 12.3. After sending the request the sender process is free to carry on working in parallel with the receiver until it needs to synchronize with the reply. It has been suggested that it might be better to enforce that the SEND-REQUEST, WAIT-REPLY primitives should be used as an indivisible pair, perhaps provided to the user as a single REQUEST-SERVICE primitive. This would prevent the complexity of parallel operation and would avoid context switching overhead in the common case where the sender has nothing to do in parallel with the service being carried out and immediately blocks, waiting for the reply, when scheduled, as shown in Figure 12.4.

There is an obvious dual with a procedural system here, as discussed in Section 11.9, in that REQUEST-SERVICE corresponds to a procedure call. This is the only mechanism provided in the Amoeba message passing kernel

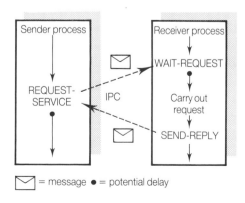

Figure 12.4
Alternative
message-based
client–server
interaction.

(Tanenbaum *et al.*, 1990). The designers argue that any communication they require can be built from these primitives and that having a single simple mechanism imposes minimum overhead.

If processes are single-threaded, the requesting process blocks until a reply is returned. If processes are multi-threaded, and threads can be created dynamically, a new thread may be created to make the request for service. We reconsider this option in Chapter 14 in the context of distributed systems.

12.5.3   Multiple ports per process

We have seen above that the primitives provided may allow a process to distinguish between request and reply messages. Let us assume a system design that does not use a single REQUEST-SERVICE primitive (which is a composite of SEND-REQUEST and WAIT-REPLY) and that a process may continue after SEND-REQUEST. Such a process may reach a point where it can either start on some new work, by taking a new message (if any) using WAIT-REQUEST, or can take the reply (if any) to its previous request for service using WAIT-REPLY. Suppose the process executes WAIT-REPLY and blocks until the reply arrives. A new request message might be available and work could proceed on it. It seems desirable that a process should be able to test whether a message of a given type is available (that is, 'poll' its message buffer(s)) before committing to a WAIT. If such a facility is not available, we do not have the flexibility we need and may as well use the composite REQUEST-SERVICE.

Extending the idea of allowing a process to select precisely which messages it is prepared to receive and in what order it will receive them, it may be possible for a process to specify a number of **ports** on which it will receive messages. With this facility, a port could be associated with each of the functions a process provides as a service to other processes and a port could be allocated to receive replies to requests this process has made as shown in Figure 12.5. With this

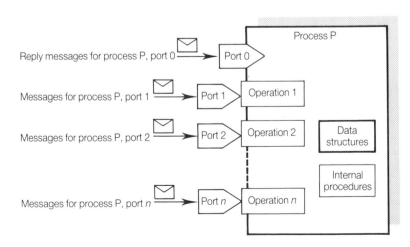

Figure 12.5
Example showing use of ports for message selection.

scheme we have come very close to the dual model discussed in Section 11.8. Each function offered on a port of a service process is the dual of a procedure exported by a monitor in a procedural system.

Again, unnecessary blocking must be avoided. This may be achieved either by allowing a process to poll its ports, in order to test for waiting messages, or by supporting the ability to specify a set of ports on which it is prepared to receive a message. A priority ordering may be possible, or a non-deterministic selection may be made from the ports with messages available. This is equivalent to a process (task) in Ada selecting which of its entry calls it is able to accept (see Section 10.4.2).

12.5.4   Input ports, output ports and channels

Within a given module a message may be sent to a local entity (named as a local program variable), which may be called an output port or a channel within a given language. Only at configuration time is it specified which other process's input port is associated with this output port or which other process is to receive from this channel. Such a scheme gives greater flexibility when a large system is to evolve. Reconfiguration can be carried out without changing the internal code of the modules concerned.

Such a scheme also allows type checking to be extended to cross address space communication. An output port could be declared as accepting a particular type of message structure and any SEND to that port could be type-checked against the port declaration. For example, a message would typically be declared as a record with appropriately typed fields: a string for a name, an integer for a size etc. An output port would typically be a structure such as an array of such records. An input port could similarly be typed and messages received from it type-checked against it. Thus type-checking of messages against input and output ports is achieved statically at compile time.

At configuration time, a configuration language could be used in which one or more typed output ports could be bound to a typed input port and type checking could again be carried out. This scheme is used in the CONIC system developed at Imperial College, UK (Sloman and Kramer, 1987). Figure 12.6

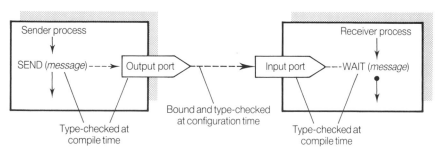

Figure 12.6
Input ports and
output ports.

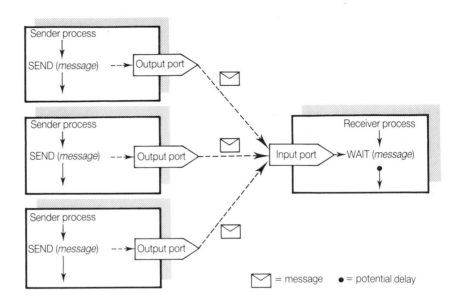

Figure 12.7
Many output ports
bound to one input
port.

illustrates the basic idea with a binding of a single output port to a single input port. Figure 12.7 shows a many to one binding.

12.5.5 Global ports

A free-standing entity called a **global port** or **mailbox** may be used to achieve (one of) many to (one of) many communication. Figure 12.8 illustrates the basic idea. Any number of processes may send to it and receive from it. Such an object

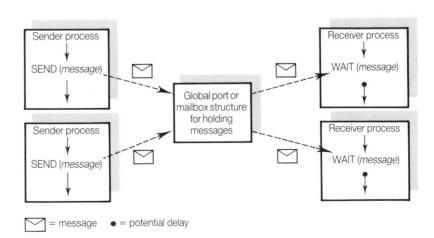

Figure 12.8
A global port.

can be used so that equivalent server processes may take request-for-work messages from it. A new server can easily be introduced or a crashed server removed. The same effect is achieved as with many to many producer–consumer buffering using a monitor (see Section 10.2.2), or programmed with semaphores (see Section 9.7). In the case of a global port the system is supporting a named object which is known to many processes. We discuss naming schemes for global objects in more detail in Chapters 14 and 22.

The Intel iAPX432 hardware supported global ports for process dispatching as well as for inter-process message passing. An idle processor could look for a runnable process at a dispatching port. If none was found the processor could wait there. Similarly, a runnable process could look for a free processor at a dispatching port. If none was available the process was added to the run queue implemented there.

The cross address space type checking described in Section 12.5.4 could be extended to global ports if each named global port was defined to accept messages of some specific type. Compile-time type checking of messages against the typed input and output ports of a single process could be carried out as before. A separate configuration phase could bind processes' ports to global ports after checking for type consistency.

12.5.6 Broadcast and multicast

Input ports, output ports, channels and global ports were introduced so that inter-process interactions other than one to one could be supported. They can all be viewed as introducing **indirect naming**. A message is sent to an intermediate, named object rather than to some specific process.

It is possible to achieve 'from anyone' (many to one) or 'to everyone' (broadcast) without introducing this indirection, simply by using a special name in the message header. What is achieved by channels etc. is the ability to **receive** messages from a specific group of processes, selected at system configuration time. What is achieved by global ports is the ability to **send** to a group of anonymous, identical processes. Global ports also support the ability to receive messages from 'anyone', or from a selected group, depending on how the name of the global port is used and controlled.

An alternative approach is to support the naming of groups of processes in a system as well as individual processes. The semantics of sending to a group name and receiving from a group name must be defined very carefully. In the previous discussion a send to a global port implied that **one** anonymous process would take the message and process it. This is a common requirement: for example, when a set of like servers offer a service. A different requirement is indicated by the term **multicast**. In this case the message should be sent to **every** process in the group. Figure 12.9 illustrates this distinction. The Isis system at Cornell University (Birman, 1985) and the V system at Stanford (Cheriton, 1984; Cheriton and Zwaenpoel, 1985) both have multicast as a basic primitive. Other

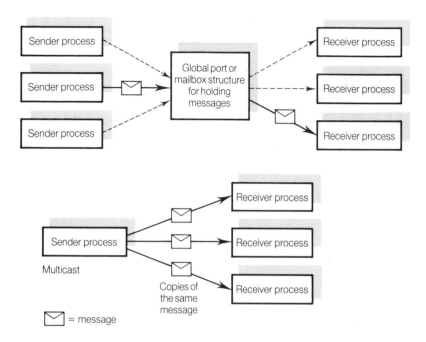

Figure 12.9
Global port
contrasted with
multicast.

systems have implemented an efficient multicast without group naming, for example, the Coda file system at Carnegie-Mellon University (Satyanarayanan *et al.*, 1990).

12.5.7 Message forwarding

Message forwarding is more appropriate for distributed systems, but is mentioned here for completeness. A message may be delivered to a process which is one of a set of processes offering the required service but which no longer has the object required. An example is that a file may have migrated from the file server which created it to some other file server. Any request associated with the file may, for a time, still be delivered to the birthplace of the file.

On receiving the request and detecting that the required object has moved, the original destination process wishes to forward the request to the correct destination but to have the reply sent to the original sender. If such a forwarding service is not offered a great deal of data could retrace the path of the original request in the reverse direction. Message forwarding can be useful, but is not so crucial, in a centralized system.

12.5.8 Specifying WAIT time

It might be appropriate to WAIT for a specified time only for a message rather than commit to an indefinite wait. Again, this facility is important in a distributed system, where a destination machine might have crashed or the network might be down or congested.

If such a timeout facility is available it can be used to poll for a message on a given port (using a zero timeout), or to enforce crisis times for event handling and to take action if some deadline is not met. The general point is that a timing facility can be put to good use, particularly in a hard real-time system.

12.5.9 Discarding out-of-date messages

It might be that a message contains information that should be superseded by a later message. A large industrial process could be monitored by many sensors, or some object's position could be tracked. In such cases, time would be wasted if an early message was received and processed when a more recent message was already available.

A method of achieving this is to support the declaration of input ports of finite size. A port of size 1 would thus hold only the most recent message of that type, previous messages being discarded.

12.6 Implementation of asynchronous message passing

Asynchronous message passing requires message buffer management which takes time and space.

In a shared-memory system, processes manage their own data transfers through producer–consumer buffering, supported by underlying mechanisms which bear little implementation overhead. The processes have to do more work for themselves to achieve IPC but only the processes involved in the IPC are affected by this overhead (the overhead is in the context of the processes using the mechanism).

In a system with no shared memory, messages may need to be copied twice: from process address space to system buffer, then from system buffer into destination process address space. There may be several context switches. All processes in the system are affected by this overhead and not just the processes involved in the IPC. More processor cycles are spent executing the underlying system if a complex message buffer has to be managed.

If a single large message buffer is used it is a shared data structure and synchronized access to it must be implemented using one of the methods explained in Chapters 9 and 10. Shared-memory techniques are necessary in the implementation of no-shared-memory techniques!

Operating system designers attempt to make the resident kernel data structures fixed in length. For example, there is likely to be a maximum number of processes the operating system can manage, each one represented by a fixed length descriptor. Space can therefore be allocated statically to the process structure.

In the design of the data structures for a message passing system the following must be considered:

1. *Messages*

   What do messages look like? Early systems had fixed-length messages and there is still likely to be a maximum message size for data that is passed by value; for example, the CHORUS limit is 64 kbytes. It is unacceptable to make such a restriction visible at the user level. Messages at the language level should be variable-length and typed, allowing type checking against a channel or port.

2. *Message buffers*

   What form do the message buffers take? Fixed or variable length slots may be used; see the case studies on CHORUS and UNIX System V.

   Early systems had many restrictions, such as a maximum number of messages outstanding (sent but not received) from any one process, in order to control the space used. Mach and Conic employ a scheme of this kind, but each process message buffer is specified as having a maximum size. A buffer slot used for a request message was sometimes reserved for the associated reply message to avoid contention (Brinch Hansen, 1970) .

   The amount of memory required is less of a problem now than in early systems which had both a small virtual address space and a small amount of physical memory. Current systems use a great deal of buffer space for communications messages as well as messages between local processes. Communications protocols are designed to take account of lost messages; if there is no space a message can be discarded and a reliable protocol will detect this and resend the message.

   An alternative to a large shared system buffer is to keep messages in the address space of processes, for example, in output ports. Problems here are that this part of the process address space should not be swapped out to disk and that the process should not be able to change a message after sending it. Copy-on-write memory management can be used here (see below). If messages are held at the process level it is easy to acquire more memory for the data structures which hold them by making a system call. If messages are held in a buffer in the kernel, the space allocated for this purpose may become exhausted.

3. *Memory management techniques*

   Can memory management techniques be used in order to transfer large amounts of data between processes without copying? Within a single system a segment name could be passed in a message and the segment could be mapped out of the sender's address space and into the receiver's. Alternatively, the segment could be mapped into both address spaces and the processes could synchronize their accesses to it by the shared memory techniques described in Chapters 9 and 10. This was available in the UK GEC 4000 series in the 1970s.

Another possible scheme is for the system to manage a number of pages which can be mapped into the address spaces of processes. In advance of creating a message a process asks the system for a page or pages. These pages are temporarily mapped into the sender's address space while the message is created. On SEND, the pages are unmapped from the sender and mapped into the receiver's address space. This technique is an efficient means of sending data to a network interface for transfer to a remote machine as well as for cross-address-space inter-process communication. The mechanism is used in the Wanda kernel at the University of Cambridge, UK (see Chapter 22).

Copy-on-write techniques may be used to implement message passing. For example, when a message is sent its pages may be mapped copy-on-write in both the sender's and the receiver's address space. The physical pages are not copied. If either process makes a write access to a message page a new physical copy of that page is made and each process is then given read/write access to a separate copy of the page.

12.7   Unifying messages and interrupts

It is appropriate to keep an event-handling mechanism as described in Section 6.4 for processes to synchronize with devices and to use message passing for processes to synchronize with each other. One method of unifying messages and events is to make the arrival of a message just another type of event, indicated as other events are in the process descriptor. Figure 12.10 illustrates this. Message

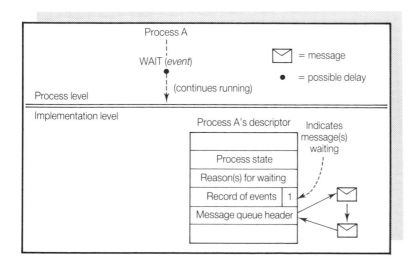

Figure 12.10
Messages and events.

chains or pointers to message structures could also start from the process descriptor.

An alternative approach is to make interaction with the hardware look like inter-process message passing. A device handler sends a message to some distinguished name (which indicates a device) in order to perform output. An interrupt arriving from the device is converted by the system into a message for the device handler. In this case it is necessary for the messages coming from devices to be given appropriate priority, either by using a priority field in the message header, or by a special port for such messages.

12.8 Synchronous message passing

A message system in which the sender is delayed on SEND until the receiver executes WAIT avoids the overhead of message buffer management. Such a system is outlined in Figure 12.11. The message is copied once (or mapped) from sender to receiver when they have synchronized. The behaviour of such a system is easier to analyse since synchronizations are explicit.

In practice, explicit synchronization is not feasible in all process interactions. For example, an important system service process must not be committed to wait in order to send a reply to one of its many client processes. The client cannot be relied on to be waiting for the reply. A device handler, for example, must get rid of its data quickly in order to be free to respond to the device. It cannot wait for a high-level client to ask for the data.

Processes with the sole function of managing buffers are often built to avoid this synchronization delay in synchronous systems. We have removed message buffering from the message passing service only to find it rebuilt at the process

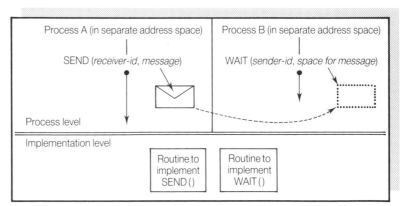

Figure 12.11
Implementation of synchronous message passing.

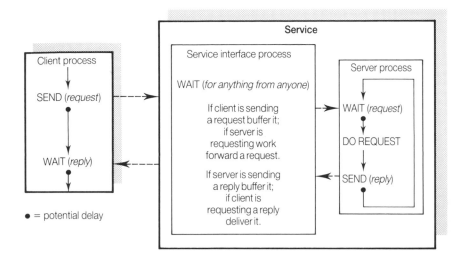

Figure 12.12
Server buffering in a synchronous message passing system.

level. The advantage of this is that the kernel has less overhead than in asynchronous systems and the time taken to manage message buffers is used only by those processes that need them, thus avoiding system overhead for others.

An outline for a buffer management scheme is given in Figure 12.12. Clients interact with the server through an interface process which manages two buffers, one for requests to the server, one for replies from the server. The interface process answers to a well-known system name for the service. Although the interface process must synchronize with the server process and its clients it never commits itself to synchronization with a specific process, and takes any incoming message. It might be possible for server messages to be given priority over client messages in the primitives provided, as discussed above in Section 12.5. Since the real service is carried out by a process which is anonymous to its clients, this scheme could be used to allow a number of server processes to perform the service, each taking work from the interface process.

12.9   Message passing in programming languages

So far we have concentrated on the implementation and interface of the message passing system rather than on a high-level language view of message passing.

Software that is to run in a single address space is likely to be developed as separate modules and to require linking, often into a single load module. The linking phase involves type checking of the parameters for inter-module calls. When processes execute in a single address space their presence and interactions need not be visible at linking and loading time since the data passed between processes is type-checked as part of the normal module linkage procedure. In shared-memory systems, this data is just procedure call arguments.

In a system where processes run in separate address spaces, the load module for each one will be created as described above. The data passed in the bodies of messages in this case passes between address spaces and we should consider whether it is type-checked.

Recall that the input ports and output ports of CONIC, described above in Section 12.5.4, were assumed to be declared in the CONIC programming language. A message sent to or received from a port is type-checked against the port declaration. A configuration language is used to set up links between ports which must be of the same type. Type-checking of the data contained in messages is therefore done both at compile time and at configuration time. Chapter 14 discusses this issue for cross-machine IPC.

Message passing can be incorporated in a high-level language directly, in the form of any of the variations of the SEND and WAIT primitives we have discussed above. We now consider two approaches which give the programmer different abstractions for message passing.

12.9.1 occam channels for synchronous communication

The concurrent programming language occam is based on synchronous communication, and processes do not share memory. occam evolved from the earlier language specification and formalism CSP (Communicating Sequential Processes) (Hoare, 1978). In CSP, named processes are the source and destination of a communication. In occam, communication takes place via a named channel.

In occam, IPC is equivalent to assignment from one process to another. An assignment statement

variable := *expression*

is distributed between two processes, one holds the variable, the other evaluates the expression. The value of the expression is communicated along a channel known to both processes.

Destination process	**Source process**
channel ? *variable*	*channel* ! *expression*

For example, $x := y+z$ could be distributed as:

channelA ? *x*	*channelA* ! *y+z*

These three kinds of statement (input, output and assignment) may be composed sequentially or in parallel using SEQ and PAR respectively. A small example is as follows (see Figure 12.13).

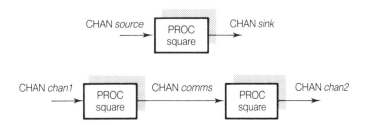

Figure 12.13
occam example.

Declare a non-terminating procedure which takes a value from channel *source* and outputs its square on channel *sink*:

PROC *square (CHAN source, sink)=*
    WHILE TRUE
        VAR *x:*
    SEQ
        source?x
        sink!x $\times$ *x*

and use the procedure, for example to create a pipeline:

CHAN *comms*:
    PAR
    square (*chan1, comms*)
    square (*comms, chan2*)

occam is intended to be a simple language with few constructs, after the philosophy of William of Occam. It is often called a high-level assembler for the transputer rather than a high-level language. It enforces a static declaration of processes and is therefore applicable to embedded systems rather than general-purpose systems. Many examples can be found in Dowsing (1988), Burns (1988) and Inmos (1984).

12.9.2 The Linda abstraction

Linda was developed in the early 1980s (Gelernter, 1985) as a concurrent programming model which aims to give a high-level, abstract view of IPC. Linda is not a complete new programming language, but a set of primitives that may be used to augment a sequential programming language, such as C, C++ or Fortran. Carriero and Gelernter (1989) evaluate Linda in comparison with other concurrent programming paradigms and give examples and references on its use. Andrews (1991) includes Linda in his overview of concurrent programming languages.

In message passing systems, the message passing mechanism is only concerned with the message header, and not the internal structure of the message (see Section 12.4). The header is used to indicate the destination(s) of the message. In Linda, tuples are used instead of messages to communicate information between processes.

A **tuple** is a series of typed fields. Unlike messages, tuples are data objects within the programming language. An example is:

('*tag*', 15.01, 17, '*a string*')

where each field is either an expression or a formal parameter of the form ? *var*, where *var* is a local variable in the executing process. The '*tag*' field is a string literal which is used to distinguish between tuples.

Tuples do not need to have a recipient's name appended as part of a header (following system-defined rules), but instead are deposited into and extracted from 'tuple space' (TS). Depositing a tuple into TS is a non-blocking operation.

A process that wishes to 'receive' a tuple does not need to know who sent it. TS is logically shared by all processes and tuples are received by an **associative search mechanism**; that is, a process can extract a tuple by giving a template of what it requires to have matched in the various fields, as illustrated below. The application programmer can decide, for example, whether one process or any process of a given type or any process that knows about a particular tag in a field of a tuple, etc. should pick up the message. A receiver blocks if there are no matching tuples.

Tuples exist independently of the processes that created them and a multi-tuple data structure in TS may have been created by many processes.

The Linda primitives are:

out   causes a tuple to be generated and deposited into TS,

in   removes from TS a tuple that matches a specified template,

rd   reads a tuple that matches a specified template but does not remove it from TS,

eval   causes a new process to be created. The process executes an assigned routine and, on termination, generates a tuple in TS.

For example, the tuple generated by:

out ('*tag*', 15.01, 17, '*a string*')

can be read by:

rd ('*tag*', ? *f*, ? *i*, '*a string*')

where *f* is a real variable and *i* is an integer variable in the executing process.

The **eval** primitive can be used by a parent to offload work onto a child and later to pick up the result in the form of a tuple. Alternatively, a child can be created in order to generate a tuple to communicate with some other process.

Exercise 12.9 invites the reader to compose a client–server interaction using the Linda primitives. In this case a server must be concerned with who deposited a tuple to make a request for service in order to return a reply tuple.

More examples can be found in the Bibliography but the flavour tends to be of small-scale computations rather than large-scale systems.

Potential problems are in the following areas:

- Naming in the form of simple, unstructured strings is used to discriminate between tuples.

- Protection is a potential problem in that all processes share TS. Any process can read or extract any tuple it can match. This is acceptable within a small-scale application but not for programming a general system, where processes do not necessarily trust each other.

- Efficient implementation is difficult to achieve, even in a centralized system. The implementation needs to be concerned with the contents of the various fields of the tuples and not just a message header, as in a message system. The distinction between a message header, of concern to the system, and a message body, of concern to the application, is clean at the IPC implementation level if inflexible to the applications above it.

- It is not clear how distributed implementation of a global shared TS abstraction would be achieved.

12.10 Multi-threaded servers

A common requirement in system design is the server that can serve many clients simultaneously; the example of a file server was taken in Chapters 7 and 8. Even if such a server receives requests for service in the form of messages, we have the same need for multiple internal threads of control: the work for one client may come to a temporary halt and work should proceed on behalf of another. All such threads may need to access the same system data structures and the shared-memory model of lightweight thread creation and access to shared data by shared memory techniques is desirable within the server.

A system design should therefore support shared-memory techniques as well as cross-address-space message passing.

When we considered shared-memory based IPC in Chapter 10 we found that the possibility of dynamic process creation should be taken into account. A child can be created to invoke the service (by procedure call) and the parent can, later, synchronize with the child to receive the results. The parent process can carry out work in parallel. The same arguments apply in message passing systems if multi-threaded processes are supported and threads may be created dynamically. A child may be created to invoke a service (by message passing) and the parent can continue with work in parallel. This may make simple message passing primitives feasible which are too inflexible for use by single threaded processes.

Further reading on the implementation and use of threads may be found in Anderson *et al.* (1992), Birrell (1991), McJones and Swart (1987) and Nelson (1991). Ousterhout *et al.* (1980) discuss the requirements for threads.

12.11 Summary

Asynchronous message passing was motivated as a general mechanism suitable for cross-address-space IPC. A number of variations in the primitives and in the detailed design and use of messages were described. Various naming schemes for the sources and destinations of messages were also considered.

Implementation was discussed in some detail. The overhead introduced into the system by buffer management and message copying can be alleviated by the use of memory mapping. Alternatively, by using ports associated with the particular processes concerned in a message exchange, the space and time overhead may be allocated to the processes using the facility.

Synchronous message passing avoids copying messages into system buffers at the expense of delaying the sender of a message as well as the receiver. Buffering processes have to be implemented to avoid important server processes being delayed, waiting for less important client processes. A synchronous system is easier to model mathematically than an asynchronous one.

The Linda approach was introduced briefly and compared with message passing. Although the Linda primitives may be convenient and flexible for the writers of concurrent applications, there are many systems issues, such as naming, protection and distribution, to be addressed before Linda can be considered as a basis for concurrent systems in general.

Message passing is a general mechanism which can be implemented with many subtle variations to satisfy the specific requirements of the system that is to use it. It can be incorporated into the programming language level and, in this case, type checking of the message contents can be carried out with the same generality as in the languages for shared memory systems. Flexiblity in system development can be offered in that the binding of modules to machines can be deferred until configuration time or even until runtime.

In a system based on message passing we still need multi-threaded server processes which can work on behalf of many clients simultaneously. The internal implementation of such a server is best done in terms of shared-memory-based communication; a system should support both shared-memory and message-based IPC. The availability of multi-threaded processes affects the choice of message passing primitives. Simple primitives may suffice in a system with multi-threaded processes and dynamic process creation, whereas more complex primitives might be required to do the same job in a single-threaded environment.

Message passing extends naturally to distributed systems and some of the examples given here have been taken from distributed operating systems. To discuss distributed message passing properly we need to consider how network communication is used. Also, processes may fail independently of each other in distributed systems. These issues are addressed in Chapter 14.

Exercises

12.1 Contrast the UNIX pipe facility for same-machine, cross-address-space IPC with message passing.

12.2 Suggest ways in which memory management hardware could be used for passing large messages between processes in separate address spaces. Consider both the case when the message is available to both sender and receiver after the message is sent and the case when the send involves only a transfer from one address space to another. Which semantics do you think should be the default and why?

12.3 Suggest two ways in which the handling of message passing between processes may be unified with process–device interactions.

12.4 What problems do you think would arise if synchronous message passing was used to implement interactions between client processes and heavily used servers? How would you solve these problems?

12.5 How can language-level type checking be included in a message passing system?

12.6 In what ways can the naming of a specific destination process be avoided in a message system design? Why is this desirable?

12.7 What is meant by multicast? What kind of naming service would be needed to support multicast?

12.8 Why might it be important to be able to specify a limit on the time that one is prepared to wait for a message?

12.9 Use the Linda primitives introduced in Section 12.9 to program the interaction between a single centralized file server and its many clients. Generalize your solution to many file servers offering a file service.

13 Crash resilience and persistent data

CONTENTS

 ## 13.1 Crashes

Part II is concerned with the execution of a single action by one process concurrently with and without interference from the execution of related actions by other processes. So far we have not considered that a system might crash at any time. In this chapter we consider this problem in relation to the execution of such a single concurrent action. In Part III higher-level actions comprising multiple lower-level actions are considered. Figure 13.1 shows an operation invocation. We are not concerned with the means by which the invocation takes place, for example, by procedure call or by message passing.

We also assume that the action of invoking the operation takes place in the same machine as the execution of the invoked operation. In this case a crash causing the loss of the contents of main memory causes all the computations to fail together. Invocation from one machine of an operation on another machine will be considered in the next chapter.

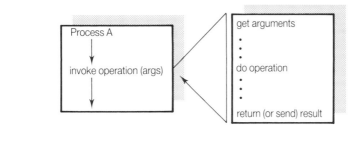

Figure 13.1
An operation
invocation.

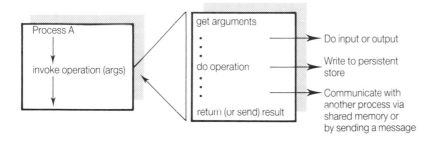

Figure 13.2
An operation
invocation with
externally visible
effects.

Figure 13.2 shows that a single operation invocation might have **externally visible effects**. It might read input, do output, cause a write to **persistent storage** or communicate with another process. A crash might happen after one or more of these effects have occurred but before the end of the operation. What, if anything, should the system do before the invocation is repeated? From the point of view of this chapter we shall consider that communication with another process brings us into the management of sets of related actions and will leave that issue for Part III. We shall therefore consider only those externally visible actions of concern to this process.

Suppose, for example, a client of a TP system invokes a *credit* operation on a bank account, as part of an electronic funds transfer, and the system replies 'done' if the credit has been performed correctly or 'not done' if there is some error such as an unknown account name. There are two externally visible effects: the updated value of the account and the response to the user. In this example these effects are related: if you tell your client you have done an operation you must first have recorded its results in persistent memory.

13.2   A model of a crash

A simple model of a crash will be taken initially a **fail–stop** model. We shall assume that a crash happens at some instant rather than over a period of time. It results in the instantaneous loss of volatile state: the processor registers, the cache and memory management unit, and the (volatile) main memory. Any changes that have been made to persistent state, for example in any non-volatile memory and disk-based storage, are assumed to be correct, but may be incomplete. By making this simplifying assumption we avoid considering how incorrect system software may behave before finally causing a crash. In Section 13.7 we take a more realistic look at the likely behaviour of failing software.

Schlichting and Schneider (1983) discuss the fail–stop model. For further reading, Lamport *et al.* (1982) present an approach to reasoning about failing distributed systems which has become the classic 'Byzantine Generals Problem'.

13.3   Crash resilience or failure transparency

If a program runs on a single machine and a failure occurs we assume that all the memory is lost; that is, all the data structures of the program are lost. If no externally visible effects have been caused by the program it is as though it had never run and it can simply be restarted. In practice, every program will eventually perform output or cause some change of permanent state or communicate an intermediate result. If a crash occurs during a program run and after such an externally visible action, we consider how to restart after the crash.

An aspect of system design is the extent to which an application is offered support to recover from system crashes. Another name for crash resilience is **crash** or **failure transparency**. In this chapter methods of achieving crash resilience are outlined. A general point is that there is a high overhead associated with these methods and some applications will not require them. Crash resilience should therefore, in most systems, be an optional extra rather than being imposed on every application.

13.4   Idempotent (repeatable) operations

In certain simple cases it is possible to ensure that an operation can be repeated without causing any errors or inconsistencies. When deciding how certain operations should be specified, for example the form their arguments should take, it may be possible to choose an idempotent implementation. For example, the repeatable method of writing a sequence of bytes to the end of a file is to specify the precise byte position at which the new bytes should be written and make this an argument of an 'append' operation. If an append operation is relative to a system-maintained pointer, the bytes could be written more than once if the operation was repeated. It is not always possible to achieve repeatable operations.

This point becomes more important in distributed systems, when a congested network may cause a reply message saying 'operation done' to be greatly delayed or lost. The invoker does not know this and repeats the request when the operation requested has already been carried out.

13.5 Atomic operations

The concept of an atomic operation is necessary for a systematic approach to analysing and solving the problem of making an operation repeatable. An atomic operation invocation is defined as follows:

- if it terminates normally then all its effects are made permanent;
- else it has no effect at all.

Note that this definition (which focuses on crash resilience) does not take into account the fact that the persistent data being accessed might be shared with other processes (that is, concurrency control is also needed). In this case we should add:

- if the operation accesses a shared data object, its invocation does not interfere with other operation invocations on the same data object.

It is essential to provide atomic operation invocations in some transaction processing (TP) systems, as argued in Section 1.1.2. They are called **transactions**, that is, the term transaction implies atomicity. Examples are banking and airline booking systems.

A programming language which supports atomic operations will provide a means of defining the start and end of a given transaction. If the operation completes successfully it is said to **commit** (and its effects are guaranteed to be permanent); if it does not complete it **aborts**. The system must make sure that all the effects of an aborted transaction are undone, as though it had never run. The result of an invocation, commit or abort, is usually notified to the invoking client (a human user or other software).

Suppose, for example, a client of a TP system invokes a *credit* operation on a bank account as part of an electronic funds transfer, and the system replies 'done' if the credit has been performed correctly or 'not done' if there has been some error such as an unknown account name. Suppose the system crashes after the invocation has started but before 'done' or 'not done' is sent to the client. The record in persistent store of the value of the bank account might or might not reflect the credit.

If *credit* is an atomic operation then the invocation which did not complete correctly must be undone; effectively it never happened. When the system comes up again the client repeats the operation. This invocation updates the account correctly and 'done' is received by the client. There is no possibility of multiple, and therefore incorrect, credits (or debits). Also, once the client has received 'done' the credit must persist, even if there is a head crash on the disk on which the account is stored.

General points are therefore:

● Computer systems crash, data in main memory is lost.
● If the system tells a client (human user or software) that an atomic operation has been done then the changes made by it must have been recorded in persistent store.

13.5.1 Volatile, persistent and stable storage

We established above that an atomic operation must write its results to persistent store before it commits. We also emphasized that this record must persist, even if there is a medium failure such as a bad block or a head crash which destroys the surface of a disk. For this reason an abstraction called **stable storage** has been established.

A single write to persistent store does not guarantee that the information written will persist. In practice, the information is typically written to at least two independent places in persistent store, so that if one copy is lost the other can be used. The phrase 'write to stable storage' is used as a shorthand for such a replicated write.

13.6 Implementation of atomic operations

Figure 13.3 illustrates the essentials for implementing an atomic operation. When the execution causes a write to persistent store, both the old value and the new value of the data must be recorded in some form, together with the identifier of the transaction that carried out the update. This is so that if a crash occurs before the operation completes, the old value can be restored. This is sometimes referred to as **rolling back** the state recorded in persistent store or **undoing** the operation.

Rolling back through input could be done by recording the input and reusing it. Depending on the application, any output might be done again if the operation is repeated, or the output that has been carried out may be recorded and repeats avoided.

This is a very general outline of atomic operations. In the context of Part II, a single operation invocation could be defined as involving only a single read, modify and write of a persistent object, and rolling back seems unnecessary at first sight.

However, if a crash occurs after the operation's single write to disk and before the operation returns, the invocation could be repeated. The final state recorded in persistent store could be affected by the first, abortive invocation, as in the *credit* example of Section 13.1.

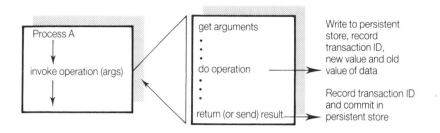

Figure 13.3
A potentially
atomic operation
invocation.

A great deal of overhead is associated with implementing atomic operations. The persistent store may be disk, in which case each write would require an acknowledged disk transfer. In some operating systems, for example UNIX, an apparent write to disk is merely a transfer into a cache in main memory and this would clearly not be good enough to implement atomic operations.

There are two basic approaches which may be used to support rollback; these are logging and shadowing.

13.6.1   Logging

The persistent store is changed (updated in place) and a record is kept in a log. The log entry must contain an identifier for the transaction, the old data value and the new data value. The log will contain a number of records for each transaction, for example, a record indicating a new transaction, a number of update records and an end of transaction (or commit) record.

After a crash the log is processed in order to restore the persistent store to a consistent state. Any partially executed transaction can be undone; that is, the persistent store is rolled back to its state at the start of the transaction using the old values recorded in the log.

An important practical point is that the log must be written to persistent store before the data in the persistent store is changed. If these operations were carried out in the reverse order, a crash could occur before the log was written and after the data was changed and the old data values would be lost. The log must therefore be a **write-ahead log**.

Details of algorithms for log processing are considered further in Chapter 19.

13.6.2   Shadowing

An alternative mechanism is to leave the persistent data unchanged until the transaction is committed but to build up a shadow data structure which will replace it on successful termination (when the transaction is committed).

An essential technique here is to make the final switch between the old and new data structures achievable in a single operation, for example by changing

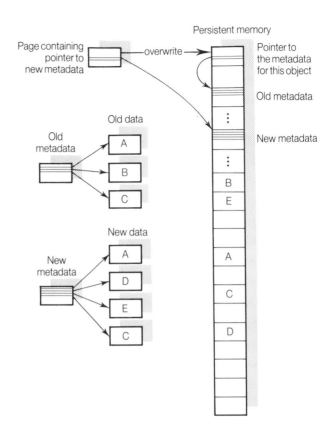

Figure 13.4
An example
illustrating
shadow paging.

one pointer. A crash can then occur only before or after the switch and not in the middle.

The implementation of shadowing may be built at the level of disk pages – a **shadow paging** mechanism. This is because the disk is written in units of fixed-sized blocks or pages. This technique can be used in filing systems where the data structures kept by the file storage service (which themselves are stored in disk pages) map the disk pages in use for storing files, directories and so on.

Figure 13.4 gives an example of one way in which a shadow paging scheme might be used. Here we see a representation of an old and new version of a given object. The figure shows the stage at which all the object's data is safely written to the disk, as are the pages containing the old and new version of the metadata. The figure illustrates a scheme where a certain disk block contains a mapping from an object's name to the location of its metadata. The change from the old version of the object to the new one is achieved by overwriting this block with one containing the new pointer.

We can make the simple assumption that the write of a single disk block is atomic. Either the new block is written, in which case we have switched to the new version of the object, or it isn't, in which case we still have the old version.

If we are not prepared to make this assumption and there is a crash during the write of this page we can read it back on restart and examine the pointer. If the crash took place before this pointer was transferred we still have the old version; if afterwards, we have the new version. This assumes that writing a single pointer is atomic.

An alternative scheme is that the object's name maps onto a particular meta-data location on disk. In this case, having written the data pages to disk, we can overwrite the old metadata with the new.

13.7   Non-volatile memory

Non-volatile RAM (NVRAM) is becoming available in reasonably large units. For example, in 1987 units up to 1 Mbyte could be purchased at about four times the cost of normal RAM; in 1990 units of up to 8 Mbytes were available at the same relative and absolute cost. There are many potential uses for NVRAM, for example:

- For caching data in a file storage service. This allows fast response to write requests, but gives the assurance that the data is stored securely, normally achieved by an acknowledged write out to disk.

- To hold the file service's data structures. When a change is made it need not be written out immediately, to achieve consistency of the stored filing system.

- To accumulate requests for writes to disk and to order them for use by an efficient disk-arm scheduling algorithm.

- If NVRAM is available to high levels of system software which have knowl-edge of the semantics of data at a fine granularity, then shadowing can be implemented at a finer granularity than disk pages. When the new data struc-ture is complete it can be written to the disks of the storage service in its entirety.

In practice, a system may not fail in the fail–stop manner described above. Wild addresses might be generated while the system is failing, causing writes to areas of memory that were not intended. This behaviour might cause the data we are carefully preserving in non-volatile memory to be corrupted. Also, we may be taking advantage of the availability of NVRAM to hold more data in main memory and deliberately delaying its write to disk. Have we made our sys-tem more vulnerable to this kind of failure behaviour by using NVRAM?

Because a very specific protocol has to be followed for writing to disk it is unlikely that failing software will write all over the disk by accident. In this respect, NVRAM is more vulnerable than disk.

Recall from Chapter 5 that filing systems may keep data in a volatile cache in memory. In some systems data may not be written out as soon as possible, but may be kept in memory until the buffer space it occupies is needed. Also, the filing system's metadata is changed in volatile main memory before being written out to disk. There is therefore the possibility that failing software might corrupt these items before they are written out. This is equally true for volatile and non-volatile memory, although we are likely to keep more data in memory for longer if we have NVRAM. To achieve crash resilience we should not only store this data in NVRAM, but also protect the NVRAM from corruption. If this is possible we shall have achieved both better response to write requests and better protection of data and metadata through using NVRAM.

One approach to protecting NVRAM is to require a simple protocol to be followed in order to write to it (Needham *et al.*, 1986). Another is to use memory management hardware to protect it. It is unlikely that failing software would accidentally change the memory management tables correctly and give itself access to NVRAM by accident.

13.8 A single operation on persistent data

For most of Part II we have considered the case where the data structures accessed by concurrent processes reside in main memory. In order to consider the effects of crashes we have started to look at the externally visible effects of operations. We have therefore begun to focus on persistent store. Figure 13.5 shows an operation (specified as part of a module's interface) operating on persistent data. An example is an implementation of an airline booking system, as used in Section 8.7.1, where we focused on the value in main memory of the variable *unbooked-seats*. In fact, the information on a particular flight would be retrieved from persistent memory before being tested and updated in main memory:

> **if** *unbooked-seats* >0
>   **then** *unbooked-seats* := *unbooked-seats* –1;

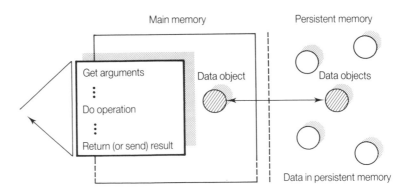

Figure 13.5
An operation on
persistent data.

The result would then be written back to persistent memory. The single operation therefore involves a read, modify, and write of persistent memory.

An obvious concern is whether another concurrent process could access the same data object in persistent store at the same time. In the next section we consider one approach to solving this problem. The basic model there is that an application-level service, such as a DBMS, manages the persistent data of the application. We assume that any service of this kind is likely to be multi-threaded; that is, several threads will be executing the service code at a given time, on behalf of different clients.

The persistent data is assumed to be stored in files and the operating system provides file-level concurrency control (see Section 5.1.1). The application service reads any required data from the relevant files into main memory. The application service is therefore in a position to carry out any fine-grained concurrency control that is required; that is, a given data object which is stored as a component of an OS file may be locked by and within the application service on behalf of a client.

In general, a concurrent program may need to access persistent data objects that are stored within operating system files. Let us first assume that the program is seen by the operating system as a single, possibly multi-threaded, process. The OS sees the process as the unit of resource allocation and will allow any thread of that process to open the files to which it has access rights. The situation is as described above for an application service.

If the concurrent system comprises several (heavyweight) processes, these are seen as separate units of resource allocation by the operating system. The access rights associated with OS files may be set up so that any of the processes comprising the application may read, write and so on. It is the responsibility of the concurrent system developer to organize any required sharing of data objects stored in these files.

The next section highlights the points raised in this discussion. A concurrent system may need to access persistent data stored within OS files and may need to implement atomic operations. Its developer must know in detail how certain functions of the operating system on which it will run are provided.

13.9   Database management systems' requirements on operating systems

When a concurrent system which must provide transactions (such as a DBMS) is implemented above a general-purpose OS, the following must be considered:

- the file buffer management policy of the OS;
- the concurrency control facilities provided by the OS.

When the DBMS makes a file-write request, and the OS says 'done', the data must have been written to persistent memory. It is not sufficient for the data to

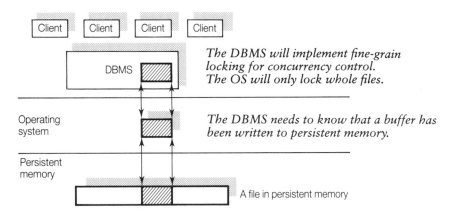

Figure 13.6
A DBMS using
an operating
system.

get as far as an OS buffer in volatile main memory. A crash could occur and the data could be lost. In the meantime, the DBMS has told its client that the operation is committed and has no means of effecting this.

As we saw in Chapter 5, a file management system provides facilities for its clients to specify who can use a given file and in what way. Assuming that several users have write access to a given file and are running processes simultaneously, there could be simultaneous requests to open the same file for writing. If the file system has **mandatory concurrency control** (see Section 5.1.1), then a multiple reader, single writer policy might be enforced, making concurrent write access, or simultaneous read and write access, impossible. The first process to open the file for writing has exclusive access to all of it.

In a centralized system this might work well enough. A client of the filing system that wished to manage a database (the client is a DBMS), and make it available to its own users in turn, would own the files holding the data and would take out a write lock on them. It would then take concurrent requests from users and manage any sharing of small parts of the data. Figure 13.6 shows such a centralized DBMS.

It might be difficult to implement a distributed DBMS in this way, since the several DBMS components would be perceived by the operating system as competing rather than cooperating users of its files. If the filing system has a more enlightened concurrency control policy it might allow its clients to build systems in which concurrent write access is allowed. Operations which lock files might be provided separate from the normal file operations. Shared locks and exclusive locks could be provided without any association with reads and writes. Distributed DBMS components could take out a shared lock and cooperate to ensure that concurrent clients did not access the same part of the data at the same time.

Operating systems may support shared or exclusive locks on whole files, but do not support fine granularity locking on small portions of files. This is done by the DBMS.

Database management systems are discussed in greater detail in Part III.

13.10   Summary

Computer systems crash and main memory is lost on a crash. If a single operation invocation takes place in the main memory of a single computer and has no externally visible effects then there is no need for crash resilience. If the operation has written to persistent store we have to decide what to do if there is a crash before it completes. We should design operations to be **idempotent** (repeatable) if it is possible to do so, but this is not always possible.

We defined **atomic operations** as a basis for studying the more general case. An atomic operation either completes successfully, in which case its results are guaranteed to persist, or the system state is restored as though the operation had never been invoked. If you tell a client an operation is done (by output, which is one form of externally visible effect of an operation) then its results must first have been written to persistent memory.

There is a great deal of overhead associated with supporting atomic operations. The system must be able to undo an incomplete operation. Approaches to achieving this were outlined, but more detail will be given in Part III.

We considered what is meant by a 'single operation' on persistent data. In Section 8.8 a read–modify–write sequence of operations on data in main memory was shown to comprise a single operation, such as 'book a seat'. The point made there was that several reads and writes of data in main memory may be necessary to achieve a change to a data object. The additional point made in this chapter is that unless the result of the operation is recorded in persistent memory a crash might destroy any record that the operation ever took place (even though the client has been notified that the seat is booked). Computers crash, so we must use persistent store to implement atomic operations.

Access to persistent data is likely to be via an operating system and concurrent write sharing of OS files (introduced in Chapter 5) was revisited. The DBMS will manage fine-grained component locking within a file whereas the OS is concerned only with whole file locking. If atomic operations are to be supported, the DBMS must know when data has been written to persistent memory by the OS.

The final chapter of Part II discusses a single operation invoked from a remote machine. In this case it is necessary to consider the possibility that either the invoking system or the system containing the invoked operation might crash at any time.

Exercises

13.1 (a) How do you think an operating system which has bugs and is about to crash might behave differently from the fail–stop model described in Section 13.2?

(b) Why is it unlikely that an operating system that is about to crash will write all over the disks it manages?

(c) Is it more likely that an operating system that is about to crash will write all over main memory? Note that such erroneous writes may be to non-volatile memory that is being used as a cache for data and metadata waiting to be written to disk. How could it be made less likely that a non-volatile cache would be corrupted in this way?

13.2   Define 'idempotent operation' and 'atomic operation'. Give examples of operations that can and cannot be made idempotent. How can an operation that cannot be made idempotent be made atomic?

13.3   How would you support atomic operations in a system which updates persistent data values 'in place'; that is, the new values overwrite the old values in the persistent store.

13.4   What is meant by a shadow copy of a portion of a filing system?

Distributed IPC

14

CONTENTS

14.1 Client–server and object models for distributed software systems

In Chapter 2 we set up a context of modular software. In Chapter 11 we explored the duality of system structures: work is done either by calling an interface procedure of a passive module or by requesting an active process to do the same job by sending it a message. In this chapter we distribute the modular software system.

We have often come across the idea of a dedicated server computer offering, for example, a file service or a mail service (see Sections 7.3 and 8.1). The **client–server model** is appropriate for these and many other distributed computations. In this model, a server maintains data objects and defines operations on them which are exported to clients. Clients invoke these operations to manipulate the data managed by the servers. This chapter focuses on the language and

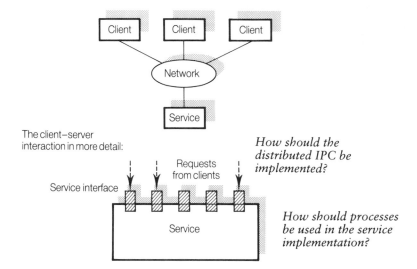

Figure 14.1
Client–server
interaction in a
distributed system,

communications support for this invocation. The issues of naming and locating services in distributed systems are discussed in Section 14.9.

Some **distributed operating systems** have taken the client–server model as the paradigm for their design, for example, the Amoeba system (Mullender and Tanenbaum, 1986; Tanenbaum *et al.*, 1990). Others are based on a more general **object model** (refer to Chapter 2 for a definition of abstract data types and objects). The **client–server model** can be seen as a special case of an object model in which data objects are managed by servers. The problem of **locating** a data object in a distributed system which is based on the client–server model reduces to locating the server that manages the object. The problem of **naming** objects is simplified by allowing an object to be named by its managing server.

In a general object model, objects are named and located in a global context and operations are invoked on them directly, rather than via a server. The underlying system must support the naming and location of objects. It is common for the system to attempt to bring an object to the invoking process, for example, to map an object into the address space of the process that invokes it. It might be the case, however, that the object is already mapped elsewhere and a remote invocation is needed. It is beyond the scope of this book to study object-oriented systems in detail.

Examples of object-oriented systems are Eden (Almes, 1985), Emerald (Black *et al.*, 1986), COOL (Habert *et al.*, 1990) and Somiw-SOS (Shapiro, 1986). Mach, which is presented as a case study in Chapter 22, is said to be designed according to an object-oriented paradigm. ANSA (1989) and Comandos (Horn and Krakowiak, 1987; Balter, 1992) define an object-oriented paradigm for distributed computing. The current release of the ANSA testbench adheres to the simpler client–server model.

In all cases, modules, abstract types and objects, we assume operations at the interface which are invoked by processes in order to carry out their computations. In this chapter we focus on how a process running on one machine can invoke an operation on an object which is on another machine. Figure 14.1 gives the general context of a number of clients invoking a service across a network. The questions that arise from the figure are:

- How should the service be implemented in terms of concurrent processes? The discussion of Sections 6.11, 7.5 and especially 8.1 are relevant here. Ideally, we should like to use a multi-threaded process with threads that are known to the operating system.

- How should the distributed service invocation be implemented? In previous chapters we have studied methods of service invocation without specifically relating them to a centralized or distributed implementation. We now focus on distributed IPC.

First, we consider how a distributed system differs from a centralized one from the point of view of software design.

Terminology: A number of different names are used in the literature to indicate a single component computer system in a distributed system, such as host, node or site. We shall use the term node, and also client and server where appropriate.

14.2 Special characteristics of distributed systems

The distinguishing characteristics of a distributed system may be summarized as follows:

1. *Independent failure modes*
   The components of a distributed program and the network connecting them may fail independently of each other.

2. *No global time*
   We assume that each component of the system has a local clock, but the clocks might not record the same time. The hardware on which the clocks are based is not guaranteed to run at precisely the same rate at all components of the system.

3. *Inconsistent state*
   It takes time for the effects of an event at one point in a distributed system to propagate throughout the system. There need not be a consistent view of the system state at every point in the system.

We consider points 1 and 2 below and point 3 is revisited at the start of Chapter 20.

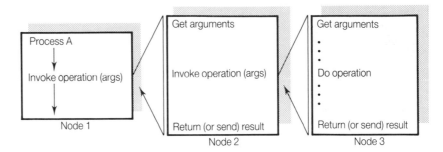

Figure 14.2
A nested
invocation.

14.2.1 Distributed operation invocation and independent failure modes

In a distributed system a process on one node may invoke an operation on another which, in turn, may invoke an operation on a third node, as shown in Figure 14.2. In Chapter 13 the notion that a single system might crash at any time was introduced. In the example illustrated in Figure 14.2 any one of these nodes may crash independently of the others at any stage in the invocations. Also, the network connections between the nodes may fail while the nodes continue to run.

14.2.2 Time in a distributed system

Figure 14.3 shows three nodes in a distributed system with a time graph for a process running at each node. An external observer can conceive of global or universal time that is the same for each of the systems, but in practice this cannot easily be implemented. Each system has a local clock which it uses for all timing purposes and such clock devices may run at slightly different rates from each other.

Figure 14.4 shows a communication from process X on node R to process Y on node S; let us assume a message is sent. We assume that messages are received one at a time at a given node. We can safely assert that X sent the message before Y received it, whatever the local clocks at R and S might indicate.

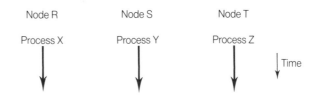

Figure 14.3
Processes in a
distributed system.

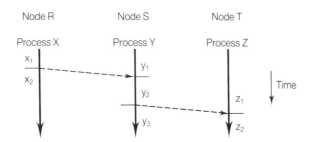

Figure 14.4
Communicating processes in a distributed system.

After receiving the message, Y does some processing and then sends a message to Z. It is clear that Y received the message from X before sending a message to Z, since both events are on the same time-scale. Z receives the message after Y sent it.

The events within a single sequential process are ordered. Communication events impose a partial ordering on events in the system as a whole. The events in process X in region x_1 happen before the events in process Y in regions y_2 and y_3. Also, the 'before' relation is transitive: the events in process X in region x_1 happen before the events in process Z in region z_2. Unless there were other messages, we cannot know and do not care about the relative ordering of the events in region x_1 in process X and those in region y_1 in process Y or region z_1 in process Z.

The classic paper by Lamport (1978) introduced and formalized this topic in a computer science context and Lamport (1990) extended the work. Einstein had, of course, already defined these concepts for a universal context.

14.2.3 Protocols for achieving a single logical system time

The time at which an event occurs only matters if the event is relevant at more than one node in a distributed system. Suppose that process X puts a time-stamp on the message it sends to process Y and that process Y finds that the reading of its local clock is earlier than that time-stamp when it receives the message. The clocks have clearly drifted apart. The clock at node S could be reset to a value greater than the time-stamp of the message to achieve correct relative ordering of the events in the two processes. Within a single process, events can be ordered by ensuring that the clock is incremented between any two communication events. The problem is that clocks are always advanced and system time may drift a long way ahead of real time. This does not matter a great deal because these timers are not used for time and date calculations. If the system became quiescent, all the clocks could be reset, but this is not feasible in a large-scale system.

The aim of the protocol is to achieve an ordering of events for the whole distributed system rather than to achieve a consistent value of time at every node that participates in communication. An alternative, or supplementary, approach is to use a protocol to synchronize the values of the clocks periodically by requiring each system component to broadcast its clock value to all the other system components. No clock can ever be put back (the values must be monotonically increasing) but clocks can be put forward to the value of the fastest clock. Alternative versions of protocols of this kind, which require fewer message exchanges than implied above, have been devised.

As distributed systems become larger, and perhaps involve satellites, stations on the moon or space probes, it may become unrealistic to aim for global time or a system-wide ordering of events. Within a reasonably small-scale system it may become feasible for each node to receive and service a time signal interrupt, from a single source such as a satellite, at a sufficiently fine time grain to keep the clocks synchronized.

14.3 Distributed processes and distributed IPC

Figure 11.7 summarizes the styles of inter-process communication mechanism that can be used for operation invocation. They were discussed in detail in Chapters 8 to 12. It is feasible to distribute any of these models. In a distributed implementation the left-hand box for each model in the figure is on one node, the right-hand box is on another, and the implementation of the interprocess communication mechanism must include cross-network communication.

A design decision for a distributed IPC scheme is whether the fact that processes are distributed is transparent to the application. We shall see an example of a non-transparent mechanism, where a connection is set up explicitly for a local communication or a remote one, in Section 21.16. In this case a network communication package was developed for a variant of UNIX and local IPC was integrated with it. We now consider how a distribution-transparent message passing mechanism might be devised.

14.3.1 Distributed message passing

Figure 12.2 shows asynchronous message passing on a single node, indicating an implementation level with routines to effect the SEND and WAIT primitives and a data structure for buffering the messages sent to process B. In a single node we can assume that the IPC implementation knows the name of the destination of any message and can deliver the message. We now develop a distributed message passing system, starting from this centralized design.

Figure 14.5 shows one approach to implementing distributed asynchronous message passing. The IPC management function is extended to invoke network

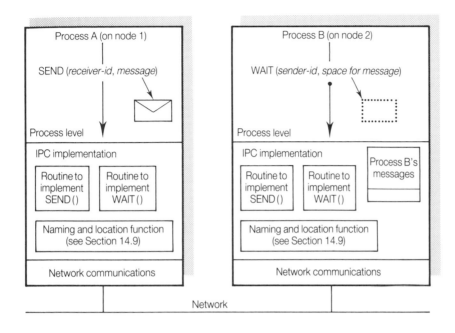

Figure 14.5
Distributed
message passing.

communication. Process A now runs on node 1 and SENDs a message to Process B which is on node 2. Process B WAITs for a message from Process A. We assume that the IPC implementation on node 1 can detect that Process B is not a local process and either knows or can find out that Process B resides on node 2. There are several ways in which this **naming and location function** can be provided in a distributed system, and we return to the topic in Section 14.9.

The implementation of a SEND message on node 1 can invoke network communication software to transmit the message to node 2. The network communication software on node 2 can receive the message from the network, and pass it to the IPC mechanism for delivery to the message buffer of process B. Figure 14.6 gives a higher-level view of the same procedure, showing virtual communication at the process level being implemented by real communication through the supporting levels and across the network. Recall that network communications software was discussed briefly in Chapter 3.

The basic approach illustrated here may be used to distribute any form of IPC transparently to the application. Here we have assumed that the kernel determines that a communication is to a non-local process and itself takes action to locate the destination. We shall see an alternative approach, which is used in the Accent and Mach kernels, in Sections 22.1 and 22.2. Here, the kernel detects a non-local communication and passes the message to a local process which is responsible for all network communication, the *NetServer* process. The basic idea is illustrated in Figure 14.7. The IPC implementation now handles only

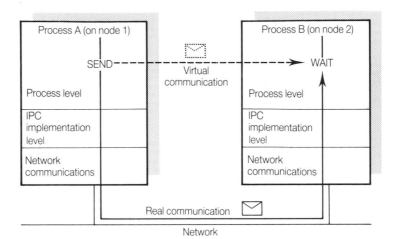

Figure 14.6
Virtual and real
communication
paths.

local communication and the *NetServer* process acts as an indirection for remote communication. An advantage of this approach is that the kernel is kept simple. A disadvantage is the extra context switching and message passing between user-level processes (A and the *NetServer*) that is needed to send a message to a non-local process. Incoming messages are passed by the communications software to the *NetServer* process, which can use a local SEND to deliver them to their intended destination.

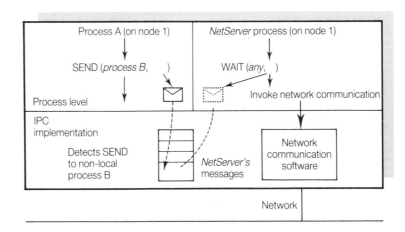

Figure 14.7
Using a process to
handle remote
communication.

14.4 Synchronous (blocking) and asynchronous communication

When a remote invocation is made it could take some time for the result to come back. It may be that the invoking process could do some work in parallel. A major design decision is whether asynchronous communication of this form will be used or whether a synchronous, or **blocking**, primitive is preferable. A general consensus is that asynchronous communication is difficult to program but it is sometimes offered as an option, see Section 14.9.3.

As shown in Chapter 8, however, we can have the best of both worlds if we have a FORK primitive available: that is, the ability to create a new process dynamically. A child process can be forked to make the remote invocation and WAIT for the result, after which it can synchronize with its parent in the usual way to pass the result. The parent can proceed with parallel work which might include forking more children to make more remote invocations. Note that it is necessary for the application to run on a kernel which supports multi-threaded processes to achieve concurrent execution of the parent with the blocked child. If the kernel sees only one process, and that process blocks for remote communication, no other component subprocess can run.

A way of viewing this model is that concurrency and distribution issues have been separated. Concurrency has been achieved by using FORK as before and the concept used for distributed programming is of a **distributed sequential process**. That is, the child process is a distributed sequential process (see Figure 14.8).

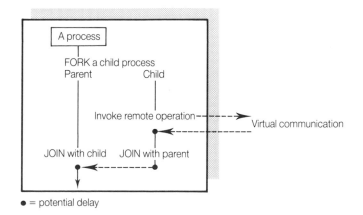

• = potential delay

Figure 14.8
Forking a child to make a synchronous call.

14.5   Distributed programming paradigms

The processes involved in a remote invocation are certainly running in separate address spaces as they are on different machines. One might therefore assume that message passing of some kind would be the best programming model for distributed IPC. We have just argued, however, that a synchronous model is preferable for manageable remote communication. This could be achieved by enforcing that a SEND request is immediately followed by a WAIT reply, perhaps by inventing a single primitive which combines them. This is done in the Amoeba distributed operating system and is the only communication paradigm supported in that system.

An alternative is to support a procedure call to a *remote* procedure. This is an attractive notion, since procedural programming languages are in widespread use. A facility for distributed sequential programming could be offered by this means for those users who do not have a requirement for concurrent programming but who need to make use of remote services. It can be incorporated into a concurrent programming language, as outlined above in Section 14.4.

For these reasons a great deal of effort has been directed towards remote procedure call (RPC) systems. Several are available, as products such as Xerox Courier and Sun RPC. Some, such as ANSA (1989), have been developed as standards to run above a wide variety of operating system and communications services. Others are part of research projects and have been integrated into high-level language systems, such as CCLU RPC, developed at Cambridge University, UK (Bacon and Hamilton, 1987) .

14.6   Remote procedure call (RPC)

An RPC system consists of a communications protocol, which typically sits on top of a transport-level service, such as the ARPA UDP/IP hierarchy, and language-level routines concerned with assembling the data to be passed by the protocol. It is also necessary to provide a mechanism for binding remote procedure names to network addresses. This is the requirement for a naming and location function that we saw when we distributed a message passing system in Section 14.3.1. Section 14.9 discusses this further. An overview of a typical RPC system will now be given, followed by a discussion of alternative ways in which this service might be provided.

14.6.1   An RPC system

Figure 14.9 outlines system components that are invoked when a remote procedure call is made. Binding remote procedure names to addresses is not shown. A request–reply–acknowledge (RRA) protocol is assumed. An alternative is

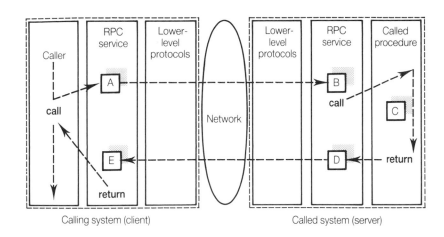

Figure 14.9
An RPC system.

request–acknowledge–reply–acknowledge (RARA). In the former case it is assumed that the reply is likely to come back sufficiently quickly to function as an acknowledgement of the request.

First the operation of the RPC protocol when client, server and network are performing well will be described. In this case a procedure call is made which is detected (by some means, which will be discussed in Section 14.7) to be a remote procedure call. Arguments are specified as usual. Control passes to point A in the diagram.

At point A:

- the arguments are packed into a data structure suitable for transfer across the network;
- an RPC identifier is generated for this call;
- a timer is set.

The data is then passed to lower protocol levels for transportation across the network. Typically, this is done by making a system call into the kernel. At the called system the lower levels deliver it up to the RPC service level.

At point B:

- the arguments are unpacked from the network buffer data structure in a form suitable for making a local procedure call;
- the RPC identifier is noted.

The call is then made to the required remote procedure, which is executed at C. The return from the procedure is to the calling environment in the RPC system, point D.

At point D:

- the return arguments are packed into a network buffer;
- another timer is set.

On arrival at the calling system's RPC service level, point E:

- the return arguments are unpacked;
- the timer set at point A is disabled;
- an acknowledgement is sent for this RPC ID (the timer at D can then be disabled).

14.6.2 The RPC protocol with network or server congestion

The systems involved in the RPC may be performing badly or the network may be congested or suffer a transient failure, causing the timers at A or D to expire. The RPC service level at the calling system, point A, may retry the call a few times without involving the application level. If the problem was network congestion the request may or may not have got through to the called system, depending on the service offered by the lower-level protocols. The RPC ID is used by the called system to detect a repeated call. If the call is still in progress it need take no action. If a reply has been sent it can be re-sent in case of loss. The actions described here can be called 'EXACTLY ONCE RPC semantics' in the absence of node crashes or prolonged network failure.

In some RPC systems the user is given a choice of RPC semantics. 'AT MOST ONCE semantics' means that as soon as the timeout at A expires, control is returned to the application level. The protocol does not retry, although the application level is likely to do so.

14.6.3 The RPC protocol with node crash and restart

In a local procedure call, caller and called procedures crash together. In a remote procedure call the following possibilities must be considered (the node containing the call is referred to as the client, that containing the called procedure, the server).

Client failure

The client may fail after sending the request. The remote call will go ahead (termed an **orphan**), as will any further related calls that it may make (more orphans), but the timer at **D** will expire and no acknowledgement will be received on prompting. The server, and other invoked servers, may have made permanent state changes as a result of the call.

Some server operations can be made repeatable (idempotent), recall Section 13.4.

The application-level client, on being restarted, may repeat the same call but the repeat cannot be detected as such by the RPC service and a new ID will be generated.

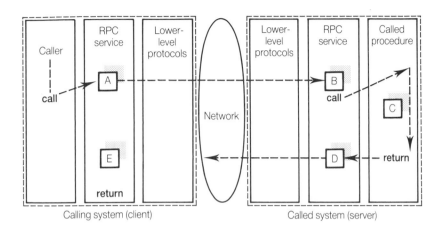

Figure 14.10
Client crash.

Most RPC systems aim to provide an efficient communication facility and make no attempt to exterminate orphans. Software at higher levels may provide atomic transactions with checkpointing and rollback facilities, as discussed in Chapter 13. The performance penalties associated with such a service can be high and should not be made mandatory for all applications.

Server failure

The server may fail before the call is received or at some point during the call (in all cases the client timeout at A will expire):

- after the RPC service receives the call but before the call to the remote procedure is made, point B;
- during the remote procedure invocation, C;
- after the remote procedure invocation but before the result is sent, D.

In all cases the client might repeat the call when the server restarts. In cases C and D this could cause problems since the server could have made permanent state changes before crashing. Again, most RPC systems do not attempt to handle rolling back state changes associated with incomplete RPCs before accepting further calls. To do this it would be necessary for the RPC service to retain RPC IDs through crashes. Some form of stable storage could be used or a time-stamp could be included in the ID so that the server could distinguish pre- and post-crash calls and could undo incomplete pre-crash calls.

14.6.4 An example: CCLU RPC call semantics

The CCLU RPC programmer has a choice of call semantics. The default is the lightweight MAYBE:

   t: *a_type* := **call** *a_remote_proc* (*<args>*)

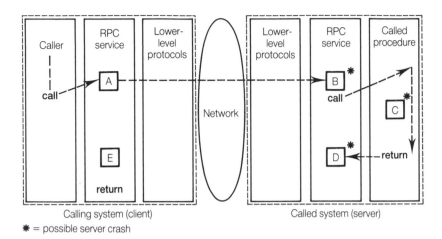

Figure 14.11
Example of a server
crash.

✱ = possible server crash

If the alternative 'reliable' EXACTLY ONCE (in the absence of node crashes) is required, the keyword **zealously** is appended to the call. For example:

call *logger* ('kernel running low on heap') **zealously**

The keyword **timeout,** followed by an integer expression representing a time in milliseconds, may be appended to any remote call. For MAYBE calls, this represents the time after which the call should be abandoned. For EXACTLY ONCE calls it represents the recommended interval between retries.

If an error occurs during execution of a remote call, the RPC will signal either the *hard_error or soft_error* exception, together with an error code. *soft_error* is only signalled by the MAYBE call mechanism and indicates that an error has occurred, such as a timeout or apparent congestion at the remote node, but that a retry may succeed. Hard error is signalled by both the MAYBE and EXACTLY ONCE options and indicates that an apparently unrecoverable error has occurred, for example, failure to contact the server node or denial by the server node that the called *a_remote_proc* is to be found there.

An exception handler for the MAYBE protocol would have the form:

begin
    .
    t: *a_type* := **call** *a_remote_proc* (*<args>*) **timeout** 2000
    .
end except
    when *problem* (*p*: *problem*):
    . . .   % exception signalled by the remote procedure
    when *hard_error* (*why*: *int*):
    . . .   % not worth retrying
    when *soft_error* (*why*: *int*):
    . . .   % worth retrying a few times
    end

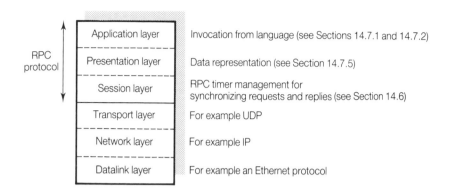

Figure 14.12
RPC in relation to
the ISO reference
model for OSI.

where *problem* is an exception signalled by the remote procedure, for example, because of an incorrect argument value. An example of a remote procedure declaration which includes this exception is given in Section 14.7.1.

14.6.5   RPC and the ISO reference model

Communications protocols were introduced in Chapter 3. Section 3.10 showed a typical division of the ISO layers between an operating system and the applications it supports. The transport level and below were located in the operating system. Similarly, in Figures 14.9, 14.10 and 14.11 the lower-level protocols are assumed to be those at transport level and below. The discussion above has assumed that the RPC protocol is built on an unreliable transport service such as ARPA's UDP (User Datagram Protocol) rather than a reliable connection-oriented protocol such as TCP (Transmission Control Protocol). Figure 14.12 shows an RPC protocol in relation to the ISO layers.

The RPC protocol described above has provided a **session-level service**: client and server were synchronized for request, reply and acknowledgement by the use of timers. We now go on to consider the application and presentation levels associated with RPC.

14.7   RPC–language integration

The previous section has described an RPC protocol in some detail. The issues involved in integrating an RPC service into the language level are now considered.

14.7.1 Distribution transparency

A design issue is the extent to which the fact that some procedures are remote is made transparent to the application. One approach is to acknowledge that remote calls are likely to take substantially longer than local ones and that parts of a distributed program may fail separately. It may be argued that distribution transparency should not be a goal. In this case changes can be made to the language, in the syntax for procedure declaration and call, to distinguish procedures that may be called by remote processes and indicate when they are being invoked.

The non-transparent approach

An example of the **non-transparent** approach taken in CCLU is as follows. The definition of a procedure which may be called from a remote node contains the keyword **remoteproc** replacing **proc** in the header. Other aspects remain the same.

> *a_remote_proc* = **remoteproc** (*<args>*)
> > **returns** (*a_type*)
> > **signals** (*problem*)
> > .
> > .
>
> **end** *a_remote_proc*

A new syntax, the call expression, is used for performing RPCs. The keyword **call** precedes the invoked procedure's name and a number of control keywords (**resignal, zealously, timeout, at**) may follow the invocation's arguments; for example:

> *v* : *a_type* := **call** *a_remote_proc* (*<args>*) **resignal** *problem*

where *problem* is an exception signalled by the remote procedure, shown in the procedure declaration. (A CLU procedure, both when returning normally and signalling an exception, may return an arbitrary number of results of arbitrary type.)

The transparent approach

The **transparent** approach means that the compiler (or a preprocessor) must detect any call to a non-local procedure. Such a procedure may be remote or non-existent, indicating an error. In order to determine which is the case it is necessary to support a naming service in which procedures available for remote call are registered and can be looked up. For each remote procedure called, a stub is generated so that a local call can be made to it, as shown in Figure 14.13. Thus the RPC support level is called transparently at runtime.

The functions carried out by the stub are required by both transparent and non-transparent RPC systems. The only difference is that when transparency is

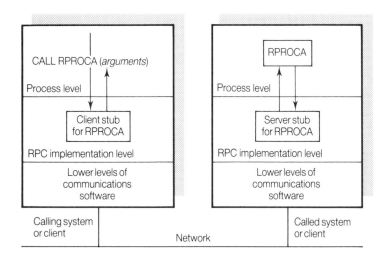

Figure 14.13
Implementation of
transparent RPC.

needed the stub is called as a local procedure with the same name as the remote procedure. The stub controls the assembling of arguments (more on this is given below) and invokes the protocol.

Even if **transparency** is achieved to this extent the call semantics for remote procedures may have to be more restricted than local calls. Some potential problems with **transparent semantics** are as follows:

● What would it mean to pass a reference parameter? In practice, RPC systems have implemented call by copy. (A brief discussion of the way object references are handled in object-oriented systems is given in Section 14.7.3.)

  If the language is such that several concurrent processes may have pointers to an object, and a reference to the object is passed as an argument in a local procedure call, all processes see any change that procedure makes. If the object is copied as an argument for a remote procedure, and the remote procedure changes the object, this is not seen by the local processes. Nor is any change made by a local process during the RPC seen by the remote process. The semantics of the language have been changed by the introduction of RPC.

● Should a call argument that is changed by the remote procedure be passed back as well as the results?

A question that is separate from transparency issues concerns large objects. It might be that only a small part of the object is used by the called procedure. In a local environment a reference parameter would typically be used in these circumstances. Should the whole object be copied and shipped across to the remote node or should it be fetched piecemeal on demand? RPC systems have tended to implement the former, but see below for object systems as well as Chapter 22.

14.7.2 Argument marshalling

Figure 14.14 shows the general approach to packing, flattening or '**marshalling**' **arguments** into a form suitable for transmission via a network buffer. The arguments are data objects that reside in the calling process's stack and heap (see Chapter 7). They must be copied into a data structure that the transmission system handles as a flat byte sequence. Any internal cross references must be preserved so that the data can be restored at the called node. Pointers (main memory addresses) within the objects must therefore be translated into pointers that are meaningful within the buffer. Any data object that is pointed to more than once need only be copied once into the buffer.

As well as the built-in data types of a language, programmers can generate their own types. Should the language allow such **user-defined types** to be passed as arguments and, if so, how does the system know how to pack them? Many RPC systems only allow the built-in system types to be transported. The Cambridge CCLU system allows almost all types, including user-defined types, to be passed as RPC arguments. This is possible because each user-defined type can be broken down successively until its component system types are reached, and the system has library routines for marshalling the language's built-in types.

When user-defined types which are to be passed as RPC arguments are declared in CCLU, the user must include a marshal and an unmarshal operation for each such type. All that is necessary is to decompose the type into lower-level components on marshalling and compose it on unmarshalling. An example

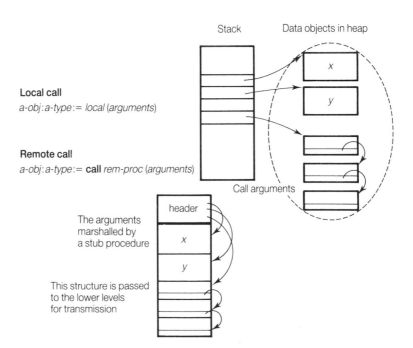

Figure 14.14
Arguments for local and remote procedures.

of an abstract data type (a cluster) *thing* with an internal representation in terms of lower-level types (**rep**) and marshal and unmarshal operations is as follows:

thing = **cluster** . . .   % abstract data type *thing*
    rep =   % the representation of *thing* in terms of lower-level
                        % (eventually built-in) types and type constructors
        record [*v*: *thing_value*,
                l: *lock*
                    ]
        .
        .

        marshal = **proc** (*t*: *thing*)   % how to marshal *thing* for RPC
                returns (*thing_value*)
            .
            .

        end *marshal;*

        unmarshal = **proc** (*tv*: *thing_value*) % how to unmarshal on return
                returns (*thing*)
            .
            .

        end *unmarshal*
    end *thing;*

14.7.3 Object-oriented systems

In Section 14.1 the client–server and object models were introduced. So far, we have followed the simpler client–server model, in which objects are created and named by a server and stay within the address space of the server. The server carries out operations on the objects in response to requests from clients. In the more general object model, objects are named and located in a global context and operations are carried out on them directly rather than via a server.

It is relevant to the discussion in Section 14.7.1 to note that object names are meaningful globally and therefore can be passed as references. It is no longer necessary to make a copy of an object which has a global name in order to pass it as an argument.

Suppose that an object-oriented system contains an object repository for storing typed objects. Suppose that a process at one node in the system invokes an object which is not in use elsewhere. Typically, that object is mapped into the address space of the invoking process (see Section 5.8). This involves converting the representation of the object into the form expected by the language system from the form in which it was stored. (Preparing a data object for storage is similar to marshalling it as an RPC argument; see Section 14.7.2.) In addition, the type operations of the object must be associated with it. They are no longer provided by a managing server.

If a process at another node in the system invokes this object, several approaches are possible:

- Only one process has an object mapped. The process which has the object mapped acts as object manager and accepts RPCs to invoke operations on the object. This is done in the Comandos system (Balter, 1992).

- Any number of processes may have an object mapped. These copies of the object are regarded as cached copies of the persistent object and a cache coherency protocol is followed by the processes. There must be a policy on how the processes may use the object. It may be that only one at a time may write to the object, or concurrent writes to different parts of the object may be allowed.

A full discussion of object-oriented systems extends beyond the intended scope of this book. This short discussion is included to show that there have been more recent approaches to passing object references than the call by copy semantics described in Section 14.7.2. Also, it should be noted that RPC may still be used within an object-oriented system.

14.7.4 Type checking and consistency checking

A language may have static, compile-time type checking, in particular of procedure call arguments. Can this be extended for an RPC system? To do so it is necessary to have a specification of any procedure which can be called remotely available for the compiler to look up. A name server or library might be used (see Section 14.9). Many systems have the concept of an interface specification where an interface contains a number of procedures.

A final point concerns the engineering and maintenance of large systems. Any component of a distributed system might be changed and recompiled. It might be that a call to a remote procedure becomes out of date and inconsistent with the new version of the procedure. This can be checked by identifying the version of the remote procedure specification that a given call was type-checked against, keeping this identification with the call and having the system check it at run-time.

14.7.5 Data representation for a heterogeneous environment

The above discussion is based on the implicit assumption that the client and server are written in the same language and run on nodes which use the same internal data representations. We have packed the RPC arguments in the client node and expect the bits to mean the same when they arrive at the server node.

This may not always be the case, particularly in large-scale distributed systems. At the lowest level of built-in language data types, from which other types are constructed, we may find differences:

- Integers may be represented differently. In CCLU one bit is used to distinguish between pointers and data. CCLU integers are therefore 31 bits in length, in two's complement representation, instead of the usual 32.

- The floating point formats may differ for different hardware floating point units.

- Characters may be represented differently: although most machines use the ASCII code, IBM favours the EBCDIC code.

- Strings are stored in words in a different order on different machines. For example, using a 32-bit word, the string 'Gulliver's Travels' could be stored either as:

Gulliver's Travels   (with so-called big-endian byte ordering), or as
lluGreviT s'evar sl   (with little-endian byte ordering)

If a filename is to be transferred from a client to a file server in a heterogeneous world, the presentation layer must be able to carry out byte reordering when necessary.

A number of external data representations have been defined, for example, Sun's XDR (eXternal Data Representation), Xerox's Courier and the ISO standard, Abstract Syntax Notation 1 (ASN.1) (ISO, 1986). The idea is to encode a standard set of data types in a way that can be recognized by all systems. Since we are not concerned here with large-scale heterogeneous systems we shall leave this topic for further study, for example, Tanenbaum (1988).

14.8   Discussion of RPC

We argued in Section 14.4 that a blocking primitive is more manageable than a non-blocking one for implementing remote operation invocation. One such primitive, RPC, was discussed in detail. We saw how to implement a single RPC. RPC maps very well onto a blocking communication paradigm.

An implementation issue is the number of RPCs that can be in progress at any time from different threads of a given process. It is important that a number of processes on a machine should be able to initiate RPCs and, in particular, that several threads of the same process should be able to initiate RPCs to the same destination. Figure 14.15 shows a common scenario which illustrates this issue. Server A is employing several threads to service RPC requests from different clients. Server A may itself need to invoke the service of another server, server B. It must be possible for one thread on server A to initiate an RPC to server B and, while that RPC is in progress, another thread on server A should be able to initiate another RPC to server B.

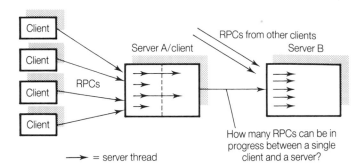

Figure 14.15
Clients, servers and
RPCs.

A system design issue is whether RPC is sufficient to meet all communications needs. Some argue that a simple, efficient RPC protocol can be used as a basis for all requirements. Others feel that a selection should be available. Examples of alternative styles of communication are:

- A simple send for event notification with no requirement for a reply.

- A version of RPC (**asynchronous RPC**) which asks the server to carry out the operation but to keep the result for the client to pick up later. An example taken from the ANSA system is given in the next section. The client continues as soon as the invocation has been made. The client may proceed with local work or may do more asynchronous RPCs. If these are to the same server it may be important for the application that they are carried out in the same order that they were sent.

- A stream protocol (based on a connection between source and destination) for users at terminals, general input and output, and transport of bulk data, including real-time voice and video.

Some systems have a real-time requirement for the transfer of massive amounts of data, for example, multimedia systems with real-time voice and video. It is unlikely that RPC will be sufficient for this purpose. RPC requires all the data to be received before the operation commences and is likely to have some maximum data size well below that of a typical video stream. Also, the overhead of marshalling is not needed for this kind of data. We do not want the RPC system to interpret a video stream as a byte sequence and to marshal the carefully counted bytes, one at a time into a buffer. We have typically obtained a block of data from a file or an on-line device and we want it sent uninterpreted (and fast). Further reading on RPC may be found in Bershad *et al.* (1990) and Birrell and Nelson (1986).

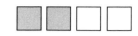

14.9   Naming, location and binding in distributed systems

So far we have assumed that a process that wishes to engage in communication with a remote process is able to name the destination of the communication.

For a single centralized system we assume that the operating system knows the names of all processes and any associated communications endpoints such as ports. A process that wishes to engage in IPC will do so via the operating system, as discussed briefly in Section 11.9.

There are a number of issues to be addressed for IPC in a distributed system:

- What objects are to be named? Recall from Chapter 12, and this chapter, that a message might be sent to a process, a port of a process, a global port or a remote procedure.

- What do object names look like?

- How does a potential client of a service, or user of an object, find out the name of that service or object in order to invoke it?

- When is a name bound to a network address?

- Is the communication controlled? (Who is allowed to invoke a given object?)

A complete discussion of these issues is beyond the scope of this book. They are at the heart of distributed systems architectures and lead on to other general issues such as security, authentication and encryption. In the sections below, an introduction is given which is sufficient for a basic understanding of how IPC may be supported in a distributed system.

Section 14.1 indicated that the distributed software system might be designed according to a client–server model or an object model. We shall use the term 'object' in the following sections to indicate anything that might be named in a remote invocation for example, service, process, port, persistent data object etc. The case studies in Part IV give examples of the use of some of the methods outlined below.

14.9.1   Naming the objects used in IPC

A convention is needed so that any object in a distributed system can be named unambiguously. A simple scheme that comes to mind is as follows.

Assume that each node has a unique network address. A naming scheme for objects, for example processes, is to name each object by (*node number, object number at that node*). Although this scheme is often used it is inflexible because an object is permanently bound to a node. If the node crashes or if it is desirable to move the object to another node, its name must be changed and all interested parties notified.

This example establishes the desirability of a **global naming scheme** comprising **location-independent names**.

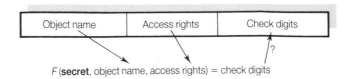

Now suppose that we decide to name objects by simple integers that are unique system-wide and location-independent. Access control is a possible problem here. Anyone might send a message to process number 123 to request a service or invoke an operation on data object number 456. This could be solved by keeping a list with each object of the processes that are allowed to access it, like the access control lists used for files. This would allow the object to reject an unauthorized access, but would not stop communications being sent to it.

An alternative to using access control lists stored with objects is to use a special kind of name that includes access rights, called a **capability** or protected name. Figure 14.16 gives an example. A number of different capability schemes have been used in distributed systems. The idea is that possession of a capability is taken to be proof that the possessor has the rights indicated in the capability to the object named in it. Possession of a capability has often been likened to having a ticket for a concert. If you can present a ticket, you can go in. The capability can be used any number of times, however (so it is more like a season ticket).

What is to stop the possessor of a capability changing the name of the object or the rights stored in it? These are protected by encryption techniques; one scheme is as follows. When an object is created a **secret** (random number) is generated and stored with the object. An encryption function, such as a one-way function, is available to the object storage service. When a capability is issued, the object name, rights and the secret are put through the encryption function and the resulting number is stored in the capability as check digits (Figure 14.16). When the capability is presented, with a request to use the object, the object name and rights from the capability and the stored secret are put through the encryption function. The resulting number is checked against that in the capability. If the capability has been changed in any way, the check fails.

This scheme allows the object name and access rights to be represented 'in clear' in the capability, that is, without encryption at the application level. This scheme can be used for file capabilities which include access rights (see Section 5.6.5). Another example is to control communication. Suppose that all communication is addressed to ports which are named and protected by capabilities. A process must have the 'send right' to send a message to a port. The communications implementation can reject a request to send a message to a port if the send right is not present in the capability presented. This prevents erroneous processes flooding the network with messages; we assume that erroneous (typically looping) processes do not accidentally give themselves send rights as well as carrying out spurious sends. A malicious process can add a send right to the capability and the communications software cannot validate it without having access to the secret asociated with the port. A scheme of this kind is used in the Accent and Mach kernels (see Chapter 22).

14.9.2   Locating named objects

In the previous section we motivated the need for a global naming scheme for various kinds of objects in a distributed system.

Let us suppose that an application process wishes to become a client of a system service and that the application program was written with a name for the service such as 'mail-service'. Before the communication can take place, the communications software, such as an RPC package, must know an address at which the required service is currently being offered. It is also likely that the communication must be addressed to a process number or port number at that network address.

How can this information be obtained? For a centralized system the operating system was assumed to manage names and extend the name spaces of the processes it supports in order to allow them to communicate (Section 11.9). The following possibilities come to mind for a distributed system:

- Every kernel maintains information on all the local objects that can be invoked from other nodes. Each kernel builds a table of all remote objects that can be invoked by local processes. The latter would be too large in practice. It would also be impossible to keep so many copies of naming data consistent, and out-of-date locations would have to be handled.

- Every kernel maintains information on all the local objects that can be invoked from other nodes. When a kernel is asked for IPC with a remote object, it locates the object by interacting with other kernels in the system, asking which one of them has the object. It is allowed to cache the locations of the objects it finds in this way.

  Some systems use methods like this, for example, the Amoeba operating system and the port mapper for SUN RPC. There is a danger that cached locations can become out-of-date and such values are used only as 'hints'. That is, the kernel is prepared for failure of communication based on a hint, in which case it will request the location of the required object afresh.

- Every kernel maintains information on all the local objects that can be invoked from other nodes. Each message is passed around the system in a logical ring. The kernel for which the destination object is local passes the message to that destination.

  This method was used in a very early distributed system experiment (Farber *et al.*, 1973). It does not scale to a reasonably large number of system components.

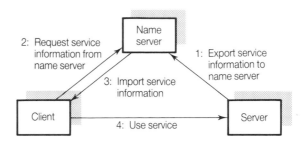

Figure 14.17
A name server in a
distributed system.

- A user-level process at each node maintains information on the local objects that can be invoked from other nodes. These processes interact with each other to locate any required object, as described above for kernels. They are requested to do so by processes attempting remote communication. This method is used in Accent and Mach (see Chapter 22).

- A **name service** is designed for the system. When a service is loaded at a given node it sends its name, location and any other information necessary for using it to the name service. When a client wishes to invoke the service, the information necessary for communication with the service may be looked up in the name service. Figure 14.17 gives the general idea. The location of the name service is assumed to be well known. It can be made available to systems on initial load.

   Many distributed systems use a name service. In a large-scale system the name service is likely to be offered by a number of servers. CDCS (Needham and Herbert, 1982), Grapevine (Birrell *et al.* 1982), Clearinghouse (Oppen and Dalal, 1983), DNS (Mockapetris and Dunlap, 1988), the DEC GNS (Lampson, 1986) and ANSA (1989) (see below), are examples. Many have greater functionality than described above. They may be involved in authentication of principals and registration of groups, for example. Details and case studies may be found in Coulouris and Dollimore (1988) and Mullender (1989). Further reading on naming may be found in Saltzer (1979, 1982) and Needham (1989).

14.9.3 The ANSA approach to distributed programming

For a full description of the ANSA Advanced Network Systems Architecture, see ANSA (1989). An example is given here to illustrate the programmer's view of how a name server, ANSA's 'interface trader', might be used for distributed programming.

   ANSA have defined a Distributed Programming Language, DPL, which, as well as a conventional range of data types, includes the types *Interface* and

InterfaceRef. DPL provides a framework in which a conventional language (typically C) is embedded and is used for programming clients and servers.

Suppose the code of a **service**, the *green* service, is to be loaded into a **server** computer and made available for use by clients. An interface specification for *green* with operations *lime* and *jade* is written in an interface definition language (IDL) and made available in an IDL file, for example:

green : *INTERFACE* =
begin
   lime : *OPERATION* (*arguments*) *RETURNS* (*arguments*);
   jade : *OPERATION* (*arguments*) *RETURNS* (*arguments*);
end.

The server must export the interface of the *green* service to the interface trader. To do this it uses an interface reference for the trader, *traderRef,* and is returned an interface reference, *green_exportRef,* for subsequent use.

! USE *green*
! DECLARE [*green_exportRef*]: *green* SERVER
 ansa_interfaceRef green_exportRef;

! [*green_exportRef*] := *traderRef$EXPORT*(*"green"*,*"/ANSA/services"*,
             \"NAME*'green'"*,NTHREADS)

The server may use the interface reference to withdraw the interface from the trader or change it. Any outstanding interface reference to that interface held by a client would then become invalid (see Section 14.7.4).

! *traderRef$withdraw* (*green_exportRef*)

A **client** which knows about and wishes to use the *green* service (its public name is *green*) will first import the green interface from the trader:

! USE *green*
! DECLARE [*green_importRef*]: *green* CLIENT
 ansa_interfaceRef green_importRef;

! [*green_exportRef*] := *traderRef$IMPORT*(*"green"*,*"/ANSA/services"*,
             \"NAME*'green'"*)

The interface reference returned by the import request to the trader can then be used to invoke the operations of the *green* interface at the server.

! [*result*] := *green_importRef* $ *lime* (*arguments*)

It is also possible to initiate an operation asynchronously and pick up the result later by using a *voucher* data type.

voucher v;
! [*v*] := *green_importRef* $ *lime* (*arguments*)
! [*result*] := *green_importRef* $REDEEM (*v*)

A preprocessor replaces the statements which are preceded by ! with calls to the runtime system to marshal arguments and invoke communications software.

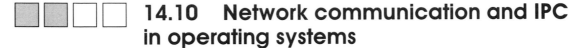

14.10   Network communication and IPC in operating systems

We have assumed that distributed IPC is an extension of local IPC; that is, requests for both local and remote IPC are made to the IPC implementation in the operating system. This approach is likely to predominate, but it should be mentioned that some operating systems have provided a separate implementation of local IPC and network communication.

UNIX System V provides messages and shared memory for local communication and integrates network communication and I/O (see Section 21.17). UNIX BSD 4.3 provides network communication via the socket abstraction, where a socket is a communication endpoint. Because UNIX Version 7 IPC (pipes and signals) is inadequate, BSD 4.3 provides a more substantial IPC implementation as a special case of network communication (see Section 21.16).

14.11   Summary of Part II

We have considered how an operation that is invoked on a data object as part of a concurrent system may be guaranteed to occur without interference from other concurrent actions. A number of methods of implementing this are available. They fall into two basic categories depending on whether the potentially interfering processes access data objects in shared memory. This formed the basis of Chapters 8 to 12. At this stage we had not considered the possibility that a system might crash at any time, causing main memory to be lost. Chapter 13 introduced crash resilience for a single system for a single operation invocation.

Chapter 14 has shown how the inter-process communication mechanisms discussed in Chapters 8 to 12 might be distributed to support remote operation invocation. We saw how IPC software and network communications software might be integrated. Once an invocation arrives from a remote system, the techniques for achieving non-interference with other invocations, both local and remote, are as described in Chapters 8 to 12. Crash resilience was included in the discussion since distributed systems are such that parts of a program can survive crashes of other parts. It is therefore important for the programmer to be aware of the possibility of crashes.

A brief introduction to the naming and location infrastructure required to support IPC in a distributed system was given. A **capability** was defined as a protected name. An in-depth study of this topic, including security, authentication, encryption and protection is left for further study in the context of large-scale distributed systems.

Having mastered the material necessary for understanding single concurrent actions we now proceed to Part III in which higher-level actions comprising a number of lower-level actions are considered.

Exercises

14.1   Compare and contrast a client–server model of distributed computation with an object model. Could a pipeline be said to adhere to either model? How would you implement a pipelined compiler in a world based on client–server interactions or object invocations?

14.2   How can the components of a distributed system agree on a value to use for system time? Under what circumstances might such a value be needed?

14.3   A process on node A invokes an operation on node B in a distributed system. How might the fact that the nodes, and the network connecting them, may fail independently of each other be taken into account in the design of the distributed invocation at the language level and at the communications level? Can you think of examples where it is desirable that the clocks at node A and node B should be kept in synchronization?

14.4   (a) For the styles of IPC studied in Part II, explain how the mechanism might be expanded for inter-node IPC.
(b) Consider how the network communication software and the local IPC support might be integrated.
(c) Focus on the naming schemes that are used by the centralized IPC mechanisms. Consider the problem of naming when the mechanisms are extended for distributed IPC. When might the name of a remote operation be bound to a network address? How could this binding be supported at kernel, local service, or dedicated remote service level?

14.5   Security involves both authentication and access control (when you invoke a remote operation you should be able to prove that you are who you say you are (authentication) and there should be a check that you are authorized to invoke that operation on that object (access control)). Consider how both of these functions are supported in a centralized, time-sharing system and in a single-user workstation. What infrastructure would be needed to support these functions in a distributed system?

14.6 (a) How can compile-time type checking be supported in an RPC system?
(b) How can an RPC system check that you are not attempting to call a remote procedure that has been changed and recompiled since your program was compiled and type-checked against it?

14.7 Can RPC be used in a heterogeneous environment?

14.8 How could you contrive to program an application in which massive amounts of data are to be transferred according to a 'stream' paradigm in a system which supports only RPC for distributed IPC? You may assume that multi-threaded processes and dynamic thread creation are available.

14.9 Is distribution transparency fully achievable in an RPC system? What software components can be used to provide this illusion? How could the independent failure modes of system components be handled in an RPC system where distribution transparency was a design aim?

14.10 Is it desirable that an RPC system should provide support for client, network and server crash and restart? Distinguish between 'exactly once' semantics in the absence of crashes and restarts and in their presence. What are the implications on the application level of providing universal 'exactly once' semantics? What are the likely implications on the performance of all RPCs?

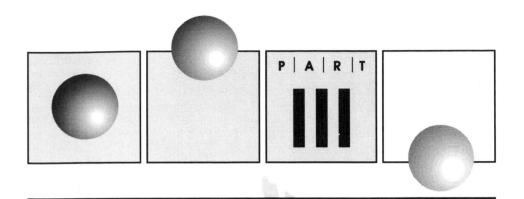

Concurrent composite actions

The issues addressed in Part II are associated with the correct execution of a single abstract operation by a sequential process which executes as part of a concurrent system of processes. We now assume this problem solved by means of the techniques described in Part II and move on to compose higher-level abstract operations. The notion of a 'high-level' operation is, again, an informal one and can be thought of as an abstract operation consisting of a number of lower-level abstract operations.

An operation hierarchy may be located entirely within the main memory of a single computer; it may span the main memories of computers in a distributed system; it may span main memory and persistent memory of a single computer or may span main memory and persistent memory throughout a distributed system. Chapter 15 gives examples from systems and applications.

Chapter 15 motivates concurrent execution of composite operations as desirable to give good system performance, such as fast response to clients. The potential problems of concurrent execution are introduced.

One of the problems that arises when processes must compete for exclusive access to a number of resources or objects is that deadlock could occur. Processes may hold on to objects while waiting for other objects, held by other processes, to become free. In certain circumstances a set of processes can reach a situation where they will wait indefinitely unless the system is designed to recognize or prevent the problem. This is discussed in Chapter 16.

Chapter 17 is concerned with the fact that a system crash could occur partway through a composite operation. In some application areas users require that either the whole operation is done or none of it is done. The definition of an atomic operation, first discussed in Chapter 13, is developed as a basis for study of systems which support this all or nothing style of composite operation execution.

The remaining chapters of Part III are concerned with methods for implementing atomic composite operations. It is necessary to be able to put the system state back to its value prior to the start of such an operation. If the system can do this it can recover from crashes. The same mechanisms can also be used to control concurrent execution of atomic operations: if interference has happened, act as though the system had crashed!

The treatment given applies equally to centralized and distributed systems. Chapter 20 discusses techniques specific to distributed systems.

Decomposable abstract operations

15

CONTENTS

15.1 Composite operations

Figures 15.1 and 15.2 show composite operation invocations: first, a simple nested invocation; then a general hierarchy of operations. We are no longer concerned with the detailed mechanism for invocation of the operations and protection of the data objects operated on. We assume that each operation is part of a concurrent system and will therefore have concurrency control associated with its invocation as discussed in Part II.

Figure 15.1 shows a simple nested operation invocation in some detail. Figure 15.2 shows a high-level operation comprising a hierarchy of operations. The

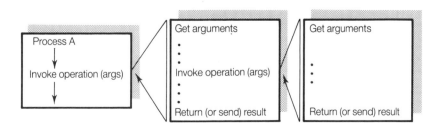

Figure 15.1
A nested invocation.

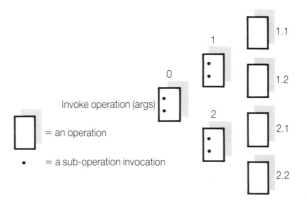

Figure 15.2
A hierarchy of operation invocations.

top-level operation (0) is invoked. Its execution involves the invocation of two operations (1 and 2), each of which involves the execution of two further operations (1.1, 1.2 and 2.1, 2.2).

The problem we address in Part III is the correct execution of general abstract operations, which decompose into sub-operations, in the presence of concurrency or crashes.

15.2 Composite operations in main memory

Consider a number of processes sharing an address space and assume that a number of monitors are available to them as the means by which shared data is protected or shared resources are allocated exclusively. The specification of the operations may be such that a process may acquire a monitor lock, then, while executing an operation of the monitor, make a nested call to another monitor (Figure 15.3). Process A has called operation *W*, assumed to be a monitor operation, and has made a nested call to operation *Y* in another monitor. Process B has called *X* and made a nested call to *Z*, at which point both hold two monitor locks. At this point process A calls *Z* and process B calls *Y* and both will wait indefinitely unless there is system intervention. This is an example of a situation called **deadlock** which is the subject matter of Chapter 16.

Figure 15.3 also shows process C attempting to make a call to *X*. The issue of whether process B should continue to hold the lock of the monitor containing *X* while making a nested call to *Z* must be addressed in a monitor-based system. In Section 10.3 we discussed the idea that a lock should be associated with the data being operated on rather than the code operating on it. This approach might help here if processes A and B are accessing different components of the data

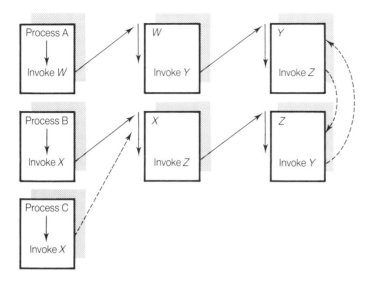

Figure 15.3
Concurrent
invocation in main
memory.

protected by the monitors containing operations W, X, Y and Z. The situation shown in Figure 15.3 would then only arise over contention for the same data items.

The situation shown in Figure 15.3 is not exclusively the problem of shared-memory based systems which use monitors for concurrency control. Each of the operations shown could be offered by a separate process in a separate address space; the objects involved could be located in main memory throughout a distributed system and invoked by remote procedure call.

15.3   Composite operations involving main memory and persistent memory

Examples of areas in which composite operations involve both main memory and persistent memory are database management systems and operating systems. Both have to handle multiple simultaneous activities.

15.3.1   Examples from operating systems

Many examples of composite operations arise within the file management subsystem of an operating system. In order to satisfy a request to write a sequence of bytes to a file an operating system might have to send more than one write request to the disk manager. A crash could occur between these associated writes.

Certain file operations require associated directory operations, as outlined in Chapter 5. When a file is deleted, the disk blocks it occupies may be made free (if there are no other paths to it) and its directory entry and metadata should be removed. A crash could occur at any time, including between these operations. If the operations were carried out in the order indicated above, the directory entryand metadata could remain, but blocks of the file would be on the free list. A number of difficulties might then arise. The disk blocks which had comprised the file might be allocated to some other, newly created file. The file system has become inconsistent (and incorrect). An important part of file system design is to avoid or detect and correct inconsistencies, particularly after a crash has occurred.

Another example is that creation of a new file has an associated directory operation to add a new entry to a directory. Disk blocks might be acquired for the file, but a crash might occur before the directory entry is made. The blocks might be lost to the filing system unless action is taken to detect this.

In a file management subsystem we are concerned with the transfer of data and metadata between main memory and persistent memory. There are many examples where a change is made to a file, such as extending it with new blocks, and these changes are recorded in file system tables in main memory. Suppose that at the time of the change the data blocks are written to disk and the new disk blocks used are recorded in tables in main memory. This metadata must also be written to disk for the persistent store to be in a consistent state, but a crash could occur at any time. Care must be taken in the file system design and in crash recovery procedures that the file system can be restored to a consistent state, with minimum loss of data. In this example consistency could be achieved after a crash by detecting that the newly written blocks are not recorded as part of any file and returning them to the free list. The unfortunate user would have to repeat the work.

These examples have emphasized that a crash can occur between the component operations of a logical operation at a higher level. Concurrent execution of component operations can have similar effects, and we shall see that it can be advantageous to consider possible actions to guard against the effects of crashes, together with those for concurrency control.

15.3.2   An example from a database system

An example of a high-level operation is to transfer a sum of money from one bank account to another:

transfer (account-A, account-B, £1000)

Two separate operations have to be invoked to achieve this. One is to access the source account, *account-A*, in order to read that there is sufficient money in there and to write the debited amount back as the new value of the account, a typical Part II-style operation. The second is to credit the destination account, *account-B*, with its updated value, another Part II-style operation.

The constituent low-level operations are therefore:

debit (*account-A*, £1000)
credit (*account-B*, £1000)

The techniques of Part II ensure that each of these separate operations can be done correctly, but do not address their composition into a correct single high-level operation.

15.4   Concurrent execution of composite operations

There is scope for concurrency in the execution of high-level, composite operation invocations.

1. Several high-level operations, invoked by different processes, could be run in parallel, their lower-level operations being interleaved.
2. It might be possible to invoke the sub-operations of a single high-level operation in parallel.

Method 2 above cannot be carried out automatically without regard to the semantics of the computation. It might be the case that some of the operations have to be invoked in a specific order. For example, *debit* might only be allowed after a *check-balance* operation but *credit* and *debit* can be carried out in parallel.

Current database programming languages tend to specify a strict sequence of operations. It can be argued, as with imperative programming languages, that the sequencing is often overspecified. To move to parallel execution of the operations of a single transaction, which is desirable for multiprocessor or distributed execution, it would be necessary to specify and enforce any necessary orderings on the operations.

Method 1 provides more obvious scope for automatic provision of concurrency. Resource contention problems are likely to arise.

15.4.1   Desirability of concurrent execution

Before looking at mechanisms for achieving concurrency we should consider whether concurrent execution is a goal worth striving for at the expense of additional complexity in the system. One approach to supporting high-level operations would be to regard them as indivisible: to acquire exclusive use of all the objects needed for the entire set of constituent operations and then to carry out the high-level operation. There are several drawbacks to such an approach:

- It could take a long time to acquire all the objects required, introducing unpredictability of service and (possibly indefinite) delay.

- All the objects would be held for the duration of all the constituent operations. This would prevent other processes from using them, even when the objects were idle and no errors could result from their use.

- A number of logically distinct operations are effectively being combined into a single large operation. Knowledge of all the objects invoked in sub-operations is needed at the outermost level.

- Deadlock could occur if the objects were acquired piecemeal (as discussed below and in Chapter 16).

In applications where it is unlikely that two processes would require simultaneous access to the same resource, either because of light use or because accesses are known to be scattered widely across a large data space, this might be a suitable approach. An example is personal data in a social security, medical or taxation database. The same individual is unlikely to be the target of multiple simultaneous queries.

In a heavily used system with frequent contention the performance could be unacceptably slow and we should aim to achieve a higher degree of concurrency. Good performance while serving multiple clients is a sufficiently widespread goal that it is important to strive for maximum concurrency in many systems.

It is worth studying the techniques for achieving concurrent execution of composite operations in order to be able to decide whether and how to provide for it in a given system design. The mechanisms that are needed for crash resilience (failure transparency) are similar to those for some methods of concurrency control, and it is desirable to consider both together.

15.5   Potential problems

We shall use the simple example of Section 15.3.2 to illustrate the problems that can occur during concurrent execution of composite operations and some approaches to their solution. Suppose:

> **process P** executes *transfer (account-A, account-B, £1000)*
>
> **process Q** executes *transfer (account-B, account-A, £200)*

In more detail:

> **P**: *debit (account-A, £1000);*   *credit (account-B, £1000)*
> **Q**: *debit (account-B, £200);*   *credit (account-A, £200)*

Showing more detail of a possible implementation for **P** (**Q** is similar):

> **P**: *debit (account-A, £1000);*
>   read the value of *account-A*

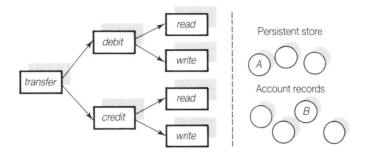

Figure 15.4
A possible hierarchy
of operations for
'transfer'.

check whether the debit can be made (value ≥ £1000), if not give an error
response, otherwise write the debited value as the new value of *account-A*
P: *credit (account-B, £1000);*
   read the value of *account-B,*
   add £1000 to the value,
   write the new value into *account-B*

15.5.1   Uncontrolled interleaving of sub-operations

Figure 15.4 shows a hierarchical decomposition for the transfer operation down
to the granularity of treating individual read and write operations on account
records as separate operations. Consider the possible consequences of having no
concurrency control whatsoever. The following sequence of operations could
occur:

   Q : completes the whole *debit* operation on *account-B*
   P : read the value of *account-A*
   Q : read the value of *account-A*
   P : check value ≥ £1000 and write back the original value minus £1000
   Q : write back the original value plus £200.

The debit of £1000 made by process **P** to account *A* has been lost, overwritten
by process **Q**'s credit to the original value of the account. This illustrates that
the *debit* and *credit* operations should be treated as abstract operations, indivisible in the sense of Part II. Their implementation in terms of individual reads and
writes should not be visible to the client of the transaction system. The reads
and writes to persistent store can be thought of in the same way as the individual reads and writes to main memory in Section 8.7.1. The data object *account-
A* can be considered as an abstract data type with operations which include
debit and *credit,* as shown in Figure 15.5. We assume that a mechanism such as
a **lock** on a data object is available to implement exclusive access to an object
for those operations which require it.

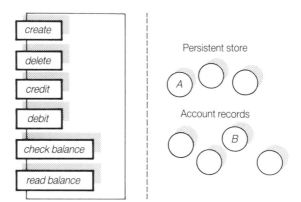

Figure 15.5
Account objects.

We shall develop a model along these lines in Chapter 17. Much database concurrency control theory in the past has been presented in terms of *read* and *write* operations only, but current thinking is that object orientation, taking into account the semantics of the operations, is a better approach. Returning to our simple example, this does not solve all our problems because interleaving operations at this level can also lead to incorrect results, as shown in the next example.

15.5.2   Visibility of the effects of sub-operations

Suppose process **R** is calculating the sum of the values of accounts *A* and *B*, and consider the following interleavings:

> **P** : *debit (account-A, £1000)*;
> **R** : *read-balance (account-A)*;
> **R** : *read-balance (account-B)*;
> **P** : *credit (account-B, £1000)*;

In this case, each of the sub-operations of the *transfer* operation is carried out correctly by process **P** but the value computed by process **R** for the sum of accounts *A* and *B* is incorrect. The problem arises because another process has been allowed to see the accounts affected by the *transfer* operation between its two sub-operations. This is a Part III problem. Its solution is addressed in Chapters 17 and 18.

15.5.3   Deadlock

If we attempt to solve the problem of Section 15.5.2 by allowing accounts to be 'locked' we could have the following interleaving of operations:

P : *lock (account-A)*;
P : *debit (account-A, £1000)*;
Q : *lock (account-B)*;
Q : *debit (account-B, £200)*;
P : *lock (account-B)*

This can't be done as **Q** already holds the lock on *account-B*. Let us assume that process **P** is obliged to wait for the lock, for example on a condition variable in a monitor.

Q : *lock (account-A)*

This can't be done as **P** already holds the lock on *account-A*. Let us assume that process **Q** is obliged to wait for the lock.

If this situation is allowed to arise, processes **P** and **Q** will wait indefinitely. They are said to be **deadlocked**. This is a Part III problem. Its solution is addressed in Chapter 16.

15.6   Crashes

In Chapter 13 we considered the effects of crashes and mechanisms that would provide crash resilience for a single operation invocation. Figure 15.6 reiterates the basic approach. In Chapter 14 we considered an operation on one host being invoked from another host in a distributed system and considered the possibility of crashes both in the invoking and invoked systems. We now generalize these ideas.

Suppose, in the simple example introduced in Section 15.5 above, that a crash occurs after the *debit* operation, which must have written its result to persistent store in order to complete, but before the *credit* operation. The fact that a transfer operation was in progress was lost, with main memory, in the crash and £1000 has been lost from the recorded values in persistent store. A system design clearly needs to take account of such a possibility.

Figure 15.7 shows the more general case of a composite operation, indicating that any component operation may involve a write to persistent memory.

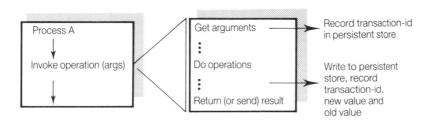

Figure 15.6
A potentially
atomic operation
invocation.

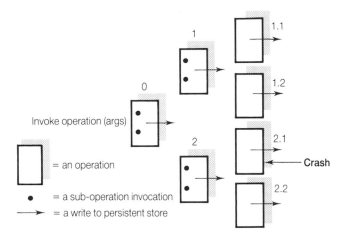

Figure 15.7
A crash during
hierarchical
operation
invocation.

Suppose that a crash occurs, as indicated, during operation 2.1. We have seen from Chapter 13 how that operation might be rolled back and restarted. We now have to consider what to do about operations 1, 1.1 and 1.2, which apparently completed successfully although the crash occurred during operation 0, the high-level invoking operation. Chapters 17 and 18 consider these issues. We should also consider a distributed implementation of such a composite operation. In this case the nodes on which the operations execute need to cooperate. This is considered in Chapter 20.

15.7 Summary

We defined composite abstract operations and looked at some examples. In some cases, concurrent execution of the component operations of high-level operations is desirable and in others it cannot be avoided. This can lead to problems. Part III will study these problems and possible solutions to them.

The general problem that can arise as a result of the uncontrolled concurrent execution of component operations is that the system state can become incorrect. A related problem is that output may be incorrect (Section 15.5.2), even if the persistent state subsequently becomes consistent. A naïve attempt to avoid these problems through locking all required resources for exclusive use can lead to bad system performance; locking piecemeal can lead to deadlock.

Incorrect system state might result from a crash part-way through a single composite operation or through uncontrolled concurrent execution of composite operations. A system must at least be able to detect that this has happened. Minimal action is to restore a consistent version of the state, possibly involving loss of information, and to warn the users affected that this has occurred. This is acceptable for some systems, typically filing systems for general-purpose operating systems.

Some systems, such as transaction processing systems, guarantee to their clients that, once a transaction is complete, its results will not be lost whatever happens. Crashes can occur, and not only must a consistent version of the system state be restored but that state must contain the results of all completed transactions. The mechanisms that must be used to achieve crash resilience without loss of the information that has been guaranteed to persist might also be used for concurrency control. It is therefore desirable to consider concurrency control and crash resilience together.

The topic of dynamic object allocation and deadlock is covered in the next chapter in some detail as general background for the specific methods discussed in later chapters.

Exercises

15.1 What problems might occur if the sub-operations of a single high-level operation are started off in parallel (for example, for running on a shared-memory multiprocessor)? Give examples. Why is it difficult to automate this approach?

15.2 Find out about the consistency checks your local operating system runs on its filing system on restarting after a crash or shutdown (an example is UNIX's *fsck* maintenance tool). Is it possible for users to lose data? If so, how are they informed of this possibility? Why is this approach not possible in a transaction processing system?

15.3 To what extent is it desirable to run the sub-operations of different high-level operations in parallel? What are the possible problems arising from uncontrolled concurrency? (Give examples of incorrect output and incorrect system state.) What are the possible consequences of attempting to solve these problems?

15.4 What are the possible effects of a crash part-way through a single composite operation? What mechanisms must be in place to allow for the possibility of a crash at any time in a transaction processing (TP) system? Are these mechanisms suitable for handling concurrent execution of composite operations as well?

15.5 Why is it important, when designing a TP system, to have estimates of the likely level of load on the system and the probability that requests for simultaneous access to the same data items will occur?

15.6 Consider how you would set up an object model for a TP system. What are possible disadvantages of treating read and write as operations on data objects?

Resource allocation and deadlock

16

CONTENTS

16.1 Requirements for dynamic allocation

We shall use the term 'object' to include resources of all kinds, including data objects, devices etc. In Chapter 15 some of the problems associated with con current execution of composite operations were introduced. A basic problem was shown to be how to maintain the appearance of consistent values across a number of distinct objects when a high-level operation may involve related lower-level operations performed sequentially on distinct objects.

An obvious starting point for solving such problems is to support exclusive use of objects by processes. This was studied in Part II, where several methods for achieving mutual exclusion of processes from shared objects were described.

Object allocation is a common requirement in concurrent systems. Physical resource management is a major function of **operating systems** and many of the managed resources must be allocated dynamically. Typical of these are disk space for users' files, buffer space in memory for disk buffers, disk space for spoolers, physical memory, tape drives and other devices which are neither spooled nor allocated statically. Certain data objects must also be managed by operating systems. Entries in fixed-length data structures, such as the central process table in UNIX, must be allocated and recovered; a new process can only be created if a free slot can be allocated. **Database management systems** have to handle requests from multiple simultaneous users to interrogate and update permanently stored data objects. **Communications protocols** require buffer space in memory for incoming and outgoing packets. It is far more common for 'loss of data' to occur through lack of buffer space when systems are congested than through errors on the wire.

16.2   Deadlock

A simple example of deadlock was given in Section 15.5. In that case, process **P** had locked object *A* for exclusive use and went on to request object *B*. Process **Q** had already locked object *B*. Deadlock occurs when process **Q** proceeds to request object *A*.

Figure 16.1 illustrates this problem. It shows the progress of processes **P** and **Q** when they are scheduled to run on a single processor, that is, only one at a time can run. Their behaviour is that each acquires one object and, while still holding it, requests the other. Paths i, j, k, l, m, n illustrate different possible dynamic behaviours of the two processes. In i and j, process **P** acquires both *A* and *B* before process **Q** requests *B*. In k and l, process **Q** acquires both *B* and *A*

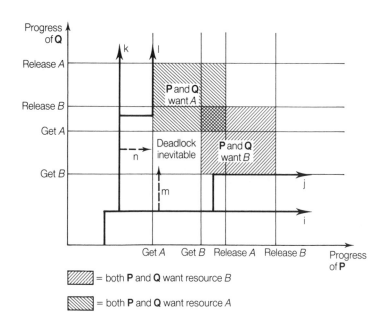

Figure 16.1
Two processes
using two
resources
(objects).

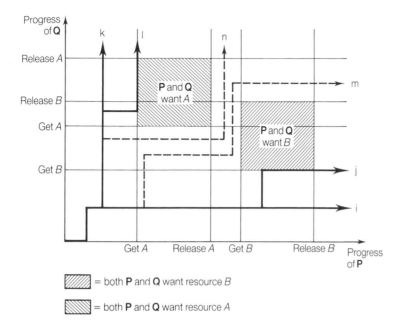

= both **P** and **Q** want resource *B*

= both **P** and **Q** want resource *A*

Figure 16.2
Two processes using
two objects without
deadlock.

before process **P** requests *A*. In paths m and n deadlock becomes inevitable *for the particular dynamic behaviour exhibited in this example* when **P** gets *A* and **Q** gets *B*.

We cannot assume that an object management system knows the semantics of the particular application. The dynamic behaviour might have been as illustrated in Figure 16.2. In this case, both processes require both *A* and *B* but process **P** releases *A* before acquiring *B*. The processes may be delayed, waiting for objects, during some dynamic patterns of resource scheduling, but deadlock cannot happen.

16.3   Livelock and starvation

Before proceeding to further investigation of the problem of deadlock it should be pointed out that processes need not necessarily be in the blocked state for there to be no possibility of progress. An example is busy waiting on a condition that can never become true. The process loops, testing the condition indefinitely. This condition is sometimes referred to as 'livelock'.

Communications protocols must be analysed to make sure they do not degenerate into an indefinite 'ping-pong' behaviour when systems are congested. If communication is attempted between two congested systems packets are likely to be discarded at both ends because buffer space is exhausted. The congestion is worsened by re-sending messages, replies, acknowledgements and negative acknowledgements, and care must be taken that an indefinite loop is not entered (Lai, 1982).

A more subtle form of a near deadlock state is due to resource starvation. A process may have large resource requirements and may be overlooked repeatedly because it is easier for the resource management system to schedule other processes with smaller resource requirements. It can happen that every time a subset of the resources the starved process wants become available they are given to some other process which can then complete. This is because system throughput looks good if processes with small requirements are scheduled and complete. The system's resource allocation policies should ensure that processes with large resource requirements are not starved, although it is reasonable to expect them to wait for longer before being scheduled than processes with small resource requirements.

An example from databases is that certain portions of the data may be hotspots: in demand by many processes. Process scheduling must take this possibility into account and a given process must not be held up unduly for this reason.

Zobel (1983) gives a classifying bibliography for the deadlock problem.

16.4 Conditions for deadlock to exist

If all of the following conditions are true at some time in a system then deadlock exists at that time (Coffman *et al.*, 1971).

1. *A resource request can be refused*
   The system's concurrency control policy is such that objects can be acquired for exclusive use or some specific shared use. It is possible for a process to be refused access to an object on the grounds that some other process has acquired it for exclusive use. It is possible for a process to be refused access to an object on the grounds that a group of processes have acquired shared access to it for a specific purpose. An example is that a process may request exclusive access to an object in order to write to it but is refused because the object is currently locked for shared reading.

2. *Hold while waiting*
   A process is allowed to hold objects while requesting further objects. The process is blocked if the request cannot be satisfied. The assumption is that the process will wait for the resource until it becomes available.

3. *No preemption*
   Objects cannot be recovered from processes. A process may acquire an object, use it and release it.

4. *Circular wait*

A cycle of processes exists such that each process holds an object that is being requested by the next process in the cycle and that request has been refused.

The processes in the cycle are deadlocked. Other processes may be able to continue but the system is degraded by the objects held by the deadlocked processes. If a process makes a request that must be refused for an object that is involved in the cycle, that process will also wait indefinitely. Further cycles could occur if a process in a cycle can have outstanding object requests that are not part of the original cycle. This would not be possible if a process had to acquire objects one at a time and was blocked as soon as a request could not be satisfied.

16.4.1 Deadlock prevention through allocation and recovery policies

All of conditions 1 to 4 above must hold for deadlock to exist. Conditions 1 to 3 are policy statements. Condition 4 is a statement about a particular dynamic behaviour of a set of processes. It might be possible to preclude some of the conditions through system policies.

1. *A resource request can be refused*

Any concurrency control policy provided by a system to assist the applications that run above it should be as flexible as possible.

An example can be taken from the concurrency control that might be provided as part of a file service by an operating system. Exclusive *write locks* and shared *read locks* were once thought to be what an operating system should provide. They are now seen to be insufficiently flexible; they force a particular view of the world on every application. Some applications may wish to have concurrent write sharing of files. For example, instances of a database management system may wish to provide their own fine-grained concurrency control to access different parts of a file at the same time. The operating system should allow them all to have the file open for writing. The provision of an exclusive lock and a shared lock could be provided so that the owners of the objects are assisted in using the object correctly in a way appropriate for the application.

Whenever concurrency control is provided, in order to ensure that the values of objects are correct, it is possible that a request to use an object in some way will be refused.

2. *Hold while waiting*

It may be possible to make a process acquire all the objects it needs at one time. This decreases utilization of, possibly scarce, objects. It may also be counter to the aim of a clean modular structure as discussed in Section 15.3. If a computation has deeply nested invocations then the outermost level would have to be aware of all the objects used at all levels.

It may not always be possible, for example, if a requirement for an object results from computations based on other objects.

3. *No preemption*

It may be possible to preempt an object and roll back the process holding it to the point at which it acquired the object that is now required by another process. This could be made transparent to the application. A policy decision is whether this should take place after deadlock is detected or at other times, such as when a process holds objects and fails to acquire another or when a high-priority process needs an object that a lower-priority process holds. This is a heavyweight mechanism and affects many aspects of program and system design. Detecting deadlock and aborting and restarting some processes might be simpler.

4. *Circular wait*

In certain applications it might be possible to require processes to request objects in a defined order. This would be less wasteful of system resources than acquiring all objects at once. This is feasible for some types of objects that are allocated; for example, a program may reasonably be required to request input devices before output devices.

An alternative is to enforce an ordering on the processes making the requests. The method of time-stamp ordering for concurrency control in database systems is deadlock free for this reason (see Section 16.5).

One method of solving the problem illustrated in Section 16.4.2 is to force processes to order their requests for resources so as to make a cycle impossible.

We use these techniques whenever we can in designing systems. We have to trade off the overhead of detecting and recovering from deadlock against the decreased resource utilization or extra complexity arising from the above policies. Knowledge of the likely behaviour of the applications to be supported should determine the policies to adopt.

16.4.2 The dining philosophers problem

The discussion above is equally appropriate to resource allocation by operating systems and data object management by a DBMS. The following example demonstrates its applicability to a small concurrent program.

This problem was posed by Dijkstra (1965) and is a classic of concurrent programming:

Five (male) philosophers spend their lives thinking and eating. The philosophers share a common circular table surrounded by five chairs, each belonging to one philosopher. In the centre of the table there is a bowl of spaghetti, and the table is laid with five forks, as shown in Figure 16.3. When a philosopher thinks he does not interact with other philosophers. From time to time, a philosopher gets hungry. In order to eat he

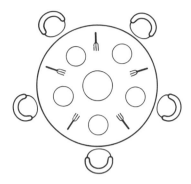

Figure 16.3
The dining
philosophers
problem.

must try to pick up the two forks that are closest (and are shared with his left and right neighbours), but may only pick up one fork at a time. He cannot pick up a fork already held by a neighbour. When a hungry philosopher has both his forks at the same time he eats without releasing them and when he has finished eating, he puts down both forks and starts thinking again.

The conditions for deadlock are set up in the problem: a philosopher acquires each fork exclusively; he must acquire one fork then hold it while waiting to acquire the second; a fork cannot be taken from a philosopher once he has picked it up. It may be possible, depending on the specification of the philosopher processes, for a cycle to occur when they execute dynamically, in which each philosopher has acquired one fork and is waiting to acquire a second: the final condition that must hold for deadlock to exist in a system.

This is illustrated by a first attempt at a solution, which is subject to deadlock. Semaphores are used for fork management:

var *fork:array*[0..4] **of** *semaphore*;

where all the elements of array *fork* are initialized to 1. Philosopher *i* may then be specified as:

```
repeat
    WAIT (fork[i]);
    WAIT (fork[i+1 mod 5]);
    eat
    SIGNAL (fork[i]);
    SIGNAL (fork[i+1 mod 5]);
    think
until false;
```

The problem arises because each philosopher process executes an identical program. One approach is to break the symmetry: make one of the philosophers, or each philosopher with an odd identifier, pick up his forks in the opposite order to the others, thus avoiding the possibility of a cycle. Another is to introduce a separate fork manager module which implements deadlock avoidance as described in Section 16.7 below: a general, and therefore heavyweight, solution. Exercise 5 outlines some approaches to solving the problem.

Although the problem is posed to explore the dangers of symmetric behaviour, it extends those we discussed in Part II because two specific shared resources must be acquired before the *eat* operation can be done. EAT is not a simple Part II-style operation. At a high level a philosopher can be specified as EAT; THINK. But the high-level EAT operation comprises five lower-level operations: *acquire fork*; *acquire fork*; *eat*; *release fork*; *release fork*.

16.5   Object allocation graphs

Figure 16.4 shows a graphical notation for describing object allocations and requests. The graph shows object types R1 and R2. The dots inside the R1 and R2 boxes indicate the number of objects of that type that exist. The directed edge from the single instance of R1 to process P indicates that P holds that object. The (dashed) directed edge from P to the object type R2 indicates that P is requesting an object of type R2. P is therefore in the blocked state. If a cycle exists in such a graph and there is only one object of each of the object types involved in the cycle then deadlock exists (this is the definition of deadlock). If there is more than one object of each type a cycle is a necessary but not sufficient condition for deadlock to exist. Examples of object types which may have multiple instances are the tape readers and printers that are allocated by a resource management module of an operating system.

A directed graph of this kind can be used as a basis for object management; for resource allocation by an operating system; for data management by a DBMS etc. The components of the graph are the set of processes which either hold or are requesting resources; the set of object types with an indication of the number of instances of each type; and a set of edges indicating allocations and requests, as described above.

Figure 16.5 shows an example of an allocation graph. Deadlock does not exist at present, but an allocation decision has to be made; there is one instance of resource type R2 and two processes are requesting it. Figure 16.6(a) shows the graph if the object of type R2 is given to Q. Deadlock does not exist. Figure 16.6(b) shows the graph if the object of type R2 is given to P. A cycle has been

Figure 16.4
Notation for resource allocation and request.

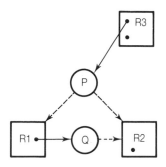

Figure 16.5
A resource
allocation graph.

created. Because there is only one object of each of types R1 and R2 deadlock
exists. Figure 16.6(c) and (d) show a similar problem except that this time there
are two instances of objects of type R2. In (c) a cycle exists but there is no deadlock. Although both objects of type R2 are allocated, process T is not
deadlocked: it may complete and release its object. In (d) we see process P with
both instances of R2. In this case there is deadlock.

We now consider data structures for holding object allocation and request
information and algorithms for detecting deadlock in a system.

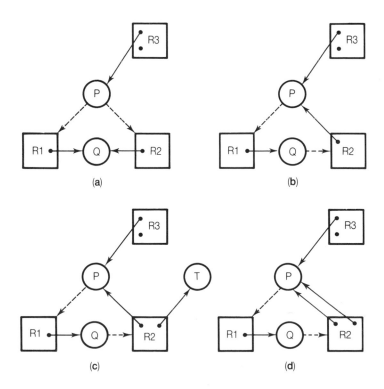

Figure 16.6
(a) Object of type
R2 allocated to Q;
(b) object of type
R2 allocated to P;
(c) a cycle but no
deadlock;
(d) a cycle with
deadlock.

16.6   Data structures and algorithms for deadlock detection

We assume a subsystem that is responsible for allocating certain objects and detecting deadlock. The object types to be managed and the number of instances of each type must be specified and the subsystem must record which are allocated and which are available. A matrix of processes against allocated objects is a suitable data structure to hold the object allocation information. Let us call it an **allocation matrix** A where a_{ij} is the number of objects of type j allocated to process i. A **request matrix** B of the same structure is suitable for holding outstanding requests by processes for objects (see Figure 16.7). We require an algorithm to detect deadlock by processing these allocation and request matrices.

16.6.1   An algorithm for deadlock detection

The algorithm below marks the rows of the allocation matrix A corresponding to processes which are not part of a deadlocked set.

1. Mark all null rows of A. (A process holding no objects cannot be part of a deadlocked cycle of processes.)
2. Initialize a working vector $W = V$, the available objects.
3. Search for an unmarked row, say row i, such that $B_i \leq W$ (the objects that process i is requesting are 'available' in W). If none is found terminate the algorithm.
4. Set $W = W + A_i$ and mark row i. Return to step 3.

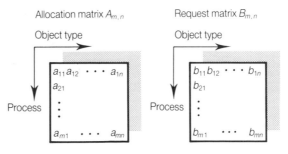

Figure 16.7
Data structures for object management.

Objects in the system being managed $= R_n = (r_1, r_2, \ldots r_n)$, the number of type i is r_i.

Objects available $= V_n = (v_1, v_2, \ldots, v_n)$, the number left of type i is v_i.
V_n can be computed from the total objects in the system, R_n minus the objects allocated.

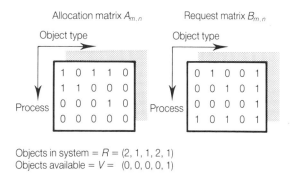

Allocation matrix $A_{m,n}$ Request matrix $B_{m,n}$

Objects in system = R = (2, 1, 1, 2, 1)
Objects available = V = (0, 0, 0, 0, 1)

Figure 16.8
Example of deadlock detection.

When the algorithm terminates, unmarked rows correspond to deadlocked processes.

The algorithm merely detects whether deadlock exists. If the object requests of a process can be satisfied it is not part of a deadlocked cycle and the objects it holds are not under contention by the deadlocked set of processes. The algorithm therefore adds them to the working pool of available objects for the purposes of the algorithm. The physical justification for this is that the process could complete its work and free its objects.

In terms of the corresponding resource allocation graph, the algorithm marks processes that are not part of a deadlocked set. If step 3 finds a process whose resource requests can be satisfied, step 4 removes the edges of the graph associated with the process; that is, its requests are assumed to be granted and the objects it holds become available for allocation.

16.6.2   Example

Figure 16.8 shows an example of a snapshot of object allocation and request at some instant.

On running the algorithm we have:

Initialize W = (0, 0, 0, 0, 1)

Mark row 4 (process 4 has no allocated objects)

Mark row 3 (process 3's requests can be satisfied from W and process 3's objects are added to W):

    W = (0, 0, 0, 1, 1)

Terminate

Rows 1 and 2 are unmarked, so processes 1 and 2 are deadlocked.

Figure 16.9(a) shows the resource allocation graph for this example. Figure 16.9(b) shows the effect of running the algorithm on (a copy of) the graph and (c) shows the cycle of deadlocked processes.

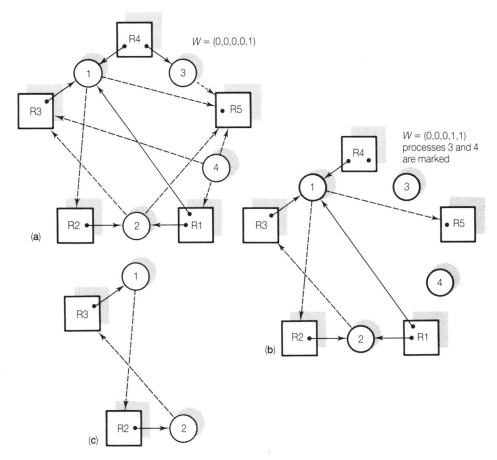

Figure 16.9
Graphs for the example in Section 16.6.2. (a) The graph at the start of the algorithm. (b) The graph when the algorithm terminates. (c) The cycle.

16.6.3 Action on detection of deadlock

The simplest action is to abort all the deadlocked processes, freeing all their objects. This could require a complete restart of these processes or a rollback to a checkpoint before the objects were acquired if the system supports this. An alternative is to abort the processes selectively, but this would require the deadlock detection algorithm to be run again, at least for the remaining processes that might still be deadlocked. Another alternative is to preempt the objects over which the deadlocked processes are contending one by one, but again the algorithm would have to be rerun.

16.7   Deadlock avoidance

It may be feasible for a process to specify its total object requirements before it runs. This information could be used by the allocation subsystem. Let us assume that a third matrix is now available, $C_{m,n}$, giving the maximum object requirements of each process as shown in Figure 16.10.

For any given request for objects that it is possible to satisfy from the objects available, the allocator can test whether

> if this allocation is made (construct A', a hypothetical allocation matrix for testing) and all the processes then request their maximum number of objects (construct B', a hypothetical request matrix) would deadlock then exist? (run the detection algorithm given above on A' and B'). If deadlock would not exist then it is safe to grant the request being tested.

This is a worst-case analysis since it is unlikely that all the processes would immediately request objects up to their maximum entitlement. It avoids the overhead of recovering from deadlock at the expense of holding an extra matrix C and constructing A' and B' before running the algorithm. It also requires this procedure to be carried out for each set of requests that might be granted. This is a matter for judgement. It might be possible to satisfy all outstanding requests, but in testing this allocation the chances of finding a potentially deadlocked state would be higher than for a more modest allocation. The safest way to proceed is to try to satisfy one process at a time. Figure 16.11 gives an example with matrices A, B and C at some instance in a system. Figure 16.12 shows the constructed matrices A' and B', supposing that process 1's request was satisfied, and the effect of running the deadlock detection algorithm on A' and B'. In this case, satisfying process 1's request would move the system to a state where deadlock did not exist and deadlock could not occur on any subsequent request: a **safe state**.

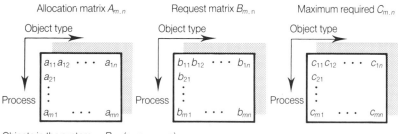

Objects in the system = $R = (r_1, r_2, \ldots, r_n)$
Objects available for allocation = $V = (v_1, v_2, \ldots, v_n)$

Figure 16.10
Data structures for deadlock avoidance.

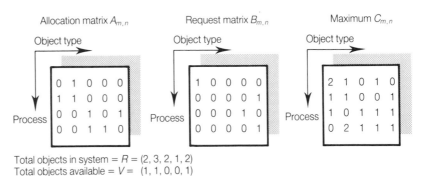

Figure 16.11
An example
for deadlock
avoidance.

Total objects in system = R = (2, 3, 2, 1, 2)
Total objects available = V = (1, 1, 0, 0, 1)

Try satisfying process 1's request. Construct A' and B' as follows:

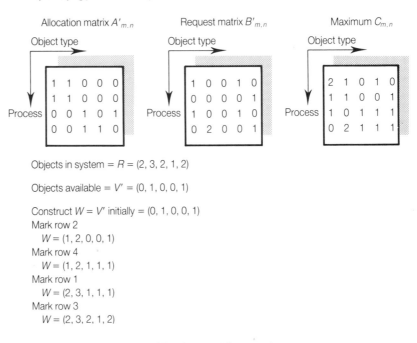

Objects in system = R = (2, 3, 2, 1, 2)

Objects available = V' = (0, 1, 0, 0, 1)

Construct $W = V'$ initially = (0, 1, 0, 0, 1)
Mark row 2
  W = (1, 2, 0, 0, 1)
Mark row 4
  W = (1, 2, 1, 1, 1)
Mark row 1
  W = (2, 3, 1, 1, 1)
Mark row 3
  W = (2, 3, 2, 1, 2)

Figure 16.12
The deadlock
avoidance
algorithm for the
example in Figure
16.11.

There would be no deadlock—it is safe to grant the request.

16.7.1 Problems of deadlock avoidance

The avoidance procedure aims to ensure that the system moves from one safe state to another on each object allocation. It could happen, however, that the algorithm finds no allocation which is guaranteed to be safe; that is, deadlock could occur when a subsequent request was made. In practice, some object allocation might have to be made eventually and the risk of deadlock run.

To carry out this form of deadlock avoidance procedure would therefore not only involve a significant overhead but could not be used in all circumstances. A fallback procedure would be needed in case of failure to find a safe state to move to. The system could then move to an unsafe state, in the terms of the algorithm.

16.8   Information on releasing objects – multiphase processes

We have seen that making information on total object requirements of processes available to the object management subsystem could allow deadlock to be avoided rather than merely detected dynamically. There are reservations, however, that the avoidance algorithm is over-cautious. It takes no account of the fact that a process might release an object at some time before it terminates. If this information could be given to the object management subsystem a more realistic model of the system could be maintained and used by a deadlock avoidance algorithm.

In order to bring in the notion of piecemeal acquiring and releasing of objects by processes we need the concept of steps in the progress of a sequential process. At the start of each step a process requests or releases one or more objects. The object management subsystem now knows the precise behaviour of the set of processes under its control. It would be possible, in theory, to schedule a combination of process steps so that the system proceeds through a sequence of safe states, a system state being defined as a step from each process being managed.

The computational overhead of such an algorithm is likely to be large and the approach is unlikely to be applicable to many application areas. The model of a distinct set of processes to be run from start to completion is not always appropriate. Some processes may run indefinitely, possibly in a cyclic fashion; some processes may terminate; new processes may be created dynamically. One area in which the model has been applied successfully is in job scheduling by operating systems. Here it may often be the case that a process will require a few resources in a specific order. It is not applicable to the scheduling of large numbers of short transactions.

16.9   Summary

Dynamic allocation of objects to processes has to be done in some systems. Operating systems, communications systems and DBMS are examples. Deadlock is possible if objects are allocated dynamically. We saw the four conditions that must hold for deadlock to exist in a system: 'exclusive access'; hold while waiting; no preemption; and circular wait. The first three conditions are basic policies of object allocation and carefully chosen system policies can go some way to help avoid deadlock. This has to be considered for the specific type of object management system to be designed.

The allocation of objects to processes was modelled by a directed graph and a cycle in an allocation graph was shown to be a necessary condition for deadlock to exist. It is also a sufficient condition if there is only one object of the object types involved in the cycle. Data structures were shown that could be used to record object allocation and availability and outstanding requests. Simple algorithms for deadlock detection and avoidance were given and discussed. These algorithms could be refined for use in specific systems.

The reader is now aware of a broad range of approaches that can be considered when resources are allocated dynamically. This material will be drawn on as a basis for subsequent chapters. It will also be extended, for example, to allow for shared locks as well as exclusive locks. We shall also consider the use of time-stamps for deadlock avoidance.

The flavour of the discussion in this chapter has been that deadlock is a rare and serious business. We shall see in later chapters that it could be expedient and desirable to provide an *abort* operation. If the ability to abort is available it can be built into many aspects of system design, including deadlock management.

Exercises

16.1   Consider a wide range of examples of objects or resources that are allocated by a system to meet the demands of the application or applications that it runs. Consider the extent to which these demands are predictable in advance. Consider real-time systems, multi-user (distributed) operating systems, database management systems etc.

16.2   What are deadlock, livelock and starvation? Give examples.

16.3   (a) What are the four conditions that must hold for deadlock to exist in an object allocation system? Which of these are system policies? Which is concerned with a specific sequence of events that happens to have occurred?
(b) Is it possible to ensure that any of these conditions can be guaranteed not to hold?

16.4   Consider the following alternative specifications of the resource requirements of a process. In each case the process makes requests dynamically for the objects it needs.

(a) No resource requirements are specified in advance.

(b) The total resource requirements are specified.

(c) The order in which the resources are required is specified.

(d) The order in which resources are acquired and released is specified.

Discuss how these levels of information on resource requirements could be used to handle the possibility of deadlock. What are the trade-offs involved in deciding on the amount of information to hold and the amount of processing to be done on it?

16.5 Devise the following solutions to the dining philosophers problem of Section 16.4:

(a) Take the semaphore program given in Section 16.4 as a starting point. Explore the use of an additional semaphore to achieve mutual exclusion, either to ensure that both forks are picked up at once or to simulate a room which the philosophers enter one at a time to eat. Adapt this latter solution to allow four philosophers at once to enter the room.

(b) Write semaphore programs which break the symmetry. Let odd-numbered philosophers pick up their forks left then right and even-numbered philosophers right then left. An alternative is that just one philosopher picks up his forks in the opposite order.

(c) Write the monitor 'solution' that is equivalent to our first attempt, given in Section 16.4, that is susceptible to deadlock.

(d) Write a solution that simulates a room in which the philosophers eat one at a time.

(e) Write a monitor solution that allocates forks so that only four philosophers at once may be attempting to eat.

(f) Write a monitor solution such that philosophers request both forks at once.

(g) The above solutions are specific to this problem. Explore the use of the general approaches to deadlock detection and avoidance described in this chapter. For example, a fork allocator monitor could run a deadlock detection algorithm whenever it could not satisfy a request for a fork. Or each process might register a claim for the total resources it might ever require before starting to run its algorithm. A fork allocator might run a deadlock avoidance algorithm. Note the length of these solutions.

17 Transactions

CONTENTS

17.1 Introduction

In Chapter 13 we considered how to make a single operation invocation crash-resilient. The idea of an atomic operation invocation was introduced, defined there as follows. An operation invocation executes **atomically** if:

- When it terminates normally all its externally visible effects are made permanent (we shall call this the property of **durability**), else it has no effect at all.

- If the operation accesses a shared data object, its invocation does not interfere with other operation invocations on the same data object. We shall extend this concept into the property of **isolation**.

If a crash occurs during the execution of an operation that has been defined to be atomic, in a system which supports atomic operations, then the system can be rolled back to the state it was in before the atomic operation was invoked and the operation can be restarted.

In Part III we consider composite operations. Figure 17.1 shows the serialization of potentially interfering operations on a single object. Part II showed how to achieve this serialization. Figure 17.2 shows a composite operation,

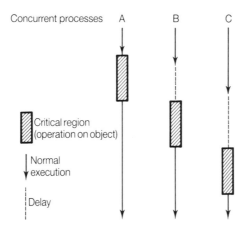

Figure 17.1
Serialization of conflicting operations on one object.

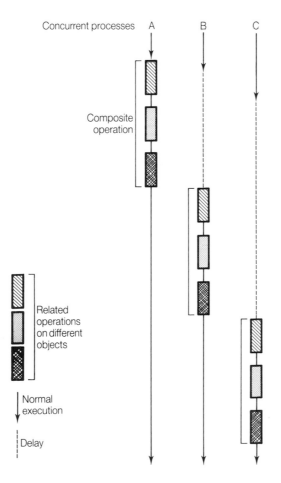

Figure 17.2
Serialization of a composite operation.

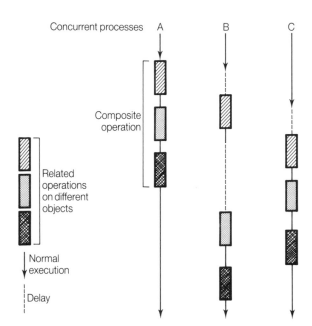

Figure 17.3
An example of interleaved (sub)operations.

comprising related, potentially interfering, operations on different objects, executed by three processes. In this case the composite operation is serialized as a single operation. In Chapter 15 we argued that it is desirable to attempt to achieve concurrent execution of composite operations by interleaving the executions of their sub-operations, as shown in Figure 17.3. Notice that the conflicting operations on individual objects are still serialized and take place in the same order within the composite operation for a given process.

17.2 Transactions

It is useful to extend the concept of atomic operation to include composite operations. We assume that it is the composite operation that has meaning to whatever application invoked it; the sub-operations are related and all or none of them must be carried out. Recall the operation hierarchy of Section 15.1 and Figures 15.4 and 15.7. It is the operation at the outermost level shown in the figures that has meaning to the application; for example, *transfer* was decomposed into *debit* and *credit*. We shall use the term **transaction** to indicate a meaningful atomic operation, such as *transfer*, that may or may not be composite.

In general, a meaningful composite operation may reside at any level in an operation hierarchy. Also, a transaction at a given level may form part of a transaction at a higher level. We shall not consider such nested transactions.

This chapter establishes a basis for studying how transactions may be implemented with concurrent execution and in the presence of crashes.

17.2.1 Commit and abort

It is useful to define a special operation to end a transaction which terminates successfully. Successful termination is called **commitment** and a successful transaction is assumed to terminate with a *commit* operation. After a successful *commit* operation, the changes that the transaction has made to the system state are guaranteed to persist. This is the **durability** property of transactions. So that we can indicate the existence of a transaction precisely we shall assume that a transaction starts with a specific *start* operation.

We shall discuss in Section 17.9 whether commitment is also the point at which those changes are allowed to become visible to other transactions. If this is the case then the transaction is said to have the property of **isolation**. It might be desirable in an implementation to make them visible earlier, thus achieving greater concurrency, but the effect on long-term system state must be as though the property of isolation was enforced.

A transaction management system must be **crash-resilient** in order to enforce the property of **atomicity** of transactions; either all or none of the operations of a transaction are carried out (see Section 15.6). If a transaction has not been committed it cannot be assumed that all its operations are complete. When the system restarts after a crash it must be able to roll back (undo) the effects of any transactions that were uncommitted at the time of the crash. This is called **aborting** a transaction. A transaction is defined to end with a *commit* or an *abort* operation.

If such a procedure is available for achieving crash resilience it may also be used for **concurrency control** by the management system. Once the possibility of undoing the effects of operations exists in a system we can, optimistically, attempt to achieve greater concurrency than is strictly safe and solve any problems that arise by undoing the effects of the operations that have turned out to be wrong.

The *abort* operation can also be made available to the application level. A transaction may then be coded to read values from a database and, depending on the values, proceed to further processing or abort, requiring any previous operations to be undone. An example is that a *check-balance* operation might find that there is insufficient money in an account to proceed with a *debit* operation.

17.2.2 Notation for transactions

It is convenient to use a concise notation for transactions and their operations. We assume that a transaction is given a unique identifying number i when it starts and that this number is associated with all its operations. We refer to the transaction as a whole as T_i, its start as S_i, a *commit* operation as C_i and an *abort* operation as A_i. The operations within the transaction will be named appropriately, such as *debit$_i$ (account-A, £1000)*.

The example from Chapter 15, of a *transfer* transaction, may be specified in some application-level programming language as follows:

> *begin transaction*
> *transfer (account-A, account-B, £1000)*
> *end transaction*;

This implies that *transfer* is defined, at a higher level of abstraction, at the programming language level. At a lower level, within a library or the transaction management system, *transfer* could be expanded in terms of operations on bank account objects as follows:

$T_i = S_i$; **if** *check-balance$_i$ (account-A, £1000)*
> **then** *debit$_i$ (account-A, £1000)*; *credit$_i$ (account-B, £1000)*; C_i
> **else** *print$_i$ ("not enough in account")*; A_i
> **fi**

We shall use the example of bank account objects again in Section 17.6 where the operations will be discussed in more detail. For more complex transactions the application level may require to interact with the transaction manager and it is returned the transaction identifier for this purpose.

17.3 Serializability and consistency

We defined a transaction as a (possibly composite) atomic operation that is meaningful to the application level; a transaction relates to some given level in an operation hierarchy. A transaction therefore causes the system to move from one consistent state at this level to another. If the possibility of crashes is ignored in the first instance, a **consistent system state** can be maintained by executing transactions **serially**.

If one process's transaction is executed to completion before any other can start there is no possibility of interference between them. We have made the transaction a single Part II-style indivisible operation (Figure 17.2). Such a procedure (single threading of all, even unrelated, transactions) could be bad for system performance, as argued in Chapter 15, and serial execution of all transactions could not be contemplated for a multiprocessor or distributed system. We must therefore consider concurrent execution of transactions.

During concurrent execution of composite operations, sub-operation executions are interleaved (see, for example, Figure 17.3). In some cases (hopefully in most cases), different transactions will access unrelated objects. An example is when transactions are associated with the data held about individuals, such as in a social security or tax-related database. The database is massive and processing is likely to be widely scattered across it.

The idea that consistent system state is maintained by serial execution of transactions is fundamental. If a specific interleaving of the sub-operations of concurrent transactions can be shown to be equivalent in some sense to some serial execution of those transactions, then we know that the system state will be consistent, given that particular concurrent execution of the transactions. Further discussion can be found in Korth *et al.* (1990).

An example illustrates the point. Consider two transactions *Sum* (*S*) and *Transfer* (*T*), with operations as defined in Section 15.5.2. The *start* and *commit* operations are not shown here. A **serial schedule** of the operations of the transactions may be achieved in two ways:

T before *S*	or *S* before *T*
T: *debit* (*account-A*, £1000);	*S* : *read-balance* (*account-A*);
T: *credit* (*account-B*, £1000);	*S* : *read-balance* (*account-B*);
S : *read-balance* (*account-A*);	*S* : *print* (*account-A* + *account-B*);
S : *read-balance* (*account-B*);	*T*: *debit* (*account-A*, £1000);
S : *print* (*account-A* + *account-B*);	*T*: *credit* (*account-B*, £1000);

The interleaving which leads to a result in which £1000 is lost from the sum:

    T: *debit* (*account-A,* £1000);
    S : *read-balance* (*account-A*);
    S : *read-balance* (*account-B*);
    S : *print* (*account-A* + *account-B*);
    T: *credit* (*account-B*, £1000);

is not equivalent to either serial schedule of operations. The problem arises because transaction *S* is seeing an inconsistent system state. We shall study how to achieve concurrent execution of transactions whilst ensuring that no transaction sees an inconsistent system state.

17.4 The ACID properties of transactions

Putting together the points made in the discussion above, a transaction may be defined as having the following properties:

Atomicity	Either all or none of the transaction's operations are performed.
Consistency	A transaction transforms the system from one consistent state to another.
Isolation	An incomplete transaction cannot reveal its result to other transactions before it is committed.
Durability	Once a transaction is committed the system must guarantee that the results of its operations will persist, even if there are subsequent system failures.

Note that these properties relate to the definition of transactions and do not imply particular methods of implementation. The effect on system state of running transactions is as defined by these properties.

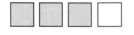

17.5 Indicating specific orderings of transactions

We assume a transaction management system with clients who may simultaneously submit a number of transactions. The system is at liberty to execute their operations in any order provided that a serializable execution is achieved, since a serializable execution of a set of transactions is defined to be correct. All serial executions are assumed by the system to be equally acceptable to the application.

If the semantics of the application require one transaction to be carried out after another they must not be submitted to a transaction management system at the same time. For example, it might be that a user must transfer money from a savings account to a current account before transferring money from the current account to some external account to make a payment. If they are submitted together, the management system may execute them concurrently and the suboperations may be scheduled in any order. The user may be told there are insufficient funds for the transfer.

This is a crude method of specifying dependencies between transactions. In Section 17.7 we explore how dependencies between the operations of transactions might be expressed, with a view to achieving a serializable execution of a number of transactions. Within a single transaction we shall assume that any two operations on the same object will be carried out in the order specified in the transaction. Unrelated operations may be carried out in any order, thus allowing for parallel execution in a multiprocessor environment.

17.6 A system model for transaction processing

Figure 17.4 shows the example of an abstract data object (a bank account) which we used in Section 15.5. We shall use the same example to study serializability. Each data object has an associated set of operations, in this case:

create a new account.

delete an existing account.

read-balance takes an account name as argument and returns the balance of the account.

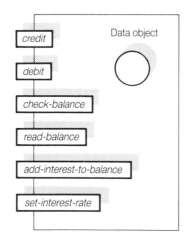

Figure 17.4
An account object.

check-balance takes an account name and a value as arguments and returns true if the balance of the account is greater than or equal to the argument value, else it returns false.

credit takes an account name and a value as arguments and adds the argument value to the balance. Note that the value of the balance is not output to the client.

debit takes an account name and a value as arguments and subtracts the argument value from the balance. Note that the value of the balance is not output to the client.

It is assumed here that the client is responsible for checking the balance before doing a debit. For example, the *transfer* transaction would contain:

if *check-balance (account-A, £1000)* **then** *debit (account-A, £1000)* . . .

set-interest-rate (*r%*) is used to set the daily interest rate to a given percentage and *add-interest-to-balance* is run daily by the system administration (probably at 3a.m., when, although cashpoints are available, not many people will be around doing transactions). This operation computes the interest accrued to the account, based on its current value, and adds the interest to the balance.

17.6.1   Non-commutative (conflicting) pairs of operations

It is possible to specify which pairs of these operations do not commute. Operations *A* and *B* are **commutative** if, from any initial state, executing *A* then *B* results in the same object state and external output values as executing *B* then

A; the order of execution does not matter. We shall use the term **conflicting** as equivalent to **non-commutative**, relating to a pair of operations.

For a given object it must therefore be specified which pairs of operations conflict. Note that it is necessary to include in the pairs each operation with itself. An example of an operation which does not commute with itself is *write*. For example:

the order: *write* $(x, 100)$; *write* $(x, 200)$ results in the final value 200 for x,

the order: *write* $(x, 200)$; *write* $(x, 100)$ results in the final value 100 for x.

In the case of the bank account object:

credit and *debit* are commutative (the final value of the account is the same whatever the order of execution and there is no external output)

credit and *credit* are commutative, as are *debit* and *debit*

read-balance and *credit* are not commutative (the value read and output for the balance is different depending on whether it is executed before or after the credit operation; the final value of the account is the same whatever the order of execution)

read-balance and *debit* are not commutative

read-balance and *read-balance* are commutative, as are *check-balance* and *check-balance*

check-balance and *credit* are not commutative

check-balance and *debit* are not commutative

set-interest-rate and *set-interest-rate* are not commutative (the final value of the interest rate depends on the order of execution of two *set-interest-rate* operations if their arguments are different)

add-interest-to-balance conflicts with *credit* and *debit* because the value computed for the interest is different depending on whether the *credit* or *debit* was done before or after *add-interest-to-balance*. It conflicts with *read-balance* and *check-balance* with respect to the value of the account output.

For example, suppose (to make the arithmetic simple and emphasize the point) that interest is computed at the (very high) rate of 0.1% per day and suppose account A stands at £10,000:

     credit (*account-A*, £5000) A=£15,000

     interest (*account-A*) A=£15,015

If the operations are executed in the other order:

     interest (*account-A*) A=£10,010

     credit (*account-A*, £5000) A=£15,010

The final state is different: the operations conflict.

17.6.2   Condition for serializability

We shall use this model with the following assumptions:

- Objects are identified uniquely in a system.

- The operations are executed without interference (in the sense of Part II); that is, the operations we are considering here are at the finest granularity of decomposition visible to the client.

- There is a single clock associated with the object which is used to indicate the time at which operations take place and therefore their order.

- The object records the time at which each operation invocation takes place with the transaction identifier (see Section 17.2.2) of the transaction that executed the operation.

It is therefore possible, for any pair of transactions, to determine the order of execution of their operations (in particular the conflicting pairs of operations) on a given object which they both invoke. This leads to the following definition of serializability of a pair of transactions (Weihl, 1984, 1989):

> For **serializability** of two transactions it is necessary and sufficient for the order of their invocations of all conflicting pairs of operations to be the same for all the objects which are invoked by both transactions.

We shall use this definition as the basis for our study of concurrent execution of transactions. In the next section we generalize from pairwise serializability to serializability of a number of transactions. Note that the definition holds for a distributed system where there can be no assumption of global time. All that is needed is time local to each object.

Herlihy (1990) takes a more general view of conflict, but we leave this work for further study.

Example

Consider again (see Section 17.3) the example of two transactions *Sum* (*S*) and *Transfer* (*T*). The serial schedules of the operations of the transactions are:

T before S	or	S before T
T: *debit* (*account-A*, £1000);		*S* : *read-balance* (*account-A*);
T: *credit* (*account-B*, £1000);		*S* : *read-balance* (*account-B*);
S : *read-balance* (*account-A*);		*S* : *print* (*account-A* + *account-B*);
S : *read-balance* (*account-B*);		*T*: *debit* (*account-A*, £1000);
S : *print* (*account-A* + *account-B*);		*T*: *credit* (*account-B*, £1000);

The pairs of conflicting operations on objects invoked by the two transactions are:

> *T*: *debit* (*account-A*, £1000) and *S*: *read-balance* (*account-A*),
> (*account-A*: *T* before *S)*

T: *credit* (*account-B*, £1000) and S: *read-balance* (*account-B*), (*account-B*: *T* before *S*).

In both of the serial schedules these pairs of conflicting operations are carried out in the same order by the transactions.

In the non-serializable schedule:

T: *debit* (*account-A*, £1000);

S: *read-balance* (*account-A*);

S: *read-balance* (*account-B*);

S: *print* (*account-A* + *account-B*);

T: *credit* (*account-B*, £1000);

The pairs of conflicting operations on objects invoked by the two transactions are:

T: *debit* (*account-A*, £1000) and S: *read-balance* (*account-A*), (*account-A*: *T* before *S*)

S: *read-balance* (*account-B*) and T: *credit* (*account-B*, £1000), (*account-B*: *S* before *T*).

 ## 17.7   Serializability illustrated by directed graphs of transactions

In this section we develop a graphical representation for schedules of operations of transactions. Any necessary ordering of the operations within a transaction is indicated in its graph. Figure 17.5 shows the transactions *Sum* and *Transfer* used above. Taking the *Sum* transaction as an example, *start* comes first, the *read-balance* operations may take place in either order or in parallel (on a multi-processor) but must precede the *write* operation, and finally there comes the *commit* operation.

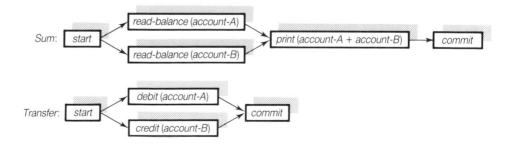

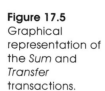
Figure 17.5
Graphical representation of the *Sum* and *Transfer* transactions.

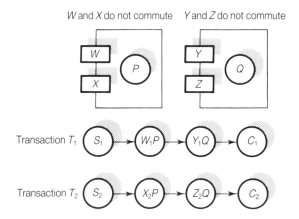

Figure 17.6
A specification of
two transactions.

In the next examples we use a more concise notation for the purposes of discussion: P and Q for objects and W, X, Y, Z for operations. Figure 17.6 specifies two transactions, both of which access objects P and Q. The operations W and X on object P are conflicting, as are operations Y and Z on object Q. In practice, an object is likely to have many operations but we consider a minimal example in order to highlight the issues. We focus on pairs of conflicting operations in order to explore the definition of serializability given in Section 17.6.2. The graphs show the operations within each transaction in serial order for simplicity. Our concern is to explore how concurrent transactions may be represented.

Figure 17.7 shows a serializable execution of the operations of the two transactions:

T_1 invokes W on P before T_2 invokes X on P (object P: T_1 before T_2)
T_1 invokes Y on Q before T_2 invokes Z on Q (object Q: T_1 before T_2)

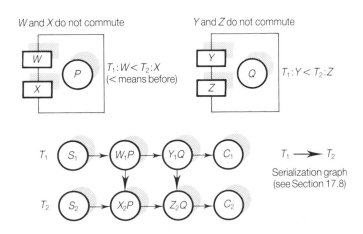

Figure 17.7
A serializable
schedule of the
transactions'
operations.

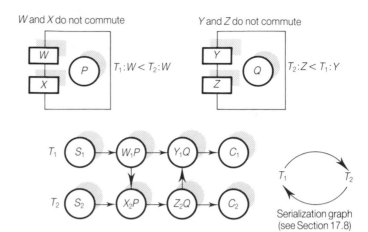

Figure 17.8
A non-serializable
schedule of the
transactions'
operations.

That is, the order of pairs of conflicting operations is the same for all the objects which are invoked by both transactions.

Figure 17.8 shows a non-serializable execution of the operations of the two transactions:

T_1 invokes W on P before T_2 invokes X on P (object P: T_1 before T_2)

T_2 invokes Z on Q before T_1 invokes Y on Q (object Q: T_2 before T_1)

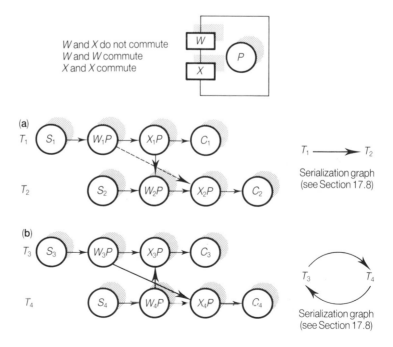

Figure 17.9
Schedules of
transactions'
operations on one
object:
(a) a serializable
schedule:
(b) a non-
serializable
schedule.

In this case, the pair of conflicting operations on P (W, X) is invoked in the order T_1 then T_2. The pair of conflicting operations on Q (Z, Y) is invoked in the order T_2 then T_1. There is no ordering of the transactions that is consistent with the order of operations at both objects.

Figure 17.9 gives an example involving a single object. Since operation W is invoked by both transactions it is necessary to know whether W commutes with W and, similarly, whether X commutes with X. We specify that W commutes with W and X commutes with X, and so we need only consider the single pair of conflicting operations W and X.

(a) T_1 invokes W on P before T_2 invokes X on P (object P: T_1 before T_2)

    T_1 invokes X on P before T_2 invokes W on P (object P: T_1 before T_2).

The schedule is not only serializable but is, in this case, serial.

(b) T_3 invokes W on P before T_4 invokes X on P (object P: T_3 before T_4)

    T_4 invokes W on P before T_3 invokes X on P (object P: T_4 before T_3).

The schedule is not serializable.

17.8 Histories and serialization graphs

A **history** is a data structure which represents a concurrent execution of a set of transactions. The directed graphs of Figures 17.7, 17.8 and 17.9 are simple examples; they show the operations within the transactions, and the order of invocation of conflicting pairs of operations by different transactions. Note that the order of invocation of all conflicting pairs of operations on all objects must be shown in the history. Figure 17.10 gives a representation of a history in which the details of the objects and operations involved are not shown.

A **serializable history** represents a serializable execution of the transactions. That is, there is a serial ordering of the transactions in which all conflicting pairs of operations at each object are invoked in the same order as in the given history.

An object is a witness to an order dependency between two transactions if they have invoked a conflicting pair of operations at that object. A **serialization graph** is a directed graph that shows only transaction identifiers and dependencies between transactions; the vertices of the graph are the transactions T_i, and there is an edge $T_i \rightarrow T_j$ if and only if some object is a witness to that order dependency. For example, $T_1 \rightarrow T_2$ is the transaction graph for the history in Figure 17.7. The serialization graph for T_1, T_2 and T_3 is shown in Figure 17.10. A transaction history is serializable if and only if its serialization graph is acyclic.

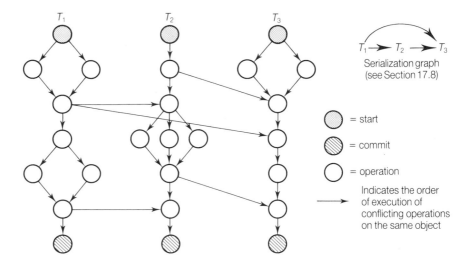

Figure 17.10
An example of a serializable history of three transactions.

Figure 17.11 gives examples of possible serialization graphs for four transactions. In both 17.11(a) and (b) every pair of transactions has conflicting operations executed in the same order (there is at most one edge between each pair of transactions). In Figure 17.11(b) the serialization graph has a cycle and the history represented by the serialization graph is not serializable.

In general we must ascertain whether a given schedule of the operations within a set of transactions is serializable. We require a total ordering of the set of transactions that is consistent with the schedule:

- Each object knows which pairs of its operations conflict.
- Each object knows which transactions have invoked conflicting operations: it is a witness to an order dependency between them.
- Provided that the order dependencies are consistent both at each given object and between objects then an ordering is determined for each pair of transac-

Figure 17.11
Examples of serialization graphs:
(a) a serialization graph for a serializable history;
(b) a serialization graph for a non-serializable history.

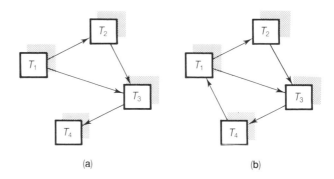

(a)   (b)

tions involved. If not, then there is a cycle in the serialization graph, say $T_1 \rightarrow T_2 \rightarrow T_1$ as in Figure 17.8, and the transaction history cannot be serializable. This information can be assembled for all the objects invoked by the set of transactions, giving rise to the serialization graph.

● To find a total ordering of the set of transactions that is consistent with the pairwise order dependencies requires a topological sort of the serialization graph. This can be done if and only if the graph is acyclic (Aho *et al.*, 1983).

Suppose that a TP system maintains a serialization graph of the transactions in progress. A new transaction is submitted and the system attempts to execute it concurrently with the ongoing transactions. Any proposed schedule of the operations of the new transaction can be tested by creating a serialization graph which is the original one extended with the operations of the new transaction. A schedule can be rejected if the serialization graph thus extended has a cycle.

17.9   Dealing with aborts: More about the property of isolation

The theory outlined above does not take into account that the operations of a transaction might be undone due to an *abort* termination. It must be possible to return the system to a consistent state as though the transaction had not taken place. The following problems could arise through concurrent execution of transactions, even if a serializable schedule of suboperations had been devised. It is demonstrated that serializability is necessary but not sufficient for correct concurrent operation.

17.9.1   Cascading aborts

Figure 17.12 shows a serializable schedule of the transactions T_1 and T_2 used above in Section 17.7. This time, T_1 happens to abort.

Suppose that the transaction scheduler, having noted the order of operations for a serializable transaction, had, in order to achieve maximum concurrency, allowed T_2 to execute operation X on object P as soon as T_1 had completed operation W and similarly for object Q. T_2 may have seen state or performed output that is now incorrect because T_1 has aborted and T_2 must also be aborted.

In general, aborting one transaction could lead to the need to abort a number of related transactions, called **cascading aborts**. This behaviour might degrade system performance so badly that it could be advisable to ensure that any state seen by a transaction has been written by a committed transaction. In other words, the effects of the sub-operations of a transaction are not made visible to other transactions until the transaction commits, thus enforcing the property of

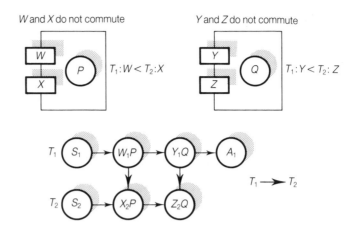

Figure 17.12
Example of
cascading abort.

isolation in the implementation. A schedule of operation invocations which
enforces this property is called a **strict** schedule. This approach would cause difficulties in systems where transactions could be long and contention was likely,
and could be deemed unnecessary if crashes and aborts are unlikely to happen.

17.9.2 The ability to recover state

The discussion here is in general terms. In the next chapter specific methods for
achieving correct (serializable) executions of transactions are described. Some of
the scenarios given below as examples might not in practice be allowed to arise,
or some of the theoretically possible system actions might be deemed too expensive to implement.

   If abort is supported it must be possible to return the system to a consistent
state, as though the aborted transaction had not taken place. Consider the following interleaving of operations within a concurrent execution of transactions
T_1 and T_2. The operations involved, several credit operations on bank accounts,
are commutative so there is no problem with serializability. Suppose that
initially A=£5000 and B=£8000.

$start_1$

$credit_1$ ($account\text{-}A$, £1000) A=£6000

$credit_1$ ($account\text{-}B$, £500) B=£8500

$start_2$

$credit_2$ ($account\text{-}A$, £200) A=£6200

$abort_1$ (A=£5200 B=£8000 should be achieved)

$credit_2$ ($account\text{-}B$, £600) B=£8600

$abort_2$ (A=£5000 B=£8000 should be achieved)

This example schedule is not strict, that is, it violates the property of isolation. If this is the case, greater care must be taken on abort or on crash recovery than merely restoring each object's state to that prior to the aborted operation. When T_1 aborts, T_2 has already done another *credit* operation on *account-A*. The value of *account-A* cannot simply be put back to that prior to $credit_1$ (*account-A*, £1000). Neither can we take no action at all; T_2 goes on to abort. We cannot then put the value of *account-A* back to what it was prior to $credit_2$ (*account-A*, £200) (this was the value after the credit by T_1 which has already aborted). If we had discarded the value prior to T_1's invocation the original state would be irrecoverable. Fortunately, we assume that a record of invocations is kept with the object and we have higher-level semantics than merely a record of state changes.

We shall assume that every operation has an **inverse** or **undo** operation. When a transaction aborts, each of its invocations must be undone. For a given object, if there have been no conflicting invocations since the one that is to be undone then we simply apply the *undo* operation to the current state (the order of invocation of commutative operations is irrelevant). In this example, the inverse of *credit* is *debit*. When T_1 aborts we can simply *debit* (*account-A*, £1000) and remove the record of the original invocation from the object.

If there has been a conflicting invocation since the invocation we require to abort then we must undo all the invocations back to the conflicting operation. After we have undone that, we can perform the undo to achieve the abort we require, then we must do the subsequent operations again. The following example illustrates this; *interest* is used as a shorthand for *add-interest-to-balance* and a (very high) daily interest rate of 0.1% is again assumed for simplicity. The point is that we cannot simply apply the inverse of $credit_1$ when T_1 aborts, for example; this would leave the account with the value £7008 which is incorrect. Note also that even though non-strict operations are allowed to go ahead, transactions which invoke them might be delayed when they request to commit because they have seen uncommitted state. Suppose that initially A=£5000.

$start_1$			
$credit_1$	(*account-A*, £1000)		A=£6000
$start_2$			
$credit_2$	(*account-A*, £2000)		A=£8000
$start_3$			
$interest_3$	(*account-A*)		A=£8008
$commit_3$	delay commit?		
$start_4$			
$credit_4$	(*account-A*, £1000)		A=£9008
$commit_4$	delay commit?		
$abort_1$			
	undo $credit_4$	(*account-A*, £1000)	A=£8008

undo *interest₃*	(*account-A*)	A=£8000

(note there is no need to undo and redo *credit₂* (*account-A*, £2000) because credits commute)

undo *credit₁*	(*account-A*, £1000)	A=£7000
redo *interest₃*	(*account-A*)	A=£7007
redo *credit₄*	(*account-A*, £1000)	A=£8007

abort₂

undo *credit₄*	(*account-A*, £1000)	A=£7007
undo *interest₃*	(*account-A*)	A=£7000
undo *credit₂*	(*account-A*, £2000)	A=£5000
redo *interest₃*	(*account-A*)	A=£5005
redo *credit₄*	(*account-A*, £1000)	A=£7005

This is a complex procedure and is the penalty to be paid for relaxing the property of isolation in an implementation and allowing non-strict conflicting operations to be invoked. In general, we shall assume a strict execution of operations to avoid this complexity, although as stated above, strictness may not be realistic in some systems. A strict execution can be enforced if each object delays any request to invoke an operation which conflicts with an uncommitted operation. An object must then be told when a transaction that has invoked it commits; this is assumed to be through a commit operation in the object's interface.

   commit (*transaction-id*)

would cause all state changes resulting in invocations on the object by the transaction to be made permanent and visible to other transactions.

   We shall return to this topic in later chapters in the context of specific methods of concurrency control. In the meantime, let us assume that each object holds information on the operations that have been invoked on it which includes the

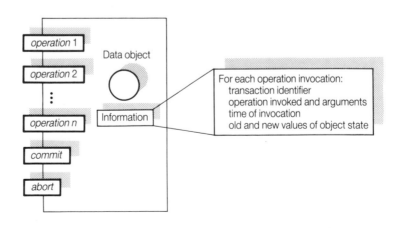

Figure 17.13
An object used in a transaction system.

transaction identifier of the invoker and the time of the invocation (Figure 17.13). It should be emphasized that this is a theoretical starting point: all relevant information is assumed to be held. It would not be possible in a practical implementation to hold an indefinite history with every object and optimizations would have to be made. We shall assume that each object has a commit operation and an abort operation.

17.10   Summary

We have extended the definition given in Chapter 13, of an atomic operation invocation in the presence of crashes, to cover atomic composite operation invocations (transactions) in the presence of concurrent transactions and crashes. The ACID (Atomicity, Consistency, Isolation, Durability) properties of transactions were motivated and discussed.

A system model to be used as a basis for reasoning about all aspects of transaction processing was introduced. The model focuses on the operations of a single object and generalizes naturally to distributed objects. Conflicting operations were defined to be those which do not commute; that is, the order in which they are executed affects the final state of the object, or the value output by an operation.

We have assumed that each object will hold information on operation invocations that have been made on it, in particular, the time of the invocation and the identifier of the invoking transaction. The order of invocation of all operations on an object can therefore be determined. We shall see how this information might be used for concurrency control and recovery purposes in later chapters. An introductory treatment of serializability was given here, based on this model.

We considered the pros and cons of relaxing the property of isolation of atomic transactions in an implementation, that is, allowing non-strict executions. In this case a transaction is able to see system state (values of objects) written by uncommitted transactions. The motivation is to allow greater concurrency, but the price to be paid is greater complexity. Cascading aborts can occur and the recovery of previous correct system state might involve a complex procedure of undoing and redoing operations. A strict execution (in which the property of isolation is enforced in the implementation) seems to be desirable to avoid this complexity. It may not be feasible to enforce strictness in practice if long transactions are common, failure is unlikely (crashes or application requested abort) and contention is likely.

Exercises

17.1 How can a serial execution of a composite operation be guaranteed? What is a serializable execution of a composite operation?

17.2 In a TP system a client submits a transaction, which is done and acknowledged to the client. What must the system guarantee when that acknowledgement is given?

17.3 What are the ACID properties of atomic transactions and how can they be ensured under concurrency and crashes?

17.4 Relate the system model based on object invocation given in Section 17.6 to the discussion of Section 14.9 on object naming, location and invocation.

17.5 How does the graph which represents the history of a set of transactions being executed differ from a serialization graph? What property of the serialization graph must hold for the transactions that it represents to be serializable?

17.6 Why might the decision to abort one transaction lead to the need to abort another? Could this happen if the property of isolation of atomic transactions was enforced at all times?

17.7 Give some practical examples of conflicting operations on an object.

17.8 Assume that every operation on an object has an inverse or undo operation. Assume that a number of operations have taken place on an object. When can an undo operation simply be applied to the current state of an object, even if there have been operations on the object since the one that must be undone?

Concurrency control

18

CONTENTS

18.1 Introduction

The main concern of this chapter is how concurrent execution of transactions can be implemented. Crash resilience, although related, is covered in the next chapter. The conceptual model based on objects, which was developed in Chapter 17, will be used again here.

A natural approach to concurrency control is to lock the objects involved in a composite operation (transaction). We shall show that locking can achieve serializability of the operations of transactions but that deadlock has to be considered. An alternative to locking is to associate a time-stamp with each transaction and to use this as a basis for enforcing one particular serializable order of execution of the operations of transactions. The methods used for concurrency control are considered in the light of the possibility that conflict may be very unlikely and having a great deal of mechanism in place to resolve it could be misplaced effort. Optimistic concurrency control may be the most suitable method for some application areas and is the final approach we consider.

First, we establish that the concurrent invocation of composite operations in main memory is subject to some of the problems that we have studied in relation to transaction systems. Then we focus on transaction processing systems (where persistent memory must be used).

18.2 Concurrent composite operations in main memory only

Assume that a concurrent program has been developed in a modular fashion. We assume that each shared data abstraction is implemented as an abstract data type, as shown in Figure 18.1, and a data object is locked for exclusive use while any of its operations is invoked. Sections 10.3 and 10.4.2 showed how this might be implemented for a single operation.

The problems of uncontrolled concurrent invocation of composite operations, discussed already in Part III, are relevant to this model. Assume in Figure 18.1 that objects *A* and *B* are operated on by one concurrent process; that is, a meaningful, high-level operation comprises both an operation on object *A* and an operation on object *B*. Similarly, another composite operation invoked by another process involves both object *B* and object *C*. We have already seen that incorrect values can result from inappropriate interleavings of the sub-operations of composite operations. This is equally true for data objects in main memory and in persistent memory.

18.2.1 Objects in the main memory of a single computer

We established the properties of transactions in Chapter 17: atomicity, consistency, isolation and durability (ACID). It is helpful to consider these properties for concurrent invocation of composite operations in main memory only: that is, when no sub-operation of a composite operation writes to persistent store. We first consider a program running in the main memory of a single computer.

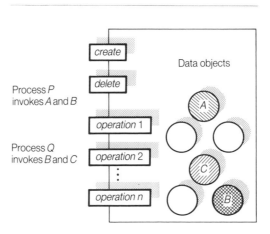

Figure 18.1
Related operations
on data objects in
main memory.

Atomicity
If there is a crash during a composite operation, all the effects of sub-operations are lost. If there is no crash the composite operation will complete. Atomicity holds without any special need for enforcement.

Consistency
We assume that a composite (high-level) operation has meaning. Invocation of a single composite operation takes the state managed by the program from one consistent value to another. We are not concerned with crashes since all state in main memory is lost on a crash. Consistency must be enforced in the presence of concurrent invocations.

Isolation
The results of the sub-operations of a composite operation should not be revealed until the operation completes. Isolation should be enforced.

Durability
If a program runs in the main memory of a single computer and a crash occurs during a composite operation invocation, all the main memory is lost. Durability is not relevant.

The properties of consistency and isolation are relevant to the correct execution of programs which contain composite operation invocations. Control of **concurrent execution of composite operations** is the central issue.

The concurrency control methods for transactions that are discussed later in this chapter might also be applicable to data in main memory only. Since locking has been the approach taken throughout Part II to ensure the correct execution of a single operation, we first consider this method briefly.

A simple example based on Figure 18.1, showing that deadlock must be considered, is as follows:

process A invokes an operation on A (thus locking A);

process Q invokes an operation on B (thus locking B);

the operation on A invokes an operation on B and P is delayed;

the operation on B invokes an operation on A and Q is delayed;

processes P and Q are deadlocked.

An alternative object management scheme is to provide separate *lock* and *unlock* operations. Deadlock can then arise when locks are acquired piecemeal. Section 15.2 set up a similar problem in a monitor-based program. The dining philosophers problem discussed in Section 16.4.2 is another example.

18.2.2 Objects in main memory in a distributed system

We now consider briefly concurrent invocations of composite operations involving objects which are located throughout the main memory of computers comprising a distributed system. We assume that there is a single copy of each object.

A given composite operation is invoked at a single node; let us call it the managing node. For any object which is not located at that node a remote invocation must be carried out. Chapter 14 showed that this might be done by a remote procedure call or by message passing. Any node or any network connection may be subject to congestion or may fail. As we discussed in Chapter 14, the protocol implementing the invocation will indicate this by returning an exception. Because the distributed program accesses data objects in main memory only, we need not be concerned, on an exception, with changes that might have been made to persistent state by a sub-operation invocation. By definition, there are none. Again, the major issue is concurrency control; in more detail:

Atomicity A number of distributed objects are invoked. If the result of every remote invocation is returned to the managing node and the local operations are also done then the composite operation is known by the manager to be complete.

   If any result is not returned (after retries by the underlying protocol) then the composite operation has failed. The significance of this depends on the application. It may be that the distributed program has to be abandoned. It may be that the program can proceed by making use of an alternative to the operation that failed.

Consistency We assume that a composite operation has meaning. Invocation of a single composite operation takes the (distributed) state managed by the program from one consistent value to another. Consistency must be enforced in the presence of concurrent invocations and partial failures.

Isolation The results of the sub-operations of a composite operation should not be revealed until the operation completes. Isolation should be enforced.

Durability If composite operations are invoked in main memory only, durability is not relevant.

Again, our main concern is to achieve consistency through enforcing isolation by some means of concurrency control. If locking is employed then, as above, we must allow for the possibility of deadlock.

18.2.3 Systematic approaches to concurrent program development

Some approaches to solving these problems in the context of a concurrent program are as follows:

1. Incorporate a transaction specification into the programming language. For example:

start transaction
invoke *operation* 1 on object *A*
invoke *operation* n on object *B*
end transaction;

The objects may or may not be persistent and may or may not be in a single local memory. This pushes the problem down into the transaction implementation. Most of this chapter is concerned with how transactions, which might be specified in this way, can be implemented.

2. Use formal techniques of program analysis to ensure that the software system is deadlock free.

3. Incorporate a general object manager in the program. Data structures and algorithms such as those described in Chapter 16 to detect or avoid deadlock could be used by the manager.

4. When designing the concurrent program, take into account the possibility of deadlock and avoid calls between operations that could lead to cycles (a systematic rather than formal approach).

For a given program the order in which locks are acquired could be specified statically in order to avoid cycles. In cases where large data objects are broken down into smaller components so that an operation on the containing object involves a nested call to the contained object this is easily achieved; the reverse direction of call is not required. Also, it may be possible to lock only the component concerned and not the whole containing object. In general it is difficult to avoid the possibility of cycles, and a systematic, informal approach is highly susceptible to error. Small problems, such as the dining philosophers example (Section 16.4.7), can be solved specifically.

5. Consider other methods of concurrency control than locking, such as time-stamp ordering (see below).

We now proceed to concurrency control in systems which support transactions on persistent data.

18.3   Structure of transaction management systems

Figure 18.2 outlines the components of an instance of a transaction processing system (TPS) in a single computer. In Chapter 20 we shall consider distributed transaction processing explicitly although much of the discussion in this chapter is relevant to distributed systems. Clients submit transactions to the TPS, which may start work on them concurrently. The transaction manager is responsible for validating the clients' submissions and for passing the component operations of the transactions to the scheduler (we assume here that the objects to be invoked are in the local database). The scheduler will use some strategy to

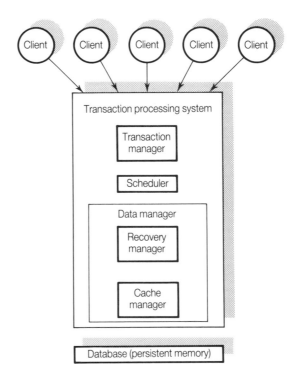

Figure 18.2
A transaction
processing system.

achieve a serializable schedule of the operations of the transactions in progress. This is the main concern of the rest of this chapter.

The data objects in persistent memory will be transferred into main memory for operation invocation and new values will be written back. This is the concern of the data manager and is discussed in the next chapter.

18.4   Concurrency control through locking

We assume a manager for each object, as discussed in Chapter 17. Figure 18.3 shows an object which is now assumed to have a *lock* and *unlock* operation as well as those previously discussed. We assume that an object can be locked and only the holder of the lock can invoke an operation on the object. Locking a single object does not solve the problems introduced in Chapter 15 since the essence of the problem is how to carry out related operations on distinct objects. A number of locks are needed for a composite operation.

We assume that the objects are located in persistent memory in a database and are accessed through a management system (a DBMS or TP system). We assume that each instance of the management system will contain a transaction

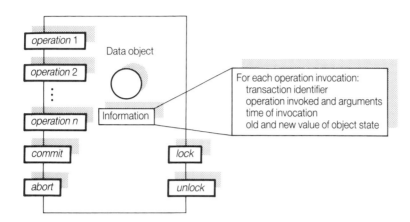

For each operation invocation:
transaction identifier
operation invoked and arguments
time of invocation
old and new value of object state

Figure 18.3
An object used in a transaction system.

scheduler and possibly a lock manager, responsible for deadlock detection or avoidance as well. Let us assume for now that the transaction scheduler will issue *lock* and *unlock* operation invocations as well as those discussed previously. A possible strategy is to lock all the objects required by a transaction at its start and to release them on *commit* or *abort*. Can we achieve better concurrency behaviour than this?

18.4.1 Two-phase locking

In two-phase locking, locks can be acquired for a transaction as they are needed. The constraint which defines two-phase locking is that no lock can be released until all locks have been acquired. A transaction therefore has a phase during which it builds up the number of locks it holds until it reaches its total requirement.

In the general form of two-phase locking, a transaction can release locks piecemeal as it finishes with the associated objects. If atomic transactions are to be supported with the property of isolation (that the effects of a transaction are not visible to other transactions before commit), a safe procedure is to release all locks on commit. This is called **strict two-phase locking**. Allowing visibility earlier allows more concurrency at the risk of cascading aborts and state which is difficult to recover, as discussed in Section 17.9.

Two-phase locking guarantees that all conflicting pairs of operations of two transactions are scheduled in the same order and thus enforces a serializable schedule of transactions. This is reasonably intuitive, but we will discuss it further after looking at an example.

It is possible for a lock request to fail because the object is locked already. In this case the transaction may be blocked for a time in the hope that the transaction holding the lock will complete and release the lock. It is possible for deadlock to occur, as shown below.

18.4.2 An example of two-phase locking

Figure 18.4 is the example used in Section 15.5.2 to illustrate the problem of inconsistent retrieval. T_1 is the *transfer* transaction which first *debit*s (D) A then *credit*s (CR) B. For conciseness we shall not show a balance check here. T_2 is a transaction which sums the values of A and B using *read-balance* (R). *Lock* (L) and *unlock* (U) operations have been inserted. When T_1 and T_2 are run concurrently, any of the following can happen:

1. T_2 locks A before T_1 locks A. T_2 proceeds to lock B and calculates and outputs A+B. T_1 is delayed when it attempts to lock A. A serializable schedule $T_2 \rightarrow T_1$ is achieved.

2. T_1 locks A before T_2 locks A. T_1 proceeds to lock B. T_2 is delayed when it attempts to lock A or B. A serializable schedule $T_1 \twoheadrightarrow T_2$ is achieved.

3. T_1 locks A before T_2 locks A. T_2 locks B. Deadlock is inevitable.

Two-phase locking ensures that a non-serializable schedule of the operations of transactions cannot occur. The method is subject to deadlock, but the occurrence of deadlock means that a non-serializable schedule has been attempted and prevented.

Discussion

Suppose two transactions have a pair of conflicting operations on object A, and another pair on object B. A particular ordering of the conflicting operations is determined as soon as one of the transactions locks one of the objects. It cannot release the object until it has locked the other object (the two-phase locking rule) which it may or may not succeed in doing. If it succeeds, it has acquired locks on both objects over which there is conflict. If it fails because the other transaction has locked the other object, deadlock is inevitable. This argument generalizes to any number of objects. It is not quite so obvious that it generalizes to any number of transactions.

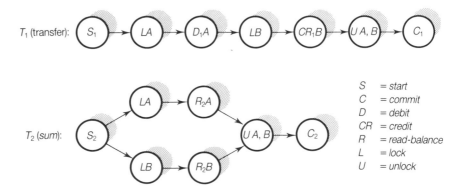

Figure 18.4
Two transactions including *lock* and *unlock* operations.

We have established that two-phase locking enforces that the conflicting operations of every pair of transactions are scheduled in the same order. It remains to argue that a cycle involving a number of transactions (see Section 17.8) is not possible. The intuition here is that if T_1 is 'before' T_2 (in the sense of Section 17.8: the operations in T_1 of all conflicting pairs are scheduled before the conflicting operations in T_2) and T_2 is before T_3, then T_1 must be before T_3: the **before** relation is transitive. At this stage we are considering a centralized system, with a single value of time, rather than a distributed one, so events can be ordered.

18.4.3 Semantic locking

The above discussion has assumed that an object is locked for exclusive use before an operation is invoked on it. For some operations, such as *read-balance*, any number of invocations could take place concurrently without interference. We could at least refine the system's locking policy to allow for shared locks and exclusive locks to be taken out.

In this case **lock conversion** might be required in some circumstances. A transaction might read a large number of object values and on that basis decide which object to update. The shared lock on the object to be updated would be converted to an exclusive lock and the shared locks on all the other objects could be released, at the time allowed by the two-phase rule. Deadlock could arise if two transactions holding a given shared lock both required to convert it to an exclusive lock.

By regarding each object as a separate entity there is maximum possible scope for indicating which operations can be executed concurrently and which cannot. Locking could be associated with each operation on an object and not provided as a separate operation. An invocation starts and a check of any degree of sophistication could be computed to determine whether to go ahead or consider the object locked against this invoker at this time and with this current object state.

18.4.4 Deadlock in two-phase locking

Allowing the objects required by a transaction to be locked separately rather than all together and allowing processes to hold their current objects while requesting further locks (the definition of two-phase locking) can lead to deadlock. That is, the rules of two-phase locking set up the conditions which make deadlock possible: (1) exclusive allocation (in the sense that a request for a resource can be refused), (2) resource hold while waiting and (3) no preemption, (see Section 16.4). An example specifically associated with two-phase locking was given in Section 18.4.2, where a cycle of processes holding some locks and waiting for others was demonstrated. Concurrency control based on two-phase locking must therefore have provision for dealing with deadlock.

The ability to *abort* a transaction is likely to be in place for crash resilience (see Chapter 19) and application requirements. Deadlock detection followed by abortion of the deadlocked transactions is likely to be a better design option than deadlock avoidance, which involves a greater overhead. Algorithms for deadlock detection and avoidance are given in Chapter 16. A simple alternative to maintaining complex data structures and running an algorithm on them for deadlock detection is to **timeout** requests for locks and to abort transactions with timed-out lock requests.

A general point is that if the ability to abort is essential in a system design for reasons other than recovery from deadlock (for crash resilience or because the applications require it) then deadlock becomes a problem that is relatively easy to deal with without introducing excessive overhead. The overhead of supporting abort was already there!

18.5   Time-stamp ordering

We are aiming to run transactions concurrently and to produce a serializable execution of their operations. An alternative approach to locking for achieving this is to associate a time-stamp with each transaction. One serializable order is then imposed on the operations: that of the time-stamps of the transactions they comprise. Assume initially that the time-stamp is the time of the start of the transaction and is recorded at the invoked object with every operation that transaction invokes. We have already assumed that an object is able to record such information.

Recall from Section 17.6.2 that for **serializability** of two transactions it is necessary and sufficient for the order of their invocations of all non-commutative (conflicting) pairs of operations to be the same for all the objects which are invoked by both transactions. Suppose a transaction invokes an operation. Suppose a second transaction attempts to invoke an operation that conflicts with it. If the time-stamp of the second transaction is later than (>) that of the first transaction then the operation can go ahead. If the time-stamp of the second transaction is earlier than (<) that of the first it is deemed TOO LATE and is rejected (the requesting transaction is aborted and restarted with a new, later, time-stamp). If this is enforced for all conflicting pairs of operations at every object then we have a serializable schedule of the operations of the concurrent transactions.

This approach enforces one particular serializable order on the operations of the concurrent transactions: that of the transactions' time-stamps. It is therefore more susceptible to transaction abort and restart than a method which allows any serializable ordering. This sacrifice of flexibility can be justified on the following grounds:

- The implementation is simple and efficient, thus improving system performance for all transactions.

- The information recorded for concurrency control is associated only with each object and is not held or processed centrally.

- Objects are not 'locked' for longer than the duration of a single operation, unlike two-phase locking, thus giving more potential for concurrent access to objects (but see Section 18.5.1 for a discussion of strictness in time-stamp ordering).

Let us consider implementation through the simple example used above in Section 18.4.2 and illustrated here in Figure 18.5. Assume the time-stamps indicate $T_1 < T_2$. Assume that objects A and B record the time-stamps of the transactions which carried out potentially conflicting pairs of operations (*debit* (D) and *read-balance* (R) are non-commutative, as are *credit* (CR) and *read-balance*). Consider the following examples of orderings of the operations of T_1 and T_2 and the corresponding actions taken by objects A and B:

1. D_1A, R_2A, R_2B, CR_1B FAILS because it conflicts with R_2B which has a higher recorded time-stamp (of T_2); T_1 is aborted.
2. R_2A, R_2B, D_1A FAILS because it conflicts with R_2A which has a higher recorded time-stamp. T_1 is aborted, even though the order $T_2 < T_1$ is serializable.

The method is simple to implement. There is no need to keep central allocation information nor to maintain a resource-wait graph and to run algorithms for deadlock detection or avoidance on it. Transactions are serialized in the order that they were submitted for execution. This means that any other serializable ordering, although correct, will fail, as in 2 above.

An early transaction fails when it attempts to invoke an operation on an object on which a later transaction has already carried out a conflicting operation. Abortion could therefore be a common occurrence if contention was likely. If contention is unlikely, the method incurs little overhead.

The following examples illustrate that the definition of conflicting behaviour must be considered carefully. Suppose a transaction to read a large number of items, process them and write a value depending on all the values read (the account to be credited is that with the lowest balance) was run concurrently

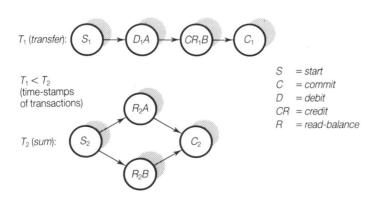

T_1 (transfer): $S_1 \rightarrow D_1A \rightarrow CR_1B \rightarrow C_1$

$T_1 < T_2$
(time-stamps
of transactions)

T_2 (sum): S_2, R_2A, R_2B, C_2

S = start
C = commit
D = debit
CR = credit
R = read-balance

Figure 18.5
Two transactions
with time-stamp
ordering.

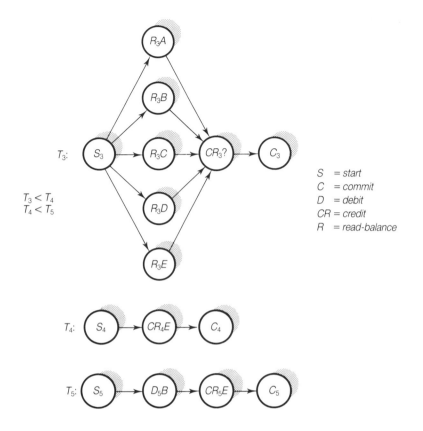

Figure 18.6
More examples of
time-stamp
ordering.

with transactions, each of which updates one of the values read. Figure 18.6 illustrates the point with a small number of objects.

1. R_3A, R_3B, R_3C, R_3D, CR_4E, R_3E: this fails because R_3E conflicts with CR_4E which has a higher recorded time-stamp. The semantics of the transaction indicate that it need not, since although the value read by T_3 relates to the state after T_4 has run, rather than before, it is not incorrect; in fact it is more relevant. Forcing serialization in the order $T_3 > T_4$ happens to be unnecessary in this case but we can only say this because we know the intention of T_3 is to invoke a credit on whichever of objects A, B, C, D and E has the lowest value.

2. R_3A, R_3B, D_5B, R_3C, R_3D, R_3E, CR_5E is allowed. Suppose T_5 has transferred £1000 from B to E. The values seen by T_3 are correct because B is read before the debit and E is read before the credit.

Two-phase locking was shown to limit concurrency more than might be strictly necessary, but delivered correct results. Time-stamp ordering may achieve a higher degree of concurrency because an object is available unless an operation is being invoked on it (but see the next section). We have seen that a large number of aborts could be made necessary by the particular serialization enforced and that no simple general definition of conflicting operations would allow us to be more flexible than this. The simple description given here has used the time of the start of a transaction as its time-stamp; it might be more appropriate to use the time of its first invocation of an operation which belongs to a conflicting pair. Refinements of the basic scheme are discussed further in Bernstein *et al.* (1987).

Time-stamp ordering can be a simple and effective scheme when conflicts are unlikely. The fact that the decision on whether an operation on an object can go ahead is made on the basis only of information recorded with the object itself makes it a suitable method for a distributed system. We shall discuss this further in Chapter 20.

18.5.1   Cascading aborts and recovery of state

Time-stamp ordering, as described above, does not enforce the property of isolation and is therefore subject to cascading aborts and complex recovery of object state as discussed in Section 17.9. Recall that it is necessary to be able to *undo* and *redo* operations.

If isolation (strict execution) is to be enforced in the implementation, an additional mechanism to that described above is needed. A transaction scheduler together with the individual object managers could achieve this. An object could ensure that a *commit* operation had been invoked for a given transaction before allowing any operation of any conflicting pair of operations to go ahead for another transaction with a later time-stamp.

Note that this does not introduce the possibility of deadlock. Circular wait is prevented by the time-stamp ordering of invocations; that is, a cycle of transactions cannot occur such that each has invoked an operation and is waiting for another transaction to commit before invoking another operation.

Strict time-stamp ordering introduces the requirement for atomic commitment. Assume that a given transaction has invoked, on a number of objects, operations which belong to conflicting pairs. All the objects must agree whether the transaction is to commit or abort. That is, all or none of the objects invoked by the transaction must commit the state changes effected by the transaction. This is not difficult to achieve in a centralized system in the absence of failures. In practice, crashes must be anticipated and distributed implementations may be necessary. Chapters 19 and 20 consider these problems.

18.6   Optimistic concurrency control (OCC)

Optimistic schemes for concurrency control are based on the premise that conflict is unlikely. We should therefore be careful to avoid heavyweight concurrency control mechanisms. We must still ensure a serializable execution. OCC

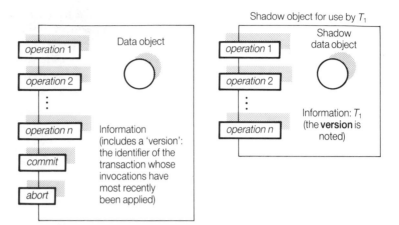

Figure 18.7
An object with a shadow.

also aims to achieve high availability of objects. The idea is to minimize delay at transaction start. OCC is therefore appropriate for certain application areas where these conditions and requirements hold: that is, for applications which need a transaction system, but where it is unusual for different transactions to touch the same objects and which need real-time response.

The strategy of OCC is to apply no changes to persistent memory during the execution of transactions. When a transaction requests *commit* its history is validated to determine whether it can be serialized along with transactions that have already been accepted. Recall Section 17.6 on serializability and Section 17.8 on histories and serialization graphs. Once a serial order of validated transactions is established, updates are applied in that order to objects in persistent memory.

The update of persistent memory must be such that in any state read from an object either all or none of the changes at that object associated with a given transaction are visible.

During transaction execution invocations are made on workspace copies, **shadow copies**, of objects. Figure 18.7 shows an object with a shadow for use by transaction T_1. Each such shadow copy has a well-defined version, which is the identifier of the transaction whose updates have most recently been applied to the object in persistent memory. Let us also assume that a time-stamp is recorded with the transaction identifier and that the time-stamp is the time when the transaction is validated and its updates are guaranteed.

Each transaction undergoes three phases:

1. **Execution (read)**   The transaction executes to completion (*commit* or *abort*) shadow copies of data objects.

2. **Validation**   Following *commit* the execution schedule is checked to ensure serializability.

3. **Update (write)**   Update invocations are applied to objects in persistent memory in serial order, transaction by transaction. It is

the responsibility of the update manager to ensure that all updates succeed. The update manager will know at any any time those transactions for which updates have succeeded. It can therefore be asserted that the updates up to those of some transaction have succeeded.

For valid execution each transaction must interact with a consistent set of shadow copies. One (heavyweight) way of achieving this is to ensure that updates are applied atomically across all objects participating in a transaction, using an atomic commitment protocol such as two-phase commit (see Section 20.9) in a distributed system. Validation can take place at each object as part of the first phase of the protocol, with update taking place only if all objects can accept the transaction. Recall that a transaction is defined to take the system from one consistent state to another. We can then make sure that a set of shadows taken at the start of a transaction is consistent; that is, we must also assume that taking a set of shadows is made atomic.

There are objections to this approach:

- The enforcement of update atomicity using a protocol such as two-phase commit reduces concurrency and is bad for performance in general. That is, there is overhead in using such an algorithm which penalizes all clients of the system. Also, specific transactions will not experience high availability of objects if they are held for the atomic commitment of some other transaction.

- At the start of transaction execution we may not know what shadows are required. Even if we enforce atomic commitment this does not help unless all shadows are taken 'at the same time'.

- More importantly, there is a mismatch of philosophy. OCC is postulated on the assumption that interference between transactions is unlikely. It is not worth going to a lot of trouble to ensure that it does not occur. The approach we are objecting to is highly pessimistic rather than optimistic!

We should therefore abandon the requirement that we take a consistent set of shadows at transaction start. We can then delay making a shadow copy of an object until an operation is invoked on it, noting the object's version so that it can be checked by the validator. There is then the risk that execution will proceed using inconsistent shadows, but this risk applies also to other schemes that aim for high concurrency, such as allowing non-strict execution in a two-phase locking approach. As in these schemes we risk rejection when we attempt to commit. We can achieve high concurrency only if we are prepared to risk abort.

The execution of the transaction continues, invoking shadow objects until either

abort: the shadow objects are simply discarded

or

commit: the validator is called.

The validator has knowledge of all transactions whose validation or update phases overlap execution of the transaction that is to be checked. When a

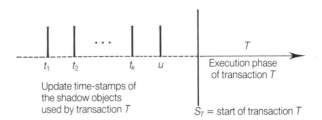

Figure 18.8
Checking for a
consistent state.

transaction involves an operation on a shadow object there may be transactions
with outstanding updates guaranteed for that object. The validator must ensure
that there has been no conflict. The information used by the validator might be
extended to take into account transactions that have started to execute since this
one, but we shall not consider this possibility further.

Two conditions need to be checked by the validator. If either cannot be met
the transaction must be aborted.

1. *The execution must be based on a consistent system state.*

   The versions of the shadow objects are available. The requirement is that
   these versions were all current at some particular transaction time-stamp.

   Figure 18.8 shows a possible scenario. Suppose that at the start S_T of
   transaction T the earliest unacknowledged time-stamp is u, and that during
   T's execution phase shadow copies are made whose version time-stamps are
   (in some order) $t_1, t_2, \ldots t_k$. If all time-stamps $t_1, t_2, \ldots t_k$ are earlier than u,
   then certainly all versions were current at the latest of the time-stamps
   recorded, say t_k.

   If interference is low it is likely that all updates to the objects involved will
   have been acknowledged before the transaction starts, and also that no further updates occur during the execution phase. Even if this precise scenario is
   not followed it is quite possible for the set of shadows to be consistent.

   If shadow validation succeeds then the execution is based on a time-stamp
   at which all the shadow versions were consistent. Let us call this the **base
   time-stamp.**

2. *The transactions must be serializable.*

   The transactions with which the given transaction must be reconciled are
   those validated for update with a time-stamp later than the base time-stamp,
   whether or not their updates have been applied. Recall that once a transaction is validated its updates are guaranteed, and that updates are applied in
   time-stamp order at each object.

   The requirement is that an ordering of these transactions can be found in
   which serial update is meaningful: that is, that the final system state reflected
   after the (serial) update of the set of transactions must be consistent with all
   of their execution phases, performed concurrently. Recall Sections 17.6 and
   17.8. Although the definitions of conflict needed can be based on non-commutativity this is unnecessarily restrictive, as we shall see in an example.

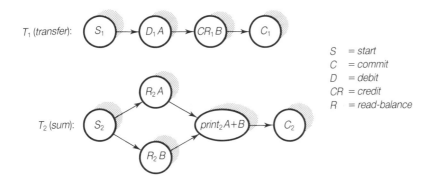

S = start
C = commit
D = debit
CR = credit
R = read-balance

Figure 18.9
The *transfer* and
sum example.

Provided that both conditions are met, the transaction can be accepted and recorded as validated. This establishes its position in the queue of validated transactions that are waiting to update. In simple cases object update is just a matter of copying a shadow object back into persistent memory. In other cases it may be necessary to reapply the operations of a transaction to a version more recent than the original shadow.

OCC has very different properties from time-stamp ordering. In the latter, transactions are scheduled in a predetermined order, usually that of transaction start. In OCC the order is determined at validation time, and in theory the validator is free to insert the current transaction at any position in the queue for update. The validation algorithm could therefore become quite elaborate, but it is probably not worth going to great lengths in an attempt to optimize. OCC is suitable only if there is little interference between transactions, and the hope is that simple validation will normally succeed.

Examples

We now consider two simple examples. In the first a consistent set of shadows is assumed. In the second only one object is involved. The examples illustrate the OCC approach and highlight some of the issues. Bear in mind that, in practice, we cannot automatically assume that the shadows are consistent and this must be checked at validation (condition 1 above).

First, consider the example we have often used, of concurrent *transfer* and *sum* transactions (see Figure 18.9), and suppose that both transactions are using shadows of the same values of A and B. Note that *sum* is a read-only transaction. It might be argued on the basis of this example that there is no point in taking shadows for a read-only transaction. The counter argument is that a number of reads might be required from a large object and taking a shadow ensures that the reads are performed on the same version of the object. We shall make the assumption that shadows are taken when an object is first invoked, either for reading or writing.

The *sum* transaction uses its shadow values of A and B quite independently of what the *transfer* transaction is doing to its shadow values of A and B. In

Section 17.6 we considered *read-balance* and *credit* (or *debit*) to be non-commutative. If consistent shadow copies are taken by both transactions this is no longer relevant. In fact, if the shadows used by a read-only transaction represent a consistent system state then that transaction cannot fail. If we allow the possibility that the shadows used by a transaction do not represent a consistent state then it can be rejected when it attempts to *commit*. A problem here is that the transaction may have performed output based on inconsistent object values. This problem is not exclusive to systems which use OCC. Whatever concurrency control scheme is used in a system there must be a policy on how to deal with aborted transactions that have performed output.

If we assume each transaction is working on a consistent set of shadows we need only be concerned with operations that are non-commutative with respect to state changes at the object. Values output by the transaction relate to a consistent version of the system state and cause no problems. The *sum* transaction will therefore be validated as correct at *commit*, whenever this is requested. It has not changed the value of *A* or *B*.

It is interesting to note that the values output by a number of transactions that are working on the same version of system state are not the same as those that would be output by a serial execution of those transactions on the persistent state; they execute in parallel on the same version. The transactions are forced to *commit* in some serial order.

When the *transfer* transaction requests *commit*, the operations it has done on *A* and *B* are **validated**. The information recorded at the persistent objects and their shadows is sufficient for the *commit* to be validated as correct or rejected. Suppose *transfer* has invoked an operation on *A* or *B* which belongs to a conflicting pair. If some other transaction has committed (since the shadow was taken for *transfer*) the result of an invocation of the conflicting operation of that pair, then *transfer* must be aborted. The validation phase checks this for all the operations that the transaction requesting *commit* has invoked on all objects.

Figure 18.10 shows transaction *abort* and restart when non-commutative *credit* and *add-interest-to-balance* operations are invoked on the same value of a bank account. Exercise 18.8 gives another example. The validation phase indicates whether *commit* is possible and the *commit* phase must ensure the correct persistent values, taking into account changes that have been committed since the shadows were taken.

In the example, T_1 invokes *credit* (£2000) on a shadow copy of *account-A*, changing its value from £5000 to £7000. A shadow copy taken from the same persistent object value has *add-interest-to-balance* invoked by T_2, changing its value from £5000 to £5005. This latter transaction T_2 is first to *commit* and the persistent value of *account-A* is updated to £5005. T_1 now requests *commit*. Because *credit* and *add-interest-to-balance* are defined to be *non-commutative*, and therefore conflicting, the *commit* is rejected. The transaction is restarted as T_3 with a shadow of *account-A* with value £5005. The *credit* (£2000) is performed at the shadow, giving £7005 for the value, and this value is then committed at the persistent copy of the object.

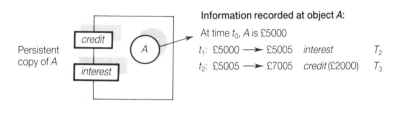

Information recorded at object A:

At time t_0, A is £5000

t_1:	£5000 ⟶ £5005	*interest*	T_2
t_2:	£5005 ⟶ £7005	*credit* (£2000)	T_3

T_1 $A =$ £5000   *credit* (£2000) $A =$ £7000 takes place in shadow taken at t_0

T_2 $A =$ £5000   *interest* $A =$ £5005 takes place in shadow taken at t_0

T_2 requests *commit*; validated and committed at time t_1.
      Information is recorded at the persistent copy of A. $A =$ £5005.

T_1 Requests *commit*.
      REJECTED at validation because *credit* does not commute with *interest*
      which has been committed since T_1's shadow copy was taken. The
      transaction is aborted and restarted as T_3.

T_3 $A =$ £5005   *credit* (£2000) $A =$ £7005 takes place in shadow taken at t_1

T_3 requests *commit*; validated and committed at time t_2
      Information is recorded at the persistent copy of A. $A =$ £7005.

Figure 18.10
Example showing
abort and restart.

Notice that when transaction T_1 requests *commit* and is rejected, applying the *credit* operation at that stage at the persistent copy of the object would yield £7005! The requirement for commutativity appears to be too strong for a case such as this. Commutativity enforces that the same result is obtained whatever the order of execution of a pair of transactions. As soon as one transaction has committed, the serialization order is defined. If the rejected transaction is aborted and restarted it is from the system state committed by the first. They are no longer running in parallel. Ideally, this should be taken into account when T_1 requests *commit*.

If invocations are carried out on shadow copies which do not conflict with subsequent updates at the persistent object, the invocations can be reapplied to the object on *commit*. For example, suppose a shadow copy of *account-A* was credited by £1000, changing its value from £4000 to £5000. Suppose at *commit*, other transactions have caused the balance to reach the value £8000 by invoking operations that commute with *credit*. The *credit* operation is redone at the object giving a balance of £9000.

Generalizing from these examples, when a transaction requests *commit* and after a consistent starting point has been ascertained (condition 1):

- The validation phase uses the information recorded with each persistent object involved and its shadow to check whether any non-commutative pairs of operations have been invoked on the object by this transaction and any other that has committed since this transaction took its shadows. As noted above, this definition of conflict may be too restrictive. See Herlihy (1990) for further reading.

- If the validation phase is successful, the transaction is committed. This may involve redoing (at the persistent copy of the objects) the operations that have changed the values of shadow objects. This can be done because the validation phase has rejected the *commit* if any of the invocations of the transaction do not commute with committed invocations.

- If the validation phase is not successful the transaction is aborted.

Optimistic concurrency control allows every operation invocation to go ahead without the overhead of locking or time-stamp checking; it achieves high object availability. The fact that shadows are taken and work proceeds without delay makes this method suitable for applications in which timing guarantees are required and in which conflict is rare. The overhead occurs when *commit* is requested. The validation phase uses the information stored locally at each object. If all the objects invoked by a transaction indicate that *commit* is possible then the updates can go ahead.

Optimistic concurrency control operates on a first come (to *commit*) first served basis. If there are several shadows of an object, the state of the first to *commit* becomes the new object state. If contention is rare the method works well. If the application is such that transactions might invoke heavily used objects (data 'hot-spots') they are likely to be aborted and restarted without regard to fairness or priority of the transaction. The method should probably not be used if this is likely to occur.

18.7 Summary

We have been concerned with methods of implementing transactions in the presence of concurrency and, in particular, with ensuring the property of serializability for correct execution. Three approaches were considered: locking, time-stamping and optimistic concurrency control.

The object model set up in Chapter 17 was used again here. To implement the locking methods of concurrency control the object was extended with *lock* and *unlock* operations. These were assumed to be invoked by a transaction manager or other agency with knowledge of all the locks held and requested by a transaction. Deadlock detection was shown to be necessary.

Two-phase locking guarantees a serializable schedule of the operation invocations of concurrent transactions. The penalty is the overhead of deadlock management. Also, objects are locked for longer than is necessary for their invocations. If the property of isolation is enforced in the implementation, locks are held until *commit*. This is called strict two-phase locking and avoids cascading aborts and complex procedures for recovering previously committed object values (at the cost of reduced concurrency).

When time-stamping is used for concurrency control, the decision to accept or reject an operation invocation is made at the object. One specific serialized order is achieved, that of the time-stamps of the transactions, and this can lead to correct transactions being rejected. A strict execution schedule can be enforced by delaying an invocation until the transaction that previously invoked an operation of a conflicting pair has committed. This cannot cause deadlock because the invocations are in time-stamp order at every object, so a circular wait is impossible.

Optimistic concurrency control minimizes the delay involved in invoking objects: each transaction works on a shadow copy of each object it invokes. It might be appropriate for the shadows to reside in the user's workstation. The shadows could be guaranteed (at heavy cost) to be taken from committed system state and therefore represent a consistent version of it. The property of isolation is manifest in such an implementation. In practice, such an approach is heavyweight and against the optimistic philosophy of the method.

There is no concurrency control until a transaction requests *commit*. A validation phase then takes place to determine whether the persistent values of the objects can be updated from the shadow copies. It may be necessary to redo operations at the persistent objects on *commit*.

The method is suitable for systems where contention is unlikely since, if no conflicting operations have been committed since the shadows were taken, *commit* is very simple. *Abort* is always very simple since it merely involves discarding the shadow objects. If contention occurs, and abortion is necessary, there is no provision for fairness in transaction scheduling. Commitment occurs on a first come first served basis.

The delay involved before work can start on the objects used by a transaction is minimized in optimistic concurrency control; shadows can be taken without delay and work can commence. For this reason the method is suitable for systems with a real-time requirement or where timing guarantees must be made.

Most practical systems are based on strict two-phase locking. Time-stamp ordering is based only on information stored at each object. It is probably more suited to distributed systems than a locking approach. We shall explore this in Chapter 20. The optimistic approach, unlike time-stamp ordering, allows work to be carried out which may later have to be discarded. It does, however, allow greater flexibility in the serialization order of transactions. Performance may degrade badly as contention increases in a system using OCC.

Exercises

18.1 (a) Why is the provision of *lock* and *unlock* operations not sufficient to ensure serializability of composite operation invocations?
(b) Why does two-phase locking ensure serializability?
(c) Why is two-phase locking subject to deadlock? (Consider the four conditions for deadlock to exist, given in Section 16.4.)

(d) Why does two-phase locking not guard against cascading aborts?

(e) In what way does strict two-phase locking guard against cascading aborts?

18.2 (a) Why might the start time of a transaction not be the best time to use for its time-stamp?

(b) Given the time-stamps of two committed transactions, can you always draw their serialization graphs? Does time-stamp ordering restrict concurrency more than locking? Discuss.

(c) Compare the overhead of implementing locking with that of time-stamp ordering.

18.3 Why are cascading aborts possible in a system with time-stamp based concurrency control? What extra mechanism could prevent it?

18.4 Is concurrency control based on time-stamp ordering (TSO) (or strict time-stamp ordering) subject to deadlock?

18.5 Why is optimistic concurrency control (OCC) potentially appropriate for use in real-time systems? Why is it potentially good for systems where contention is rare?

18.6 (a) What is involved in aborting a transaction in a system which uses OCC?

(b) Describe the validation and commitment phases of an OCC scheme. Consider the case where the objects to be committed have had updates committed since the shadow copies were taken. Consider the cases where the updates are the result of operations which do and do not belong to conflicting pairs. What actions should be taken in both these cases?

18.7 Suppose that two transactions use copies of the same objects under an OCC scheme. Suppose that both transactions generate output and are both committed. Does the output reflect a serial ordering of the transactions? Does it matter?

18.8 Consider the example shown in Figure 18.11. What happens when T_3 requests *commit*? What happens when T_1 then requests *commit*?

18.9 A particular application is known to comprise almost entirely read-only transactions. Discuss the three approaches to concurrency control for such a system.

18.10 For a particular application, transactions are either read-only or have a phase in which they read and compute followed by a phase in which they write their results back to the database. Discuss the three approaches to concurrency control for this application.

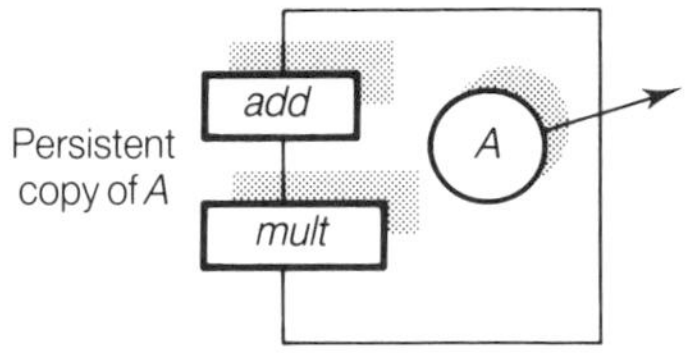

Information recorded at object *A*:

At time t_0, $A = 1$

t_1: A, $1 \longrightarrow 4$ *add* (3) T_2

T_1	$A = 1$	*add* (2)	$A = 3$	takes place in shadow taken at t_0
T_2	$A = 1$	*add* (3)	$A = 4$	takes place in shadow taken at t_0
T_3	$A = 1$	*mult* (2)	$A = 2$	takes place in shadow taken at t_0

T_2 requests *commit*; validated and committed at time t_1.

Information is recorded at the persistent copy of A. $A = 4$.

T_3 Requests *commit*

T_1 Requests *commit*

Figure 18.11
Example involving
non-commutative
operations.

18.11 In OCC we defined the version number of an object as the time-stamp of the transaction whose validated invocations were most recently applied to the object. The transaction's time-stamp is therefore that of its commit time instead of its start time. Contrast TSO and OCC with respect to the time-stamps allocated to transactions and the schedules that are allowed to execute.

19 Recovery

CONTENTS

19.1 Requirements for recovery

There are a number of reasons why recovery procedures are required in a system which supports atomic transactions:

1. *System crash*: the contents of main memory are lost, perhaps because of a power failure, but persistent store is not affected. This kind of system crash was discussed in Chapter 13 and a fail-stop model was assumed for simplicity. Any transaction in progress (that has not completed commit processing) will be affected by the loss of data structures in main memory and must be aborted. The effects of any committed transaction must persist and the system software must be designed to ensure this.

2. *Media failure*: for example, a disk head crash. Part of the database will be lost and it must be possible to restore it. If transactions in progress are using

that part of the persistent store they must be aborted and the persistent state prior to the transactions must be recoverable. There must be more than one copy of all persistent data, including any system management data. If the system guarantees to retain the state resulting from every committed transaction then two independent copies must be written during commit processing.

We assume that a **dump** of all the database is taken periodically, for example overnight, as part of normal operating system file backup procedures. The database application is responsible for recording all subsequent changes.

3. *Transaction abort*: an *abort* operation may be available to the transaction programmer. A transaction might not be able to complete for some application-level reason, such as insufficient money in an account to continue with a transfer operation.

    A transaction management system may be designed to use *abort* followed by restart of the transaction to solve problems such as deadlock, as discussed in previous chapters. This type of failure can be transparent to the user except that it might detect slower than expected performance.

In general, the transaction is taken to be the unit of recovery.

Figure 18.2 showed the components of a transaction processing system. The concern of this chapter is the data management module which includes the **cache manager** and the **recovery manager**. The cache manager is responsible for moving information between main memory and persistent memory. The recovery manager is responsible for carrying out recovery procedures after a crash.

19.2 The object model, object state and recovery

Throughout Part III we have used an object model for reasoning about atomic transactions. In this chapter we focus on object state and how and when it is recorded in persistent memory. Clients of a TP system are not concerned with object state explicitly, but with the results of operation invocations. The TPS implementation must ensure that the states of the objects comprising the system together present a consistent system state to its clients.

In Section 17.9 we assumed that an object records all relevant information on the operations that are invoked on it, for example, the transaction identifier and time of invocation. In Chapter 18 this was used for concurrency control. We assumed, as a theoretical starting point, that a complete history of invocations is held by every object. In theory, an object's state is defined as a sequence of invocations on an object starting from a *create* operation. In theory, any state can be recovered by starting again from the initial state on *create* and performing some required sequence of invocations, for example, to exclude an operation of an aborted transaction. In practice, this procedure would take too much time and space and a suitable optimization must be devised.

A basis for such an optimization is that an object may make a **checkpoint** of its state. It may even record its state before and after every invocation that changes its state. We justify this recording of state as follows: if it is impossible to distinguish between an object state derived from the application of the invocations which comprise its history and the recorded value, then recording that value is a valid optimization. Practical implementations are based on recording object state, while theoretical models are based on histories of invocations. In this chapter we are concerned with implementation issues, but we must be able to reason about the behaviour and correctness of our implementations.

If we base our recovery procedures on recorded state *instead of* a history of invocations we should consider whether we have lost the ability to recover some required previous state. By dispensing with the full history and recording state we have introduced a requirement that operations should be UNDO-able. We can no longer reason from a basis of invocations (forwards) from *create* so must be able to go backwards from some recorded value of state; that is, starting from a value of state, it should be possible to UNDO an operation to recover the state previous to its invocation. In Chapter 18 we assumed that any operation could be undone; that is, every operation has a corresponding UNDO operation. If this is the case, the UNDO operations may form the basis of recovery; any transaction can be aborted by undoing its operations.

19.3 Concurrency, crashes and the properties of transactions

The ACID properties of transactions must be guaranteed by a TPS in the presence of concurrency and unpredictable failures.

Atomicity   Either all or none of the transaction's operations are performed. This must be ensured by the recovery manager. A crash may occur part-way through a transaction and the invocations of any incomplete transactions must be undone.

Consistency   A transaction transforms the system from one consistent state to another. This is achieved through concurrency control, provided that atomicity is guaranteed by the recovery manager in the presence of crashes.

Isolation   An incomplete transaction cannot reveal its result to other transactions before it is committed. This is achieved through concurrency control.

Durability   Once a transaction is committed the system must guarantee that the results of its operations will persist, even if there are subsequent system failures.

This is the responsibility of the recovery manager, based on general data management policies. As we discussed in Chapter 13, the system can make the probability of losing information arbitrarily small by replicating its storage. We used the 'stable storage' abstraction to indicate this.

We have used the concept of system state comprising the state of all objects in the system. We now proceed to discuss the implementation of recovery. We shall assume that objects record their state (as discussed above) and the terms 'object value' and 'object state' are used in this practical sense.

19.4   Logging and shadowing to support a crash-resilient TPS implementation

Two basic approaches to achieving crash resilience were outlined in Chapter 13, logging and shadowing. Our concern there was to make a single invocation atomic in the presence of crashes. In Part III we have moved on to transactions comprising a number of related invocations and should reconsider the approaches from this perspective.

Logging   Persistent object values are updated in place and all changes are recorded in a log. The method is based on recorded state and a fundamental assumption is that it is possible to undo an invocation at an object. This is necessary when a crash occurs part-way through a transaction. The pre-crash invocations of the uncommitted transaction must be undone. We shall explore this approach in more detail in the next section.

Shadowing Persistent object values are not updated in place. The new and old values of each object comprising a transaction are maintained in persistent store and a switch is made from old to new values on *commit*.

Note that this requires *commit* to be atomic over all the objects involved in a transaction. The objects must participate in a protocol and a single point of decision is necessary for transaction *commit*. If a crash occurs during *commit*, the objects participating in *commit* must be able to find out the decision for the whole transaction and act accordingly.

We shall study an atomic commitment protocol in Chapter 20. In that chapter we are concerned with distributed objects and partial failures of (components of) a system. In this chapter we focus on centralized systems where the whole TPS is assumed to fail when main memory is lost. Our concern here is to be able to ensure the consistency of the persistent memory on restart after a failure.

In both cases, the aim is to record securely the values before and after operation invocations. The difference is in implementation detail.

An alternative approach is to **defer invocations** until *commit*. Recall our discussion of optimistic concurrency control (Section 18.6) where invocations which have been carried out on shadow copies are first validated, then committed at the database. The approach might be used more generally, depending on the requirements of applications. It might, however, be impossible to defer invocation of operations for some transactions, for example, if they require intermediate results in order to proceed with their computations.

An extension of this approach is explored in the context of distributed systems in Yahalom (1991). We leave this for further reading and consider use of a recovery log in more detail.

19.5   Use of a recovery log

As noted in Section 19.1, it is assumed that a daily dump of the system's persistent state is taken and that the DBMS must make a record of subsequent activity if complete crash resilience is to be achieved at any time.

An outline of the general approach is that, on an invocation, the object value is updated in persistent store and a record of the invocation is made in a log. We have already assumed that every object keeps information (for concurrency control purposes) of the kind we require to be logged and we can require objects to write log records. In order to achieve a recoverable state we must consider when the update to persistent object state is made and when the corresponding log record is written to persistent store (see Section 19.5.1). Points to bear in mind which relate to an efficient implementation are as follows:

- Writing to a log is efficient; it requires an append to a file and involves records from all active transactions.

- Writing values of objects to persistent store is inefficient; the objects are likely to be scattered throughout the database. We should take care not to require object values to be updated in place at a very fine time grain. A long queue of updates can be ordered to exploit an efficient disk arm scheduling algorithm, for example. Also, object values written by committed transactions may be read from the cache in main memory.

19.5.1   Log records and their use in recovery

We require an object to write a log record for all the invocations on it. Depending on the use that is to be made of the log, it might only be necessary to log the invocations that have changed object state. A log record might take the following general form:

Transaction id, object id, operation, arguments, state prior to invocation, state after invocation

We also assume that *start*, *commit* and *abort* are recorded in the log with the appropriate transaction identifier.

If a failure of any kind occurs the log can be used in the recovery procedure by the recovery manager. We assume that the log is written to stable storage so that if a medium failure causes one copy of the log to be lost another copy exists.

The effects of any transaction that committed before the failure must persist and the recovery manager can use the log to ensure this. If a transaction has not committed at the time of the failure it must be aborted and any changes made to object values in the database by any of its operations must be undone by the recovery manager.

If a transaction has simply to be aborted as in case 3 of Section 19.1, its operations can be undone using the information in the log. If a medium failure occurs (case 2) the database can be reloaded from the latest dump. The recovery manager can then REDO the operations of all committed transactions since the time of the dump and UNDO the effects of any uncommitted transaction.

19.5.2 Log write-ahead

Two distinct actions are associated with effecting an invocation of a transaction:

1. update the value of an object in the persistent store;
2. write the log record of the change to persistent store.

A failure could occur at any time including between the two actions. Once the object value is changed its previous value is lost. The log record contains both the old value and the new value.

● The log record must be written to persistent store before the object value is changed.

When a transaction *commits*, the system guarantees that the changes it has made to the database become permanent.

● It is necessary for all the log records of a transaction to be written out to the log before *commit* is completed.

Note that we need not insist that all the object values are written to persistent store on *commit*. There is sufficient information in the log records to update the object values if a failure occurs. The point made above, that it could be inefficient to write out object values on the *commit* of every transaction, is relevant here.

19.5.3 Checkpoints and the checkpoint procedure

It can be seen from the above that the log is very large. Processing a large log might be tolerable on media failure but transaction abort must be efficient and recovery after a crash should be reasonably fast. A **checkpoint** is therefore taken at 'small' time intervals, for example, every five minutes or after a specified number of items have been logged.

A checkpoint procedure would be as follows:

1. Force-write any log records in main storage out to the actual log on persistent store.

2. Force-write a 'checkpoint record' to the log which contains a list of all the transactions which are active at the time of the checkpoint and the address within the log of each transaction's most recent log record.

3. Force-write any database updates which are still in memory (in database buffers) out to persistent store.

4. Write the address of the checkpoint record within the log into a 'restart file'.

It must be possible to know that data has been written out to disk. Figure 19.1 shows that data objects are initially invoked in main memory and log

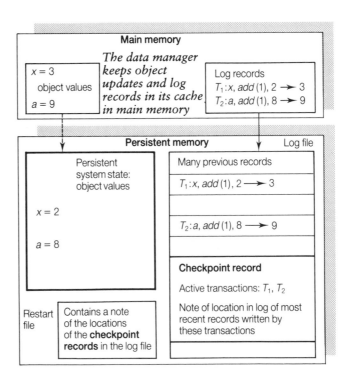

Figure 19.1
A recovery log with a checkpoint record.

records are initially written in main memory. It also shows the log file and restart file in persistent memory. Not only does the DBMS cache data in main memory (to avoid many writes to disk of small items of data), but the operating system on which the DBMS runs may also cache data in memory. Chapter 21 gives a detailed example. It is essential that an operating system over which a DBMS runs should allow an application to request that data is written out to persistent store and should acknowledge that this has been done.

19.6   Idempotent undo and redo operations

A transaction can make a number of different types of change to a database, for example:

delete an existing object

create a new object

invoke an operation which changes an object's state.

A crash might occur at any time, including in the middle of undoing or redoing invocations during failure recovery. No assumptions should therefore be made about whether the object has its old or new value and the UNDO and REDO operations must be made idempotent (repeatable) by some means.

We have made the simplifying assumption in this chapter that an object's state before and after an invocation is recorded in the log record associated with the invocation. If this is the case, an idempotent UNDO operation can simply set the object value to that before the invocation, and an idempotent REDO operation can set the object value to the state after the invocation.

It could be argued that a more general approach should be taken which is closer to our abstract object model. In some application areas object state is large and recording pre- and post-invocation state might take up an excessive amount of space. Perhaps we should instead expect each object to specify an undo operation for every operation. In the case of the bank account object, for example, a *debit* operation undoes a *credit* operation. Unfortunately, *debit* and *credit* are not idempotent and one would be very pleased, or very angry, depending on which was executed repeatedly on one's bank account object.

In general, operations and their inverses are not idempotent. A recovery procedure based on log records without both pre- and post-invocation state would have to use other techniques to achieve atomic invocation of UNDO and REDO in the presence of crashes.

For simplicity, we shall continue to use our state-based implementation model, which gives us idempotent UNDO and REDO.

19.7 Transaction states on a failure

In Figure 19.2 a checkpoint is taken at time t_c and the system fails at time t_f.

T_1 has already committed at the time of the checkpoint. All its log records will have been written to the log on commit. Any remaining changes to data items will be written out at the time of the checkpoint. T_1 will not be recorded as active in the checkpoint and no recovery action is needed.

T_2 was recorded as active at the time of the checkpoint. Its log records and database updates at that time are written out. T_2 commits before the crash. All its log records are written out before commit completes. T_2 must be REDONE by the recovery procedure since it has committed.

T_3 was recorded as active at the time of the checkpoint. Its log records and database updates at that time are written out. T_3 is still in progress at the time of the crash. It must be UNDONE because it is incomplete. The log records are the basis for this.

T_4 was not recorded as active at the time of the checkpoint. It has completed commit processing, however, and must therefore be REDONE since all the changes it made are guaranteed to persist. All its log records were written out on commit.

T_5 was not recorded as active at the time of the checkpoint. T_5 is still in progress at the time of the crash. It must be UNDONE because it is incomplete. The log records are the basis for this.

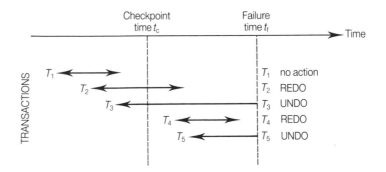

Figure 19.2
Transaction categories for recovery.

19.8   An algorithm for recovery

An algorithm for the recovery procedure is as follows
The recovery manager keeps:

an UNDO LIST   which initially contains all the transactions listed as active in
                          the checkpoint record

a REDO LIST   which is initially empty

It searches forwards from the checkpoint record to the end of the log (that is,
the most recently written record at the time of failure):

- if it finds a START TRANSACTION record it adds that transaction to the
  UNDO LIST
- if it finds a COMMIT record it moves that transaction from the UNDO LIST
  to the REDO LIST.

It then works backwards through the log from its end,

- UNDOing transactions on the UNDO LIST

Finally, it works forwards again from the checkpoint record to the end of the
log,

- REDOing transactions on the REDO LIST

An example of the recovery algorithm for T_1 to T_5 above is shown in Figure
19.3. It is assumed that the transactions have the property of isolation and their
executions are strict. The columns of the table indicate a partial ordering of the
operations and the associated writing of log records; for example, T_3 cannot
access x until after T_2 has committed. For conciseness the operations invoked
and their arguments are not shown. The figure shows only the object states
before and after each invocation.

At the checkpoint, T_2 and T_3 are recorded as active. After the crash, at the
start of the recovery procedure:

UNDO LIST = T_2, T_3

REDO LIST is empty

After searching forwards through the log to the end:

UNDO LIST = T_3, T_5 (T_2 is removed, T_4 is added then removed)
REDO LIST = T_2, T_4

While working back through the log from the end to the checkpoint, UNDOing
transactions on the UNDO list (T_3, T_5) the following data values are established:

$z = 8$ (T_5), $x = 3$ and $b = 5$ (T_3)

				Checkpoint time t_c				Failure time t_f
T_2	S_2	$x, 2 \to 3$	$y, 3 \to 4$	$z, 6 \to 7$	C_2			
T_3		S_3	$a, 2 \to 4$	$b, 5 \to 7$		$x, 3 \to 5$		
T_4				S_4	$c, 3 \to 4$	$z, 7 \to 8$	C_4	
T_5					S_5			$z, 8 \to 9$

Figure 19.3
Example of a recovery algorithm.

The checkpoint record can then be used to locate the most recent record of an operation invoked by T_3 and to complete the UNDOing of T_3.

While working forwards through the log from the checkpoint to the end, REDOing transactions on the REDO list (T_2, T_4) the following data values are established:

$$z = 7 \ (T_2), \quad c = 4 \quad \text{and} \quad z = 8 \ (T_4)$$

Note that these operations are repeatable, allowing for a crash during the recovery procedure. The previous value of each data item does not matter.

19.9 Summary

Any system which supports atomic operations must be able to recover from failures of all kinds at any time. In Part II we studied single atomic operations; in Part III we studied atomic composite operations (transactions).

Throughout Part III we have used a general object model for reasoning about transactions. In theory, object state may be regarded as the result of a sequence of invocations starting from *create*. In theory, any state can be recovered by starting again from *create* and making any required sequence of invocations. In practice, our recovery procedures have to be efficient and have to allow for a crash at any time. We took a simple, state-based model for recovery in which object state was assumed to be recorded before and after an invocation. This allows any operation to be undone and redone, and these UNDO and REDO operations are idempotent.

When a transaction has committed, its effects must be guaranteed to persist. In this chapter we studied one specific system implementation of recovery based on a recovery log. The approach here is to update the database in place and to record all the changes that have been made in a recovery log.

The method is efficient because the log records of all transactions are appended to one place on the disk, the log file. Since log records must be guaranteed to have reached the disk before a transaction is acknowledged as committed, log writes must take place on a fine time grain. Database updates can be done on a coarser time grain and any transaction which needs the committed object values can read them from main memory buffers. The state of all objects affected by committed transactions can be computed from the log if a crash occurs before the object values are updated. Gleeson (1989) makes the following point:

Once the log records of committed transaction are written to persistent store, the persistent store may be regarded as in a consistent state. When all object values are updated from the log, the persistent store is restored to not only a consistent state but a canonical state.

All this is based on the assumption that the operating system allows the DBMS application to force writes out to the physical disk or to some other form of persistent memory. Many operating systems cache data in main memory until they need the buffer space that it occupies. A TP application cannot be built on an operating system with such semantics.

Our main area of concern is concurrency control. Although crash recovery is not central to this study, the implementation of concurrency control and crash recovery are often inextricably related. Date (1983) and Bernstein *et al.* (1987) are recommended for further reading.

Exercises

19.1 Consider a TP system crash, in which main memory is lost at the following times:
   (a) A transaction has completed some but not all of its operations.
   (b) A client has received acknowledgement that a transaction has committed.
   (c) The system has decided to commit a transaction and has recorded the fact on stable storage, but there is a crash before the client can receive the acknowledgement of commit.
   Discuss what the system must do on restart for each of these cases. Consider for each case where the data values that have been or are about to be committed might be stored. Why is it essential for the TP system to know? Why might a conventional operating system not make this information available?

19.2 A recovery log is very large and it may be used for transaction abort as well as crash recovery. How can a periodic checkpoint procedure help to manage this complex process?

19.3 Why must undo and redo operations be idempotent?

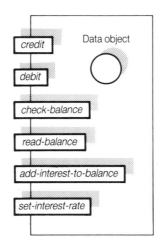

Figure 19.4
An account object.

19.4 Consider a TP system based on the bank account objects used as an example in Section 17.6 and shown in Figure 19.4. For each operation define an undo operation.

Suppose that a recovery log record contains:

Transaction id, object id, operation, arguments, state prior to invocation

Define recovery procedures for transactions in all the states shown in Figure 19.2 when a crash occurs. Consider the possibility of a crash during the recovery procedures.

Distributed transactions

20

CONTENTS

20.1 Properties specific to distributed systems

A brief discussion of the special properties of distributed systems was given in Chapter 14. The concern there was to implement a single remote operation invocation. The characteristic properties are as follows:

1. **Independent failure modes.** The components of a distributed system and the networks connecting them may fail independently. Some parts of a distributed computation may fail while others continue to run; all components may be running but some may not communicate; some components may fail and some network connections may fail.

   Chapter 14 described a protocol for remote operation invocation that allows for network or server congestion and network, client or server failure.

2. **There is no global time.** The components of a distributed system each have a local clock. We cannot assume a consistent value of time throughout a distributed system.

   Chapter 14 introduced a model for time, clocks and the ordering of events in a distributed system (see also Lamport, 1978, 1990). Each system has a local clock which it uses for all timing purposes, including time-stamp generation, and such clock devices run at slightly different rates from each other.

We have seen in Chapters 17 and 18 that the knowledge of whether a given object invocation happened before or after some other is central to serializability theory.

3. **Inconsistent state.** It takes time for the effects of an event at one point in a distributed system to propagate throughout the system. There may not be a consistent view of the system state at every point in the system. This is discussed briefly in the next section.

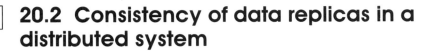

20.2 Consistency of data replicas in a distributed system

Point 3 above is most relevant to large-scale systems. Here, data that is needed to support the smooth operation of the system is often **replicated**. An example is the naming data held by name servers that was discussed in Section 14.9. Replication of data ensures that if a single computer that holds such data fails, another copy exists. Replication may also be used to ensure that there is a copy reasonably near to all points of the system. Data is therefore replicated for reasons of availability and performance.

When data replicas exist in a system there must be a policy about how changes to such data are handled. Alternative policies are as follows:

- A change made to one of the replicas is visible immediately. The system will propagate the change to the other replicas in due course, but in the meantime the system has become inconsistent.

- Another approach is to attempt to make the change to all the copies before allowing the data to become visible again. The problem here is that even if all the computers holding the replicas are available, the process is much slower than updating one nearby copy.

  If any replica is on a system which is not available we have either to forbid the update or handle the inconsistency when the system becomes available again. It has been said that distributed computing means that the fact that a computer you have never heard of has crashed means that you can't get on with your work!

  Another scenario is that all the replicas may be on systems that are running but the network has become partitioned. There is the possibility of inconsistent updates being made within the separate partitions.

  An approach to alleviating the problem of contacting every replica is to allow an update to take place when a **majority** of the replicas can be assembled to take part in the process. This is called a **write quorum**. A **read quorum** is also defined and its value is chosen to ensure that at least one of them contains the most recent update. If there are *n* replicas a write quorum *WQ* and read quorum *RQ* are typically defined to be:

$$WQ > n/2$$

$$RQ + WQ > n$$

For example, if *n*=7, you may have to assemble and write to three replicas and assemble five for reading. On reading you check the time of last update of all of them and use the most recent. The system software is likely to attempt to bring all the replicas up-to date behind the scenes.

A great deal of work has been carried out to address these kinds of problem in the context of large-scale distributed systems. For Part III we should note the similarities in the problems to be solved. We shall study how to make related changes (atomically) to different objects in Section 20.9. The same kind of protocol is needed to change many replicas of the same object.

20.3   An object model for distributed systems

In Section 17.6 a model of objects was set up as a basis for studying transaction processing systems. We now consider this model with specific reference to distributed systems. Figure 20.1 is given here for completeness. We assume each object is invoked through operations appropriate to its type. The figure also shows some object management operations such as *commit, abort, lock* and

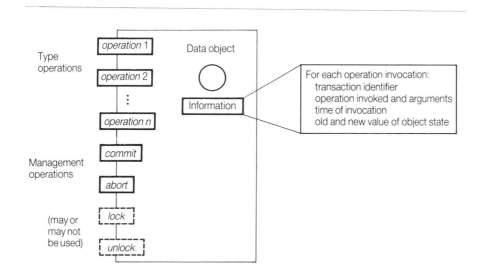

Figure 20.1
An object in a distributed transaction system.

unlock which may be needed for practical implementation of a transaction processing system (TPS).

The assumptions stated in Section 17.6 were as follows:

- Objects are identified uniquely in a system.
- The operations are executed atomically (in the sense of Part II); that is, the operations we are considering here are at the finest granularity of decomposition.
- There is a single clock associated with the object which is used to indicate the time at which operation invocations take place and therefore their order.
- The object records the time at which each operation invocation takes place and the transaction identifier of the transaction that executed the operation.

The model is appropriate for a distributed system. We now consider object invocation in the context of a distributed TPS.

20.4   Distributed transaction processing

Figure 20.2 shows two instances of the transaction processing system (TPS) described in Section 18.3 such as would occur at two nodes in a distributed TPS. The following points and assumptions are relevant to an implementation of a distributed TPS, extending the assumptions about objects stated above:

- A client submits a transaction at one node only, which we shall call the **coordinating node**.
- A given object resides at one and only one node; that is, we assume there is no object replication. An object invocation takes place at this **home node**.
- There are mechanisms for locating an object, given its unique identifier.

The TPS instances comprising the distributed TPS must cooperate. A client submits a transaction to one TPS. The transaction manager identifies and locates the objects invoked by the transaction. Local object invocations are passed to the local scheduler; remote object invocations are passed to the (scheduler of the) appropriate remote TPS.

A TPS must therefore handle both transaction requests from local clients and requests from remote TPSs to invoke operations on its local objects. For this latter type of request we assume initially that the TPS does not have a specification of the whole transaction. The scheduler at each node is passed operations which come from both local and remote transaction submissions. As before, the scheduler is at liberty to invoke the operations in any order, subject to the concurrency control algorithm it implements.

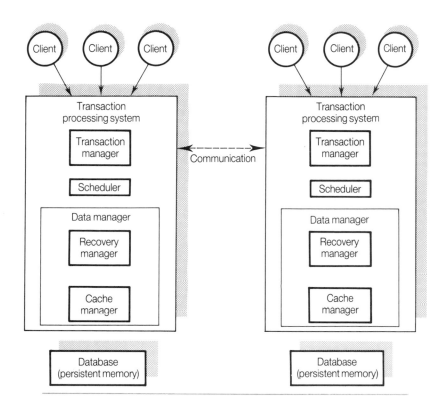

Figure 20.2
A distributed transaction processing system.

We must consider:

- **Concurrency control:** how a serializable schedule is achieved in a distributed TPS. The methods introduced in Chapter 18 (locking, time-stamping and optimistic concurrency control) will be reconsidered for a distributed system.

- **Commitment:** The transaction manager at a single node receives a client request for a transaction and initiates local and remote operation invocations. It must be notified of the results of attempted invocations: whether an invocation was accepted and done, or rejected, or perhaps that a *lock* request has been outstanding for some specified timeout period, depending on the method used to achieve concurrency control. Assuming that all the transaction's invocations (at all the nodes) have been notified as 'done' to the initiating transaction manager the transaction must then be committed. We shall study how this can be achieved in a distributed system in the presence of partial failures.

As in Chapter 18 we shall assume that the property of isolation is enforced: a transaction can only see committed object values.

20.5   Communication

The above discussion assumes communication between TPS instances. In some cases specific application protocols are needed, for example, an atomic commitment protocol. Application protocols are implemented above general communications protocols such as remote procedure call (Section 14.6) or some form of message passing. Specific examples are a clock synchronization protocol (Section 14.2) and a two-phase commit protocol (Section 20.9.1).

Communications protocols are designed to allow for the possibilities of congestion and failure of the network and the communicating nodes. The mechanism used is the timeout (see Section 14.6). If a timeout expires the protocol may immediately inform the higher level which invoked it or may retry a few times to allow for congestion. We shall assume the latter here for simplicity. The higher level may therefore receive a 'success' notification or an exception, indicating a failure. The application protocol must be designed on this basis, as we shall see in Section 20.9.1, for atomic commitment in the presence of failures.

20.6   Concurrency control: two-phase locking (2PL)

In Section 18.4 two-phase locking was shown to enforce a serializable order on the object invocations of transactions. Each object is assumed to have *lock* and *unlock* operations (see Figure 20.1). We should consider how the two phases, of acquiring and releasing locks, can be implemented in a distributed system. In a centralized system the transaction manager knows when locks on all the objects of a transaction have been acquired and the operations done. The *unlock* operation can then be invoked on all the objects.

In a distributed system, all the schedulers involved in a transaction must inform the transaction manager at the coordinating node that the requested locking and invocation of objects is done. Only then can the unlock operations be sent back to the schedulers concerned. Notice that use of a protocol of this kind prevents timing problems. The phases are defined at one node: the coordinating node of the transaction. For a strict execution that enforces the property of isolation in the implementation, the locks are not released until the transaction is committed.

The method is subject to deadlock, and we assumed in Chapter 18 that deadlock detection and recovery would be carried out by a component of a (centralized) TPS.

This component (let us call it the lock manager) maintains information on the objects that have been locked by transactions and the outstanding lock requests. The implicit assumption in Chapter 18 was that all the objects concerned were local to the TPS, so that complete information on all transactions was available.

A deadlock detection algorithm could be run and action taken, such as aborting some or all of the deadlocked transactions.

In a distributed TPS the lock manager at any node can maintain the same information as described above for invocations by local transactions. It can be told about requests for remote invocations by local transactions. It can also know about the requests for local invocations by remote transactions. What it does not know is the remote locks held by these remote transactions and their outstanding requests, and so on until the transitive closure of locks and requests is computed. This information is needed for deadlock (cycle) detection (Section 16.6).

The overhead of two-phase locking is large, particularly when extended for use in a distributed system. Each node must maintain a great deal of information to detect and recover from deadlock, and the method scales badly. In practice a simpler approach based on timeout might be adopted. If a transaction fails to acquire a lock in a given time it is aborted and all the locks it holds are therefore freed.

20.7 Concurrency control: time-stamp ordering (TSO)

Time-stamp ordering was described in Section 18.5. Each transaction is given a unique time-stamp and their executions are serialized in the order of their time-stamps. In the general model, each object maintains information on its invocations. In time-stamp ordering, the operation invoked and the time-stamp of the invoking transaction are recorded at the object. The object knows which pairs of its operations conflict.

Assume that one operation of a conflicting pair has been carried out (and committed) at an object and the information described above has been recorded. Assume that a subsequent request for the other operation of the conflicting pair is made. If the transaction identifier associated with the request is greater than that recorded, the invocation goes ahead and is recorded. If it is less, the transaction must be aborted and may be restarted with a new time-stamp.

The major advantage of this method for a distributed implementation of concurrency control is that only information held at each object is used to achieve serialization. Contrast this with the overhead described above for the distributed deadlock detection associated with distributed two-phase locking.

At first sight it seems that there might be a problem associated with time in using the method in a distributed TPS. In a centralized system the time-stamps have a serial order because they are generated from a single clock. In a distributed system a system-wide ordering of time-stamps is needed for correct serialization of transactions. This is quite easy to achieve. The essential requirement for correctness is that every object takes the same decision about the relative order of two time-stamps. First, suppose that we use the local time of the coordinating node of the transaction for the time-stamp. Except for the case of identically equal times, these values could be used to achieve a correct serializable execution. To deal with the case of equal times we just need a system-wide policy to achieve the arbitration. The node-identifiers could be used, for example.

Although this method of generating and using time-stamps achieves correctness it favours nodes with fast-running clocks when arbitration between equal times is needed.

20.8   Optimistic concurrency control (OCC)

The premise on which the use of OCC is based is that conflict is unlikely to happen. It is also assumed that transactions require high availability of objects, such as in systems which have some degree of real-time requirement. A transaction is allowed to proceed without delay on shadow copies of objects. No changes are applied to persistent object states until the transaction requests *commit*. The transaction is then validated in order to ascertain whether its shadow copies represent a consistent system state and whether its history is serializable with the histories of transactions that have already been validated. Once a transaction is validated, its updates are guaranteed to be made. If the validation fails, the transaction is aborted. This simply involves discarding its shadows. It might then restart with new shadows.

In Section 18.6 we argued that it would be pessimistic, rather than optimistic, to ensure at transaction start that the shadow copies of objects used by the transaction during the **execution phase** represent a consistent system state. To achieve this consistency we should have to sacrifice guaranteed high availability of objects since an object might be held during commit of some transaction when required by another. It would be necessary to enforce atomic commitment over all the objects invoked by a transaction and to take shadow copies of all the objects needed by a transaction atomically. Section 20.9 shows how atomic commitment can be carried out in a distributed system. This is too heavyweight when we optimistically assume that conflict is unlikely. Also it is not always possible to know at transaction start all the objects that will be needed by a transaction.

As in time-stamp ordering, the decision on whether a transaction may *commit* is based on information recorded at each object. The decision is made during the **validation phase**, after a transaction requests commit. Objects vote independently to *accept* or *reject* the transaction, and this aspect of OCC is therefore appropriate for a distributed system. There is a need to ensure that the local contexts for validation at the objects participating in a transaction are consistent.

The discussion of Section 18.6 was equally applicable to a centralized and a distributed implementation. An essential requirement in a distributed system is that transactions are validated for update in a well-defined serial order. Decisions on validation must be communicated to the participating objects atomically, and we shall sketch a protocol to achieve this in Section 20.9.2.

In Section 18.6 we required that in the **update phase** of a transaction update invocations are applied to objects in persistent memory in serial order, transaction by transaction. It is the responsibility of the update manager to ensure that all updates succeed. The update manager will know at any time those transactions for which updates have succeeded. It can therefore be asserted that the updates up to those of some transaction have succeeded.

This places a requirement on the underlying communications system used for making remote object invocations. There are issues specific to a distributed implementation that are associated with the independent failure modes of its components. It is necessary to assume that the invocations are made at the object in the order they are sent by the update manager and that these invocations are acknowledged to the update manager. We require that messages are not lost without notification and are not received in a different order from that in which they are sent. This can be achieved by selecting an appropriate communications protocol.

20.9 Commit and abort in a distributed system

Let us assume in the case of 2PL and TSO that the transaction manager at the coordinating node has received a request to *commit* a transaction. We have to ensure:

Atomicity   Either all nodes commit the changes or none do, and any other transaction perceives the changes made at every node or those at none.

Isolation   The effects of the transaction are not made visible until all nodes have made an irrevocable decision to commit or abort.

We have set up the conditions that no scheduler will refuse to *commit* the transaction on correctness grounds. In 2PL and TSO we have avoided this possibility by only allowing serializable invocations to take place. For these pessimistic methods there are two remaining issues to consider:

● Nodes or network connections might fail during *commit*.

● Other nodes may be attempting to carry out distributed commit at the same time and this might involve an intersecting set of objects.

Atomic commitment protocols address these issues. The two-phase commit protocol is discussed in Section 20.9.1.

In 2PL and TSO we can ensure isolation by holding locks until after *commit* (see Sections 18.4.1 and 18.5.1), thus guaranteeing *strictness*. If strictness is enforced we can assume that all the objects that were invoked by the transaction to be committed are available to the *commit* procedure for it. To achieve this we have introduced a possible additional delay when an object is invoked in 2PL and TSO. Once again we are restricting concurrency (object availability) in order to ensure that transactions see a consistent system state.

In the case of OCC we have made no attempt to ensure the correctness of an executing transaction, preventing harmful consequences by invoking operations on shadow objects. After an executing transaction has issued *commit* we have to ensure during validation:

Consistency   The execution has been based on shadow objects derived from a consistent system state, and there has been no interference at any object from transactions executing concurrently.

We have argued against the atomic commitment of updates for OCC, but its use has definite advantages. Herlihy (1990) proves the correctness of OCC algorithms that are based on a two-phase protocol for update in which validation is performed at each object during the first phase. In this paper he also shows that optimistic and pessimistic methods can be mixed on a per-object basis. Should we wish to enforce strictness (execution based on consistent system state only) for OCC it would be necessary not only to commit updates atomically but also to take the shadow copies needed by a transaction atomically. The drawback of this in a distributed system is that it can greatly reduce object availability, which was one of the goals when OCC was introduced.

On the other hand, we have to ensure a serializable execution, which means that a consistent serial order of committed transactions must be established system-wide. Global consistency is enforced during validation, and locks held during this phase relate only to the process of validation, not to the objects themselves. Once a transaction has its updates guaranteed these can be applied asynchronously at the participating objects, and executing transactions merely read whatever version the object has reached when creating a shadow object. Objects are therefore available except at the moment of version change. The drawback is loss of strictness, with the result that a transaction may be rejected simply because its shadow objects were inconsistent. Since transactions always execute to completion there can be a considerable waste of system resources. A protocol for atomic validation is described in Section 20.9.2.

We shall now look at a widely used atomic commitment protocol: two-phase commit (2PC). Other such protocols have been defined which vary with respect to the failures they can tolerate and the number of communications that are needed. Further reading on the topic may be found in Bernstein *et al.* (1987), Ceri and Pelagatti (1985) and Bell and Grimson (1992).

20.9.1 The two-phase commit protocol

We assume a number of participating nodes and a *commit* manager at the coordinating node of the transaction (see Figure 20.3(a)). Each participating node 'votes' for *commit* or *abort* of the transaction. Ultimately, all the nodes must make the same decision and the purpose of the protocol is to ensure this. The two phases involved are, broadly:

phase 1: the *commit* manager requests and assembles the 'votes' for *commit* or *abort* of the transaction from each participating node;

phase 2: the *commit* manager decides to *commit* or *abort*, on the basis of the votes, and propagates the decision to the participating nodes.

Showing more detail of the steps involved:

1. The *commit* manager sends a request to each participating node for its vote.

2. Each node either votes *commit* and awaits further instructions, or votes *abort* and stops (exits from the algorithm). Note that a *commit* vote indicates that both the new value of the data object and the old value are stored safely in stable storage so that the node has the ability to *commit* or *abort*.

3. The *commit* manager receives the votes and adds its own vote. If all the votes are to *commit* it decides *commit* and sends *commit* to every participating node. If any vote is *abort* it decides *abort* and sends *abort* to all the nodes that voted *commit* (the others have already stopped). The *commit* manager stops.

4. The participating nodes that voted *commit* are awaiting notification of the decision. They receive this notification, decide accordingly and stop.

We assume that the decision indicated in step 3 above is permanent, guaranteed to persist; there is a point of decision in the algorithm at the *commit* manager.

We must consider how the protocol might handle congestion and failures in the nodes and connections involved. As discussed in Section 20.5 above, the two-phase commit protocol is an application protocol which is implemented above lower-level protocols. Each communication involved in two-phase commit will have a success indication or an exception returned from the level below. We shall assume that the lower levels have made allowance for congestion (by retrying after timeouts) and that an exception indicates a failure of some kind. The protocol must be designed on this basis. Bear in mind that a decision cannot be reversed; once a decision is made, failure recovery procedures must ensure it is implemented.

Suppose that an RPC from the coordinating node to each participating node is used to implement steps 1 (request for vote) and 2 (reply with vote). A failure of any one of these RPCs is assumed to indicate a failure of that participating node. The vote from that node might have been abort; an abort vote is the only safe assumption, so the transaction is aborted.

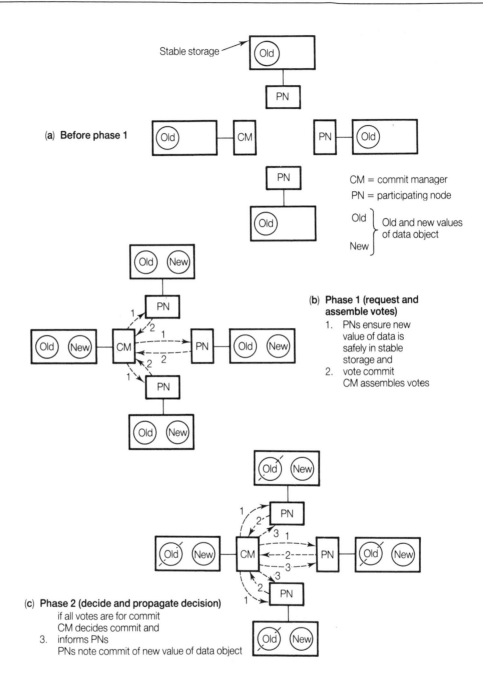

Stable storage

(a) **Before phase 1**

CM = commit manager
PN = participating node

Old ⎫
⎬ Old and new values
⎭ of data object
New

(b) **Phase 1 (request and assemble votes)**
1. PNs ensure new value of data is safely in stable storage and
2. vote commit CM assembles votes

(c) **Phase 2 (decide and propagate decision)**
    if all votes are for commit CM decides commit and
3. informs PNs PNs note commit of new value of data object

Figure 20.3
The two-phase commit protocol when all nodes vote *commit*.

Suppose that step 3 (send the decision to nodes that voted *commit*) is also implemented by RPC, the reply indicating just an acknowledgement of receipt. A failure of any one of these RPCs indicates that the decision to *commit* or *abort* may still need to be effected at that node. The decision cannot be changed;

it has been made and put into effect at the management node and at the nodes which have received the decision from the manager. Recovery from failure at any node must therefore involve terminating correctly any two-phase commit that was in progress when the node failed and sufficient information must be stored in persistent storage to make this possible. On restarting, the node could ask the manager for the decision. The manager knows that node failed and can expect the request.

The above discussion has outlined how failure resilience might be approached in two-phase commit if one or more of the participating nodes fail. The manager might also fail:

1. After sending requests for votes but before deciding. All the participating nodes that voted *commit* will time out (at the two-phase commit level) waiting for a decision.

2. After deciding (and recording the decision in persistent store) but before sending the decision to any participating nodes. All the participating nodes that voted *commit* will time out waiting for a decision.

3. After deciding (and recording the decision in persistent store) and after sending the decision to some but not all participating nodes. Some of the participating nodes that voted *commit* will time out waiting for the decision.

Any one participating node which times out cannot distinguish between these three possibilities. So far we have assumed that the participating nodes know about the manager but not about each other. It would be easy to add a list of participating nodes to the request for vote. Any node that timed out could attempt to find out the decision from the other nodes. Bell and Grimson (1992) and Bernstein *et al.* (1987) give detailed termination protocols for 2PC and also discuss three-phase commit (3PC) protocols.

20.9.2   Two-phase validation for optimistic concurrency control

We assume a number of participating nodes and a *validation manager* at the coordinating node of each transaction (see Figure 20.4). In addition there is a single logical agent in the system, the *update manager*, which is responsible for the queue of transactions that have been validated for update. Each transaction involves a number of participating objects, and each object votes independently *accept* or *reject* on whether there has been conflict. In addition, any object that votes to accept a transaction notifies the validation manager of the version time-stamp of the shadow object that was created for the execution phase.

In the figure, transaction T is being validated by validation manager 2, the participating objects being A, D and X. Another transaction involving objects C and X has just issued *commit*, and validation manager 3 is to validate it. Two-phase validation has much the same general structure as the two-phase commit protocol described in Section 20.9.1, but there are two important differences.

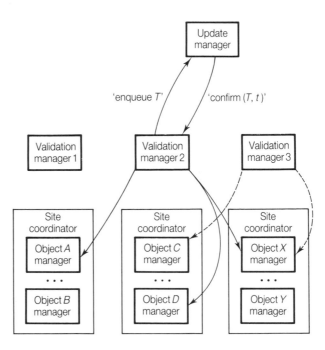

Figure 20.4
Distributed
validation for OCC.

First, an object may be involved in several transactions concurrently; one transaction may issue commit when the object is already participating in the validation phase of some other transaction. It would be possible to block the newly requested validation, but such a policy would run the risk of deadlock. A better approach is to ask the validation manager to try again later if the object's vote is still of interest. Secondly, if all participants vote *accept* at the first phase and the transaction is validated successfully, they do not need to apply the updates during the second phase. Instead the validation manager applies to the update manager for a time-stamp for the transaction, and at this point the serialization order is determined. This interaction is atomic. The validation manager must then inform each participating object of the decision, so that any subsequent validation takes place in a consistent context.

Interaction between the validation manager and participating objects follows the general pattern shown in Figure 20.3, but the details of the protocol must take account of the above differences. The two phases involved are, broadly:

Phase 1: the *validation manager* requests and assembles the 'votes' for *accept* or *reject* of the transaction from each participating object, except those that say *busy*;

Phase 2: the *validation manager* decides to *commit, reject* or *retry*, on the basis of the votes, taking account of shadow object consistency. If the decision is *commit* it applies to the *update manager* for a time-stamp. The decision is propagated to participating objects.

Considering the steps involved in more detail:

1. The *validation manager* sends a request to each participating object for its vote on the transaction execution.

2. Any object that is performing validation of some other transaction replies *busy* and awaits further information. Other objects either vote *accept* (indicating the shadow object version time-stamp) and await further instructions, or vote *reject*, record rejection locally and discard the shadow object. Objects that vote *reject* need not be contacted further.

3. The *validation manager* receives the responses and determines what action to take.

   If any vote is *reject* it decides *reject* and sends *reject* to all the objects that replied *accept* or *busy* (the others have already stopped).

   Otherwise, if any vote is *busy* it asks all the objects to suspend validation for a subsequent *retry*. Objects which voted *accept* are then free to validate other transactions. *The validation manager* will retry after a suitable interval. Objects which voted *accept* originally may then vote *reject*.

   If all the votes are *accept* the *validation manager* decides whether to *commit* on the basis of shadow object consistency. If the versions were inconsistent (see Section 18.6), it decides *reject* and sends *reject* to all the objects; the *validation manager* stops.

4. If the decision is *commit*, the *validation manager* applies to the *update manager* for a time-stamp for the transaction. The decision is propagated to all participating objects, together with the time-stamp. The *validation manager* stops.

The point of decision in the above algorithm occurs when the update manager issues a time-stamp for the transaction. At that point all participating objects have voted *accept* in a two-phase protocol, and they must be prepared to apply updates at some later stage.

It is worth considering the extent to which concurrent execution is sacrificed, and the consequences for object availability. First, the interaction to obtain a time-stamp from the update manager is atomic, and requests must be serviced by a single queue manager. Secondly, when a validation manager receives a *busy* reply from an object it abandons the attempt to validate for a while. Objects will service only one request to validate at a time. Both of these restrictions apply to the **validation phase** of a transaction. The *busy* reply may increase the chance that a transaction is rejected, thus wasting system resources. On the other hand there are no bad implications for object availability at the **execution phase**, since updates are applied locally at each object during the **update phase**, without a protocol that involves external sites. Shadow objects can therefore be created except when a request is received during a change of object version (essentially a rename operation).

This discussion has not considered how the protocol might handle congestion and failures in the nodes and connections involved. Two-phase validation, like two-phase commit, is an application protocol which is implemented above lower-level protocols. The considerations outlined in Section 20.9.1 apply equally here.

20.10 Summary

We considered multiple cooperating instances of the TPS described in Chapter 18 and reiterated, in the context of a distributed system, the general object model that was set up in Chapter 17.

Much of the discussion of concurrency control in Chapter 18 was equally applicable to distributed systems. In this chapter a short discussion on each method highlighted the points specific to distributed systems. There is as yet little practical experience of distributed implementations.

Two-phase locking has the overhead of deadlock detection which is more complex and imposes greater overhead in a distributed system than in a centralized one. A simple timeout approach, in which a transaction that does not succeed in acquiring a lock in a given time is aborted and restarted, is preferable.

Time-stamp ordering has the advantage that information held locally at an object is the basis on which an invocation is accepted or rejected so the method is potentially good for distributed systems. The absence of system-wide time is not a problem provided that there is a policy which ensures that all objects reach the same decision on the relative order of any two transaction timestamps.

Optimistic methods are also potentially well suited to distributed systems. Operations are invoked on copies of all the objects involved in a transaction and the results of the transaction are incorporated into the database when it requests *commit*. In OCC the order in which transactions' updates are made at each object is determined by the update manager. A time-stamp, issued by the update manager, is associated with the transaction and the updates are made in timestamp order at each object.

For simplicity, we assumed in 2PL and TSO that strictness was enforced in the implementation of the transaction executions. Greater concurrency might be achieved at the expense of greater complexity by relaxing strictness. We argued that atomic commitment and taking shadow copies atomically would reflect a pessimistic, rather than optimistic, approach and is therefore unsuitable for OCC.

We discussed atomic commitment for 2PL and TSO. The independent failure modes of the components of distributed systems are relevant here. The same decision on transaction *commit* or *abort* must be made for all objects invoked by the transaction. A two-phase commit protocol was described and discussed in some detail. Finally, we discussed a two-phase validation protocol for OCC. In this case, the single point of decision on whether the transaction is to be committed is when the update manager issues the transaction time-stamp. Updates are then guaranteed to be made in time-stamp order at each object.

Exercises

20.1 In what ways do distributed systems differ from centralized ones?

20.2 How can the components of a distributed system agree on a basis for establishing system time? Under what circumstances might system time be needed?

20.3 Relate the object model in Section 20.3 and the distributed TPS of Section 20.5 with the discussion on the implementation of naming, binding, locating and invoking objects of Section 14.9.

First, consider the component TPSs as a distributed application that a client may wish to invoke. The components may be named as a set of application servers. The objects they manage are named internally by the TPS. This is the client-server model.

A more general object model might support global naming and invocation of the data objects. How might this be managed in a system?

20.4 Describe the operation of a distributed TPS from the point at which a client submits a transaction to a single component of the TPS.

20.5 Why are the time-stamp ordering (TSO) and optimistic concurrency control (OCC) approaches to concurrency control potentially more suitable for distributed implementation than two-phase locking? How can 2PL be simplified?

20.6 What is involved in the validation phase of OCC in a distributed system?

20.7 (a) Why is a complex protocol required to *commit* a transaction atomically in a distributed TPS?

(b) What happens in the two-phase commit protocol if the transaction manager fails? Discuss its failure at all relevant stages in the protocol.

(c) Suppose a participant fails after voting for *commit* of a transaction. What should it do on restart?

What are the advantages and disadvantages of letting the nodes participating in a two-phase commit know about each other?

20.11   Summary of Part III

The model of an object with abstract operations is used throughout the book. Part II is concerned with implementing a single abstract operation correctly in the presence of concurrency and crashes. Part III is concerned with implementing a number of related operations comprising a single higher-level abstract operation.

The problems arising from uncontrolled concurrent execution of composite operations are incorrect results arising from certain interleavings of sub-operations, and deadlock arising from some approaches to controlling this. Deadlock is discussed in Chapter 16. The concept of atomic transaction is developed in Chapter 17 and the ACID properties of transactions (atomicity, consistency, isolation and durability) are discussed. Concurrency control procedures must ensure consistency and isolation; storage management policies and crash recovery procedures must ensure atomicity and durability.

For concurrency control purposes we assume that information is stored at each object, including the time at which each invocation was made and by which transaction. The object also specifies which of its pairs of operations are conflicting (non-commutative).

On this basis the implementation of transactions in the presence of concurrent transactions and failures can be studied. Chapter 18 focuses on concurrency control; two-phase locking (2PL), time-stamp ordering (TSO) and optimistic methods (OCC) are discussed in general terms.

In Chapter 19 we are concerned with crash recovery. If a crash occurs it must be possible to recover any desired system state and therefore any desired state for any object. We have already set up the recording of a history of invocations at each object for concurrency control purposes. In theory, object state may be regarded as the result of a sequence of invocations starting from *create*. In theory, any state can be recovered by starting again from *create* and making any required sequence of invocations. In practice, our recovery procedures have to be efficient and have to allow for a crash at any time. We took a simple, state-based model for recovery in which object state was assumed to be recorded before and after an invocation. This allows any operation to be undone and redone, and these UNDO and REDO operations must be idempotent to allow for crashes during recovery.

Concurrency control and recovery are closely related because the mechanisms that must be in place for crash resilience in a transaction system can be used by a concurrency control method to achieve *abort*.

The object model used throughout Part III is not restricted to a centralized implementation. Most of the discussion in Chapters 15 to 19 is relevant to both centralized and distributed systems. Chapter 20 focuses on the issues specific to distributed systems; their special properties are discussed and the various methods for achieving concurrency control are reconsidered. Time-stamp ordering and optimistic concurrency control are shown to be immediately applicable to distributed systems; two-phase locking involves a good deal of extra work to distribute the deadlock detection procedure. In practice, if distributed two-phase locking was used for concurrency control, a timeout mechanism would be used. Any transaction which fails to achieve a lock in a given time is aborted.

In pessimistic methods commitment must be implemented atomically over all objects invoked by a transaction. In a centralized system the whole TPS is assumed to fail together. The recovery procedures must ensure the consistency of persistent memory on restart after a failure. In a distributed system we are concerned with the atomic commitment of distributed objects in the presence of partial failures of (components of) a system. We studied a two-phase commit protocol and outlined the recovery procedures of nodes that fail during the protocol.

In optimistic methods, we strive for high concurrency, that is, high availability of objects. If objects are involved in the atomic commitment of one transaction they are unavailable to others. We studied a two-phase validation protocol for distributed OCC during which shadow objects may still be taken by new transactions.

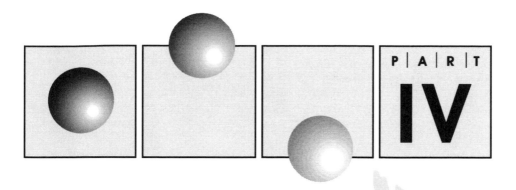

System case studies

CHAPTERS

We have studied how processes are implemented and how they may interact to carry out the goals of a concurrent system. We have considered different approaches to the design of interprocess communication facilities in the context of system structure. In Part IV we look at the design choices that were made in some real systems, in order to see a consistent set of choices for a given application area with the technology available at the time. An overview of each system is given, but the emphasis is on concurrency control. Aspects of the naming infrastructure which was introduced in Section 14.9 are also relevant. The evolution from a conventional closed operating system dating from the 1970s, through microkernels dating from the 1980s, to current research systems is traced.

Many papers, and sometimes books, have been written on the systems we consider. A short case study cannot do full justice to any system and, for greater insight, the papers written by those involved in the design and everyday use of the systems are referenced.

Although fragments of UNIX have been used as examples throughout the book, UNIX is the first case study in Chapter 21. An outline of the design of Bell Research Laboratory's Edition 7 UNIX kernel is given, followed by a discussion of its good and bad points. The modifications and extensions offered by Berkeley UNIX BSD 4.3 and AT&T's System V.4 are then given. The attempt to unify these potentially diverging versions of UNIX made by the IEEE POSIX committee is then outlined.

The microkernel approach is illustrated in Chapter 22. A microkernel does not itself support a program development environment and a common approach is to emulate an existing operating system, such as UNIX. Any software that runs on UNIX can then be run on the microkernel. We consider Mach, which supports UNIX BSD 4.3, and CHORUS, which supports UNIX System V.4. The evolution of the Mach kernel design is given from RIG through Accent. The CHORUS system is described briefly. Many of the topics discussed in Part II can be seen in practice in these systems.

Next, we trace the development of the distributed systems research at the University of Cambridge, UK. An issue of current interest is how to design microkernels so that they can give quality of service guarantees to real-time applications. The real-time criteria have come into prominence in general purpose operating systems because of the requirement to support continuous media in multimedia workstations. Current networks can deliver voice and video in real time, and the software in the workstations must be designed to offer equally good performance. The Cambridge research projects include a persistent implementation of C++ which supports distributed, nested transactions. Optimistic concurrency control is used, thus providing a practical example of a topic covered in Part III.

Chapter 23 first discusses how transaction processing systems might be implemented in terms of processes and IPC. We then outline some TP systems in the area of electronic funds transfer (EFT). The international automatic teller machine network is then described in some detail. Security issues and some approaches to their solution are outlined.

UNIX

CONTENTS

21.1 Introduction

This chapter outlines the design of the UNIX operating system kernel. The first widely known UNIX design, that of Bell Telephone Laboratory's Seventh Edition of 1978, is described and evaluated. The two major current UNIX systems, AT&T's System V and Berkeley Software Distribution (BSD) 4.3 are then described. Emphasis is given to the ways in which some of the shortcomings in the original UNIX kernel design have been addressed in these later systems.

There is a massive amount of literature on UNIX, including some books on the kernel design and others on the environment above the kernel. Classic references are Ritchie and Thompson (1974), and a collection of papers in the July–August 1978 issue of the *Bell System Technical Journal*. More recent books which give a comprehensive treatment of the kernel design are Bach (1986) which emphasizes System V and Leffler *et al.* (1989) for BSD 4.3.

The aim of this chapter is not to give explicit UNIX syntax for every system call or kernel function. These are widely available in books and manuals. Rather, the reader should understand the basic modular structure of UNIX and how it supports the execution of user-level processes and is itself executed procedurally in response to users' requests and actions. Good and bad aspects of its design are highlighted.

21.2 Evolution of UNIX

UNIX dates from 1969. Bell Telephone's Research Laboratory had been involved in the US project MAC Multics project in collaboration with MIT and General Electric. The aim was to build a large, complex, general-purpose time-sharing system. Bell pulled out of the collaboration in the late 1960s and Ken Thompson, soon joined by Dennis Ritchie, set about building a computing environment which became UNIX.

UNIX was soon moved to the PDP11 architecture and was implemented in the high-level language C in 1973. This was unusual at the time and made it possible to port UNIX relatively easily to other architectures. UNIX therefore had the advantage of being independent of any computer manufacturer and potentially available on any architecture.

In the early years, UNIX was a small, simple, easily understandable system. It was originally developed as a single-user programming environment, but was soon extended to support multi-access use. Its designers opted for a simple and comprehensible design, even if this was at the expense of efficiency. UNIX became popular within the Bell Labs research environment, particularly for text processing. Bell was not able to market, advertise or support UNIX in the 1970s but its use spread to some 500 sites by 1977, partly as a result of being made available free to universities for educational purposes. The fact that it was written in a high-level language and the source code was made available made it popular as a vehicle for teaching operating systems. Also, much software was written for it and shared among its users.

A comprehensive description of the evolution of the many versions of UNIX can be found in the books mentioned above. Figure 21.1 shows some of the major milestones to give a context for the systems described in this chapter.

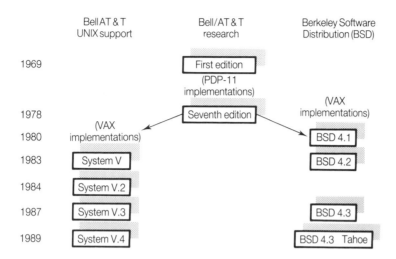

Bell AT & T
UNIX support

Bell/AT & T
research

Berkeley Software
Distribution (BSD)

Figure 21.1
Some versions of
UNIX.

21.3 A summary of UNIX design features

In 1974 a paper was published by Ritchie and Thompson in the
Communications of the ACM in which the following were highlighted as the
main design features of UNIX:

1. a hierarchical file system incorporating demountable volumes (see Sections
   21.5, 21.6);

2. compatible file, device and inter-process input and output (21.5, 21.6, 21.9);

3. the ability to initiate asynchronous processes (21.8);

4. a system command language selectable on a per-user basis (21.8);

5. over a hundred subsystems, including a dozen languages;

6. a high degree of portability.

21.4 Overview of kernel modules

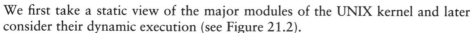

We first take a static view of the major modules of the UNIX kernel and later
consider their dynamic execution (see Figure 21.2).

The file subsystem manages the UNIX naming graph. Because files, directories, and devices are all named here, system calls concerned with these items
will be handled here in the first instance. For example, input and output are
handled through the 'file' subsystem.

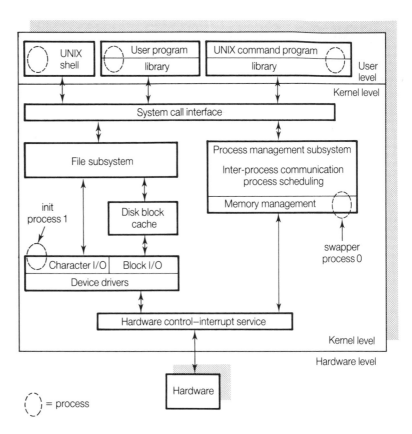

Figure 21.2
Outline of UNIX
kernel modules.

Since our major concern is the dynamic execution of a system by processes we will take a brief look at this before proceeding to an outline of UNIX functions. Figure 21.2 shows that UNIX has very few dedicated system processes. *Process 0* is concerned with swapping processes between main memory and backing store and must therefore always be guaranteed to be resident in main memory (later systems also have a process to handle paging). *Process 1*, the *init* process, is concerned with responding to new users when they become active at terminal devices. After the new user has been put through the logging-in procedure, a user-level process is created to receive and interpret the user's commands. Three examples of user-level processes are shown in the figure.

The *init* process is therefore the ancestor of all user processes. More details will be given when system initialization is considered. Processes may be created (forked) dynamically and a process may create any number of child processes, subject to exhaustion of system resources. A UNIX process is heavyweight, occupying a separate address space, and a UNIX system will have some maximum number of processes that it can suppport.

When a user-level process makes a system call it becomes a (privileged) system process and enters the kernel. It may run without preemption until it chooses to block.

21.5 The file system interface

UNIX supports a hierarchical file system as described in Chapter 6. A simple example is shown in Figure 21.3. From a distinguished root directory, a naming tree with directory files at the interior nodes and normal files (or special files) at the leaves is supported. A normal file is just a sequence of bytes as far as UNIX is concerned, and is named by a pathname from the root. Devices are named as 'special files', each device having an entry in a device directory (*/dev*).

There are a small number of system calls provided for both normal file and device input and output. The file's pathname is given when a file is opened for use. If all is well, a small integer, the *file-id* (indicated below) for the open file, is returned for use in subsequent calls. A pointer into the file is maintained by the system for reads and writes. This can be manipulated explicitly by the user, but for sequential reads and writes the system will remember where you got to.

file-id = **open** (*pathname, mode*)

reply = **close** (*file-id*)

bytes = **read** (*file-id, where-to-in-memory, byte-count*)

count = **write** (*file-id, where-from-in-memory, byte-count*)

reply = **seek** (*file-id, where to position the pointer in the file*)

reply = **create** (*pathname*)

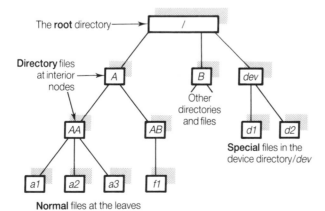

Figure 21.3
A filing system.

21.5.1 Graph navigation and the current directory

It is inconvenient to use the full pathname, starting from the root, every time a filename is used. For this reason, UNIX allows a current or working directory to be specified and filenames may be interpreted relative to that. In Figure 21.3:

/A/AA/a1 is a pathname starting from the root, '/'

a1   is the same file's name if *AA* is the current directory.

Each user has an entry in a file called */etc/passwd* which has the form:

> *user-name : encrypted password : user-id : group-id : full-name : home-directory : shell*

The *home-directory* component allows an initial working directory to be established at login. After that, the user may change current directory at any time, using a system call, **chdir**.

UNIX also allows navigation of the naming graph upwards from the current directory. Each directory contains an entry for itself named '.' and an entry for its parent named '..'

If *AA* is the current directory, .. / *AB* / *f1* is a pathname up to directory *A* (the parent of *AA*) then down to directory *AB*, then file *f1*. It is often more convenient to change working directory than to construct long pathnames of this kind.

21.5.2 An aside: the readable password file

We saw in the previous section that the file */etc/passwd* contains an entry on each user. This file is readable by anyone and, in particular, the encrypted form of everyone's password can be read there. The encrypted password is generated as follows:

> *password → one-way-function → encrypted password*

where the one-way function is an encryption function which does not have an inverse; that is, given the encrypted password, there is no function which can be used to generate the password. At login the password the user gives is put through the one-way function and the result is compared with that indicated in the user's entry.

The disadvantage of this scheme, as described, is that someone with a lot of processing power could do work off-line to find passwords. The one-way function is well known and the password file is readable. The would-be intruder could put a large number of guesses for passwords through the one-way function and compare the results with the encrypted passwords. If a single match is found, one password is known and the intruder can login. Stoll (1989) describes a systematic penetration of UNIX systems using this technique. More sophisticated encryption techniques have been introduced to combat this approach.

21.6 The file system implementation

UNIX keeps a metadata table for each of its filing systems in which each file (normal, directory or special) in that filing system has an entry. An entry is called an index node or **inode** and contains information on the corresponding file. By convention, the inode of the root of a filing system is the first entry in the table.

Figure 21.4 outlines the information held in an inode, and Figure 21.5 emphasizes that the inode table is held in persistent storage. Although special files have

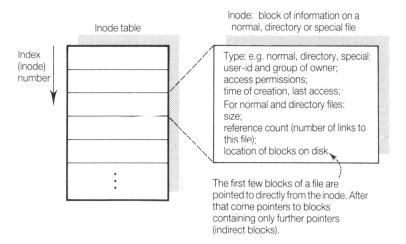

Figure 21.4
The inode table for a filing system.

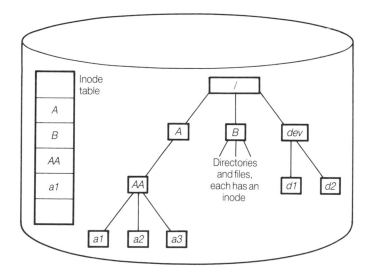

Figure 21.5
A filing system on a single device.

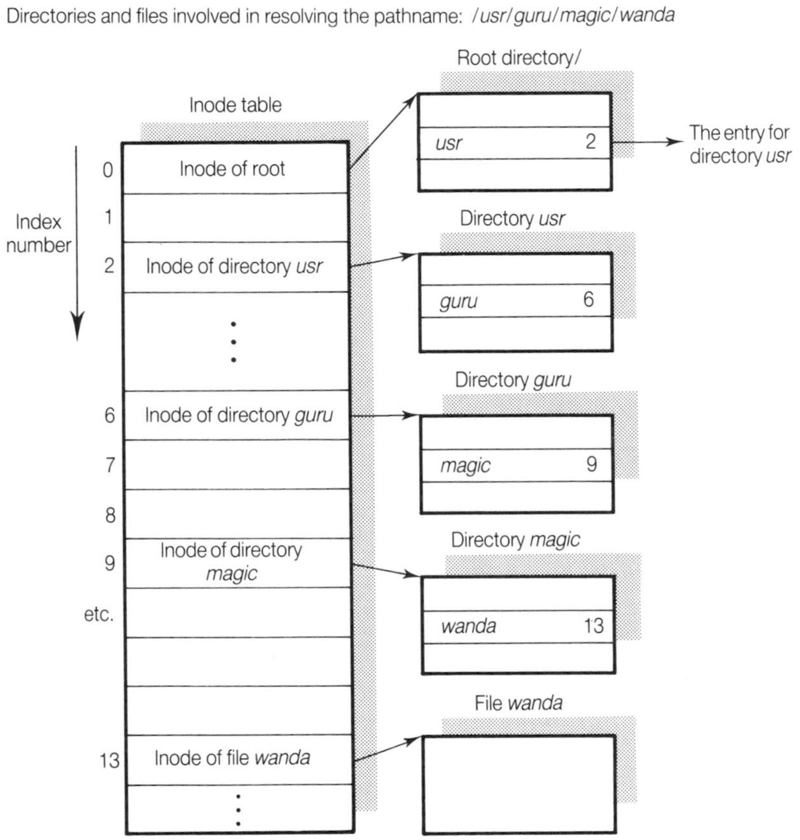

Directories and files involved in resolving the pathname: /usr/guru/magic/wanda

Figure 21.6
Pathname resolution.

an inode they do not occupy disk storage. The disk blocks occupied by normal and directory files are recorded as a table of pointers in the inode. The first few pointers, typically 12, point directly to disk blocks used for the file. Small files can therefore be accessed efficiently. After the direct pointers come (two) pointers to disk blocks which contain only pointers to blocks of the file (indirect blocks). After these comes a pointer to a block which contains pointers to further blocks of pointers (double indirect blocks). UNIX systems differ in the disk block size and the number of direct and indirect pointers, but all use this general approach (see Exercise 21.3). Figure 21.6 gives an example of a pathname lookup.

Keeping the information on files together in a table is convenient. An alternative is to use a disk block as an indirection on the path to each file, thus scattering the information and leading to many more disk reads. Algorithms for checking the consistency of the filing system are easy to implement using the inode table (see Section 21.6.5).

The disadvantage of an inode table is that it is vulnerable to head crashes or bad blocks in that area. For that reason, the table is replicated.

21.6.1 Mounting and unmounting filing systems

The complete on-line filing system is typically large and constructed from a number of separate filing systems on separate devices. A filing system can be mounted into the existing naming tree, its root replacing some specified directory (file in early versions of UNIX), using the **mount** system call (see Figure 21.7). For example:

> **mount** ("/A" "/dev/disk32" R/W)

causes the filing system which is on device *disk32* (with special file */dev/disk32*) to be mounted over the directory */A*. *R/W* indicates that it can be read and written. The file *a1* shown on a mounted file system becomes */A/a1* after mounting.

The inode of a directory over which a filing system is mounted is called a mount point and information on the mounted filing system is noted there, for example, the name of the special file of the device on which it resides (see Figure 21.8). There is also a system call to **unmount** a filing system. When UNIX is loaded a number of filing systems are mounted to form the online filing system. The **mount** system call can also be used to mount a user's private filing system.

Each separate filing system has its own inode table and space allocation. A filing system resides on a logical device which is either a separate physical device or a self-contained partition of a physical device.

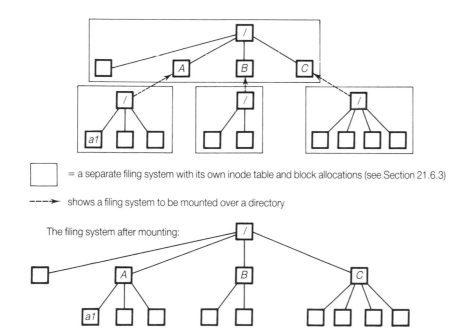

☐ = a separate filing system with its own inode table and block allocations (see Section 21.6.3)

----> shows a filing system to be mounted over a directory

The filing system after mounting:

Figure 21.7
An on-line filing system showing separate mounted filing systems.

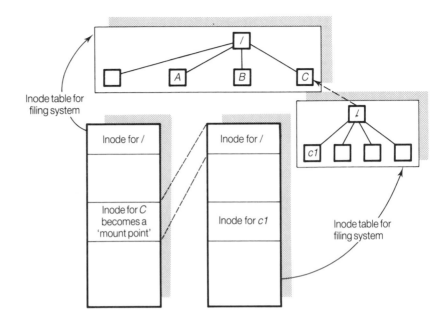

Figure 21.8
Inodes as 'mount
points'.

21.6.2 Access protection

Access control information is kept in each inode. This indicates, in broad categories, who can access the file and in what way. Three categories are used: owner, group (typically used for a class of students or a project team) and others. The types of access that can be specified for a normal file are read, write and execute. This information is coded as shown in Figure 21.9. The same coding is used for directory files, but the interpretation of the access types is appropriate for directories: read, add or remove an entry, search for a name and access the corresponding inode.

An additional permissions bit, called the **set user-id** bit, allows access by program to be specified as well as access by categories of user. When this bit is set for a program file, any user having permission to execute the program inherits the privileges of the owner **while executing the program**. It is therefore possible for a given user to write to some data file (accessible to the owner of the program being executed) while executing a set-uid file, but not otherwise.

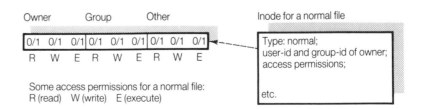

Figure 21.9
Access permissions
for a normal file.

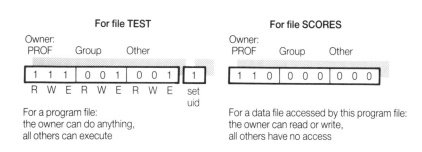

Figure 21.10
Use of the set-user-id facility.

Figure 21.10 gives an example. A user named PROF has written a program called TEST which students must run in order to be assessed. The program gives them some tasks to carry out and writes their scores into the file SCORES. A student has no access to the file SCORES except when running the program TEST so she cannot bypass the test procedure and write a high score into it; nor can she read the scores of her fellow students.

Another aspect of this facility is that while running the set-uid program the user has her original *real-id* and an *effective-id* (of the owner of the program). These are available to the program through system calls and may be used to ensure that only a certain group of users carry out the TEST in the example above. More generally, any set-uid program can keep a hate-list and refuse to run for blacklisted individuals. It may also enforce access controls related to time of day, for example, the students may have to run the TEST before a certain deadline or in a certain room at certain times so that collaboration can be prevented.

A set-uid program can therefore enforce arbitrarily fine-grained access controls and is a protected interface to the data files it accesses. The facility can be used for programs owned by the system for reading and writing system files which are not generally accessible.

We should also consider whether a set-uid program could be a danger to the users that execute it. When the program runs in your address space can it access your files? Can TEST, after testing you, delete all your files? The answer should be NO because both the *effective-id* and *real-id* are available to the code which enforces access control. The program is running as PROF, and we assume that you have not given PROF the right to delete all your files. If however, UNIX were to allow the *effective-id* to be changed to the *real-id* then TEST could test you, change its *effective-id* to your ID and inherit all your privileges.

21.6.3 Allocation of disk blocks to a filing system

A disk can be represented as an array of blocks. Early systems typically used a block size of 512 bytes. Current systems use larger block sizes, typically 4 kbyte, for greater efficiency.

- Block 0 of a disk which holds a filing system is reserved for bootstrapping UNIX and is not used by the filing system.

- Block 1 is called the **super-block** and is used for management purposes. It contains information such as:

    the number of blocks in the filing system;

    the number of free blocks in the filing system;

    a list of (some of the) free blocks;

    the size of the inode table;

    the number of free inodes;

    a list of (some of the) free inodes;

    together with flags to prevent race conditions over access to free blocks and free inodes.

- Blocks 2 to N contain the inode table.
- Blocks $N+1$ to the end contain blocks allocated to files and free blocks.
- The free blocks are maintained in a structure which is a chain of tables of free blocks. One disk read gives a table of free blocks and a pointer to the next table.

Figure 21.12 includes a diagram of this block layout.

21.6.4 File system data structures in main memory

When a system is up and running, information about the files that have been opened by the active users is held in main memory. Figure 21.11 shows some of the data structures involved. Each user has an open file table. Recall that all I/O

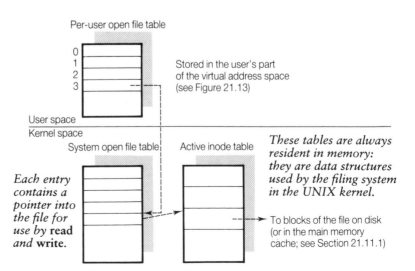

Figure 21.11
Main-memory data structures used by the filing system.

is handled through the filing system so the user's terminal device as well as normal files that are open will be represented here. This table is held in a user data area rather than in the kernel, and may be swapped out.

There are also tables held in the kernel which are resident in main memory. One is the system open file table. Each open file has at least one entry in this table and an entry in the per-user open file table points to an entry in this table. One piece of information in this table is the file pointer for each file (see Section 21.5).

The active inode table contains a 'copy' of the inode of each open file. In fact the information will differ from that held in the inode on disk in a number of ways. The active inode must identify its corresponding inode uniquely within the entire filing system; the mode of use must be indicated (read only or read/write); and the location of information on disk may change if the file is open for writing and this is first recorded in the active inode. There are therefore potential Part III style problems if a crash occurs, as discussed in Chapter 15. When a file is closed the inode is written to disk if any changes have been made. A design issue is how frequently inodes which have been changed should be written to disk while the file is in use.

Suppose a file has been opened by two different users. If the users are independent they each need a separate pointer. This is achieved by having an entry of the system open file table for each independent sharer of an open file, but a single active inode. One assumes that such sharers are likely to be reading only. UNIX does not enforce exclusive write locks however. UNIX assumes that related processes, for example parent and child, will be cooperating closely and enforces that they share a file pointer. This is discussed below in the context of process creation.

21.6.5 Consistency issues

Let us consider the separate actions involved in deleting a file:

rm (*pathname*)

Figure 21.12 shows the data relevant to the delete operation in main memory and on disk.

- *Remove the directory entry*
  If the access check indicates that the user has the right to delete the file, the directory service will remove the entry from the directory specified by the pathname, first noting the inode of the file. The change to the directory is first made in main memory and the changed directory is later written to disk.

- *Check the reference count in the file's inode*
  The inode is read into main memory. Let us assume the reference count is 1 so the inode and the blocks of the file can be freed.

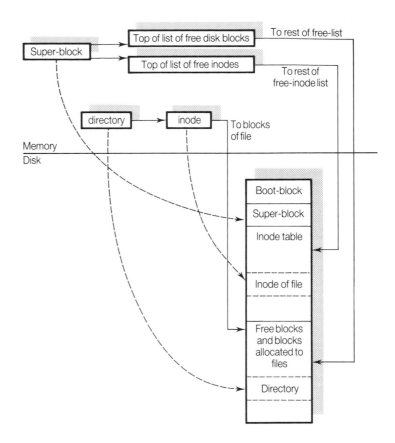

Figure 21.12
Memory and disk
copies of data
used when deleting
a file.

- *Free the material and the inode*
  The blocks that were allocated to the file are added to the free-list. Recall
  from Section 21.6.3 that the free-list and the free-inode list start from the
  memory copy of the super-block. The changed super-block must later be
  written to disk.

This example shows that a typical operation will involve a number of related
changes to the filing system on disk. If there is no crash, all the changes will
eventually reach the disk, reflecting the state after the successful completion of
the operation. If there is a crash which causes main memory to be lost, after
some but not all of the data is written out to disk, the filing system is inconsistent. For this reason, a consistency check is carried out on the filing system when
UNIX is restarted after a crash.

The fact that the blocks allocated to files can be ascertained just from reading
the inode table (without reference to the directory structure) is convenient for
consistency checking. Each block must be allocated to a file or be on the free-
list. The check will detect whether any block is lost to the filing system or
doubly allocated: both to a file and on the free-list.

21.7 The execution environment of a process

A basic requirement that a user places on the operating system is to load some specified program and have it executed by a process. The code may be the binary resulting from compilation of a user's program, a system utility or the code comprising an operating system command. Figure 21.13 shows the address space that is set up for a process by UNIX. The UNIX kernel, which is always resident in memory, occupies part of (typically half) the address space of every process. As well as code and data the execution environment of a process includes such things as register values and open file status.

The user-level part of the address space is set up with three segments: text (code), data and stack. The text segment is write-protected and may be shared with other users. The data and stack segments are private to an individual user. The information held by UNIX for the purpose of managing the process is divided into two portions. That which must remain resident in memory at all times is held in a process descriptor in the central process table in the UNIX kernel. Information that must be held here includes signals that have been sent to the process. That which only needs to be in memory when the process is executing is held in a 'per-process data area' at the start of the data segment.

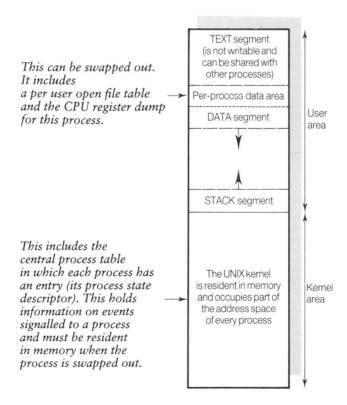

*This can be swapped out.
It includes
a per user open file table
and the CPU register dump
for this process.*

*This includes the
central process table
in which each process has
an entry (its process state
descriptor). This holds
information on events
signalled to a process
and must be resident
in memory when the
process is swapped out.*

Figure 21.13
The address space
of a process.

This aspect of the design shows UNIX's age. The PDP11, UNIX's major host machine in the early days, had a 64 kbyte address space and kernel space was very tight. Today, a typical UNIX machine might have a 4Gbyte address space and tens of megabytes of physical memory.

21.8 Process creation and termination

UNIX has very few permanent system processes, as outlined in Section 21.4 and shown in Figure 21.2. There is a process to manage the swapping into and out of memory of segments of the address spaces of processes and a process to monitor the input devices which users might activate. All other processes come into existence as a result of the **fork** system call which takes the form:

process-id = **fork** ( )

This causes a new address space to be created which is a replica of that of the process executing the **fork** system call (the parent process). The *process-id* returned to the parent is that of the child which has been created. The *process-id* returned to the child is zero. After **fork** the parent and child can take different paths by testing this value.

Notice that **fork** is heavyweight, since a new address space is created for the new process. This mechanism should be contrasted with the lightweight fork discussed in Chapters 7 and 10, where a new process shares an address space with its parent and only a new stack needs to be created.

21.8.1 Loading and execution

The **execve** system call specifies a program to be loaded and executed:

execve *(program-name <argument-list>)*

The existing code (text) segment of the process is replaced by the executable program. The data segments are lost apart from the per-process data area. The argument list is made available to the new program through the per-process data area.

It is very common that a new process is created for the purpose of executing a new program. The work involved in replicating the address space on **fork** is largely wasted in this case.

21.8.2 Parent–child synchronization on process termination

The parent process created the child process for a purpose. The parent needs to know when the child has finished its task. If the child executes a single program

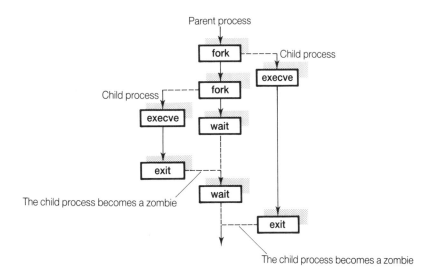

Figure 21.14
Process
management
system calls.

and hits the end rather than **execve**ing some other program, it should tell its parent it has finished on or before committing suicide. This is achieved by the **exit** system call:

> **exit** (*address of a byte of status information*)

The address space of the process which has executed **exit** is removed from the system but the process descriptor in the central process table is kept. The byte of status information is stored there for the parent to pick up. This is called **zombie** state – the process is dead but not buried.

The parent can synchronize with the death of a child by executing the system call

> *process-id* = **wait** (*address for a byte of status information*)

If the process has more than one child it may not specify which particular death it is waiting for. The system returns the *process-id* concerned (the first child to execute **exit**) and the associated status information. If termination of two children is awaited, two **wait** calls are executed and the *process-id*s examined to determine the order of death. Figure 21.14 shows the general scheme.

21.8.3   Process creation during system initialization

At system initialization the kernel is loaded from the filing system and starts to run. Data structures are initialized, the filing system is mounted, *process 0* is created and control is passed to it. *Process 0* creates *process 1* and becomes the *swapper* for the lifetime of the system. *Process 1 (init)* is the terminal monitor and login initiator (see Figure 21.15). It finds out which terminal lines are active and creates a child for each of these.

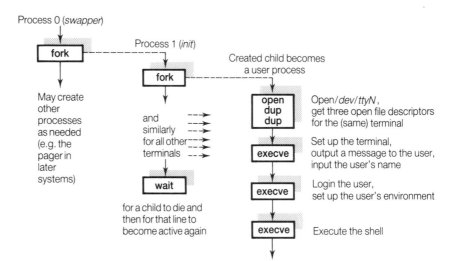

Figure 21.15
System initialization.

The process created by *init* to manage an active terminal device is the only process that needs to know the characteristics of the device and the name of the special device file for that terminal. It opens the special file for the terminal (*/dev/ttyN*). One file descriptor (indicating an entry in the per-user open file table) is insufficient for handling terminal input, output and error diagnostic output, so three are created for the terminal via the **dup** system call. These files remain open across all subsequent **execve** system calls.

The next **execve**d program (*/etc/tty*) causes a message to be output to the user and the login name to be read. The next **execve**d program (*/bin/login*) carries out the login procedure: inputs, encrypts and checks the password. The user's entry in the password file contains information such as the *user-id* and *group-id* which is set up in the process descriptor for this process. The user's preferred working directory (home directory) is also stored there and is now set up as working directory for this process. Finally, the shell (command interpreter program) is **execve**d (*/bin/sh* or the user's preferred shell indicated in the password file entry).

21.8.4 Process creation by the command interpreter

We have seen that a command interpreter or shell is loaded and executed by a process for each logged-in user. Figure 21.16 shows what happens next. The shell reads a command from the user by using a **read** system call on the terminal input file descriptor (opened as described in the previous section). It might be that the command requires a short system call to be made by the shell on the user's behalf; more generally the command might indicate that an executable

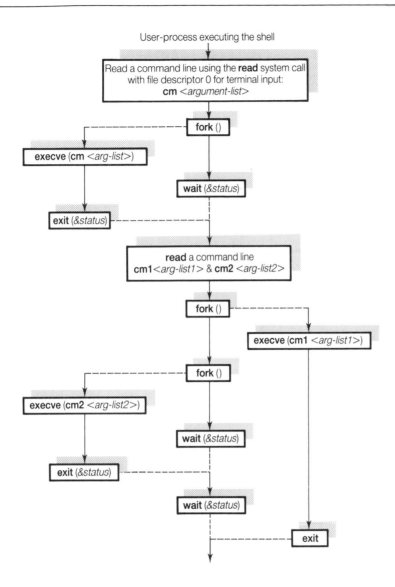

User-process executing the shell

Read a command line using the **read** system call
with file descriptor 0 for terminal input:
cm <*argument-list*>

fork ()

execve (**cm** <*arg-list*>)

wait (&*status*)

exit (&*status*)

read a command line
cm1<*arg-list1*> & **cm2** <*arg-list2*>

fork ()

execve (**cm1** <*arg-list1*>)

fork ()

execve (**cm2** <*arg-list2*>)

wait (&*status*)

exit (&*status*)

wait (&*status*)

exit

Figure 21.16
Process creation
used by the shell.

user program or system program should be loaded from the file store and executed. In this case the shell **fork**s a child process which **execve**s the required program. The shell process **wait**s for termination of the child.

The user's shell process then goes on to read another command. This time two commands are input, separated by &. This indicates that the two commands are to be run in parallel. The shell forks a process to execute each command. Only when the complete command, which in general may have any number of parallel components, has been obeyed does the shell process wait for the children it has created to die.

 ## 21.9 IPC: Pipelines of processes

21.9.1 Redirection of standard input and output

We have seen that a process starts life with three open files for terminal input, output and error diagnostic output. The shell will allow the standard terminal input and output to be redirected by the user for the duration of a command, so that standard input is taken from a file instead of the terminal, and standard output is written to a file. For example:

ls	lists the current working directory to the terminal
ls *>there*	lists the directory to the file called *there*
ed	runs **ed** which takes input from the terminal
ed *<script*	runs **ed** which takes input from the file called *script*

A pipeline of processes could be set up using the standard output of one command as the standard input for another. For example:

cm1 *>temp1*

cm2 *<temp1 >temp2*

cm3 *<temp2*

If the files *temp1* and *temp2* are not required after the processing is complete the user must delete them explicitly.

This flexibility is possible because file and device input and output are designed to be compatible and the UNIX commands are designed to produce output which is suitable for input to other commands. The output from commands therefore tends to be somewhat terse and unembellished by headings and summaries. In the next section we see how inter-process communication was made compatible with file and device I/O and a more convenient way of setting up a pipeline of processes.

21.9.2 Pipes

In order to achieve compatibility between file and device I/O, devices are considered as 'special files' and are accessed through the same naming graph as normal files. In order to make inter-process communication compatible with file and device I/O, the concept of a pipe is used. A pipe may be thought of as another kind of file. Like normal files, directory files and special files, each pipe is used through file identifiers in the communicating processes' open file tables (see Figure 21.11). A pipe has an inode but, in the original UNIX design, pipes did not have a pathname; a pipe exists as long as the processes which have its descriptors in their open file tables. It is assumed that one process puts bytes

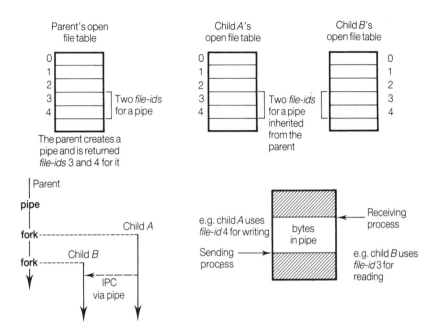

Figure 21.17
Example of use of a pipe file.

into the pipe and another takes bytes out; that is, a pipe is typically used as a one-way, one to one byte stream (see Figure 21.17).

Notice the differences between pipes and normal files:

- There are two pointers, for input (reading) and output (writing).

- There is a separate system call to create a pipe:

  pipe(*fildes*)

  where *fildes* is an integer array with two elements. **pipe** returns a read and write file descriptor, used as *fildes*[0] and *fildes*[1] respectively.

- The pointers cannot be manipulated explicitly using seek. Once bytes have been read they cannot be read again.

- If a process reads from an empty pipe it is blocked until bytes are available to satisfy the read. There is a notion of a 'full' pipe so that a pipe file stays small enough to be kept in main memory. If a process writes to a full pipe it is blocked until some bytes are removed by the reader. The pipe file is therefore a synchronized byte stream between a writing process and a reading process.

Notice the similarities between normal files and pipes:

- Once a pipe file is created with two open *file-ids* it is read and written as though it was a normal file.

- The pipe *file-ids* are passed down from parent to child on process creation (like all other *file-ids*). They are indistinguishable from other file descriptors in the process's open file tables. Figure 21.17 shows an example. Descendants of a common ancestor may therefore be programmed to use a pipe to communicate in a similar way to using an open file, but with the restrictions noted above.

The pipe mechanism is therefore not a general IPC mechanism in that it may only be used between processes with a common ancestor.

21.9.3 Named pipes in later systems

Current versions of UNIX support both unnamed and named pipes. A named pipe has a pathname and exists permanently in the file system hierarchy. The semantics of a named pipe are the same as those of an unnamed pipe, as described above. Processes may open a named pipe in exactly the same way as a normal file, and therefore unrelated processes can use them to communicate. Their use must of course be coordinated by the processes concerned. The system call for opening a named pipe for reading may block (unless a no delay option is specified) until the pipe is opened for writing.

21.9.4 Pipes between commands

When the shell, instanced on behalf of a user, creates processes to carry out in parallel the commands specified by the user it is the common ancestor of all these processes. It is therefore possible for pipes to be used between commands which are running in parallel on behalf of a user process. The shell will create pipes for use between the command programs if requested as follows:

command1 | command2 | command3

A pipe is created for IPC between command1 and command2 before processes are created to execute them. Its descriptors are inherited by the processes which are forked. Similarly another pipe is created for IPC between command2 and command3.

Note that pipes may be used in this way without any changes within the programs that take the input or deliver the output. The command programs are such that their input and output may use standard terminal I/O, I/O redirected to or from normal files, or pipes. To this extent, device, file and inter-process I/O are compatible (see Section 21.3).

21.10 IPC: Signals, sleep and wakeup

Although these basic mechanisms have been retained for BSD 4.3 and System V and in the POSIX standard interface (see Section 21.18), they are not discussed again in the later sections of this chapter. The description here includes the extended use of signals in these later versions.

21.10.1 Signals

Signals inform processes of the occurrence of events. They are typically concerned with terminating a process when an error has been detected or an abort character has been typed by the user. They are not a general mechanism for inter-process synchronization since a process does not, in general, wait for a signal, but just tests at certain times to see if a signal has been sent. The exception to this rule is that a parent may **wait** for the death of a child, on **exit**; this mechanism has been included with the signals only in later versions of UNIX. Signals are not for synchronizing with devices or waiting for resources: we shall see how this is done in the next section. The mechanism for sending a signal is as described in Section 6.4, where we saw a bit set in the process descriptor to indicate the occurrence of the associated event. Only one signal of a given type can be recorded and subsequent events of that type are lost if the process does not detect the first signal in time.

The use of the signal mechanism has been extended in later versions of UNIX to allow user-level processes to send signals to each other as well as to allow errors detected in the kernel to be signalled and handled by user-level processes. There are 20 kinds of signal in UNIX BSD 4.3 and 19 in System V.4 and in the POSIX interface.

We shall not study every signal in detail, but broad categories of signals are as follows:

process termination on **exit** and **wait** (see Section 21.8.2);

process-induced exceptions (see Section 3.3.1), for example arithmetic overflow;

unrecoverable conditions during a system call, such as insufficient memory for an **execve** call;

errors associated with system calls, such as illegal call numbers or parameters;

signals between user-level processes, sent by the **kill** system call;

signals related to terminal interaction such as a 'break' which requires the program execution to be aborted;

signals for tracing the execution of a process.

Many of these signals are recorded when a process executes in kernel mode and an error is detected. When a process is about to return to user mode, it checks whether any signals are outstanding and handles them.

We shall see below that a process waiting for a low-priority hardware event or system resource is allowed to handle outstanding signals before waiting, on waking up, or may be woken up to handle the signal then sleep again.

A signal sent from a user process to another user process will only be detected when that process has cause to enter the kernel or is interrupted. Before returning control to the interrupted user-level process a check is made for signals, which are then handled.

21.10.2 Sleep and wakeup

When a process is executing in the kernel it may need to wait for an event to occur, or a resource to become available: for example, for a device to input some data or for a buffer or inode to become free. To achieve this condition synchronization the process executes the *sleep* routine, which transfers it from the runnable state to the blocked state. The thread of control that was the process that has become blocked then enters the scheduler and another process is selected to run. At some stage the thread of control 'becomes' a permanent system process, the swapper; that is, the stack of the swapper is used instead of that of the process that has blocked. Note that the UNIX kernel is being executed procedurally through being entered by user-level processes.

When the event occurs or the resource becomes free the *wakeup* routine is executed. If the event is signalled by an interrupt, the interrupt handler executes *wakeup*. If the event occurs as a result of an action by some process, such as freeing a locked resource, that process executes *wakeup*. Again, we see the procedural method of kernel invocation.

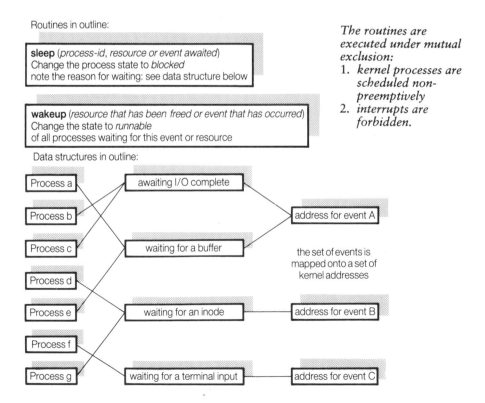

Figure 21.18
Processes sleeping on events and event addresses.

The *wakeup* routine changes the state of any process that was blocked (waiting for the event or resource) to runnable. A number of processes may wait for the same event and all are made runnable. Figure 21.18 illustrates the mechanism. Rather than record the events waited for and occurring in process descriptors, the implementation maps the set of events to a set of kernel addresses. There is not even a one to one mapping of events to addresses, so processes waiting on different events which map to the same address will be awakened when that address is used by the *wakeup* routine.

Non-preemptive scheduling of kernel processes ensures that a process can complete the execution of *sleep* or *wakeup* without interference from another process. An interrupt could occur, however, so interrupts are disabled while the *sleep* and *wakeup* routines manipulate the event–wait data structures. This is to avoid the possibility of 'race conditions' such as the event occurring after the process has decided it must wait but before it is recorded as waiting for the event.

Recall that in Section 6.6 we saw that the priority of a process could be dynamic and could depend on its reason for blocking. This approach is taken here. The kernel sets the priority of the sleeping process according to its reason for sleeping. An additional complexity is that if a process is sleeping with low priority it may be woken up temporarily in response to the arrival of a signal. If it is sleeping at high priority it must wait until the event for which it is waiting occurs.

21.10.3 IPC: summary

Figure 21.19 gives the context for the UNIX IPC mechanisms. It shows a pipe for communication between user-level processes which execute in separate address spaces. It also shows that kernel-level processes execute in shared memory and may therefore communicate through shared data structures.

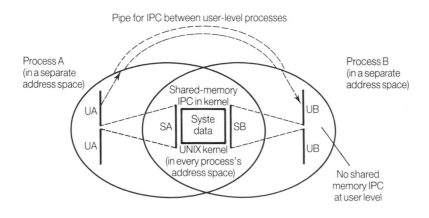

Figure 21.19
UNIX IPC: for user-level and kernel processes.

User-level processes

For user-level processes signals and pipes are available for IPC.

- Signals convey very limited information: that the particular type of event named by the signal has occurred. In the case of death of a child, a byte of status information is passed from the dying child to the waiting parent.
- Only one outstanding signal of a given type can be recorded.
- A process only checks for the occurrence of signals at certain times, such as when it is about to leave the kernel and return to user level. There can be a long delay before a process detects a signal.
- Pipes also offer a limited facility. A pipe is an unstructured byte stream between processes with a common ancestor. This latter restriction is removed by the named pipe facility.
- A process may use a number of different pipes, but is blocked as soon as it attempts to read from an empty pipe, even if its other pipes are not empty.

The model of parallel processing supported is the pipeline and tools are not provided for building server processes which can take requests from many clients.

Kernel processes

- Kernel processes use signals, see above.
- Processes execute the kernel procedurally and use shared data structures for sharing information about resources managed by the kernel. Non-preemptive scheduling prevents interference between processes and no semaphores are needed. Forbidding interrupts, as described for the sleep routine above, prevents race conditions, that is, interference between hardware-driven access to data structures and processes.
- A process will sleep in order to wait for a specific event to occur. Many processes may wait for the same event and all are woken when it occurs. They must therefore re-test the availability of the resource when they are scheduled again and may need to sleep again if some other process has acquired the resource first. The priority of a sleeping process depends on its reason for sleeping. Signals may be handled by low-priority processes when they are about to sleep, are sleeping (they are temporarily wakened), or on awaking.

21.11 Aspects of I/O implementation

Figure 21.20 gives an overview of the kernel modules involved in I/O. I/O management is divided into two separate systems, block I/O and 'character' I/O. Block I/O is used for the disks of the filing system. All other I/O is deemed to be

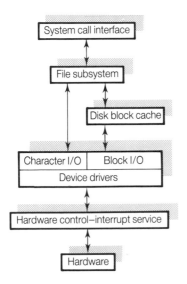

In order to avoid reading and writing the physical disk, blocks which have been used recently are kept in memory in a cache. The cache is always examined first for reads and writes and only if the required blocks are not in the cache does a request go down for disk I/O.

Figure 21.20
I/O handling.

character I/O and this can include block-structured devices with a non-standard block size, for example.

We have already seen that every device is represented in the filing system and has a 'special file' and an inode associated with it. The inode for a special file identifies the associated device driver (major device number) and individual device (minor device number) and indicates whether that device is programmed by block or character I/O.

21.11.1 The disk block cache

For reasons of efficiency, in order to avoid reading and writing the physical disk, blocks which have been used recently are kept in memory in a disk block cache. The cache is always examined first for reads and writes, and only if the required blocks are not in the cache does a request go down to the block I/O system for real disk I/O.

The cache is a shared data structure, accessed by processes which are executing the kernel. Its design must take into account possible concurrent access by processes and by DMA devices as discussed in Part II. Each block in the cache has an associated header which indicates which block of which disk it is and other status information, which includes:

- Is the block busy, that is, currently being read or written (locked for concurrency control)?
- Has the block been written to since it entered the cache? (Is the 'dirty' bit set?)
- Is the block reserved but not yet in receipt of its intended data?

Various pointers are also used to chain the blocks for rapid access by the cache management algorithm.

On a read request the cache is searched for the required block and it is read from the cache if present. If it is not present a cache block must be allocated for the new block. First, a free block is sought from the free block chain. If all blocks are in use a policy is needed to decide which block should be taken over. Typically, the system attempts to reallocate the 'least recently used' block. If the chosen block has been written to (if the dirty bit is set) it must be written out to disk before being overwritten by the new data.

On a write request the cache is searched for the required block. If it is present it is written to and marked dirty. Note that it is not immediately written out to disk. If it is not in the cache a new block must be found as described above for a read.

A substantial disk block cache in main memory increases system performance by reducing the number of disk accesses. A summary of potential problems is as follows:

- It is possible that output which has been acknowledged as done to the process concerned is still in the cache when a crash occurs.

- An application may have ordered the writes to disk carefully. The order may be changed by the cache management algorithm. Data structures on disk may become inconsistent and may be visible to other processes while inconsistent.

- The system cannot give error reports to applications resulting from failed writes to disk since the writes have been decoupled from the associated requests. User-level processes therefore cannot include error handling for this kind of I/O.

For these reasons the implementors of applications may wish to have more control over disk writes than indicated here. UNIX has always included a primitive to flush the cache for a given file and later versions have allowed greater control by the application level. Various strategies have been employed, such as writing dirty blocks to disk at specified times: when a user logs off, or every 30 seconds for example. In some versions of UNIX, changed metadata is written to disk synchronously, leaving the associated changed data to be written asynchronously. Non-volatile memory could be used for implementing the cache.

21.11.2 Device drivers

Device driving will not be discussed in detail since UNIX is not of special interest in this respect. System V's stream facility was designed to provide greater modularity and efficiency in the I/O subsystem and to incorporate network I/O (see Section 21.17.5).

A **disk driver** takes requests from a queue and carries them out. Each request takes the form of a 'transaction record' which indicates whether a read or write should be done and the disk and memory addresses and data sizes involved. The queue will have been sorted into an order which optimizes the head movements, allowing the heads to sweep across the disk surface and back. If the transaction originates from the block I/O system the memory address will indicate a block in the cache. A user area data block may be indicated otherwise.

UNIX maintains a pool of character blocks (c-lists) for **terminal drivers** rather than an input buffer and output buffer per process. Again, terminal handling does not merit detailed discussion.

21.11.3   Low-level exception and interrupt handling

Much of UNIX exception handling is standard, or machine-dependent, as described in Chapter 3. It is worth noting that even exception handling routines are written in the (relatively) high-level language C rather than in assembler. This introduces a small overhead per exception.

The main point of interest to us in the context of concurrent systems and their structures is that interrupts are serviced in the context of the interrupted process. Since there are no dedicated device handler processes there is no process that could be switched to, to take an interrupt from a device.

21.12   Execution of the system by processes

Figure 21.21 shows the situation where three user-level processes have made system calls. As described in Section 3.3, a software interrupt or trap mechanism is used to effect the transfer from user code to system code and the process changes state from user mode to kernel mode. The process number is not changed so, for example, user process 25 becomes system process 25 when it makes a system call and proceeds to execute the kernel.

At this point it seems possible that we might have many processes executing UNIX concurrently. The UNIX design imposes restrictions to ensure that at any time at most one process is runnable and executing the kernel; that is, UNIX is single-threaded.

- A kernel process may run without preemption until it blocks (sleeps), waiting for an event (see Section 21.10.2).
- Any interrupt that occurs is handled in the context of the currently executing process. If a kernel process is interrupted, control is always returned to it; that is, **kernel processes are scheduled non-preemptively.** If a user process is running and the interrupt frees some process then a reschedule is done.

Figure 21.21 indicates that the dedicated kernel processes 0 and 1 are blocked (waiting for swapping to be required and for a terminal line to become active). Two of the user-level processes which have entered the kernel via system calls have blocked, waiting for I/O or other events, by executing the *sleep* routine.

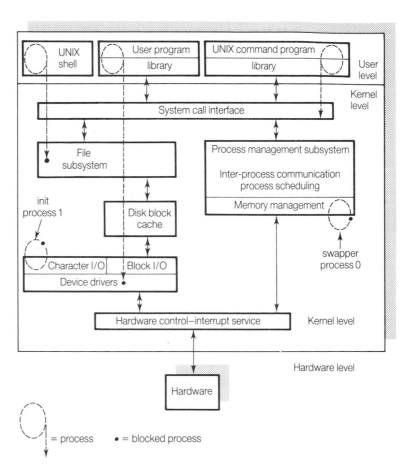

Figure 21.21
UNIX kernel
modules executed
by processes.

The justification for these restrictions is that UNIX is designed for a uniprocessor. Context switching between processes does not get more processing done; indeed, it imposes system overhead. Also, the kernel algorithms may be written to avoid much of the complexity of the kind of concurrency control described in Chapter 10. The assumption of uniprocessor operation underlies the UNIX kernel design and a major rewrite would be needed for a multiprocessor version in order to incorporate fully general, shared-memory concurrency control.

Access to shared kernel data structures by processes executing the kernel is therefore no problem in UNIX. Each process can run until it waits voluntarily and therefore can be guaranteed to execute a critical region without interference from another process. An interrupt could occur, however, while a process is in a critical region. If there is the possibility that a process is accessing a data structure that could be modified by an interrupt handler, interrupts are disabled for that source for the duration of the critical code.

21.13   Process scheduling and swapping

21.13.1   Process scheduling

The previous section has described some aspects of process scheduling; in particular, kernel processes are scheduled non-preemptively. Process scheduling is done on the following basis:

- System processes (executing the kernel) are of higher priority than user processes.

- The priority of a blocked system process is associated with the event it awaits.

- User processes are scheduled with a time quantum. If all processes were to use up their quantum they would execute on a round-robin basis. The scheduling algorithm takes account of the amount of CPU time the process has used in its recent time slices, weighting the most recent highest, and associates a number, effectively a dynamic priority, with each process based on this.

Notice that the scheduling algorithm, like most of the UNIX kernel, will run 'in process'. The final stage of setting up the selected process's registers and passing control to it (dispatching the process) is carried out by the swapper, since that process is guaranteed always to be resident in memory. By the time a process is being dispatched, the previous process that ran the scheduler to select it may have become a candidate for swapping out. Figure 21.22 shows the possible states and state transitions of a UNIX process

21.13.2   The swapping algorithm

UNIX systems always employ swapping in some form. Early systems did not have paging, but this is now commonly available.

Process 0, the swapper, lives throughout the lifetime of the system and is resident in main memory. It runs when an event occurs (the *wakeup* routine is executed) and a process waiting for that event is swapped out. The swapping-in might then be initiated, if appropriate. The swapper also runs periodically, say once a second, to review the processes in main memory and swapped out, and to determine whether any swapping should be started. The original design was simple and aimed to avoid unnecessary transfers.

The algorithm looks for the longest swapped-out process that is runnable and considers swapping it in. If there is free store or a blocked process it can swap out it proceeds. If this is not the case and the process has been swapped out for less than three seconds nothing else happens this time round. If the process has been swapped out for three seconds a runnable process is considered as a candidate for swapping out. If the process has been in main memory for less than two seconds nothing happens at this stage. Otherwise the swapping out and in is initiated.

This simple algorithm means that an event could be signalled to a process that has just been swapped out and the process might be unable to respond for three seconds. Together with the non-preemptive scheduling of kernel processes this property made UNIX unsuitable for any application with real-time response requirements.

21.14 Process states and transitions

Figure 21.22 shows the possible states and transitions of a single UNIX process from creation on **fork** to death on **exit**.

First, a process is created and (eventually) scheduled:

c-rbm: A newly created process is allocated some main memory.

rbm-rk: The process is scheduled according to some arbitrarily assigned initial priority.

rk-ru: The process transfers from kernel to user state.

Then, from user state the process may be interrupted or may make a system call:

ru-rk: A process running in user state makes a system call and becomes a system state process, executing the kernel (see Section 21.12); or an interrupt occurs, such as a device interrupt or the clock, and is

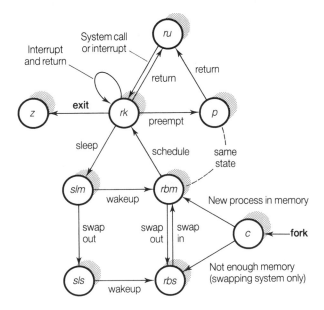

Figure 21.22
UNIX process state transitions.

serviced in system state in the context of this process (see Sections 21.11, 21.12).

rk-ru: Return from system to user state after an interrupt when the interrupt has not made a kernel process runnable or 'timed out' this process, or return to user state after a system call (either immediately or after sleeping, waking up and being scheduled, for example *rk-slm-rbm-rk*).

rk-p: The process is preempted when it is about to transfer to user state. A kernel process may have been made runnable as a result of an interrupt, or a timer interrupt may have caused this process to run out of time.

p-ru: No process in system state is runnable and the preempted process is scheduled to run in user state.

rk-rk: An interrupt occurs and is serviced in the context of the interrupted process. If the process is executing in user state when the interrupt occurs the interrupt mechanism changes the process state to system state.

rk-slm: A process executing kernel code sleeps to wait for an event (see Section 21.10.2).

slm-rbm: The awaited event occurs and the process is made runnable (see Section 21.10.2).

rbm-rk: The process is scheduled according to the priority at which it slept (see Section 21.10.2).

slm-sls: A sleeping process is swapped out (see Section 21.14).

sls-rbs: The awaited event occurs and the process is made runnable, but is still swapped out.

rbs-rbm: The process is swapped in (see Section 21.14).

rbm-rbs: A runnable process is swapped out (see Section 21.14).

c-rbs: There is insufficient main memory available to allocate to a newly created process.

rk-z: The process executes the **exit** system call (*ru-rk*) and is removed from the system. It remains a zombie until its exit code is picked up by its parent (see Section 21.8.2).

A check for signals is made during *rk-slm* and *rbm-rk*, and signals are checked and handled when a process is about to transfer to user state, *rk-ru* and *p-ru* (see Section 21.10.1).

The state diagram again shows the procedural nature of UNIX. System calls are executed in-process (with a change of privilege state). There are no device handler processes so interrupts are handled in the context of the interrupted process. The interrupt mechanism ensures that interrupt processing is done in system state. Notice that a user process never blocks. Doing I/O, IPC or terminating requires a system call and the kernel is entered.

 **21.15 Discussion of basic UNIX, Edition 7**

Many design features are good, particularly for 1970. These include the points listed in Section 21.3. The fact that powerful programs can be composed from UNIX commands is worthy of note. The interchangeability of file, device and inter-process I/O allows generality in programming and flexibility in use of programs, but means that the inter-process communication facility is an unstructured byte stream.

A summary of unsatisfactory aspects of the original UNIX design is now given. A brief indication of how each problem is handled in two major versions of UNIX now available is given when appropriate. These points are expanded in the rest of this chapter. In the next chapter the approach of emulating UNIX (that is, supporting the UNIX system calls above a completely different kernel) is described.

1. The interprocess communication facilities are inadequate as discussed in Section 21.10.3.

    BSD 4.3 provides a general communication facility based on the socket abstraction in which local and remote IPC are integrated. Pipes are supported as part of this new facility.

    The System V shared-memory facility allows processes to share writeable data and provides semaphores for synchronization. Messages are provided to allow processes to send formatted data streams to arbitrary processes (in separate address spaces) on the same machine. Network communication is integrated with a new I/O stream mechanism.

2. Memory management uses only swapping for historical reasons associated with the PDP-11 architecture.

    BSD 4.3 was the first UNIX implementation to provide demand paging (Section 4.8). System V also supports demand paging.

3. Process creation (on **fork**) involves the creation of a new address space for the created process which is a replica of that of the creating process. This involves a great deal of copying and is slow. The created process very often sets up new code and data as soon as it starts to run making all this effort unnecessary.

    BSD 4.3 and System V use the copy-on-write technique (Section 4.9.2).

4. The use of a main memory cache of file buffers with no guarantee that a write to disk has been done on a file write is inadequate for some application areas such as transaction processing.

    A system call which requests an acknowledged, synchronous write to disk is now provided in UNIX systems.

5. UNIX is unsuitable for implementing multi-threaded servers. This is because each process runs in a separate address space, processes cannot share data and system calls are synchronous. If a thread package is used within a single process any thread might block for I/O and block the whole process.

System V provides shared memory. BSD networking provides support for client–server interactions. Synchronous system calls remain a problem.

6. It is impossible to guarantee real-time response because non-preemptive scheduling is used. Also, because UNIX is executed procedurally a good deal of code may be executed 'in process' on behalf of other processes, for example, on returning from kernel mode to user mode after being scheduled. These factors make it difficult to bound the delay between the occurrence of an event and the process that is awaiting it starting to run in user mode.

These problems can only be solved by a complete rewrite of the kernel, as has been done in SunOS 5.0 (Khanna *et al.*, 1992). Processes may be assigned a priority by the application and preemptive scheduling has been implemented. This makes it necessary to protect shared data structures by semaphores. The possible delay on waiting on these semaphores is bounded by using the technique of priority inheritance (see Section 9.5.2).

An alternative to rewriting the kernel is to emulate UNIX above a microkernel, as described in Chapter 22.

7. The kernel cannot run on a multiprocessor because it uses the technique of forbidding interrupts to implement critical regions.

This can only be solved by a complete rewrite of the kernel.

21.16 UNIX BSD 4.3

The University of California at Berkeley were funded by DARPA to add virtual memory management and support for networking to UNIX.

21.16.1 Memory management

Demand paging and page replacement algorithms are described in Chapter 4 and will not be discussed further here. As in original UNIX, BSD UNIX does not allow processes to share their data segments. As always, code may be shared in the form of the text segment.

Memory-mapped files

Data sharing could be achieved by using memory-mapped files (see Section 5.7). A number of system calls, comprising the *mmap* interface, were specified for BSD 4.2 but were not implemented. The *mmap* interface was revised and implemented on SunOS by Sun MicroSystems (Gingell *et al.*, 1987) and a new interface has been proposed for BSD 4.3 (McKusick and Karels, 1987) which supports semaphores and calls to achieve synchronization through them.

The BSD 4.2 *mmap* interface comprises a number of system calls which allow a process to map a file or portion of a file into its address space. Read, write and execute access may be specified for the mapping as well as map-private or map-shared. In the latter case any changes made by a process will be seen by sharing processes.

Copy-on-write

Process creation (on **fork**) is expensive in UNIX. The address space of the creating process is replicated for the created process. Although the text segment can be shared, the data segments were originally copied. This could often be very wasteful since a child process might **execve** a new program immediately after creation and then commit suicide using **exit**. Much of the copied data will be overwritten or unused.

Memory management hardware that allows copy-on-write is useful in these circumstances. When a child is created, the pages of the data segments are no longer copied, but parent and child process each have page tables for these segments. Both processes are given copy-on-write access to these pages. If a process attempts a write access to one of these pages, a copy of that page is made and its location replaces that of the shared page for the writing process. Write access can then be recorded to that page for both processes.

21.16.2 Sockets

BSD 4.3 has integrated local and remote IPC. For compatibility, the pipe can still be used as a special case of a more general facility based on sockets.

The basic concepts are:

socket: an endpoint of communication;

domain: within which sockets are named and communication takes place. A socket operates in a single domain and the address format of the socket depends on that domain. Each domain employs a single protocol suite.

The domains available at present are:

- UNIX (AF-UNIX) for local communication, in which case the address format of a socket is the file system pathname.
- The Internet domain (AF-INET) in which the DARPA protocols such as TCP and UDP over IP are used (see Section 3.10). The address formats are Internet addresses comprising a 32-bit host identifier and a 32-bit port identifier.
- Xerox network services (AF-NS).

Figure 21.23 shows a process with a socket for each of these domains.

There are several types of socket. Each type may or may not be implemented in a given communication domain.

- A **stream socket** provides a reliable duplex data stream, a 'virtual circuit' in communications terminology. There are no record boundaries within the byte stream. In the UNIX domain a pipe may be implemented as a pair of sockets of this type (two communication endpoints). In the INET domain the TCP

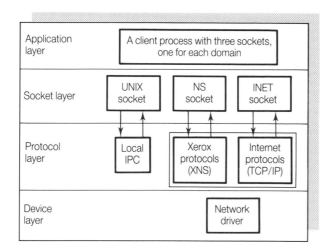

Figure 21.23
Sockets and
domains in UNIX
BSD 4.3.

protocol supports this socket type.

- A **sequenced packet socket** is used in the NS domain, supported by the sequenced packet protocol. These sockets are like stream sockets but, in addition, record boundaries are provided.

- A **datagram socket** will transfer a message of variable size in either direction. This is an unreliable datagram service; that is, there is no guarantee that the order of sending will be preserved on receipt and a datagram might be lost. This type is supported by UDP (the user datagram protocol) in the Internet domain.

- A **reliably delivered message socket** is defined to provide a reliable datagram service and guarantees delivery of a message.

- A **raw socket** allows direct access by processes to the protocols that support the other socket types. This is intended for use in developing new protocols. For example, a new protocol suite to support lightweight connections (a service between streams and datagrams) for multimedia working could be developed above the Ethernet protocol.

Like files, devices and pipes, a socket is used via a descriptor which is a small integer index into the process's 'open file table' (see Figure 21.11).

A socket is created by:

socket-descriptor= **socket** (*domain, socket type, protocol*)

The newly created socket must have a name for another process to use it.

bind (*socket-descriptor, pointer to name, length of name in bytes*)

Two processes which wish to communicate must each create sockets and bind names to them. To establish connection:

> **connect** (*socket-descriptor, pointer to name, length of name in bytes*)

indicates a local descriptor and remote socket name. When both processes have executed **connect** the communication can proceed.

An example of a one-to-one communication is as follows:

ProcessA:

> *sA-id* = **socket** (*AF-INET, stream, default-TCP*)
>   **bind** (*sA-id, <A-socket-name>*)

ProcessB:

> *sB-id* = **socket** (*AF-INET, stream, default-TCP*)
>   **bind** (*sB-id, <B-socket-name>*)

ProcessA:

>   **connect** (*sA-id, <B-socket-name>*)

ProcessB:

>   **connect** (*sB-id, <A-socket-name>*)

In the case of a client–server interaction, the client will know the name of the server but not vice versa. Two additional system calls are provided:

> **listen** (*socket-descriptor, queue-length*)

which the server executes to tell the kernel that it is ready to accept calls for service. It also indicates how many requests the kernel should allow to accumulate.

> *new-socket-descriptor* = **accept** (*socket-descriptor*)

which allows the server to take a single request for connection from a client. A new socket is created for that client. The server process may fork a child process to service the request although parent and child cannot share memory. In this case, the server will continue to listen for new requests at the well-known address.

An example of a client–server interaction is as follows:

Client processC:

> *sC-id* =   **socket** (*AF-INET, stream, default-TCP*)
>   **bind** (*sC-id, <Client-socket-name>*)

Server processS:

> *sS-id* =   **socket** (*AF-INET, stream, default-TCP*)
>   **bind** (*sS-id, <Server-socket-name>*)

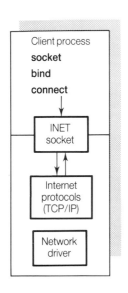 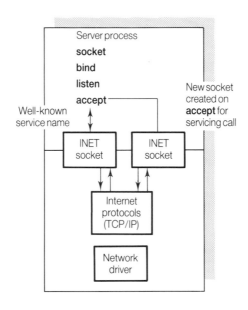

Figure 21.24
Client–server
interaction using
sockets.

ProcessC:

> **connect** (*sC-id*, *<Server-socket-name>*)

ProcessS:

> **listen** (*sS-id*, *<queue-length>*)
> *sN-id* =   **acccpt** (*sS-id*)

Figure 21.24 shows a client–server interaction. The server creates and names a socket to function as the 'well-known' address of the service. A client **connects** to that well-known name.

The **close** system call closes a connection and destroys a socket, whereas the **shutdown** call allows one direction of the duplex connection to be closed. There are other calls such as **getsockname, getsockopt** and **setsockopt**.

The above discussion relates to connection-oriented communication. Connectionless communication using datagram sockets is achieved by

byte-count = **sendto**   (*socket descriptor, data-buffer-pointer and length,*
                          address-buffer-pointer and length)
byte-count = **recvfrom**   (*socket descriptor, data-buffer-pointer and length,*
                          address-buffer-pointer and length)

The number of bytes transferred is returned in each case. The address buffer contains the destination address on **sendto** and the source address is supplied by the system on **recvfrom**.

21.17 UNIX System V.4

The facilities for inter-process communication and networking are outlined here. Full details of their use and implementation can be found in Bach (1986). Other extensions and improvements will not be discussed. Again, memory management based on paged segments has been incorporated and a copy-on-write mechanism is used to make process creation more efficient.

21.17.1 Messages

There are four system calls to support message passing between arbitrary processes on the same machine.

$$
\begin{aligned}
msgqid = \quad &\textbf{msgget} \quad (key, flag) \\
&\textbf{msgsnd} \quad (msgqid, msg, count, flag) \\
count = \quad &\textbf{msgrcv} \quad (id, msg, maxcount, type, flag) \\
&\textbf{msgctl} \quad (id, cmd, mstatbuf)
\end{aligned}
$$

Messages are buffered in the kernel. A table of message queue headers is maintained as shown in Figure 21.25 and a message is sent to or received from a message queue. A message queue is identified by a user-specified integer key which is recorded in the message queue header. A process effectively 'opens' a message queue using the **msgget** system call which returns a small integer descriptor, the *msgqid*. This call is also used to create a new queue. A *msgqid* must be specified when a message is sent and received.

The queue header indicates which process created the queue, which processes may send messages to and receive messages from the queue and other information. The implementation can impose restrictions on the maximum message size and the maximum number of bytes that a queue may buffer.

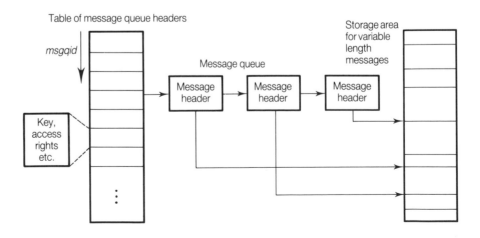

Figure 21.25
System V support for message passing.

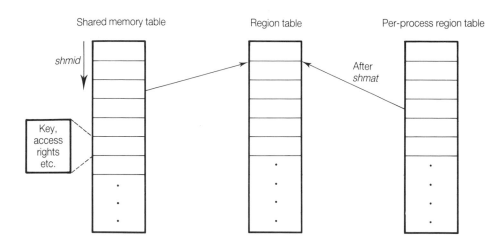

Figure 21.26
System V support
for shared memory.

21.17.2 Shared memory

The system calls for using shared memory are similar to those for messages. The **shmget** system call creates a new region of shared memory or returns an existing one. The **shmat** call logically attaches a region to the virtual address space of a process. The **shmdt** detaches a region from the virtual address space of a process and **shmctl** is concerned with manipulating various parameters. After a region of shared memory is attached to the virtual address space of a process it is read and written like any other memory, and not via system calls.

As for the message mechanism, a region of shared memory is identified by a user-specified key and used via a small integer descriptor (see Figure 21.26). An entry in the shared memory table contains the key and access control information on which processes may access the region. An access check is made on **shmget** and, if it is successful, the descriptor *shmid* is returned.

The system calls are:

$shmid$ =   **shmget** (*key, size, flag*)
$virtaddr$ = **shmat**   (*shmid, addr, flags*)
              shmdt   (*addr*)
              shmctl (*shmid, cmd, shmstatbuf*)

The virtual address returned by **shmat** may or may not be that specified by the address parameter.

21.17.3 Semaphores for shared user-level memory

Semaphores are needed so that processes may synchronize their activities. System V semaphores are a generalization of those defined in Chapter 9. An array of semaphores can be manipulated atomically; that is, the specified

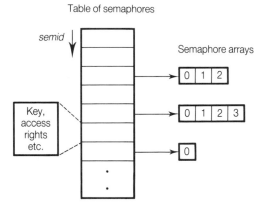

Table of semaphores

Figure 21.27
System V support
for semaphores.

operations will be done on all the elements of a semaphore array or none will be done. Each semaphore in an array is implemented by:

- an integer value;
- the process identifier of the last process to manipulate the semaphore;
- the number of processes waiting for the value to increase;
- the number of processes waiting for the value to equal 0.

The system calls are **semget** to create and gain access to an array of semaphores, **semctl** to carry out various control operations and **semop** to manipulate the semaphore values. As for messages and shared memory regions, each semaphore array is identified by a user-specified key and used via a small integer descriptor (see Figure 21.27).

$$semid = \quad \textbf{semget} \quad (key, count, flag)$$
$$oldval = \quad \textbf{semop} \quad (semid, oplist, count)$$
$$\textbf{semctl} \quad (semid, cmd, shmstatbuf)$$

21.17.4 Discussion of System V IPC

The IPC package has introduced a new type of name for messages, memory regions and semaphores: the key. These integers can be made to identify objects uniquely within a single system, but do not generalize for use in distributed systems. System V integrates device and network I/O, rather than integrating local and remote IPC (see below).

The tools provided are powerful, and can be used effectively by special-purpose applications.

A criticism of the basic design is that there is no equivalent to a **close** system call so the kernel has no record of which processes are accessing a given item. Processes are therefore able to bypass the **get** system calls and guess and use an ID, provided that they satisfy the access control specification. Also, the kernel cannot detect and remove unused IPC items.

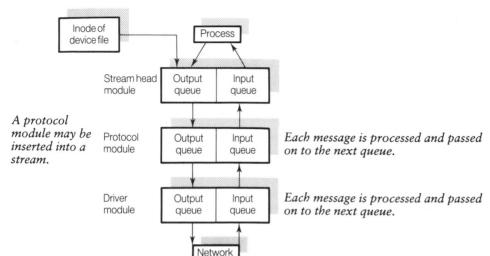

A protocol module may be inserted into a stream.

Each message is processed and passed on to the next queue.

Each message is processed and passed on to the next queue.

Figure 21.28
System V streams
for network I/O.

Some of the facilities offered can be achieved by other mechanisms, such as pipes, files and signals.

21.17.5 Streams for networking in System V

The UNIX I/O subsystem has been restructured in System V to provide greater modularity, flexibility and efficiency.

A stream is a full duplex connection between a process and a device driver which may contain a protocol to process data *en route*.

A stream consists of a number of linearly linked queue pairs, one member of each pair for input and the other for output (see Figure 21.28). Each queue pair is associated with a kernel module such as a device driver. Each queue contains a list of messages which are processed and passed on to the next queue in the stream.

The driver modules manipulate the data passsed through the queues by calling operations on the queues. Each queue is an abstract data type with operations:

open, called during an **open** system call;
close, called during a **close** system call;
put, to pass a message into the queue;
service, called when a queue is scheduled to execute;

and data:

a pointer to the next queue in the stream;
a pointer to a list of messages awaiting service;
a pointer to a private data structure that maintains the state of the queue;
flags etc. for managing the queue size, flow control and scheduling.

21.18 The POSIX standard

The ideal for an application programer is that a program written for one of the many versions of UNIX should run on any other. We have seen an apparent divergence rather than this desirable uniformity.

UNIX has been subject to several standardization initiatives, the most notable being that of the IEEE POSIX committee. This committee has produced a standard (IEEE 1003.1) for UNIX system calls (library functions) (see IEEE, 1988). Other documents published by the committee relate to the standardization of features of UNIX such as networking, the shell and utility programs, real-time extensions, security extensions and system administration.

POSIX achieves a reasonable degree of compatibility with BSD and System V by, on the whole, including the system calls they have in common and excluding their differences. It therefore bears a strong resemblance to Edition 7. It deviates from Edition 7 in the support for signals, which is close to BSD's, and terminal handling, which is new. POSIX has been adopted by both the AT&T-led UNIX International (UI) and the Open Software Foundation (OSF).

21.19 Summary

The original UNIX design was small and comprehensible. Some of its features were dictated by the PDP-11 architecture with which it was closely associated in its early years. If a design decision required a choice to be made between simplicity and efficiency, the former was chosen.

We studied the original design, including its well-known deficiencies. We then looked at how some of the major deficiencies have been addressed in the two most commonly used versions of UNIX: Berkeley's BSD 4.3 and UNIX System Laboratory's System V.4. In both cases a very large system has been produced with several ways of achieving any given task. The design is no longer clean and simple.

The assumption that UNIX will run on a uniprocessor permeates the design of the kernel. There have been some rewrites of the kernel for multiprocessor and real-time systems, for example SunOS 5.0. The UNIX system call interface is supported (emulated) by a number of microkernels. We shall study two of these in the next chapter (Mach and CHORUS), which are fully compatible with BSD 4.3 and System V.4 respectively.

Exercises

21.1 (a) What is meant by saying that UNIX is a procedural system? How might the hardware support or assume this style of system design (see Sections 8.3 and 4.11 for an example)?
(b) How does procedural execution of the kernel affect the design of the mechanism for synchronization between the hardware and processes?
(c) How might a procedural design make it difficult to guarantee a bound for the time between an event occurring and a process that was waiting for it running at user level?

21.2 Assume that all the directories and files in the following pathname and all the inodes except that of the root are on disk rather than in main memory. Assume that each directory may be read by a single disk access. How many disk reads would it take to resolve the pathname:

/usr/guru/examples/C-examples/C-prog

21.3 (a) Suppose a filing system uses a 4 kbyte block size and a block pointer occupies 4 bytes. What size of file can be accessed from 12 direct pointers in an inode? What size of file can be accessed from 12 direct pointers and 2 indirect pointers (see Section 21.6)? What size of file could be accessed with an additional triple indirect pointer?
(b) Figure 21.11 shows the system open file table. Each entry contains a pointer into an open file for use in reading and writing. If the table is designed so that this pointer occupies 4 bytes, how large can a file be?

21.4 Suppose that an instructor has written a skill-testing game program called */usr/boss/tester*. Her pupils are to run the program which will record their scores in a file called */usr/boss/scores*.

How should the instructor set up the access permissions of the two files so that the scores of the pupils can be recorded but only by running the program */usr/boss/tester*?

Are the pupil's files accessible to the *tester* program while they are running it?

21.5 What are the advantages and disadvantages of using process-relative names, such as small integers, for open files, pipes, sockets etc?

21.6 Contrast the effect of the UNIX **fork** system call with that of the language-level fork described in Sections 7.4.1, 10.2.4 and 11.8.

21.7 (a) The UNIX command interpreter (shell) is run as a user-level process. Explain how the shell sets up a process to execute a command and how the command's arguments might be passed to it.

(b) How would you arrange to run your own command interpreter instead of the standard shell?

21.8 UNIX keeps a pool of character buffers of a defined size (say, 32 characters) for terminal I/O. Work out in some detail how a character would be delivered by a device, accepted by an interrupt handler, checked to see whether any special action should be taken (for example on a break or flow control character) and put in a buffer.

21.9 UNIX keeps a cache of disk block buffers. Each buffer has a data area which is the size of a disk block and a header for control information. What information would you keep in the header to control the use of the buffers and to ensure mutually exclusive access to them?

21.10 A process creates and opens a file and a pipe then creates two child processes. Which system calls can the children use to access both the file and the pipe? Which system calls can be used for the file but not for the pipe?

21.11 Extend Figure 21.11 to show two independent sharers of an open file and two sharers of a file which have inherited it from a common ancestor.

21.12 Are UNIX signals a general inter-process synchronization mechanism? Discuss.

21.13 Why is there no need for semaphores in the UNIX kernel?

21.14 How might a crash make a UNIX filing system inconsistent? Consider a sequence of events that might lose a block to the filing system or might cause a block to be recorded as allocated both to a file and to the free list. How does the way UNIX records the blocks allocated to files help to make consistency checks relatively easy?

21.15 Find a list of UNIX commands. Outline how a spelling checker program could be written by composing UNIX commands in a pipeline.

Microkernels

CONTENTS

Conventional operating systems have become large and unwieldy. They are difficult to comprehend, develop and maintain. The addition of new facilities often means that a given task can be done in a number of different ways. Section 2.4 introduced the microkernel approach: it is argued that the kernel should have the minimum functionality necessary to support:

- the management of the hardware interface;
- processes (or whatever term is used to indicate the unit of computation and scheduling on a processor);
- inter-process communication;
- minimal memory management: handling MMU exceptions for example.

Other functions such as the file service and much of memory management and communications handling can be provided above the kernel and run as user-level processes. The efficiency penalty of offering services at user level is offset by the greater efficiency of a streamlined kernel.

There is a vast amount of existing software that runs on conventional operating systems such as UNIX. If a microkernel is to form the basis of a workstation programming support environment as well as high-performance special-purpose servers, it must be possible to run existing applications software above it. Several microkernel projects have emulated the UNIX interface; that is, servers running at user level above the microkernel will accept UNIX system calls and translate them into calls on the microkernel. In theory, it should be easy to use the simple abstractions provided at the microkernel interface to build higher-level services. In practice, emulating an existing system is a huge undertaking and some aspects of the existing design may impose undesirable constraints on the new one.

A number of microkernels have been developed within university computer science departments. Some of the research projects have gone on to seek funding for development as standards or commercial products. It is interesting to see how long this process takes. In the last chapter we traced the evolution of UNIX from a research activity within Bell Telephone Research Laboratories, starting in 1969, to a worldwide commercial success 15–20 years later. In this chapter we examine some research activities that started in the late 1970s and early 1980s in the area of kernel design for distributed systems.

Other microkernels could have been selected for description here, for example, V (Cheriton, 1984; Cheriton and Zwaenpoel, 1985), Amoeba (Mullender and Tanenbaum, 1986; Tanenbaum *et al.*, 1990), Sprite (Ousterhout *et al.*, 1988) and the object-oriented systems mentioned in Section 14.1. Mach and CHORUS were chosen because they are closely associated with the two versions of UNIX that were described in the last chapter. In each case their evolution is traced, showing the lessons learned, the integration of research results in the field and the developments that became possible as technology improved.

The case studies in this chapter are **distributed** operating system **microkernels**. Underlying architectural support for naming, location, protection and authentication are needed before IPC can take place in a distributed system. The same requirements were highlighted in Chapters 14 and 20, and Section 14.9 discussed these issues.

The final case study is taken from the work at the author's Laboratory. This shows an evolution of network technology and the distributed systems built to exploit it. Current research directions are outlined in order to show the kinds of requirements that will be placed on the next generation of microkernels.

22.1   The evolution from RIG through Accent to Mach

The University of Rochester's Intelligent Gateway (RIG) was designed to support access to external networks. This kernel design dates from the late 1970s and uses asynchronous message passing as the basic IPC mechanism (Rashid, 1986; Ball *et al.*, 1976; Lantz *et al.*, 1982). Abstractions supported were (refer to Chapter 12 and Figure 22.1):

- **process** A protected address space with a single thread of program control. Each process had an identifier comprising its host identifier and an identifier within the host system.

- **port** A RIG port was a kernel-provided queue for messages and was referenced by a global identifier (process number, port number) where the process number includes a host identifier. A RIG port was protected in the sense that it could only be manipulated by the RIG kernel, but it was unprotected in the sense that any process could send a message to a port.

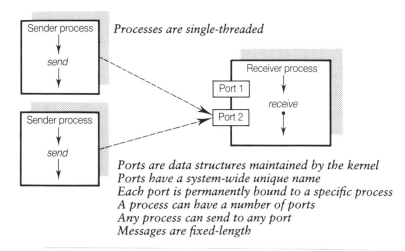

Figure 22.1
RIG (1980–1986)
IPC.

- **message** A RIG message comprised a header followed by data. Messages were of limited size (up to 2 kbyte) and could contain at most two scalar data items or two array objects. Port identifiers were passed in messages as simple integers for interpretation by the receiving process.

A client-server style of interaction was used and a request for service was sent to a port of a process. Processes were single-threaded. RIG was heavily used for networking and aspects of the design that caused problems were seen to be:

- Because ports were tied explicitly to processes it was not possible to move a service at a well-known port from one process to another without notifying all parties. Also, a port identifier contained a host identifier as part of its process identifier field. This made it difficult to move a service to a new host if its existing host failed.

- The limited message size was a source of inefficiency: it increased the message traffic and made client–server interactions more complex than necessary.

- The fact that ports were represented as global identifiers that could be constructed and used by any process meant that a process could not limit the set of processes that could send it a message. Each process had to be prepared to accept any possible message from any process in the system. A single faulty process could flood the entire system with messages.

- The fact that ports were represented as global identifiers that were passed as simple integers meant that the system could not determine the dependencies between processes. Processes had to register their dependencies explicitly in order to receive event-driven failure notifications.

RIG ran until 1986 and the experience gained was used in the design of the Accent kernel at Carnegie-Mellon University (CMU). The Accent design dates from the early 1980s when a kernel was needed for the Spice distributed personal workstation project at CMU.

22.1.1 Accent

The Accent design (Rashid and Robertson, 1981; Fitzgerald and Rashid, 1987) retains the port abstraction but enforces protection on ports. It also uses virtual memory techniques to overcome the limitations in handling large objects. A client–server style of interaction is supported based on asynchronous message passing. A port is no longer bound permanently to a process and a message is addressed to a port instead of to a port of a process. Processes are single-threaded. The Accent abstractions are as follows (refer to Chapter 12 and Figure 22.2):

- **process** A 4 Gbyte paged address space with a single thread of program control. Processes may send and receive messages according to their access rights for ports. When a process is created, the kernel also creates a port, the kernel port of the process, to represent it. The state of the process and its virtual memory can be manipulated by sending messages to its kernel port, for example to stop or kill it. By default, only a process and its parent have access to its kernel port.

- **port** A port is a kernel-protected queue for messages. At any time it has a maximum queue length, but this can be changed. Several options are open to a process that attempts to send to a full port; it may block and be notified by

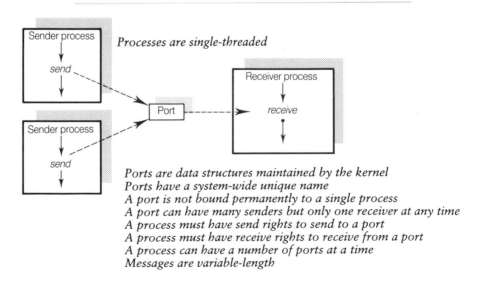

Figure 22.2
Accent IPC.

Processes are single-threaded

Ports are data structures maintained by the kernel
Ports have a system-wide unique name
A port is not bound permanently to a single process
A port can have many senders but only one receiver at any time
A process must have send rights to send to a port
A process must have receive rights to receive from a port
A process can have a number of ports at a time
Messages are variable-length

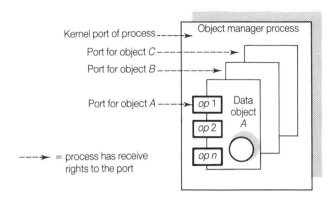

Kernel port of process ----
Port for object *C* ----
Port for object *B* ----

Port for object *A* ----

---→ = process has receive
       rights to the port

Object manager process

op 1   Data
          object
op 2   *A*

op n

Figure 22.3
Accent process
(and Mach task) as
object manager.

the kernel when space is available or may request the kernel to buffer one message, but no more.

Ports may have many senders, but only one receiver. Access to a port is granted by receiving a message containing a port capability to either send or receive.

A port has a global name which does not bind it permanently to a specific process or host.

Ports are used by processes to represent services or data abstractions; that is, a process can act as the manager of data objects and has receive rights for the ports of the objects it manages (see Figure 22.3). The port is a global name for the data object (refer to Sections 14.9 and 20.3).

● **message** An Accent message consists of a fixed-length header and a variable-sized collection of typed data objects. Messages may contain port identifiers and references to data provided they are properly typed. The maximum message size for by-value data is an entire address space, 4 Gbyte.

Messages can be sent asynchronously or synchronously. The default semantics of message passing are that the data is copied and available to both sender and receiver. Memory mapping is used to avoid physical copying; above a certain message size the message is mapped copy-on-write for sender and receiver (see Section 4.9.2). If asynchronous message passing is invoked, the message is mapped copy-on-write in the sender's address space on *send* and is mapped into the kernel's address space. On *receive* it is mapped copy-on-write into the receiver's address space and removed from the kernel's.

● **memory object** A kernel-provided repository for persistent data. A memory object is any object which supports data read and write operations. It is held in persistent storage.

Each entry of an Accent process's virtual memory table maps a contiguous region of the process's virtual memory to a contiguous portion of a memory object.

The Accent kernel can itself be viewed as a process with its own 4 Gbyte paged virtual address space and port access rights. The main purpose of the Accent

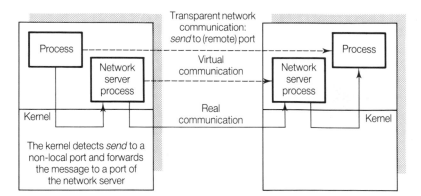

Figure 22.4
Accent (and
Mach) network IPC.

kernel is to provide an execution environment for user processes and an IPC facility.

The kernel's IPC facility provides communication only between processes on the same machine. However, its IPC facility and virtual memory support are designed to be extended by user-state, server processes.

- **Page servers** may handle the paging in and out of the pages of memory objects; for example, a new page reference is trapped by the kernel which sends a message to the appropriate port of the paging server for that memory object. That is, a process can provide virtual memory for a mapped object in a way appropriate to the application. The kernel provides minimal memory management in the form of a default pager.

- **Network servers** handle external communication. When a message is sent to a port which the kernel detects is not local, the message is passed to a network server process. This process is responsible for locating the remote port and managing the communication to it. This method is described in Section 14.9.2 and shown in Figure 22.4.

  Note that a message can be sent across a network 'copy-on-reference'. On *send*, the message is mapped into the address space of the local network server which can act as a remote page server and transfer the pages of the message as they are referenced by the destination process.

  Note that all file access is provided through the memory management system; there is no separate file I/O (see Section 5.7). A process making a request for a large file will receive the whole file in a single message from a file server process and will receive pages on access as described above.

A package was provided for Accent to enable software that had been developed to run above UNIX to run in the Spice environment. Accent's single threaded processes make it unsuitable for multiprocessors.

22.2 Mach

The previous section on the Accent kernel should be read before this section on the Mach kernel. Many features of Accent were retained when the time came for a successor to be developed for new generations of hardware. As discussed in Chapter 21, UNIX could only be made to run on multiprocessors by a complete rewrite of the kernel. Mach was chosen for support by DARPA to emulate the BSD 4.3 UNIX interface and to provide multiprocessor operation. Mach was also selected by the Open Software Foundation to form the basis of their operating system OSF/1. Mach release 2.5 has many UNIX services still integrated with the Mach kernel. Mach release 3.0 has all UNIX functionality moved up to the application level.

Mach is fully binary compatible with BSD 4.3 and also offers the following facilities:

- Support for tightly coupled and loosely coupled general-purpose multiprocessors, not available in UNIX or Accent.

- Support for large, sparse virtual address spaces, 'copy-on-write' virtual copy operations and memory-mapped files (Rashid *et al.*, 1987; Tevanian *et al.*, 1987). Memory-mapped files were proposed for UNIX BSD 4.2 but not implemented. Accent used memory-mapping techniques for IPC and these have been extended in Mach.

- Provision for user-supplied memory objects and user-level page managers for them. This approach is familiar from Accent and assists in the kernelization of any operating system.

- Multiple threads of control within a single address space. Not available in Accent or UNIX.

- A message-based IPC facility which is integrated with memory management and allows large amounts of data to be transferred using the 'copy-on-write' technique, the approach taken in Accent.

- Transparent network IPC. As in Accent, this is achieved by a user-level network server, and also by port names which are independent of 'processes' (Mach tasks) and network addresses.

- Protection of interprocess communication which extends across network boundaries. As in Accent this is achieved through protected port names and send and receive rights for ports. Mach also has security extensions which are not covered here. Encryption is available for network communication (Sansom *et al.*, 1986).

- An internal, symbolic kernel debugger. A new facility.

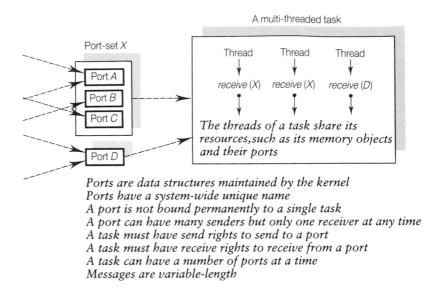

A multi-threaded task

Port-set *X*

Port *A*
Port *B*
Port *C*

Port *D*

Thread   Thread   Thread

receive (*X*)   *receive* (*X*)   *receive* (*D*)

*The threads of a task share its
resources, such as its memory objects
and their ports*

*Ports are data structures maintained by the kernel
Ports have a system-wide unique name
A port is not bound permanently to a single task
A port can have many senders but only one receiver at any time
A task must have send rights to send to a port
A task must have receive rights to receive from a port
A task can have a number of ports at a time
Messages are variable-length*

Figure 22.5
Mach IPC.

22.2.1   The Mach basic abstractions

It can be seen from the above that Mach, like Accent, is a message-passing
kernel. The Mach kernel supports six basic abstractions (see also Figure 22.5):

- **task** An execution environment and the basic unit of resource allocation.
  This includes a paged virtual address space and access to the system
  resources such as processors, ports, capabilities for using ports and virtual
  memory.

- **thread** The basic unit of execution. A thread executes in the address space
  of a single task. A thread shares the resources allocated to the task with
  other threads in the task.

- **port** A one-way communication channel implemented as a message queue
  managed by the kernel. All communication takes place via ports.

- **port set** A group of ports that are treated as a logical unit. The port set has
  a single queue.

- **message** A collection of typed data objects used in communication between
  threads. Data may be contained by value or by reference. Port rights are
  obtained in this way.

- **memory object** An object usually residing in secondary storage that is
  mapped into the address space of a task.

Note that the 'process' of RIG and Accent has been replaced by the two concepts 'task' and 'thread'.

22.2.2 Mach IPC

As in Accent, message passing is the essential service of the system and is used both for communication between threads of different tasks and between a thread and the kernel. Ports, port names and port rights are similar to those of Accent. In order to use a port it is necessary to have the appropriate access rights. The *send* right indicates that a thread may send a message to a port. The *receive* right indicates that a thread may de-queue messages from a port.

The port name is a capability (see Section 14.9). The use of a random component in the port name, and encryption techniques for generating and checking port names, ensures that a port name cannot be guessed or forged, and that *send* and *receive* rights cannot be forged. The security measures in Mach are discussed in Sansom *et al.* (1986).

The new concept of port set allows ports to share a single message queue and a thread running in a task to service a number of ports. The thread can determine from the specific port to which the message was sent, which object should be invoked or which service done. If a port belongs to a set it may not also be addressed directly by a *receive*.

As in Accent both synchronous and asynchronous message passing are supported. Mach also supports an RPC (request–response) primitive, with the ability to specify timeouts for *send* and *receive* (compare Amoeba, Cambridge and Chorus V3). Higher-level RPC can easily be built on this.

Like Accent, Mach uses virtual memory techniques to allow large amounts of data to be transmitted. When a thread in a task *send*s a large message, the data is mapped into a special address space used by the kernel, called the *ipc-map*. The data is also remapped copy-on-write in the sender's address space so that if the sender writes to the data new pages are generated, leaving the message intact. When a thread of the destination task performs a *receive* operation, the data is mapped into the receiver's address space. If many large messages are in transit, the *ipc-map* address space could become full.

The tight integration of the Mach IPC and VM systems gives high performance for large, intra-node messages. Small messages are costly due to the large VM manipulation overhead. This has been identified as an area for further study by the Mach developers.

Messages destined for ports on a different machine suffer a level of indirection through the network server task, as explained above for Accent and as shown in Figure 22.4. This penalty could be reduced by putting such servers in the kernel.

22.2.3 Memory objects and object sharing in main memory

The Mach design is object-oriented. A port is the means by which an object is referenced. An operation on an object is invoked by sending a message to the port which represents the object; see Figure 22.3. When an object is mapped into the address space of a task, the object is a resource of the task and therefore shared by all its threads. Only one task may have receive access rights to a given port at any time, but any thread in that task may use the port to receive messages.

The primary role of memory management in the microkernel is to manage physical memory as a cache of the contents of persistent memory objects. If an object has been mapped into the address space of a task and a thread of another task requests to map the same object, two problems must be solved. First, the kind of sharing that is required must be specified: private copy or single copy. If each task wants a private copy of the object, the copy-on-write technique is used to minimize data copying. An example of this situation is when a child is forked and a new address space is created for it (see Section 21.8). Second, if two or more private copies of an object exist in main memory, which have diverged from the copy on disk, then these versions must be managed. Mach uses shadow copies of objects for this purpose. Details can be found in Tevanian *et al.* (1987).

22.2.4   Task and thread creation

Task creation is similar to UNIX process creation (see Section 21.8). A task is created as a result of a **fork** system call, but there is finer-grained control of the inheritance of memory. Instead of the whole virtual address space being replicated for the child, the parent may specify which regions are to be inherited and whether they are to be shared or private (implemented as copy-on-write). A task is created with a single thread which, as in UNIX, starts execution at the instruction after fork. When a task is suspended, all its threads are suspended. A new task is created with a kernel port.

22.2.5   The C threads package

Like UNIX, Mach is written in C. A threads package has been provided for C which provides shared variables, mutual exclusion for critical regions and condition variables for synchronization (see Chapter 10).

Threads are managed via calls to the following routines:

cthread-fork: creates a new thread within a task. It is given a function to execute and a parameter, or a pointer to parameters, as input (see Sections 7.4.1, 10.2.4 and 11.8). The created thread executes concurrently with the creating thread. The creating thread is returned the *thread-id* of the created thread.

cthread-exit: destroys the calling thread. If the thread is not detached a value is returned to the thread which originally created it (see Section 21.8.2).

cthread-join: waits for a child thread to terminate and to receive a value (see Section 21.8).

cthread-detach: the parent disowns the child – it will never be joined.

cthread-yield: the thread yields the processor – it indicates to the scheduler
                     that another thread should be run at this time.

Mutual exclusion is achieved through the use of 'spin locks' (see Section 9.2);
that is, the thread busy waits for the lock to become free (repeatedly tests the
lock) instead of being suspended. The calls available are:

mutex-alloc: creates a variable for use as a mutual exclusion lock.

mutex-free: deallocates the specified variable.

mutex-lock   requests to lock the specified mutex variable. If the mutex was
                     unlocked it will be locked. If the mutex was already locked
                     the thread will spin (busy wait). The package does not guar-
                     antee bounded delay or freedom from deadlock.

mutex-unlock: unlocks the specified mutex variable; similar to a *signal* opera-
                     tion on a semaphore.

Condition variables are used for condition synchronization. A familiar example
is that a producer thread may achieve exclusive access to a bounded buffer only
to find that the buffer is full. A condition variable may be associated with a
mutex variable to implement a monitor-like program structure. The calls available are:

condition-alloc: creates a condition variable.

condition-free: deletes the specified condition variable.

condition-wait: unlocks the associated mutex variable and suspends the
                     thread on the condition variable until it is signalled. The
                     implementation does not guarantee that the condition sig-
                     nalled still holds when the freed thread is scheduled and runs
                     again. The freed thread must therefore be resumed at its exe-
                     cution of *condition-wait* and with the associated mutex
                     locked.

condition-signal: signals the condition variable.

Further information on the C threads package may be found in Cooper and
Draves (1987).

22.2.6   Real-time extensions

There have been several attempts at providing real-time extensions to the microkernel. The Advanced Real-Time Technology (ART) group at CMU is developing a real-time version of the Mach microkernel and a real-time toolset for
system design and analysis (Tokuda *et al.*, 1990). This new microkernel includes
an integrated, time-driven scheduler, real-time synchronization and memory-
resident objects. Nakajima *et al.* (1991) describes real-time extensions to the
microkernel specifically to support multimedia applications.

22.3 CHORUS

CHORUS was started as a research project at INRIA in France in 1979. It was conceived as a small communications-oriented multiprocessor kernel with both system and application services exchanging messages via ports. CHORUS has evolved from version V0 to the current version V3 (Rozier *et al.*, 1988). The first two versions were concerned with research into a message passing kernel design. V2 saw the start of the attempt to provide UNIX compatibility and distribution of UNIX services. An implementation of UNIX System V, called CHORUS/MIX, has been built on top of CHORUS. CHORUS is now developed by CHORUS Systèmes Inc. and, under an agreement with UNIX System Laboratories Inc., CHORUS/MIX and System V Release 4 will evolve in step.

The CHORUS V2 IPC abstractions (location transparency, untyped messages, asynchronous and RPC protocols, ports and port groups) were found to be well suited to the implementation of distributed operating systems and applications. As we have seen in other kernels developed at this time, only single-threaded 'actors' were supported in V2. CHORUS is written in C++. A detailed evaluation of V2 and rationale for the design of V3, can be found in Bricker *et al.* (1991).

The experience gained with V2 led to work on version V3 which has the general aim of demonstrating the commercial feasibility of the microkernel approach to distributed operating system design, and specific aims as follows:

- **portability** This aim motivated the design of an architecture-independent memory management system (V2 was hardware-specific).

- **generality** The primitives provided by the microkernel should be sufficiently general that a number of operating systems could be built above it. Some UNIX-specific features were removed from V2.

- **compatibility** V2 was source-compatible with UNIX. V3 is binary compatible both for applications and device drivers.

- **real-time** The microkernel should be usable for process control and telecommunications applications which have requirements for responsiveness.

- **performance** is essential for commercial viability. The modular structuring and message passing approach should not reduce performance below that of a monolithic operating system.

22.3.1 The CHORUS V3 basic abstractions

The basic abstractions of CHORUS V3 are as follows (see also Figure 22.6):

- **actor** An address space, the unit of resource allocation. The kernel distinguishes between two types of actor, system actors and user actors. Some kernel services can only be executed by threads belonging to system actors and system actors may be created so that they use the kernel address space instead of a separate address space. These are called **supervisor actors**.

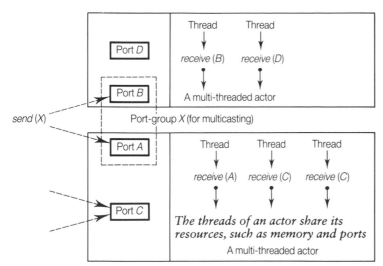

Ports are regions within actors that are maintained by the kernel
Ports, port-groups and actors have system-wide unique names
A port is not bound permanently to a single actor, but can migrate
A port can have many senders but only one actor receiver at any time
An actor can have a number of ports at a time
Messages are variable-length and untyped

Figure 22.6
CHORUS IPC.

Supervisor actors are, however, separate entities and are compiled, link edited and loaded independently. They are seen to be the most fundamental enhancement of V2 (Bricker *et al.*, 1991). It is interesting to note the experimental removal of functions from the kernel in V2 and their return for reasons of efficiency in V3.

- **thread** The basic unit of execution. A thread executes in the address space of a single actor. The kernel provides facilities for thread synchronization and the allocation of priorities to threads (a 'real-time' feature). It is possible to arrange that a number of threads run on the same processor and also to arrange that threads are scheduled to run on different processors of a multiprocessor (see Section 6.7).

- **message** An untyped string of bytes.

- **port** A region within an actor where messages for that actor are received. Any thread having knowledge of a port can send messages to it. A port is attached to a single actor at any time, but can migrate from one actor to another (as a result of a system call), with or without the messages it contains.

- **port group** Ports may be grouped together dynamically to form port groups. This supports multicasting (see Section 12.5.6) in that a message sent to the port group is sent to each port of the group.

Actors, ports and port groups were found to be basic abstractions that should be provided in a microkernel. V2 had experimented with providing some aspects of their management above the kernel.

- **UIs** Actors, ports and port groups all have **unique identifiers** which are global, location-independent and unique in time and space. (In V2 global names were not made available to actors. Local, actor-relative names were used and were found not to be effective, as in RIG (see Section 22.1 above).)

- **capability** The use of resources is controlled by capabilities, which are issued by individual servers.

- **segment** A backing store object.

- **region** A contiguous range of virtual addresses within an actor that map a portion of a segment into the actor's address space.

22.3.2   CHORUS IPC

Abrossimov *et al.* (1989) describe a CHORUS V3 message (body) as an untyped string of bytes of variable but limited size (64 kbyte). A sender may optionally join a fixed size string (64 bytes) as a message header. When present, this header is copied to the receiver's address space. By default, the message body is sent with copy semantics but a transfer option is also available. As described above, messages are sent to location-independent ports which are identified by global protected UIs.

Originally, the implementation of CHORUS IPC was decoupled from memory management. The kernel implementation used a special segment called the IPC buffer segment which is managed as a pool of fixed-size 64 kbyte slots. A message was therefore limited to 64 kbyte in size. When a message was sent the kernel copied its contents into one of these slots and when it was read it was copied again into the context of the receiving thread. This was a source of inefficiency and a more recent paper (Bricker *et al.*, 1991) indicates that memory mapping is now used for the transfer of message bodies between actors on the same machine. As in Mach, copy-on-write is used if a message is to be copied rather than transferred.

The main communications facility is a lightweight RPC. In addition, for applications that require basic low-level communication, asynchronous message passing is provided. This facility is minimal, being unidirectional with no flow control or error control. Higher-level protocol layers may be built on top of this nucleus function.

22.3.3   CHORUS system structure

A (single machine) host is referred to as a **site** and a **node** comprises a number of sites connected together by a single physical medium.

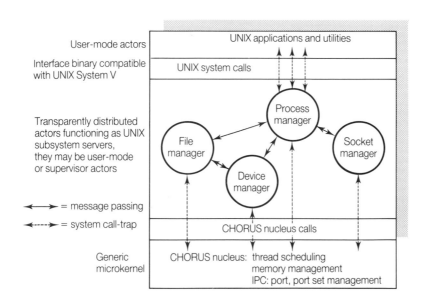

User-mode actors

Interface binary compatible
with UNIX System V

Transparently distributed
actors functioning as UNIX
subsystem servers,
they may be user-mode
or supervisor actors

◄───► = message passing

◄----► = system call-trap

Generic
microkernel

Figure 22.7
CHORUS/MIX–V3
architecture.

The CHORUS microkernel or 'Nucleus' has four components:

CHORUS **Supervisor:**   handles all exceptions delivered by the hardware;

CHORUS **Real-Time Executive:** controls processor allocation and provides synchronization and scheduling;

CHORUS **IPC Manager:**   supports asynchronous message passing and RPC facilities;

CHORUS **VMM:**   responsible for memory management.

Figure 22.7 shows the CHORUS/MIX-V3 architecture. At the top level, UNIX processes are implemented as user actors. At the next level are four transparently distributed UNIX subsystems: file management, process management, device management and socket management, implemented as supervisor actors. UNIX system calls are taken by the process manager, a supervisor actor which uses message passing to invoke the services of the other subsystems as required.

Supervisor actors are similar to user actors except that they share the kernel address space and their threads execute in privileged state and may therefore execute privileged instructions. Like user actors, they make calls on the nucleus interface to invoke IPC and other services. They are loaded dynamically and are paged like user actors.

Supervisor actors alone are allowed direct access to the hardware event facilities. Using the nucleus interface, a supervisor actor may dynamically establish a 'connected' handler for any hardware interrupt, system call trap or program exception. This connected handler is called as a procedure from the low-level handler in the nucleus and may take actions such as processing a hardware event and/or awakening a thread in the device manager actor. Only actors that process device interrupts are required to be implemented as supervisor actors. Other device-handling functions may be implemented as user-mode actors, in which case there is message passing and context switching overhead.

This use of supervisor actors has the following advantages:

- The nucleus need not be modified each time a new type of device is to be supported on a given machine.

- Interrupt processing time is greatly reduced. This contributes towards the ability to support real-time applications. The main consideration for real-time support is, however, bounded time rather than possibly very short but unknown time.

22.3.4 CHORUS memory management

CHORUS memory management considers the address space of a task as a number of non-overlapping regions. Secondary storage objects called segments are mapped into these regions. A region may map a whole segment or part of one, in which case it serves as a window onto the segment which may 'slide down the segment' for sequential access. As in Mach, segments of memory may be managed by external (user-level) servers called mappers. Mappers are responsible for synchronizing access to and maintaining the consistency of segments which may be mapped into different actors on several sites. Like Mach, CHORUS employs copy-on-write sharing techniques and maintains history objects to manage multiple versions in main memory of a single backing store object. It has been found that the copy-on-write mechanisms in CHORUS are simpler and more efficient than those in Mach. Again, a full discussion is not appropriate here and more information can be found in Abrossimov *et al.* (1989 a, b).

22.4   Distributed systems at Cambridge

As a final case study I will outline the distributed systems research projects at the University of Cambridge Computer Laboratory. The emphasis here is on the provision of an environment for research rather than a commercial programming development environment. The final section focuses on current research directions. Although this book is not attempting to give an advanced research course in distributed systems, a brief look at current research projects helps to show the direction that concurrent software design must take.

22.4.1 The Cambridge Distributed Computing System (CDCS)

CDCS (Needham and Herbert, 1982) was designed in the late 1970s and was in everyday use as the main research environment at Cambridge throughout the 1980s. It was based on the Cambridge Ring (CR) local area network and employed the 'pool of processors' approach to distributed computing. CDCS provided a number of common services such as file storage and printing, which were invoked from the heterogeneous systems running in processor bank machines. CDCS was a distributed system architecture and included a communications, naming and authorization infrastructure as well as management of the processor bank (see Figure 22.8). An overview of the CDCS environment and the distributed systems research projects carried out in it is given in Bacon *et al.* (1989).

Typical usage of CDCS is for a user, via a terminal server, to ask the Resource Manager for a processor from the processor bank. The user specifies a software system to be loaded into the acquired processor, is authenticated to this system

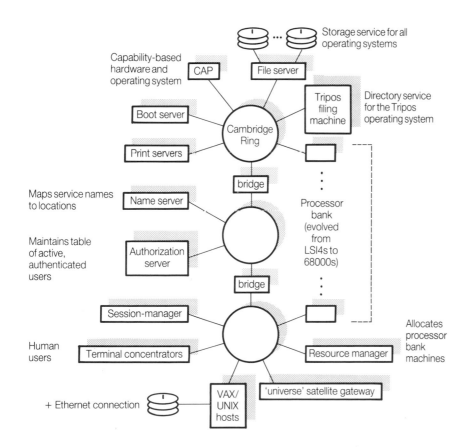

Figure 22.8
CDCS 1980-1989

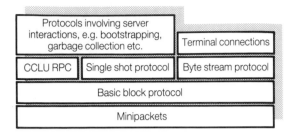

Figure 22.9
CDCS protocols.

and to CDCS and then runs applications on this single machine. Although the user is free to acquire more than one machine, CDCS originally provided virtually no support for users to spread a task across a number of machines.

Processor bank machines may be loaded with public operating systems or private research systems. The Tripos operating system (Richards *et al.*, 1979) was used originally and the Mayflower kernel (Bacon and Hamilton, 1987) was developed as a research system, then provided for public use. The CAP capability machine and operating system (Wilkes and Needham, 1979) was also used through CDCS.

The Cambridge File Server (CFS)

This 'universal file server' (Birrell and Needham, 1980; Dion, 1980) was designed to be used by any number of different clients' file directory servers, each with its own text-naming conventions and access control policies. CFS supported a general naming graph, existence control and mandatory concurrency control (see Chapter 5). The CFS existence control policy, that an object exists while it is reachable from the root, was supported by a garbage collection mechanism which CFS initiated to run asynchronously in a processor bank machine. The clients of CFS were Tripos, Mayflower and CAP. It could also be used directly by services or utilities such as mail servers.

LAN medium and protocol hierarchy

Cell-based LANs were pioneered at Cambridge in the 1970s. The Cambridge Ring is a slotted, 10 Mbit s^{-1} ring with anti-hogging and indication of success or failure of delivery at the lowest (minipacket) level (Wilkes and Wheeler, 1979). A protocol hierarchy was designed for CDCS with a Basic Block protocol above the CR and a choice of a Single Shot (request–response or transaction) Protocol and a Byte Stream Protocol at the next level (see Figure 22.9). Above this, specialized application protocols were developed for service bootstrapping, file service and garbage collection above SSP and for terminal connections above BSP. CDCS was an early example of the use of lightweight protocols in a reliable, high-speed, high-bandwidth LAN environment.

Evolution of CDCS

CDCS was initially implemented on a single Cambridge Ring and was extended to operate over three bridged Cambridge Rings on two sites. Project Universe (Leslie *et al.*, 1984) further extended the basic system design to seven CR-based systems connected by satellite over a wide area.

In 1982 the **Mayflower** project was set up to develop a language and environment for programming distributed services and applications. A concurrent programming language Concurrent CLU (CCLU), including a language-level remote procedure call (RPC) facility (see Chapters 10 and 14), was produced and used for development of a number of services, tools and applications (Bacon and Hamilton, 1987).

The Mayflower kernel was designed for implementing high-performance services for distributed systems. It supported lightweight processes, known to the operating system, running in a shared address space (a Mayflower domain); that is, it supported the multi-threaded processes we have studied throughout the book.

After some ten years of use of CDCS, a new distributed systems research environment, based on new high-speed networks and a new microkernel (Wanda), had evolved.

22.4.2 A multi-service ATM network environment

Like the Cambridge Ring, the new ring networks are based on a fixed cell size, this time containing 32 bytes of data. Section 3.8 describes the network interfaces. All follow the Asynchronous Transfer Mode (ATM) of operation; that is, attached computers may insert cells onto the network in an interleaved fashion, as opposed to a pair of stations acquiring exclusive use of the network for the transfer of a synchronous stream of data between them. The Cambridge networks were designed and in use well before the B-ISDN standard (Broadband-Integrated Services Data Network) was published, or the name ATM was coined. The standard is a specific instance of the ATM approach and employs 48 byte cells.

The new research network environment comprises Cambridge Fast Rings (CFR), a 100 Mbit s^{-1} ATM network (Hopper and Needham, 1988), linked by the Gbit s^{-1} Cambridge Backbone Ring (CBR) (Greaves *et al.*, 1990). Prototypes are operating at 75 Mbit and a half Gbit respectively. A switch-based network (Fairisle) is also being built and a 'desk area network' (Hayter and McAuley, 1991) is one project that will make use of this switch (see below). Fairisle employs 48-byte cells.

Software development takes place on Ethernet-based UNIX host systems but a new kernel was needed for the target environment. A specific requirement was a kernel on which efficient services, including storage services and gateways, could be built. Figure 22.10 outlines the components of the new environment.

Figure 22.10
The Cambridge
multi-service
network
environment.

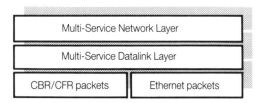

CFRs supporting UNIX-based
multimedia workstations
and Wanda-based storage
and other services

Cambridge
Fast Ring

Cambridge
Backbone
Ring

Ethernets
supporting
UNIX host
systems

Wanda-based gateways

Figure 22.11
The Multi-Service
Network
Architecture
(MSNA).

| Multi-Service Network Layer |
| Multi-Service Datalink Layer |

| CBR/CFR packets | Ethernet packets |

Olivetti Research Limited (ORL) at Cambridge shares an active interest in ATM network and applications research. The Pandora project (Hopper, 1990) is a joint undertaking between ORL and the Computer Laboratory. The project aims to provide multimedia facilities integrated into the workstation environment as described in Section 1.1. It uses the CFR for voice and video transport. By late 1990 Pandora workstations were deployed and in everyday use at three sites in Cambridge. A protocol hierarchy was developed for this multi-service environment (McAuley, 1989) (see Figure 22.11).

The basic design concepts are that lightweight connections are used and multiplexing is avoided above the lowest level. Lightweight connections can easily be broken and reformed and data can be transmitted as soon as the first hop of a route is set up; there is no need to wait for end-to-end connection set-up. If there is no multiplexing above the lowest level, the packets that arrive in an interleaved (multiplexed) fashion from the network can be allocated to a connection (and therefore the final destination process) and no further decoding is required at higher levels. The aim is to make it possible to transfer continuous media such as voice and video as well as conventional data.

The Wanda microkernel

Wanda is a vehicle for research into kernels for high-performance services and is not intended to support a program development environment. Like Mach and CHORUS, Wanda supports multi-threaded processes and multiprocessor thread scheduling.

The design philosophy is that multiple protocol hierarchies can be supported in a Wanda system. Currently, MSNA and TCP-UDP/IP are available in Wanda (and in our UNIX systems). There is a socket-like interface for invoking communications services. The ANSA testbench (ANSA, 1989), which includes an RPC facility and a name server ('interface trader'), see Section 14.9.3, runs on Wanda and UNIX machines at the Laboratory, thus facilitating interworking between the host and target environments. Sun RPC is also installed above Wanda.

Memory management is based on paged segments, and page mapping and unmapping is used for efficient inter-process (cross-address-space) communication and for network I/O. A kernel extension for mapping files into the address spaces of processes has been developed (Mapp, 1991). Semaphores are supported and are used both in the kernel and for user-level inter-thread communication within an address space.

Wanda runs on VAX-based machines, including MicroVAXIIs and the multiprocessor Firefly; on the MC68000 series with and without memory management, on Acorn ARM2 and 3s; and on the LR33000 development card, which is effectively a MIPS R3000 without an MMU. Wanda machines run on the CFR and on Ethernet and are also used for gateways between the CFR and the CBR.

The Multi-Service Storage Architecture (MSSA)

Current storage services are unable to meet the requirements of emerging application areas. An open storage service hierarchy is being developed to run above the Wanda kernel (Bacon *et al.*, 1991). Prototypes of a low-level storage service (LLSS) and a high-level storage service (HLSS) are operational. The LLSS supports a byte sequence storage abstraction and special-purpose versions of LLSS will be used as media stores. The HLSS supports structured data, at an acceptable cost, for those clients that require this service; for example, a structured multimedia document can be represented on the HLSS. The HLSS provides existence control and arbitrarily fine-grained concurrency control. Filing systems, database systems and multimedia systems make use of these components.

A persistent extension to C++ (PC++) which supports transactions has been developed for programming services and applications. The HLSS is used by PC++ for storage and retrieval of structured objects. Optimistic concurrency control is used in this distributed environment where conflict is expected to be rare and where real-time quality of service requirements may be important (see Sections 18.6 and 20.8).

Fairisle and the desk area network

The **Fairisle** switch-based network provides 100 Mbit s^{-1} data links between hosts and switches, and between switches and switches. The links are currently made of coaxial cable and can be up to 200 metres in length, but they could be made from optical fibre which would allow links of a few kilometres. Each link is full duplex, allowing simultaneous transfers of 48–byte cells to and from a switch. Figure 22.12 gives a simple picture of a 4×4 switch. In practice, a network would comprise many switches and a cell would be routed from switch to switch as well as across a single switch. A 16×16 switch is currently being built.

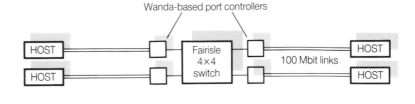

Figure 22.12
A Fairisle 4×4 switch.

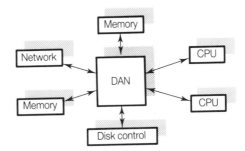

Figure 22.13
A multiprocessor
built as a desk area
network.

To allow experimentation, ARM3 computers running Wanda are used to control the transmission of cells into and out of the switch fabric.

Host interfaces exist for the TurboChannel allowing connection to DecStation 5100s and HP-375s and for the Archimedes podule bus. The MSNA protocols (see McAuley (1989)) are used on the Fairisle network, and since there is also an implementation of IP over MSNL, all standard UNIX traffic can be carried (for example, that to the NFS file servers).

The **desk area network (DAN)** project (Hayter and McAuley, 1991) aims to investigate the use of an ATM interconnection network for use within a machine as well as externally. The main argument for doing this is that data is then shipped internally in the same way as externally on the LAN or WAN; no translation is needed. In the sort of machine we use today, the cells (or network packets) of a video stream arrive at the network interface, are converted for transporting over the bus, are changed into another form for writing into the frame buffer and finally are displayed.

A simple multiprocessor, DAN-based machine can be made from a Fairisle switch with associated software (see Figure 22.13). One idea is to have a processor node with a large cache but no local memory. A cache miss causes a cell to be sent across the DAN to a memory server.

Figure 22.14 shows a multimedia workstation. One of the main problems with the support of multimedia in a workstation is the management of real-time streams of data. In a workstation based on a DAN, the switch is used to deliver real-time streams directly to the relevant devices, while their control streams are routed to a controlling processor. The DAN project has built an ATM camera which produces a stream of ATM cells directly.

The DAN idea is based on our belief that the correct thing to do is to keep the ATM-cell nature of the connection visible all the way to the endpoints. We are

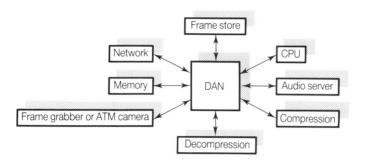

Figure 22.14
A multimedia
workstation built as
a desk area
network.

therefore concerned that the international standards for wide area ATM, the B-ISDN, should allow this use, instead of imposing one specific mechanism.

Real-time requirements

Research into and development of high-speed networks will continue and will provide the technology that the protocols and operating systems must exploit on behalf of the applications. The networks make it possible to support applications that use real-time continuous media. Current operating systems and protocols are unsuitable for this kind of application. A theme of several research topics is therefore that the application must be able to specify the **quality of service** it requires and the system must be able to guarantee this quality with a specified probability.

Only the application knows which of its threads have real-time requirements. A real-time version of Wanda is being developed which includes periodic threads (threads which are guaranteed to run for a certain proportion of a given time period), dynamic priority and user-specified thread management.

In order to deliver a multimedia object to a workstation it is necessary to synchronize its different components. Sometimes the components are on special-purpose storage servers, sometimes they are coming from devices in real time. Timing requirements cannot be met by an operating system alone in a distributed system. It is necessary for the communications system also to give timing guarantees (Dixon, 1991).

22.5   Summary

We considered two microkernels which support the two major UNIX systems, BSD 4.3 and System V.4. By this means, existing UNIX applications can take advantage of multiprocessor architectures and the new features such as memory-mapped files which provide for greater efficiency. UNIX was started around 1970; Mach and CHORUS were both started around 1980. A great deal of time is needed to incorporate good research ideas into commercial products, particularly when the abstractions of an existing operating system, good or bad, must be emulated.

Mach and CHORUS V3 both support multi-threaded 'processes' and map files into virtual memory to avoid the inefficiency of copying to and from I/O buffers. Mach uses memory mapping for intra-machine IPC. CHORUS first copied data with a maximum message size of 64 kbyte but now uses memory mapping akin to that of Mach. The network server tasks of Mach allow large messages to be transferred across the network 'copy-on-reference'. They introduce the overhead of an extra context switch and message receive and send on every external communication, however, as they are implemented at user level. CHORUS claims that its supervisor actors provide a good compromise, as they run in privileged mode and share the kernel's address space while being separate entities, akin to user-mode actors, in other respects.

Both Mach and CHORUS use a port abstraction where ports have location-independent, globally unique, protected identifiers. The port set of Mach allows ports to share a queue and threads to receive from one of a number of ports. The port group of CHORUS is designed to support multicast.

The evolution of microkernel design that we saw in Mach and CHORUS has been repeated elsewhere. There are many other operating systems research projects and a number of different systems could have been covered as case studies. References to several systems were given in Chapters 10, 11 and 12 when system structure and IPC was discussed, and some were mentioned at the start of this chapter.

We concluded the chapter with an outline of the distributed systems that have been built at the University of Cambridge UK. The aim here is to provide a research environment rather than a commercial product. An outline was given of past and present distributed systems research projects. Current research issues include how to design communications systems and microkernels that can exploit current and projected network performance to support applications which use real-time continuous media.

Exercises

22.1 How is a port transferred from one task to another in Mach and from one actor to another in CHORUS?

22.2 What is the difference between Mach and CHORUS port sets?

22.3   What functions have been implemented inside the microkernel in Mach and CHORUS? Which functions are implemented as servers above the kernel?

22.4   To what extent do Mach and CHORUS support real-time execution?

22.5   What are the implementation languages of Mach and CHORUS?

22.6   How are memory management techniques used to avoid physical copying of data in Mach and CHORUS?

22.7   Which objects in Mach and CHORUS are given globally unique identifiers? How are the objects referenced by these identifiers located in each system?

Transaction processing monitors and systems

CONTENTS

We first discuss systems aspects of transaction processing (TP) monitors. TP applications impose requirements on the underlying system in the following areas:

- the operating systems in the various computers involved, in particular, their support for processes, with or without multi-threading and inter-process communication (IPC);

- the communications support for the messages which flow to effect transactions;

- the higher-level transaction support to ensure correctness of stored data in the presence of failures in systems and communications;

- the requirements for transaction throughput, particularly in large-scale systems. Average, peak and emergency load should be considered.

We then look at some examples of transaction processing systems which are taken from the general area of electronic funds transfer (EFT). This application area is usually described from the viewpoint of security, since EFT systems are an obvious focus for criminals who want to steal money. Here, we are more concerned with general systems aspects and will leave a detailed study of encryption techniques for more specialized texts, for example Davies and Price (1984) and Meyer and Matyas (1982).

Terminology

In this chapter ATM stands for automatic teller machine and an ATM network allows you to obtain banking services internationally. In Chapter 22 an ATM network was one employing the asynchronous transfer mode of communication. We are suffering from a coincidence of TLAs (three-letter acronyms). Perhaps the term 'cashpoint machine' would be better.

23.1   Transaction processing monitors

Transaction processing applications were introduced in Chapter 1 and the theory underlying the correct execution of transactions was the core topic of Part III. A TP monitor coordinates the flow of information between users at terminals who issue transaction requests and TP applications that process the requests. Much of the integration of the software components (operating systems, communications and database management systems (DBMS)) that are used by TP applications is done by the TP monitor. Figure 23.1 gives a model for a TP monitor, which follows Bernstein (1990). It is assumed that each transaction selects a pre-specified application service program. This is in contrast with a database transaction, which is composed in response to a query.

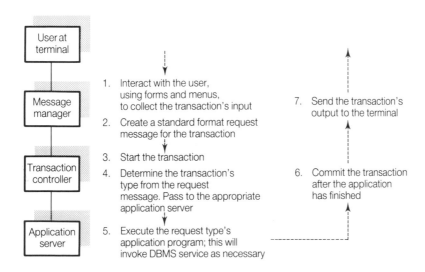

Figure 23.1
Components of a
TP monitor.

The figure shows the functions of the components of the TP monitor in the execution of a single transaction. In a typical TP system there are many instances of each of the components. Bernstein (1990) discusses the functions of each component in detail, together with standard message formats etc. We shall focus on operating systems aspects.

23.1.1   Use of processes and IPC

A TP monitor is responsible for creating and managing the processes which execute the components shown in Figure 23.1. Design issues include the following:

● Should the components execute together in a single address space or separately in different address spaces?

● Is each process single-threaded or multi-threaded?

Multi-threaded processes were discussed in Section 6.11, throughout Chapters 7 and 8, in Sections 12.10 and 21.15 and in the context of the microkernels of Chapter 22.

It is necessary to know the process model of the operating system and the IPC it provides when making these design decisions. We now consider the various options.

Single address space, single-threaded processes

The components are linked together into a single load module and are executed by a single process (see Figure 23.2(a)). The control flow between the components is effected by a simple procedure call within the process. A simple strategy

Figure 23.2
TP modules in a single address space: (a) single-threading; (b) multi-threading,

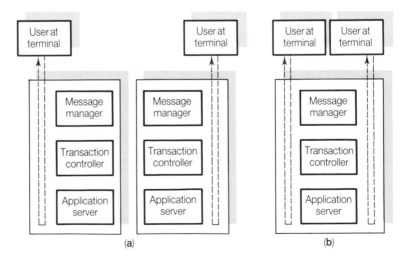

(a)   (b)

is to create such a process for each terminal. This model is used in small TP systems, but it does not scale well. A TP system may have a large number of active terminals. Even if the operating system is, in theory, able to support a large number of processes it may perform badly when a large number exist. This is because of the overhead of handling a large number of process descriptors for scheduling purposes, context switching overhead and memory overhead per process leading to the possibility of paging etc. If the TP system is distributed there may be a process per terminal on each computer involved in a given transaction (see Chapter 20).

It is not clear how times of high activity, and therefore high load on the system, could be managed. An approach that is used in practice is to lower the priority of some request types. An example from a stock control system is that new orders would be given priority over requests from a management information system for the current stock level. We can assume the existence of a process dedicated to monitoring the load on the system. We can assume that each process, on decoding a request, could determine the current level of the load. We should then need a process to be able to request that its priority is lowered if the load is high and its request type is deemed unimportant. It may not be possible to do this and the crude approach of rejecting or aborting terminal transactions, whatever their type, might have to be used.

Single address space, multi-threaded processes

The components are linked together into a single load module and are executed by a multi-threaded process (see Figure 23.2(b)). Each terminal is assigned a thread and each thread has a private data area for its local variables. We assume that a strongly typed language would offer protection of the private data.

The threads may be managed by the operating system or by a threads package in the TP monitor (see Chapter 7). In the latter case, the operating system must offer asynchronous system calls for this scheme to work effectively. Recall that a synchronous system call which results in blocking will block the whole process if the operating system is not aware of the separate threads of the process. This problem was discussed in the UNIX case study in Chapter 21 and the microkernels in Chapter 22 were shown to support multi-threading.

If the system is to run on a shared-memory multiprocessor, multi-threading implemented by the operating system allows the threads to run concurrently.

As we noted above, scheduling parameters may need to be adjusted at times of high load. The area of scheduling multi-threaded processes is still under active research and this is a requirement that should be taken into account.

TP monitors that use a single address space in practice use multi-threading. Examples are IBM's CICS (Customer Information Control System) (see Yelavitch, 1985) and Digital's DECintact. Note that both IBM and Digital have proprietary network architectures to provide communications support for these products: IBM has System Network Architecture (SNA) and Digital has DEC-NET.

Multiple address spaces, single-threaded processes

It is desirable to implement the components of the TP monitor as separate processes in the following circumstances:

- The system may comprise a large, geographically dispersed network of terminals. It is convenient to locate a message manager in a machine which is close to a group of terminals.

- The users submit transactions at workstations. The message manager component is best located in the workstation.

- The system may be partitioned so that some application servers execute specific request types. This may be because different parts of a business are concerned with different types of transaction and the business may most conveniently be served by such an arrangement.

We now require IPC between the components of the TP monitor which is executing a given transaction. This may take the form of message passing or remote procedure call (RPC). Figure 23.3 shows the approach in general terms.

The modules shown there may be located in separate address spaces in the same computer or in separate computers. The IPC may be between different address spaces on the same machine or inter-machine. A wide area network may separate some of the components.

Connection-oriented message passing is used in some systems (see Section 3.9.2). A process establishes a session, or virtual circuit, with another process after which they can exchange messages. In IBM's CICS, for example, a permanent half-duplex connection is set up and there is explicit transfer of con-

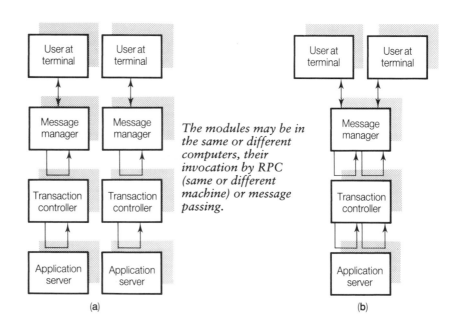

Figure 23.3
TP modules in separate address spaces: (a) single-threading; (b) multi-threading.

The modules may be in the same or different computers, their invocation by RPC (same or different machine) or message passing.

trol between the processes at the connection endpoints to form a conversation. Conversations are intended to be long-lived and to span many transactions. With this model a single transaction comprises a chain of processes. When each component process in the chain has finished its processing the transaction may be committed. Only then can the chain of connected processes start work on the next transaction.

When message passing is used between some components of the TP monitor and procedure call is used to invoke other components the system configuration is made explicit in the programs. For example, the message manager might be in a dedicated machine, but the other components might run in a single address space. This could not be changed without reprogramming. The argument against using a separate address space for every component, even when they run on the same machine, is that the IPC would then be less efficient than procedure call.

We have seen that an RPC mechanism implements a client–server style of interaction. Each component of the TP monitor could be implemented as a separate process and RPC could be used for invocation. Some components are invoked as a server, then become a client of the next component in the line. The components could be invoked by same-machine RPC or cross-network RPC transparently to the application. This would make programming easy and reconfiguration possible without reprogramming. Digital's ACMS and Tandem's Pathway TP monitors use the client–server model.

Increasing the efficiency of general message passing and RPC is an active research area, as we have seen in Chapter 22. If cross address space IPC can be made efficient it is preferable for the components of TP systems to be implemented as separate processes running in separate address spaces for the reasons mentioned above. However, if each of these processes is only single-threaded a large number of processes is needed when a large number of transactions must be handled. As we discussed for single address space implementations, this imposes a high overhead on the operating system and leads to a large amount of context switching overhead.

Multiple address spaces, multi-threaded processes

Here we again have the TP monitor's components in separate address spaces but this time they are executed by multi-threaded processes (see Figure 23.3(b)). The context switching overhead between threads is much lower than between processes. Problems may arise (as discussed for single address space, multi-threaded processes) if the operating system does not support threads and has synchronous system calls.

Digital's ACMS and Tandem's Pathway TP monitors support an 'application service class' abstraction to avoid this problem. The application service modules (which make potentially blocking system calls) are single-threaded and run as separate OS processes. A new transaction which requires an application service can make a request to the class and not to a specific instance of the application service. Any free application service process of this class can service the request. Similar mechanisms were discussed in Section 12.5.

23.1.2 Buffered transaction requests

The implication in the above discussion has been that a transaction is executed while the user waits. This may be the case in some applications. In others it may be convenient for the system to accumulate a batch of requests before carrying out processing. For example, a shop may record the items that have been sold during the day as a batch of transactions and may update the stock database overnight. Orders for new stock are then made on a daily basis. The shop may record the cheque or credit card purchases made by its customers as a batch of transactions to be sent to its bank for settlement.

A batch mode of working is natural for many systems. In others it may be that a transaction that would normally be executed on-line, such as an order to dispatch an item to a customer, might not be able to complete for some reason. A network connection or remote database system might be unavailable. In this case, it might be possible to enter the transaction into the system and have it guaranteed to execute but after some delay. The crucial requirement is that once the transaction is accepted it is not lost.

The TP monitor may therefore provide for messages to be stored securely and executed later. This allows batch working as described above and also allows the system to be used if there has been a network or server failure.

23.1.3 Monitoring system load and performance

TP systems are large and complex. Human managers or automated management systems need information on the throughput in transactions per second and the response times that are being achieved. This information allows the system to be expanded when it becomes necessary. It also allows parameters to be tuned dynamically to improve system performance.

A typical system will grade its transaction request types in priority, for example, into those which must, if possible, be carried out immediately and those which may be batched or delayed for a short time. When load becomes high, low-priority request types might be rejected or queued to ensure good response to high-priority types. The operating system may help or hinder, as we discussed briefly in Section 23.1.1. A general requirement is that the OS should allow the application to specify the relative priorities of its threads and should be able to change these priorities dynamically to respond to changing load levels.

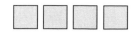

23.2   Introduction to some electronic funds transfer (EFT) applications

An outline of some of the transaction processing which is carried out within EFT systems is now given.

23.2.1   Paying by cheque

Figure 23.4 outlines what is involved when goods are paid for by cheque.

I have bought a television and have paid the shop by cheque. My handwritten signature on the cheque is used to authenticate me, but only in the event of a dispute at a later stage.

1. The shop presents my cheque (and many others) to its bank.
2. The shop's bank transmits a file containing a batch of transactions to a central clearing house. A central clearing house service is used to avoid the necessity of every bank interacting with every other bank. One of these transactions corresponds to my cheque. The transactions are called **debit transfers** because they are requests to debit various accounts. The clearing house will need to interact with many different banks to establish whether the transactions can be carried out. These interactions are likely to be batched per bank rather than on-line.
3. For each transaction, the clearing house asks the bank concerned whether the cheque can be honoured; whether there is enough money in the account. This

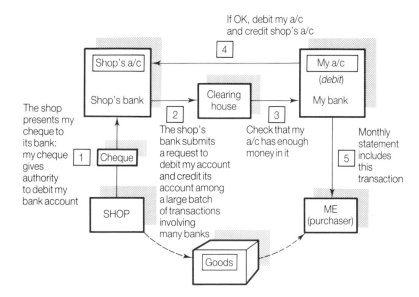

Figure 23.4
Payment by cheque.

process will involve a batch of transactions for each bank. The figure may imply something more interactive and immediate. The bank sends back bounced cheques after a day or two. Let us assume that I can pay for the television.

4. My account is debited and the shop's account is credited with the amount specified in the cheque. The mechanism for achieving this is again likely to involve a batch of accumulated transactions from my bank. This time, the transactions are credit transfers; they are a list of authorized credits.

5. I get a monthly bank statement which includes a record of this transaction.

Note that while the cheque is being cleared I cannot safely use the money represented by the cheque, nor can the shop that I have paid with it. The mechanism takes of the order of days because very large numbers of cheques are involved and the batch mode of working is used. This system therefore favours the banks since they can make use of the money in transit. Customer pressure and competition between banks will provide the motivation for developing more interactive systems.

We avoided discussing cheques that bounce. In practice, in Britain and some other countries, the shop would have insisted that I cover my cheque with a bank card which guarantees that the cheque will be honoured. It is then my bank's problem if the cheque bounces (to recover the money from me), and not the shop's. In this case, interaction 3 would merely pass the requirement to make the debit to my bank, whether my account could cover the cheque or not. Banks will not cover very large sums of money in this way, without a fee being paid, and other payment mechanisms are needed. For example, the goods might be held until the cheque is cleared, as described in 1 to 5 above.

The following points are relevant to an implementation of such a system:

- That the long time taken to clear a cheque by this means is tolerable to users of the system.

- A file transfer protocol is used to transfer the files of transactions. Copies of the various transaction files are kept so that any problems can be resolved. Early systems used magnetic tape to transfer batches of transactions.

- Encryption is used for security (see below).

- When transactions are being carried out at my bank, a transaction log records the debit to my account. If the system crashes during transaction processing, the log has a record of the old and new value of the account (see Chapter 19).

- When transactions are being carried out at the shop's bank, a transaction log records the credit corresponding to my cheque. This prevents the credit being made more than once, or not at all.

It must be ensured that each transaction is carried out exactly once, even when the systems or the networks connecting them fail. The use of a log for recovery was described in Chapter 19.

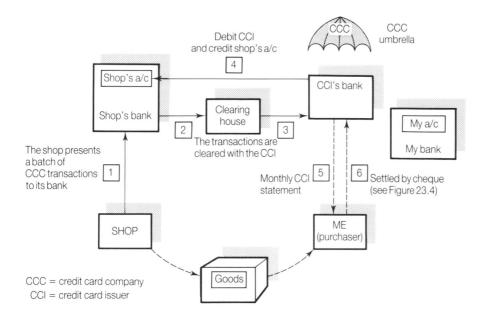

Figure 23.5
Payment by credit card.

23.2.2   Paying by credit card

Figure 23.5 outlines what is involved when goods are paid for by credit card. This time, the shop is guaranteed payment by the credit card company (CCC). My credit card is issued by a member of the CCC which we shall call the credit card issuer (CCI). The CCI may be associated with a bank, for example.

My CCI notifies me of a batch of transactions in my monthly statement and I then pay the CCI for all of them (or pay to borrow money from the CCI). The CCC acts as a large, secure, high-level guarantor for the money involved in the transactions, shown as an umbrella in Figure 23.5. It is less likely to go broke than any one of its member CCIs and a card with its endorsement is more likely to be trusted by vendors of goods and services.

23.2.3   Paying by debit card: point of sale transactions

A debit card is also likely to be guaranteed by an umbrella organization as described above for credit cards. If a debit card is used together with a hand-written signature on a payment slip, the procedure is similar to that described above for cheques. The debit card also acts as a guarantee that the issuer will cover the payment. At present there is no on-line interaction between the point of sale and the card issuer: the card merely functions as a cheque that is easy to clear. The card is put through the point of sale machine to check against a list of stolen card numbers (see below).

Most point of sale systems currently use handwritten signatures for authentication but are likely to move towards more secure methods in future. These are discussed in Section 23.4.

Note that so far, a batch mode of working has been used to avoid the complexity of myriad interactive transactions between the many banks of purchasers, vendors and card issuers. The requirements on the operating system and communications support are less demanding for this batch mode of working than for online TP (OLTP). Interactive working implies that all parties wait in real time for accounts to be checked and authority to be given. When a batch mode is used, a system or communications line can go down for a short time without affecting the financial operations. If we move to interactive working, systems must be fault-tolerant. It would be intolerable for purchases etc. to be held up when failures occur.

23.2.4 Some security issues

Cheque-books and cards can be stolen and forged. One of the critical issues for the financial card industry is the rate of loss due to fraud and forgery. In the USA, for example, this amounts to over 1.5% of the turnover of signature-based credit card transactions. For many issuing institutions this is over half of the profit made on credit card business. Much of the effort in designing EFT systems is therefore directed towards preventing and detecting both crime external to the EFT system (by its users), and internally (by those operating it).

After you have reported that your card is stolen, the credit card company is responsible for covering subsequent use of the card. It is in the company's interest to propagate information on stolen cards, so-called 'hot card numbers', as widely and rapidly as possible.

When a file of transactions is recorded it must be ensured that all these transactions are genuine and have not been augmented by transactions in favour of bank employees, nor have any transactions been changed to achieve this end. It must be guaranteed that only the intended transactions are processed when the file reaches its destination. Also, transactions must not be changed during transmission. In general, the requirement is that attacks on the transaction data must be prevented. An attack seeks to change data for the benefit of the attacker.

Security policies and mechanisms to achieve these aims are described in Davies and Price (1984) and Meyer and Matyas (1982).

23.3 International inter-bank payments: S.W.I.F.T.

The discussion in the previous section has given some indication of the immense volume of EFT traffic. The implicit assumption was that the banks concerned were located in a single country, but many transactions involve the transfer of funds between countries. If you can find a garage when on holiday in the high Pyrenees it will almost certainly allow you to pay for your petrol by credit card. The supermarket in the provincial French town where you buy your holiday provisions will give you a choice of using a debit or a credit card.

The previous section described methods that are used for transactions involving a small amount of money. The methods described above would not be used for large sums. In the past, telephone or telex would have been used to arrange such transfers, but these methods are subject to misunderstandings and fraud. Increasingly, telecommunications are being used for this purpose, a major example being the Society for Worldwide Inter-bank Financial Telecommunications (S.W.I.F.T.). S.W.I.F.T. was formed in 1973 as a bank-owned, non-profit cooperative society, directed by about 1000 shareholding member banks which are located in about 50 countries worldwide. It has been operational since 1977. The costs of its message transfer service are paid for by members using a tariff based on the numbers of connections, their addresses and the volume of traffic.

Chapter 10 of Davies and Price (1984) covers the operation of S.W.I.F.T. in detail and its interaction with the clearing houses of its member nations

23.4   Authentication by PIN

In Section 23.2 we considered payment by cheque, credit card and debit card. In all of these cases a handwritten signature was the basis for authenticating the purchaser. In the next section we consider automatic teller machines (ATMs) which are EFT terminals which give cash dispensing and other banking services. For these machines a handwritten signature is not used. Before going on to the design of an ATM system we first consider authentication by personal identification numbers (PINs), a method suitable for banking and other applications. As well as being an authentication mechanism that is easier to automate than handwritten signatures, the PIN method has also been found to be very much less subject to fraud.

A PIN is a secret number assigned to, or selected by, the holder of a credit card or debit card. It authenticates the cardholder to the EFT system. The PIN is memorized by the cardholder and must not be recorded in any way that could be recognized by another person. At the time when the cardholder initiates an EFT transaction, the PIN is entered into the EFT terminal using a keyboard provided for this purpose. Unless the PIN, as entered, is recognized by the EFT system as correct for this particular account number (which is also recorded on the card) the EFT system refuses to accept the transaction.

This approach ensures that if someone steals a card or finds a lost card, he or she is unable to use it because the PIN is not known to them. Also, if a counterfeit copy of a card is made, it is useless without the corresponding PIN.

Chapter 10 of Meyer and Matyas (1982) discusses PINs in detail. The issues discussed there are summarized briefly below.

PIN secrecy

It is important that the users of the EFT system have confidence in its security. For example, if an applicant for a card were to be asked to specify a PIN on an application form it would be obvious that many employees of the card issuer would have access to the PIN. For this reason, we are issued with PINs instead of specifying our own.

Certain policies should hold, such as:

● A PIN should not be transmitted across a network connection 'in clear', that is, without first being encrypted.

● A clear PIN should never reside in a mainframe computer or database, even momentarily when in transit.

● A clear PIN should not be seen by an employee of the company at any time, including when it is being issued.

● Employees should not have access to the encryption keys used in the system.

PIN length

We are exhorted to use non-alphanumeric characters in our login passwords, whereas PINs are restricted to numeric characters to keep the EFT terminal's keyboard simple. As with computer passwords, the longer the PIN, the more difficult the system is to crack: the more unlikely it is that a guessed PIN will be correct. However, the method of guessing at random is thought to be infeasible for a would-be thief. It would be necessary to stand at an EFT terminal for many hours and this would not go without detection; see also 'allowable entry attempts' below.

Cardholders are required to memorize their PINs. The longer the PINs, the more likely we are to forget them. Four digits allow 10 000 different PINs, 5 digits give 100 000 and 6 digits 1 000 000. Four-digit PINs are often used, in order to be easy to remember, but this means that a lot of people will share a given PIN (each with a different account number of course), and occasionally they are found to live in the same house. In general, short PINs can be used because we do not tell them to each other.

Allowable PIN entry attempts

Notice a significant difference in the way passwords at login and PINs are used. When the card is inserted and a PIN is typed, the EFT system can monitor the process and can count the number of attempts which are made to type the correct PIN. The system typically refuses to allow more than a small number of

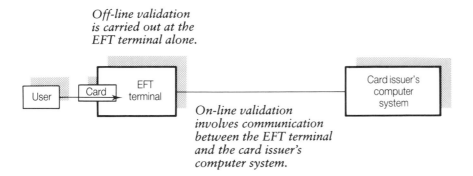

Off-line validation is carried out at the EFT terminal alone.

On-line validation involves communication between the EFT terminal and the card issuer's computer system.

Figure 23.6
PIN validation.

attempts. A login procedure could do the same, but this would not prevent other methods of attempting to break a computer system's security. These often involve off-line computation; for example, a password file could be copied and many artificially constructed passwords could be put through the known encryption function and compared with the encrypted passwords in the file. The stored, encrypted PINs are not available to users of the EFT system. Off-line attacks on the master PIN key (see below) are still feasible, however.

The PIN validation mechanism

Suppose that the EFT terminal is owned by the card issuer. The two approaches to PIN validation are outlined in Figure 23.6. Either the PIN is validated off-line in the EFT terminal alone or it is validated on-line by an interaction between the EFT terminal and the card issuer's computer system.

Figure 23.7 gives a simplified view of one method of off-line validation. When the card and PIN are issued, the account number and a secret random number

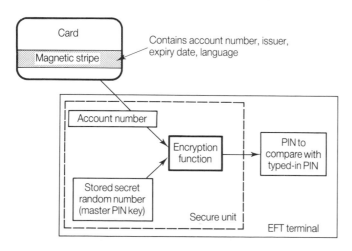

Figure 23.7
Off-line PIN validation at the EFT terminal.

(the Master PIN key) are put through an encryption function, giving the PIN as result. The PIN is not stored anywhere in the system and no bank employee sees it: it emerges in a sealed, addressed envelope.

When the card is used at an EFT terminal, the terminal must have the computing power and the information necessary to carry out the same encryption process. This information resides in the tamper-proof secure unit shown in the figure. The account number from the card's magnetic stripe and the stored secret random number (the master PIN key) are put through the encryption function and the result is compared with the typed-in PIN. The reader is referred to Meyer and Matyas (1982) for details of this and other methods.

If an off-line validation method is used, some of the EFT services, such as cash dispensing, can still be offered when the EFT terminal is disconnected from the rest of the network. The EFT terminal must have stable storage to record the transactions. Other services, such as determining the balance of the account, may not be available.

Changing a PIN interactively

Some machines allow you to change your PIN. How can this be possible if PINs are not stored in the system? The method used is to store the difference between the original PIN and the new one the user has chosen. This stored information must be available to any EFT terminal. On-line validation is more appropriate for systems which offer a 'change PIN' service.

23.5   The international automatic teller machine (ATM) network service

Early ATMs were essentially cash dispensers. Their single function was to deliver cash in the form of bank notes and debit the corresponding bank account. Further facilities have now been added to these automatic tellers. You can enquire about the status of your bank accounts. You can move money between your own accounts and sometimes may be allowed to credit another person's account. It may be possible for travellers' cheques to be dispensed (in countries where these are needed). There may also be a simple deposit facility.

We have become used to the convenience of being able to put a card into an ATM anywhere in the world in order to draw cash from a bank account. You can now set off on holiday or on business with very little concern about how much cash to take with you.

This has happened recently and the design of the systems that support the service tends not to be discussed in the standard systems literature. When they are described, the emphasis is on the security aspects of their design. We give a short

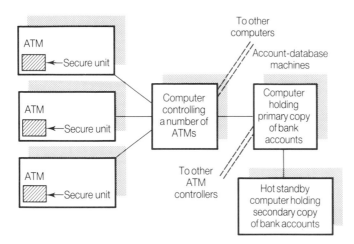

Figure 23.8
Local control of
ATMs.

case study here which does not involve a deep discussion of security issues. An introduction to PINs and their validation was given in the previous section.

23.5.1   How bank accounts are held

A bank's account database is likely to be held on a relatively small number of large computer systems. Any given account is held at a primary site and a backup site, the 'hot standby' shown in Figure 23.8. As transactions involving the accounts are carried out at the primary site a log is kept as described in Chapter 19. If this computer should fail the bank accounts it holds should not become unavailable. This is the reason for the 'hot standby'.

One approach to maintaining the hot standby would be to carry out each transaction on both machines but this would slow down the rate at which transactions could be processed. The log of transactions on the primary site is not lost on a crash, however, and it is therefore not necessary to keep the accounts exactly in step. The hot standby tends to be updated at a granularity of about ten minutes and the log can be used after a crash to bring the standby right up to date. With this approach, during normal working, a batch of transactions can be sent from the primary to the standby machine, thus optimizing both use of communication services and transaction processing at the standby.

23.5.2   Local control of ATMs

Figure 23.8 shows a number of ATM machines in a local area. The machines must be physically secure because they contain money. A secure authentication mechanism will not protect the machine from a brute force attack by heavy lifting gear. They therefore tend to be built into the foundations of the buildings where they are located. Each ATM has a keyboard through which the customer requests services and a screen to display information. Authentication of the customer is of primary importance and different approaches to achieving this were outlined in Section 23.4. Once the customer is authenticated, the transactions are carried out.

An ATM is typically owned and managed by a single bank, but the banks cooperate to allow transactions from each others' ATMs (not illustrated). The figure shows a small computer which controls a number of local ATMs in addition to the main computers at which bank accounts are held. The rationale for the local computer is that while at work, for example, I regularly use the same few ATM outlets of my bank. The local computer can manage a large proportion of ATM traffic without interacting with the large account database storage systems. The functions of the ATM controller include the following:

- To keep a copy of information on selected local bank accounts. Hopefully, most transactions can be satisfied from this information. The less frequent cases are when a stranger uses this machine and when a local person goes elsewhere and uses a remote machine (see Section 23.5.4).

  The values of the various copies of a bank account (on the account database machines and on the local ATM controller) are guaranteed to be synchronized on a 24–hour basis. In practice, transactions are carried out at a finer time grain and synchronization is more likely to be achieved after ten minutes or so. The information at the local controller can become out of date if the account is accessed remotely.

  The most recent value of each local account is remembered so if only local transactions are carried out, this value is up to date.

  All transactions are recorded in stable storage and a batch is sent to the account-database machine periodically, for example, every ten minutes.

- To keep a list of 'hot cards': those which have been notified as missing, presumed stolen. This is updated at least on a daily basis.

- To keep information on cards which have been used recently. This allows any attempt to use a stolen card repeatedly to be detected. It also allows a policy to limit the number of transactions per day or the amount of cash that can be withdrawn per day to be enforced.

- To cache information that may be useful in satisfying future requests.

- To communicate with other computers when requests cannot be satisfied from information held locally.

From the above it is clear that a local request is satisfied on the basis of the information held in the local controller.

23.5.3 Remote use

The following issues arise when an ATM is used by someone whose account information is not held by the ATM's controller.

The user belongs to the same bank or card issuer (CI) as the ATM's owner

- The ATM's stored encryption keys, the encryption function it uses and the encoding of the card are uniform for the CI. The PIN typed by the user at the ATM can therefore be validated.

- After PIN validation the ATM can carry out some services, such as dispensing cash. The transaction is recorded and in due course is passed to the account-holding database machine and the account is debited.

  If that user makes use of his or her local ATM on the way home, the value stored there for the balance of the account will not, in general, reflect this transaction.

- Certain services, such as giving the value of the account, may not be available. To provide such a service, it would be necessary to support interactive querying of the account database from this ATM's local controller. It might be that the account database is queried to ascertain and enforce the user's credit limit and the balance might or might not be divulged depending on the bank's policy for remote use.

Interactive TP is likely to become available increasingly in the future.

The user belongs to a different bank or card issuer (CI) from the ATM's owner

It is necessary for the user's CI and the ATM owner to have an agreement that their cards can be used in each others' machines. They may agree to use the same method of PIN validation (see Section 23.4), but the 'secret random number' (key) that is input to the encryption function when the card is issued, and when the PIN is validated, will be different for the two CIs. It must be possible for these secret numbers to be inserted into the tamper-proof secure unit in the ATM without being disclosed to the cooperating CIs. The program in the ATM which reads the card can detect the bank number and select the appropriate secret on that basis. An alternative method is to encrypt the information and transmit it for remote validation by the CI.

The service offered may differ slightly from that given to a customer of the owner's bank. It might be necessary that the account database is interrogated to enforce a 'no overdraft' policy, but the value is unlikely to be disclosed.

23.6 Load and traffic in TP systems

The above descriptions were presented in general terms. In order to understand the likely load on TP systems and the volume of traffic involved in this application area, knowledge of typical transaction sizes and the rates at which they are invoked is needed. If one is to design a TP system it is essential to know these values for the application areas it is intended to serve.

An example from ATM systems of the rate at which transactions can be executed is that a recent reimplementation of a widely used system has increased the potential transaction rate from 50 per second to 400 per second. The transaction rate could be limited by the line speed used for the connection between the ATM controller and the customer's host system, but is most often software-limited.

Another factor to bear in mind is peak load both in normal and exceptional circumstances. For example, ATM machines are used most heavily on Fridays and Saturdays around midday. The international stock exchanges' systems were unable to cope with the load generated on 'Black Monday' in October 1987. A TP system should have management procedures to cope with predicted high loads and projected emergency loads.

The size of a transaction depends on the number of instructions executed (the 'pathlength') and the number of input and output instructions it performs. Studies of real workloads have shown that pathlength provides a reasonable basis for comparison. Sharman (1991) classifies typical workloads as simple, medium and complex:

simple: pathlength < 100 000 instructions

medium: 100 000< pathlength <1 000 000

complex: >1 000 000 instructions.

A typical mixed workload comprises simple and medium transactions. Complex transactions typically occur in applications which involve complex query analysis on a database, expert systems inference applications or very large components databases (such as the components involved in manufacturing various parts of an aircraft).

It is difficult to compare systems with widely varying transaction mixes. Figures indicating the number of transactions per second are quoted, but the transaction sizes must be known for these rates to mean anything. The non-profit Transaction Processing Performance Council (TPPC) was set up for this purpose in 1989. Its aim is to define standard benchmarks upon which both the industry and its customers can rely (see Gray, 1991). TPPC will define benchmarks based on typical applications and will specify the configurations which are needed to run them.

One benchmark, TPC-A, is based on a simplified banking transaction known as debit/credit which has a pathlength of 100 000 instructions. Typical prices of systems that can achieve one TPC-A transaction per second are in the range $20 000 to $40 000 (Sharman, 1991).

A customer may wish to purchase a TP system that will scale, for example, to handle from 0.1 to 1000 transactions per second. Different departments of the company may require different mixes and different rates, and any given part of a company will wish to be able to allow for growth of the system.

In addition to supporting some specified transaction rate a TP system (comprising the hardware and software of the attached computers and the network connections) is required to be highly available, to operate continuously and to be secure.

23.7 Summary and trends

This brief study of transaction processing systems has shown the relevance to them of the topics that we studied in the earlier parts of the book. We saw that it is necessary to know the process model and IPC facilities of the operating system over which a TP system is implemented. Ideally, the OS should support multi-threaded processes. The TP system can then be programmed naturally and without artificial restrictions. If only single-threaded processes are supported, and system calls are synchronous, the TP system implementor has to go to a great deal of trouble to program around the potential problems. We saw that multiple address spaces containing multi-threaded processes using RPC for communication could be used to provide a general and flexible implementation.

Examples of TP systems in the area of electronic funds transfer were given. They can be divided into those which use handwritten signatures for authentication and those which use personal identification numbers (PINs). The latter are more convenient to automate and more secure. The trend is therefore towards the use of PINs, and PIN validation is likely to come into use at point of sale terminals. IBM, however, go for signature verification.

We saw that file transfer and batched transaction processing are often used. This method uses processing power and communications efficiently, but is subject to delay. The trend is towards increasingly widespread use of on-line transaction processing (OLTP), associated with the more conveniently automated PIN-based authentication.

Large distributed systems of this kind require management: configuration management and evolution in response to failures and bottlenecks and parameter tuning in response to varying load. At present, monitoring processes may report to human managers but the trend is towards increased automation of management processes. An example is that the transactions issued by one company to order goods from another may be input directly to the control mechanisms of the manufacturing processes of the supplying company.

Exercises

23.1 What problems arise from using one operating system process per user terminal?

23.2 How do the problems which arise when single-threaded processes are used for building multi-threaded servers apply to TP system implementations? How have these problems been addressed in practice?

23.3 Why is connection-oriented communication between the components of a TP system less elegant than an RPC system? Why might it be more efficient?

23.4 Why is the use of a separate process for each component of a TP system more flexible than a shared address space solution?

23.5 Indicate where buffered transaction processing is used when goods are paid for by cheque, credit card and debit card. How could on-line TP be brought into point of sale applications?

23.6 (a) What are the factors affecting the design of PIN-based authentication?
(b) What would be the problems arising from a 12 digit PIN?
(c) Why shouldn't I choose a PIN and tell my card issuer by writing it on a form that includes my unencrypted name and address?

23.7 What would be involved in keeping the bank accounts in the bank account database computers and the ATM controllers completely up to date?

23.8 Why are TP benchmarks needed?

Summary and conclusions

24

CONTENTS

24.1 Requirements for implementing concurrent systems

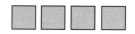

Section 1.5 summarized the requirements that had been drawn from an initial study of a wide range of concurrent systems as follows:

1. Support for separate activities. Examples are:
   the monitoring and control activities in a process control system;
   the running of users' programs by an operating system;
   the handling of devices by an operating system;
   the transactions of the customers of a banking system;
   the concurrent computations executing an application.

2. Support for the management of separate activities, in particular, the ability to create, run, stop and kill them and possibly to indicate their relative priorities.

3. Support for related activities to work together. Examples are:
   parallel activities each generating part of a solution to a problem;
   device handling programs which deliver input data to, or take output data from, user programs;

booking clerks making airline bookings on behalf of clients, when many clerks can interact with the booking database concurrently.

4. The ability to meet timing requirements. Examples are:
   that an alarm might require a response in a specified time;
   the weather forecast must be ready before the time of the forecast arrives;
   users must hear clear, smooth, recognizable speech and see non-jittering video; users should get response in a 'reasonable' time from systems.
   If a real-time application runs above an operating system the application must know what the operating system can guarantee and with what probability. Note that it might be necessary for the application level to indicate the priorities of its separate activities to the underlying operating system in order that timing requirements can be met. This is not possible in most current operating systems.

5. Support for composite tasks. A single task may have several components which are executed concurrently with other tasks. The system may fail after the completion of some of the subtasks but before the whole task is complete.

24.2   Part I

We established a basis for considering the static structure and dynamic behaviour of systems. We described structure in terms of modules, each with an abstract interface and a concrete implementation. We generalized this into an object model which we have used throughout the book. We argued that to understand a system's behaviour we need more than a specification of its structure. We have used object invocations by processes as the means by which dynamic execution of a system is achieved.

Since most concurrent systems will either form part of an operating system or will run above one, making use of its services, we looked at some typical operating system functions and structures. We introduced the ideas of a closed operating system and a microkernel-based, open operating system.

Chapter 3 set up some of the fundamental problems that were to be studied later. Devices, including communications devices, are sources of events in a concurrent system. We studied devices and I/O handling in order to introduce the concept of **synchronization** through a concrete example. We saw how hardware events are handled 'bottom-up' in a system and the need for hardware–process synchronization. We then saw the need for synchronization between application processes, making requests 'top-down' for I/O, with 'bottom-up' physical I/O handling by processes. We saw data **buffers** used between the application processes and the device handler processes to smooth out the data rates of the hardware and the application requiring I/O. This introduced the need for processes to synchronize their accesses to the buffers in order to avoid interference.

We considered devices dedicated to a single user and the more general case of shared devices, such as disks. The software for network handling is similar in function to that for a shared device, but it must often meet more demanding requirements for concurrency and throughput. Communication between different computers is likely to generate more data at a higher rate than that between a computer and a peripheral. Also, systems which differ in their hardware and software may wish to communicate. We studied the ISO reference model as an example of a layered structure. Each layer creates an abstraction and can hide any differences in the implementations of the layers below it. For example, the underlying network might be a ring or an Ethernet, but this is not apparent above the data link level. Communications handling was used as an example of a concurrent system with a specific structure. Also, when we program distributed services or applications, we need to know what communications services are available. This depends both on the underlying hardware characteristics and the communications services and protocols.

The aim of Chapter 4 was to look at the hardware basis of how processes share data. It described memory management functions and introduced the **address space** of a process. We looked at the memory hierarchy, including a processor's hardware-controlled cache. Later we were concerned with whether shared data might be cached by several processors of a multiprocessor; that is, multiple copies of the data might exist rather than a single copy in main memory. Memory management hardware was described so that we could understand how parts of the address space of a process might be shared. Some detailed examples of memory management units were given and mechanisms for sharing and copying data were considered.

We studied filing systems as providers of persistent storage for a system. A file server with many simultaneous clients is a rich source of examples of many aspects of concurrent systems. We looked at the internal implementation of filing systems. We saw that a given operation invoked by an application, such as 'delete a file', may lead to several separate invocations at a lower level within the filing system. This sets up an example of a high-level, composite operation for use in Part III. It also prepares the ground for studying the implications of system crashes when main memory is lost. You had better write a result to persistent store before you tell a user you have done the work. You also need to know whether you can trust the file service you use to write your results to persistent store and not just to a buffer in main memory.

We used the directory service and directory objects as an example of abstraction. A directory may only be accessed through its type operations via the directory service. It may not be read and written arbitrarily by its owner.

Chapter 6 shows how processes are supported by an operating system. Again, we emphasized abstraction and implementation. The implementation of processes is concerned with such things as the data that is held on them and how they may share the processors in a system.

We discussed process scheduling for conventional systems and saw that pre-emptive scheduling is needed for rapid or predictable response to events. Even this may not be sufficient to meet the particular requirements of some real-time systems. Chapter 1 had introduced statically analysable real-time systems, such as process control systems. We studied how a schedule might be devised for such a system, taking into account both periodic and unpredictable events.

We saw how processes might be used within systems. We looked at operating systems with processes dedicated to carrying out operating system functions. An alternative is to use very few dedicated system processes and to have the operating system executed procedurally by applications. We took a first look at multi-threaded processes at the end of Chapter 6.

Chapter 7 is concerned with how a concurrent system is programmed and in particular how concurrency is supported in programming languages. We looked at the functions of the runtime systems of sequential and concurrent programming languages. Again we were concerned with abstractions such as 'coroutine' or 'process' and their implementations.

A sequential programming language might have concurrency extensions. These might be provided as library routines which make operating system calls if and when necessary. Mach's 'C threads package' is an example. This approach is system-dependent and porting a concurrent system to a different operating system could be difficult.

The chapter emphasized that the processes you use in a concurrent programming language may not be processes that are run by the operating system. Real concurrent execution of language-level processes can only be achieved with the cooperation of the operating system. If the operating system supports **multi-threaded processes**, a concurrent program can be written to exploit real concurrency, such as in a multiprocessor architecture.

Part I showed how the abstraction of a concurrent system as a set of concurrent processes is supported by operating systems and language systems. It showed that the processes you write in a language system must be known to and scheduled by the operating system if timing requirements are to be met by the system. **Preemptive process scheduling** is a necessary, but not sufficient, condition for real-time response to be achieved. Special **real-time scheduling** approaches were introduced.

Requirements 1, 2 and 4 were covered in Part I.

24.3 Part II

Part II is concerned with interactions between concurrent processes: requirement 3. We focused on the ability of a system to support the invocation of a single interface operation on an object by concurrent processes, without interference. The object to be invoked might be in the same address space as the invoking processes, in a separate address space on the same machine or in a machine across a network.

There is a need for both shared-memory IPC and separate address space IPC in many concurrent systems. If a requirement is to build servers that can have the requests of many clients in progress at the same time, the ideal arrangement is to have multi-threading within the server and shared memory for inter-thread communication.

If it is desirable for processes to run in separate address spaces for protection purposes, memory management techniques can be used to avoid copying data between address spaces.

We saw how communications software is used to augment IPC when cross-network object invocation is needed.

We can assume that the name of an object in the same address space as a process is known. If the object is in another address space on the same machine we assume that the operating system can support the required naming and location. The operating system extends each process's name space for the purpose of IPC. When the object to be invoked can be on a remote machine, a global naming scheme must be supported by the system. At the end of Part II we considered some approaches to providing a global naming service, for example the use of dedicated name servers, and the case studies in Chapter 22 gave further examples. Naming, location, binding and protection of objects in a global context is part of the subject matter of an advanced course in distributed systems design.

The fact that components of a distributed system may fail independently leads to a need for transactions.

24.4   Part III

Part III's concern was concurrency control when processes carry out related operations on a number of objects, requirement 5. Each separate invocation can be assumed to be atomic, but the composite operations must also be made atomic. The so-called ACID properties of transactions were motivated. Examples were given to illustrate that concurrent composite operations occur in systems and applications other than transaction processing systems.

We used an object model as a basis for reasoning about transactions and a definition of conflict based on non-commutativity. We assumed that, in theory, a complete history of invocations starting from *create* is recorded at each object as a correct representation of its state.

We studied three approaches to concurrency control: locking, time stamping and optimistic concurrency control. Although most existing systems use some form of two-phase locking, other methods may be more suitable for distributed systems because they are based on information recorded at each object rather than centrally. As distributed systems become more widespread these methods may become more widely used.

We contrasted the pessimistic (strict two-phase locking and strict time-stamp ordering) and optimistic approaches to concurrency control. Pessimistic methods are simpler and therefore easier to comprehend, but they reduce potential concurrency. This is because an object used by a transaction is not available to other transactions until the first transaction commits or aborts. Optimistic methods provide high availability of objects based on the premise that conflict is unlikely and therefore a great deal of mechanism to prevent it is misplaced and bad for system performance. There is a risk of greater complexity in ensuring a consistent system state if conflict does occur. The choice of a concurrency control method for a given system must take into account the requirements of the applications that will use it and the assumptions on which the method is based.

When we came to reason about crash recovery we made the assumption that, in practice, a reduced form of an object's state would be used instead of a full invocation history. We had to allow for crashes at any time, including during crash recovery procedures. This made it necessary to discuss idempotent operations. The existence of a record of an object's state before and after an invocation makes this easy to achieve. In general, operations are not idempotent.

We outlined how transaction processing systems might be distributed, but left a full treatment of this topic for further study. It was easy to extend the object model for distributed systems. We looked at an atomic commitment protocol, two-phase commit. This gives the flavour of how the characteristics of distributed systems must be taken into account when we attempt to distribute concurrency control or commitment. The concept of transaction is fundamental to an understanding of distributed systems.

A transaction processing system must know whether the operating system on which it runs has written data to persistent store and not just to a buffer in volatile main memory.

24.5   Part IV

Seventh edition UNIX is the ancestor of all current UNIX systems and was described in some detail. The heavyweight process model of UNIX makes it difficult to build servers above it. A UNIX process runs in a separate address space, can share no data with other processes and makes synchronous, and therefore potentially blocking, system calls. User-level IPC is based on the pipe: an unstructured, synchronized byte stream between processes with a common ancestor, which adds to this difficulty. Later versions have provided completely new IPC and we looked at this aspect of BSD 4.3 and System V. The latter also provides shared memory and we saw how shared writeable data might be used in that system.

Processes executing the UNIX kernel are scheduled non-preemptively. There is no way of achieving guaranteed real-time response, or multiprocessor operation, without a rewrite of the kernel. SunOS 5.0 is the result of such a rewrite (Khanna *et al.*, 1992). A vast amount of software has been written to run above UNIX and there is commercial interest in at least supporting the UNIX system call interface in future systems.

Chapter 22 described the Mach and CHORUS microkernels, which are binary compatible with UNIX BSD 4.3 and System V.4 respectively, but also support multiprocessor operation. Many other microkernels have been developed, often in university research environments, but the evolution of Mach and CHORUS highlighted the integration of established research results as the designs evolved. It is interesting to see how similar they have become.

It is also interesting to see the time it takes for a research system to become a commercial product. The UNIX design dates from 1969 and the Mach and CHORUS designs from about 1979. Sustained effort and massive funding are needed as well as a good basic design.

These and other systems have demonstrated the feasibility of the microkernel approach. There is a trade-off between modularity and efficiency. If you provide services above the kernel there is IPC overhead in invoking them. If you integrate services into the kernel you have a massive, closed, inflexible, difficult to maintain system, but you have avoided the overhead of user-level services.

Both systems support multi-threaded processes; both use message passing as the basic IPC mechanism; both employ globally named ports as the destinations for messages. Although both implement the microkernel as processes invoked by message passing instead of having it in each process's address space, invoked procedurally, CHORUS has the concept of supervisor actors which are claimed to be a compromise, avoiding separate address space and context switching overhead, but retaining modularity of the kernel. Both systems employ memory mapping techniques to provide efficient IPC and data sharing.

The current generation of networks are capable of supporting high, sustained data transfer rates. This has led to interest in using them as a basis for multimedia working. The challenge for designers of communications and operating systems software is to provide real-time guarantees to the application level. Chapter 22 concludes with a description of projects in my own laboratory which are based on networks of this kind.

Chapter 23 first discussed the implementation of transaction processing monitors. It was shown that it is necessary to know the process model of the underlying operating system and the IPC facilities provided. Single threaded processes and synchronous system calls were again shown to cause problems and multithreaded processes and RPC were shown to provide a general and flexible model for implementing a system.

Electronic fund transfer systems are examples of TP systems. The use of batched transactions and the trend towards on-line transaction processing were noted. Typical transaction sizes and rates were given and the need for benchmarks was discussed.

24.6 Hardware developments and their implications for software

System designers must exploit technology. A motivation for studying concurrent systems is to be in a position to exploit current and future processors, memories, storage devices and communications media.

For this reason, a technology-driven order of presentation was chosen, starting from devices and networks. It is important to be aware of current and projected hardware performance characteristics and some examples were included of device and network interfaces and MMUs. In all cases references were given to sources of detailed information.

RISC processor design seems likely to dominate the market for general purpose systems for reasons of price–performance, simplicity of design and time to the marketplace. Measurements of RISC machines are based on sequential programs running on uniprocessors. Part II highlighted the implications for shared memory IPC of multiprocessors comprising processors without test-and-set or equivalent instructions and designed to exploit caching of data values. A concurrent program on a uniprocessor RISC could forbid interrupts while a flag was tested and set but a multiprocessor implementation would require a complex algorithm to be run. Marking semaphore values as non-cacheable would also affect performance. The area of processor and multiprocessor support for concurrency requires further research and experiment. It is not clear that shared-memory multiprocessors will become commonplace, rather than networked uniprocessors, but if they do, we shall need to consider these issues. The correctness of concurrency control procedures must be ensured because they are at the heart of every system, and in particular those that are safety-critical.

An 'I/O bottleneck' is likely to occur because of the divergence of processor and network speeds compared with those of electromechanical storage devices. Increasing memory sizes could alleviate the problem, for example by using a large read cache for files, but when data must be guaranteed to be stored securely on stable storage before its receipt is acknowledged, main memory will not suffice. Non-volatile memory (NVRAM) tends to cost about four times as much as volatile RAM but is likely to be used for write caches. RAM disks (memory accessed through a block-level interface) of about 200 Mbyte are already available and although the storage they provide is volatile they may have a backup power supply and disk in case of power failure. Disks may become obsolete in twenty years or so.

Copying data in main memory is a source of inefficiency which is always undesirable and sometimes intolerable, for example when very high-speed networks are delivering large amounts of data. We have seen how memory management techniques such as remapping and copy-on-write can be used to avoid data copying, and this is likely to become a standard approach. A less obvious way of avoiding data copying is to integrate file I/O and memory management to map files into the virtual address spaces of processes, as described in Section 5.7.

The desk area network (DAN) project, which was described briefly in Section 22.4, is investigating whether the ATM network cell may be used internally as the unit of data transfer within a single system as well as for network transmission. It is important that the international standards for wide area ATM, the B-ISDN, should allow this use.

It is disquieting to see that some processor designs are assuming that operating systems are invoked procedurally, no doubt influenced by UNIX. In Section

8.3 we saw a design that allocates half a process's address space to three operating system segments. This is unfortunate at a time when message passing, to operating systems which occupy a separate address space, is beginning to predominate.

24.7 A design consensus?

A microkernel approach to operating system design is established as feasible. It has all the software engineering advantages following from modularity and allows special-purpose systems, such as dedicated communications or storage servers, to be built, as well as workstations. The extra overhead of providing services at user rather than system level has been found to be tolerable, although certain communications, device control and memory management functions have been tried outside the microkernel and have been put back inside it.

Increasingly, systems are supporting multi-threaded processes. Shared memory IPC is used between the threads of a process (within a single address space) and message passing is used between threads in different address spaces. Coping with very large numbers of threads is a new problem and some simplification may be appropriate for some application areas.

Complexity must be avoided in the kernel design, particularly if an application-level thread which is waiting for a hardware event must be scheduled in a guaranteed time after the event occurs. We must know what is on the path through the kernel to the point at which control passes to the application. A design aim is that the kernel should provide simple thread-scheduling mechanisms, and any complex algorithms, such as those to determine the relative priorities of threads within and between applications, should run above the kernel. They could then be executed at lower priority than certain applications.

Memory management techniques are now used routinely to avoid copying data. Even these techniques, although designed to reduce overhead, are themselves quite expensive. The approach of providing simple mechanisms in the kernel and more complex ones, appropriate for specific applications, at user level is being used in some systems. The integration of virtual memory and file I/O seems to have become accepted after an uneasy history, starting from Multics in the mid 1960s. The best paging algorithms for mapped files are unlikely to be those based on the principle of locality of program execution.

Much of computer science is concerned with **managing complexity** by creating abstractions. This enables systems to be modelled at different levels of detail so that at a high level of abstraction the behaviour of an entire system can be comprehended, while at a low level we can focus on the details of a specific component and its immediate surroundings. Some degree of object orientation as a design methodology or a system architecture has become accepted. It is claimed that programmers prefer to work with a higher-level interface than mapped files, and persistent object-oriented programming languages may come to fulfil this need.

24.8   Further study

We have not studied naming, location and protection of objects in a distributed system in depth. An advanced course on distributed systems would cover these topics and also authentication of principals, encryption for secure communication and the problems of **very large-scale systems**. In large-scale systems naming and location data is replicated for high availability. When data replicas are made a new range of problems arises associated with the system's policy on updating the data replicas. Should every replica be updated before anyone can read any replica or should we live with inconsistency, and the possibility of reading out-of-date information, for the sake of high availability of the service? We studied the two-phase commit protocol in Chapter 20. Should such a protocol be used to update a set of replicas and, if so, what should be done about replicas that reside on systems that are not available when the protocol is run?

New issues have arisen in the area of scheduling because operating systems that can run on multiprocessors support multi-threaded processes. If timing requirements must be met by the system it is necessary for the applications to be able to specify the priority of their threads. How best to manage large numbers of threads and many priorities and how to make and meet timing guarantees is still to be determined.

Thread scheduling is just one aspect of meeting **quality of service (QOS)** requirements. New high-speed networks have made it possible for multimedia applications to be developed for general-purpose systems. The distinguishing characteristic of these applications is that the requests they make for system service are **dynamic**. This is in contrast with conventional real-time systems, where a process schedule can be worked out in advance. Another difference is that in static real-time systems a schedule can be worked out so that processes meet their deadlines with a high probability. An unmet deadline could cause catastrophe procedures to be invoked. In a dynamic real-time system it might not be possible to meet users' requests which arrive in bursts. It is possible to arrange for the system to **degrade gracefully** or for some users to be delayed.

In order to meet QOS requirements for a number of applications of this kind it is necessary:

- For the application to be able to specify its requirements in detail.

- For the operating system (microkernel) to be able to determine, and specify, the time it takes to respond to any event.

- For resource requirements, such as storage, to be available, and for the time taken to provide them to be determined and guaranteed. This requires the cooperation of services provided above a microkernel.

- For the communications time between the various hosts which must cooperate to provide a service to be deterministic and bounded.

We have studied where concurrency control is needed in systems. Many published algorithms for concurrency control have later been shown to be incorrect. Although readers have sometimes been encouraged to try their hand at concurrent algorithm design, it was emphasized that they are very likely to make mistakes and should compare their algorithms with those proved correct elsewhere. Further study in the area of formal methods is recommended for anyone who must design concurrent algorithms.

24.9   Conclusions

There is a need to understand some high-level, abstract principles of system design to avoid being overwhelmed by the complexity of the low-level detail. Modularity and concurrency capture the notions of static structure and dynamic execution of software systems.

A modular system structure is usually discernible in an existing system and one can then explore how the functions provided are invoked dynamically by concurrent processes. We have explored a procedural approach to invocation, exemplified by UNIX at a large-system level and by monitors at a fine granularity, and a separate address space approach, exemplified by Mach and CHORUS, at the system level. Above the operating system we have used either an object model or a simple client–server model for the software systems we have studied.

The microkernel designs presented here are adequate for today's systems but there are already new requirements to be met. These result from developments in network technology making new application areas feasible and the need to give guarantees of quality of service to these applications. Some of the techniques that have been developed for real-time systems will be needed in mainstream operating systems.

We have seen the time lag, measured in decades, between research projects and commercial systems based on them. We have also seen the enormous investment of time and human effort involved in this process, particularly when compatibility with previous systems must be ensured. It is easy to say that it would be a good thing to allow the researchers the resources to get the ideas right in the first place, but this seems to be impossible to achieve politically. It could be made easier for future system designers to spend a period carrying out research.

Concurrency is hard to comprehend and we get it wrong. One's instinct is often to restrict concurrency in order to achieve a simple algorithm and this should be done where appropriate. The author's experience in writing Part III provides an example. We discussed optimistic and pessimistic approaches to concurrency control. Pessimistic methods restrict and simplify the issues and are relatively easy to describe. One has to be more careful that one has reasoned correctly if one adopts an optimistic method. The sections on optimistic methods required many iterations of exposition. You think you finally see the problem clearly; next day you see the algorithm from another angle and realize it is flawed. It is not surprising that published algorithms are later found to contain errors! The object model is a good basis for reasoning, but more formal models are also needed.

Unfortunately, we shall need to write highly concurrent systems if we are to exploit future computer systems. Programmers have to work to deadlines and incorrect algorithms will be implemented.

If the lowest level of concurrency control, such as the implementation of the signal and wait operations on a semaphore, is not implemented correctly, people will die as a result. We rely on computer systems to control our medical equipment, the planes we fly in, and our industrial, commercial and financial infrastructure. We are past the stage of being able to remove computer systems from these processes. We must strive for correctness ensured by mathematical modelling based on sound systems assumptions. It is dangerous to implement concurrency control without mathematics. It is futile to build models of concurrency without systems knowledge.

As computer science has grown, each of its areas has acquired more specialized knowledge. We have seen a divergence of closely related specialisms, such as operating systems, real-time systems, communications, transaction processing and databases. This can result in an unfortunate tendency to reinvent wheels and avoid the questioning of assumptions. The curriculum at undergraduate level should work against this divergence rather than reinforce it.

Appendix: Two case studies with exercises

CONTENTS

A.1 *N*-process mutual exclusion for shared memory and distributed systems

A.1.1 Requirements

Section 9.2 discussed how processes can achieve mutually exclusive access to shared data. There we emphasized the use of hardware support in the form of a composite instruction and discussed the option of forbidding interrupts inside the kernel of a uniprocessor. We now return to the case of a shared-memory multiprocessor comprising processors without support for concurrency. We have seen that RISC processors may be like this.

A great deal of research effort has been directed towards this problem. It was first discussed by Dijkstra (1965) and the Dutch mathematician Dekker was the first to publish a correct algorithm, for two processes. This algorithm was generalized to *n*-processes by Dijkstra. Subsequently, versions with greater efficiency and alternative algorithms were devised. We shall study two of these algorithms.

Each process contains a critical region (CR) of code which it may execute any number of times. The phases of a process's execution may be represented as follows:

execute non-critical code
    execute an **entry protocol** for the critical region
        execute the critical region
    execute an **exit protocol** for the critical region
execute non-critical code

The requirements on an algorithm implemented by the entry and exit protocols are as follows:

- The processes may run on a multiprocessor, so we cannot forbid interrupts to achieve mutual exclusion.
- The processors may not have a composite read–modify–write instruction. We must solve the problem by software alone.
- The processes are not identical and no assumption can be made about their relative speeds. It is not satisfactory to arrange that they enter their critical regions in some specific order.
- A process may halt in its non-critical region. This must not affect the other processes. It may not halt in its critical region nor in the entry and exit protocols for it.
- The algorithm must be free from deadlock. If some processes are attempting to enter their critical region then one of them must eventually succeed.
- The algorithm must be free from starvation for every process. If a process commences execution of the entry protocol it must eventually succeed.
- In the absence of contention for the critical region the overhead of executing the entry protocol should be minimal.

A.1.2 The *N*-process mutual exclusion protocol of Eisenberg and McGuire (1972)

Let us assume n processes, $P_0,...,P_{n-1}$ which share two variables:

procphase: **array**[0..*n*–1]**of**(*out-cr, want-cr, claim-cr*);
turn: 0..*n*–1;

Initially, all entries in the array *procphase* are set to *out-cr* (no process is in the critical region or seeking entry to it) and *turn* has some arbitrary value, say *turn*=0. Figure A.1 gives an example to illustrate how *procphase* and *turn* are used and how they must be manipulated by the entry and exit protocols. In the algorithms i indicates the process identifier and j is a local variable of each process P_i.

The entry protocol for process P_i expresses the intention of entering the critical region by setting *procphase*[*i*]=*want-cr*. If no other process P_k for some k between *turn* and i (in circular order) has expressed a similar intention, then P_i asserts its right to enter the critical region by setting *procphase*[*i*]=*claim-cr*. Provided that P_i is the only process to have asserted its right, it enters the critical region by setting *turn*=*i*; if there is contention it restarts the entry protocol.

The exit protocol for process P_i examines the array *procphase* in the order $i+1, i+2,..., n-1,0,1,..., i-1$. If a process is found which has the value *want-cr* (or possibly *claim-cr*) in *procphase*, then *turn* is set to the identifier of that process. In the example in Figure A.1, P_2's exit protocol would set *turn*=3. If every

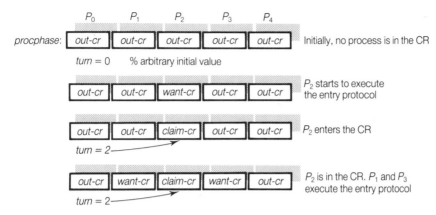

Figure A.1
An example of the use of *procphase* and *turn* by five processes to achieve mutual exclusion.

The exit protocol executed by P_2 will choose a successor, if possible, and will set *turn* to that process's ID and *procphase*[2] = *out-cr*.

process, other than *i* itself, has *value out-cr* in *procphase*, then *turn* remains at value *i*. Finally, P_i sets its own value in *procphase* to *out-cr*.

The algorithm depends on scanning the list of processes in circular order (see Figure A.2). While process P_i is executing the critical region *turn=i*; if at its exit from the critical region no other process has expressed an intention of entering then *turn* remains set to *i*, otherwise P_i sets *turn* to the identifier of the first interested process.

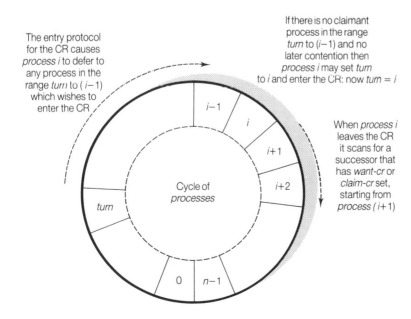

Figure A.2
Scanning *n* processes in circular order.

We introduce the notation $j\oplus 1$ for $(j+1 \bmod n)$. The complete algorithm is as follows:

non-critical code

```
% entry protocol for process i
repeat
    procphase[i]:=want-cr;
    j:=turn;
    while j≠i                              % no check if turn=i
        do if procphase[j]=out-cr
            then  j:= j⊕1
            else j:=turn;                  % restart scan
        procphase[i]:=claim-cr;            % no prior claimant
        j:=i⊕1;
        while (procphase[j]≠claim-cr)do j:= j⊕1;   % contention ?
    until (j=i) and (turn=i or procphase[turn]=out-cr);
    turn:=i;
```

critical region (CR)

```
% exit protocol for process i
    j:= turn⊕1;         %    turn=i
    while (procphase[j]=out-cr)do j:= j⊕1;          % any interest ?
    turn:=j ;
    procphase[i]:=out-cr;
```

non-critical code

Suppose that a process has finished its turn but has found no successor waiting to enter (see Figure A.2). Later, process i starts its entry protocol. procphase[i] will be reset to out-cr only after process i has been through its critical region; hence only processes to which process i defers can obtain right of entry before it does. Any such process on exit will detect that process i is waiting to enter, unless some other process intermediate in the cycle is also waiting, At worst, process i will be given its turn after a single critical region execution by each such intermediate process.

In order to understand the entry protocol we shall use an example with five processes and consider some simple cases, followed by parallel execution of the entry protocol.

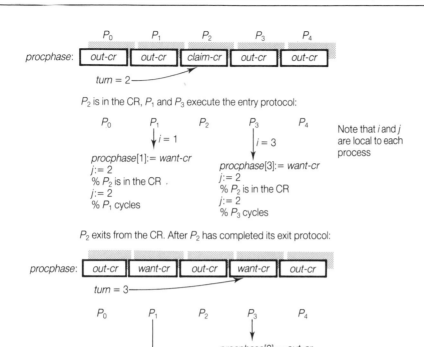

Figure A.3
An example illustrating the entry protocol.

Figure A.3 illustrates the case where two processes are waiting to enter the critical region when P_2 exits from it. P_3 detects that P_2 has left the region and that *turn*=3. It therefore proceeds to set *procphase*[3]=*claim-cr* and (eventually) *turn*=3.

Exercise

A.1 What happens if P_1 runs before P_3 after P_2 exits from the critical region?

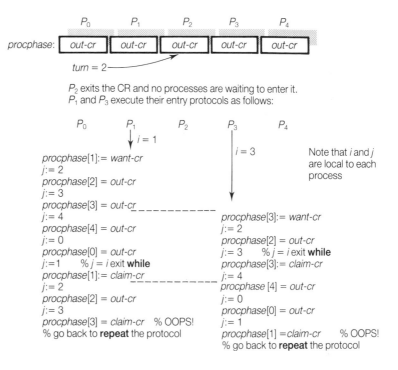

Figure A.4
Parallel execution
of the entry
protocol.

Figure A.4 illustrates the case where P_2 exits from the critical region and no processes are waiting to enter. Later P_1 and P_3 execute the entry protocol with instruction execution in parallel as shown in the figure.

Exercises

A.2 (a) What happens when P_1 and P_3 restart their entry protocols? Why do they not cycle indefinitely as shown in the figure?
(b) What happens if P_2 attempts to re-enter the critical region while P_1 and P_3 are executing the entry protocol as shown? Recall that *turn* still has value 2 when P_2 has finished the exit protocol in this example.
(c) What happens if P_0 and P_4 start to execute the entry protocol?
(d) How many turns can P_1 have to wait between starting its entry protocol by setting *want-cr* and entering its critical region?

Some general **questions** on the Eisenberg–McGuire algorithm are as follows:

A.3 Can you argue (informally) that the algorithm preserves mutual exclusion?

A.4 Is it the case that once a process has expressed an interest in entering the critical region it will not be delayed indefinitely? (Is the algorithm free from starvation?)

A.5 If several processes want to enter the critical region will one of them succeed eventually? Is the algorithm free from deadlock?

A.6 What is the overhead of executing the algorithm in the absence of contention? Express the number of tests made as a function of *n*.

A.1.3 The *N*-process bakery algorithm

In 1974 Lamport published an algorithm based on the method used in bakeries, shoe shops etc. for achieving service in first come first served order. The idea is that a process which wishes to enter the critical region takes a ticket and it is arranged that the processes enter the critical region in the order of the number on their tickets.

The shared data structures are:

taking: **array** [0..*n*–1] **of** *boolean*;   % initialized to *false*
ticket: **array** [0..*n*–1] **of** *integer*;   % initialized to 0

In order to express the algorithm concisely we use a 'less than' relation on ordered pairs of integers, so that:

$(a,b) < (c,d)$ if $a < c$ or if $a=c$ and $b < d$

The bakery algorithm is as follows:

non-critical code
    critical region (CR)

```
% entry protocol for the critical region for process i
    taking[i]:=true;
    ticket[i]:=max(ticket[0],ticket[1],...,ticket[n–1])+1
    taking[i]:=false;
    for j:=0 to n–1
        do begin
            while taking[j]do no-op;
            while ticket[j] ≠ 0 and (ticket[j],j) < (ticket[i],i) do no-op;
        end
```

non-critical code

```
% exit protocol for the critical region for process i
    ticket[i]:=0;
```

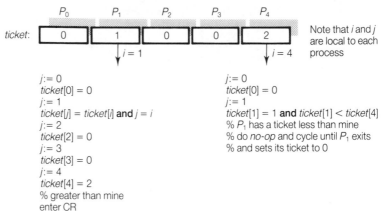

Figure A.5
Parallel
execution of the
bakery protocol.

Suppose that P_1 has taken a ticket with number 1 and P_4 then takes a ticket with 2

Exercises

A.7   Figure A.5 gives a simple example. Work through this case and complete the entry protocol for P_4. If P_4 completes its exit protocol, what will be the value of the ticket taken by the next process to enter the critical region?

A.8   Under what circumstances will the values of the tickets increase indefinitely? Is this likely to be a problem?

A.9   Notice that it is possible for processes to have tickets with the same value. How does the entry protocol ensure that only one process at a time enters the critical region?

A.10   Can you argue (informally) that the algorithm preserves mutual exclusion?

A.11   Is it the case that once a process has expressed an interest in entering the critical region it will not be delayed indefinitely? (Is the algorithm free from starvation?)

A.12   If several processes want to enter the critical region will one of them succeed eventually? Is the algorithm free from deadlock?

A.13   What is the overhead of executing the algorithm in the absence of contention? Express the number of tests made as a function of n.

A.14   Compare the two algorithms with respect to scheduling of processes (order of entry into the critical region), overhead, ease of comprehension and programming. Consider how each behaves under heavy contention.

A.15 In Section 9.5 we discussed the implementation of semaphore operations. Section 9.5.1 concluded: 'This is a difficult and crucial area of system design. When we have built atomic and correct WAIT and SIGNAL operations which are guaranteed to terminate we can build the rest of the concurrent system above them'. Discuss how the algorithms presented here could be used to implement atomic WAIT and SIGNAL in the kernel of a multiprocessor based on hardware without support for concurrency control. Is the overhead involved in executing the algorithms acceptable for this purpose? Is the overhead acceptable for implementing user-level semaphore operations?

A.1.4 Distributed *N*-process mutual exclusion

Consider *n* processes executing on *n* processors with no shared memory. A problem discussed in the literature is to devise an algorithm to implement a critical region within each process. As discussed in Chapters 14 and 20 any such algorithm must take into account the possibility of independent failures of the components of distributed systems, the absence of global time and the delay involved in communications between components.

In order to explore the characteristics of applications for which a distributed mutual exclusion protocol may be appropriate we shall start from an example of a **centralized data object** with **distributed processing**.

Assume that *n* processes are cooperating to process data in a shared file and that the processes must use a conventional file server which sees a file as an unstructured byte sequence. Processes read the data in fixed size records, of size *k* bytes, process it, write it back to its original place in the file, read another record, and so on (see Figure A.6). The processes may run at different speeds and the processing of the records may involve variable amounts of computing.

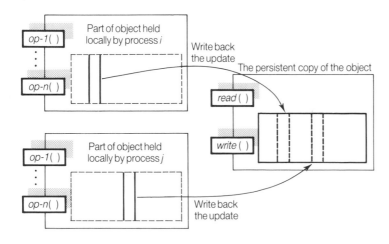

Figure A.6
Centralized object, distributed operation invocation.

The problem is to ensure that no record of the file is processed by more than one process and that all records are processed by some process.

If a process requests to read 'the next k bytes' (relative to some system-maintained pointer) the file server delivers a unique portion of the file to each process. Unfortunately, the process is unable to write back the record because it does not know the position of the record in the file; other processes may change the position of the pointer. If, instead, each process asks for a specific range of bytes, it is possible that more than one process will read a given range (or that some records will be missed) unless they coordinate their activities.

The file service interface does not provide the functionality required by the cooperating processes. We may adopt two approaches to solving this problem:

- A centralized approach: provide an 'access coordination server' (or coordinator) which tells the processes which record they may process.

  Note that we must avoid introducing extra data transfers into the distributed system. We must not put the coordinator on the data transfer path between the file server and the processes. Instead, each free process should ask the coordinator for a byte range in the file which is may process.

  Note that we are not implementing the coordinator as a server which functions as an object manager. It does not perform operation invocations on the object; we wish to have these done in parallel by the processes. Our coordinator is part of the process of assessing the object, similar to an object location server which is transparent to client (object invoker) and server (object manager).

- A distributed approach. The processes execute a protocol to ensure that no record of the file is processed by more than one process and that all records are processed by some process. Before going into the details of such protocols we first consider some more general examples.

Replicated or distributed data objects

In the example above there is a single copy of the data object, and we arranged carefully that no part of it would be acquired by more than one process. We now consider the possibility that multiple copies of objects or parts of objects might exist in a distributed system.

For example, suppose that a system supports object mapping. Suppose that several processes have mapped a given object in their address spaces (see Figure A.7). When process i wishes to invoke an operation on its local copy of the object it must first coordinate with the other processes to ensure that it has exclusive access to the object or some specified part of it.

Another example is a distributed game with n players. Suppose each player has a copy of the game's data and that only one player at once may make a change to the data. The change is propagated to all the other players.

Another example is a multimedia, on-line conferencing system. Each delegate sees some replicated objects and some private objects. A participant may only make a change to a replicated object after executing a distributed mutual exclu-

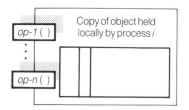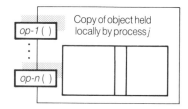

Figure A.7
A replicated or
distributed object.

sion protocol. A similar situation arises when a participant wishes to speak. It is agreed that only one person may speak at once and obtaining permission to speak requires a mutual exclusion protocol.

A.1.5 Approaches to implementing distributed *N*-process mutual exclusion

Three approaches to implementing *n*-process distributed mutual exclusion are now outlined. The exercises which follow guide the reader in exploring the trade-offs and potential problems. Raynal (1986) contains these and other algorithms. The fully distributed approach was discussed in Lamport (1978) and the algorithm presented below was devised by Ricart and Agrawala (1983).

Centralized algorithm

This approach is similar to that described above for a centralized access coordination server or coordinator. The idea is that one of the *n* processes is elected as coordinator. Each process sends a request to the coordinator before entering its CR. The coordinator checks whether any process is in the CR and, if so, accumulates a queue of requests. When the CR becomes free the coordinator sends a reply to a process, selected according to some specified scheduling policy, and this process receives the message and proceeds into its CR. On exit from its CR it sends a release message to the coordinator.

Token passing in a virtual ring of processes

The processes are ordered into a virtual ring and a 'token' is devised. The token comprises a message which all processes recognize as permission to enter the CR. The token is passed from process to process in the order specified. When a process receives the token it may, if it wishes, enter its CR. In this case it keeps the token and passes it on to the next process on exit from the CR. Otherwise it passes on the token immediately. Notice the similarity of the scheduling policy to that of the Eisenberg–McGuire algorithm for shared-memory systems.

A distributed algorithm

The aim is to implement a first come first served scheduling policy. Recall the discussion of Section 14.1 on the ordering of events in distributed systems.

When a process wishes to enter its CR it sends a request message to all processes, including itself, and includes a time-stamp with the message. The system has a policy for global ordering of time-stamps: for example, if any time-stamps are equal, the associated process *id*s are used to achieve a unique global ordering of the request messages. On receiving a request message a process may reply immediately or may defer sending a reply as follows:

- If a process is in its CR it defers sending a reply.
- If a process does not want to enter its CR it sends a reply immediately.
- If a process wants to enter its CR but has not yet done so then it compares the time-stamp on its own request with the time-stamp of the incoming request. If its own time-stamp is greater than that of the incoming request it sends a reply immediately (the other process asked first). Otherwise it defers its reply.

A process that has received a reply from all the other processes may enter its CR. On exit from the CR the process replies to any requests that it has deferred. Notice the similarity of the scheduling policy to that of the bakery algorithm.

Exercises

A.16 How many messages are required for the entry and exit protocols for the three methods described above?

A.17 Consider each of the above algorithms in the absence of failures. Is mutual exclusion achieved and is each free from deadlock and starvation?

A.18 Discuss the susceptibility to failure of each of the three algorithms. First, consider the effect on the algorithm as stated. Then consider how it might be adapted to take account of failure. You may assume that the system provides an 'aliveness and notification service'. You register an interest in certain processes with the service. It tells you if any of these processes fail.
(a) Consider death of the coordinator for the centralized algorithm. Also consider death of any other process at any time.
(b) Consider death of any process at any time and loss of the token for the token passing algorithm.
(c) Consider death of any process at any time for the distributed algorithm. Note that the algorithm is designed to expect delay.

A.19 For each of the three algorithms:
(a) How many processes does each process need to know about?
(b) How easy is it for a new process to join the existing group?

A.2   Management of a disk block cache

A.2.1   Disk read and write and the requirement for buffers and a cache

We shall assume a conventional file I/O model rather than files mapped into virtual memory. A **read** or **write** request from a client of a filing system typically specifies a byte sequence. Let us assume that such a request has been converted by the filing system into a request to read or write a sub-sequence of bytes from or to some disk block. In practice a requested byte sequence may span more than one disk block, but we can generalize to this from the single block case.

It is necessary to have **buffers** to hold blocks of information on their way to or from the disk. The client program requires a subsequence of a block, DMA transfers between disk and memory deliver a block. We therefore assume a pool of disk buffers is available, each one with a data area large enough to hold a disk block and a header to hold information about the block. A block could be delivered directly into user space, but for several reasons it is more usual for the filing system to maintain a pool of buffers.

Once a disk block is read into a buffer for some client program, a number of read requests might be satisfied from that buffer. Having read from a buffer, the client may wish to change the data and write it back. The filing system may detect that the disk block needed for the write is still available in a buffer. Also, files can be shared, so it is possible that read and write requests from any client program might be satisfied from a buffer already in memory. We are moving towards using our pool of buffers as a **cache**.

Exercise

A.20   What are the advantages and disadvantages of having a system-maintained cache of disk blocks in volatile main memory?

In more detail, on a client **read** or **write**:

- The cache is searched to see if the required block is already there. If so the request is carried out via the cache. Note that when a cache block has been modified by a **write** the data on disk is no longer up to date, and the cached block must at some point be written to disk.

On a **read**:

- If the required block is not in the cache a free buffer must be acquired and filled by a disk read.

On a **write**:

- If the required block is not already in the cache a free buffer must be acquired. If that block of the file already exists it must be read from disk so that the subsequence of bytes may be written into it, to change some existing bytes or to append to the end of a previously written area. If the block does not already exist it is sufficient to acquire a new buffer.

Having outlined the client requirements we now focus on the buffer management that is needed to satisfy them.

A.2.2   Allocated and free buffers

As a first attempt at buffer management let us propose:

- An *available* list which contains buffers that do not hold any valid data. When a new buffer is needed it is taken from the head of this list. When a buffer is no longer required it is put back at the head of the list. This requires only a singly linked list data structure. We extend this definition after the discussion below.

- An *in-use* data structure which provides access to buffers which hold valid data. Whenever a client issues **read** or **write** this structure must be searched to determine whether the disk block is in the cache, so access must be efficient. A simple solution is to use an open hash table: we hash on the disk block number to find the bucket that would contain the buffer. Hash table slots use little memory compared with a disk buffer, so it is fair to assume that there are about as many buckets as buffers. On this assumption it is efficient to organize each bucket as a simple list.

In the previous section we argued that the buffer should be used as a cache for data on disk, and we do not release buffers as soon as each transfer is complete. In this case, we must decide on a policy for recovering blocks that are *in-use*. An obvious case is when a file is closed by a client and no other client has the file open. Any of its buffers *in-use* can be added to the *available* list. Any that contain new data must first be written out to disk.

We also have to solve the problem of what to do if there are no free buffers when we need one. A reasonable strategy is to attempt to find buffers that have fallen out of use. We can implement an approximate 'Least Recently Used (LRU)' policy over all the blocks in the buffer pool. It is proposed that the *available* list should be defined as follows:

- Any free block and any buffer that is allocated but not locked should not be on the *available* list. The hash lists of the *in-use* data structure contain buffers that are both *locked* and *unlocked*. They also contain blocks that have fallen out of use in the cache, for example when a file is closed, but have not yet been reassigned. When a buffer is locked for use by some process it is detached from the *available* list. When a buffer is no longer required by any process and is unlocked it may be replaced in the *available* list, at the *head* if it does not hold valid disk data, at the *tail* if it does. When a new buffer is needed it is taken from the *head* of the *available* list; it will either be free, or it should be LRU.

To implement such a policy requires that we organize the *available* list as a doubly linked list. We must be able to determine the status of the data held in the buffer from information kept in the header. It may be that the data in a buffer in the *available* list has not been written out to disk. This must be done before the buffer can be reused, and the write to disk is initiated. In the meantime we continue the scan from the head of the list in search of a buffer that is not dirty.

A.2.3   The structure of a buffer

A disk buffer comprises a header and a data field which is sufficiently large to hold a disk block. A disk block is identified uniquely by the identifier of a filing system and its number within that filing system. This information is held in the buffer header. We shall use a simple integer to identify each block in the examples.

Figure A.8 shows the contents of a buffer header. The disk block held in the buffer is identified; two pointers link the buffer in the *available* list, and a further one indicates the next buffer in the same bucket of the *in-use* data structure.

The status field indicates the current status of the buffer. Several of these conditions may hold at a given time:

- The buffer is *locked* (so that a change to the header and/or data can be made). The *lock* operation must be atomic.

- The buffer contains valid data. It could be that the buffer is allocated to a certain block but the block has yet to be read into it.

- The data area must be written to disk before the buffer is reused. This is sometimes referred to as a 'dirty' condition; the data has been changed since being read from disk.

- The buffer's data area is in the process of being written to disk or read from disk by a DMA transfer.

- A process is waiting to use this buffer.

In general, processes should be able to WAIT for a specific buffer or for any, as appropriate, and must be SIGNALled when a buffer is *unlocked*.

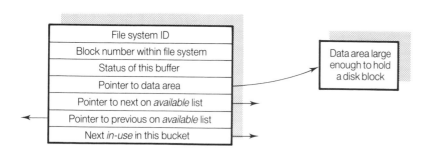

| File system ID |
| Block number within file system |
| Status of this buffer |
| Pointer to data area |
| Pointer to next on *available* list |
| Pointer to previous on *available* list |
| Next *in-use* in this bucket |

Data area large enough to hold a disk block

Figure A.8
A disk buffer header.

Exercise

A.21 Outline the procedure for reading data into a newly acquired buffer. Assume that a process has found a free buffer. What information should it record in the header, and in what order, to achieve a read without interference? Can you ensure that two processes do not acquire a buffer for the same block at the same time?

A.2.4 Outline of the algorithms for buffer access

Figure A.9 shows the overall data structure. Once a buffer has been allocated for a specific disk block it is added to the list of blocks *in-use* in the appropriate bucket. If the data it holds becomes invalid (for example, if it is part of a file that is deleted) then it is moved to the head of the *available* list. Otherwise it will be removed from the *in-use* data structure only if the buffer is acquired for reallocation under the LRU strategy.

The following situations might arise when a buffer is to be accessed:

1. The block is *in-use* and is not *locked*. The process may *lock* the buffer, detach it from the *available* list and proceed to use it.

2. The block is *in-use* but is *locked*. The process must WAIT for this specific buffer.

3. The block is not *in-use* and the *available* list is not empty. Provided that the buffer does not contain *dirty* data, the process may use the buffer at the head

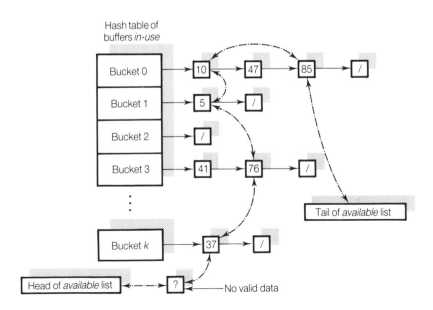

Figure A.9
An example of hash queues of buffers allocated to blocks.

of the *available* list. The buffer is removed from the *available* list and reassigned within the *in-use* data structure.

If the data is dirty, the buffer must be written out to disk. This is initiated and the process continues its search of the available list.

4. The block is not *in-use* and no free buffer is found in the *available* list. The process must WAIT for any buffer.

Event handling: WAIT and SIGNAL

Alternative policies for managing processes waiting for one specific or any buffer are as follows:

(a) When a buffer is unlocked:
  (i) If there are processes waiting for this specific buffer, select one of them and SIGNAL to it. It awakens and proceeds to use the buffer.

or

  (ii) If there are processes waiting for this specific buffer, awaken all of them. The scheduling algorithm of the system determines which process acquires the buffer.

  If there are no processes waiting for this buffer but there are processes waiting for any buffer, awaken one (i) or all (ii) of them as above.

(b) When a buffer is unlocked:
  Awaken all processes that are waiting for this specific buffer or for any buffer.

The choice of policy depends on the mechanisms available for waiting for events and signalling events. It may be that it is only possible to specify 'waiting for a buffer'. In this case, every process waiting for a specific buffer which is not the one that has become unlocked will also be awakened.

Concurrent execution

We assume a multi-threaded file server or procedural execution of file service codes by user processes. It is therefore possible that the algorithms for accessing the buffer pool are executed concurrently. We have implied a degree of concurrency control in the above discussion. The following issues are relevant to concurrent execution of the algorithms:

● A *lock* in the buffer header is provided so that only one process at once may use a given buffer. That is, exclusive access is assumed, rather than a multiple reader, single writer policy. The *lock* operation must be *atomic*.

● The *in-use* data structure and the *available* list are shared, writeable data structures. It is necessary to ensure that they are manipulated under mutual exclusion.

- An interrupt might occur at any time to indicate that a DMA transfer between a buffer and disk is complete. The interrupt may free a waiting process at a time when the cache is being accessed by some other process.

The exercises invite further consideration of these issues.

Exercises

A.22 Sketch the event handling mechanisms that are needed to support policies (a) and (b) above.

A.23 Evaluate the policies, taking into account the possibilities of unfair scheduling and starvation.

A.24 We have discussed the implementation of the *in-use* and *available* shared writable data structures. Define interfaces for these data objects. Specify the concurrency control requirements on execution of the interface operations.

A.25 A file may be open either for reading only or for reading and writing. In the former case access at file level is shared, and it seems reasonable to allow simultaneous read access to a buffer which holds a block of that file. Outline how this facility could be incorporated into the buffer design and the access algorithms.

A.26 (a) Outline a design for a buffer management module. What is the interface of this module? Assuming that multi-threaded execution is supported, where can concurrent execution be allowed and where must single threading be enforced? What happens when a process must WAIT within the module?

(b) Consider any race conditions that may arise because of concurrent execution of the buffer management module. Assume that any process may run out of time or be pre-empted from its processor at any time.

(c) Consider the possibility that, at any time, an interrupt may occur which may free a waiting process. Suppose that the system's scheduling policy is such that it is possible that this process may run immediately, pre-empting some process that was accessing the cache. Describe in detail when and how this could cause problems.

(d) When a process runs again after waiting for a specific buffer does it need to re-test the buffer identifier before proceeding to use it? Can errors occur if a process proceeds, when it is awakened, on the assumption that it now has a specific buffer?

A.27 (a) In the design outlined above buffers are written to disk only when a file is closed, unless the buffer reaches the head of the *available* list and is detected as *dirty* when required for reassignment. What are the advantages and disadvantages of this policy?

(b) Sketch an alternative design in which a separate *scribe* process is responsible for writing all cache buffers to disk. When any file is closed a message is sent to the *scribe*, which in addition scans the *available* list from head to tail looking for dirty buffers. What should be done when some other process issues a **read** or **write** request for a buffer while the *scribe* is writing it to disk? What steps might be taken to reduce contention of this kind?

Bibliography

Abrossimov V., Rozier M. and Gien M. (1989a). Virtual memory management in CHORUS. In *Proc. Progress in Distributed Operating Systems and Distributed Systems Management*, Berlin 1989. *Lecture Notes in Computer Science* **433**, pp. 45–59. Berlin: Springer.

Abrossimov V., Rozier M. and Shapiro M. (1989b). Generic virtual memory management in operating systems kernels. In *Proc. 12th ACM Symposium on Operating Systems Principles*, Dec. 1989.

Aho A.V., Hopcroft J.E. and Ullman J.D. (1983). *Data Structures and Algorithms*. Reading MA: Addison-Wesley.

Aho A.V., Sethi R. and Ullman J.D. (1986). *Compilers: Principles, Techniques and Tools*. Reading MA: Addison-Wesley.

Almasi G.S. and Gottlieb A. (1989). *Highly Parallel Computing*. Redwood City CA: Benjamin/Cummings.

Almes G.T. (1985). The Eden System, a technical overview. *IEEE Trans SE* **11**(1).

AMD (1985). Advanced Micro Devices, Local Area Network Controller (Lance) *Am7990*.

Anderson T.E., Bershad B.N., Lazowska E.D. and Levy H.M. (1992). Scheduler activations: effective kernel support for the user-level management of parallelism. *ACM Trans. on Computer Systems*, **10**(1).

Andrews G.R. (1991). *Concurrent Programming, Principles and Practice*. Redwood City CA: Benjamin/Cummings.

Andrews G.R. and Schneider F.B. (1983). Concepts and notations for concurrent programming. *ACM Computing Surveys* **15**(1).

ANSA (1989). *The Advanced Networks Systems Architecture (ANSA) Reference Manual*. Castle Hill, Cambridge, UK: Architecture Projects Management.

Bach M.J. (1986). *The Design of the UNIX Operating System*. Englewood Cliffs NJ: Prentice-Hall.

Bacon J.M. and Hamilton K.G. (1987). Distributed computing with RPC: the Cambridge approach. In *Proc. IFIPS Conference on Distributed Processing* (Barton M. *et al.*, eds.). Amsterdam: North-Holland.

Bacon J.M., Leslie I.M. and Needham R.M. (1989). Distributed computing with a processor bank. In *Proc. Progress in Distributed Operating Systems and Distributed*

Systems Management, Berlin 1989. *Lecture Notes in Computer Science* **433**, pp. 147–61. Berlin: Springer.

Bacon J.M., Moody K., Wilson T.D. and Thomson S.E. (1991). A multi service storage architecture. *ACM Operating Systems Review* **25**(4).

Ball J.E., Feldman J.A., Low J.R., Rashid R.F. and Rovner P.D. (1976). RIG, Rochester's Intelligent Gateway, System Overview. *IEEE Trans SE* **2**(4), 321–8.

Balter R. (1989). Construction and management of distributed office systems – achievements and future trends. In *Proc. ESPRIT 89 Conference* Brussels. Amsterdam: North Holland.

Balter R., Cahill V., Harris N. and Rousset de Pina X. (eds.) (1993). *The Comandos Distributed Application Platform.* Berlin: Springer.

Bayer R., Graham R.M. and Seegmuller G., eds. (1978). Operating Systems – An Advanced Course. *Lecture notes in Computer Science* **60**. Berlin: Springer.

Bell (1978). *Bell Systems Technical Journal,* Special Issue on UNIX **57**(6), part 2.

Bell D. and Grimson J. (1992). *Distributed Database Systems.* Wokingham: Addison-Wesley.

Ben Ari M. (1990). *Principles of Concurrent and Distributed Programming.* Englewood Cliffs NJ: Prentice-Hall.

Bensoussan A., Clingen C.T. and Daley R.C. (1972). The Multics virtual memory: concepts and design. *Comm. ACM* **15**(5), 308–18.

Bernstein P.A. (1990). Transaction processing monitors. *Comm. ACM* **33**(11).

Bernstein P.A., Hadzilacos V. and Goodman N. (1987). *Concurrency Control and Recovery in Database Systems.* Reading MA: Addison-Wesley.

Bershad B.N., Anderson T.E., Lazowska E.D. and Levy H.M. (1990). Lightweight remote procedure call. *ACM Trans on Computer Systems* **8**(1).

Bertsekas D.P. and Tsitsiklis J.N. (1989). *Parallel and Distributed Computation, Numerical Methods.* Englewood Cliffs NJ: Prentice-Hall.

Birman K. (1985). Replication and fault tolerance in the ISIS system. In *ACM 10th Symposium on Operating Systems Principles,* Dec.

Birrell A.D. (1991). An introduction to programming with threads. In Nelson G., ed. *Systems Programming with Modula-3.* Englewood Cliffs NJ: Prentice-Hall.

Birrell A.D. and Needham R.M. (1980). A universal file server. *IEEE Trans. SE* **SE-6**(5).

Birrell A.D. and Nelson B.J. (1986). Implementing remote procedure calls. *ACM Trans. on Computer Systems* **2**(1).

Birrell A.D., Levin R., Needham R.M. and Schroeder M.D. (1982). Grapevine: an exercise in distributed computing. *Comm. ACM* **25**(4), 260–74.

Black A., Hutchinson E.J., Levy H. and Carter L. (1986). Object structure in the Emerald system. In *Proc. Conference on Object Oriented Programming Systems.* October 1986 and *ACM SIGPLAN Notices,* **21**(11).

Bricker A., Gien M., Guillemont M., Lipkis J., Orr D. and Rozier M. (1991). A new look at microkernel based UNIX operating systems: lessons in performance and compatibility. *Chorus Systèmes.* CS/TR-91-7.

Brinch Hansen P. (1970). The nucleus of a multiprogramming system. *Comm. ACM* **13**(4).

Brinch Hansen P. (1973a). *Operating System Principles*. Englewood Cliffs NJ: Prentice-Hall.

Brinch Hansen P. (1973b). Concurrent programming concepts. *ACM Computing Surveys* 5(4).

Brinch Hansen P. (1977). *The Architecture of Concurrent Programs*. Englewood Cliffs NJ: Prentice-Hall.

Brinch Hansen P. (1978). Distributed processes: A concurrent programming concept. *Comm. ACM* 21(11).

Brownbridge D.R., Marshall L.F. and Randell B. (1982). The Newcastle connection, or UNIXs of the world unite! *Software, Practice and Experience* 12, 1147–62.

Burns A. (1988). *Programming in occam 2*. Wokingham: Addison-Wesley.

Burns A. and Davies G.L. (1993). *Concurrent Programming*. Wokingham: Addison-Wesley.

Burns A. and Wellings A. (1989). *Real-Time Systems and their Programming Languages*. Wokingham: Addison-Wesley.

Burr W.E. (1986). The FDDI optical data link. *IEEE Communication Magazine* 25(5).

Bustard D., Elder J and Welsh J. (1988). *Concurrent Program Structures*. Englewood Cliffs NJ: Prentice-Hall.

Bux W., Janson P.A., Kummerle K., Muller H.R. and Rothauser E.H. (1992). A local area communication network based on a reliable token ring system. In *Proc. IFIP TCG Symposium on LANs*, Florence (Ravasio P.C., Hopkins G. and Naffah H., eds.). Amsterdam: North-Holland.

Campbell R.H. and Haberman N.A. (1974). *The Specification of Process Synchronization by Path Expressions. Lecture Notes in Computer Science* 16. Berlin: Springer.

Campbell R.H. and Kolstad R.B. (1980). An overview of Path Pascal's design and Path Pascal user manual. *ACM SIGPLAN notices* 15(9).

Carriero N. and Gelernter D. (1989). Linda in context. *Comm. ACM* 32(4).

Ceri S. and Pelagatti G. (1985). *Distributed Databases, Principles and Systems*. McGraw-Hill.

Cheriton D.R. (1984). The V kernel, a software base for distributed systems. *IEEE Software* 1(2).

Cheriton D.R. and Zwaenpoel W. (1985). Distributed process groups in the V kernel. *ACM Trans. on Computer Systems* 3(2)

Chou W., ed. (1977). *Computer Communications Vol II: Systems and Applications*. Englewood Cliffs NJ: Prentice-Hall.

Ciminiera L. and Valenzano A. (1987). *Advanced Microprocessor Architectures*. Wokingham: Addison-Wesley.

Coffman E.G. Jr., Elphick M.J. and Shoshani A. (1971). System deadlocks. *ACM Computing Surveys* 3(2).

Comer D.E. (1991). *Internetworking with TCP/IP: Principles, Protocols and Architecture*, Vol 1, 2nd edn. Englewood Cliffs NJ: Prentice-Hall.

Cook R.L. and Rawson F.L. III (1988). The design of OS/2. *IBM Systems Journal* 27(2), 90–104.

Cooper E.C. and Draves R.P. (1987). *C Threads*. Technical Report, Carnegie-Mellon University.

Corbato F.J. and Vyssotsky V.A. (1965). Introduction and overview of the Multics system. In *Proc. AFIPS FJCC*.

Coulouris G.F. and Dollimore J. (1988). *Distributed Systems, Concepts and Design*. Wokingham: Addison-Wesley.

Date C.J. (1983, 1986). *An Introduction to Database Systems* Vol. 1, 4th edn. *(1986),* Vol. 2 (1983). Reading MA: Addison-Wesley.

Davari S. and Sha L. (1992). Sources of unbounded priority inversion in real-time systems and a comparative study of possible solutions. *ACM Operating Systems Review* **26**(2).

Davies D.W. and Price W.L. (1984). *Security for Computer Networks*. Chichester: Wiley.

DEC (1986). *DEQNA Ethernet: User's Guide*. Digital Equipment Corporation.

Denning P.J., Comer D.E., Gries D., Mulder M., Tucker A., Turner A.J. and Young P.R. (1989). Computing as a discipline. *Comm. ACM* **32**(1).

Dijkstra E.W. (1965). Solution of a problem in concurrent programming control. *Comm. ACM* **8**(9).

Dijkstra E.W. (1968). The structure of THE operating system. *Comm. ACM* **11**(5).

Dijkstra E.W. (1975). Guarded commands, nondeterminacy and the formal derivation of programs. *Comm. ACM* **18**(8).

Dion J. (1980). The Cambridge File Server. *ACM Operating Systems Review* **14**(4).

Dixon M.J. (1991). *System Support for Multiservice Traffic*. PhD Thesis, University of Cambridge and TR 245.

Dowsing R. (1988). *An introduction to concurrency using occam*. London: Van Nostrand Reinhold.

Eisenberg M.A. and McGuire M.R. (1972). Further comments on Dijkstra's concurrent programming control problem. *Comm. ACM.* **15**(11).

Farber D.J., Feldman J., Heinrich F.R., Hopwood M.D., Larsen K.C., Loomis D.C. and Rowe L.A. (1973). The distributed computing system. In *Proc. 7th IEEE Comp. Soc. Int. Conf. (COMPCON)*, February 1973.

Fitzgerald R. and Rashid R.F. (1987). The integration of virtual memory and IPC in Accent. In *Proc. 10th ACM Symposium on Operating Systems Principles*, Dec. 1987.

Gelernter D. (1985). Generative communication in Linda. *ACM Trans. Prog. Lang. and Sys.* **7**(1).

Gingell R.A., Moran J.P. and Shannon W.A. (1987). Virtual memory architecture in SunOS. *Proc. USENIX Assoc.* 81–94.

Gleeson T.J. (1989). *Aspects of abstraction in computing*. PhD Thesis, University of Cambridge.

Goodenough J.B. and Sha L. (1988). The priority ceiling protocol: a method for minimising the blocking of high priority Ada tasks. *Ada Letters, Special Issue: Proc. 2nd International Workshop on Real-Time Ada Issues VIII*, 7, Fall 1988.

Gray J., ed. (1991). *The Benchmark Handbook for Database and Transaction Processing Systems*. San Mateo CA: Morgan Kaufman.

Greaves D.J., Lioupis D. and Hopper A. (1990). *The Cambridge Backbone Ring*. Olivetti Research Ltd. Cambridge, Technical Report 2. Feb.

Habert S., Mosseri L. and Abrossimov V. (1990). COOL: kernel support for object-oriented environments. *Proc. ECOOP/OOPSLA,* Oct. 1990.

Halsall F. (1992). *Data Communications, Computer Networks and OSI*, 3rd edn. Wokingham: Addison-Wesley.

Hayes I., ed. (1987). *Specification Case Studies*. Englewood Cliffs NJ: Prentice-Hall.

Hayter M.D. and McAuley D. (1991). *The Desk Area Network*. University of Cambridge Computer Laboratory Technical Report 219, May 91, and *ACM Operating Systems Review* **25**(4).

Hennessy J.L. and Patterson D.A. (1990). *Computer Architecture, A Quantitative Approach*. San Mateo CA: Morgan Kaufman.

Herlihy M. (1990). Apologizing versus asking permission: optimistic concurrency control for abstract data types. *ACM Transactions on Database Systems* **15**(1).

Hoare C.A.R. (1974). Monitors: an operating system structuring concept. *Comm. ACM* **17**(10).

Hoare C.A.R. (1978). Communicating sequential processes. *Comm. ACM* **21**(8).

Hoare C.A.R. (1985). *Communicating Sequential Processes*. Englewood Cliffs NJ: Prentice-Hall.

Hopper A. and Needham R.M. (1988). The Cambridge Fast Ring networking system. *IEEE Trans. Computers*. **37**(10).

Hopper A. (1990). Pandora – an experimental system for multimedia applications. *ACM Operating Systems Review*. **24**(2).

Hopper A., Temple S. and Williamson R. (1986). *Local Area Network Design*. Wokingham: Addison-Wesley.

Horn C. and Krakowiak S. (1987). Object Oriented Architecture for Distributed Office Systems. In *Proc 1987 ESPRIT Conference*. Amsterdam: North-Holland.

IEEE Std 1003.1 (1988). *IEEE Standard Portable Operating System Interface for Computer Environments (POSIX)*. IEEE.

Inmos (1984). *occam Programming Manual*. Englewood Cliffs NJ: Prentice-Hall.

ISO 7498 (1981). *ISO Open Systems Interconnection, Basic Reference Model*. ISO.

ISO (1986). *OSI: Specification of Abstract Syntax Notation 1 (ASN.1)*. ISO/DIS 8824.2.

Jacky J. (1990). Risks in medical electronics. *Comm. ACM* **33**(12).

Janson P.A. (1985). *Operating Systems, Structures and Mechanisms*. London: Academic Press.

Kane G. (1989). *MIPS RISC Architecture*. Englewood Cliffs NJ: Prentice-Hall.

Khanna S., Sebree M. and Zolnowskey J. (1992). Real-time scheduling on SunOS 5.0. *Proc. USENIX*. Winter 1992.

Kilburn T., Edwards D.B.G., Lanigan M.J. and Sumner F.H. (1962). One level storage systems. *IRE Trans. Electronic Computers*. *EC(11)* April 1962.

Kogan M.S. and Rawson S.L. III (1990). The design of Operating System/2. *IBM Systems Journal* . **27**(2), 90–104.

Korth H.F. and Silberschatz A. (1991). *Database System Concepts*, 2nd edn. New York: McGraw-Hill.

Korth H.F., Kim W. and Bancilhon F. (1990). On long-duration CAD transactions. In *Readings on Object-Oriented Database Systems*. (Zdonik S.B. and Maier D., eds.). San Mateo CA:Morgan Kaufmann.

Lai W.S. (1982). Protocol traps in computer networks. *IEEE Trans. Commun. 30(6)*.

Lamport L. (1974). A new solution of Dijkstra's concurrent programming problem. *Comm. ACM.* **17**(8).

Lamport L. (1978). Time, clocks and the ordering of events in a distributed system. *Comm. ACM.* **21**(7).

Lamport L. (1987). A fast mutual exclusion algorithm. ACM *Trans. on Computer Systems.* **5**(1).

Lamport L. (1990). Concurrent reading and writing of clocks. ACM *Trans. on Computer Systems.* **8**(4).

Lamport L., Shostak R. and Peace M. (1982). The Byzantine Generals Problem. *ACM Trans. on Prog. Lang. and Systems.* **4**(3).

Lampson B. (1981). Atomic transactions. In *Distributed Systems: Architecture and Implementation. Lecture notes in Computer Science* **105**, 246–65. Berlin: Springer.

Lampson B. (1986). Designing a global name Service. In *Proc. 5th ACM Symposium on Principles of Distributed Computing*.

Lampson B. and Sproull R.F. (1979). An open operating system for a single user machine. In *ACM 7th Symposium on Operating System Principles*, Dec. 1979.

Lantz K.A., Gradischnig K.D., Feldman J.A. and Rashid R.F. (1982). Rochester's Intelligent Gateway. *Computer* **15**(10), 54–68.

Lauer H.C. and Needham R.M. (1978). On the duality of system structures. *ACM Operating Systems Review* **13**(2).

Leffler S.J., McKusick M.K., Karels M.J. and Quarterman J.S. (1989). *The Design and Implementation of the 4.3 BSD UNIX Operating System*. Reading MA: Addison-Wesley.

Leslie I.M., Needham R.M., Burren J.W. and Adams G.C. (1984). The architecture of the UNIVERSE network. *Proc. ACM SIGCOMM '84*, **14**(2).

Littlewood B. and Strigini L. (1992). *Validation of Ultra-High Dependability for Software-based Systems*. City University, London, Technical Report.

Liskov B.H. (1972). The design of the VENUS operating system. *Comm. ACM.* **15**(3).

Liskov B.H. (1988). Distributed programming in Argus. *Comm. ACM.* **31**(3).

Liskov B.H., Moss E., Schaffert C., Scheifler R. and Snyder A. (1981). *CLU Reference Manual. Lecture Notes in Computer Science* **114**. Berlin: Springer.

McAuley D. (1989). *Protocol Design for High Speed Networks*. PhD Thesis, University of Cambridge and TR 186.

McJones P.R. and Swart G.F. (1987). *Evolving the UNIX System Interface to Support Multithreaded Programs*. DEC SRC Technical Report Sept.

McKusick M.K. and Karels M.J. (1987). *A New Virtual Memory Implementation for Berkeley UNIX*. Berkeley Technical Report.

Manber U. (1989). *Introduction to Algorithms, A Creative Approach*. Reading MA: Addison-Wesley.

Mapp G.E. (1991). *An Object-Oriented Approach to Virtual Memory Management*. PhD Thesis, University of Cambridge and TR 242D.

Metcalfe R.M. and Boggs D.R. (1976). Ethernet: distributed packet switching for local computer networks. *Comm. ACM*. **19**(6).

Meyer B. (1988). *Object-oriented Software Construction*. Englewood Cliffs NJ: Prentice-Hall.

Meyer C. H. and Matyass M. (1982). *Cryptography: A New Dimension in Computer Data Security*. Wiley.

Milenkovic M. (1990). Microprocessor memory management units. *IEEE Micro*, April.

Milner R. (1989). *Communication and Concurrency*. Englewood Cliffs NJ: Prentice-Hall.

Mockapetris P.V. and Dunlap K.J. (1988). Development of the Domain Name System. *ACM SIGCAMM'88*, California Aug. 1988.

Morris D. and Detlefsen G.D. (1969). A virtual processor for real-time operation. In *Software Engineering: COINS III, Vol. 1, Proc. 3rd Symposium on Computer and Information Sciences*, Miami Beach, Florida, Dec. 1969. New York: Academic Press.

Morris D. and Ibett R.N. (1979). *The MU5 Computer System*. Basingstoke: Macmillan.

Mullender S.J. ed. (1989). *Distributed Systems, an Advanced Course*. Wokingham: ACM Press/Addison-Wesley.

Mullender S.J. and Tanenbaum A.S. (1986). The design of a capability based operating system. *Computer Journal*. **29**(4).

Nakajima J., Yazaki M. and Matsumoto H. (1991). Multimedia/real-time extensions for the Mach operating system. In *Proc USENIX Summer Conference*, June 1991.

Nelson G., ed. (1991). *Systems Programming with Modula-3*. Englewood Cliffs NJ: Prentice-Hall.

Needham R. M. (1989). Naming and protection. In *Distributed Systems: an Advanced Course* (Mullender S.S., ed.). Wokingham: ACM/Addison-Wesley.

Needham R.M. and Herbert A.J. (1982). *The Cambridge Distributed Computing System*. Wokingham: Addison-Wesley.

Needham R.M., Herbert A.J. and Mitchell L.J.G. (1986). How to connect stable storage to a computer. *ACM Operating Systems Review*. **17**(1).

Oppen D.C. and Dalal Y.K. (1983). The Clearinghouse: a decentralized agent for locating named objects in a distributed environment. *ACM Trans. Office and Information Systems*. **1**(3).

Ousterhout J.K., Scelza D.A. and Sindum P.S. (1980). Medusa: an experiment in distributed operating system structure. *Comm. ACM*. **23**(2).

Ousterhout J.K., Cherenson A.R., Douglis F., Nelson M.N. and Welch B.B. (1988). The Sprite network operating system. *IEEE Computer* 21(2). February.

Pike R., Presotto D., Thomson K. and Trickey H. (1990). Plan 9 from Bell Labs. *Proc. Summer 1990 UKUUG Conference*. London July 90, p1–9.

Pike R., Presotto D., Thomson K. and Trickey H. (1991). Designing Plan 9. *Dr Dobbs Journal*. **16**(1).

Quarterman J.S. and Hoskins J.C. (1986). Notable computer networks. *Comm. ACM.* **29**(10).

Quinn M.J. (1987). *Designing Efficient Algorithms for Parallel Computers.* McGraw-Hill.

Rashid R.F. (1986). From RIG to Accent to Mach: the evolution of a network operating system. In *Proc. ACM/IEEE Fall Joint Conference*, November 1986.

Rashid R.F. and Robertson G. (1981). Accent: a communication oriented network operating system kernel. In *Proc. ACM 8th Symp. on Operating Systems Principles*, December 1981.

Rashid R.F., Tevanian A., Young M.W., Golub D.B., Baron R., Black D. and Chew J. (1987). Machine independent virtual memory management for paged uni- and multiprocessor architectures. In *Proc. ACM 2nd Symp. on Architectural Support for Programming and Operating Systems*, Palo Alto CA.

Raynal M. (1986). *Algorithms for Mutual Exclusion.* Cambridge MA: MIT Press.

Redell D.D., Dalal Y.K., Horsley T.R., Lauer H.C., Lynch W.C., McJones P.R., Murray H.G. and Purcell S.C. (1980). Pilot, an operating systems for a personal computer. *Comm. ACM.* **23**(2).

Reed D.P. and Kanodia R.K. (1979). Synchronization with eventcounts and sequencers. *Comm. ACM.* **23**(2).

Ricart G. and Agrawala A.K. (1981). An optimal algorithm for mutual exclusion in computer networks. *Comm. ACM.* **24**(1).

Richards M., Aylward A.R., Bond P., Evans R.D. and Knight B.J. (1979). TRIPOS: A portable real-time operating system for minicomputers. *Software Practice and Experience* **9**, June.

Ritchie D.M. and Thompson K. (1974). The UNIX operating system. *Comm. ACM.* **17**(7).

Ross F.E. (1986). FDDI – a tutorial. *IEEE Communication Magazine.* 25(5). 25 May.

Rozier M., Abrossimov V., Armand F., Bowle I., Giln M., Guillemont M., Herrman F., Kaiser C., Langlois S., Leonard P. and Neuhauser W. (1988). CHORUS distributed operating systems. *Computing Systems Journal.* **1**(4). The USENIX Assoc.

Saltzer J.H. (1974). Protection and control of information sharing in Multics. *Comm. ACM.* **17**(7).

Saltzer J.H. (1979). On the naming and binding of objects. In *Operating Systems: An Advanced Course. Lecture Notes in Computer Science*, 60, 99–208. Berlin: Springer.

Saltzer J. (1982). On the naming and binding of network destinations. In *Proc. IFIP/TC6 International Symposium on Local Computer Networks*, Florence, Italy, 1982.

Sansom R.D., Julin D.P. and Rashid R.F. (1986). *Extending a Capability Based System into a Network Environment.* Technical Report CMU-CS 86 116, Carnegie-Mellon University.

Satyanarayanan M., Howard J., Nichols D., Sidebotham R., Spector A and West M. (1985). The ITC distributed file system: principles and design. In *Proc. 10th ACM Symposium on Operating Systems Principles*, December 1985.

Satyanarayanan M., Kistler J.J., Kumar P., Okasaki M.F., Siegal E.H. and Steere D.C. (1990). Coda, a highly available filing system for a distributed workstation environment. *IEEE Trans. on Computers.* **39**(4).

Schlichting R.D. and Schneider F.B. (1983). Fail-stop processors: an approach to designing fault tolerant computing systems. *ACM Trans. on Computer Systems.* **1**(3).

Sha L., Rajkumar R. and Lehoczky J.P. (1990). Priority inheritance protocol: an approach to real-time synchronization. *IEEE Trans. Computers.* 38(9).

Shapiro M. (1986). Structure and encapsulation in distributed systems: the proxy principle. In *Proc. 6th Int. Conf. on Dist. Comp. Sys.* Boston MA, May 1986.

Sharman G. C. H. (1991). The evolution of online transaction processing systems. In *Aspects of Databases* (Jackson M.S. and Robinson A.E., eds.). Guildford: Butterworth Heinemann.

Siewiorek D., Bell G.B. and Newell A., eds. (1982). *Computer Structures: Readings and Examples*, 2nd edn. McGraw-Hill.

Silberschatz A., Peterson J. and Galvin P. (1991). *Operating Systems Concepts*, 3rd edn. Reading MA: Addison-Wesley.

Sloman M. and Kramer J. (1987). *Distributed Systems and Computer Networks*, Englewood Cliffs NJ: Prentice-Hall.

Sommerville I. (1989). *Software Engineering*, 3rd edn. Wokingham: Addison-Wesley.

Stankovic J. A. and Ramamritham K., eds. (1988). Tutorial – Hard real-time systems. *IEEE Computer Society* no. 819, cat. EHO276–6.

Stefano C. and Pelagatti G. (1987). *Distributed Database: Principles and Systems*. McGraw-Hill .

Stoll C. (1989). *The Cuckoo's Egg*. London: Bodley Head.

Tanenbaum A.S. (1987). *Operating Systems, Design and Implementation*. Englewood Cliffs NJ: Prentice-Hall.

Tanenbaum A.S. (1988). *Computer Networks*, 2nd edn. Englewood Cliffs NJ: Prentice-Hall.

Tanenbaum A.S. (1992). *Modern Operating Systems*. Englewood Cliffs NJ: Prentice-Hall.

Tanenbaum A.S. and Van Renesse R. (1985). Distributed operating systems. *ACM Computing Surveys.* **17**(4).

Tanenbaum A.S., von Renesse R., van Staveren H., Sharp G.J., Mullender S.J., Jansen J. and van Rossum G. (1990). Experiences with the Amoeba operating system. *Comm. ACM.* **33**(12).

Tevanian A. Jr, Rashid R.F., Young M.W., Golub D.B., Thompson M., Bolosky W. and Sonzi R. (1987). *A UNIX Interface for Shared Memory and Memory Mapped Files under Mach*. Technical Report, Carnegie-Mellon University.

Thacker C., Stewart L. and Satterthwaite E. Jr. (1987). *Firefly: A Multiprocessor Workstation*. DEC Systems Research Centre Technical Report 23, Dec. 1987.

Thakaar S.S., ed. (1987). *Selected Reprints on Dataflow and Reduction Architectures*. IEEE Computer Society Press (order number 759).

Tokuda M., Nakajima T. and Rao P. (1990). Real-time Mach: towards a predictable real-time system. *Proc. USENIX Mach workshop*, Burlington, Vermont. USENIX Assoc.

Treese G. W. (1988). Berkeley UNIX on 1000 workstations, Athena changes to 4.3BSD. *Proc. USENIX,* Winter 1988.

Tucker A.B., ed. (1991). A summary of the ACM/IEEE-CS joint curriculum task force report Computing Curricula 1991. *Comm. ACM.* **34**(6).

Welsh J. and Lister A. (1981). A comparative study of task communication in Ada. *Software, Practice and Experience.* **11**, 256–90.

Weihl W. E. (1984). *Specification and Implementation of Atomic Data Types.* Technical Report MIT/LCS/TR-314, MIT Lab for Computer Science, March 1984.

Weihl W. E. (1989). Local atomicity properties: modular concurrency control for abstract data types. *ACM Trans. Prog. Lang. and Sys.* **11**(2).

Whiddett D. (1987). *Concurrent Programming for Software Engineers.* Chichester: Ellis Horwood.

Wilkes M.V. and Needham R.M. (1979). *The Cambridge CAP Computer and its Operating System.* Amsterdam: North-Holland.

Wilkes M.V. and Wheeler D.J. (1979). The Cambridge Digital Communication Ring. In *Local Area Networks Communications Symposium* (sponsors Mitre Corp. and NBS), Boston MA, May 1979.

Yahalom R. (1991). *Managing the Order of Transactions in Widely Distributed Data Systems.* PhD Thesis, University of Cambridge and TR 231.

Yelavitch B. M. (1985). Customer information control system: an evolving system facility. *IBM Systems Journal.* **24**(3/4).

Zdonik S.B. and Maier D., eds. (1990). *Readings on Object-Oriented Database Systems.* San Mateo CA: Morgan Kaufmann.

Zimmerman H. (1980). OSI reference model – the ISO model of architecture for open systems interconnection. *IEEE Trans. Computers* **28**(4).

Zöbel D. (1983). The deadlock problem, a classifying bibliography. *ACM Operating Systems Review,* **17**(4).

Glossary

ADT	Abstract Data Type
AIX	IBM's version of UNIX
ANSA	Advanced Networked Systems Architecture
ANSI	American National Standards Institute
ARM	Acorn RISC Machine
ASCII	American Standard Code for Information Interchange
ASN.1	Abstract Syntax Notation one
ATM	1. Asynchronous Transfer Mode 2. Automatic Teller Machine
BSD	Berkeley Software Distribution (of UNIX, for example BSD 4.3)
capability	A name for an object which includes access rights to the object
CBR	Cambridge Backbone Ring
CCITT	Comitée Consultatif International Télégraphique et Téléphonique
CDCS	Cambridge Distributed Computing System
CFR	Cambridge Fast Ring
CISC	Complex Instruction Set Computer
client	A computer program for which a *server* performs some computation; compare *user*
COW	Copy-On-Write
CR	Cambridge Ring
DAN	Desk Area Network
DARPA	Defence Advanced Research Projects Agency
DEQNA	An Ethernet network interface of Digital Equipment Corporation
DMA	Direct Memory Access
DRAM	Dynamic Random Access Memory
EBCDIC	Extended Binary Coded Decimal Interchange Code
FCFS	First Come First Served

FDDI	Fibre Distributed Data Interface
FID	File IDentifier
FIFO	First In First Out
FTP	File Transfer Protocol
garbage	Inaccessible object occupying storage resources
GNU	GNU's Not UNIX, a recursive acronym. The name of a project to make freely available UNIX-compatible software
GUI	Graphical User Interface
host	A computer attached to a network, in particular, an IP network
HP-UX	Hewlett-Packard's version of UNIX
ID	IDentifier
IEEE	Institute of Electrical and Electronics Engineers
inode	In the UNIX file system a file's *index node* or *inode* stores the file's metadata
Internet	A global network connecting many commercial, academic and government sites, especially institutions engaged in research. The internet is an aggregate of many independently managed networks. The unifying factor is the Internet Protocol
IP	Internet Protocol
IPC	Inter-Process Communication
ISDN	Integrated Services Digital Network
ISO	International Standards Organization
LAN	Local Area Network
LANCE	Local Area Network Controller for Ethernet
MAN	Metropolitan Area Network
MIPS	1. Millions of Instructions Per Second – an indicator of processor speed. 2. A RISC processor made by MIPS Computer Systems Inc.
MMU	Memory Management Unit

MS-DOS	Microsoft Disk Operating System. A single user OS for the Intel 8088 microprocessor and its successors
MSNA	Multi-Service Network Architecture
MTBF	Mean Time Between Failures
multi-threaded process	Used in systems where a process is the unit of resource allocation and a thread is the unit of execution on a processor. The threads of the process share its resources
NFS	SUN's Network File System
node	A component computer of a distributed system, like *host*
NVRAM	Non-Volatile Random Access Memory
OCC	Optimistic Concurrency Control, a method of concurrency control for transactions
OSF	Open Software Foundation
OSI	Open Systems Interconnection: a consortium of vendors led by IBM, DEC and Hewlett-Packard
POSIX	IEEE Standard 1000.3, Portable Operating System Interface for Computer (UNIX) Environments
PTT	Post, Telephone and Telegraph: the bodies within a country that are licensed to provide public data transmission services
QOS	Quality Of Service
RISC	Reduced Instruction Set Computer
RPC	Remote Procedure Call
SAP	Service Access Point
SAR	Segmentation And Reassembly
SCSI	Small Computer System Interface. A standard I/O bus.
server	A computer or program designed to perform computations on behalf of other programs, its *clients*
SFID	System File IDentifier
site	1. A component computer of a distributed system, like *host* and *node* 2. A local internetwork at some geographical locality, such as the Cambridge site
socket	An abstraction for a communication end-point

SPARC	Scalable Processor ARChitecture, a RISC architecture
TAS	Test-And-Set
TCP	Transmission Control Protocol
thread	A name for a unit of execution on a processor; see *multi-threaded process*
TLB	Translation Lookaside Buffer
TSO	Time-Stamp Ordering, a method of concurrency control for transactions
UDP	User Datagram Protocol
UFID	User File IDentifier
UI	UNIX International: a consortium of vendors led by AT&T
ULTRIX	Digital Equipment Corporation's version of UNIX
UPS	Uninterruptable Power Supply – used to maintain a supply of power to equipment when the mains has failed
user	A human operator of a computer system; compare *client*
VAX	A CISC processor proprietary to the Digital Equipment Corporation
VC	Virtual Circuit
VME	A backplane bus standard, IEEE standard 104
WAN	Wide Area Network
Wanda	An experimental microkernel operating system under development at the University of Cambridge Computer Laboratory
WORM	Write Once Read Multiple, an optical storage technology
XDR	External Data Representation. A standard for representing data types so that they can be exchanged between different types of computer
2PL	Two-Phase Locking: a method of concurrency control for transactions
2PC	Two-Phase Commit: an atomic commitment protocol
3PC	Three-Phase Commit: an atomic commitment protocol

Author index

Subject index